T0204613

The Economic Sociology of Capitalism

The Economic Sociology of Capitalism

Edited by
Victor Nee and Richard Swedberg

PRINCETON UNIVERSITY PRESS

PRINCETON AND OXFORD

Copyright © 2005 by Princeton University Press

Published by Princeton University Press, 41 William Street, Princeton, New Jersey 08540
In the United Kingdom: Princeton University Press, 3 Market Place, Woodstock,
Oxfordshire OX20 1SY

All Rights Reserved

Library of Congress Cataloging-in-Publication Data

The economic sociology of capitalism / edited by Victor Nee and Richard Swedberg.
    p. cm.
  Includes bibliographical references and index.
  ISBN 0-691-11957-0 (cl : alk. paper)—ISBN 0-691-11958-9 (pbk. : alk. paper)
    1. Capitalism—Social aspects.   2. Economics—Sociological aspects.   I. Nee, Victor,
  1945– II. Swedberg, Richard.

  HB501.E2565 2005
  306.3'42—dc22   2004043151

British Library Cataloging-in-Publication Data is available

This book has been composed in Galliard

Printed on acid-free paper. ∞

pup.princeton.edu

Printed in the United States of America

10 9 8 7 6 5 4 3 2 1

WE DEDICATE THIS BOOK

to the memory of Robert K. Merton

Contents

Institutions, Markets, and Games

Avner Greif

CAPITALISM IS THE BACKBONE of contemporary economies in both developed and many developing countries. At the center of this socioeconomic system are incentives based on private ownership of the means of production, profit, and the voluntary, market-based exchange of ideas, information, labor, and products. Contemporary capitalism comes in various forms and varieties, and despite broad commonalities, capitalist economies, such as those of the U.S., UK, Germany, and Japan, differ in many ways from each other. They differ along dimensions that are central to the capitalist system, such as the nature and extent of direct state interventions in the allocation of economic resources and the structure of the capital market. Their distinctions notwithstanding, the prosperity of capitalist economies stands in sharp contrast to those economies in which alternative systems prevail. Indeed, the failure of the great social experiments of the twentieth century—communism and fascism—in developing alternative economic systems left capitalism with no viable alternatives. Poverty is the hallmark of countries in which the heritage of these experiments still lingers, or in which dictators and their cronies are central to the socioeconomic system.

Comprehending economic and social outcomes in the contemporary world thus requires understanding capitalism, its nature, origin, variety, the evolution of particular capitalist economies, and the system as a whole. Despite the triumph of capitalism, we have surprisingly little understanding of this kind. Sociology has a particularly long and sophisticated tradition of studying capitalism and its emergence, dating back to the pioneering works of Marx and Weber. In contrast, neo-classical economics has held for a long time that markets are organisms that emerge spontaneously (e.g., Hayek 1960). State protection of property rights and private contracting is necessary and sufficient for market economy to emerge. This

This foreword draws on my forthcoming book, Institutions: Theory and History. Comparative and Historical Institutional Analysis. It also benefited from comments by Victor Nee and Richard Swedberg.

conviction, however, has been undermined when it has been tested in guiding the transitions of previously socialist economies to market economies.

It has become widely accepted in economics, sociology, and political science that studying the origin, nature, and dynamics of various economies—including capitalist ones—requires studying their institutional underpinnings.[1] Indeed, numerous empirical papers using proxies of institutions, such as the degree of the rule of law, property rights security, and openness to trade on the national and international levels have found that they matter.[2] The challenge is to go beyond proxies and get a better micro-level understanding of the institutions that manifest themselves in such societal features as the rule of law, property rights security, and the extent of the market.

Yet, social science does not currently provide a coherent conceptual, theoretical, and analytical framework for studying institutions. Indeed, one of the obstacles to advancing the study of the institutional underpinnings of capitalist economies is the elusive nature of the concept of institutions. There are many, seemingly alternative, definitions of the term institutions. Among the most common, many of which are used in this book, are:

- "The rules of the game" in a society (North 1990: 4) and "the sets of working rules" that "contain prescriptions that forbid, permit, or require some action or outcome," and that are "actually used, monitored, and enforced" (Ostrom 1990: 6).
- Organizations such as parliaments, tribes, families, communities, and universities (e.g., Weingast 1996; Granovetter 1985; Nelson 1994).
- Beliefs. Shared beliefs about others' behavior or about the world around us and the relationships between actions and outcomes in it (e.g., Durkheim [1895] 1982; Weber [1904–1905] 1958; Denzau and North 1994; Greif 1994; Calvert 1995; Aoki 2001).
- Norms of behavior that were internalized by members of the society and hence influenced their behavior (e.g., Parsons 1951; Ullmann-Margalit 1977; Elster 1989; Platteau 1994).
- Regularities of behavior or "social practices that are regularly and continuously repeated" and which include contractual regularities that can express themselves in organizations such as firms (Abercrombie et al. 1984: 216; see also Berger 1977; Schotter 1981; Williamson 1985; Young 1998: preface).

The main approaches to institutional analysis in the social sciences differ in more ways than in how they define their object of study. They also differ in their basic presuppositions regarding the nature, dynamics, and origins of institutions and how they relate to rationality and the complexity of the world within which individuals interact.

Some approaches have adopted an agency perspective on institutions while others have advanced a structural perspective. Those that adopted the agency perspective place the individual decision-maker at the center of their analysis and study institutions as reflecting the interrelationships among individuals' objectives, possibilities, and the environment within which they interact. Institutions are therefore considered as reflections of human actions and social processes and are postulated not to endure beyond the conditions that led to their emergence. Politicians, for example, aspire to create the rules that serve their political and economic objectives best. If these objectives or the political process of rule formation changes, so will the resulting rules. Similarly, conventional rules of behavior emerge sponta-neously through the interactions of individuals in a given environment and will therefore change following an environmental change. The point of departure for such institutional analysis is therefore at the micro-level of the individuals whose interactions in a particular environment give rise to an institution.

Approaches that have adopted the structural perspective emphasize that institutions do not reflect agents' needs and possibilities, but shape these needs and determine these possibilities instead. Institutions structure human interactions, mold individuals, and constitute the social and cultural worlds within which they interact. They therefore transcend the situation that led to their emergence and are part of a society's historical heritage. Beliefs, norms, organizations, and social structures that were crystalized in the past, for example, are part of the structure within which individuals in-teract. The point of departure for such institutional analysis is thus at the macro-level of the historically determined structure within which individ-uals interact.

These two perspectives—the agency and the structural—separate the main approaches to institutional analysis in the social sciences. Within so-ciology, works in the tradition of Weber (e.g., 1949) maintain that institu-tions reflect the interactions among individuals. In contrast, Durkheim considered institutions as societal features which "impose themselves upon" individuals ([1895] 1982: 2) and "consist of cognitive, normative, and reg-ulative structures and activities that provide stability and meaning to social behavior" (Scott 1995: 33). Within economics, transaction cost economics assumes that institutions are instrumental transaction costs optimizing re-sponses to environmental conditions (e.g., Williamson 1985), but in eco-nomic history and evolutionary economics it is common to identify insti-tutions with history-dependent behavior (e.g., North 1990; Hodgson 1998). Rational choice analysis in political science examines institutions as instrumental outcomes, while historical institutionalism emphasizes that they reflect a historical process (Thelen 1999).

Various approaches to the study of institutions also invoke particular, and often contradictory, assumptions regarding their origins and func-tions. For Hayek (1960) and many others (e.g., Hodgson 1998; Young

1998), institutions emerge spontaneously and unintentionally. They reflect human actions but not human intentions because individuals have limited knowledge and rationality. For many others, however, intentional attempts by individuals to improve their lot underpin the processes through which institutions emerge (e.g., Williamson 1985; North and Thomas 1973).

Similarly, various approaches to institutional analysis rest on distinct assumptions regarding the function that institutions fulfill. For North (1990: 6) and many others, "the major role of institutions in a society is to reduce uncertainty." For Williamson (1998: 37) and others, institutions foster efficiency. They are the "means by which order is accomplished in a relationship in which potential conflict threatens to undo or upset opportunities to realize mutual gains." For Knight (1992), the main function of institutions is to affect the distribution of gains. Finally, various definitions of institutions invoke contradictory assumptions regarding human nature. Parsons (1951), for example, assumes that individuals are capable of internalizing rules, and that institutions are internalized behavioral standards. Williamson's (1985) institutional analysis, however, rests on the opposite assumption: Individuals are assumed always to act opportunistically unless constrained by external forces. For Aoki (2001) and Young (1998), *institutions* reflect limited knowledge regarding the environment within which they interact while others, such as Calvert (1995) and Williamson (1985), initiate the analysis assuming that individuals have a comprehensive knowledge of this environment.

Given these differences in how institutions have been defined and the basic presuppositions underpinning their analysis, it is not surprising that the various approaches to institutional analysis have been treated in the literature as mutually exclusive. This, however, curtails our ability to advance the study of such issues as capitalism, which requires a multidisciplinary and multidimensional perspective as advocated in this book. A key to further advancing institutional analysis is understanding the common aspects of the various definitions of institutions, developing a unifying concept of the object of study, and exploring the complementary relationships between various definitions and perspectives. Each definition and presupposition is appropriate for addressing particular issues, but fails to provide a comprehensive understanding of the social underpinnings of regularities of behavior and their dynamics.

Although the above definitions are considered alternatives in the literature, they nevertheless have much in common. Indeed, they have enough in common to advance a concept of institutions that transcends these definitions and distinctions. All the above definitions relate to the behavioral implications of social factors: man-made, nonphysical factors that are exogenous to each individual whose behavior they influence.[3] Examples of such factors include shared beliefs regarding the relationships between behavior and outcomes, internalized norms, cognitive systems, socially articulated and distributed rules, and formal and informal organizations (social structures).[4] Each of the above definitions of institutions (and others) concentrates on a particular social factor. Yet, as further discussed below, these various factors have distinct roles in generating regularities of behavior. Hence, it is appropriate to define an institution, roughly speaking, as a system of such social factors ("institutional elements") that conjointly generate a regularity of behavior. An institution motivates, enables, and guides individuals with particular social positions to follow one rule of behavior among the many technologically feasible ones.

This definition encompasses the many, seemingly alternative, definitions of institutions as special cases. It covers, for example, the definition of institutions as rules imposed by the state, but it also encompasses the definition of institutions as social norms that reflect the interdependencies among the interacting individuals. Similarly, this definition bridges the "agency" and the "structural" dichotomy in institutional analysis by noting that institutions are man-made yet exogenous to each of the individuals whose behavior they influence. The definition commits institutional analysis neither to any postulate regarding the origin, function, or dynamics of institutions, nor to a particular view regarding human nature and ability. Furthermore, the definition captures the assertion that advancing institutional analysis requires bridging the conceptual divide between studying them as rules as is common in economics, and studying them as cultural, social, and organizational phenomena, as is common in sociology. Indeed, the importance of integrating both the "cultural" and "social" into institutional analysis has been recognized by many students in economics, sociology, and political science (e.g., North 1990; Williamson 2000; Scott 1995; Hall and Taylor 1996).

The artificiality of differentiating between the study of rules, on the one hand, and cultural and social features, on the other, is well reflected in the concept of institutions as rules supported by, for example, legal sanctions imposed by the state or social or economic sanctions imposed by one's peers. As a first approximation, one can assert, as is common in economics, that individuals follow rules because there are other rules specifying punishment if they do not. It is in the self-interest of a person to follow rules because otherwise he will be punished. This implies, however, that a claim regarding the effectiveness of rules in influencing behavior is an assertion about beliefs regarding the relationships between one's actions, others' responses, and the implied consequences. Studying the rules of behavior followed in a society therefore requires examining the beliefs shared among its members. Similarly, if one asserts that rules are followed based on internalized norms or social embeddedness, it amounts to an assertion regarding socialization processes and beliefs about others' behavior and feelings in social interactions.

Understanding regularities of behavior therefore requires, in addition to examining the process through which rules are stipulated, studying why some behavioral rules are followed while others are not. Rules are behavioral instructions that can be ignored, implying that for any prescriptive rules of behavior to have an impact, individuals must be motivated to follow them. Motivation (incentives)—provided by beliefs, internalized norms, or social relationships—mediates between the environment and behavior, whether individuals act rationally, imitatively, or habitually.[5]

The importance and difficulties of studying endogenous motivation has long been recognized in sociology. Durkheim ([1895] 1982: 45) defined institutions as "all the beliefs and modes of behavior instituted by the collectivity"; Parsons (1951: 38–40) took the position that full institutionalization of a behavioral standard requires its internalization, namely, its transformation into an internalized norm. Wrong (1961, 1999) and Granovetter (1985) have argued that the motivating impact of personal relationships (embeddedness) is central to generating regularities of behavior.

Studying endogenous motivation, however, is difficult because shared beliefs, internalized norms, and the strength of personal relationships are not directly observable and hence any behavior can be justified based on ad hoc assertions regarding motivating beliefs, norms, and relationships. Advancing the analysis requires bridging the divide between the structural and the agency perspectives and between studying rules and motivation based on shared beliefs, internalized norms, and social relationships. Advancing institutional analysis requires an analytical framework that links behavior on the individual level and the reproduction of societal features, such as shared beliefs, internalized norms, and social networks. This framework has to delineate the causal mechanism leading to reproduction of these societal features by the behavior on the individual level that these societal features induce. In short, it has to delineate the mechanism for the reproduction of institutional elements and the conditions under which this mechanism is effective.

Until recently, however, the lack of such an analytical framework limited our ability to study institutions and the endogenous motivation central to them. Neither Durkheim nor Parsons provided a theory limiting the set of shared beliefs and internalized norms that can prevail in a given situation, and in discussing embeddedness, Wrong (1961, 1999) noted that invoking the human propensity to seek either social acceptance or internalized norms as the deus ex machina of social order is partial at best. More generally, Powell and DiMaggio (1991: 2) argued that promising institutional research—from Veblen and Commons in economics to Parsons and Selznick in sociology—"fell into disfavor, not because they asked the wrong questions, but because they provided answers that were either largely descriptive and historically specific or so abstract as to lack explanatory punch." There was no analytical framework with which to study beliefs and norms as institutional elements exogenous to each individual yet generated by the actions of each.

In recent years game theory has emerged as a useful analytical framework for studying beliefs and norms as institutional elements exogenous to each individual yet generated by the actions of each. More generally, it bridges the structural and agency views by delineating a particular mechanism for self-enforcing behavior that reproduces itself and exposes the distinct roles and complementary interrelationships among various institutional elements. Game theory is not widely used in sociology and accordingly the following emphasizes its conceptual and analytical benefits.[6] Instead of demonstrating this theory's benefits by providing examples of positive game-theoretic analyses of particular institutions, the discussion centers around its contribution to an assertion central to the economic sociology of capitalism. This assertion is that economics alone is insufficient for studying the institutions underpinning capitalism. Indeed, game theory highlights the limitations of our deductive theories of institutions and the need to incorporate substantiative issues central to sociology into economic analyses. Game theory provides an analytical framework that both exposes this need and provides a means for beneficial exchange between economics and sociology.

Game theory examines decision-making in strategic situations, namely, those in which the optimal behavior for a decision-maker depends on the behavior and expected behavior of others. Because it is a theory of decision-making in strategic situations, it enables examining how institutional elements—man-made, nonphysical factors exogenous to each of the interacting individuals—influence behavior in a particular interaction (transaction). The game-theoretic framework is very flexible in accommodating situations in which the number of interacting individuals is large, such as one's decision about which side of the road to drive on, or small, such as a lender's decision whether to give a loan to a particular borrower. It can capture such realistic features of the environment as asymmetric information, hidden actions, uncertainty, and the importance of knowledge. At the same time, game theory enables us to study behavior while evaluating and accommodating various assumptions regarding human cognitive and computational abilities and capturing within the same framework economic, social, moral, and coercive considerations.

A major contribution of game theory to positive, empirical institutional analysis has been its ability analytically to restrict the set of beliefs regarding behavior that can be shared among members of a society and that lead to behavior corresponding to these beliefs. When beliefs that members of the society hold are identical and commonly known and each player plays his or her best response to them, the set of permissible beliefs is restricted to those that correspond to a game-theoretic equilibrium. Behavior satisfies the game-theoretic equilibrium condition when each individual finds it optimal to follow this behavior, expecting that everyone will follow it. Shared beliefs that each individual takes as exogenous to his or her actions lead this individual—under the assumption that he or she chooses his best response to these beliefs—to behave as expected. When this is the case, we refer to this behavior and beliefs as self-enforcing. Behavior is followed in the absence of exogenous enforcement.

Game theory enables deductively restricting behavior in this manner, even in situations that would not actually transpire, given the expected behavior. Hence, it can restrict, for example, the beliefs that can prevail in a given environment regarding how people will respond to cheating although, given their beliefs, cheating will not actually occur. Intuitively, game theory restricts admissible behavior and beliefs in such situations to those involving credible threats and promises—those that one would actually carry out if the need arose given others' expected behavior.

The benefit of this analytical framework for positive institutional analysis has been demonstrated in numerous studies.[7] Equally important, game theory, particularly that of repeated games, highlighted the limitations of a deductive approach to institutions and the necessity of incorporating considerations long emphasized by sociologists into the analysis. Game theory, as a theory of behavior, revealed that in situations of interest to institutional analysis—strategic, recurrent situations—multiple equilibria, and hence institutions, generically exist. Even if we assume that individuals are perfectly rational and the rules of the game are common knowledge, there is no one-to-one mapping from the environment to institutions—namely, to the outcomes of interests. Multiple outcomes are consistent with the theory.

The finding that there is no one-to-one mapping from the environment to outcomes of interests amounts to a conceptual break from neoclassical economics, whose general equilibrium theory asserted that unique allocation and prices would prevail as an equilibrium outcome in a given situation. In contrast, game theory suggests that the failure to develop a deductive theory of institutions so far reflects an inherent indeterminacy of institutions: multiple behaviors and beliefs can be self-enforcing in a given environment. The ultimate selection of one institution over another critically depends on the social environment—norms, culture, cultural beliefs, identity, social networks, who has a legitimate say over what behavior is to be followed—phenomena that are in fact the conceptual and empirical lifeblood of sociology.

Similarly, game theory and the associated economics of information revealed the importance of information in influencing possible self-enforcing behavior. Who knows what and when generically has a substantial impact on the set of self-enforcing beliefs and behavior in strategic situations.

Hence, just exactly how information is transmitted in a society and by whom is important. This generic insight highlights the indispensability of integrating factors long emphasized in sociology into institutional analysis, such as social, business, ethnic, cultural, and immigrant information networks, and the asymmetry between information based on personal and social relationships and that obtained outside such relationships. This type of game-theoretic analysis is presented, for example, in Greif (1989). He has noted the importance of informal social structures in changing information flows, thereby altering the set of self-enforcing behavior and beliefs that could prevail among merchants and their overseas agents. The game-theoretic framework exposed the details of the underlying environment and agency relationships, which made these beliefs and behavior self-enforcing, and how the resulting economic institution reproduced the social network that initially supported it.

At the same time, the generic insight regarding the importance of information highlights the informational function of formal, business organizations, such as credit bureaus, business associations, consumer reports, and stock exchanges. Such organizations can substitute and complement socially based mechanisms for reliable information transmission. Studying informal and formal social structures using the same analytical framework fosters the ability to study their relationships and the historical evolution of distinct structures.

More generally, game theory has facilitated our ability to investigate the interrelationships among organizations—formal and informal social structures—and economic institutions. These relationships have been traditionally examined mainly from three perspectives, to which game theory contributed greatly. The first, common in political science and political economy, considers organizations as bodies for collective decision-making, such as a Congress or a Parliament. Institutions are rules specified by members of these organizations and reflect their interactions and interests. The second perspective considers an organization to be a group "of individuals bound by some common purpose to achieve objectives" (North 1990: 5). Such organizations—interest groups, courts, labor unions, etc.—influence politically determined rules by participating in the political decision-making process. They often reflect existing rules that motivate those who benefit from them to get organized collectively to ensure that these rules persist.

The third perspective, which has been advanced in organizational theory, also holds that organizations are "collectivities oriented to the pursuit of relatively specific goals and exhibiting highly formalized social structures" (Scott 1998: 26). This perspective maintains, however, that organizations reflect the options and constraints implied by institutions conceptualized as systems of meaning and regulatory processes (enforcement mechanisms).

The sociological branch of organizational theory emphasizes that organizations reflect the meaning, objectives, and identities provided by institutions (e.g., Scott et al. 1994: 74; Scott 1995, chaps. 5–6). The economic branch of organizational theory emphasizes that institutions influencing the costs and benefits of various actions and organizations are optimal—transaction cost minimizing—responses to these incentives (Coase 1937; Williamson 1985, 2000).

In the above three perspectives, organizations are considered as either arenas for political rule-making, players in the political rule-making process, or private responses to institutions. Furthermore, they either determine institutions or are determined by them. Game theory has been used to study such interrelationships for a long time. In the first case, we study the process of rule-making as a game; in the second, we consider a game in which individuals can form organizations in response to existing rules and these organizations can labor through the political system to maintain or change these rules; in the last case we study the game spanned by existing institutions and how it provides individuals with the motivation to establish organizations to foster the pursuit of an economic objective.

But organizations and institutions interrelate in one more important way. Organizations are institutional elements that alter the situation from the perspective of each of the interacting individuals engaged in the central interaction or transaction of interest (e.g., between merchants and agents and lenders and borrowers). Hence, organizations change the set of self-enforcing behavior in that interaction. Such organizations—exogenous to each of the individuals whose behavior they influence—neither determine institutions nor are determined by them. Rather, they are an integral part of institutions: as institutional elements they change the set of self-enforcing behavioral beliefs in the central transaction under consideration by providing coordination, circulating information, and directly changing payoffs.

On a deeper level, this perspective on organizations relates to the relationships between transactions and the rationale for considering organizations as institutional elements. Institutional analysis focuses on central interactions or transactions and explores the factors generating regularities of behavior in them. Organizations alter the set of self-enforcing beliefs and behavior possible in these transactions by linking them to other (auxiliary) transactions. This linkage influences the set of self-enforcing behavior and beliefs in the central transaction. Game theory provides the analytical framework to study such linkages among transactions and their implications.

Consider, for example, the case of institutions facilitating exchange. Suppose that in the absence of contractual problems, an exchange is mutually beneficial. Yet, even for such exchange to be carried out, the inherent credible commitment problem has to be mitigated. This credible commitment problem is inherent to every exchange relationship because all exchange is sequential and hence the party that moves second has to be able to commit ex ante not to renege on its obligations ex post. (The basic game is a One-sided Prisoner's Dilemma game, or the game of trust. See, Greif 2000.) Generically, commitment is achieved by linking this central exchange transaction with other transactions (Greif and Kandel 1995). This linkage can be between the same transactions over time, when the transacting individuals condition their behavior in future periods on conduct from the past; it can be between the same transactions among different individuals, as was the case among the Maghribi traders examined in Greif (1989) where transactions between a merchant and an agent were conditioned on the outcomes of the agent's past transactions with other merchants. But the linkages can also be between various transactions.

In any of these cases, commitment in the central transaction was achieved by linking it to another transaction, and this resulting linkage altered the equilibrium set—the set of self-enforcing beliefs and behavior—relative to a situation without the linkage. When this linkage sufficiently increased the cost of reneging (or the benefit of compliance), it became possible for the transacting individuals to commit ex ante not to renege ex post. The linkage rendered the belief self-enforcing so that the interacting individuals would comply.[8] Organizations that are institutional elements—exogenous to each of the individuals engaged in the central transaction—are mechanisms for, or are a reflection of, the ways that a central transaction is linked with other transactions, thereby altering the set of self-enforcing beliefs in that transaction. Such organizations can intentionally be established or unintentionally emerge. They can be formal or informal, intentional or unintentional, and examples of them include groups, social networks, courts, firms, credit bureaus, escrow companies, and credit rating companies

We study the relationships among organizations and institutions using game theory by first considering the "benchmark" game that captures the essence of the central transaction under consideration without the organization whose impact we want to explore. We then examine the set of self-enforcing beliefs and the associated outcomes. We proceed by considering an augmented game in which the organization of interest is incorporated by changing the action sets, information, and payoffs. Organizations are modeled as constituting a new player (the organization itself), changing the information available to players, or changing payoffs associated with certain actions (Greif 1994: 915–16). Then we can explore self-enforcing beliefs and outcomes in the central transaction.

Game theory also exposed the importance of socially articulated and transmitted rules through which "socially-sanctioned-facts-of-life . . . that-any-bona-fide-member-of-the-society-knows" are distributed (Garfinkel

1967: 76). Such "institutionalized" rules—rules that are institutional elements—are shared among members of a society, everyone knows them and everyone knows that others know them. They are transmitted in diverse forms, such as laws, regulations, customs, taboos, conventional rules of behavior, and constitutions. They are transmitted by individuals with diverse social positions such as parents, teachers, peers, priests, and a tribe's elders, and are conveyed using such means as teaching, training, public announcements, manuals, and ceremonies.

While such institutionalized rules have no role in the neoclassical framework, game theory revealed to economists the need to study the multiple roles of institutionalized rules while providing a unifying framework in which to do so and contributing to our understanding of their nature as well. In particular, game theory exposed the coordinative, informative, and cognitive roles of these rules. Multiple equilibria, and hence institutions, imply the need to coordinate behavior among the interacting individuals. Institutionalized rules facilitate the task of each individual in forming beliefs regarding what behavior, among the many possible ones, will be followed by others. But rules only assist in forming beliefs and do not determine them because retrospective individuals compare outcomes with expectations. Individuals' beliefs are reproduced only if they are confirmed by observing the behavior of others. Socially articulated and distributed rules that can establish themselves and be followed—that can become institutionalized—are therefore those which correspond to an equilibrium.

This reproduction process and the requirement that institutionalized rules constitute an equilibrium imply that these rules also aggregate the dispersed information that each individual has and transmit it in a compressed form. Institutionalized rules both provide individuals with the information they need to make decisions regarding how to act, and also aggregate the information privately held by each of them. In doing so, institutionalized rules of behavior direct individuals to play an equilibrium outcome in the underlying game, although the assumptions held in classical game theory regarding common knowledge and rationality do not hold. Because such rules correspond to an equilibrium, individuals are seemingly rule-followers, following the rules associated with the social position they occupy.[9]

Institutionalized rules are therefore equivalent to prices in market situations. They inform each individual about the expected behavior of others and the only behavioral rules that can prevail and correspond to actual behavior are those in which each individual, basing his decision on his private information, finds it optimal to follow. Hence, in an institution, behavioral rules aggregate the private information of all the agents, providing each of them with sufficient statistics to make an informed decision.

Last but not least, game theory highlights the role of institutionalized rules in circulating a cognitive system among members of the society and the importance of this system. A cognitive system embodies, transmits, and propagates knowledge, reflecting the accumulated experience and innovativeness of past and present members of the society. It provides members of the society with typification, classifications, and meaning, using symbols such as words and signs. A cognitive system provides the terms for describing socially recognized and created items, ideas, actors, events, and possible actions to which the system also imputes meanings. Whether evolving over time or created intentionally, once such a cognitive system has established itself in a society, it provides the foundation for behavior in social situations (D'Andrade 1984; Searle 1995; Scott 1995).

In game theory, we capture a cognitive system and examine its behavioral implications by specifying and analyzing a game. Defining a game is making a statement regarding the cognitive system that the relevant actors share. It is a statement regarding the socially constructed shared understanding of a situation. Specifying the rules of the game makes a claim about the perceptions of agents regarding the situation that reflects their shared cognitive system and understanding of their physical environment. A game-theoretic model of a trading network based on a distinct social identity and norms, for example, captures the traders' shared idea of their separate identities, that they are able to cognitively recognize each other and share a common understanding of appropriate behavior. The implied behavioral rules—which we study as an equilibrium outcome—rely on this shared cognitive system. By exposing the complexity of decision-making in strategic situations, game theory fosters our understanding of why and how institutionalized rules are a "device for coping with our ignorance" (Hayek 1976: 29).

Socially articulated and distributed rules help individuals know how to act in a complex, uncertain, and potentially inhospitable environment. Institutionalized rules distribute cognitive systems and behavioral rules that circulate knowledge, create common knowledge, aggregate private information, and coordinate beliefs and behavior. At the same time, the institutionalized rules that can prevail and are followed in a society are restricted by the responses of individuals to the rules themselves. This view bridges the gap between the sociologists' emphasis on the importance of socially articulated and distributed rules and the economists' emphasis on individualistic behavior and choice. Institutionalized rules facilitate individualistic behavior while simultaneously being constrained by it. Social processes of rule formation are thus important, and in studying institutions one has to address issues central to sociology. For example, who can influence the beliefs of others? Who has legitimacy in the process of rule formation, socialization, and the relationships between institutions and endogenous experimentation that can lead to new rules of behavior?

Although the discussion so far has been conducted as if individuals' preferences are exogenously given, game theory has exposed the need and provided an analytical framework for studying these interests as social outcomes. That individuals have social propensities—the capacity to value social relationships, to internalize norms, to have emotions, and to care about others' welfare—is intuitive. While the potential importance of such factors in motivating behavior has been argued by many scholars, substantiating their importance is elusive because their exact nature is difficult to discern based on empirical observations. If one forgoes an opportunity to cheat, for example, it may be difficult to determine whether this behavior reflects an altruistic inclination, an internalized norm of behavior, a fear of God, or the desire to enhance an economically valuable reputation. Experimental game theory, however, has been used recently to devise experiments that enable differentiating among these alternative hypotheses. The tentative results have enhanced our ability to identify and explicitly formulate various manifestations of human social propensities, such as altruism, inequality-aversion, emotions, and the force that social rules have in shaping preferences.[10]

Furthermore, the game-theoretic framework is flexible enough to incorporate into the same model the assumption that individuals are selfish and materialistic with the assumption that humans have social propensities. Indeed, it provides an analytical framework for restricting statements regarding the behavioral implications of social propensities in a given environment. We can impose analytical restrictions and examine the endogenous formation of, for example, friendships, internalized norms, and social statuses. This is the case because game theory is flexible enough to capture explicitly how preferences are endogenously generated through social interactions (e.g., Holländer 1990). Because game theory enables us to capture how materialistic, social, and normative considerations influence behavior, it provides a framework that does not assume that a particular consideration predominates, but instead fosters looking at the factors determining the prominence of one consideration over another, and when and how such considerations can complement and substitute for each other.

Although game theory is a theory of equilibrium, it fosters the study of institutional dynamics when we appropriately differentiate between the object of study—institutions—and the analytical framework used to study it—game theory. The study of institutional dynamics in economics has gone through three phases, the most recent bringing it closer to beneficially interacting with the sociological study. Traditionally, economic institutions have been considered immutable cultural features of a society. In the 1970s, neoinstitutional economics challenged this view. Employing the tools of microeconomic theory and considering institutions as either rules, organizations, contractual forms, or patterns of behavior, it argued that institutions change in response to environmental changes. Property rights, organizations, and behavior, for example, would adjust to changes in relative prices in an optimal manner or in a way that best served those who dictate rules or choose organizations and behavior. More recently attention has been given to factors causing past institutions to influence the trajectory of institutional change and exhibit path-dependence. Using political economy and contractual frameworks, it has been argued that once a particular institution prevails, it tends to perpetuate in a changing environment because of such factors as sunk costs in specifying rules, interest groups that emerge in response to and have an interest in the maintenance of existing rules, and learning effects.

The game-theoretic perspective further enhanced our understanding and analysis of institutional path-dependence. Analytically examining institutions as self-enforcing—using the perspective of game-theoretic equilibria—highlights how particular beliefs and behavior can reproduce each other. As mentioned before, beliefs motivate behavior and observed behavior confirms the relevance of beliefs. Taken together, self-enforcing beliefs and behavior are in a steady-state equilibrium: The observed behavior causes each individual to believe that others will behave in a particular manner, and given these beliefs, it is optimal for each person to behave in the expected way. At the same time, by making explicit the parameter set under which this is the case, game theory highlights what and how exogenous change will terminate the processes through which an institution is reproduced. With an exogenous change to the parameters, the relevant rules of the game can cause the current behavior to no longer be self-enforcing.

In addition, however, the above perspective also highlighted how institutions can and do endogenously change. An institution reinforces itself when its implications, beyond behavior in the interaction it governs, (weakly) increase the range of situations (parameters) in which the behavior associated with the institution is self-enforcing.[11] Reinforcing processes can reflect, for example, individuals' intentional responses to the incentives the institution entails or the unintentional feedback from behavior to preference and habit formation, knowledge, information, demography, ideology, wealth distribution, political power, or social networks.

To illustrate the idea, consider the following example. Suppose that beliefs in collective punishment within a community lead to a particular regularity of behavior. To study this institution, we have to examine the community, beliefs, and behavioral rules as a self-enforcing system of institutional elements generating the behavior. We have to examine why each member of the community is endogenously motivated to retain membership in it, hold these beliefs, follow the behavioral rules, and participate in a collective punishment. But even if this is true at a particular point in time, the institution can still undermine itself. For example, the economic success of the community implied by the collective punishment may lead it to grow over time. Growth can undermine the self-enforceability of beliefs in collective punishment because information transmission within a larger group may be too slow to deter deviation. Similarly, each member of the community can become, over time, sufficiently wealthy that the threat of communal punishment will no longer be strong enough to make past patterns of behavior self-enforcing.

Self-reinforcing institutions influence their rates of change. Reinforcement implies that an institution is self-enforcing—and hence past behavior will prevail—in a larger parameter set. The institution is less likely to cease being self-enforcing following a given exogenous shock to this parameter set. Marginal environmental changes will not undermine past patterns of behavior. Indeed, behavior can prevail even in situations in which it would not have emerged to begin with.

The opposite is true, however, when negative self-reinforcement transpires. Then institutions are self-destructing or self-undermining: They foster processes that, over the long run, undermine the self-enforceability of the associated behavior. The institution is thus less likely to remain self-enforcing for a given exogenous parametric change and can even cease to be self-enforcing without any exogenous change.

Similarly, the concept of institutions, which emphasize the nature and distinct roles of institutional elements, provides the basis for studying how past institutions influence the direction of institutional change in a manner consistent with the sociological tradition. Even if a particular institution is no longer self-enforcing—its past institutional elements no longer generating a particular behavior—its constituting institutional elements still influence the direction of institutional change. Institutional elements inherited from the past, such as shared beliefs, communities, political and economic organizations, internalized norms, and cognitive systems embodied in rules transcend the situations that led to their emergence. They reflect and embody shared, common beliefs and knowledge among members of the society; they constitute mechanisms to coordinate their actions and expectations; and they embody in their utility functions a cognitive understanding of their social and physical environment. Institutional elements that were crystalized in the past constitute part of the historical heritage of a society. Past institutional elements provide the foundation for, and influence the processes leading to, new institutions (e.g., Greif 1994).

Hence, new institutions do not emerge reflecting only environmental conditions and the interests of relevant decision-makers. They evolve over time and their transactions occur in a spiral-like manner, building on existing institutional elements. For example, communities and political organizations that were formed in the past constitute part of the ("endogenous") rules of the game in new situations. Cultural beliefs that were crystalized in the past and are embodied within existing institutions are part of the initial conditions present in the process leading to one among the many alternative self-enforcing behavior and beliefs in new situations.

The inherently static framework provided by game theory thus fosters the study of institutional dynamics as an inherently historical process in which past institutions influence the rate and direction of institutional change. This requires, however, making the appropriate differentiation between the subject of study—institutions—and the analytical framework—game theory—used to study it. In empirically studying institutional dynamics we should and can benefit from going beyond imposing theoretical restrictions on the set of admissible institutions by using, for example, game theory. We should also impose restrictions based on our knowledge of past institutional elements; these elements are part of the initial conditions in the process of institutional change. Studying institutional dynamics, therefore, necessitates conducting an interactive, context-specific analysis that generates and evaluates theses by combining theoretical restrictions with those based on our knowledge of past institutions. In particular, we can use the knowledge of past institutional elements as input when constructing a game-theoretic model that facilitates examining the process of institutional change.

Past institutional elements direct but do not determine new institutions. If they do not become part of a new self-enforcing institution, they will decay over time and vanish. Institutions are outcomes emerging from within and interacting with the legacy of past institutional elements. For past institutional elements to persist, they have to become part of the new institutions. This is the case because environmental factors and functional considerations, such as simplicity, efficiency, and distribution, also direct institutional change. The extent of their influence, in turn, is not exogenous to existing institutions. Existing institutions determine the transaction costs involved when institutions change to accommodate such concerns.

The spiral-like evolution of institutions implies that they will form institutional complexes: sets of institutions governing various transactions that share institutional elements and are complementary to each other. The exact attributes of such complexes, in turn, also influence both the rate and direction of institutional change. They determine, for example, the speed and scope of institutional change when it occurs, whether or not the change will be continuous and encompass many institutions, and whether new institutions will be more or less likely to include past institutional elements. This implies the need to study a society's institutions from a holistic, systemic perspective. The book following this foreword conducts such an analysis with respect to the institutional complexes that constitute capitalist economies.

It is appropriate therefore to bring this long foreward to conclusion by commenting on the large extent to which economics and economic sociology seem to be poised for an extended dual journey along the path of institutional analysis. The attempt—motivated by and based on game theory—to study institutions while considering more behavior to be en-dogenous than before, suggests the merit of pursuing a socioeconomic perspective on institutions.[12] As is common in economics, it makes the causal relationships between the exogenous and endogenous features of the situation explicit. At the same time, it accommodates the four main distinctions between the (traditional) economic and the sociological views on institutions as summarized by Smelser and Swedberg (1994: 4–8) in the *Handbook of Economic Sociology*.

The socioeconomic perspective does not presuppose methodological in-dividualism (namely, that actors' preferences can always be studied as though they weren't influenced by the actions of others), that the allocation of re-sources reflects only "formal rationality," that social structures and meaning are not important in constraining behavior, or that the economy is not an in-tegral part of the society. As a matter of fact, the perspective adopted here—as is now so common in economics—accepts that preferences and rationality are socially constructed, that social structures and meaning are important, and that the economy is an integral part of the society.

It is not surprising then that the above discussion touches upon the main traditions of sociological institutionalism: the tradition associated with Durkheim, which focuses on socially constituted codes of conduct and beliefs; the tradition associated with Parsons, which focuses on nor-mative behavior; and that associated with Wrong, Granovetter, March, and Olsen, which focuses on social structures and relationships; and finally the cognitive tradition associated with the works of Weber, Berger, Luck-mann, Searle, Powell, and DiMaggio, which focuses on organizations, the cognitive foundations of behavior, and the social construction of reality.

The chapters in this book do not, by and large, explicitly draw on the game-theoretic analytical framework or its insights. Yet, it lends support to the overarching argument behind the book project: studying economic systems, and particularly the capitalist, more rational one, requires draw-ing on sociological lines of research, not as complements to the economic approaches for institutional analysis, but as an integral and indispensable part of the research agenda. The study of capitalism, its origin, nature, and variety is central to our understanding of why some economies are rich and others are poor. There is a need for a new and better way to study cap-italism, and this is what this book presents.

NOTES

1. North (e.g., 1990) has long advocated such a research agenda. For recent statements to this effect and contributions to the study of capitalist economies, see, for example, Greif 2000, Aoki 2001 (economics); Fligstein 2001 (sociology); and Hall and Soskice 2001 (political science).

2. For recent reviews and contributions, see Knack and Keefer 1995; Barro 1997; Hall and Jones 1999; Easterly 2002; Rodrik et al. 2002.

3. The term man-made here designates any or all members of the human race regardless of their gender, as in the principal sense of the word in Old English. See the *American Heritage Dictionary of the English Language*, 4th ed., 2000.

4. Rules, beliefs, and norms are more primitive institutional elements than organizations because organizations are also combined of rules, norms, and beliefs. Hence, whether it is appropriate to consider an organization as an institutional element in a particular analysis depends on its objective. While we focus on the institutional elements generating behavior in a particular "central transaction," we can take relevant organizations as institutional elements and examine their endogenous behavior and perpetration whenever needed. See further discussion below.

5. I use the term "motivation" rather than "enforcement," as is common in economics, because the latter term explicitly implies that action is induced only by the fear of punishment rather than, for example, by reward. Studying enforcement is therefore one aspect of studying motivation.

6. For notable exceptions and discussion, see, for example, Holländer 1990; Petersen 1994; Hechter and Kanazawa 1997; Macy and Boone 1999; Swedberg 2001.

7. For a review of topics and findings, see Greif 1997, 2004, and forthcoming. For a more technical presentation, but one that touches explicitly on capitalist economies, see Aoki 2001.

8. Because of multiple equilibria, however, such organizations are necessary but not sufficient for commitment.

9. Hence, rules enable individuals to choose behavior in complicated situations while devoting their limited cognitive resources to decision-making in non-institutionalized situations. Simon (1962: 88–89) has argued that habits similarly serve the function of directing attention to selected aspects of a situation.

10. For surveys, see Camerer 1997; Fehr and Fischbacher 2001; Greif forthcoming.

11. An institution that is self-enforcing and reinforcing is a self-reinforcing institution.

12. The particular interpretation of the still evolving approach presented here draws on Greif 1994, 1997, 1998, 2000, forthcoming. For related interpretations, see Shepsle 1992; Calvert 1995; Gibbons 2001; and Aoki 2001.

REFERENCES

Abercrombie, Nocholar, Stephen Hill, and Bryan S. Turner, eds. 1994. *Penguin Dictionary of Sociology*. 3rd ed. London: Penguin Books.

Aoki, Masahiko. 2001. *Toward a Comparative Institutional Analysis.* Cambridge, Mass.: MIT Press.

Barro, Robert J. 1997. *The Determinants of Economic Growth: A Cross-Country Empirical Study.* Cambridge: Cambridge University Press.

Berger, Peter L. 1977. *Invitation to Sociology.* Harmondsworth: Penguin Books.

Calvert, Randall L. 1995. "Rational Actors, Equilibrium, and Social Institutions." In *Explaining Social Institutions,* ed. Jack Knight and Itai Sened. Ann Arbor: University of Michigan Press. 57–93.

Camerer, Colin F. 1997. "Progress in Behavioral Game Theory." *Journal of Economic Perspectives* 11(4): 167–88.

Casella, Alessandra and James E. Rauch. 2002. "Anonymous Market and Group Ties in International Trade." *Journal of International Economics* 58(1): 19–47.

Coase, Ronald H. 1937. "The Nature of the Firm." *Economica* n.s. 4: 386–405.

D'Andrade, Roy G. 1984. "Cultural Meaning Systems." In *Culture Theory: Essays on Mind, Self, and Emotion,* eds. R. A. Shweder and R. LeVine. New York: Cambridge University Press. 88–122.

Denzau, Arthur T. and Douglass C. North. 1994. "Shared Mental Models: Ideologies and Institutions." *Kyklos* 47: 3–30.

Durkheim, Emile. [1895]1982. *The Rules of Sociological Method.* New York: Free Press.

Easterly, William. 2002. *The Elusive Quest for Growth: Economists' Adventures and Misadventures in the Tropics.* Cambridge, Mass.: MIT Press.

Elster, Jon. 1989. "Social Norms and Economic Theory." *Journal of Economic Perspectives* 3(4): 99–117.

Fehr, Ernst and Urs Fischbacher. 2001. "Why Social Preferences Matter—The Impact of Non-Selfish Motives on Competition, Cooperation, and Incentives." Working Paper 84, University of Zürich.

Fligstein, Neil. 2001. *The Architecture of Markets: An Economic Sociology of Twenty-First-Century Capitalist Societies.* Princeton: Princeton University Press.

Garfinkel, Harold. 1967. *Studies in Ethnomethodology.* Englewood Cliffs, N.J.: Prentice-Hall.

Gibbons, Robert. 2001. "Trust in Social Structures: Hobbes and Coase Meet Repeated Games." In *Trust in Society,* ed. Karen Cook. New York: Russell Sage.

Granovetter, Mark S. 1985. "Economic Action and Social Structure: The Problem of Embeddedness." *American Journal of Sociology* 91(3): 481–510.

Greif, Avner. 1989. "Reputation and Coalitions in Medieval Trade: Evidence on the Maghribi Traders." *Journal of Economic History* 49(4): 857–82.

———. 1994. "Cultural Beliefs and the Organization of Society: Historical and Theoretical Reflection on Collective and Individualist Societies." *Journal of Political Economy* 102(5)(October): 912–50.

———. 1997. "Microtheory and Recent Developments in the Study of Economic Institutions through Economic History." In *Advances in Economics and Econometrics,* ed. David M. Kreps and Kenneth F. Wallis. Cambridge: Cambridge University Press. Vol. 2, 79–113.

———. 1998. "Historical and Comparative Institutional Analysis." *American Economic Review* 2 (May): 80–84.

———. 2000. "The Fundamental Problem of Exchange: A Research Agenda in Historical Institutional Analysis." *Review of European Economic History* 4(3) (December): 251–84.

———. 2004. "The Emergence of Institutions Securing Property Rights." In *The Handbook of New Institutional Economics*, ed. Claude Ménard and Mary M. Shirley. Norwell, Mass.: Kluwer Academic.

———. Forthcoming. *Institutions: Theory and History: Comparative and Historical Institutional Analysis.* Cambridge: Cambridge University Press.

Greif, Avner and Eugene Kandel. 1995. "Contract Enforcement Institutions: Historical Perspective and Current Status in Russia." In *Economic Transition in Eastern Europe and Russia: Realities of Reform*, ed. Edward P. Lazear. Stanford: Hoover Institution Press. 291–321.

Hall, Peter A. and David Soskice, eds. 2001. *Varieties of Capitalism: The Institutional Foundations of Comparative Advantage.* Oxford: Oxford University Press.

Hall, Peter A. and Rosemary C. R. Taylor. 1996. "Political Science and the Three New Institutionalisms." *Political Studies* 44(5): 936–38.

Hall, Robert and Charles I. Jones. 1999. "Why Do Some Countries Produce So Much More Output per Worker Than Others?" *Quarterly Journal of Economics* 114: 83–116.

Hayek, Friedrich A. von. 1960. *The Constitution of Liberty.* Chicago: University of Chicago Press.

———. 1973. *Law, Legislation, and Liberty: A New Statement of the Liberal Principles of Justice and Economy.* Vol. 1, *Rules and Order.* Chicago: University of Chicago Press.

———. 1976. *Law, Legislation, and Liberty: A New Statement of the Liberal Principles of Justice and Economy.* Vol. 2, *The Mirage of Social Justice.* Chicago: University of Chicago Press.

Hechter, Michael and Satoshi Kanazawa, "Sociological Rational Choice Theory." *Annual Review of Sociology* 23: 191–214.

Hodgson, Geoffrey M. 1998. "The Approach of Institutional Economics." *Journal of Economic Literature* 36(1)(March): 166–92.

Holländer, Heinz. 1990. "A Social Exchange Approach to Voluntary Cooperation." *American Economic Review* 80(5) (December): 1157–67.

Knack, Stephen and Philip Keefer. 1995. "Institutions and Economic Performance: Cross-Country Tests Using Alternative Institutional Measures." *Economics and Politics* 7: 207–27.

Knight, Jack. 1992. *Institutions and Social Conflict.* Cambridge: Cambridge University Press.

Macy, Michael W. and R. Thomas Boone. 1999. "Unlocking the Doors to Prisoner's Dilemma: Dependence, Selectivity, and Cooperation." *Social Psychology Quarterly* 62: 32–52.

McMillan, John and Christopher Woodruff. 1999. "Interfirm Relationships and Informal Credit in Vietnam." *Quarterly Journal of Economics* 114(4): 1285–1320.

Nelson, Richard R. 1994. "The Co-evolution of Technology, Industrial Structure, and Supporting Institutions." *Industrial and Corporate Change* 3: 47–63.

North, Douglass C. 1990. *Institutions, Institutional Change and Economic Performance*. Cambridge: Cambridge University Press.

———. 1991. "Institutions." *Journal of Economic Perspectives* 5(1) (Winter): 97–112.

North, Douglass C. and Robert P. Thomas. 1973. *The Rise of the Western World*. Cambridge: Cambridge University Press.

Ostrom, Elinor. 1990. *Governing the Commons: The Evolution of Institutions for Collective Action*. Cambridge: Cambridge University Press.

Parsons, Talcott. 1951. *The Social System*. London: Routledge and Kegan Paul.

Peterson, Trond. 1994. "On the Promise of Game Theory in Sociology." *Contemporary Sociology* 23(4): 498–502.

Platteau, Jean-Philippe. 1994. "Behind the Market Stage Where Real Societies Exist. Part II: The Role of Moral Norms." *Journal of Development Studies* 30(3)(July): 753–817.

Powell, Walter W. and Paul J. DiMaggio, eds. 1991. *The New Institutionalism in Organizational Analysis*. Chicago: University of Chicago Press.

Rauch, James E. 2001. "Business and Social Networks in International Trade." *Journal of Economic Literature* 39(December): 1177–1203.

Rodrik, Dani, Arvind Subramanian, and Francesco Trebbi. "Institutions Rule: The Primacy of Institutions over Geography and Integration in Economic Development." Working paper, JFK School of Development, Harvard University.

Schotter, Andrew. 1981. *The Economic Theory of Social Institutions*. Cambridge: Cambridge University Press.

Scott, W. Richard. 1995. *Institutions and Organizations*. Thousand Oaks, Calif.: Sage.

———. 1998. *Organizations: Rational, Natural, and Open Systems*. Upper Saddle River, N.J.: Prentice-Hall.

Scott, W. Richard, John W. Meyer, and Associates. 1994. *Institutional Environments and Organizations: Structural Complexity and Individualism*. London: Sage.

Searle, John R. 1995. *The Construction of Social Reality*. New York: Free Press.

Shepsle, Kenneth A. 1992. "Institutional Equilibrium and Equilibrium Institutions." In *Political Science: The Science of Politics*, ed. Herbert F. Weisberg. Cambridge: Cambridge University Press.

Simon, Herbert A. 1976. *Administrative Behavior*. 3rd ed. New York: Macmillan.

Smelser, Neil J. and Richard Swedberg. 1994. "The Sociological Perspective on the Economy." In *The Handbook of Economic Sociology*, ed. Neil J. Smelser and Richard Swedberg. Princeton: Princeton University Press. 3–26.

Swedberg, Richard. 2001. "Sociology and Game Theory: Contemporary and Historical Perspectives." *Theory and Society* 30(3): 301–35.

Thelen, Kathleen. 1999. "Historical Institutionalism in Comparative Politics." *Annual Review of Political Science* 2: 369–404.

Ullmann-Margalit, Edna. 1977. *The Emergence of Norms*. Oxford: Clarendon Press.

Weber, Max. [1904–1905]1958. *The Protestant Ethic and the Spirit of Capitalism*. New York: Scribner's.

———. 1949. *The Methodology of the Social Sciences*. Glencoe, Ill.: Free Press.

Weisberg, Herbert F., ed. 1992. *Political Science: The Science of Politics*. Cambridge: Cambridge University Press.

Weingast, Barry R. 1996. "Political Institutions: Rational Choice Perspectives." In *A New Handbook of Political Science*, ed. Robert Goodin and Hans-Dieter Klingemann. Oxford: Oxford University Press.

Williamson, Oliver E. 1985. *The Economic Institutions of Capitalism*. New York: Free Press.

———. 1998. "Transactional Cost Economics: How It Works: Where It Is Headed." *Economist* 146(1): 23–58.

———. 2000. "The New Institutional Economics: Taking Stock, Looking Ahead." *Journal of Economic Literature* 38(September): 595–613.

Wrong, Dennis H. 1961. "The Oversocialized Conception of Man in Modern Sociology." *American Sociological Review* 26(2) (April): 183–93. Reprinted as chapter 2 in Wrong 1999.

———. 1999. *The Oversocialized Conception of Man*. New Brunswick, N.J.: Transaction Publishers.

Young, H. Peyton. 1998. *Individual Strategy and Social Structure*. Princeton: Princeton University Press.

ACKNOWLEDGMENTS

IN PRODUCING THIS BOOK we have accumulated many debts. We are first of all grateful to Cornell University for so generously supporting and funding the Center for the Study of Economy and Society. The Center sponsored the initial conference, at which most of the chapters in this volume were presented for the first time. We also would like to celebrate this volume as the first of a series of works that our Center will produce. Finally, we are also enormously grateful for the work by the Executive Administrator of the Center, Diane E. Masters. It is no exaggeration to say that without her skill, energy, and professionalism, this book would not have materialized.

Victor Nee and Richard Swedberg

DURING THE LAST DECADES of the twentieth century, capitalism expanded its global scope and dominance over economic activity. The diffusion of its economic institutions accelerated following the collapse of central planning as an institutional model. New markets, investment opportunities, and production sites contributed to fueling an exceptionally long period of sustained economic growth. Freed from the constraints of Cold War competition with state socialism, global capitalism has entered a new millennium, yet paradoxically in this new era of unfettered capitalism it has confronted what appears to be the most challenges to the world economy since the Great Depression of the 1930s. The early stages of a global economic downturn are manifest in numerous interrelated events: the largest asset bubble crashes in financial history, scandals, global overcapacity in manufacture, competitive currency devaluation, disaffection with market ideology and institutions (especially evident in Latin America), and the fear of a descent into deflation with its attendant high unemployment, protracted contraction of economic activity, and high social costs. In the past the economic institutions of capitalism revealed their interconnectedness most clearly during periods of rapid expansion followed by cyclical downturns. Presently, the inner workings of modern capitalism as an institutional order seem once again to demand analysis and reformulation of past theories. This book seeks to stimulate interest in the comparative institutional analysis of capitalism.

It is imperative, we think, to advance social science understanding of the distinctive features and dynamics of capitalist economic institutions. As a discipline founded on the comparative study of institutions, sociology is well positioned to contribute to this effort. The greatest advances in understanding the underlying organization and dynamics of modern society came during the classical era when the discipline's founders studied the emergent institutional order of capitalism (Swedberg 1998, 2003a). Since the classical era, sociologists have tended simply to assume the existence of institutions in their studies of economic life, in part because the institutional framework of capitalism congealed following World War II in a stable equilibrium. It was possible to study the underlying constitution of economy and society without explaining the origin and development of its institutional order (Parsons and Smelser 1956).

Within this stable equilibrium, economic sociology pioneered the study of how social networks structured economic life (White 1970; Granovetter 1974; Burt 1982; Baker 1984). Network analysis of economic life generally focused at the meso-level where personal connections serve as ties cementing trust, channeling information and sponsoring economic transactions. In his seminal essay, Granovetter (1985) identifying this network embeddedness as the New Economic Sociology, criticized the new institutional economics for its functionalism in viewing institutions as efficient solutions to the problem of trust. His decision to focus the causal analysis of economic action on the role of social networks was in part motivated by an interest in distancing economic sociology from that functionalism, especially evident in Oliver Williamson's (1975) transaction cost economics. However, this gave rise to a singular focus on proximate causes, while overlooking the deeper distal causes that are located in large institutional structures.

The eclipse in analytical interest in the classical themes of comparative institutional analysis pioneered by Max Weber and Karl Polanyi, who coined the concept of embeddedness, limited the New Economic Sociology largely to descriptive studies of economic life. The problem with focusing solely on specifying proximate causes stems from overlooking the deeper underlying causes of institutional change (Miller 1987). As an approach to the study of economic life, Granovetter's network embeddedness could not escape the limitations of causal indeterminacy evident in the difficulty in determining ex ante the effect of personal ties on economic action. Granovetter acknowledges the problem in his discussion of embezzlement, which can only be accomplished by trusted agents. An economic sociology of capitalism needs to move decisively beyond the network embeddedness approach, incorporating the focus on social networks into an explanatory framework that takes into account the deeper distal causes of institutional change, which are located in the larger social structures of the core economic institutions governing economic life (Nee and Ingram 1998; Nee 2005).

Like the New Economic Sociology, sociological studies of organizations also assumed the underlying institutional framework of modern capitalism in analyzing the effect of the institutional environment on the behavior of organizations. John Meyer and Brian Rowan (1977) argued persuasively that organizations are actors driven by the need to secure legitimacy through conformity to myths and rituals of the institutional environment or sometimes through efforts to decouple from them as a means to accomplish tangible objectives. Their theory assumed the modern myths and rituals and focused attention on institutional effects in shaping the behavior of organizations. Similarly, in addressing the question as to why there is so much homogeneity in organizational forms and practices, Paul

DiMaggio and Walter Powell (1983) extended organizational theory to elaborate the deeper distal mechanisms of isomorphism in organizational fields. Importantly, their extension of neoinstitutional organizational theory specified the causal mechanisms implicit in Meyer and Rowan in their analysis of isomorphism, which they attributed to state regulation, mimicking behavior among firms, and normative pressures stemming from professionalism. Although their essay represented a significant theoretical advance in neoinstitutional organizational sociology, as with the Stanford school, they assumed the institutional framework of advanced capitalism and instead focused analytic attention on specifying the effects of the institutional environment under equilibrium conditions.

Although much progress has been made by economic sociology and organizational theory, we contend that important new advances will come from the renewal of the study of institutions and institutional change. Rather than assuming that institutions are important, economic sociologists need to explain how and why institutions provide a framework or arrangements that facilitate economic action and specify the mechanisms that account for continuity and discontinuity in institutional structures.

This task entails directing attention to the comparative analysis of the political and economic institutions that provide the foundation and scaffolding for modern capitalism. Polanyi's economic sociology highlighted two central pillars of the institutional foundations of modern capitalism, the centralized state—especially its legal and regulatory systems—and the market as an institution of exchange ([1944] 1957). These two institutions are interconnected with all the other key institutions of capitalism, playing a crucial role in determining the structure of property rights, the quality of financial institutions—banks and capital markets, and the incentives for capital accumulation, investments and entrepreneurship. An economic sociology of capitalism needs to endogenize the state and market by examining the concrete interconnections between political and economic actors and the manner in which, actors compete and cooperate to shape the structure of property rights, influence the workings of financial institutions, and give form to incentives for investment and entrepreneurship through the tax laws, interest rates, and other regulatory mechanisms governing economic activity. An economic sociology of capitalism also needs to direct attention to endogenizing institutional change as a process that is not simply reducible to changing relative prices, but fundamentally rooted in the organizational dynamics of firms and in opposition norms mobilized by networks and social movements (see Nee, this volume).

The contemporary era of global capitalism is characterized by far-reaching institutional change, not only in the former state socialist societies, now undergoing transitions to market economies, but in the advanced societies of capitalism where assumptions about the role of the welfare state and the constitution of society are being challenged by ongoing societal transformations stemming from globalization. Economic sociology, with its tradition of theory-driven empirical research, is well positioned to advance understanding of the economic institutions of modern capitalism. Toward this objective, we suggest that much can be gained not only through debate, but more importantly through productive exchange of ideas and research findings between economics and sociology. Advances in the economic sociology of capitalism, we think, will necessarily entail work contributed by these two disciplines. Although the starting assumptions of sociology and economics differ, this book aims to demonstrate the utility of moving beyond a debate over first principles between economic sociology and economics to join in the cross-disciplinary effort to advance social science understanding of institutions and institutional change.

For an economic sociology of capitalism to make advances in explaining the role of institutions and institutional change, it is important, we think, to have a definition of institutions appropriate for analysis from the sociological perspective, which emphasizes the causal effect of social structures. Institutions are not disembodied rules that specify the incentive structure of social action, as in the new institutional economics approach; fundamentally they involve actors, whether as individuals or organizations, who pursue real interests in concrete institutional structures. The utility of a realist definition of institutions is readily evident in the recent corporate scandals in the United States wherein corporations are revealed as institutional arrangements where powerful men and women both conform and bend the rules in their strivings to secure tangible interests (Swedberg 2003b). Hence, we define institutions as a web of interrelated informal and formal norms governing social relationships within which actors pursue and fix the limits of legitimate interests. In this view, institutions are not just humanly devised constraints but social structures that provide a framework and conduit for collective action by shaping the interests of actors and specifying and enforcing the principal agent relationship. It follows from our definition that institutional change entails not simply altering the formal rules, but the fundamentally realignment of interests and power through contentious politics, social movements, and warfare.

We think this conception of institutions and institutional change provides analytic leverage in understanding large-scale institutional change—for instance, the transition from state socialism, whether in the former Soviet Union or China. Institutional economists generally view institutions as rules of the game which structure the incentives for economic actors. When western economists traveled to Eastern Europe and the former Soviet Union to advise reformers at the onset of market reforms, their advice consistently emphasized big bang approaches to instituting capitalism by designing sweeping changes in the formal rules governing property rights, capital, and labor markets. Such efforts at capitalism by design usually led to ineffectual, if not counter-productive, outcomes because the emphasis on writing and legislating new rules of economic action overlooked the realities of power and interests vested in institutional arrangements. By contrast, the trial-and-error approach taken by reformers in China has allowed for a more evolutionary approach to economic transition. The insight we infer from China's approach to market transition is that institutional change was driven not so much by change in the formal rules as by bottom-up realignment of interests and power as new organizational forms, private property rights, and new market institutions evolved in an economy shifting away from state control over economic activity (Nee 1992). In China, changes in the formal rules governing the emerging market economy tended to follow ex post changes in the informal business practices, and were therefore more in keeping with the real interests of economic actors and politicians. As in the former Soviet Union, however, efforts to reform state-owned enterprises through formal rule changes in China proved largely ineffectual, as Victor Nee's chapter details, because, in part, ex ante changes in formal rules often ran counter to the vested interests and power of the communist party organization entrenched in state owned firms.

In his foreword to this volume, Avner Greif outlines a framework for promoting intellectual trade between economics and sociology, identifying substantive problems that provide a basis for fruitful intellectual exchange and highlighting the use of game theory in comparative institutional analysis. The chapters in the book are organized around three broad themes. Part I brings together chapters that address core issues and problems in the new study of capitalism. Part II assembles a series of chapters on a variety of topics focusing on American capitalism, the leading capitalist economy of the world. Part III focuses attention on the question of convergence stemming from the global transformation of capitalism and the challenge of explaining institutional change. The chapters need not be read in sequence; readers may choose a sequencing that conforms to their own interests. The individual contributions do not attempt to provide a unified approach to the economic institutions of capitalism. Instead, the aim is to bring together contributions by leading scholars in economic sociology who represent current approaches and research programs that reflect the new interest in the study of capitalism as an ensemble of interconnected economic and political institutions. Our purpose in assembling these chapters is to bring together the elements of theory and lines of empirical research that we think comprise the basis for the next stage in the development of economic sociology. They point to the outlines of a new institutionalism in economic sociology which we will elaborate further in subsequent publications.

The theme of intellectual exchange between economics and sociology is picked up by Richard Swedberg in his essay outlining an agenda for economic sociology in the study of capitalist institutions. Swedberg emphasizes that economic sociology needs to draw on a mix of ideas from economics and sociology in broadening its focus to study modern capitalism as an institutional framework in which exchange (the market) and the feedback loop of profits into production operate as the principal mechanisms in the organization of the economy. He emphasizes the importance of understanding the interconnectedness of economic institutions and suggests a conception of institutions as embodiment of concrete interests and social relations, which he argues should replace the definition of institutions as a system of incentives used by Douglass North. Nevertheless, institutions conceived as congealed interests and as a system of incentives are broadly speaking complementary, since both features of institutional structures can account for why institutions matter in shaping economic action.

The second chapter of Part I is an essay by Douglass North, the Nobel laureate in economics whose work integrated classical themes in sociology with transaction costs economics to explain economic performance. The main issue that North addresses in his essay is what accounts for dynamic economic growth; why do some countries advance quickly, while others fall behind? To the answer that North has supplied in earlier writings—that the key is to be found in an institutional structure that has the kind of incentives that lead to increases in productivity—he now also adds that is of a cognitive sort. This is that once the human mind has settled for one type of evidence, it will have difficulty in switching over to another type of evidence, even if the latter is superior, as exemplified by the difficult transition from personal to impersonal exchange. North also discusses William Baumol's ideas about modern capitalism as an innovation machine, and he especially applauds Baumol's critique of modern growth theory for completely ignoring institutions.

North's theory of institutional change elaborated in his seminal *Structure and Change in Economic History* (1981) arguably is the centerpiece of the New Institutional Economics. It provides a parsimonious and elegant explanation that specifies two clusters of causal mechanisms, the state and market. However, North's theory of institutional change has not fared well in explaining the large-scale institutional transformations stemming from the transitions from state socialism. Victor Nee argues in his own chapter that the problem stems from North's assumption that organizational actors respond unproblematically to market incentives. A more adequate explanatory account of institutional change, Nee suggests, must take into account a different conception of organizational dynamics, one based on sociological understanding of the structural inertia of organizations and oppositional norms in networks arising from responses to rapid changes in the institutional environment. His analysis of the limits of North's theory of institutional change is grounded in an examination of recent efforts to institute state capitalism in China, which, through the Company Law enacted in 1994, changed the structure of property rights for state-owned firms in the image of Western corporate governance. Nee extends insights integrating economic sociology and organizational ecology to argue that it is not the existing stock of organizations but new organizations and new organizational forms that adapt most readily to rapid changes in the institutional environment.

The revitalization of institutionalist thinking in economics has had a growing influence on development economics, especially evident in the World Bank, where North's theory has become the mainstream approach to development. Peter Evans engages what he identifies as the "institutional turn" in the economic analysis of development by asking what sociological new institutionalism can offer to help resolve limitations in the economic theory of development. Evans argues that the problem with mainline economics was capital fundamentalism, the theory that by increasing savings and opening capital markets to attract foreign investments, poor countries can catch up with the developed economies. The problem is that capital fundamentalism didn't work when applied to development policy. Nor did its replacement, the new growth theory, which emphasized the role of technology and human capital. According to Evans, the institutional turn in development economics came in reaction to the realization that mainline development economics was unable to generate effective policies for poor countries.

Francis Fukuyama observes that Max Weber was wrong in his pessimistic expectation that capitalist development would result in humanity being locked in an "iron cage" of centralized bureaucracy. He also criticizes the neoclassical economic assumption of rational optimization, which he argues cannot account for central elements of modern postindustrial capitalism. Fukuyama acknowledges that the iterated prisoner dilemma games in rational choice theory provide a persuasive account of norms of reciprocity based on strategic interactions, but the cooperation and trust upon which much of modern institutional life is built have nonrational origins in religion, tradition and history. Fukuyama concludes that an adequate explanation of the institutional order of modern capitalism is outside the scope of neoclassical economics and is only accessible through an economic sociology.

In Part II we include chapters that provide analytic descriptions of some of the main economic institutions of contemporary American capitalism. One of the most important of these is clearly the state, and we therefore begin with a chapter by Neil Fligstein that addresses this very issue. Even when we look at the most "pure" of market phenomena, he argues, we will find that the state plays a crucial role. This thesis is illustrated by two examples: the emergence of the "shareholder value" conception of the firm and the creation of Silicon Valley. No modern market can exist without the state, Fligstein concludes.

The global dominance of the modern American corporation to no small degree stems from its superior ability to build formal organizations well adapted to the needs of a high technology economy (Fukuyama 1999). Not surprisingly, organizational sociologists have been important contributors to the economic sociology of advanced capitalism. John Freeman provides an analytic description of venture capital as an economic institution that has played a central role in generating the dynamic growth of new industries arising from the application of science and technology, especially in the U.S. Venture capitalists direct capital to start-up firms and industries through sponsoring and managing entrepreneurship. As Freeman points out, a distinctive feature of modern American capitalism is that new firms are built to be sold for profit. Because a characteristic feature of modern capitalism is the speed with which new firms and industries are formed, the venture capital firm, argues Freeman, is important for understanding the workings of American capitalism. Drawing on his research on venture capitalism in California's Silicon Valley, he describes how the venture capital firm works in managing the risk of investing capital in new firms, its interconnectedness with tax law and other financial institutions, its history as an organizational form, its internal organization, and the central role venture capitalists play in modern capitalist entrepreneurship.

James Baron and Michael Hannan report findings from the Stanford Project on Emerging Companies (SPEC) where they interviewed founders and executives of 200 technology start-ups, just the type of firms that venture capitalists help to launch by providing them with capital and initial guidance in developing and implementing business plans. Baron and Hannan formulate a typology of organizational models based on classifying the forms they undercover through their field research. Rather than homogeneity stemming from uniform cultural templates, as predicted by DiMaggio and Powell (1983), they found remarkable diversity in organizational models and practices. Moreover, founding organizational blueprints tend to sustain enduring patterns of reliability and accountability in organizational behavior.

A key economic institution of American capitalism is unquestionably the Federal Reserve, which has charge of overseeing monetary policy through its control over money supply and discount rates charged to banks. In the past, Federal Open Market Committee (FOMC) meetings of the Federal Reserve Bank's governors were cloaked in secrecy. But recently the transcripts of past meetings have been opened to public access by the Freedom of Information Act. Mitchel Abolafia's chapter analyzes the FOMC transcripts for meetings held between 1982 and 1992. The result is a remarkably rich and detailed account of the deliberation of the Federal Reserve governors as they sought to make sense of the economic data considered in shaping monetary policy. Elaborating a process of deliberation and debate that conforms surprisingly well to the conception outlined by Mary Douglas in her influential book, *How Institutions Think* (1986), Abolafia depicts the Federal Reserve's ad hoc theorizing and the political and economic considerations that shape the signals it sends to economic actors about changes in monetary policy. He shows how institutional categories frame the discussion and debate of Committee members, how a shifting mix of preferences are negotiated in the course of meetings on monetary policy, and how the twelve Committee members, following stylized rituals of turn-taking, try collectively to make sense of diverse streams of economic data and practical, administrative, and political considerations. Abolafia confirms that the Federal Reserve strategically frames the signals it issues to the public in terms of their likely influence—intended and unintended—on market psychology.

Two chapters in Part II add to the economic sociology of the Internet, arguably the most important application of knowledge technologies in American capitalism, which has extended its dominance of the global economy by greatly expanding the boundaries of markets, accelerating a global division of labor, and enabling instantaneous worldwide diffusion of information. Paul DiMaggio and Joseph Cohen argue that economic sociology needs to pay attention to goods that have what the economists call "network externalities,"—their value to a user depends on how many other users there are. The more of your friends have e-mail, for example, the more important it is for you to have it as well. In using the concept of network externalities in economic sociology, however, it is imperative to add a sociological dimension, since the diffusion of a technology, such as the Internet, depends on the social structure of the users. DiMaggio and Cohen's analysis is capped off by a comparative analysis of the early diffusion of the television (1948–57) with that of the Internet (1994–2002). Ko Kuwabara aptly analyzes data from eBay, the largest on-line auction site, and shows how the impersonality of the electronic marketplace gives rise to the institutional design of feedback provisions which aim to manufacture on-line the informal basis of trust, personal reputation, and emotions found traditionally in transactions in local markets. While the technology that is being used is hypermodern, the institutional structure of eBay consequently consists of elements that are part of most markets.

An argument for the need to incorporate sentiments into the economic analysis and to show that these are by no means antagonistic to it can also be found in Viviana Zelizer's chapter. In contrast to the earlier chapter on eBay, she chooses her examples from sectors at the margins of the modern capitalist economy: those parts of the economy where local currencies are being used and where care is being dispensed. We also signal the presence of an evocative concept in Zelizer's analysis: that or circuits or the interactional patterns that currencies of different kinds tend to create when they are being used.

Part III includes chapters on globalization and the challenge of explaining institutional change. The forces of globalization—manifest in rapid changes in the sites of production, turnover in dominant technologies, flow of investment capital, and high volume international migration to advanced capitalist societies—have ushered in a new era in the development of the world capitalist economy. AnnaLee Saxenian's study documents the way in which the global diffusion of high technology has evolved through transnational networks of immigrant entrepreneurs and engineers who integrate firms in California's Silicon Valley with specialized high technology production sites in Taiwan and China, bringing their experience and knowledge to their home country. Rather than compete directly with Silicon Valley firms, these immigrant entrepreneurs and engineers deftly construct specialized niches that complement the U.S. high technology industry. In doing so, Taiwan and now China acquire the capacity for autonomous technical development within their specialized niches by building on the information technologies and organizational blueprints developed by American firms.

Advances in information technology have facilitated the globalization of production in virtually all industrial sectors that gain comparative advantages from cheaper skilled and unskilled labor. This driving mechanism of the global diffusion of modern capitalism has been accompanied by the international integration of financial markets through lowering the barriers to the free movement of investment capital and the increase in foreign firms listed on stock exchanges in the U.S. Gerald Davis and Christopher Marquis examine the validity of arguments proffered by economists that U.S. financial markets operate as wheels of change advancing the global diffusion of the American model of shareholder capitalism. Specifically, Davis and Marquis ask whether foreign firms listed on the New York Stock Exchange and Nasdaq show a tendency to adopt the American model of corporate governance. Their findings generally support the view of organizational and institutional structures as much more resistant to changes leading to adoption of the American model of shareholder capitalism, even in the face of positive market incentives to do so and regulatory pressures that ought to induce isomorphism with American corporate governance. Thus, neither the arguments of economists nor neoinstitutional organizational sociologists about market incentive and isomorphism are supported by analysis of the governance structures of foreign listed firms. Instead their findings are broadly complementary to those reported by

Nee, Baron, and Hannan, confirming the structural inertia of organizations and institutional structures. These findings are not inconsistent with Saxenian's account of the diffusion of high technology production, since the processes she analyzes entail the establishment of new organizational forms by immigrant entrepreneurs rather than the adaptation of the existing stock of firms to Silicon Valley's organizational blueprints and technologies.

John Campbell's chapter focuses on a central economic institution of capitalism, taxation, and asks whether global market forces are inducing convergence in national tax policy. He takes issue with globalization theorists who argue that global market forces induce national states to reduce their marginal tax rate in order to compete better with other states for investment capital and trade. His analysis of tax regimes in the advanced capitalist economies does not confirm the globalization argument. Instead, he shows that national tax regimes have been resistant to change and are not on the path of convergence. As with the other chapters in this volume that analyze institutional change, Campbell argues that institutional structures do not adapt readily to changing relative prices in the world economy, as North's theory suggests. Rather, like organizations, institutional structures are a product of national politics and local business interests. Once in place, they tend to be inert.

An important dilemma facing both economic and sociological institutional approaches has been the problem of deriving causal inferences from the comparative analysis of institutions and institutional change. This is the problem that Mary Brinton's analysis of the school-to-work institutional arrangement in Japan focuses on. She shows that analysts commonly have attributed Japan's sustained economic growth in the post–World War II period to its distinctive institutional structures, from the Japanese keiretsu-based corporate structures to the widespread reliance on networks. Now that Japan's economy has endured more than a decade of deflation and stagnation, the question Brinton asks is "What are the exogenous and endogenous forces that are giving rise to pressures for institutional change?" This question, she contends, should lead analysts away from the easy assumption of cause-effect implicit in the functionalist view of institutions.

By way of summarizing our argument in this introduction, we would like to emphasize again that it is our belief that economic sociologists can add to the analysis of contemporary capitalism in a number of substantial ways. Over the last two decades economic sociologists have developed a series of concepts and approaches that have proven very helpful in analyzing a number of middle-range economic phenomena. Many of these, we argue, can just as well be used to illuminate various aspects of a macro-phenomenon such as capitalism.

That the concept of institution will have to stand at the center of this type of enterprise is obvious—but also that efforts have to be made to create a much more powerful and hard hitting concept of institution than the ones that are currently in use, be it in economics or in sociology. Sociologists, in all brevity, may need to abandon their exclusive concern with social relations and make much more room for interests in their analyses. And economists may need to introduce social relations into their analyses in a much more solid and organic manner than they currently do. What is at stake today, in the analysis of capitalism, is to develop an approach that is centered around the following two aspects of modern society: the role that is being played by profit-making interests, and the web of social structures that is being created and used in attempts to realize these interests.

REFERENCES

Baker, Wayne E. 1984. "The Social Structure of a National Securities Market." *American Journal of Sociology* 89: 775–811.

Burt, Ronald S. 1982. *Toward a Structural Theory of Action: Network Models of Social Structure.* New York: Academic Press.

DiMaggio, Paul and Walter W. Powell. 1983. "The Iron Cage Revisited: Institutional Isomorphism and Collective Rationality in Organizational Fields." *American Sociological Review* 48: 147–60.

Douglas, Mary. 1986. *How Institutions Think.* Syracuse: Syracuse University Press.

Fukuyama, Francis. 1999. *The Great Disruption: Human Nature and the Reconstruction of Social Order.* New York: Free Press.

Granovetter, Mark S. 1974. *Getting a Job: A Study of Contacts and Careers.* Cambridge, Mass.: Harvard University Press.

———. 1985. "Economic Action and Social Structure: The Problem of Embeddedness." *American Journal of Sociology* 91(3): 481–510.

Miller, Richard W. 1987. *Fact and Method: Explanation, Confirmation, and Reality in the Natural and the Social Sciences.* Princeton: Princeton University Press.

Merton, Robert K. [1949]1968. *Social Theory and Social Structure.* New York: Free Press.

Meyer, John W. and Brian Rowan. 1977. "Institutionalized Organizations: Formal Structure as Myth and Ceremony." *American Journal of Sociology* 83: 340–63.

Nee, Victor. 1992. "The Organizational Dynamics of Market Transition: Hybrid Forms, Property Rights, and Mixed Economy in China." *Administrative Science Quarterly* 37(1): 1–27.

———. 1998. "Sources of the New Institutionalism." In *The New Institutionalism in Sociology,* ed. Mary C. Brinton and Victor Nee. New York: Russell Sage. 1–16.

———. 2005. "The New Institutionalisms in Economics and Sociology." In *The Handbook of Economic Sociology,* ed. Neil J. Smelser and Richard Swedberg. 2nd ed. Princeton: Princeton University Press. 49–74.

North, Douglass C. 1981. *Structure and Change in Economic History.* New York: W.W. Norton.

Parsons, Talcott and Neil Smelser. 1956. *Economy and Society: A Study in the Integration of Economic and Social Theory.* Glencoe, Ill.: Free Press.

Polanyi, Karl. [1944]1957. *The Great Transformation: The Political and Economic Origins of Our Time.* Boston: Beacon Press.

Swedberg, Richard. 1998. *Max Weber and the Idea of Economic Sociology.* Princeton: Princeton University Press.

———. 2003a. *Principles of Economic Sociology.* Princeton: Princeton University Press.

———. 2003b. "A Nation of Shareholders: Conflicts of Interest and the Corporate Scandals of 2001–2002." Paper presented at CSES Inaugural Symposium, Center for the Study of Economics and Society, Cornell University, February 19.

White, Harrison C. 1970. *Chains of Opportunity: System Models of Mobility in Organizations.* Cambridge, Mass.: Harvard University Press.

Williamson, Oliver E. 1975. *Markets and Hierarchies: Analysis and Antitrust Implications.* New York: Free Press.

PART 1

The New Study of Capitalism

The Economic Sociology of Capitalism: An Introduction and Agenda

Richard Swedberg

CAPITALISM IS THE dominant economic system in today's world, and there appear to be few alternatives in sight. Socialism, its main competitor, has been weakened immeasurably by the collapse of the Soviet Union. Where socialism still prevails, such as in the People's Republic of China, serious attempts are made to turn the whole economic system in a capitalist direction so that it will operate in a more efficient manner. "It doesn't matter if the cat is white or black as long as it catches mice," to cite a famous line by Deng Xiaping (e.g., Becker 2000: 52–53).

While the superiority of capitalism as an economic system and growth machine has fascinated economists for centuries, this has not been the case with sociologists. For sociologists capitalism has mainly been of interest for its *social* effects—how it has led to class struggle, anomie, inequality, and social problems more generally. Capitalism as an economic system in its own right and as a generator of wealth has been of considerably less interest. Some of this reaction has probably to do with the unfortunate division of labor that developed between economists and sociologists in the nineteenth century: economists studied the economy, and sociologists society minus the economy. In this respect, as in so many others, sociology has essentially been a "left-over science" (Wirth 1948).

This division of labor between economists and sociologists, however, has not gone unchallenged. In the 1980s sociologists, especially in the United States, turned their attention to the study of the economy itself, asking questions such as the following: Where do markets come from? How is economic action embedded in social relations? What role do norms and trust play in the economy? (e.g., White 1981; Stinchcombe 1983; Coleman 1985; Granovetter 1985).

That this set of questions heralded something new soon became clear. A huge amount of research—known as "New Economic Sociology"—soon came into being. By the mid-1990s enough work had been done to put together a handbook in economic sociology, with chapters on such topics as "business groups," "a rational choice perspective on economic sociology" and "networks and economic life" (Granovetter 1994; Coleman 1994;

Powell and Smith-Doerr 1994). This trend has continued very strongly, and as of today economic sociology represents one of the strongholds of American sociology.

In all of these writings by sociologists on the economy, the emphasis has primarily been on middle-range phenomena, and few efforts have been made to analyze capitalism. Why this is the case is difficult to say. One answer might be that capitalism is taken for granted, and this would seem to be especially true for the business schools, where a number of important economic sociologists are currently to be found. Another may be that new economic sociologists (with a few exceptions) do not seem to have been very interested in politics—and the concept of capitalism is by tradition among sociologists associated with a political critique of capitalism. The contributions to the study of capitalism that one can find in Marxist sociology have, for example, not been much explored by contemporary economic sociologists.[1]

If we now turn to the economists, these used to stay away from analyses of capitalism as an economic system and instead focus on the workings of the price system and show how this led to an efficient allocation of resources. The word "capitalism" was rarely used by economists during the twentieth century until they suddenly embraced it (e.g., Sombart 1930; Block 2000). Since this time, however, the economists have made quick strides forward. As a result, the leading academic scholars on the subject of capitalism are no longer sociologists but economists—from Friedrich Hayek and Milton Friedman, who started the trend, to Douglass North, Oliver Williamson, and others who have continued it.

In this opening chapter an effort will be made to present an agenda for a sociological study of capitalism. There are two reasons why this type of study may be called *an economic sociology of capitalism*. First, the main emphasis is not on the social effects of capitalism, but on capitalism as an economic system in its own right—on the firms, the banks, the markets, and the other economic institutions that make up the core of the economy. This is where the "economic" in "economic sociology" comes in. Second, whereas we already have several economic theories of capitalism, we need one which sufficiently takes the social dimension of the capitalist machinery into account—and this is where the "sociology" in "economic sociology" comes in.

A study of capitalism as an economic system should consist of two parts. First of all, studies of individual, middle-range phenomena need to be made. Indeed, this constitutes by far the most important task of an economic sociology of capitalism and cannot be replaced by macro-level studies of capitalism. But while studies of capitalism itself should not predominate, they do have their own distinct raison d'être. One of these is that studies of this type outline the basic connections between the different parts of the economy—how the whole economic process hangs together. Related to this, they also show how the study of the various parts of the economy need to be interrelated. In studying each individual part of the capitalist system it is furthermore important to be clear about what drives the system as a whole. And finally, as already the classics were well aware of, there exists an overall logic to capitalism as an economic system, which the individual actors are not aware of. Through the logic of unintended consequences capitalism not only produces individual wealth but also social wealth (Smith), not only advances for some but also setbacks and hard times for others (Marx, Weber).

A Basic Model of Capitalism

The reference to Adam Smith, Marx, and Weber leads in a natural way to the next step in this argument, namely, to the analytical point of departure for an economic sociology of capitalism. This consists of the proposition that *interests* drive the actions of the individuals, and that these interests come together in a very specific way in capitalism. The actors in society are driven by a variety of interests—political, economic, legal, and so on. It is important to insist here on *the plurality of interests* since this makes the analysis realistic as well as flexible. Interests of the same type, as well as of different types, may reinforce each other, counterbalance each other, block each other, and so on. Interests, very importantly, are what supply *the force* in the economic system—what make millions of people get up in the morning and work all day. Interests also explain why banks, financial markets, and similar institutions are so powerful: they can mobilize and energize masses of people into action through their control over economic resources.

At this point it should be noted that sociologists have often tended to ignore interests and focus exclusively on social relations and the impact that these may have. This exclusive emphasis on social relations can to some extent be explained as the professional myopia of the sociologist. It is matched, in the economic profession, by a similar overemphasis on the purely economic side of things—on economic interests and their effects, *minus* social relations as well as other types of interests. A hardhitting economic sociology would attempt to draw on the best of sociology and economics, and to *unite* interests and social relations in one and the same analysis. Interests, in all brevity, are always socially defined, and they can only be realized through social relations.[2]

Our definition of institutions can be used to exemplify this need for drawing on both interests and social relations in the analysis. Institutions are often defined in sociology—especially in the approach that has been developed by various experts on organization theory at Stanford University—in exclusively social terms, that is, as rules, models, social constructions, and so on. Everything, from this perspective, can be an institution, from a hand-shake and a dance to the state and the firm. The individuals with their inter-ests are somehow abstracted away, to make room for a vision of institutions as pure and empty structures which are imitated, duplicated, and so on in a fairly effortless manner.

In contrast to this approach, institutions will here be defined as *durable lock-ins or amalgamations of interests and social relations*. This view of in-stitutions is currently being developed, but still has some way to go (e.g., Swedberg 2003b). According to this perspective, the interests of individuals as well as of corporate actors must always be explicitly taken into account. A business firm, for example, does not exist unless you also include the cap-ital of the firm and the interests that are associated with this. Similarly a family does not exist unless you take into account the forces (interests) that draw the members together—be they emotional, sexual, and/or eco-nomic. To this may be added that there is not only a time dimension to institutions—they tend to last for some time—but also a normative element: they tell you *how* interests should be realized in society, be they family, political, economic, or some other type of interest. The more legitimate an institution is, the more this normative element tends to be taken for granted—and this gives the institution legitimacy and makes it stronger. Finally, as a sign of the importance of institutions to society, they are typi-cally also regulated in law.

A basic model for capitalism will now be presented which draws on a mix-ture of sociology and economics. Our general point of departure is the con-ventional definition of economics as consisting of production, distribution, and consumption. To cite a well-known textbook: "Economics is the study of how men and society end up *choosing*, with or without the use of money, to employ *scarce* productive resources which could have alternative uses, to produce various commodities and distribute them for consumption, now or in the future, among various people and groups in society" (Samuelson 1970: 4).

This definition describes the economy as a process: all economies start with *production*, continue with *distribution*, and end with *consumption*. Now all economies can be organized in what amounts to two fundamen-tally different ways. Weber expressed this with the help of his two cate-gories "householding" (*Haushalten*) and "profit-making" (*Erwerben*): you produce either for consumption or for profit (Weber [1922] 1978: 86–100). Marx alluded to the same phenomenon when he spoke of "use value" versus "exchange value" (Marx [1867] 1906: 42–43). And so did Aristotle, with his famous distinction between *oekonomia* (household management) and *chrematistica* (moneymaking; Aristotle 1946: 18 ff., cf. Finley [1973] 1985: 17).

The key to the different ways of organizing the economy, I suggest, is to be found in the way that the economic product is *distributed* in the sense of being passed on in the economic process. As the reader will notice I am here departing from the way that the term distribution is often used in economics—as the division of what has been produced—and instead focusing on the different social mechanisms through which what has been produced is being passed on.

To show the fruitfulness of this approach, one may refer to Polanyi's three concepts of *redistribution, reciprocity,* and *exchange* (Polanyi [1957] 1971). Following Polanyi, it is clear that one way of distributing or passing on what has been produced is through *redistribution.* The agent who does the redistribution is typically the state or some other political authority. The modern socialist state is an example of an economic system that is primarily based on redistribution. Other examples can easily be found, for example, in antiquity. What has been redistributed is then consumed. Some part of what has been produced is always set aside for future production; the size of this part is decided by the political authority. An economy which is primarily based on redistribution is capable of growth—but not the dynamic type of growth that is characteristic of capitalism. It is a growth that rather follows and mirrors political decisions than an internal and independent logic.

The second way of distributing or passing on what has been produced, according to Polanyi, is through *reciprocity.* This means some horizontal form of distribution, as is common in a family or in a kin-based economy. Again, some part of what is being produced, is always set aside for future production. And, again, the result of proceeding in this manner is not going to lead to a dynamic economy. An economy which is based on reciprocity tends toward traditionalism and some form of equity.

Only the third way of distributing or passing on production—through *exchange*—can lead to a truly dynamic economic system, with an ever growing economy. The reason for this is that this system is driven not exclusively by the eternal human interest in consumption but also by the powerful interest of *profit.* The latter activates people in a very different way from what redistribution or reciprocity do. And on the assumption that the profit is also reinvested in production, a dynamic economic system—*capitalism*—will now come into being.

What is unique about capitalism, as compared to economic systems based on redistribution and reciprocity, is that it alone is primarily driven by the profit motive. The two most important social mechanisms in capitalism are consequently *exchange* and *the feedback of profit into production* (see figure 1). Complexity is added to the capitalist type of economy by the fact that it also contains several sectors or local (but interconnected) economies, which are based on reciprocity and redistribution. What can

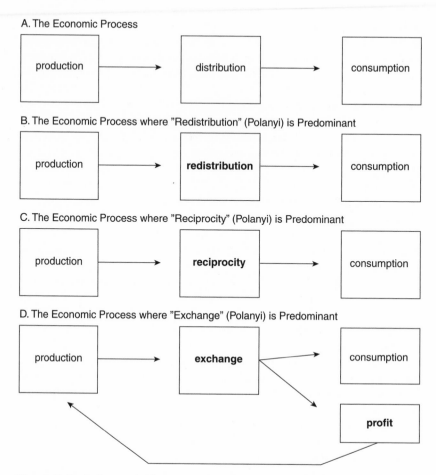

Figure 1 Capitalism and other ways of organizing the economic process and economic interests.

Comment: The economic process in any society can be defined as consisting of *production, distribution* and *consumption.* The act of distribution or passing on of what has been produced can be organized in fundamentally three ways; and which of these is chosen will have an enormous impact on the productivity of the economy as well as its social structure and relationship to the rest of society. Following Polanyi, we may call these *redistribution* (by eg. the state), *reciprocity* (in eg. a family), and *exchange* (in a market). Exchange characterizes the capitalist organization of the economy; and this type of economy derives its dynamic from the fact that the end goal of the economic process is not exclusively consumption, but also *profit.* The more that this profit is reinvested into production, the more dynamic the economy will be. The two key mechanisms in capitalism, in other words, are *organized exchange (the market)* and *the feedback loop of profit into production.* It is the use of these two, it should be stressed, that makes the organization of economic interests in the form of capitalism into such an effective machinery for transforming economic reality.

be called *the state economy* is, for example, based on redistribution, while *the household economy* is based on a mixture of redistribution and reciprocity. *The nonprofit economy* is based on exchange but does not aim at profit. The only sector that is squarely based on exchange and profit is consequently *the corporate economy*.

Following this model, the modern capitalist economies can be said to consist of several sectors or local (but interconnected) economies. There is, first of all, the corporate economy, where exchange dominates. There is also the nonprofit sector, which is based, among other things, on redistribution. The state accounts for a huge part of GNP (30–50 percent), and what can be called the state economy is primarily based on redistribution. The household economy is based on a mixture of redistribution and reciprocity.

The rest of this chapter is devoted to an attempt to spell out what it would mean for economic sociology to set this model of capitalism at the center of its analyses. It is clear that this would have important consequences for what may be seen as the central task of economic sociology—namely, to produce studies of production, distribution, consumption and profit-making (the first four sections of the chapter). Added to this are the following three crucial topics: the impact on the economic process by *law, politics,* and *culture* (the next three sections). For all of these topics it is also imperative to investigate how they can *speed up, slow down,* or *block* economic growth. Still, our model obviously remains highly simplistic and is in its current shape silent on a number of important economic phenomena, from savings to the dynamics of the business cycle. The focus in this chapter is on the macroeconomic level of the economic process. The reasoning on which the model is based, however, may also be used to capture essential aspects of what happens in the economy on the micro- and meso-level.

Finally, there exist a number of theories of capitalism in social science; how these can add to the approach that is being presented in this chapter will be explored in the next section. Special attention will be paid to the works of Marx, Weber, Schumpeter, Douglass North, and advocates of the varieties of capitalism-approach. The chapter ends with a discussion of some ways to bring more complexity to the model of capitalism which is advocated here.

THE SOCIOLOGY OF DISTRIBUTION

While the capitalist system consists of three basic processes which are all interdependent and shaped by the fact that they are parts of a dynamic system—production, distribution, and consumption—one of these is especially important: *distribution*, in the form of exchange on the market. This is also the main reason why it is preferable to start with distribution rather than with production (which otherwise comes "first" in the economic process).

Once it has been decided to start with distribution in the form of exchange, it immediately becomes clear that there exists an important precondition for exchange to take place in the first place, namely private property. From a sociological perspective, Weber explains, property can be conceptualized as a specific form of a closed social relationship. More precisely, it represents a relationship that allows the actor to exclude other actors from the opportunity to use some item or some person. This right is also alienable and can be inherited. Property is typically legally protected, which means that if it is infringed upon, a staff will use coercion to restore it (Weber [1922] 1978: 22, 44).

This view of property is close to the economists' view of property as a collection of enforceable property rights (e.g., Barzel 1989). The main difference is that the element of social relations is given a much more prominent and visible form in the sociological view of property. That there nonetheless exists a basic compatibility between the economic and sociological view of property can be illustrated by the fact that during the last few years a number of sociological studies have appeared, which draw on the notion of property rights (e.g., Campbell and Lindberg 1990; Nee 1992; Oi and Walder 1999).

What is crucial about private as opposed to collective property is that the former appeals directly to the individual, and in doing so, activates him or her in a manner that collective property is unable to do. Some might argue that people should in principle be as motivated by the prospect of acquiring and using collective property as they are by the prospect of acquiring and using private property. The reason why this is rarely the case, however, has much to do with the free rider problem (Olson 1965). It is also very easy for a few individuals to misuse or destroy collective property.

Once private property exists, exchange becomes possible. The driving force in an exchange is always that both parties will be better off by trading with each other than by not doing so. Actor A may value her bike at $50 and Actor B at $70; and if an exchange takes place both will be better off—and social wealth will have increased by $20. For an exchange to take place, it is not necessary that one party becomes better off while no-one is worse off (Pareto optimality). What rather is needed is that both parties become better off by X, without a third party being worse off by more than X, according to the so-called Kaldor-Hicks concept of efficiency. This latter concept of efficiency is often used in economics because its demands are less stringent than those of Pareto optimality. The reason for referring to it here, however, is that it explains the nature of exchange very nicely, especially what drives the two parties to engage in an exchange in the first place.

Sociologists and economists have developed different approaches to markets—to the role that these play in the economic process, to what is typically regulated in a market, and so on. To economists, markets are primarily processes for price formation, in which the price helps to allocate scarce resources in an efficient manner. By tradition, economists have neglected the institutional dimension of markets, such as rules for exchange, the enforcement machinery, and so on (e.g., North 1977: 710; Coase 1988: 7).

Sociologists, on the other hand, tend to emphasize the role of social relations and institutions in markets. Today's sociologists will typically analyze the networks which are created by interacting market actors (e.g., Baker 1984; Uzzi 1997). Weber noted that markets consist not of repeated acts of exchange, but also of competition among the actors for who will be the one to sell and who will be the one to buy (Weber [1922] 1978: 82–85, 635). This idea of "competition for opportunities of exchange" is perfectly compatible with a networks approach, as Ronald Burt has shown in his theory of structural autonomy (Weber [1922] 1978: 635; Burt 1983, 1992).

Given the fact that economists and sociologists each hold half of the truth, so to speak, when it comes to markets, it seems natural that they should try to coordinate their efforts. Economists need to better understand the role of the social relations in the market, and sociologists need to better understand how prices are formed and what effect these have on the economy. Prices drive many economic changes in capitalism, as Douglass North has made clear—but they do so via a social structure in which interests are embedded, and where quite a bit else is going on as well (North and Thomas 1973; cf. Hayek 1945).

An economic sociology of markets should also study what changes in the exchange mechanism make the capitalist wheel spin faster as well as what slows it down and makes it grind to a halt. According to the theory of transaction costs, lower costs for market deals are a sign of a more efficient exchange mechanism. This is true indeed, and there are economic reasons for it. Lower transaction costs in this context, however, are typically accomplished through changes in social relations and in social mechanisms—and this is where the sociologist can be of help (e.g., Hedström and Swedberg 1998). Take, for example, the clause of bona fide or the fact that if the buyer is in good faith it does not matter if the seller did not acquire the goods in question in a proper manner. Bona fide naturally lowers the transaction costs—but is also a fact of such social complexity that the sociologist may be better equipped than the economist to analyze it. The same is true for many other forms of trust in economic life (e.g., Fukuyama 1995).

But economic sociology is not only interested in what makes the wheels of capitalism spin faster; there is the equally challenging question of what makes them slow down or grind to a halt. Again, Weber's work can be used for illustrations. If bureaucrats in a firm gain power at the expense of the entrepreneur, for example, profit-making will be slowed down since bureaucrats are by nature somewhat alien to the idea of profit-making. One reason for this, Weber says, has to do with the fact that people on a fixed income often find it dishonorable to be swayed exclusively by economic considerations (Weber [1922] 1978: 1108–9). But there is also the fact that if individual firms and capitalists are not stopped in their attempts to create monopolies, capitalism may wither away because there will be no competition to keep it alive (Weber [1922] 1978: 202–5). Recent scandals in corporate America have also shown how dishonest and false accounting can slow down economic growth and block new investments.

All in all, the market is *the* central institution in capitalism. To this should immediately be added that this is only true on condition that most of the production passes through the market. In the great majority of societies throughout history, markets have indeed played a role, but usually a marginal one. It is only since the late nineteenth century, in countries such as England and the United States, that the great bulk of production—food, clothes, and so on—has been produced in the form of commodities which are exchanged in the market. In 1790, for example, 80 percent of all clothing in the United States was made in the home, while a century later 90 percent was made outside the home (Boorstin 1974: 97–99).

When most of production passes through the market, it can be added, the competition for exchange that Weber speaks about as characteristic of the market will also dominate what happens in the economy *outside* of the market. That is, instead of just bringing a few surplus items to the market, as peasants often did in the Middle Ages, the producers in a modern capitalist economy must start the competition and think about the market long before they enter the market. When one speaks of a market economy, in other words, what is meant is an economy where the market is not only used for exchange; it also dominates production (and consumption, as we shall soon see).

Before leaving the topic of distribution, something also needs to be said about *money* since this is the place in the economic process where money enters into the picture. There are primarily two reasons for this: money is the medium of exchange par excellence and it is also a facilitator of credit (e.g., Menger 1892; Ingham 2004). The historical step from barter to exchange with money extended the number of goods that could be exchanged against each other enormously. Money, more generally, also helps the process exchange to proceed smoothly and lowers the cost of exchange. Many other financial innovations—such as the bill of exchange, certificates of deposit and so on—have similarly helped to lower transition costs and were developed in close touch with markets.

While money, like any other economic phenomena, has a cultural dimension (a point I shall return to), it is its place within the overall economic process that is of most interest to economic sociology. In economies based on reciprocity, money often plays a subordinate role since other values than "the cash nexus" decide who should get what. In economies based on redistribution, money is often in use, as recent examples of state socialism are a reminder of. Political interests, however, dominate the operations of money in this type of societies, and socialist states have usually failed in their attempts to simulate effective market or exchange prices.

In capitalism, in contrast, money and markets are protected by the existence of "credible commitments" from the political rulers, that is, by assurances of the rulers that they will not unduly intervene in the workings of the market. Money, in brief, is allowed to operate "freely" and can therefore help the market to operate more smoothly and cheaply. Money also plays an important role in the capitalist process in the form of capital, that is, as resources devoted to profit-seeking. Money and markets, in brief, belong together and therefore need to be studied together.

The Sociology of Production

The next major area within the economic sociology of capitalism is that of *production*. No society can live without production, and all production involves social coordination—a sociological element. Nonetheless, an economic sociology of production may want to start from the following well-known economic premise: that production consists of combinations of some or all of the traditional factors of production (land, labor, capital, technology, and "organization"; Marshall [1890] 1961). The sociologist may want to add that all of these factors of production have their own distinct sociological profiles—before they enter into production as well as once they interact in the firm. In relation to the basic model of capitalism, the factors of production can be conceptualized as inputs into production (see figure 2).

It should also be emphasized that it is not the organizational form itself (or capital or technology) that is the sole determinant of productivity. It represents a common error among organization theorists, for example, to think that organizations are what matters the most—just as Marxists think that labor is the key to all production, engineers (and many economic historians) that technology is the cause of all economic growth, and so on. *All* of these factors contribute to productivity, individually as well as in combination.

This is also where entrepreneurship in its Schumpeterian sense comes in. Entrepreneurship is classically defined by Schumpeter as the putting together of *"new combinations"* (Schumpeter 1934: 65–66; emphasis

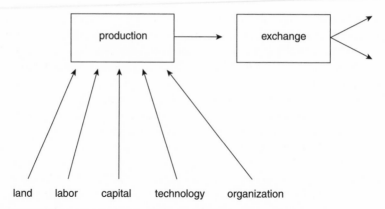

Figure 2 The factors of production in capitalism.
Comment: Following economics, the economic sociology approaches the study of production in terms of its five factors: land, labor, capital, technology and organization (Marshall). All of these factors—not only technology—influence the level of productivity.

added). An innovation may consist, for example, of a new kind of commodity or some novel way of lowering the price, and it will typically result in high profit for the entrepreneur. Soon, however, there will be more entrepreneurs and lower profit, until a stage is reached where overinvestments are made. When this happens to a number of innovations, according to Schumpeter, a business cycle is set off which works itself out in the economy—until there is a new wave of innovations and the whole process is repeated.

Factor of Production # 1: Labor

When factors of production were discussed in the nineteenth century, land was usually assigned a prominent place. In today's capitalism, however, land is of much less importance for the economy as a whole, and the average household is not dependent on working the land for its livelihood. Land as a factor of production will therefore be passed over in this chapter, and I shall proceed directly to labor, which has retained its central importance for the process of production.

Labor as a modern factor of production typically passes through two stages. There is the first stage, which takes place *before* labor enters into production; it is followed by the stage once labor has entered the market and the workplace. Two institutions which are central to labor before it enters into production are the home and the school. In the home children learn values, discipline, and how to interact (what some analysts refer to as social capital, and others as cultural capital). They also get to live in a household economy and become influenced by its values. In school, various skills are taught, some of which are of value in production, from reading, writing, and elementary mathematics in school to engineering, computer programming, and nuclear physics at the university (what some analysts refer to as human capital; for a discussion of the different forms of capital, see, e.g., Bourdieu 1986; Coleman 1990).

According to a well-known strand of sociological theory, when labor is distributed via the market it tends to form into large and loose groups of people with similar economic interests and life-chances (*classes*). When there is no market, or the market is being controlled by, say, a profession, labor instead tends to form into small and cohesive groups centered around honor and consumption (*status groups*; e.g., Weber [1922] 1978: 302–7). Whatever the exact relationship is between class and status, on the one hand, and class and labor, on the other, it is imperative for economic sociology to attempt to theorize the link between the economic process and the formation of classes and status groups in society. This is where economic sociology needs to connect with stratification theory—and perhaps also where stratification theory can get some inspiration from economic sociology.

At this point it is important to make clear that for many people who are part of the capitalist process the economy basically represents pain and difficulties. While profit-seeking brings excitement and wealth to the successful entrepreneur, a large number of people suffer from the everyday workings of capitalism. Max Weber and Pierre Bourdieu have tried to theorize this situation with the help of the concept of theodicy ("why is there suffering in the world, and why do some people suffer more than others?"; e.g., Weber 1946; Bourdieu et al. 1999). Weber, for example, refers to what he calls "the theodicy of good fortune" or the fact that people who are successful also want to feel that they deserve their good fortune, and therefore develop and seek out various accounts to this effect (Weber 1946: 271). There also is the equivalent "theodicy of suffering" which explains to those who are misfortunate why they suffer and why they should put up with a harsh world. While the concept of theodicy originally was religious in nature, it has become secular in the works of Weber and Bourdieu as well as increasingly applicable to the world of the economy.

In modern capitalist society labor tends to form into three broad categories: workers, professionals, and managers. Sociology is by tradition skillful in tracing the structure of groups as well as the mentalities of their members, while economists often tend to use a nondifferentiated concept of labor and emphasize the crucial role played by the productivity of the worker (according to the standard formula of marginal productivity theory; but see also the different approach of personnel economics in, e.g., Lazear 1995). Again, it would appear that both sociology and economics can benefit from the insights of the other science.

To what extent can labor, before as well as after entering the process of production, add to, slow down, or block the wheels of capitalism? What happens in the home and the school, in terms of creation of values and skills, is clearly of great relevance for an answer to this question. And so is what happens at the workplace, where informal norms and groups are formed and where trade unions may be active. It is also important if the element of status or class predominates. Status groups, Weber argues, are inherently anticapitalist since they set honor and other noneconomic values before profit-making. They are antagonistic to the market since the market disregards the values that its members hold dear. The more labor feels the impact of the market, on the other hand, the more the element of class will be predominant. In this situation individual actors typically accept the logic of the market: the need for efficiency, profit-making, and constant reinvestment. Honor of the type that exists in a status group can be characterized as an ideal interest—but an ideal interest that is closely allied with material interests.

Factor of Production # 2: Capital

Economists pay by tradition much attention to the role of capital in the process of production; while sociologists, if they study capital at all, tend to analyze its role outside of production, in the form of so-called wealth (e.g., Keister 2000). Again, the two approaches may want to draw on each other's insights in order to get a full picture of what is going on. To this can be added that the groups in society who control the economic resources have different attitudes to wealth—how it should be acquired, what it can be used for, and so on. Aristocrats, for example, have traditionally had contempt for merchants, and so have warriors. There is also the fact that certain groups of merchants take larger risks than others, and this will naturally have an important impact on the generation of wealth and capital. Merchants furthermore deal in different types of goods, as exemplified by the historical appearance of *the businessman*—a term that was first used in the U.S. in the 1830s to denote a new type of merchant, who traded not only in goods but also in land and whatever else could result in a profit (Boorstin 1974: 115).[3]

Control over capital is often delegated by the owner to some other actor, and this creates for the owner the well-known problem of corporate control. A flexible type of analysis that economists use to handle this type of situation is agency theory, which is based on the idea that the owner (the principal) has a different interest from that of the one to whom he or she assigns some specific task (the agent). This means that something has to be done about the divergence of interest. One solution is direct observation of the agent (monitoring); another is to give the agent an incentive to act in the interest of the owner (alignment of interests). The former is less easy to carry out when it comes to managers as opposed to workers; there is also the problem of "who will monitor the monitor" (e.g., Alchian and Demsetz 1972).

Agency theory can enrich economic sociology by adding to its analyses, especially when it comes to the question of how the owner can maintain control over his or her capital, once a manager is in place. According to Harrison White, for example, the advantage of agency theory is that "it is intensely social in its mechanisms, since it gets one person to do something for another vis-à-vis a third person but only with heavy reliance on the lay of the social landscape" (White 1985: 187; cf. White 1992: 245–54). James Coleman has a similarly positive view of the sociological potential of agency theory, as is clear from the following quote from *Foundations of Social Theory*: "once a transaction has been made, in which the principal satisfies interests of the agent (for example, through a monetary payment) in return for the agent's using his actions to pursue the principal's interests, a social system has been created" (Coleman 1990: 152).

A corporation can acquire capital in a variety of ways—from banks, venture capitalists, the capital market, and so on. Each of these institutions has its own distinct social structure and history which sociology can help to analyze. Pension funds and other mutual funds which have become key players in the modern capital market are often managed by single individuals; very little is currently known about these. Agency theory, in combination with economic sociology, represents one way of approaching this type of issue.

The way that capital is brought to production will also affect the generation of economic value. Risk taking, as already mentioned, is a crucial factor at this point of the process, closely related to the profit level. But risk taking itself is also affected by social relations, as the historical emergence of venture capital in the United States a few decades ago illustrates (see the chapter by John Freeman in this volume). What characterizes venture capitalists is typically an intimate knowledge of the business in which they invest, often in combination with some form of control over the firm that is being targeted. Together, these two measures make risk taking more manageable—and thereby also increase the chance to make a high profit. Again, this is a topic where economic sociology can be of assistance.

Factor of Production # 3: Technology

Contemporary capitalism is heavily dependent on technology, primarily because it helps to increase productivity (e.g., Rosenberg and Birdzell 1986; Mokyr 1990). Exactly how this is done, however, is something that neither economists nor sociologists understand very well. The concept of productivity, for example, is in need of much clarification. Economists realize well the importance of technology in this context, but have difficulty in theorizing it (e.g., Solow 2002). A sign of this is the discussion about the role of computers in the economic growth in the United States in the 1990s. "You can see the computer age everywhere but in the productivity statistics," to quote a famous line by Robert Solow (Solow 1987).

Another difficulty with the economists' view of technology is that they often see technology as the one and only reason for growth in productivity. While innovations in technology may well be *the* major reason for growth in productivity in modern capitalism, it is by no means the only one, and it most surely could not operate in isolation. Social organization, in particular, affects productivity, a fact that industrial sociology made clear many decades ago (e.g., Roy 1952; cf. Roethlisberger and Dickson 1939).

Sociologists differ from economists in that they rarely note that technology is of great importance to productivity and the generation of profits. Sociologists of science of the old school view science primarily as a public good, which may once have been true but is less so today. Modern sociologists of science, on the other hand, argue that science and technology essentially are to be understood as forms of social construction, a position which may well be true from a philosophical perspective but which is of limited relevance to an understanding of the role science and technology play in the economic process.

From historians of technology we know that economically relevant technology for a long time emerged in a slow, evolutionary manner—as evidenced by the history of boat, the ax, the plow, and so on. At the time of the Industrial Revolution, and even more so during the second half of the nineteenth century, however, a historical meeting took place between capitalism and science. This alliance has continued till today and has become ever more important to the dynamic growth of capitalism.

It has often been pointed out that social organization can accelerate or impede the emergence of new technology, which in turn will affect the economy. In his study of religions in India, for example, Weber notes that the caste system blocked innovations by forbidding changes in the tools of the artisans (Weber [1921] 1958: 103; cf. Schroeder and Swedberg 2002). Since the penalty for a change of this type was religious, Weber's example also illustrates how a religious interest (in this case successful reincarnation) can be used to block an economic interest (in this case improved productivity). In today's society, to use a more contemporary example, we are witnessing an important change in the property rights to science, which has helped to speed up production. While science until recently was seen as a common good, ways are now increasingly found to turn it into a private good (e.g., Mirowski and Miriam-Sent 2002). The forces that have caused this change are obvious enough. A new pharmaceutical drug can, for example, be worth billions of dollars in profit. It currently also costs some 800 million dollars to develop a new drug.

Factor of Production # 4: Organization (Marshall)

Alfred Marshall sensed the limits to the economics of his days and argued, in *Principles of Economics* [1890] (1961), that not only land, labor, and capital but also "organization" should be considered a factor of production. By organization Marshall meant a number of phenomena, including the individual firm as well as a dynamic collection of firms in the same geographical area, which he termed "industrial district" (Marshall [1890] 1961, 1: 138–39, 240–313). The insight that organization is crucial to profit-making is also at the heart of what is known as organizational economics, which draws on a mixture of agency theory, game theory, transaction cost analysis, and law and economics—but not on sociology (e.g., Barnes and Ouchi 1986; Milgrom and Roberts 1992).

Nonetheless, sociologists have developed a series of conceptual tools that can be used to analyze the way the factors of production come together in the profit-making firm. Sociologists, however, are to a certain extent held back from making the contribution they should be able to make by their belief that the central unit of analysis is the generic organization and not the corporation (cf. Davis and McAdam 2000). When sociologists do research on firms this is typically translated into knowledge about organizations in general (e.g., Perrow 2002). The following facts about the modern firm are consequently ignored: (1) that the firm has its own institutional history; (2) that the firm is treated differently from other organizations in laws and regulations; and (3) that firms in modern society control more economic resources than any other type of organization, except for the state.

Regardless of this critique, it is clear that several of the concepts and middle-range theories that have been developed in organization theory can be of considerable help in analyzing corporations, and to some extent they have already been used for this purpose. This is true, for example, for population ecology and for resource dependency (e.g., Burt 1983; Carrol and Hannan 1995). Networks are another helpful tool which can be used, for example, to trace the relations between corporations that are a result of their attempts to make a profit (e.g., Ebers 1997). There is also the insight that work groups can develop norms that go counter to the goals of the corporation, so-called opposition norms (Nee 1998).

It is obvious that the way a corporation is organized will speed up, slow down, or block profit-making. What was once thought to represent the ideal design for a firm—the huge, bureaucratically organized firm with much of the knowledge and power to decide concentrated at the top (Weber, Chandler)—has fallen out of favor. It is indeed true that certain new technologies as well as new ways of appealing to the interests of the employees can replace monitoring with interest alignment, and that this has led to changes in the old type of corporation. What modern firms strive for, however, is not to so much to create a decentralized or a less formal corporation per se, but to do what it takes to make a profit.

THE SOCIOLOGY OF CONSUMPTION

Consumption, to cite *The Wealth of Nations*, represents the end product of production: "consumption is the sole end and purpose of all production" (Smith [1776] 1976: 660). From the viewpoint of the model of capitalism that has been presented in this chapter, however, things are not that simple. For one thing, how income at the end of the process is divided between consumption and profit is of crucial importance. The more profit that is taken out by the owners and fed back into production, the faster the wheels of capitalism tend to spin.

There is also the fact that consumption will affect the productivity of labor. If we return to figure 1, it is possible to imagine a line that goes from consumption to production, via labor as a factor of production. Adequate food and some amount of leisure, fueling body and mind, are examples of this. Education that is paid by private means would be another.

But even if consumption does have an indirect effect on production, as just exemplified, its main contribution to capitalism is that it takes place in the first place. The fact that human beings must satisfy their material needs may sound like a triviality. And so it is—except that consumption always has to increase in capitalism, in contrast to economies based on redistribution or reciprocity. If this does not happen, profits stagnate and capitalism loses its vitality. This means that efforts always have to be made, as part of the process of *production*, to encourage consumption as much as possible. Advertisement is one way to accomplish this, but there are many more. In modern capitalist society whole settings in the form of shopping centers and the like have been created, precisely for this purpose. One observer refers to these as "means of consumption" (Ritzer 1999).

Consumption can be speeded up, slowed down, or blocked through the impact of various forces—and thereby affect the capitalist machinery. The United States, for example, has for a long time been a commercial society, with a population with a strong desire for democratic "comfort" as opposed to aristocratic "luxury"; this clearly greases the wheels of capitalism (e.g., Tocqueville [1835–40] 1945). Immediately after September 11, to use another example from the United States, shopping was nearly proclaimed a patriotic duty so that the economy would not slump. Examples also exist of societies which have tried to block consumption. One example is Florence in the fifteenth century, when the city was ruled by Savonarola, who staged the famous "bonfires of vanities"—public burnings of expensive dresses, sensual paintings, and the like which were judged to detract from a pious life (for sumptuary laws, see, e.g., Hunt 1995).

THE SOCIOLOGY OF PROFIT

The fact that the level of profit is directly related to how much is set aside for consumption has already been mentioned. To this can be added that profit, according to economists, can in principle not be affected by social forces. Sociologists, however, see things differently. To sociologists productivity is notoriously difficult to measure, and the theory of marginal productivity is very hard to apply empirically. It is also clear, as noted earlier, that the social relations of an employee will affect productivity. A worker may, for example, be more or less productive depending on the work group he or she is part of (e.g., Granovetter 1988). The size of the wages, of course, also affects the profit level and depends, among other things, on the strength of the unions.

Regardless of the actual size of the profit, however, it is *the opportunity for more profit* that drives the capitalist process forward. According to Weber, capitalism is primarily characterized by "the pursuit of profit, and forever *renewed* profit" (Weber [1904–5] 1958: 17). Marx expressed the same idea in his well-known formula M-C-M′, where M stands for money, C for commodity, and M′ for money plus an increment, equaling surplus value (Marx [1867] 1990: 247–57). In a similar vein, the capitalist process is set in motion by the search for profit and—equally important—kept in motion by the continuous reinvestment of profit in production.

It is clear that while the size of the profit in relation to consumption is one thing, how much of the profit is reinvested is another. It is also obvious that the level of reinvestment is influenced by social forces. In a discussion of Latin America in the 1960s, S. M. Lipset noted, for example, how successful businessmen in Chile, Argentina, Paraguay, and some other countries often withdrew their earnings from industry and invested it in land, to acquire the status of landowners (Lipset [1967] 1988). Puritan businessmen in Weber's *Protestant Ethic*, on the other hand, used very little of their profit for their own consumption and reinvested the bulk. They had contempt for the aristocrats and their consumption of luxuries. The religion of the Puritans allowed them to make a profit since this meant that God looked favorably at their activities. They were not, however, allowed to indulge their senses—just as they were not allowed to enjoy sex, even if they were allowed to procreate.

According to Weber, accounting grew out of the need to calculate profit, as exemplified by the need to know exactly how much was due to each party in a commenda (e.g., Weber [1923] 1981: 206–7). To this can be added that profit is a social construction, in the sense that what is presented as profit in, say, an annual report may differ quite a bit from what is reported to, say, the tax authorities. As any newspaper reader knows after Enron, the way that accounting rules are applied will also affect the level of profit. "Aggressive accounting" is the term currently used for accounting practices in the United States which are in the gray zone between legality and illegality, and which are used to artificially increase profits.

Among the factors that may block profit and profit-making, religion is of special historical importance. Most religions have been negative to business, since profit-making has been seen as negative to the attempt to lead a life according to religious principles. "You cannot serve both God and Money" (Matthew 6:24). But exceptions also exist not only where religion and profit-making have coexisted, but where religion has actually *encouraged* profit-making. The most famous case of this is obviously ascetic Protestantism, as analyzed in *The Protestant Ethic*. One may possibly also add contemporary America, since the United States both is a very religious country and has the most vigorous capitalism. I say "possibly" because neither sociologists of religion nor economic sociologists have addressed this issue squarely, so we consequently do not know what role religion really plays in contemporary American capitalism (cf. Inglehart and Baker 2000; Barro 2002).

ADDITIONAL FACTOR # 1: THE ROLE OF LAW

In addition to the factors that make up the basic model of capitalism, which is discussed in this chapter, a few more must be added: *law, politics (including the state)*, and *culture*. Law is typically part of the political machinery, but it deserves to be singled out and treated in a separate section. One reason for this is that law introduces an extra layer, so to speak, between political decisions and their execution (Swedberg 2003a; cf. Edelman and Stryker 2005). To become reality, political decisions often have to be translated into legal language and interpreted by legal experts. Individual actors also needs to orient their actions to the law itself and comply with it, in order for it to have an effect on their behavior. Another reason why law deserves to be treated separately from the state is that courts can be more or less independent of the rest of the state. American courts, for example, are to a large extent peopled by judges who have been elected, as opposed to courts in Europe, where judges are appointed and essentially civil servants. Furthermore, all laws in the United States are subject to judicial review and can in principle be overturned. The European Union, it can be added, seems to be moving in a similar direction.

The basic relationship between law and the economy is as follows. Since private property is a precondition for a capitalist economy, so is the law about private property. Conflicts always emerge in society, including the economy, and law represents a legitimate way to settle conflicts. Law also helps to ensure predictability, which is essential for an advanced capitalist economy. In general, the economy thrives on peace, and law is essential for there to be peace in society.

Sociologists have often noted that law is necessary to *prevent* certain economic actions from taking place. Law, for example, is used to stop the formation of monopolies and discrimination against women and minorities in the labor market (e.g., Fligstein 1990; Edelman 1992). Sociologists have also pointed out that law can be used to *punish* economic actors who engage in the wrong type of behavior, from petty thievery in the workplace to the kind of economic wrongdoing that is policed by the SEC (e.g., Shapiro 1984; Tucker 1999).

What has not been much explored by sociologists, however, is that law can play an *enabling* role in the economy (Swedberg 2003a). Law can, for example, help to "release [economic] energy," to cite the famous expression of James Willard Hurst (e.g., 1956). Judges can be encouraged to use wealth maximization as a guide in their legal questions (e.g., Posner 1981). In general, contracts also provide actors with a new tool through which they can create economic relations of their own (e.g., Weber [1922] 1978: 667).

From what has just been said it is clear that law can further the capitalist process and make it operate in a more efficient manner. It is also clear that it can block economic development, by forbidding certain kinds of economic actions. One historical example of this is the labeling of certain loans as usury. To this should be added, however, that businesspeople often choose to disregard the law—they often ignore it, whether it operates in their favor or not (e.g., Macaulay 1963). Another elementary insight from the sociology of law is that major economic transformations can take place without any equivalent change in the legal system (e.g., Weber [1922] 1978: 333–34; Renner [1904] 1949).

ADDITIONAL FACTOR # 2: THE ROLE OF POLITICS (INCLUDING THE STATE)

The role of politics and the state in the economy is complex. In general, the state in a capitalist economy has less power over the economy than does the state in a redistributory one. In the latter the state controls the great bulk of the economic resources and also decides what rules to follow; in a capitalist economy the state has the power only to set the rules and to channel certain resources from one point in society to another, not to decide how economic

24 • Swedberg

Control of Resources for Production

		YES	NO
Capacity to Set Rules	**YES**	Socialist state	Capitalist state
	NO	Patrimonial states in early history	Libertarian non-state

Figure 3 Capacity of the state to control resources for production versus capacity to set rules in the economy.
Comment: The state can have different types of control over the economy: control of resources for production is one of these, and the capacity to set the rules in the economy is another. In modern capitalism the state typically lacks control of resources for production but can set rules in the economy. In socialism, on the other hand, the state has control of economic resources as well as the capacity to set rules.

resources are to be used for purposes of production. This last situation, as has often been pointed out by economists, is actually more complex than it may at first appear. The capitalist state has to solve what has been called "the fundamental political dilemma of an economy," namely that the state has to be strong enough to enforce private property rights but still refrain from using its strength to expropriate private property (e.g., North et al. 2000: 21; see figure 3).

That the capitalist state has no or little say over the use of the economic resources when it comes to production does not mean that it is without economic power. No state can exist without economic resources of its own, especially the modern capitalist state, which has a number of tasks to fulfill: defense, education, health care, welfare, regulation, and so on. The capitalist state finances its expenses primarily by seizing part of what has been produced, from what otherwise would have gone to consumption or to profit. The decision to tax consumption or profit is an important political question. The sociological study of the generation and spending of the state's resources belongs to a much neglected field of study, known as fiscal sociology (Schumpeter [1918] 1991; see also Campbell, this volume).

A question which has been much discussed in contemporary social science is the relationship between democracy and capitalism. Several different opinions exist on this issue. There is, on the one hand, S. M. Lipset's assertion that prosperous countries tend to be democratic, which has led to a huge amount of research (Lipset 1960; for a stronger version of this thesis, see, e.g., Friedman 1962). One insight which has grown out of the discussion of Lipset's thesis is that it is very difficult to pinpoint the exact social mechanisms that account for the relationship between prosperity and democracy (for a review of the literature, see Diamond 1992). Weber, in contrast, considers the relationship between capitalism and democracy to be much more problematic, and he has recently been backed up by various studies by Robert Barro (e.g., Weber [1916] 1994: 68–70; Barro 2000). A third theory states that countries which have been industrialized under the leadership of the bourgeoisie tend to become democratic, in contrast to countries which have been industrialized under the leadership of a class of landowners (Moore 1966; cf. Rueschemeyer et al. 1997).

Democratic or not, it is clear that the capitalist state can steer the economy in various ways. Two traditional ways of doing so are through fiscal and monetary policy—two topics on which economists, as opposed to sociologists, are knowledgeable. To this should be added that the state can also influence the economy through regulation and industrial policy, and that especially the former is extremely important in modern society. While economists worry that these last two ways of influencing the economy may sap capitalism of its vitality, sociologists tend to see them as positive and much needed (see, e.g., Stigler 1971 versus Fligstein 2001). Regulations as well as industrial policy, in brief, can be used to speed up the economy as well as slow it down—and so can monetary and fiscal policy.

ADDITIONAL FACTOR # 3: THE ROLE OF CULTURE IN THE ECONOMY

Culture is a difficult and complex topic for economists as well as sociologists. In sociology, the traditional concept of culture draws heavily on Weber and essentially covers two topics which are overlapping but not identical: *valuation* and *sense-making* (e.g., Weber [1904] 1949: 76, [1907] 1977: 109; cf. [1922] 1978: 98). Or to put it into more concrete language, the cultural element of an economic action has to do with the fact that (1) anything economic is typically viewed as being either positive or negative, and (2) economic phenomena, like all human phenomena, have somehow to be pieced together in the human mind in order to make sense and acquire a distinct *Gestalt*.

To cite one of Weber's examples that deals with the first point, profit-making can be seen as negative in a religion (e.g., Catholicism) or as positive (e.g., ascetic Protestantism). And to cite one of Weber's examples which illustrates how people make sense of an economic phenomenon with the help of culture: the act of passing around little pieces of metal only becomes an exchange of money under certain conditions (Weber [1907] 1977: 109).

It can be added that whether trade in money is seen as positive or negative is also a question which involves culture, from a Weberian perspective. In nearly all cultures this type of activity has been looked down upon and been associated with various outcast groups, such as the Jews in medieval

Europe. This is much less the case in modern capitalism—where nonetheless traces of these earlier beliefs still linger on, as illustrated by the instinctive hostility to someone like Soros or to financial capital more generally.

Attempts have recently been made to import some insights from cognitive psychology into the sociological concept of culture (e.g., DiMaggio 1997). To what extent this will succeed is too early to tell. What remains true, however, is the fruitfulness of the Weberian approach, namely of equating culture with values as well as with sense-making. A series of studies of economic culture, from Tocqueville's analysis of nineteenth-century America to Clifford Geertz's analysis of Indonesia in the twentieth century, testify to this (e.g., Tocqueville [1835–40] 1945; Geertz 1963; see also, e.g., Lipset [1967] 1988, 1996).

Some of these studies also describe how economic culture can speed up the economic process. This, for example, is what Tocqueville claims that American culture did for the economy in the nineteenth century or, for that matter, what Weber claims that ascetic Protestantism did for certain parts of Western Europe a few centuries earlier. Indeed, Tocqueville's *Democracy in America* can be seen as a sequel to *The Protestant Ethic* in this respect, and his theory of the role played in the U.S. economy by religion (tempering immediate interest into "interest properly understood") parallels Weber's ideas about the impact of the Puritans.

That economic culture also can dampen and block capitalist development can similarly be illustrated by referring to the works of Tocqueville and Weber. The culture in the American South, according to *Democracy in America*, devalued labor by associating it with slavery, and this led to a stagnant economy. The same was true according to Weber for societies with a dualistic economic ethic, according to which members of the in-group should be treated fairly, while dishonesty and trickery were allowed in dealing with outsiders. This attitude made it hard for rational capitalism to emerge.

Finally, special mention should be made of a recent attempt to revive a classical cultural concept in the analysis of capitalism, namely Weber's notion of "the spirit of capitalism." In *Le nouvel esprit du capitalisme* (1999) Luc Boltanski and Eve Chiapello look at the major types of ideologies that have been used to justify capitalism, from the nineteenth century till today. Their definition of the spirit of capitalism is as follows: "we have labeled as a 'spirit of capitalism' the ideology that justifies people's commitment to capitalism, and which renders this commitment attractive" (Boltanski and Chiapello 2002: 2). During much of the twentieth century the spirit of capitalism was centered around big organizations and stability, but it is now in the process of being replaced by "a new spirit of capitalism." The heart of this new spirit, they argue, mainly consists of arguments that justify and glorify a decentralized economic world in which flexibility and networks play a key role. Running a corporation is seen as conceiving and executing a never ending series of "projects," each of which has its own network (the "Project World").

ON DIFFERENT ATTEMPTS TO ANALYZE CAPITALISM

The main message in this chapter so far is that profit-making is at the center of the capitalist enterprise and should also be at the center of analyses of capitalism. Related to this, it has been suggested that economic sociology should study the factors that favor profit-making as well as the factors that slow it down or block it. A number of competing theories of capitalism exist—by the classics, by economists, and by sociologists. Something can be learned from many of these, especially from the theories of Weber, Schumpeter, and North. Some of them, however, are passé and not very useful.

One theory of capitalism which seems less relevant today is that of Marx, which is also the one that has been the most popular among sociologists (e.g., Berger 1986, 1987). There are several reasons why sociologists of today may want to replace Marx's theory with a new one. One of these has to do with Marx's view of culture and law as a part of the so-called superstructure, which is created by economic forces and which is unable to influence the economy on its own. This is plainly wrong—as is Marx's theory that what drives history in capitalist society is the production of surplus value, translated into class struggle. More generally, Marx's view of capitalism is closely modeled on nineteenth-century capitalism in Europe, with its abject misery in the cities and often violent clashes between the classes. This state of affairs, however, turned out *not* to be a permanent feature of capitalism. The general economic situation is very different in many countries today, and the working class has more to lose than its chains.

Much of what Weber and Schumpeter have to say about capitalism, on the other hand, is still relevant for an understanding of capitalism. Weber's *General Economic History*, for example, remains unsurpassed as a concentrated history of capitalism. *Economy and Society* is similarly instructive on many points—and so is Schumpeter's masterpiece, *Capitalism, Socialism and Democracy*.

One important suggestion that Weber makes a propos capitalism is that one should speak of capitalism not in the singular (as Marx did), but in the *plural*—of different types of capitalism. His own typology in *Economy and Society*—rational, political, and traditional capitalism—is a case in point (Weber [1922] 1978: 164–66). While this typology is well known in sociological circles, it has been little used in concrete studies.

It should also be emphasized that even if much of value can be learned by a closer textual reading of the classics, the real challenge that faces today's economic sociologists is to incorporate the insights of the classics about capitalism into a new and more hard-hitting theory which can be used to analyze contemporary capitalism. Similar to the way that classical political economy once became transformed into neoclassical economics, classical sociology needs to be transformed into a more effective type of sociology.

How this can be done can be illustrated with the help of *The Protestant Ethic*, a work which is typically seen by sociologists as a study of how ascetic Protestantism helped to create the spirit of modern capitalism. Weber's argument on this point has, for example, been fleshed out by James Coleman in his famous model of macro-micro-macro relations in chapter 1 of *Foundations of Sociology* (Coleman 1990: 6–10). The doctrine of Protestantism affects the attitudes of individual believers, who gradually transfer the methodical scheme of their new religious beliefs onto their economic activities, helping thereby to create, together with other individuals in a similar position, the spirit of modern capitalism.

While this emphasis on the link between religious and economic attitudes was no doubt part of Weber's story, *The Protestant Ethic* can also be read—and more effectively, I would argue—as an analysis centered around *interests* and their relationship to social structures. Ascetic Protestantism had such an impact on the individual, according to this view, because it deeply affected his or her religious interests (*Heilsgüter*), not just his or her religious attitudes. As Coleman indicates, Weber goes below the surface—but to the interests of the individual. When the believer began to think that his or her achievements in the area of the economy could also influence his or her chances in the next world, the force of economic interests was wedded to the force of religious interests, and this created an extremely powerful force. Indeed, it was a force that was so powerful that it could break through the old hold of traditional religion and traditional capitalist ideology. *The Protestant Ethic*, from this perspective, can be seen as a textbook case for how to carry out an effective interest analysis with the help of sociology.

If we now leave the sociologists for a moment and switch to the economists, it is clear that these have not been very interested in producing theories about capitalism. One reason for this is that from the turn of the nineteenth century till the mid-1970s, when New Institutional Economics had its breakthrough, economists did not pay much attention to institutions. Another is that economists associated the term "capitalism" with the political ideology of socialism and avoided the term as much as they could.[4] One important exception to this whole trend is the work of Schumpeter, which deserves special mention (cf. Galbraith [1952] 1956; Hayek 1954; Mises 1956; Friedman 1962).

Schumpeter's general theory of capitalism can be found in a series of work, the most important of which are *Theory of Economic Development* (1911, 1934), *Business Cycles* (1939) and *Capitalism, Socialism and Democracy* (1942; e.g., Swedberg 2002). The heart of Schumpeter's argument is that capitalism stands and falls with entrepreneurship: if capitalism continuously presents new opportunities for profit it will thrive, otherwise it will die out and be replaced by some some form of bureaucracy and socialism. "Creative destruction," or the replacement of old businesses with new businesses, is the very essence of the capitalist process (Schumpeter [1942] 1994: 81–86). In Schumpeter's last major statement on capitalism—an article he wrote for *Encyclopaedia Brittanica* in 1946—he defines capitalism as follows: "a society is called capitalist if it entrusts its economic process to the guidance of the private businessman" (Schumpeter [1946] 1951: 184). Capitalism, he also argues in this article, has gone through a series of different periods, from "Early Capitalism" to the "Modern Phase." Of all of these periods, Schumpeter notes, the one that had been the most favorable to capitalism was "Intact Capitalism." During this period, which was set off by the Industrial Revolution and lasted until the end of the nineteenth century, the elements of free trade and laissez-faire were very strong; taxes were low and there was little protectionism.

Of contemporary economists who have written about capitalism, Douglass North may well be the most important (e.g., North 1970; North and Thomas 1973). It can be argued that North's early theory of capitalism as primarily driven by changes in relative prices, which lead to efficient property rights, is less realistic than his later theory of capitalism, with its strong emphasis on institutions and rules. This is a view that goes well with the model of capitalism as a special mixture of interests and social relations which has been presented in this chapter.

To this should be added that North's works are filled with ideas that have turned out to be very helpful in analyzing capitalism. These include his theory of the state as an institution which maximizes the wealth (or utility) of the ruler; his ideas about the positive role played by errors in history; and his analysis of how reputation, under certain conditions, can replace coercion as a means of reinforcing legal decisions about the economy.

There also exist a few theories of capitalism which have been created by other social scientists than economists. Immanuel Wallerstein and his followers have, for example, created a theory of capitalism as a world system, and they should be credited with having carried out research on many countries which have attracted little attention from the average academic in the West (cf. Wallerstein 1974–89; e.g., Hall 2000). Wallerstein's idea that capitalism is unique insofar that it is the first economic system which does not coincide with a distinct political territory is another useful insight that has been generated by this perspective. Capitalism, in brief, is a system that goes beyond the boundaries of empires and nation-states. As a general theory of capitalism, however, the idea of capitalism as a world-system with a center, a periphery, and so on is less useful. Since its creation in the 1970s world-system theory has also followed its own distinct course and more or less ignored what has happened in economics and economic sociology.

Another theory of capitalism, or more precisely, of advanced Western capitalism, is the one that is associated with the work on "flexible production" (e.g., Piore and Sabel 1984; Zeitlin 1990). Two major contributions of this theory are to have drawn attention to the existence of industrial districts and to the decentralizing impact of some new technologies. On the negative side, this type of theory tends to overplay the impact of technology. It also has a strong normative tone, as do many studies in political economy. Finally, Sabel, Piore, and so on take no position on a number of issues which are central to a full theory of capitalism.

Since the end of the 1980s a literature has also emerged which is known as "varieties of capitalism" (e.g., Berger and Dore 1996; Crouch and Streeck 1997; Hollingsworth and Boyer 1997; Hall and Soskice 2001; cf. Kitschelt et al. 1999). The main idea here is to outline the institutional and social structure of the economy in industrial countries, and then compare these, in the spirit of political economy. Many valuable insights and empirical facts can be found in this literature, which currently represents the most important competitor to North's theory of capitalism.

On the negative side is the fact that much of the literature on the varieties of capitalism is perhaps better described as studies of the political and economic history of individual Western countries and how these compare to each other, than as studies of capitalism and its special dynamic. Two further drawbacks with this approach are its normative undertone and its general tendency to disregard the fact that capitalism has to be understood as a social system centered around profit-making, and not as a collection of social, economic, and political institutions for governance. Social relations (in the form of institutions) rather than interests are at the center of this approach.

Concluding Remarks

> *Material and ideal interests directly govern men's behavior.*
> —Max Weber, *The Sociology of Religion* (1946: 212)

An attempt has been made in this chapter to outline a model of capitalism that can be of help in setting an agenda for an economic sociology of capitalism. According to the argument that has been presented, production, exchange, consumption, and profit constitute the four main themes in an economic sociology of this type; to these should also be added the impact that law, politics, and culture may have on these.

More has been left unsaid than said in this chapter, as is often the case when vast topics are addressed. Nonetheless, it is hoped that the core of the argument will prove useful, namely, the need to set interests and the way that these are played out in social relationships at the center of the analysis. Economic sociology, I argue, should not exclusively look at social relations—be they in the form of networks, organizations, institutions, or whatever—it also has to take into account what drives social action, namely *interests* (cf. Swedberg 2003b, 2005).

Before concluding this chapter, two important topics need to be addressed. The first has to do with the relationship of the theory that has just been presented to rational choice theory, and the second with the need to take ethnicity and gender into account. Rational choice theory draws on methodological individualism and strongly emphasizes the element of choice. The economic actor, in all brevity, chooses what is best for him or her. In this chapter I part company with many economists by emphasizing the role played by interests much more than the role of choice. I also disagree with the assumption that the actor knows his or her interests and automatically chooses the best way to proceed.

The position I argue for is as follows. Actors sometimes do not know their own interests, and if they do know them, they may still not know how to realize them. More generally, economic reality is often such that whatever the actors do, they will fail or only partially succeed in realizing their interests. That this description of the role of interests answers to reality is something that lost investments, bankruptcies, bad career choices, and so on are a daily reminder of. What Erving Goffman has said about game theory applies, as I see it, just as well to interests:

> persons often don't know what game they are in or whom they are playing for until they have already played. Even when they know about their own position, they may be unclear as to whom, if anybody, they are playing against, and, if anyone, what his game is, let alone his framework of possible moves. Knowing their own possible moves, they may be quite unable to make any estimate of the likelihood of the various outcomes or the value to be placed on each of them. . . . Of course, these various difficulties can be dealt with by approximating the possible outcomes along with the value and likelihood of each, and casting the result in a game matrix; but while this is justified as an exercise, the approximations may have (and be felt to have), woefully little relation to the facts. (Goffman [1961] 1972: 149–50)

A second point that needs to be addressed in this chapter has to do with the role of ethnicity and gender in capitalism. Both of these phenomena are deeply influenced by culture. While Weber's two rules of thumb about culture are simple enough—culture involves valuation and sense-making—cultural phenomena are difficult to analyze empirically, and ethnicity and gender illustrate this more than well. While there is a tendency among sociologists to study and discuss these two phenomena apart from capitalism, I would strongly argue that it is crucial for economic sociology to try to include them in one and the same analysis as economic phenomena.

How this is to be done is something that needs to be discussed. There already exists an important sociological literature on ethnicity and the economy, as well as on women and the economy (e.g., Light and Karageorgis 1994; Milkman and Townsley 1994; England and Folbre 2005). From this it is clear that the activities of minorities and women are typically devalued in various manners—through prejudices, stereotypes, and the like. Still, interests drive the actions of majorities and males vis-à-vis minorities and women, and the way that a number of different interests are aligned, set against one another, and so on, will have an important impact on what happens in ethnic and gender-related relations. To analyze gender and ethnicity without taking interests into account may result in analyses that portray these as free-floating social constructions; and this is something that should be avoided. Here as elsewhere in economic sociology a useful starting point for the analysis may be the following maxim: *follow the interests!*

Notes

1. For exceptions, see especially the work of Fred Block and Erik Olin Wright. Both of these authors have a distinguished list of publications in the area of Marxist sociology. Their main contributions has been to de-dogmatize the Marxist theory of the state (Block) and to turn the Marxist analysis of class in an empirical direction (Wright; see, e.g., Block 1987; Wright 1997). In his current work, it should be mentioned, Block draws mainly on the work of Karl Polanyi, especially *The Great Transformation*.

2. For an elaboration of this argument, see my *Principles of Economic Sociology* (Swedberg 2003b).

3. The Oxford English Dictionary lists only two references to "business woman"—one dated 1844 and the other 1958 (Oxford English Dictionary Online 1989).

4. The term capitalism has its origin in the Latin word "caput," which means "head" as in "head of cattle" (Braudel [1979] 1985: 232–39; cf. Weber [1922] 1978: 95–96). An early meaning of the word "capital" is that of wealth as well as the principal sum of a loan. The term "[money] capital" is first found in medieval Italy. The word "capitalist" was used many centuries later and never in a friendly sense. The term "capitalism" can be traced back to the nineteenth century and

probably to Louis Blanc; it was, however, probably used already in the eighteenth century. Marx never used the term "capitalism" in his published writings. In academic circles the term "capitalism" was popularized by Werner Sombart around the turn of the twentieth century (cf. Sombart 1930). Sombart notes, however, that while "capitalism" was used by the members of the German Historical School, other economists did not use it (Schumpeter being a lone exception). In the 1950s Hayek and Galbraith helped to brake this trend by both using the term capitalism in their works. Both also commented on the negative connotations of the term. According to Hayek, the reason for economists avoiding the term capitalism was clear: "it [that is, capitalism] is connected with the idea of the rise of the propertyless proletariat, which by some devious process have been deprived of their rightful ownership of the tools for their work" (Hayek 1954: 15). Galbraith simply noted that "for many years this term [that is, capitalism] . . . has been regarded as vaguely obscene. All sorts of euphemisms—free enterprise, individual enterprise, the competitive system and the price system—are currently used in its place" (Galbraith [1952] 1956: 4). The history of the term "capitalism" in more recent times has been traced by Fred Block. In the 1960s in the United States, according to Block, the term capitalism was associated with Communist propaganda and studiously avoided by the establishment. "It is impossible to exaggerate how much has changed over the intervening thirty years. . . . [Today] the businessmen routinely talk about capitalism, and the term has lost any hint of connection to a critical discourse" (Block 2000: 84–85).

REFERENCES

Alchian, Armen and Harold Demsetz. 1972. "Production, Information Costs, and Economic Organization." *American Economic Review* 62(5): 777–95.

Aristotle. 1946. *The Politics of Aristotle*. Trans. Ernest Baker. New York: Oxford University Press.

Baker, Wayne E. 1984. "The Social Structure of a National Securities Market." *American Journal of Sociology* 89: 775–811.

Barnes, Jay and William Ouchi, eds. 1986. *Organizational Economics*. San Francisco: Jossey Bass.

Barro, Robert J. 2000. "Democracy and the Rule of Law." In *Governing for Prosperity*, ed. Bruce Bueno de Mesquito and Hilton Root. New Haven: Yale University Press. 209–31.

———. 2002. "Religiosity and Economic Variables in a Panel of Countries." Talk given at Weatherhead Center, Harvard University.

Barzel, Yoram. 1989. *The Economic Analysis of Property Rights*. Cambridge: Cambridge University Press.

Becker, Jasper. 2000. *The Chinese*. New York: Oxford University Press.

Berger, Peter L. 1986. *The Capitalist Revolution: Fifty Propositions about Prosperity, Equality, and Liberty*. New York: Basic Books.

———, ed. 1987. *Modern Capitalism*. Vol. 1, *Capitalism and Equality in America*. New York: Institute for Educational Affairs.

Berger, Suzanne and Ronald P. Dore, eds. 1996. *National Diversity and Global Capitalism*. Ithaca: Cornell University Press.

Block, Fred. 1987. *Revising State Theory: Essays in Politics and Postindustrialization*. Philadelphia: Temple University Press.

———. 2000. "Deconstructing Capitalism as a System." *Rethinking Marxism* 12(3): 83–98.

Boltanski, Luc and Eve Chiapello. 1999. *Le nouvel esprit du capitalisme*. Paris: Gallimard.

———. 2002. "The New Spirit of Capitalism." Paper presented at the Conference of Europeanists, Chicago, March 14–16. See also http://www.sociologia.unimib.it/mastersqs/rivi/boltan.pdf.

Boorstin, Daniel. 1974. *The Americans: The Democratic Experience*. New York: Vintage.

Bourdieu, Pierre. 1986. "The Forms of Capital." In *Handbook of Theory and Research for the Sociology of Education*. Westport, Conn.: Greenwood Press. 241–58.

Bourdieu, Pierre, Alain Accardo, et al. *The Weight of the World: Social Suffering in Contemporary Societies*. Stanford: Stanford University Press.

Braudel, Fernand. [1979]1985. *The Wheels of Commerce*. Vol. 2, *Civilization and Capitalism, 15th–18th Century*. London: Fontana Press.

Brinton, Mary C. and Victor Nee, eds. 1998. *The New Institutionalism in Sociology*. New York: Russell Sage.

Burt, Ronald S. 1983. *Corporate Profits and Cooptation: Networks of Market Constraints and Directorate Ties in the American Economy*. New York: Academic Press.

———. 1992. *Structural Holes: The Social Structure of Competition*. Cambridge, Mass.: Harvard University Press.

Campbell, John L. and Leon N. Lindberg. 1990. "Property Rights and the Organization of Economic Activity by the State." *American Sociological Review* 55(5): 634–77.

Carroll, Glenn R. and Michael T. Hannan, eds. 1992. *Organization in Industry: Strategy, Structure, and Selection*. New York: Oxford University Press.

———. 2000. *The Demography of Corporations and Industries*. Princeton: Princeton University Press.

Coase, Ronald H. 1988. *The Firm, the Market, and the Law*. Chicago: University of Chicago Press.

Coleman, James S. 1985. "Introducing a Social Structure into Economic Analysis." *American Economic Review* 74(2): 84–88.

———. 1990. *Foundations of Social Theory*. Cambridge, Mass.: Belknap Press of Harvard University Press.

———. 1994. "A Rational Choice Perspective on Economic Sociology." In *The Handbook of Economic Sociology*, ed. Neil J. Smelser and Richard Swedberg. Princeton: Princeton University Press. 166–80.

Crouch, Colin and Wolfgang Streeck, eds. 1997. *Political Economy of Modern Capitalism*. London: Sage.

Davis, Gerald F. and Doug McAdam. 2000. "Corporations, Classes, and Social Movement after Managerialism. *Research in Organizational Behavior* 22: 195–238.

Diamond, Larry. 1992. "Economic Development and Democracy Reconsidered." *American Behavioral Scientist* 35(4/5): 450–99.

DiMaggio, Paul. 1997. "Culture and Cognition." *Annual Review of Sociology* 23: 263–87.

Ebers, Mark, ed. 1997. *The Formation of Inter-Organizational Networks*. Oxford: Oxford University Press.

Edelman, Lauren. 1992. "Legal Ambiguity and Symbolic Structures: Organizational Mediation of Civil Rights." *American Journal of Sociology* 97: 1531–76.

Edelman, Lauren and Robin Stryker. 2005. "A Sociological Approach to Law and Economy." In *The Handbook of Economic Sociology*, ed. Neil J. Smelser and Richard Swedberg. 2nd ed. Princeton: Princeton University Press. 527–51.

England, Paula and Nancy Folbre. 2005. "Gender and Economy in Economic Sociology." In *The Handbook of Economic Sociology*, ed. Neil J. Smelser and Richard Swedberg. 2nd ed. Princeton: Princeton University Press. 627–49.

Finley, M. I. [1973]1985. *The Ancient Economy*. London: Hogarth Press.

Fligstein, Neil. 1990. *The Transformation of Corporate Control*. Cambridge, Mass.: Harvard University Press.

———. 2001. *The Architecture of Markets: An Economic Sociology of Twenty-First-Century Capitalist Societies*. Princeton: Princeton University Press.

Friedman, Milton. 1962. *Capitalism and Freedom*. Chicago: University of Chicago Press.

Fukuyama, Francis. 1995. *Trust: The Social Virtues and the Creation of Prosperity*. London: Penguin Books.

Galbraith, Kenneth. [1952]1956. *American Capitalism: The Concept of Countervailing Power*. Rev. ed. Boston: Houghton Mifflin.

Geertz, Clifford. 1963. *Peddlers and Princes: Social Development and Economic Change in Two Indonesian Towns*. Chicago: University of Chicago Press.

Goffman, Erving. [1969]1972. "Strategic Interaction." In Goffman, *Strategic Interaction*. New York: Ballantine Books. 83–145.

Granovetter, Mark S. 1985. "Economic Action and Social Structure: The Problem of Embeddedness." *American Journal of Sociology* 91(3): 481–510.

———. 1988. "The Sociological and Economic Approaches to Labor Market Analysis: A Social Structural View." In *Industries, Firms, and Jobs: Sociological and Economic Approaches*, ed. George Farkas and Paula England. New York: Plenum Press. 187–216.

———. 1994. "Business Groups." In *The Handbook of Economic Sociology*, ed. Neil J. Smelser and Richard Swedberg. Princeton: Princeton University Press.

Hall, Peter A. and David Soskice, eds. 2001. *Varieties of Capitalism: The Institutional Foundations of Comparative Advantage*. Oxford: Oxford University Press.

Hall, Thomas, ed. 2000. *A World-Systems Reader*. Lanham, Md.: Rowman and Littlefield.

Hannan, Michael T. and Glenn R. Carroll. 1992. *Dynamics of Organizational Populations: Density, Legitimation, and Competition*. Oxford: Oxford University Press.

Hayek, Friedrich von. 1945. "The Use of Knowledge in Society." *American Economic Review* 35: 519–30.

————, ed. 1954. *Capitalism and the Historians*. Chicago: University of Chicago Press.

Hedstrom, Peter and Richard Swedberg, eds. 1998. *Social Mechanisms: An Analytical Approach to Social Theory*. Cambridge: Cambridge University Press.

Hollingsworth, J. Rogers and Robert Boyer, eds. 1997. *Contemporary Capitalism: The Embeddedness of Institutions*. Cambridge: Cambridge University Press.

Hollingsworth, J. Rogers, Philippe C. Schmitter, and Wolfgang Streeck, eds. 1994. *Governing Capitalist Economies: Performance and Control of Economic Sectors*. New York: Oxford University Press.

Hunt, Alan. "Moralizing Luxury: The Discourse of the Governance of Consumption." *Journal of Historical Sociology* 8(4): 352–74.

Hurst, James Willard. 1956. *Law and the Condition of Freedom in the Nineteenth Century*. Madison: University of Wisconsin Press.

Ingham, Geoffrey. 2004. *The Nature of Money*. Cambridge: Polity Press.

Inglehart, Ronald and Wayne E. Baker. 2000. "Modernization, Cultural Change, and Persistence of Traditional Values." *American Sociological Review* 65: 19–51.

Keister, Lisa. 2000. *Wealth in America: Trends in Wealth Inequality*. Cambridge: Cambridge University Press.

Kitschelt, Herbert, Peter Lange, Gary Marks, and John D. Stephens, eds. 1999. *Continuity and Change in Contemporary Capitalism*. Cambridge: Cambridge University Press.

Lazear, Edward P. 1995. *Personnel Economics*. Cambridge, Mass.: MIT Press.

Light, Ivan and Stavros Karageorgis. 1994. "The Ethnic Economy." In *The Handbook of Economic Sociology*, ed. Neil J. Smelser and Richard Swedberg. Princeton: Princeton University Press. 647–76.

Lipset, Seymour M. 1960. *Political Man: The Social Basis of Politics*. New York: Doubleday.

————. [1967]1988. "Values and Entrepreneurship in the Americas. In Lipset, *Revolution and Counterrevolution: Change and Persistence in Social Structures*. New Brunswick, N.J.: Transaction Books. 77–140.

————. 1989. *Continental Divide: The United States and Institutions of the United States and Canada*. Washington, D.C.: Canadian-American Committee.

————. 1996. *American Exceptionalism: A Double-Edged Sword*. New York: W.W. Norton.

Macaulay, Stewart. 1963. "Non-Contractual Relations in Business: A Preliminary Study." *American Sociological Review* 28: 55–67.

Marshall, Alfred. [1890]1961. *The Principles of Economics*. 9th (variorum) ed. 2 vols. London: Macmillan.

Marx, Karl. [1867]1990. *Capital: A Critique of Political Economy*. Vol. 1. London: Penguin Books.

Marx, Karl and Friedrich Engels. [1848]1978. "Manifesto of the Communist Party." In *The Marx-Engels Reader*, ed. Robert C. Tucker. 2nd ed. New York: W.W. Norton. 473–500.

Menger, Carl. 1892. "On the Origin of Money." *Economic Journal* 2: 239–55.

Milgrom, Paul, Douglass C. North, and Barry R. Weingast. 1990. "The Role of Institutions in the Revival of Trade: The Law Merchant, Private Judges, and the Champagne Fairs." *Economics and Politics* 2 (1): 1–23.
Milgrom, Paul and John Roberts. 1992. *Economics, Organization, and Management.* Englewood Cliffs, N.J.: Prentice-Hall.
Milkman, Ruth and Eleanor Townsley. 1994. "Gender and the Economy." In *The Handbook of Economic Sociology,* ed. Neil J. Smelser and Richard Swedberg. Princeton: Princeton University Press. 600–619.
Mirowski, Philip and Esther-Mirjam Sent, eds. *Science Bought and Sold: Essays in the Economics of Science.* Chicago: University of Chicago Press.
Mises, Ludwig von. 1956. *The Anti-Capitalist Mentality.* Princeton: Van Nostrand.
Mokyr, Joel. 1990. *The Lever of Riches: Technological Creativity and Economic Progress.* New York: Oxford University Press.
Moore, Barrington. 1966. *Origins of Democracy and Dictatorship.* Boston: Beacon Press.
Nee, Victor. 1992. "The Organizational Dynamics of Market Transition: Hybrid Forms, Property Rights, and Mixed Economy in China." *Administrative Science Quarterly* 37(1): 1–27.
———. 1998. "Norms and Networks in Economic and Organizational Performance." *American Economic Review* 88(May): 85–89.
North, Douglass C. 1970. "An Economic Theory of the Growth of the Western World." *Journal of Economic History* 23: 1–17.
———. 1977. "Markets and Other Allocation Systems in History: The Challenge of Karl Polanyi." *Journal of European Economic History* 6: 703–16.
North, Douglass C., William Summerhill, and Barry Weingast. 2000. "Order, Disorder, and Economic Change: Latin America versus North America." In *Governing for Prosperity,* ed. Bruce Bueno de Mesquito and Hilton Root. New Haven: Yale University Press. 59–84.
North, Douglass C. and Robert P. Thomas. 1973. *The Rise of the Western World.* Cambridge: Cambridge University Press.
North, Douglass C. and Barry R. Weingast. 1989. "Constitutions and Commitment: The Evolution of Institutions Governing Public Choice in Seventeenth-Century England." *Journal of Economic History* 49: 803–32.
Oi, Jean C. and Andrew G. Walder, eds. 1999. *Property Rights and Economic Reform in China.* Stanford: Stanford University Press.
Olson, Mancur. 1965. *The Logic of Collective Action: Public Goods and the Theory of Groups.* Cambridge, Mass.: Harvard University Press.
Oxford English Dictionary Online. 1989. "Business 24. Business Woman." 2nd ed.
Perrow, Charles. 2002. *Organizing America: Wealth, Power, and the Origins of Corporate Capitalism.* New Haven: Yale University Press.
Piore, Michael J. and Charles F. Sabel. 1984. *The Second Industrial Divide: Possibilities for Prosperity.* New York: Basic Books.
Polanyi, Karl. [1957]1971. "The Economy as Instituted Process." In *Trade and Market in the Early Empires: Economies in History and Theory,* ed. Karl Polanyi, Conrad M. Arensberg, and Harry W. Pearson. Chicago: Henry Regnery. 243–69.

Posner, Richard. [1972]1998. *Economic Analysis of Law*. 5th ed. Boston: Little, Brown.

———. 1981. *The Economics of Justice*. Cambridge, Mass.: Harvard University Press.

Powell, Walter W. and Laurel Smith-Doerr. 1994. "Networks and Economic Life." In *The Handbook of Economic Sociology*, ed. Neil J. Smelser and Richard Swedberg. Princeton: Princeton University Press. 368–402.

Renner, Karl. [1904]1949. *The Institutions of Private Law and Their Social Function*. Boston: Routledge and Kegan Paul.

Ritzer, George. 1999. *Enchanting a Disenchanted World: Revolutionizing the Means of Consumption*. Thousand Oaks, Calif.: Pine Forge Press.

Roethlisberger, Fritz and William Dickson. 1939. *Management and the Worker*. Cambridge, Mass.: Harvard University Press.

Rosenberg, Nathan and L. E. Birdzell. 1986. *How the West Grew Rich*. New York: Basic Books.

Roy, Donald. 1952. "Quota Restrictions and Goldbricking in a Machine Shop." *American Journal of Sociology* 57: 427–42.

Rueschemeyer, Dietrich, Evelyne Huber, and John D. Stephens. 1992. *Capitalist Development and Democracy*. Cambridge: Polity Press.

Samuelson, Paul. 1970. *Economics*. 8th ed. New York: McGraw-Hill.

Schroeder, Ralph and Richard Swedberg. 2002. "Weberian Perspectives on Science, Technology and the Economy." *British Journal of Sociology* 53: 383–401.

Schumpeter, Joseph A. 1911. *Theorie der wortschaftlichen Entwicklung*. Leipzig: Duncker and Humblot.

———. [1918]1991. "The Crisis of the Tax State." In Schumpeter, *The Economics and Sociology of Capitalism*, ed. Richard Swedberg. Princeton: Princeton University Press. 99–140.

———. 1934. *The Theory of Economic Development*. Cambridge, Mass.: Harvard University Press.

———. 1939. *Business Cycles: A Theoretical, Historical, and Statistical Analysis of the Capitalist Process*. 2 vols. New York: McGraw-Hill.

———. [1942]1994. *Capitalism, Socialism and Democracy*. London: Routledge.

———. [1946]1951. "Capitalism." In Schumpeter, *Essays*. New York: Addison-Wesley. 184–205.

Shapiro, Susan. 1984. *Wayward Capitalists: Target of the Security and Exchange Commission*. New Haven: Yale University Press.

Smith, Adam. [1776]1976. *An Inquiry into the Nature and Causes of the Wealth of Nations*. 2 vols. Oxford: Oxford University Press.

Solow, Robert M. 1987. "We'd Better Watch Out." *New York Times Book Review*, July 12, 36.

———. 2002. *Growth Theory: An Exposition*. 2nd ed. New York: Oxford University Press.

Sombart, Werner. 1930. "Capitalism." In *Encyclopaedia of the Social Sciences*, ed. Alvin Johnson and Edwin R. A. Seligman. New York: Macmillan. Vol. 3: 195–216.

Stigler, George. 1971. "The Theory of Economic Regulation." *Bell Journal of Economics* 2(Spring): 3–21.

Stinchcombe, Arthur. 1983. *Economic Sociology.* New York: Academic Press.

Streeck, Wolfgang. 1992. *Social Institutions and Economic Performance.* London: Sage.

Swedberg, Richard. 1994. "Markets as Social Structures." In *The Handbook of Economic Sociology,* ed. Neil J. Smelser and Richard Swedberg. Princeton: Princeton University Press. 255–82.

———. 2002. "The Economic Sociology of Capitalism: Weber and Schumpeter." *Journal of Classical Sociology* 2(3): 227–55.

———. 2003a. "The Case for an Economic Sociology of Law." *Theory and Society* 32: 1–37.

———. 2003b. *Principles of Economic Sociology.* Princeton: Princeton University Press.

———. 2005. *Interest.* London: Open University Press.

Tocqueville, Alexis de. [1835–40]1945. *Democracy in America.* Trans. Henry Reeve. 2 vols. New York: Vintage Books.

Tucker, James. 1999. "Worker Deviance as Social Control." *Research in the Sociology of Work* 81: 1–16.

Uzzi, Brian. 1997. "Social Structure and Competition in Interfirm Networks: The Paradox of Embeddedness." *Administrative Science Quarterly* 42: 35–67.

Wallerstein, Immanuel. 1974–1989. *The Modern World System.* Vols. 1–3. New York: Academic Press.

Weber, Max. [1904]1949. " 'Objectivity' in Social Science and Social Policy." In *The Methodology of the Social Sciences.* New York: Free Press, 49–112.

Weber, Max. [1904–1905]1958. *The Protestant Ethic and the Spirit of Capitalism.* New York: Scribner's.

———. [1907]1977. *Critique of Stammler.* New York: Free Press.

———. [1916]1994. "Between Two Laws." In Weber, *Political Writings,* ed. Peter Lassman and Ronald Speirs. Cambridge: Cambridge University Press. 75–79.

———. [1921]1958. *The Religion of India.* New York: Free Press.

———. [1922]1978. *Economy and Society: An Outline of Interpretive Sociology.* 2 vols. Berkeley: University of California Press.

———. [1923]1981. *General Economic History.* New Brunswick, N.J.: Transaction Books.

———. 1946. *From Max Weber.* Ed. Hans Gerth and C. Wright Mills. New York: Oxford University Press.

Weingast, Barry R. 1996. "Political Institutions: Rational Choice Perspectives." In *A New Handbook of Political Science,* ed. Robert Goodin and Hans-Dieter Klingemann. Oxford: Oxford University Press. 167–90.

White, Harrison C. 1981. "Where Do Markets Come From?" *American Journal of Sociology* 87: 517–47.

———. 1985. "Agency as Control." In *Principals and Agents: The Structure of Business,* ed. John Pratt and Richard Zeckhsuser. Boston: Harvard Business School. 187–212.

————. 1992. *Identity and Control: A Structural Theory of Social Action.* Princeton: Princeton University Press.

Wirth, Louis. "American Sociology, 1915–47." *American Journal of Sociology,* Index to vols, 1–52: 273–81.

Wright, Erik Olin. 1997. *Classes.* London: Verso.

Zeitlin, Jonathan. 1990. *Industrial Districts and Local Economic Regionalism.* Geneva: International Institute for Labour Studies.

Capitalism and Economic Growth

Douglass C. North

KARL MARX'S FAMOUS CELEBRATION of the dynamics of a capitalist society in the Communist Manifesto remains to this day a testimonial to the potential of capitalism. But with more than a century and a half perspective, the results of capitalism's spread around the world have been a mixed bag at best. In parts of the world it has produced growth that would have astonished even Marx. In sub-Saharan Africa it has resulted in absolutely declining levels of per capita output and throughout much of the rest of the world the results have varied from "stop and go" growth in Latin America to spectacular expansion in parts of Asia and most surprising (to Marx's ghost anyway) in nominally communist China. How do we account for this extraordinary outcome?

• • •

In this chapter I shall explore both the very special historical conditions that produced the capitalist engine in the West and just why capitalism has failed to produce growth in much of the rest of the world; I will then specify the relationship between institutions and economic performance. I am then in a position to specify the economic institutions and the unique conditions that produced "the free market innovation machine." In conclusion, I shall set this discussion in time to demonstrate the essential contribution that economic history can make to our understanding of economic performance.

The rise of the Western world was the ascendancy of a relatively backward part of the world to world hegemony in the millennium after the tenth century. But it was more than that. It was part of a fundamental shift in the focus of institutional change, from dealing with the uncertainties of the physical environment to dealing with those of the increasingly complex human

This chapter is drawn from and is an extension of the paper, "The Institutional Bases of Capitalist Development," prepared for the conference "Entrepreneurship, Innovation, and the Growth Mechanism of Free Market Economies," honoring Will Baumol, New York, 2003.

environment. The conquest of the physical environment with the growth of scientific knowledge entailed a far more complex human environment; a necessary prerequisite was a social, political, and economic structure of interdependence, ubiquitous externalities, and impersonal exchange. The Western world evolved gradually to provide the necessary structure to realize, very imperfectly, the potential of the application of this growing knowledge to solve problems of human scarcity. Adam Smith was correct that the wealth of nations was a result of specialization, division of labor, and the size of the market. But he could only dimly have envisioned the complex societies that would result. The shift from personal to impersonal exchange requires a political, economic, and social structure that runs counter to the genetic predispositions of millions of years of hunter/gatherer heritage.[1] Realizing the potential of human well-being possible with this scientific knowledge entails a fundamental restructuring of societies. The necessary political and economic structure developed over centuries.[2] The essential condition is the creation of an incentive structure that rewards productive activity and discourages anti-social behavior in the specific setting of impersonal markets, both political and economic. But the institutional changes necessary to create such an incentive framework must overcome innate genetic predispositions that evolved with a hunter/gatherer environment.

The widening gap between rich and poor countries that we are observing in modern times is a reflection of our inability to reproduce the necessary conditions in countries with a heritage of personal exchange. Most of these countries are (at least nominally) capitalist but in no way reflect the "free market" that we associate with a vigorous capitalist society. Rather they reflect an inability to restructure their political and economic frameworks to reap the benefits of the productive potential which we possess. Table 1 gives a capsule summary of the contrast.

While the figures exaggerate the difference for all the reasons we are familiar with in national income accounting, they are nevertheless startling, even more so because of the persistence of the difference. In figure 1, trends of per capita income as a percentage of U.S. per capita income not only show the persistence of the gap in Latin America but in the case of Argentina show a country which in 1940 was the sixth highest income country in the world and its subsequent decline. We know the sources of productivity growth and we even know the essential institutions, political and economic, to produce the desired results. We have only a very imperfect understanding of how to get those conditions.

The key to positive economic performance is to structure human interaction to reward productive activity. Institutions are the incentive structure of societies and therefore it is necessary to understand just "how they work" and why they work "imperfectly." We are some distance from having a complete theory of institutions that would explain their formation,

TABLE 1
The World in 2000. Per-Capita Income as a Percentage of U.S. Per-Capita
Income Rank in 2001 (*Index of Economic Freedom* in Parentheses)

Rich Countries		Poor Countries	
Britannica		*Latin America*	
UK (7)	68.1	Bolivia (35)	8.2
Australia (9)	76.3	Chile (13)	29.2
Canada (14)	80.7	Uruguay (34)	28.9
Ireland (3)	76.4	Argentina (29)	32.9
Europe		*Africa*	
Switzerland (9)	79.2	Ethiopia (124)	2.0
Denmark (14)	80.1	Kenya (87)	3.7
Luxembourg (5)	137.5	Zimbabwe (146)	7.3
Asia		*Asia*	
Hong Kong (1)	78.3	Indonesia (114)	11.3
Japan (14)	72.8	China (114)	10.8
Singapore (2)	80.4	India (1333)	7.5

Source: Penn World Tables; (2001).

just how they influence performance and the process of change, and their
integration with neoclassical (price) theory. But we have made a good deal
of progress and the thriving development of the International Society of
the New Institutional Economics (ISNIE) promises substantial further improvement. Recent studies that have contributed to our understanding are
those dealing with the movement from personal to impersonal exchange
(Greif 1994; Milgrom, North, and Weingast 1990), the structure of property rights (Barzel 1997), and the interplay between the mind and the environment (Donald 1991; Hutchins 1995).

Institutions are composed of formal rules, informal constraints, and their
enforcement characteristics. Formal rules are constitutions, laws, rules, and
regulations; informal constraints are made up of conventions, norms of behavior, and self-imposed constraints on conduct. Enforcement is either first
person (self-imposed), second person (retaliation), or third person (ranging
from peer pressure to governmental enforcement). Together these components determine the way the game is played.

Let me illustrate from professional team sports. Professional football is
played on the basis of formal rules, informal constraints (such as not deliberately injuring the quarterback of the opposing team), and umpires

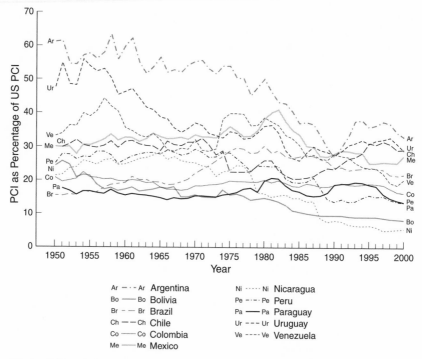

Figure 1 Trends in per capita income relative to the United States: Latin America, 1950–2000 (*source:* Penn World Tables).

and referees to enforce both formal rules and informal norms. Enforcement is always imperfect and accordingly it frequently pays to violate the rules or norms. Obviously the way the game is in fact played is a function of the degree of imperfection of enforcement, which is in turn a function of the strength of norms of behavior, the effectiveness of the umpires, and the severity of penalties for violation. But beyond that, the rules themselves were devised by interested parties so that even the fundamental characteristics of the game can be understood only by examining the interests of the parties structuring the game.

In essence, understanding the performance of political/economic systems entails analysis of the same issues, including the imperfect nature of enforcement. Formal economic rules are made by polities, and therefore we must be able to model polities as a first requirement. Ever since James Madison's insightful comments in Federalist Paper 10, we have been aware of the fundamental dilemma of polities. If a polity is strong enough to enforce the rules of the game, it is strong enough to be employed by special interests to pursue their own objectives at the expense of the society as a whole. Creating a polity that is strong but "limited" is an essential condition. In the economy, it is competition that turns the interests of the individual producer into a social "good." But what kind of competition? It must be competition that gets the players to compete via price and quality rather than at some other margin such as killing one's competitor (as a Russian banker cheerfully confided to me in the 1990s) or some other socially undesirable behavior. Norms of behavior may constrain the players, but where do they come from and how strong are they? Indeed, the last sentence gets to a fundamental issue. Where do the beliefs, norms, and institutions come from? Economics is a theory of choice, but what is the source of choices? This may be easy to answer when one goes to the supermarket, but it is vastly more complicated when one tries to account for the institutions in various societies. The incentive system implicit in neoclassical theory is dependent on a specific belief system. Widely different belief systems throughout history and in the present day produce different incentive systems and accordingly different choices when confronting the same source of uncertainty. It should not be necessary to belabor this point in the aftermath of 9/11. We have a way to go in cognitive science before we have sufficient understanding of the operation of the mind and brain to provide definitive answers to the issues of consciousness which can produce on the one hand a Mozart or Einstein and on the other hand a Savonarola or Hitler. But such understanding is crucial to our survival in a world that can produce weapons that can destroy whole societies. The crucial issue to be confronted is not just the individual's belief but the existence of belief systems that will provide widespread support for violence and terrorism.

The institutions essential to a dynamic capitalism must create a polity that will in turn put in place and maintain economic rules of the game that will provide the incentive structure for continuous innovation, including a competitive structure to get the players to compete at socially productive margins. It requires a belief system that will provide the necessary incentives. More than that, with changes in technology, information costs, and relative prices the essential political and economic entrepreneurs must adjust the institutions to continue to provide the appropriate incentives in the face of such alterations. An additional dilemma is that we are evolving political/economic/social structures that are radically different and more complex than any in our past and therefore the evolving human environment has no historical precedent from which to derive theoretical inspiration. The degree to which the decision-makers understand the changes in this novel environment and act accordingly is problematic. And even if they do have an understanding they may find that the necessary changes threaten their survival, as the self-destruction of the Soviet Union bears witness. The relative success of the United States and other developed economies has entailed a flexible institutional structure that encourages the kind of trial and error structure argued by Friedrich Hayek as an essential prerequisite for survival in a world of ubiquitous uncertainty. Such adaptively efficient structures have evolved over a long time period and depend on the development of strong informal norms that will constrain the players in the face of the ubiquitous drive of economic and political actors to engage in rent seeking and eventually produce the stagnation and inefficient societies that Mancur Olson (1982) thought were inevitable without periodic revolutions.

We tend to "get it wrong" when the accumulated experiences and beliefs derived from the past do not provide a correct guide to future decision making. The reason is twofold: (1) The set of mental models, categories, and classifications of the neural networks that have evolved in our belief system through which the new evidence gets filtered has no existing pattern that can correctly assess the new evidence. (2) In cases where conflicting beliefs have evolved, the dominant organizations and their entrepreneurs may view the necessary changes as threats to their survival. To the degree that the entrepreneurs of such organizations control decision-making they can thwart the necessary changes. The first factor stems from our not correctly comprehending what is happening to us; the second from an inability to make the necessary institutional changes.

The shift from personal to impersonal exchange has produced just such a stumbling block both historically and in the contemporary world. Personal exchange relies on reciprocity, repeat dealings, and the kind of informal norms that tend to evolve from strong reciprocity relationships. Impersonal exchange requires the development of economic and political institutions that alter the payoffs in exchange to reward cooperative behavior even when the other party is a complete stranger. The creation of the necessary institutions requires a fundamental alteration in the structure of the economy and the polity which is frequently not in the feasible set given the historically derived beliefs and institutions of the players. The unique development of the western world, from the relative backwardness in the tenth century to world hegemony by the nineteenth century, gives us a glimpse of the kind of long run historical evolution that made such change possible. But we do not know how to create those conditions in the short run.

• • •

We can explore those conditions by examining the sources of the dramatic growth of transaction costs in the American economy over the past century, an increase that largely reflected the increasing complexity of the economy. Between 1870 and 1970, the transaction sector of the American economy increased from 25 percent to 45 percent of the GNP, reflecting the dramatic alteration of an economy shifting focus from the uncertainties associated with the physical environment to the increasingly complex human environment (see Wallis and North 1986). The most dramatic part of the increase reflected growing specialization and division of labor along with the growing size of the market. Multiplying the number of exchanges with growing specialization entailed an overall increase in transacting. The increase in transaction costs arose as a result of the costs of

1. measuring the multiple valuable dimensions of a good or service;
2. the protection of individual property rights;
3. the enforcement of agreements;
4. the integration of the dispersed knowledge of the society.

Let me elaborate on each:

1. Goods and services typically have multiple dimensions that have utility to the individual. To the degree that these individual dimensions can be measured, we can define property rights more precisely and thereby increase the utility to the individual and reduce the overall costs of exchange.
2. The development of effective third party enforcement with all that it entails in terms of institutions and organizations is always supplemented by re-sources the individual devotes to protecting his or her property.
3. Enforcement of agreements involves the cost of monitoring and metering exchanges to see that the terms of exchange are being lived up to and developing effective punishment for violations.
4. The greater the specialization and division of labor in a society, the more dispersed is the knowledge in the society and the more resources must be devoted to integrating that dispersed knowledge.

Improving economic performance means lowering production and transaction costs; the key is modifying institutions to accomplish this objective. This includes the development of a uniform system of weights and measures (and technological research to achieve better measurement), the creation of an effective judicial system and enforcement mechanisms, and the development of institutions and organizations to integrate the dispersed knowledge in a society as well as to monitor and meter agreements and adjudicate disputes. The overall consequence is a dramatic increase in the overall costs of transacting that is much more than offset by dramatic decreases in production costs.[3]

• • •

The unique condition that has produced a dynamic capitalism has been most carefully described by Will Baumol in his study *The Free Market Innovation Machine* (2002). Let me set out to evaluate Baumol's account. His description of the free market innovation machine poses a distinct challenge.

Just what kind of an institutional structure will support such a machine? He provides a number of clues including a thoughtful discussion of productive activity in the thirteenth to fifteenth centuries, the trading of property rights to constituents for income which was the initial source of representative government, and other factors leading to the rule of law (chapter 5). Indeed he asserts in discussing the critical role of the entrepreneur that: "How entrepreneurs act at a given time and place depends heavily on the prevailing "rules of the game"—i.e. the reward structure in the economy" (61). The chapter on the historical evidence (chapter 14) tells a story full of "implicit" institutions in which it would appear that they are dependent variables in the story and therefore not worth independent attention. But such free market institutions do not evolve automatically, as Baumol himself implies in the following passage: "The historical episodes that will be reviewed also underscore a critical point. The availability of human capital may be necessary but is surely not sufficient by itself to insure a firm connection between invention and economic growth. This requires, in addition, a set of powerful incentives, such as the free market provides to insure a continuous flow of inventions and their transformation through the innovation stage into a direct contribution to productivity and output growth" (246). And that is exactly what institutions are—incentives.

Let me see if we can be more specific. Just what incentive structure will produce the dynamic features of Baumol's model?

Beyond the rule of law which he does specify (68), "Capitalism requires markets in which the participants can have confidence in any agreement arrived at" (69). Such confidence comes from enforcement mechanisms which at low cost of transacting will assure that agreements are met. But personalized exchange runs counter to such a structure. One has only to witness the legal system in most Latin American countries to be acutely aware of this dilemma. It is not just that it is not a "level playing field" for all participants, but also that altering the judicial actors at the whim of political actors is a recurring phenomenon, as the history of Argentina (to take but one of many examples) abundantly illustrates. (see, e.g. Alston 2003).

But beyond a set of property rights and enforcement mechanisms much more is required to provide the essential underpinnings of Baumol's "machine." Baumol lists them as follows:

1. "Oligopolistic competition among large high-tech business firms with innovation as a prime competitive weapon ensuring continued innovative activity and, very plausibly, their growth."
2. "Routinization of these innovative activities, making them a regular and even ordinary component of the activities of the firm and thereby minimizing the uncertainty of the process."

3. "Productive entrepreneurship encouraged by incentives for entrepreneurs to devote themselves to productive innovation rather than to innovative rent seeking."
4. "The rule of law."
5. "Technology selling and trading, in other words, firms' voluntary pursuit of opportunities for profitable dissemination of innovations and rental of the right to use them, via licensing, even to direct competitors." (Baumol 2002: 4, 5)

Moreover, a persistent oligopolistic structure in which the kind of collusion that Baumol considers essential is only possible with a particular antitrust policy, as he states (114–15). Both productive entrepreneurship, which must be encouraged by incentives, and the rule of law are essential requirements. But the truly innovative part of Baumol's argument stems from his disenchantment with the traditional building blocks of neoclassical theory. After acknowledging Solow's pioneering argument, he explores the subsequent development of the "new growth economics" and finds that literature not completely satisfactory. "The central point is that each of these models employs a production function that contains a growth component, but that none of them has any attribute uniquely related to free-enterprise economies rather than some other economic form. That is what makes these models ahistorical. Moreover, when they do take account of innovation, the mechanisms of the activity enter only implicitly. There is no equation or other relationship that attempts to describe, for example, the incentive structure that leads to determination of the magnitude of this activity" (265).

We are some distance from understanding the complex structure that underlies the Baumol engine of progress. Nathan Rosenberg and David Mowery in their *Paths of Innovation* describe the changes as follows:

> Changes in the structure of the U.S. intellectual property system in the early 20th century, as well as the treatment of intellectual property by the judiciary, thus enhanced firms' incentives to both internalize industrial research and to invest in the acquisition of technologies from external sources. Against the backdrop of tougher federal enforcement of antitrust statutes, judicial decisions affirming the use of patents to create or maintain positions of market power also created additional incentives to pursue in-house R&D. Stronger, more consistent intellectual property rights also improved the operation of a market for intellectual property, making it easier for firms to use their in-house research facilities to acquire technology." (Mowery and Rosenberg 1998: 19–20)

But there is more to the story than a changing judiciary and antitrust policy. The integration of the dispersed knowledge of the complex human environment that we have created takes more than a "well oiled" price system to produce the desired results. Integrating the dispersed knowledge requires a much more complex structure. Paul David describes the issues:

> Nor has economics yet had much to say about what types of contractual arrangements, institutional forms, and organizational policies have proved to be especially conducive (or inimical) to the process of "knowledge transfer." Until very recently most economists studying the inside of the "black box" of private sector R&D have not thought it important to understand the variety of mechanisms responsible for the "spillovers" that theoretical analysis holds would result in industrial innovators reaping private benefits from the work of publicly supported academic and governmental research organizations. (David 1991: 6, 8)

Indeed Baumol's argument would be strengthened by devoting specific attention to the necessary growth of transaction costs that accompanies the innovation machine and permits it to operate.

•   •   •

Baumol is right on track when he criticizes the new growth economics for being ahistorical. Indeed his account is an enormous improvement over the purely theoretical, noninstitutional, nonhistorical accounts that pervade the growth literature.[4] The key to this overall explanation for the "innovation machine" is an incremental account through time of the evolution of the essential institutional/organizational complex that has produced these results in particular settings. This must be an analytical narrative that in the case of American economic history begins with the transfer of beliefs and institutions into colonial America and follows their development in the context of the resource rich environment of the new world and the institutional changes that resulted from the turbulent social upheaval in the nineteenth century. It would include the growth of higher educational investment with the enactment of the Morrill Act of 1862 and the subsequent expansion of the competitive structure of universities in the United States (in contrast to Europe) that eventually led to their preeminent position in supporting and integrating knowledge and specifically providing the context for the innovations of the twentieth century.[5] It would of necessity integrate the story with the development of antitrust legislation and its evolution—and beyond that, integrate it with the rich historical context of twentieth-century political and economic events. For Europe, Japan, and other developed economies, each would be a particular historical narrative but with common denominators of the essential institutions that underlie the innovation machine.[6] It is only thus that we can do justice to explaining Baumol's innovation machine. If economic history is to fulfill its promise of adding the dimension of time to economic (and political) analysis, the analytical historical narrative is the proper vehicle. A beginning has already been made with the above cited works of Nathan Rosenberg and Paul David. Joel Mokyr's *The Gifts of Athena* (2002), with its emphasis on the historical origins of the knowledge economy, is a further contribution. But we have a way to go before we can properly provide the dimension of time to economic analysis, a necessary development if we are to enrich our understanding of economic performance.

NOTES

1. There is a rich treasure trove of experimental research currently being undertaken to give us a better understanding of human behavior. An up-to-date summary can be found in McCabe 2003.

2. See the studies by Milgorm, North, and Weingast 1990; North and Weingast 1989; and Greif 1994 for description of the institutional changes that were an essential part of this transformation.

3. It is important to emphasize that not all transaction costs have been associated with productivity increases, even in the past century of dramatic growth. Institutional changes which have gone in the other direction, such as the long run consequences of the Interstate Commerce Commission for railroad productivity, are also part of the story.

4. See, e.g, the symposium on New Growth Theory in *Journal of Economic Perspectives* (Winter 1994).

5. See Rosenberg 2000, chap. 3, "American Universities as Endogenous Institutions."

6. It is important to stress that the key is to create the necessary incentive structure, not slavishly to imitate the institutions of the developed countries. China's accelerated development from the Household Responsibility system to TVEs has created the essential incentive system with unique specific institutions.

REFERENCES

Alston, Lee S. 2003. "The Erosion of the Rule of Law in Argentina, 1930–1947: An Explanation of Argentina's Economic Slide from the Top 10." Working paper, University of Illinois.

Barzel, Yoram. 1997. *Economic Analysis of Property Rights.* 2nd ed. Cambridge: Cambridge University Press.

Baumol, William J. 2000. *The Free Market Innovation Machine: Analyzing the Growth Miracle of Capitalism.* Princeton: Princeton University Press.

David, Paul A. 1991. "Positive Feedback and Research Productivity in Science: Reopening Another Black Box." In *Economics of Technology,* ed. Ove Granstrand. Amsterdam: Elsevier Science.

Donald, Merlin. 1991. *Origins of the Modern Mind: Three Stages in the Evolution of Culture and Cognition.* Cambridge, Mass.: Harvard University Press.

Greif, Avner. 1994. "On the Political Foundations of the Late Medieval Commercial Revolution: Genoa during the Twelfth and Thirteenth Centuries." *Journal of Economic History* 54(2): 271–87.

Hutchins, Edwin. 1995. *Cognition in the Wild.* Cambridge, Mass.: MIT Press.

McCabe, Kevin. 2003. "Reciprocity and Social Order: What Do Experiments Tell Us about the Failure of Economic Growth?" Working paper, Experimental Economics Laboratory, George Mason University.

Milgrom, Paul, Douglass C. North, and Barry R. Weingast. 1990. "The Role of Institutions in the Revival of Trade: The Law Merchant, Private Judges, and the Champagne Fairs." *Economics and Politics* 2 (1): 1–23.

Mokyr, Joel. 2002. *The Gifts of Athena: Historical Origins of the Knowledge Economy.* Princeton: Princeton University Press.

Mowery, David C. and Nathan Rosenberg. 1998. *Paths of Innovation: Technological Change in 20th-Century America.* Cambridge: Cambridge University Press.

North, Douglass C. and Barry R. Weingast. 1989. "Constitutions and Commitment: The Evolution of Institutions Governing Public Choice in Seventeenth-Century England." *Journal of Economic History* 49: 803–32.

O'Driscoll, Gerald P., Jr., Kim R. Holmes, and Melanie Kirkpatrick, eds. 2001. *2001 Index of Economic Freedom.* Washington, D.C.: Heritage Foundation.

Olson, Mancur. 1982. *The Rise and Decline of Nations: Economic Growth, Stagflation, and Social Rigidities.* New Haven: Yale University Press.

Rosenberg, Nathan. *Schumpeter and the Endogeneity of Technology: Some American Perspectives.* London: Routledge.

Wallis, John Joseph and Douglass C. North. 1986. "Measuring the Transaction Sector in the American Economy, 1870–1970." In *Long Term Factors in American Economic Growth*, ed. Stanley L. Engerman and Robert E. Gallman. Chicago: University of Chicago Press.

Organizational Dynamics of Institutional Change: Politicized Capitalism in China

Victor Nee

TRANSITIONS FROM STATE SOCIALISM offer rich natural experiments allowing for a better understanding of the dynamics of large-scale institutional change in newly emerging capitalist economies. Market transitions entail the shift from one distinct institutional form to another. In a state socialist redistributive economy, goods and services are allocated through central direction by nonmarket means. By contrast, in a market society, decentralized market exchange serves as the main mechanism that allocates goods and services. In this chapter I examine institutional transformation in an economy undergoing a rapid shift from central planning to reliance on markets. Through the theoretical lens of new institutional economics and economic sociology, I examine the ongoing organizational dynamics in China's industrial economy shaped by the rapid emergence of hybrid ownership forms and private enterprises and persistent displacement of the market share of state-owned firms. I show that Douglass North's (1990) theory of institutional change encounters difficulty in accounting for the organizational dynamics of large-scale institutional change because it assumes that organizational actors respond unproblematically to incentives stemming from changing relative prices. A more adequate explanatory account of the dynamics of institutional change, I argue, integrates hypotheses from economic sociology explaining the structural inertia facing organizational actors and the emergence of oppositional networks and norms limiting the scope and direction of transformative change.

North's theory of institutional change assigns to the state a central role. His starting point is a neoclassical theory of the state, which assumes that states exchange the provision of security and justice for revenue from their constituents, and devise property rights to maximize this revenue. North's theory argues that states are constrained in their revenue

I gratefully acknowledge research assistance provided by Wubiao Zhou, as well as Rachel Davis, Sonja Opper, Alexei Waters, and Geoff Woodley for providing useful comments and careful readings of the manuscript.

maximizing activity by competition with other states and political rivals; hence, they have an interest in structuring property rights that will secure the support of constituents against possible rivals, including other states and competitors within the same political order. North's theory offers two important insights into the role of the state in large-scale institutional change. First, when rival states threaten the state's survival and force "the choice of extinction or of modifying the fundamental ownership structure" (North 1981: 29), rulers are confronted with powerful incentives to initiate institutional innovations aimed at devising more efficient property rights to improve economic performance and to better compete with their rivals in inter-state competition. Second, institutional innovations will come from states rather than constituents because the state does not have a free rider problem, whereas individuals and organizational actors are limited in their capacity to implement large-scale changes due to the problem of free riding.

A still more fundamental mechanism of institutional change in North's theory is changing relative prices, which arise from changes in the ratio of factor prices (e.g., cost of labor), changes in the cost of information (e.g., stemming from the internet), and changes in technology, especially military technology. In North's view entrepreneurs act as agents of change and organizational actors as the players who respond to changes in relative prices in order to adapt to enhance survival and profit-making. An example of the latter is the rush of manufacturers from advanced capitalist economies to China to take competitive advantage of its huge supply of skilled low-cost compliant labor. Manufacturers facing intense competition in the global economy are irresistibly drawn toward skilled Chinese labor eager to work two full days for the price of one hour or less of an American or European or Japanese laborer's time. As a result, even long-standing institutionalized commitments to local labor—in the Japanese case, lifetime employment—are altered, in order to gain marginal profits otherwise not attainable.

Thus North's theory turns on two clusters of causal mechanisms: the market, with the incentives stemming from changes in relative prices, and the state, as a revenue maximizer, devising, initiating, and implementing large-scale institutional change. By means of laws and regulations, the state specifies the fundamental rules of competition and cooperation in devising the system of property rights. As a revenue maximizer, the state has an incentive to lower transaction costs in order to stimulate the productive output of society and by this means increase tax revenue. But, as North emphasizes, states seldom get it right, and more commonly institute and maintain arrangements that are inefficient.

North was the first new institutional economist to highlight the importance of informal norms, customs, and conventions, arguing that informal and formal constraints operate together in providing an underlying structure for economic activity. In his framework, institutions are defined as humanly constructed constraints, the formal and informal elements that structure incentives for economic and political actors. "Formal rules are an important part of the institutional framework but only a part. To work effectively they must be complemented by informal constraints (conventions, norms of behavior) that supplement them and reduce enforcement costs" (North 1993: 20). He acknowledges, however, that economics currently understands "very little about how informal norms evolve" and how they combine and interact with formal rules to structure incentives. "What is it about informal constraints that gives them such a pervasive influence upon the long-run character of economies? What is the relationship between formal and informal constraints?" (North 1991: 111). Williamson (2000) also recognizes that economists encounter difficulty in understanding the powerful effect of networks and norms on economic action: "We are still very ignorant about institutions. . . . North does not have an answer . . . nor do I" (2000: 596).

Informal networks and norms, operating in combination and interaction with the formal rules of the game, can both limit and facilitate economic performance. They can give rise to inefficient allocation of resources when interest groups collude to secure resources from government, resulting in structural rigidities and stagnation (Olson 1982). They can also promote the growth of a new industry by providing a framework for trust and collective action (McGuire et al. 1993). Economic sociology has made progress in accounting for how informal and formal institutional elements combine and interact in an institutional environment (Nee 2005). Its contribution to a cross-disciplinary understanding of institutional change is to focus analytic attention on explaining why networks and norms can have powerful effects in shaping economic and social behavior. Networks and the informal norms can play a decisive role in rendering formal rules ineffectual or effectual (Nee and Ingram 1998). If formal rules are in alignment with the informal norms, identity, and interests of actors in networks, then monitoring and enforcement of formal rules will be to a large extent assumed by social networks, giving rise to transaction cost economizing. On the other hand, if the formal rules are aligned against the identity and perceived interests of members of close-knit groups, oppositional norms are likely to emerge to counter the formal rules.[1]

Although North's theory asserts that organizations are important players in institutional change, there is surprisingly little said about organizations per se. The main references are to Coase's (1937) transaction cost theory of the firm, and to the extension of this theory by Williamson (1975). Otherwise, North assumes organizations behave like rational actors in their response to market incentives, adapting readily and unproblematically to

changing relative prices. This may provide an accurate model of organizational actors in a stable institutional environment where existing rules and
procedures provide a reliable guideline for organizational response, and
where the corporate governance is structured so that management is accountable for the firm's performance. But it provides at best a faulty model
in the context of a rapidly changing institutional environment in which the
existing repertoire of rules and procedures no longer works to provide a
helpful roadmap for effective organizational action. Under such circumstances, the customary roadmaps of appropriate organizational responses do
not yield their expected utility because established rules and procedures no
longer work as ready guidelines. Indeed, I argue that under conditions of
transformative change, the old rules and procedures frequently become, instead, sources of oppositional norms, which in turn reinforce organizational inertia to the extent they lock organizational actors into routines that are
at odds with the path of institutional change. The naive view of efficient organizational adaptation to change in relative price in North's theory is, I
maintain, a serious limitation.

Organizational analysts proffer a theory of structural inertia of organizations, which specifies just why they are unable to adapt quickly and effectively to changes in their institutional environment. Learning and
adapting by organizations is relatively slow due to structural inertia, defined as a slower speed of adaptation than the rate of change in the institutional environment (Hannan and Freeman 1984). Organizations are
complex entities that require resources to build and maintain, which are
costs sunk in the organizational structure. Not only is the cost of building
an organization nontrivial, but organizations require resources just to
maintain and reproduce their structure, apart from performing collective
action. Organizations that manage to survive competitive pressures in
their niche have invested considerable resources to ensure reliability of
performance, secured by maintaining reliability in compliance to rules and
procedures. Moreover, organizations gain legitimacy by producing internally consistent accounts showing that appropriate rules and procedures
are in place to produce rational allocations of resources and appropriate
organizational action. Thus organizations possess relatively fixed repertoires of rules and procedures. Resistance to change is a "by-product of
the ability to reproduce a structure with high fidelity: high levels of reproducibility of structure imply strong inertial pressures" (Hannan and Freeman 1989: 77). Because selection pressures favor organizations with a
high level of inertia, successful organizations tend to be those that carry
with them the strongest inertial forces.

As organizations age, they face stronger inertial pressures. Hannan and
Freeman (1989) observe that "nothing legitimates both individual organizations and forms more than longevity" (81). Older organizations develop

strong attachments to established rules and routines and dense network ties to centers of power. Their capacity for reliable and accountable action ironically slows their ability to adapt to environmental threats and opportunities. In contrast, new organizations and new organizational forms have lower levels of reproducibility. This gives rise to the "liability-of-newness," defined as a greater risk of failure faced by new organizations (Stinchcombe 1965). However, new organizations and organizational forms are more able to adapt quickly and effectively to changes in their environment. By extension, they are more able to champion new institutional arrangements because long-standing routines and rules encumber them less (Ingram 1998).

The claim that structural inertia renders the existing stock of organizations slow to adapt to change in their environment poses a challenge to North's theory of institutional change. This challenge, moreover, cannot be readily solved from within the theoretical logic of transaction cost economics which assumes that firms adapt efficiently to changes in relative prices, though, as North maintains, the state as an actor often institutes inefficient property rights and formal rules. However, the structural inertia hypothesis is consistent with and complementary to my argument that oppositional norms rooted in close-knit networks pose an incorrigible challenge to state-initiated institutional change because they significantly reinforce organizational inertia. Rapid changes in formal rules threaten established repertoires of organizational routines and identities, which gives rise to both manifest and latent opposition to the new rules of the game. Opposition norms often evolve out of the preexisting organizational rules and practices, which in the past structured incentives to benefit powerful networks in the firm.

Both the opposition norm and structural inertia hypotheses specify social mechanisms that claim broad explanatory power in understanding the organizational constraints on state-initiated institutional change. They suggest that new organizations and organizational forms are more capable of robust action in championing institutional change than old organizational forms, which are more vulnerable to lock-in and path-dependence stemming from oppositional networks and norms. Hence new organizations and organizational forms adapt more readily to rapid changes in the institutional environment.

In the next sections, I will examine institutional change in China, first through the lens of North's theory of institutional change, and then from the vantage point of insights from economic sociology. Changing relative prices stemming from advances in technology, especially military technology, in the advanced capitalist countries compelled communist reformers in state socialist economies to "sleep with the enemy" and launch large-scale institutional change to remake their economic institutions by expanding the role of markets (Nee and Lian 1994). These changes were initiated by the state as a means to maximize state revenues through improved economic performance, in large measure in response to a perceived intensification of interstate competition with rival states at a time when state socialist economies experienced declining economic performance due to inefficiencies in central planning. In China, as the enormous pool of cheap unskilled and skilled labor became available to international capital and as investments and global markets opened up to Chinese entrepreneurs and managers, the state initiated a series of innovations aimed at instituting the foundations of state capitalism. In the next section, I summarily describe very cursorily the decline of redistribution as an institutional form and the emergence of a market economy in China in order to document the rapidity of large parameter shifts in the institutional environment.

Decline of Socialist Redistribution and Emergence of Markets

In the 1980s, the Chinese economy shifted decisively away from nonmarket mechanisms for coordinating economic activity. The departure from reliance on central planning entailed a broad-based dissolution of the redistributive mechanisms controlled by the central government. First, a dramatic decline took place in the proportion of factor resources that were subject to allocation by central planning. This declined from 70 percent in 1980 to 14 percent in 1991. With respect to the distribution of manufactured goods, the categories of products subject to mandatory distribution through nonmarket channels decreased from 120 in 1980 to 50 in 1988, to make up only 16.2 percent of the total value of industrial output. By 1991, the number of categories dropped to only 21. Parallel to this, the number of commodities distributed by the state supply bureaucracy declined from 256 in 1980 to only 19 by 1989. These massive shifts away from central planning led to significant declines in the redistributive role of the central state. Although the state continued to set the prices for key agricultural and industrial products, by the early 1990s state regulation was no longer the dominant mechanism determining the prices of goods and services in the Chinese economy.

Rapid growth and diversification of domestic market institutions accompanied China's opening to the global market economy. The number of marketplaces more than doubled from 1978 (33,302) to 1991 (74,675). The volume of transactions in these markets increased at an even more rapid rate (over 20 times) from an initial small base in rural free markets. By the 1990s, there was a wide variety of market arrangements, including many types of commodity markets, labor markets, realty markets, financial markets, and lending institutions. Regional and provincial market centers that flourished prior to the revolution quickly reemerged. In the southeastern provinces of Guangdong and Fujian, for example, dense multiplex regional marketing networks linked to the economies of Hong Kong and Taiwan created the central places of a new capitalist economy. Foreign direct investments increased rapidly for more than two decades, with overseas Chinese, Taiwan, Japan, and the United States providing the largest sources of foreign capital. As multinational corporations moved manufacturing to China to take advantage of its huge supply of cheap unskilled and skilled labor, China emerged as the fastest growing economy in the world. Since 1980, China's GDP grew at an average annual rate of 8.6 percent. The sustained two-decade surge in China's exports was accompanied by an unexpectedly swift movement up the product chain in the goods manufactured in China, from cheap low-technology to high quality high technology products.

The resulting growth and diversification of a market economy in China have implications for the behavior of political and economic actors. The number and variety of markets and the dramatic increase in the sheer volume of market transactions comprise a significant source of discontinuous change in the institutional environment, especially for state-owned firms. These firms can no longer depend on the state for their inputs and for the distribution of their products. Instead, they find subcontractors outside of the state-managed economy, or go directly to wholesale markets and even international markets in competitive bids to gain price advantages and market share. Also, with the emergence of regional marketing networks, competition is no longer limited to local markets, but is regional and global in scope. In short, due to rapid parameter shifts driven by the transition to a market economy, the old rules and procedures of state-owned enterprises do not provide useful roadmaps for effective responses to competitive pressures. Yet because the old organizational rules and routines are enmeshed with the interests and identity of individuals in powerful networks entrenched inside the state-owned firms, organizational inertia is reinforced, resulting in structural rigidities that lock these firms into inefficient economic performance.

THE INSTITUTIONAL FOUNDATION OF STATE CAPITALISM

Changing relative prices, driven by an expanding market economy, motivated the state to redefine its relationship to state-owned firms (Naughton 1995; Steinfeld 1998; Keister 2000). North's theory finds support in the sequence of state-crafted institutional innovations directed at motivating improvements in these firms' economic performance. New institutional arrangements diffused quickly to provide a variety of hybrid governance structures for local government-owned industrial firms (Oi 1995; Nee and

Cao 1999). They helped to improve the economic performance for township and village enterprises by specifying property rights over rural industry under local government ownership (Walder 1995). New profit-sharing arrangements opened the way for informal forms of privatization based in local networks (Nee and Su 1996).

However, state-crafted institutional innovations that proved favorable to township and village enterprises could not be readily extended to reform large state-owned enterprises, which continued to operate at a loss and hence to drain state resources. In an attempt to address the problem, in the mid-1990s the Chinese government initiated an ambitious series of institutional innovations aimed at reforming the governance structure of state-owned enterprises. The main legislation was the Company Law, which was enacted by the Fifth Session of the Standing Committee of the Eighth National People's Congress of China on December 29, 1993 and promulgated on the same day. Outlined in eleven chapters and specified in 230 articles, this complex state-crafted institutional innovation provided the formal rules of a "modern enterprise system" (*xiandai qiye zhidu*) to enable state-owned enterprises to adapt to a rapidly expanding market economy by means of conversion to profit-maximizing capitalist firms.

In drafting this legislation, reform economists in Beijing borrowed extensively from the legal framework of corporate governance and shareholder rights in the West, principally corporate and securities laws of the United States and Australia (Wang and Tomasic 1994). The Company Law elaborates and specifies the formal rules specifying the corporate governance to be adopted by state-owned enterprises as they reorganize themselves into for-profit public corporations. The Law lays out the rules and procedures by which state-owned enterprises change their legal status to that of a "limited-liability company" (*youxian zeren gongsi*) or a "joint-stock company" (*gufen youxian gongsi*); foreign and joint-venture firms are regulated by different laws and regulations. The Company Law specifies the rights of shareholders and creditors. It confers to the joint-stock company the right to be listed on the stock exchange, and presumably to partially privatize through issuing securities.

As in the West, the firm has the rights of a legal person in regard to its property, where liability is limited to the amount of capital contributed by each shareholder in a limited-liability company and the amount of shares held by a shareholder in the joint-stock company. The new status of the firm as a legal person represents significant progress over earlier reform laws in clarifying the structure of property rights for state-owned enterprises (Wang and Tomasic 1994). Previously, the enterprise's property rights were limited to possessing, utilizing, and disposing of property which the state authorized it to operate and manage, leaving no clear legal separation between the company's property rights and those of the state. The Company Law instead provides a legal basis for the partitioning of rights of shareholders—principally the state—and the firm. Reflecting the partitioning of rights, the Company Law stipulates that the enterprise is legally responsible for its own profits and losses and the state may not intervene in the management of the firm. Furthermore, it limits the state to exercising macro-economic adjustments and controls. As long as the company conducts its business within the framework of the law and government macro-economic policy, it has the right to make its own decisions in accordance with market conditions. The Company Law stipulates that the firm must conform to the separation of authority between the manager and board of directors. And it must lawfully safeguard the rights of shareholders.

The broad outlines of the Company Law are laid out in its General Provisions. To my mind, the defining feature of state capitalism in China is specified by Article 17, which recognizes the right of the Communist Party to carry out its activities in the enterprise. This article cements the political orientation of the state as integral to its economic institutions. In the main body of the Law there are 211 articles detailing every aspect of corporate governance. These include careful specification of how limited-liability and joint-stock companies are to be set up with respect to the number of shareholders, their rights, the purpose of shareholders' meetings, their frequency, the disposition of start-up capital, the company's name and organizational structure, and the company's physical plant. The Company Law requires firms to have a board of directors, and specifies through its articles the composition, selection procedures, organization, term of office, responsibilities, and rights of this board. As in Western corporate governance, the chairman of the board is the legal representative of the firm. The board of directors is charged with the responsibility for appointing and dismissing the firm's management.

In keeping with its intent to impose formal constraints on the state's involvement in the firm, the Company Law states that government employees are disqualified from serving as directors or managers of a company. The Law also clarifies the limits of the authority of directors and managers. It definitively spells out legal restrictions against patrimonial uses of the company's resources and funds. Furthermore, it explicitly forbids directors and managers to engage in business activity in competition with their company, or to disclose company secrets, and specifies their liability to compensate the firm for damages if they violate the law and regulations of the state.

Viewed from the lens of North's theory of institutional change, the promulgation of the Company Law appears to follow his story line. Changing relative prices, both preceding and accompanying deepening shifts to reliance on markets and the decline in central planning, forced the hand of the central state. As a revenue maximizer, the state has a powerful interest

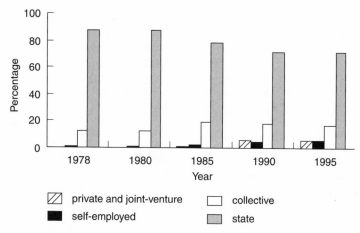

Figure 1 The structure of government revenue by ownership (*source:* State Statistical Bureau 1998: 272).

in devising a new structure of property rights that can promote needed improvements in the economic performance of its main assets, state-owned enterprises. Figure 1 shows that through the course of economic reform and the enactment of the Company Law, the state's revenues overwhelmingly derived from state-owned enterprises, even though the percentage declined from nearly 90 percent at the start of economic reform to a little over 70 percent by 1995. Hence it remained very much in the state's interest to devise a structure of property rights that could turn the loss-making state-owned enterprises into profitable businesses. The state's strategy was to convert state-owned enterprises into profit-maximizing capitalist firms by instituting Western corporate governance structures in China. The attraction of this to reformers is obvious: it provided guidelines legitimated by the success of public corporations in advanced capitalist economies of the West, which conveniently allows the state to maintain formal ownership rights in enterprises, while specifying corporate governance that reformers believed would enable managers of the restructured state-owned firms to compete with foreign firms, capitalist hybrids (joint-venture firms), and private enterprise in the emerging market economy.

By the mid-1990s, the institutional foundation of state capitalism was in place in China. As North's theory would predict, in a global context of changing relative prices, the revenue maximizing interests of China's rulers, competition with rivals, and the lobbying activity of managers of state-owned enterprises all contribute to explaining the institutional changes embodied in the enactment of the Company Law. But difficulties with North's theory begin to emerge when one examines the state's enforcement of the Company Law and the response of enterprise managers. Here is where economic sociology has much to contribute to explaining the organizational dynamics of institutional change—specifically, first, organizational ecology's argument that structural inertia makes organizations slow to adjust to changes in their institutional environment (Hannan and Freeman 1984); and second, study of the relationship between informal and formal institutional constraints, pointing to oppositional networks and norms to the formal rules (Nee and Ingram 1998).

In Shanghai, China's largest industrial and commercial city, shortly after the implementation of the Company Law, interviews with managers of state-owned enterprises show that they were aware of the Company Law, but uncertain about how it would concretely effect their firm (Guthrie 1999). Firms that applied to the municipal agency charged with overseeing the implementation of the Company Law were casually granted permission to change their legal status into a limited-liability or joint-stock company without clear interpretation of the rules to provide practical guidelines for conversion of state-owned enterprises into public corporations. Management often operated within the same de facto rules and procedures as those that were in place when they were state-owned enterprises (Li 1998; Ye and Liang 1999). The firm's party committee frequently continued to appoint the heads of companies and to intervene in the company's management. Managers often appointed the members of the board of directors, rather than the board of directors appointing the manager. Moreover, the company's party secretary commonly served as the chairman of the board. Initially at least, the board of directors had little authority over the firm's management (Li 1998; Ye and Liang 1999). Though the Law stipulates that the same person cannot hold simultaneously the positions of chairman of the board and CEO, firms were frequently in violation of this rule. In 1999, 18 percent of firms listed on the Shanghai Stock Exchange showed that the CEO and chairman of the board was the same person (Opper et al. 2002). In short, despite the formal rules specified by the Company Law, much of the old repertoire of organizational rules and procedures remained in place, giving rise to decoupling between the rules of corporate governance specified in the Company Law and the actual organizational routines and practices of firm.

Court records reveal very few cases litigating the Company Law, and these involved prosecutions of traditional economic crimes such as bribery, embezzlement, and other forms of corruption. Despite the weak and sporadic nature of state enforcement, however, the interest of managers in gaining legitimacy accounted for increased formal compliance with the Company Law. Guthrie's (1999) analysis indicates that voluntary formal compliance appeared in firms he surveyed in Shanghai because managers actively seek the mantel of legitimacy associated with being viewed as a modern Western-style corporation. As DiMaggio and Powell (1983) persuasively argue, organizations come to comply with rules institutionalized and legitimated by central states because they gain better access to resources by being perceived as legitimate; further, organizations respond to uncertainty by mimicking or copying legitimatized procedures and models; and last, professionals experience normative pressures to accept and act on models of appropriate behavior. These studies of state-owned firms in Shanghai appear to support these hypotheses.

By 2000, a study of the corporate governance structure of 257 companies listed on the Shanghai Stock Exchange confirms that the formal rules and procedures specified by the Company Law in fact shaped corporate governance and decision making (Opper et al. 2001). In compliance with the Law, shareholders' meetings were held annually and substantive decisions were made at the meetings. Boards of directors were organizationally important—deciding on the selection and dismissal of managers, setting their remuneration, calling board and shareholder meetings and setting their agendas, formulating the company's strategic plan, organizing training for members of the board and management, electing and dismissing the chairman secretary of the board and, and making a wide range of decisions regarding strategic investments by the firm. Overall, the survey shows that formally the board of directors has the widest range of decision-making power, followed by the manager, the shareholders' meeting, the board of supervisors, and last the communist party branch.

Notwithstanding the formal changes in decision-making, the informal decision-making power embedded in party-controlled networks perpetuates the organizational culture of the state-owned enterprise. This is especially the case in companies where the chairman of the board is the same person as the party secretary. Meyer and Rowan (1977) argue that such decoupling between formal rules as myths and rituals and the actual organizational practices enables the firm to conform to expectations emanating from the institutional environment while allowing actors in the firm to pursue practical objectives. The same survey of 257 listed companies confirms that the communist party continues to intervene in the management of the firm through informal governance structures that operate in the shadows of the formal rules and procedures (Opper et al. 2002). In sum, despite impressive evidence of formal compliance to the formal rules and procedures of corporate governance specified by the Company Law, opposition norms rooted in the culture of party-controlled networks in the firm continued to be manifest in a wide range of organizational practices.

A different type of oppositional norm is manifest in widespread asset stripping in state-owned companies following the promulgation of the

Company Law (Li 1998). Prior to the enactment of the Law, state agencies monitored the financial accounts of state-owned enterprises; by eliminating monitoring, the new structure of property rights opened the door to asset stripping. Widespread asset-stripping can take place only if management tacitly cooperates and even profits from such activity, through lax monitoring of the informal economy that operates in the shadows of the formal economy of the firm. A common practice in firms is for entrepreneurs to organize a work group of employees and bid for contracts on the open market. Although they may work on the project during off-hours, they nonetheless use the firm's equipment and plants without compensating the firm for the costs of depreciation of physical capital. Once incorporated into a firm's organizational culture, the informal economy becomes a source of oppositional norms to management's effort to utilize the firm's human and physical capital to pursue profit-making that accrues to the firm rather than to individual entrepreneurs and members of work groups. Moreover, it is not uncommon for management to join close-knit networks comprising the firm's informal economy. A more serious form of asset stripping stems from outright illegal sale of physical capital and assets, which can result in costly losses for state-owned companies.

Oppositional norms are also evident in welfare-maximizing expenditures whereby management lavishly allocates the firm's investment capital to build new housing for employees and to provide other nonwage benefits. Such expenditures are not based on productivity gains, but are driven by the clientelist politics of the party organization, a long-standing feature of the organizational culture of state-owned enterprises (Walder 1986). Party leaders use their redistributive power to build a coterie of loyal employees to whom they can turn for support, especially during campaigns led by the party organization in the firm. They seek to promote welfare-maximizing expenditures aimed at augmenting nonwage benefits that can placate workers' discontent over wages falling relative to private, foreign, and joint-venture firms. One common welfare-maximizing practice is to defer the layoff of workers even when the company continues to sustain losses. The norm of lifetime employment becomes an oppositional norm in the context of the company's formal goals of profit-maximization. Similarly, the long-standing practice of late arrival and early departure, long lunch breaks, and rest periods also becomes a source of oppositional norms in state-owned companies. By contrast, the work rules of new private firms, foreign branch firms, and even joint-venture firms conform to the conventions of capitalist firms elsewhere.

Even after the restructuring of property rights and the formal adoption of corporate governance structures that came with the implementation of the Company Law in the mid-1990s, the share of the total industrial output of private and joint-venture firms and self-employed entrepreneurs

66 • Nee

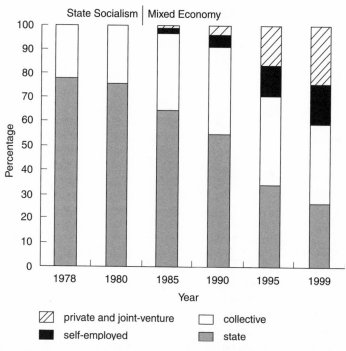

Figure 2 The structure of industrial output value (*source:* State Statistical Bureau, http://www.stats.gov.cn/sjjw/ndsj/zgnj/2000/M03c.htm). Economic types of enterprises and their output values were adjusted for comparison among historical years after 1998.

continued to displace that of state-owned enterprises, as figure 2 shows. By 1999, the state-owned companies account for only slightly over 25 percent of the value of industrial output, declining from almost 80 percent in 1978 at the start of China's economic reforms. The pace of decline in the share of industrial output accelerates as the broader institutional environment shifts away from a centrally planned economy to a mixed market economy in the late 1980s.

New organizations and organizational forms adapted more effectively and quickly to changes in the institutional environment stemming from the shift to market coordination than the state-owned firms. This can be inferred from the rapid growth in the number of new private firms in the rural industrial sector alone, shown in figure 3. If new organizations and organizational forms more readily endorse the new rules and procedures, then they will be the first to display organizational behavior that most fully reflects private property rights. That the old organizational form of state-owned enterprises is slower to adapt to the new rules of a market economy,

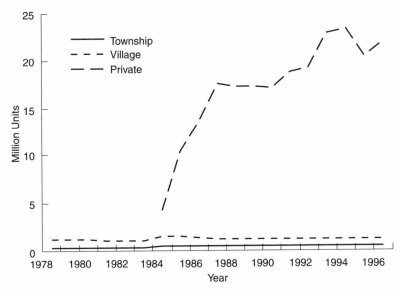

Figure 3 Property forms in rural industry (*source:* State Statistical Bureau, 1991: 377; 1997: 399).

despite efforts to change the structure of property rights by mimicking Western corporate governance structures, can be inferred from the superior performance of new organizations and organizational forms reported in figure 2. It is also reflected in the exponential growth in the number of private industrial firms in the mid-1980s, although as organizational ecology predicts, the growth levels off when density intensifies competition by the late 1980s (Hannan and Freeman 1989). The declining economic performance of state-owned enterprises is unmistakably clear when we examine the net profits and net profits plus tax revenue to the state for state-owned enterprises (figure 4). Decline in profits and tax revenues is especially steep during the recession of the late 1980s; economic recovery is evident in the early 1990s, but around the time of the enactment of the Company Law, profits and taxes fall off again. Data on the economic returns to investments in state-owned companies (figure 5) also show a continuous decline in economic performance, beginning at the time of the start of rapid change in the institutional environment. This is consistent with the view that state-owned companies have persistent problems of organizational inertia. Even if not all state-owned firms were corporatized, there should have been signs of improving economic performance as more of them adopted modern corporate governance. The data from both figures show that through much of the 1990s there was no discernible positive effect of change in the structure of property rights and corporate governance on

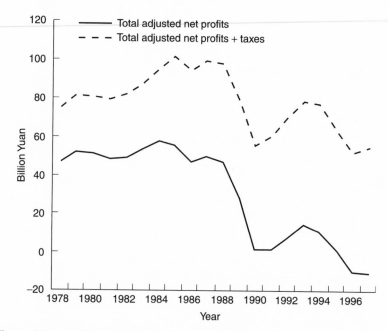

Figure 4 Economic performance of state enterprises (*source:* State Statistical Bureau 1998: 461). All numbers are adjusted by General Retail Price Index (1999: 294).

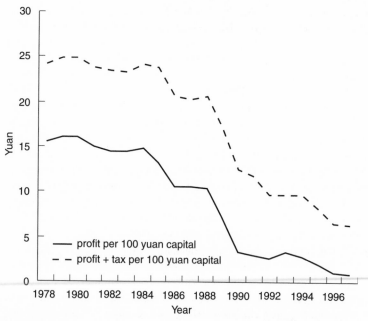

Figure 5 Economic performance of state enterprises (*source:* State Statistical Bureau, 1991–1998).

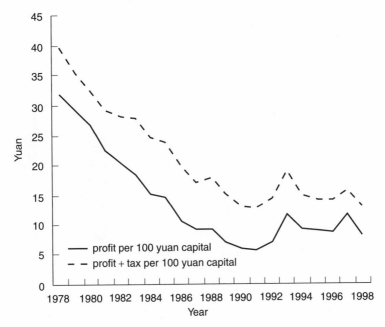

Figure 6 Economic performance of local state-owned firms (*source:* State Statistical Bureau, 1991–1999).

the performance of state-owned companies. In other words, whether governed by modern corporate structures or not, older industrial firms in the aggregate were unable to respond effectively to the changes in their institutional environment. The economic performance of township and village enterprises also declined (figure 6). There is evidence that this begins to level off in the 1990s, perhaps due to extensive informal privatization in the rural industrial sector (Nee and Su 1996; Peng 2001); nonetheless, the data show that the rural industrial sector is experiencing stagnation in productivity gains.

Finally, figure 7 reveals a trend that suggests why state-crafted institutional innovations aimed at building state capitalism in China might not result in a stable institutional framework for capitalism in China. It shows a dramatic reversal in returns on investment capital, which were already low during the pre-reform period of extensive economic growth, but which grow seriously in deficit by 1993 and the years immediately following the enactment of the Company Law. This trend is consistent with the problems that were experienced by East Asian capitalist economies in confronting the limits of extensive economic growth. Compounding the problem, state-owned banks in China are lending investment capital to

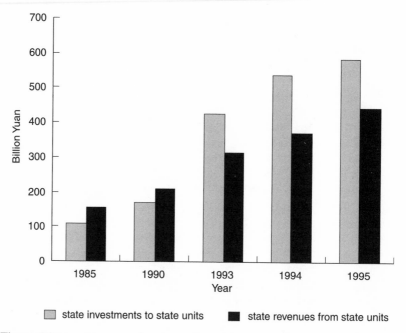

Figure 7 Investments to and revenues from state units: 1985–1995 (*source:* State Statistical Bureau, 1998: 272; 1996: 143). Here state investment includes capitals from both state budgets and extra-budget funds.

state-owned companies, likely to become problem loans in light of their continuing poor economic performance.

The paradox of China's rise as a major manufacturing power in the global capitalist economy is that it is both the fastest growing economy in the world and also among the most inefficient. Symptomatic of the problem is the sorry state of China's banking system, which has a bad loan ratio of 50 percent, arguably the highest of the major economies in the world. Bank loans make up 98 percent of the total financing of Chinese firms. As the economist Weijian Shan observes: "Standard & Poor's estimates that it will cost some $518 billion, or more than 40 percent of China's GDP, to clean up China's banking system. These costs plus the equity write-off of those companies that will go bankrupt without continued funding from banks translate into years of negative growth. China's growth therefore can be regarded as being borrowed at a very high cost—which will need to be repaid sooner or later" (Shan 2003). This analysis is consistent with my view that the 1990 institutional innovations to establish the institutional framework of state capitalism in China are unlikely to succeed, and will be followed by new reform measures aimed at building a capitalist economy not dissimilar to the pattern established elsewhere in East Asia. Indeed, in 2002, the Communist Party Congress instituted new rules to privatize state-owned firms, pave the way for loss-making firms to declare bankruptcy, and clean up bad loans held by banks.

Conclusion

The structure of property rights specified by the Company Law formally partitioned rights in a manner not dissimilar to corporate governance in advanced capitalist economies. It is reasonable to assume that if property rights were the main culprit in a persistent trend of declining firm performance, then as more and more firms adopted modern corporate governance structures, there should have been a discernible reversal in the trend of declining economic performance of state-owned companies by the late 1990s. Clearly this has not occurred. Thus a property rights interpretation does not by itself explain the observed trends. We need also to consider the social mechanisms explaining structural inertia in organizational responses and oppositional norms embedded in longstanding networks in the firm, as discussed earlier. Furthermore, property rights are themselves fundamentally a bundle of informal and formal rules governing the use of resources (Demsetz 1967). Despite formal changes embodied in the Company Law, informal rules reflecting path dependent norms and entrenched practices from the earlier era of state-owned enterprises can and do operate as oppositional norms, which combine to cause organizational inertia in these older forms. Hence a property rights interpretation is not incompatible with arguments that emphasize the importance of social mechanisms in explaining the organizational dynamics of large-scale institutional change we have witnessed in the departures from central planning in postsocialist societies.

North's account of institutional change is the centerpiece of the New Institutional Economics. It won him the Nobel Prize in Economics, and interest in his theory has diffused widely in political science, understandably, because North's theory has revitalized interest in classical themes of political economy. His theory achieves parsimony and generality by integrating a neoclassical theory of the state with standard marginalist theory in economics. Its strength is its robustness in explaining the role of the state in making institutional innovations and the incentives stemming from changing relative prices in motivating both organizational actors and the state. Its weaknesses stem from its attempts to explain the organizational dynamics of institutional change solely by reference to derivations from standard economic theory. Because the identity and network-based interests of members of close-knit groups matter, oppositional norms rooted in path-dependent practices of older firms can be expected to undermine and severely constrain their ability to respond effectively to rapid parameter shifts in the institutional environment. Structural inertia stems from success in reproducing procedures and routines with high fidelity, which in the past enhanced firms' (and states') ability to survive competitive pressure; thus North's theory is far too optimistic about the adaptive capacity of the existing stock of organizations. In contrast, economic sociology emphasizes not the existing stock of old organizations as players in large-scale institutional change, but the role of new organizations and new organizational forms.

NOTE

1. These prepositions explaining the nature of the relationship between informal and formal norms are grounded in case studies of close-knit groups in a variety of organizational and institutional settings (Homans 1950; Blau 1963; Shibutani 1978; Ellickson 1991).

REFERENCES

Blau, Peter. 1963. *The Dynamics of Bureaucracy: A Study of Interpersonal Relations in Two Government Agencies.* 2nd ed. Chicago: University of Chicago Press.
Coase, Ronald H. 1937. "The Nature of the Firm." *Economica* n.s. 4: 386–405.
Demsetz, Harold. 1967. "Toward a Theory of Property Rights." *American Economic Review* 57: 347–59.
DiMaggio, Paul and Walter W. Powell. 1983. "The Iron Cage Revisited: Institutional Isomorphism and Collective Rationality in Organizational Fields." *American Sociological Review* 48: 147–60.
Ellickson, Robert C. 1991. *Order without Law: How Neighbors Settle Disputes.* Cambridge, Mass.: Harvard University Press.
Fligstein, Neil. 1990. *The Transformation of Corporate Control.* Cambridge, Mass.: Harvard University Press.
Guthrie, Doug. 1999. *Dragon in a Three-Piece Suit: The Emergence of Capitalism in China.* Princeton: Princeton University Press.
Hannan, Michael T. and John Freeman. 1984. "Structural Inertia and Organizational Change." *American Sociological Review* 49: 149–64.
———. 1989. *Organizational Ecology.* Cambridge, Mass.: Harvard University Press.
Homans, George C. 1950. *The Human Group.* New York: Harcourt Brace Jovanovich.
Ingram, Paul. 1998. "Changing the Rules: Interests, Organizations, and Institutional Change in the U.S. Hospitality Industry." In *The New Institutionalism in Sociology*, ed. Mary C. Brinton and Victor Nee. New York: Russell Sage. 258–76.

Keister, Lisa. 2000. *Chinese Business Groups: The Structure and Impact of Interfirm Relations during Economic Development*. Oxford: Oxford University Press.

Li, Zinai, ed. 1998. *Shiji zhijiao de gongjian: xin yijie zhongguo zhengfu zhengce zhuanti jiangzuo* (China's Dilemmas in the Turn of the Century: Topics on the Public Policies of the New Administration of the State Council). Beijing: China Fiscal Economic Press.

McGuire, Patrick, Mark S. Granovetter, and Michael Schwartz. 1993. "Thomas Edison and the Social Construction of the Early Electricity Industry in America." In *Explorations in Economic Sociology*, ed. Richard Swedberg. New York: Russell Sage. 213–48.

McMillan, John and Barry Naughton, eds. 1996. *Reforming Asian Economies: The Growth of Market Institutions*. Ann Arbor: University of Michigan Press.

Meyer, John W. and Brian Rowan. 1977. "Institutionalized Organizations: Formal Structure as Myth and Ceremony." *American Journal of Sociology* 83: 340–63.

National Bureau of Staistics of China. 1998. *China Statistical Yearbook*. Beijing: China Statistics Press.

Naughton, Barry. 1995. *Growing out of the Plan: Chinese Economic Reform, 1978–1994*. Cambridge: Cambridge University Press.

Nee, Victor. 2005. "The New Institutionalisms in Economics and Sociology." In *The Handbook of Economic Sociology*, ed. Neil J. Smelser and Richard Swedberg. 2nd ed. Princeton: Princeton University Press. 49–74.

Nee, Victor and Paul Ingram. 1998. "Embeddedness and Beyond: Institutions, Exchange, and Social Structure." In *The New Institutionalism in Sociology*, ed. Mary C. Brinton and Victor Nee. New York: Russell Sage. 19–45.

Nee, Victor and Peng Lian. 1994. "Sleeping with the Enemy: A Dynamic Model of Declining Political Commitment in State Socialism." *Theory and Society* 23: 253–96.

Nee, Victor and Sijin Su. 1996. "Institutions, Social Ties, and Commitment in China's Corporatist Transformation." In *Reforming Asian Economies: The Growth of Market Institutions*, ed. John McMillan and Barry Naughton. Ann Arbor: University of Michigan Press. 111–34.

Nee, Victor and Yang Cao. 1999. "Path Dependent Societal Transformations." *Theory and Society* 28: 799–834.

North, Douglass C. 1981. *Structure and Change in Economic History*. New York: W.W. Norton.

———. 1990. *Institutions, Institutional Change, and Economic Performance*. Cambridge: Cambridge University Press.

———. 1991. "Institutions." *Journal of Economic Perspectives* 5(1)(Winter): 97–112.

———. 1993. "Institutions and Credible Commitment." *Journal of Institutional and Theoretical Economics* 149: 11–23.

Oi, Jean C. 1995. "The Role of the Local State in China's Transitional Economy." *China Quarterly* 144: 1132–49

Olson, Mancur. 1982. *The Rise and Decline of Nations: Economic Growth, Stagflation, and Social Rigidities*. New Haven: Yale University Press.

Opper, Sonja, Sonia M. L. Wong, and Ruyin Hu. 2001. "On the Power-Structure in China's Listed Companies: The Company Law and Its Enforcement." Unpublished paper.

———. 2002. "Party Power, Market, and Private Power: Chinese Communist Party Persistence in China's Listed Companies." In *The Future of Market Transition*, ed. Kevin T. Liecht. *Research in Social Stratification and Mobility* 19 (special issue): 105–38.

Peng, Yusheng. 2001. "Chinese Villages and Townships as Industrial Corporations: Ownership, Governance, and Market Discipline." *American Journal of Sociology* 106(5): 1338.

Shan, Weijan. 2003. "Living on Borrowed Growth." *Wall Street Journal*, October 7.

Shibutani, Tomatsu. 1978. *The Derelicts of Company K: A Study of Demoralization*. Berkeley: University of California Press

Steinfeld, Edward S. 1998. *Forging Reform in China: The Fate of State-Owned Industry*. Cambridge: Cambridge University Press.

Stinchcombe, Arthur I. 1965. "Social Structure and Organization." In *Handbook of Organizations*, ed. James G. March. Chicago: Rand McNally.

Walder, Andrew G. 1986. *Communist Neo-Traditionalism: Work and Authority in Chinese Industry*. Berkeley: University of California Press

———. 1995. "Local Government as Industrial Firms: An Organizational Analysis of China's Transitional Economy." *American Journal of Sociology* 101: 263–301.

Wang, Guiguo and Roman Tomasic. 1994. *China's Company Law: An Annotation*. Hong Kong: Butterworths Asia.

Williamson, Oliver E. 1975. *Markets and Hierarchies: Analysis and Antitrust Implications*. New York: Free Press.

———. 2000. "The New Institutional Economics: Taking Stock, Looking Ahead." *Journal of Economic Literature* 38(September): 595–613.

Ye, Zhengpeng and Liang Shangmin, eds. 1999. *Zhongguo caizheng gaige er'shi nian huigu* (Twenty years of fiscal reform in China). Beijing: China Fiscal Economic Press.

Still Disenchanted? The Modernity of Postindustrial Capitalism

Francis Fukuyama

MODERN SOCIOLOGY IS BUILT on an interlocking series of assumptions about the nature of modernity, and in particular about the capitalist economic system on which it is based. In Maine's (1875) view, "status" relationships built around personal loyalties would be replaced by impersonal "contracts," developing Marx's observation that modern capitalism turned wage labor into a commodity; Tönnies ([1887] 1955) argued that the intimate norms of *Gemeinschaft* (community) would be replaced by a broad *Gesellschaft* (society) characterized by formal law; Durkheim ([1893] 1933) described the shift from mechanical or organic solidarity; while Weber ([1904] 1930) held that modernity would see an increasing rationalization of all aspects of life, and the steady displacement of religion, magic, and other nonrational perspectives by that of modern science.[1] This latter point was crystalized in Weber's famous observation at the end of *The Protestant Ethic and the Spirit of Capitalism* about the "disenchantment" of the modern world: while there were still "ghosts of dead religious beliefs" haunting late capitalism in the form of social habits like thrift and work, modern man had nonetheless built for himself an "iron cage" of rationalism from which there was no escape.

The classical sociologists were aware, however, that the rationalization of modern economic life had to contend with powerful nonrational sources of behavior. Durkheim wrote about anomie and suicide as byproducts of the shift into industrial society, and Weber foresaw the return of charismatic authority precisely as a response to the iron cage of modern capitalism. The same has not generally been true of contemporary neoclassical economics, which takes assumptions of rationality even farther and tends to have a more optimistic view of human history. Not only is human behavior instrumentally rational, but the embedded norms of classical sociology that define community and often establish the ends of human activity can themselves be decomposed into individual preferences that are the object of rational pursuit. For modern economics, the most important forms of agency are individual rather than collective: group norms concerning behaviors like reciprocity and honesty are the product of game-theoretic interactions between rational individuals who enter into "society" to satisfy their purely individual preferences.

In the world of neoclassical economics, informality, religion, magic, custom, and other nonrational sources of behavior—the sphere of culture—have relatively weak explanatory power. Indeed, certain neoclassical economists like Becker (1993) argue that not just modern capitalism but the whole of human behavior can be understood as the outcome of rational optimization. In the law and economics literature, there is often an overt hypothesis that there will be an evolution toward economic efficiency over time as firms and institutions compete with one another (Roe 1996).

It is hard to doubt that modern science, rationalism, and secularism have all made great strides over the past several centuries, and that a social science predicated like modern economics on an assumption about the rationality of human behavior will in fact successfully describe much of today's economic world. But such explanations ultimately confront the problem that important areas of economic behavior remain nonrational in origin, based on religious belief, inherited social habit, or what Weber labeled charismatic authority. Social norms and values whose origins and staying power cannot be explained as the result of any functional or game-theoretic interaction among rational individuals continue to shape the economies around the globe, including those of the postindustrial world. Religion and other deeply embedded cultural values have not disappeared and affect the way traders and investors operate in the global economy.

But it is not simply a matter that the ghosts of dead religious beliefs have not yet been fully exorcised. Capitalism itself does not fully dictate a single, optimal set of institutions on which all societies will necessarily converge as a result of ever more ruthless competition. There is a degree of variance among functionally efficient institutions, and the choice that any given society makes among them is often the result of norms or path-dependencies that economics as a science cannot explain. Indeed, it is possible to argue with Platteau (1994 a, b) that the *most* efficient forms of contemporary capitalism rest on prior social givens like the existence of a generalized system of morality that are ultimately noneconomic in origin. Whether or not the latter assertion is true, it appears that Weber's iron cage is actually made of a somewhat more flexible material.

Cultural Explanations in Historical Perspective

The view that economic behavior needs to be explained by reference to religion and other historically determined noneconomic sources of behavior—that is, that it has cultural determinants—has traced a complex trajectory since the publication of Weber's *Protestant Ethic*, the *locus classicus* of this genre. Through the middle of the twentieth century, such explanations were quite common, with analysts like Parsons (1951), Lewis (1955), McClelland (1961), and Hagen (1962) arguing that modernization required the adoption of certain enabling cultural values distinct from those found in "traditional" societies.

This view came under sharp attack in the 1960s and 1970s from two sources. The first came from the political Left. Some were neo-Marxists like the *dependencia* theorists (Cardoso and Faletto 1969), who argued that poverty was the result not of poor cultural values, but of structural biases in the global economy. Others were postmodernists who argued that modernization theory was ethnocentric and privileged Western over non-Western values.

But a second source of criticism of culturalist explanations came from the political right, in the form of neoclassical economists arguing that their growth models were sufficient to explain all but a small residual in observed economic behavior (Solow 1956). This group maintained that the outcomes typically ascribed to cultural factors were actually better explained by political or economic factors within the scope of those models, and accused those promoting cultural factors of methodological sloppiness (Becker 1993).

In the last two decades of the twentieth century, cultural explanations of economic behavior have made a comeback of sorts and, if not fully established within the mainstream of the discipline of economics, have found a more secure niche in the social sciences more broadly. One of the sources for this change came with the rise of a new subdiscipline within economics labeled the "new institutionalism," associated with economic historian Douglass North (North 1990, 1994).

North does not contest the foundations of neoclassical economics as far as they relate to microeconomic theory. He argues, however, that models like price theory fail when scaled up to the level of the macroeconomy, because the latter introduces a host of noneconomic variables like political institutions and path-dependent cognitive structures that inhibit the adoption of optimal economic policies (North and Denzau 1994). Institutions, for North, are formal or informal rules that regularize and make predictable economic behavior, thereby reducing transaction costs. Many institutions are thus efficient, and economists have developed a huge body of game theory to explain how they arise. But North would be the first to admit that societies can get trapped in suboptimal equilibria where the rationality of individual actors provides no obvious way out. That societies ever do overcome such obstacles is thus often a matter of historical accident, culture, luck, leadership, or other factors that economists with less of an institutionalist bent generally tend to disregard.

Further impetus for thinking about nonrational sources of economic behavior outside the standard neoclassical model came from the real world. The East Asian "miracle" was seen by many to reflect not simply good economic policies and sound institutions—"getting the fundamentals right" in the words of the World Bank's report on Asian development (1993)—but also some culturally distinctive micro-institutions like the Japanese seniority wage system, lifetime employment, and the *keiretsu* system of business networks, the South Korean *chaebol*, or the bank-financed Chinese family business. The force of these arguments diminished considerably after the 1997–1998 Asian economic crisis, when these same culturally distinctive institutions were seen as one of the sources of the crisis and were in the process of being dismantled as part of post-crisis reform (Lanyi and Lee 1999).

But closer examination of the East Asian case reveals that culture and values remained an important component of the "miracle." It is widely conceded that one of the reasons why Asia grew faster economically than other parts of the world in the postwar period was the fact that many countries there had superior institutions and quality of governance for economic policymaking (World Bank 1997; Haggard 2000; Fukuyama and Marwah 2000). Those countries with the strongest institutions, like Japan, South Korea, and Taiwan, ran ambitious and relatively successful industrial policies for several decades; those with weaker institutions, like China, Malaysia, Indonesia, and Thailand, intervened less heavily. To assert that good governance was important is not necessarily to provide an explanation falling within the domain of traditional economics, however, but rather to beg the question of how certain societies develop superior institutions, since it is clear that they cannot be imported like technology or physical capital. There was, in other words, something in these country's cultural backgrounds and historical experiences that permitted them to create effective governance institutions when historical conditions were right. Conversely, Argentina's persistent failure to manage macroeconomic policy properly over a period of several generations suggests that poor policy and weak institutions reflect a deeper cultural problem.

A similar observation can be made about the former socialist world, which tried to develop both democratic political institutions and market economies in the post-1989 period. There was a huge variance in postcommunist transition outcomes, a variance that is very difficult to explain using the normal tools of neoclassical economics. The standard neoclassical growth models led to predictions that countries like Ukraine and Russia should have done best after communism, since they had the largest stocks of physical and human capital at the time of communism's collapse. In fact, the best predictor of postcommunist transition outcomes was the cultural distance between the country in question and Western Europe, with Protestant Estonia coming out on top, followed by Catholic Poland and Hungary, followed by Orthodox Russia, Ukraine, or Bulgaria, followed in turn by Muslim Central Asia. Here as in East Asia, the speed with which societies were able to rebuild post-communist institutions correlated with success in economic and political transition, but the former was clearly a dependent and not an independent variable.

The idea that shared cultural values and embedded social relationships could have a significant impact on economic development and growth has been most intensively discussed in recent years under the rubric of social capital. Social capital is defined as a form of capital that arises out of the ability of people to cooperate in groups (Coleman 1988; Putnam 2000; Woolcock 1998). The concept of social capital has been around at least since the time of Tocqueville's observations that American democracy rested on an American "art of association" that inclined citizens to work together in a broad variety of voluntary associations. The economic impact of social capital was most evident in countries like Italy that shared a common system of formal law but experienced wide variation in economic and political outcomes (Putnam 1993). The origin of these interregional differences was held to be cultural factors like Banfield's (1958) "amoral familism," which discouraged trust and cooperation outside the boundaries of the nuclear family.

The concept of social capital remains controversial among economists (see, e.g., Arrow 2000; Solow 2000), perhaps understandably in light of the fact that there is still no generally agreed definition of what it is, and particularly how it is to be measured. Most would not deny, however, that institutions (understood in North's sense) were critical for economic growth, and that the cooperative norms that characterize social capital are also important.

There is, however, a substantial gulf separating economists from other social scientists concerning the origins of norms. A great deal of economic theory has been developed to address the problems of collective action (Olson 1965; Hardin 1968) and the spontaneous generation of cooperative norms (Sugden 1989; Ellickson 1991). Since Axelrod and Hamilton's (1981) pioneering work, it has been clear that norms of reciprocity and honesty will emerge spontaneously out of an iterated prisoner's dilemma game. Ostrom (1990) has documented a number of empirical examples of the emergence of cooperative norms providing solutions to problems of shared common-pool resources like fisheries and forests, which earlier economic theory suggests should have led to either a "tragedy of the commons" outcome or state regulation. More recent analysts (Posner 2000) have tried to use a rational-choice framework to explain how social norms are generated more broadly, in what at times appears to be a sophisticated updating of functionalist theories of culture.

The problem with this approach, however, is that while some norms do indeed arise out of a strategic interaction between individual rational agents, a great many others do not (Fukuyama 1999). Sociologists have tried to give functional explanations for norms like the Muslim limit of four wives per husband or the Hindu ban on eating cows, but neither the origin nor the survival of these practices has a fully convincing economic explanation. While social capital is generated daily in modern postindustrial societies through the kinds of rational, game-theoretic processes described by economists, in other cases it arises as an externality or byproduct of activities with completely different purposes. Religion and religious belief, for example, are sources of shared values and social capital that have always resisted functional or rational-choice explanations (or have been incorporated into such interpretations at the cost of a trivializing reductionism). It is not true, as Hirsch (1977) has suggested, that modern societies are living off of the social capital generated during bygone eras of religious enchantment, and will inevitably collapse of their own internal contradictions. But it is also not the case that a society's full stock of social capital is generated or renewed automatically as a result of the everyday economic activity. The realm of values and culture remains to an important degree autonomous from the realm of the economy.

SOCIAL VALUES AND POSTINDUSTRIAL CAPITALISM: THREE CASES

While many people would grant that cultural values are important in explaining economic behavior in historical preindustrial or contemporary developing countries, most assume with the social theorists cited at the beginning of this chapter that the importance of such factors declines with modernization. Cultural norms that value leisure at the expense of work, or that attach social status to rentiers rather than industrialists, or that dictate that clerics rather than markets should set interest rates, are seen as cultural obstacles to modernization which need to be overcome if growth is to occur. The modern economic world that results once these barriers are surpassed is one in which rational optimization is sufficient to account for most behavior.

This view is problematic because there are still several key areas where rational optimization, and therefore the analytical tools based on the assumption of rational optimization, are insufficient to explain economic behavior. Certain preexisting cultural norms are necessary to the successful functioning not just of premodern economic societies, but of postindustrial ones as well. The two most important areas in which this is evident are in firms and organization and in the question of how societies control political corruption.

The Black Box of the Firm

One of the areas in which neoclassical economics seems the least satisfying is organizational theory, that is, the microeconomic theory of what goes on inside individual firms and how the latter are optimally organized. There is, of course, a highly developed neoclassical theory of the firm that explains the existence of firms in terms of transaction costs, bounded rationality, and the need to control opportunism (Coase 1937; Williamson 1981, 1985). The neoclassical approach to organizations sees them as bundles of individual labor contracts: the authority relationship described by Coase is actually just another form of voluntary labor contract and can be analyzed like other contractual relationships (see Alchian and Demsetz 1972; Jensen and Meckling 1976; Fama 1980). The fact of the matter is that models that see firms as no more than bundles of labor contracts or that try to extend the individualistic premises of markets into the inside of the "black box" of organizations almost always miss an important part of what is actually going on. Miller (1992) shows that neither hierarchies nor decentralized authority constitute optimal forms of decision-making under all circumstances, which means that managers have considerable latitude in designing organizations. (For a fuller account of the weaknesses of the principal-agent framework by which hierarchical relationships are chiefly understood, see Fukuyama 2004.)

The limits of traditional economic theory in explaining how firms and organizations operate is evident when one considers the role of information in them. Economists have long understood that information is a peculiar commodity insofar as the first copy is often very costly or difficult to produce, while subsequent copies are essentially free. A firm owns the property rights to all the information generated within it, in theory, and therefore should be able to move that information costlessly from wherever it is generated to wherever it is potentially useful. But this never happens in any real-world organization: information owned by the firm is distorted, delayed, or otherwise used strategically by employees whose individual interests are never fully aligned with those of their fellows or of the organization as a whole. A great deal of economic theorizing about organizations has sought to solve such principal-agent problems by aligning the interests of individuals better with the organization through changing the incentive structure that they face.

These principal-agent problems can never be fully solved, however, if the agents behave like *homo economicus* pursuing narrowly defined individual interests. A survey of the management literature over the past generation shows an emphasis not so much on structuring individual incentives, as on factors like leadership (Schein 1988), the building of corporate and organizational cultures (Wilson 1989), and motivating workers through loyalty and norms (Malone and Davidow, 1992). Successful organizations build social capital by bolstering worker loyalty, either to the firm as a whole or to fellow workers, and having the workers internalize group goals as their own. The extensive literature on the Japanese firm emphasizes the important of norms and social bonding to their success (Rohlen 1973; Abegglen and Stalk 1985; Dore and Aoki 1994). Organizations that build a high degree of internal cohesion and mutual trust are able to achieve certain cooperative outcomes far more easily than those that are riven by individualistic internal competition. This is most obvious in military organizations that live or die by the amount of unit cohesion they are able to achieve (Marshall 1947), but it is also evident in modern economic organizations.

Many recent productivity-enhancing managerial innovations have exploited the informational advantages and incentive structures accruing to group-oriented, high-trust workplaces. The flattening of formerly hierarchical organizations in effect substitutes informal social capital for formal organization (Fukuyama 1999). Another example is just-in-time or lean manufacturing, which has replaced Taylorite forms of factory organization throughout much of the North American automobile industry (Womack et al. 1991). Taylorism, or scientific management, was a real-life embodiment of Weberian bureaucratic rationality, in which complex production was organized hierarchically and incentives were purely individual economic ones. Lean manufacturing by contrast rests on the delegation of responsibility to groups of workers who build horizontal relationships and learn to trust one another. This type of organization produces huge gains in worker productivity because it makes use of social capital.

There are, of course, drawbacks to organizations that are too tightly bonded internally, from nepotism, inbreeding, and corruption to resistance to innovation (Granovetter 1973). But social capital in the form of shared norms is a critical element that is necessary to the proper functioning of modern capitalism's microlevel institutions.

Reciprocity, Regions, and High-Tech Research and Development

Informal norms of reciprocity turn out to be critical not just inside the black box of the firm, but outside it as well, in regions and industrial districts. The fact that certain regions like the British Midlands in the nineteenth century, or central Italy and Silicon Valley in the twentieth, have been the loci of particularly intensive economic development has been a subject of interest to economists from at least the time of Alfred Marshall ([1890] 1920) to the present (Porter 1998). Most of these studies tend to focus on externalities like education or complementarities in skill sets to explain this phenomenon. But social capital and informal norms of reciprocity are also a critical part of the story.

Saxenian (1994), for example, points out that, despite the apparent competitiveness and atomization of the information technology industry, there are a large number of social networks linking engineers and managers in Silicon Valley. These networks facilitate the informal sharing of valuable intellectual property between ostensibly competing firms. There is of course a great deal of sharing of intellectual property through formal mechanisms like cross-licensing and other types of contracting. But most accounts of the way that the Valley does business stress the importance of informal ties, which economize on transaction costs and greatly facilitate the movement of new ideas and practices within the broader R&D community. It is also the case that contracts between IT firms in Silicon Valley tend to be thinner than those negotiated between similar firms in other parts of the United States, because the parties tend to trust one another more and therefore feel that there is less of a necessity insure themselves against different contingencies involving opportunism and cheating.

In most cases the ties on which such trust relationships are based are modern and voluntary rather than ascriptive, such as common educational background (e.g., attending the same electrical engineering department), common past employment (many leaders of the U.S. semiconductor industry in the 1980s and 1990s once worked for Fairchild Semiconductor in the 1950s and 1960s), or in other cases participation in the Bay Area counterculture of the 1960s. In other cases, however, the moral bonds are more traditional. Shared religion (Mormonism) has played a role in the development of the software industry around Provo, Utah, and shared ethnicity has promoted a high volume of trade and investment between Silicon Valley and regions in both Taiwan and India (Saxenian 1999). Regions remain important despite the "death of distance" said to be brought about by the information revolution (Cairncross 1997) because networks of reciprocity are strongest when there is physical contact and contiguity. If two engineers who are friends but work for competing companies don't have the opportunity to meet at a bar or attend the same workshops or health clubs, they are much less likely to share information.

In other cases, however, technology has facilitated the growth of so-called "communities of practice" that transcend geographical limits (Brown and Daguid 1991). These communities are built around individual technologies and involve informal sharing of intellectual property based on reciprocity. Brown and Daguid point out that in such communities, a great deal of knowledge cannot be formalized (i.e., written down) because it is not possessed by any one individual and only emerges as a consequence of their interaction. The open-source software movement is based on an explicit norm of reciprocity and the rejection of individual property rights, and has led to among other things the development of the Linux operating system, a product whose market value is measured in the billions of dollars.

CORRUPTION AND THE RULE OF LAW

The 1990s saw a great increase in the awareness of the development policy community of the importance of political corruption as an obstacle to economic development. A decade that began with the so-called "Washington consensus" neoliberal approach to development emphasizing markets ended with a realization that in the absence of effective state institutions, no development would be possible. This new consensus on the importance of what came to be called "governance" was reflected in the World Bank's 1997 and 2001 World Development Reports (World Bank 1997, 2001).

The new emphasis on institutions simply begs the question, however, of how effective institutions are created. A great deal of thought has been put in recent years into the question of institutional design, and of the proper sequencing of institutional reform. As Klitgaard (1988) notes, controlling corruption is often a question of shifting the incentive structure facing bureaucrats so that there is a better chance they will be rewarded for doing their jobs honestly and a greater likelihood of being monitored and held accountable if they do not.

Most studies of political corruption conclude, however, that institutional reforms like professionalism in training, higher pay for public sector workers, and monitoring by outside agencies go only so far in controlling official wrongdoing. In particular, if leaders at the top of the government's various hierarchies (and especially the judicial hierarchy) are themselves corrupt, then no amount of institutional rejiggering will be sufficient to solve the problem. Controlling corruption, in other words, has a moral component as well: if the entire political and/or business elite in a country shares norms that tolerate bribery and nepotism, then even the best-designed institutions won't work.

As noted earlier, the iterated prisoner's dilemma game suggests that honesty and reciprocity (or, at least, the *appearance* of honesty and reciprocity) are not exogenous to a market-based economic system, since repeatedly interacting agents will develop a stake in good reputations. Adam Smith made a similar point when he talked about the civilizing effects of *doux commerce* (Smith [1776] 1981; Hirschman 1982). But while some forms of honesty and reciprocity will arise spontaneously in a commercial society, what cannot be taken for granted is the existence of a generalized system of morality that will extend trustworthy behavior to public officials more generally. There are plenty of equilibrium outcomes in which public officials maximize their individual payoffs by accepting bribes or otherwise shortchanging the public interest. That one should want to exercise public office impartially, that a bureaucratic position is not an opportunity to steal on behalf of one's family, that politics is not simply a game for redistributing wealth, are all moral and political ideas that do not necessarily arise spontaneously.

The rule of law has traditionally been understood to act as a bridge between strangers, one that allows them to engage in market transactions. But how does one implement a rule of law if those responsible for creating it themselves do not trust one another, or behave opportunistically? There is a chicken-and-egg problem here that many developing and transitional countries face today: they need clean and transparent legal institutions in order to create a generalized system of trust that extends beyond a narrow circle of family and friends, and yet they cannot create those institutions because of their inability to cooperate. Historically, modernizing societies in Europe and North America overcame this problem only as a result of cultural factors exogenous to the economic system. Whether such modernized, rule-of-law systems become self-sustaining once created is another question. Platteau (1994b) argues that they are not; as evidence one might point to the fact that even within the modernized European Union there remains a gradient of levels of corruption from north to south that correlates strongly with religion.

Conclusions

A century after Max Weber's gloomy conclusion that modern societies would be trapped within an iron cage of bureaucratic rationalism, we find that postindustrial economies have evolved in a rather different direction. He was proven the most wrong with regard to his view about the importance of centralized bureaucracy: decentralized markets and individuals within those markets have proven to be much more efficient allocators of resources than rational bureaucrats, a fact that has helped to keep bureaucracy in check in the latter decades of the twentieth century.

But Weber's predictions about the disenchantment of modern economic society have not proven correct either. The contemporary global economy has its share of discontents, from inequality and insecurity to environmental and social damage. But the particular nightmare of Weber's age, that modern workers would be trapped as voiceless cogs in a gigantic, heartless Taylorite machine, has not materialized. A postindustrial economy's dependence on education and skills, and the difficulties of coordination in a high-tech, knowledge-intensive environment, have guaranteed the need for human judgment and creativity in the workplace, as well as the survival informal norms of reciprocity, trust, and shared values among workers. The latter are not just anachronistic holdovers from a bygone age of enchantment, but necessary to the efficient functioning of an information economy.

There is a further methodological implication. Modern neoclassical economics, with its focus on rational optimization, will never be able to fully explicate the functioning of a modern economy. Embedded social norms, path dependencies, and moral commitments that come not from rational calculations of individual self-interest but from received authority, religion, history, and tradition will be important to a full understanding of the economy, and yet remain outside of the scope of the science of economics as currently understood. These necessary aspects of modern economic life are accessible only through an economic sociology.

NOTE

1. By nonrational, I mean not rational in the sense that economists use the term rationality, that is, consciously optimizing behavior. Nonrational behavior can in fact serve rational economic aims (e.g., the Protestant work ethic or the Asian emphasis on education), and is not the same as irrational behavior.

REFERENCES

Abegglen, James C. and George Stalk, Jr. 1985. *Kaisha: The Japanese Corporation.* New York: Basic Books.

Alchian, Armen A. and Harold Demsetz. 1972. "Production, Information Costs, and Economic Organization." *American Economic Review* 62(5): 777–95.

Arrow, Kenneth J. 2000. "Observations on Social Capital." In *Social Capital: A Multifaceted Perspective*, ed. Partha Dasgupta and Ismail Serageldin. Washington, D.C.: World Bank.

Axelrod, Robert and W. D. Hamilton. 1981. "The Evolution of Cooperation." *Science* 211: 1390–96.

Banfield, Edward C. 1958. *The Moral Basis of a Backward Society.* Glencoe, Ill.: Free Press.

Becker, Gary S. 1993. "Nobel Lecture: The Economic Way of Looking at Behavior." *Journal of Political Economy* 101: 385–409.

Brown, John Seely and Paul Daguid. 1991. "Organizational Learning and Communities-of-Practice: Toward a Unified View of Working, Learning, and Innovation." *Organization Science* 2: 40–57.

Cairncross, Frances. 1997. *The Death of Distance: How the Communications Revolution Will Change Our Lives.* Boston: Harvard Business School Press.

Cardoso, Fernando H. and Enzo Faletto. 1969. *Dependence and Development in Latin America.* Berkeley: University of California Press.

Coase, Ronald H. 1937. "The Nature of the Firm." *Economica* n.s. 4: 386–405.

Coleman, James S. 1988. "Social Capital in the Creation of Human Capital." *American Journal of Sociology* Supplement 94: S95–S120.

Denzau, Arthur and Douglass C. North. 1994. "Shared Mental Models: Ideologies and Institutions." *Kyklos* 47(1): 3–31.

Dore, Ronald P. and Masahiko Aoki. 1994. *The Japanese Firm: The Sources of Competitive Strength*. Oxford: University Press.

Durkheim, Emile. [1892]1933. *The Division of Labor in Society*. New York: Macmillan.

Ellickson, Robert C. 1991. *Order without Law: How Neighbors Settle Disputes*. Cambridge, Mass.: Harvard University Press.

Fama, Eugene F. 1980. "Agency Problems and the Theory of the Firm." *Journal of Political Economy* 88(2)(April): 288–307.

Fukuyama, Francis. 1999. *The Great Disruption: Human Nature and the Reconstruction of Social Order*. New York: Free Press.

———. 2004. *State-Building: Governance and World Order in the 21st Century*. Ithaca: Cornell University Press.

Fukuyama, Francis and Sanjay Marwah. 2000. "Comparing East Asia and Latin America: Dimensions of Development." *Journal of Democracy* 11(4)(October): 80–94.

Granovetter, Mark S. 1973. "The Strength of Weak Ties." *American Journal of Sociology* 78: 1360–80.

Hagen, Everett E. 1962. *On the Theory of Social Change: How Economic Growth Begins*. Homewood, Ill.: Dorsey Press.

Haggard, Stephan. 2000. *The Political Economy of the Asian Financial Crisis*. Washington, D.C.: Institute for International Economics.

Hardin, Garrett. 1968. "The Tragedy of the Commons." *Science* 162: 1243–48.

Hirsch, Fred. 1977. *Social Limits to Growth*. London: Routledge and Kegan Paul.

Hirschman, Albert O. 1982. "Rival Interpretations of Market Society: Civilizing, Destructive, or Feeble." *Journal of Economic Literature* 20: 1463–84.

Jensen, Michael C. and William A. Meckling. 1976. "Theory of the Firm: Managerial Behavior, Agency Costs, and Ownership Structure." *Journal of Financial Economics* 3: 305–60.

Klitgaard, Robert. 1988. *Controlling Corruption*. Berkeley: University of California Press.

Lanyi, Anthony and Young Lee. 1999. "Governance Aspects of the East Asian Financial Crisis." IRIS Working Paper 226. Center for Institutional Reform and the Informal Sector, Department of Economics, University of Maryland.

Lewis, W. Arthur. 1995. *The Theory of Economic Growth*. Homewood, Ill.: Richard D. Irwin.

Maine, Henry. 1875. *Lectures on the Early History of Institutions*. London: J. Murray.

Malone, Michael S. and William H. Davidow. 1992. *The Virtual Corporation: Structuring and Revitalizing the Corporation for the 21st Century*. New York: HarperCollins.

Marshall, Alfred. [1890]1920. *The Principles of Economics*. 8th ed. New York: Porcupine Press.

Marshall, S.L.A. 1947. *Men against Fire: The Problem of Battle Command in Future War*. New York: William Morrow.

McClelland, David C. 1961. *The Achieving Society*. Princeton: Van Nostrand.

Miller, Gary J. 1992. *Managerial Dilemmas: The Political Economy of Hierarchy.* New York: Cambridge University Press.

North, Douglass C. 1990. *Institutions, Institutional Change and Economic Performance.* Cambridge: Cambridge University Press.

———. 1994. "Economic Performance through Time." *American Economic Review* 84: 359–67.

Olson, Mancur. 1965. *The Logic of Collective Action: Public Goods and the Theory of Groups.* Cambridge, Mass.: Harvard University Press.

Ostrom, Elinor. 1990. *Governing the Commons: The Evolution of Institutions for Collective Action.* Cambridge: Cambridge University Press.

Parsons, Talcott. 1951. *The Social System.* Glencoe, Ill.: Free Press.

Platteau, Jean-Philippe. 1994a. "Behind the Market Stage Where Real Societies Exist. Part I: The Role of Public and Private Order Institutions." *Journal of Development Studies* 30(3)(April): 533–77.

———. 1994b. "Behind the Market Stage Where Real Societies Exist. Part II: The Role of Moral Norms." *Journal of Development Studies* 30(4)(July): 753–817.

Porter, Michael E. 1998. "Clusters and the New Ecomomics of Competition." *Harvard Business Review* 76(6): 77–90.

Posner, Eric A. 2000. *Law and Social Norms.* Cambridge, Mass.: Harvard University Press.

Putnam, Robert D. 1993. *Making Democracy Work: Civic Traditions in Modern Italy.* Princeton: Princeton University Press.

———. *Bowling Alone: The Collapse and Revival of American Community.* New York: Simon and Schuster.

Roe, Mark J. 1996. "Chaos and Evolution in Law and Economics." *Harvard Law Review* 109: 641–68.

Rohlen, Thomas P. 1973. "'Spiritual Education' in a Japanese Bank." *American Anthropologist* 75: 1542–62.

Saxenian, AnnaLee. 1994. *Regional Advantage: Culture and Competition in Silicon Valley and Route 128.* Cambridge, Mass.: Harvard University Press.

———. 1999. *Silicon Valley's New Immigrant Entrepreneurs.* San Francisco: Public Policy Institute of California.

Schein, Edgar H. 1988. *Organizational Culture and Leadership.* San Francisco: Jossey-Bass.

Smith, Adam. [1776]1981. *An Inquiry into the Nature and Causes of the Wealth of Nations.* Indianapolis: Liberty Classics.

Solow, Robert M. 1956. "A Contribution to the Theory of Economic Growth." *Quarterly Journal of Economics* 70: 65–94.

———. 2000. "Notes on Social Capital and Economic Performance." In *Social Capital: A Multifaceted Perspective,* ed. Partha Dasgupta and Ismail Serageldin. Washington, D.C.: World Bank.

Sugden, Andrew. 1989. "Spontaneous Order." *Journal of Economic Perspectives* 3: 85–97.

Tönnies, Ferdinand. [1887]1955. *Community and Association.* London: Routledge and Kegan Paul.

Weber, Max. [1904]1930. *The Protestant Ethic and the Spirit of Capitalism.* London: Allen and Unwin.

Williamson, Oliver. 1981. "The Economics of Organization: The Transaction Cost Approach." *American Journal of Sociology* 87: 548–77.

———. 1985. *The Economic Institutions of Capitalism.* New York: Free Press.

Wilson, James Q. 1989. *Bureaucracy: What Government Agencies Do and Why They Do It.* New York: Basic Books.

Womack, James P., Daniel T. Jones, and Donald Roos. 1991. *The Machine That Changed the World: How Japan's Secret Weapon in the Global Auto Wars Will Revolutionize Western Industry.* New York: HarperPerennial.

Woolcock, Michael. 1998. "Social Capital and Economic Development: Towards a Theoretical Synthesis and Policy Framework." *Theory and Society* 27(2): 151–208.

World Bank. 1993. *The East Asian Miracle: Economic Growth and Public Policy.* Oxford: Oxford University Press.

———. 1997. *The State in a Changing World.* Oxford: Oxford University Press.

———. 2001. *Building Institutions for Markets.* Oxford: Oxford University Press.

The Challenges of the "Institutional Turn": New Interdisciplinary Opportunities in Development Theory

Peter Evans

DEVELOPMENT THEORY IS READY for new departures. Economic analysis of development has taken an "institutional turn." Setting out the opportunities and challenges presented by the institutional turn is the goal of this chapter. My discussion will start with the displacement of "capital fundamentalism" from the theoretical core of development economics. I will then go on to discuss the institutional turn itself. While the institutional turn has taken a variety of forms, I will focus on only a few.[1] The "new growth theory," whose implications have been least effectively exploited by non-economists, will be a primary focus. Sen's "capability approach," which, despite its carefully measured formulations, is arguably the most radical version of the institutional turn, will also be a focus. North's historical institutional approach will be used as a bridge between the two. I will end with a challenge to institutionally oriented analysts with roots in other social sciences to step forward and contribute to the resolution of the new puzzles being generated by the institutional turn coming out of economics.

The issues raised by the institutional turn are theoretical, but they have implications for policy and politics.[2] Theories that focused on capital accumulation had the virtue of projecting consistency between established institutional interests and the requirements of developmental success. Newer approaches undermine this comfortable correspondence. If the contradictions between existing institutional interests and developmental goals can be resolved, it will only be through a more sophisticated approach to the politics of institutional change, an approach which connects power and culture and focuses on distributional issues. This chapter does

This chapter has benefited from the careful reading and comments of the editors, Fred Block, Marion Fourcade-Gourinchas, Nathan Newman, and Anna Wetterberg. Its flaws and failings remain entirely mine. The sections on the capability approach and institution possibilities for expanding capabilities draw heavily on Evans 2002, 2003.

not claim to offer such a resolution. It rests content to point out the extent to which the frontiers of development theory have shifted to new, inevitably interdisciplinary, theoretical terrain.

THE INSTITUTIONAL TURN

"Capital fundamentalism" assumed that solving the problem of underdevelopment was primarily about increasing poor countries' stock of capital.[3] It was a vision with strong intuitive appeal. From the point of view of poor countries, it also lent itself to optimistic projections of future growth. Poor countries could become rich if they could increase their domestic savings, which would then become investments, producing a proportionate expansion of future incomes. If domestic savings rates couldn't be increased, external financing could fill the gap. Rich countries should suffer from diminishing returns to capital. Capital should flow from where it is relatively abundant and therefore gets lower returns (rich countries) to where it is relatively scarce and should get higher returns (poor countries). "Catch-up" becomes a reasonable expectation.

Unfortunately, capital fundamentalism did not work—either theoretically or empirically. Almost fifty years ago, Robert Solow (1957) pointed out that capital fundamentalism neither made theoretical sense nor accounted for the long-term trajectory of American growth. Given that capital, especially physical capital, is subject to diminishing returns, additions to the stock of capital could not possibly account for long-term growth of the kind experienced by the United States.[4] Relying on increases in the capital stock to solve development problems in the global South didn't work very well either. Capital tended to flow among rich countries rather than from rich to poor. International institutions, trying to compensate with loans and grants, found to their frustration that more capital often did little good. Visions of capital accumulation as a "magic bullet" persist, despite all, even in academic discussion.[5] Nonetheless, the consensus has moved capital off its throne as magic bullet.[6] Today, most would agree with Hoff and Stiglitz (2001: 428, 389) that "shortage of capital must be a symptom, not a cause, of underdevelopment."

Hoff and Stiglitz (2001: 389) summarize the impact of what they call "modern economics" on the study of development with a simple assertion: "Development is no longer seen primarily as a process of capital accumulation, but rather as a process of organizational change." This is one way of flagging the institutional turn, but it doesn't fully capture the extent of the change. Along with organizations, culture and norms are also involved. The role of power in shaping both organizational structures and culture is central.

There are a variety of "institutionalisms" with a variety of ways of defining "institutions."[7] Only a small subset will be dealt with here.[8] What is essential to my argument is only that turning the focus to institutions brings a gamut of new considerations to the analysis of development. Preferences depend on beliefs and expectations rooted in shared cultural understandings. Relationships among economic agents that are based on loyalties and identifications not easily reduced to the pursuit of material ends enter into the mix. Technological change is shaped by incentives as well as shaping them. Development theory becomes a brave new world, full of intriguing but ornery conceptualizations.[9]

Moving the study of development in the direction of such a brave new world was probably not the goal of most of the theorists who produced the institutional turn. Increasing the consistency and elegance of existing theoretical formulations and bringing predictions more in line with empirical observations was the goal. The institutional turn was a by-product. The "new growth theory" exemplifies the process.

THE NEW GROWTH THEORY

The new growth theory, which has become an established part of conventional theoretical discussions of growth in the last twenty years, started from Solow's argument that "technological change" must account for most growth, then went further by making the production of new ideas "endogenous."[10] Instead of being something whose explanation lay outside the bounds of economic growth models, the emergence of productive new ideas ("rate of technological change") was seen as depending on economic incentives which were in turn shaped by institutional contexts.

In principle, the implications of the new growth theory are optimistic. Underlying this optimism is the simple idea that the dismal logic of diminishing returns, which limits the prospects of development strategies based on machinery and other physical capital, does not apply to ideas. Ideas are "nonrival" goods, simultaneously useable by any number of different people at the same time. Once a useful idea or piece of knowledge has been created—the proverbial design for a better mousetrap—the cost of using it again is essentially zero. Returns therefore expand with the scope of its use, without corresponding increase in costs (Romer, 1993a: 63). New ideas that spur the rate of technological change can lead to increased growth even if people are unable to shift income from consumption to savings. Increasing returns to ideas can compensate for diminishing returns to other factors of production.[11]

In the abstract, the implications for the global South might seem even more optimistic. There is, after all, already a monumental stock of productive ideas available in the North. At first glance, transporting them to the global South looks easy. If they can be effectively inserted into productive processes in the South, rapid growth should result. Optimistic possibilities are easiest to see if we focus on the set of ideas that are traditionally identified as "technology"—ideas that transform physical processes of production. These kinds of ideas are, in principle, easiest to move across national boundaries, increasing poor countries' stock of productive ideas and therefore their growth rates. Since technology, narrowly defined, can be embodied in machinery, it creates the possibility that foreign direct investment or the import of capital goods by local firms might generate increasing returns by facilitating the transport of ideas. Ideas may also "leak" (that is, be emulated by actors other than their owners), creating positive spillovers within and between countries.

Sometimes, things do work this way and growth follows. In most cases, however, the flow and the utilization of ideas are complicated and difficult processes. Garnering returns from ideas depends on being able to put them together with complementary inputs—physical capital and skilled labor—as well as with complementary ideas (cf. Easterly, 2001a: 150–51). If prospects of increasing returns draw these complementary inputs to better endowed locales, then being poor remains a trap, despite the apparent transportability of ideas.

The case of skilled labor is a good example. Skills are essential complements to technology and returns to any particular skill are likely to increase as a result of the agglomeration of complementary skills. Concentrations of skilled workers are likely to attract capital. Skilled workers are likely to want to move to places where they can combine their knowledge with those of other skilled workers (see Kremer 1993; Hoff and Stiglitz 2001: app. A; Easterly, 2001: 155–60). All of this works against poor countries. They will suffer triply: from having lower concentrations of skilled workers to begin with; from the natural tendency of skilled workers to move to better endowed countries where the returns to their skills will be greater; and from the fact that citizens who plan to stay in their homelands will have lower incentives to invest in training than workers in rich countries.

Other problems are equally obvious. If ideas are assets, their owners will do their best to maintain control over the returns that ideas generate. Since owners are concentrated in the rich countries of the North, to the degree that they succeed in maintaining control, the returns will flow back to the North. When the focus was on diminishing returns from physical capital, the expectation that growth rates would converge was reasonable. When the focus is on ideas, countries that have accumulated the larger stock of ideas are likely to grow faster than those with smaller stocks. Indeed, one of the advantages of the new growth theory over capital fundamentalism is that it makes the failure of poor countries to catch up more theoretically comprehensible.[12]

By fostering a more sophisticated understanding of why "catch-up" is difficult, the new growth theory has helped shift attention to institutional issues but the new growth theory's contribution to the institutional turn is more fundamental. Once growth is seen as centered around ideas, not as an exogenous factor, but as resulting from the actions of forward-looking economic agents responding to incentives, institutions come to the center of the development stage. Because they shape the incentives to develop ideas, institutional arrangements are central to determining the rate of growth. The fact that institutions not only mold the incentives to generate new ideas but can be seen themselves as essentially constituted by "ideas" completes the logic that binds the new growth theory to the institutional turn.

INSTITUTIONS AND IDEAS

Most development theorists would agree that the genre of ideas most influential in explaining why some countries develop and others stagnate are not the "technologies" associated with changes in physical processes of production, but rather the more complex concatenations of ideas that form the basis for organizations and institutions. At the simplest level, ideas embodied in institutions range from double-entry bookkeeping to a McDonald's franchise operations manuals, from congressional committee rules to research universities. Since they all have the "non-rival" character that is fundamental to "ideas," the returns they generate will grow with the scope of their application.

The potential for generating returns from institutional technologies is most obvious when we look at the returns to organizational technologies in firms. Having developed a system of organizational ideas, Wal-Mart, McDonald's, or Starbucks can use it to generate returns in thousands of locations all around the world. The organizational manual has the same non-rival property as the plan for a wheelbarrow; the additional cost of having many people use it simultaneously is trivial. These sorts of "organizational technologies" can be as powerful in generating returns as the conventional technological ideas that come more immediately to mind as illustrations—like MSDOS or Linux.

More fundamental still are the institutionalized ideas that operate at the level of the society as a whole—like administrative norms, legal rules, and other governance mechanisms. They are ideas themselves, but they also generate (or fail to generate) the incentives for the production of new ideas of all kinds, and thereby help determine the overall rate of growth. They are what Romer (1993c) calls "meta-ideas." By arguing that the quality of the ideas embodied in these kinds of governance institutions provides the best historical explanations for differential rates of development, the institution-alist analysis of Douglass North (1981, 1986, 1990) converges with the new growth theory and pushes the institutional turn further in the direction of sociopolitical analysis.

One of the principal effects of North's contribution is to make institutional politics a central determinant of growth. In the new growth theory, politics enters growth equations because political variables may influence the incentives of economic agents to develop new ideas.[13] In North's analysis the political characteristics of institutions do more than create incentives. They become embedded in the assumptions and behavior of economic actors with a thoroughness that makes them likely to persist in "path-dependent" ways. The "institutional frameworks" that North considers "the underlying determinant of the long-run performance of economies" (1990: 107) are analogous to what sociologists might call "a normative order." They explicitly include informal norms and customs as well as formal rules and procedures. The scope of a "normative order" goes far beyond guaranteeing property rights by punishing force and fraud. Even if we limit ourselves to the aspects of "institutional frameworks" most central to economic growth, for example, providing predictable guarantees of property rights, the necessary framework involves a complex combination of legitimation, social learning, and coercive power.

North's version of historical institutionalism, like the new growth theory, does remain conventional in one important respect: growth of incomes, as measured by market valuations, continues to be the fundamental metric of development. However generous the disclaimers about the importance of other social and political goals, these remain complementary, implicitly subordinated to the fundamental income metric. The full flowering of the institutional turn depends on escaping this restrictive vision. Amartya Sen's capability approach best exemplifies the logic of escape.

THE CAPABILITY APPROACH

Sen defines "capabilities" as the set of valued things that it is feasible for person to do. The range of capabilities is enormously variegated—from having dependable access to adequate nourishment to having the possibility of being a respected participant in community life. Taken together, capabilities define the extent to which people can "lead the kind of lives they value—and have reason to value" (Sen 1999a: 18).

The contribution of the capability approach is really two inseparably interconnected contributions. First, it is the most elegant and effective effort, among a long series of attempts, to impose on conventional economics the proposition that enhancing human capabilities is the only legitimate measure of development and that income growth is only an intermediate measure, imperfectly correlated with the real goal.[14] At the same time, the capability approach argues convincingly that democratic deliberation is not only a feasible method for orienting efforts to expand human capabilities, but the only defensible method.[15]

Most economists would probably acknowledge that the expansion of human capacities is the ultimate goal of development. Where they would differ from Sen is in their conviction that, while indicators of health, education, or for that matter civil rights and security, are all important, there is no way to weight and sum them that can provide a means of comparing a collectivity's overall level of utility or welfare, either across nations or over time. Therefore, the best (and really the only) effective overall metric we have for measuring the expansion of capabilities is the expansion of real incomes.[16] What sets Sen apart is his refusal to accept this proposition. He argues that real incomes are an analytically inadequate metric for making welfare comparisons (1999a: 79–80), and that utilitarian efforts to reduce well-being to "one homogeneous good thing" (real incomes) are equally inadequate.[17]

Sen's refusal to accept real incomes as the "one good thing" capable of providing a proxy for development brings the question of social choice at the heart of "what development is about" (cf. Sen 2001). For the capability approach to work, it must be possible to arrive at a legitimate weighting of many different capabilities. From this it follows that "There is a strong methodological case for emphasizing the need to assign explicitly evaluative weights to different components of quality of life (or of well-being) and then to place the chosen weights for open public discussion and critical scrutiny" (1999a: 81). In other words, "a proper understanding of what economic needs are—their content and their force—requires discussion and exchange" (1999a: 153).[18] The capability approach entails then a political process that is "democratic," in the thick sense of continuous deliberative involvement of the citizenry. Better institutions don't just improve our ability to achieve ends given by economic theory (as in the new growth theory). Deliberative decision-making institutions are the only means of adequately defining what the desired ends of development might be.[19]

Post-Sen, it is hard to resurrect either the anonymous aggregation of individual exchanges via the market or top-down technocratic analysis of needs as sufficient summaries of society's economic goals.[20] As long as development models assumed that preferences had to be taken as exogenous and avoided questions of social choice, a technocratic definition of the means for attaining a plausible end, which in practice meant growth in real incomes, made sense. Even though "getting preferences right" was logically prior to figuring out how to realize them, there was no way of even beginning to figure out what "right" might mean. Sen's elegant and persuasive argument that "right" means "arrived at through open public discussion" changes the nature of the argument. Figuring out concrete institutional mechanisms for instantiating "open and public discussion" becomes the central problem of development.

Just as the new growth theory turned technological change and idea creation into something that had to be dealt with inside economics (rather than left conveniently exogenous), the capability approach makes the process of collective preference formation irretrievably endogenous.[21] Not only do preferences become the endogenous results of institutional arrangements, but a particular type of institutional arrangements, namely those that promote public discussion and exchange is specified as the sine qua non of legitimate preference formation.

The capability approach shifts the focus to the institutions which facilitate choices of developmental goals. It puts the institutions of collective decision-making at the center of any economic theory of development, not just of social or political theories of development but of any economic theory of development. On reflection, this makes sense. Dani Rodrik (1999) comes to the same conclusion from a very different epistemological direction.[22] The ability of communities and societies to define their goals is certainly the most basic kind of institutional technology. Without it, the acquisition of other institutional techniques is unlikely to bear fruit. Accepting this basic fact ratchets up the level of challenge to those who would try to build on the institutional turn.

The Challenges of the Institutional Turn

One of the reasons ideologues and policymakers cling to capital fundamentalism is that its policy prescriptions are consistent with the existing global structure of economic power. The theoretical presumption that inputs of capital are the key to increased well-being is thoroughly congruent with the preferences of those who control capital. The institutional turn threatens this congruence. Its implications for policy are complex and often ambiguous. It draws attention to ways in which the interests of the powerful may conflict with those of ordinary citizens, particularly in poor countries. Of most immediate concern here, however, is another effect of the institutional turn. It challenges social scientists outside of economics, who have traditionally claimed to be institutionally oriented, to engage with the new perspectives coming out of economics and demonstrate how their own approaches can help resolve some of the complications created by the institutional turn.

The nature of the challenge will be illustrated here with three examples of issues raised by the institutional turn that I consider to be particularly crucial to the theory, policy, and politics of development. First, I will set out some disquieting extensions of the new growth theory: the implications of focusing on the economic power of ideas for global concentration of income and for the institutional preferences of those with major proprietary interests in ideas. Then I will discuss, equally briefly, pessimistic implications of North's "non-functionalist" vision of basic institutions for the evolution of economic governance. Finally, I will explore possible extensions of the capability approach that have implications for both inequality and governance.

IDEAS AND INEQUALITY

The new growth theory brings the analysis of governance institutions to the core of even the most economistic analysis of growth. At the same time, it predicts an increasingly important role for a particular set of economic actors. These actors, who might be called (following Negroponte 1996) "bit-based" entrepreneurs, are corporations whose most important assets are "collections of bits rather than collections of atoms," which is to say ideas or images rather than machines or natural resources. Bit-based entrepreneurs have distinctive advantages and distinctive institutional preferences, both of which are potentially problematic.

The exciting possibilities for growth generated by increasing returns from ideas are epitomized by the expansion of bit-based economic empires. At the same time, when growth is bit-based the absence of an argument for the eventual predominance of diseconomies of scale leaves tendencies toward concentration of incomes and economic power unchecked by "market forces." Given that political power cannot really be insulated from economic power, this implies increasing political as well economic inequality.

Unhampered by the normal diseconomies of scale that flow from dependence on physical capital and consequently unconstrained by the U-shaped cost curves that are a major pillar of competitive equilibria, those whose primary assets take the form of ideas and images are in an enviable position. Bit-based entrepreneurs can enjoy increasing returns from even a single product for as long as the scope of the market continues to expand. The possibility of returns that increase indefinitely with the size of the market applies not just to "technology," like the program for MSDOS, but to ideas and images more generally—everything from the formula for Coca-Cola to the image of Mickey Mouse to the image of Michael Jordan dunking a basketball. "Network externalities" and what might be called "cultural externalities" magnify the effects of increasing returns.[23] The incentives to secure "first mover advantages" and "lock-in" are very large (cf. Williamson 1975, 1985; Arthur 1990, 1994). All of this magnifies possibilities for the concentration of income and power well beyond what they would be in an economy based on physical production of simple tangible goods.[24]

None of this negates the tremendous promise of growth based on the generation and exploitation of new ideas to improve the well-being of ordinary citizens in rich and poor countries alike.[25] Nor does it negate the fact that bit-based entrepreneurs should, in principle, have an interest in institutional contexts that foster the generation of ideas. What this perspective suggests, however, is that interests in the production of ideas are always accompanied by equally powerful interests in being able to appropriate returns from ideas. As current North-South struggles over intellectual property rights indicate, it is the South that is confronted by demands to strengthen the institutions of appropriability while suffering from the full effects of the inegalitarian distribution of existing property rights.

This analysis suggests that global extensions of Northern property rights protection are more likely to exacerbate current inequalities than to redress them and underlines the importance of building institutions capable of compensating for the inegalitarian downside of bit-based growth. Two kinds of institutional responses can be imagined. First, governance institutions capable of restraining the inegalitarian tendencies themselves might be constructed. Alternatively, inequality could be allowed to increase but attention directed toward means of compensating for the negative political, social, and economic effects of increased inequality. If, however, we move from desirability to likelihood, prediction of the trajectory of change in economic governance institutions must start with the probable agenda of bit-based entrepreneurs themselves.[26]

Even if the home country agendas of bit-based entrepreneurs include an interest in generating new ideas, their global institutional agendas must almost inevitably center on the problem of appropriating returns. Ideas are easier to steal than tangible assets. In addition, the extent to which information is "private property" is often ambiguous (e.g., the human genome). Bit-based entrepreneurs need political and legal structures that will maximize the difficulty of stealing ideas whose ownership has been established and facilitate the transformation of ideas that might be considered part of the "commons" into private property.

Markets which deal in bits must be regulated more intensely than any homogeneous commodity market; otherwise it is too easy for interlopers to threaten returns by copying the ideas or images.[27] From aggressive U.S. efforts to keep entrepreneurs in the South from pirating copies of Titanic or Windows to the court-ordered closure of Napster, the centrality of regulation to "free" markets has never been clearer than in the contemporary global economy.[28]

Developing institutions that will more effectively prevent the theft of ideas and images is the defensive half of the bit-based agenda. The expansive part of the agenda involves expanding the definition of what ideas and images can be privately owned. Transforming ideas previously considered part of the natural or cultural "commons" into private property is an obvious strategy for generating new assets and returns. The process is most dramatic when nature is transformed. Shared seed-stocks which have emerged out of millennia of experimentation by communities of anonymous agrarian producers are further transformed to make them private property. Or, in an even more extreme example, the name "basmati rice" is patented so that a particular entrepreneur can appropriate the returns from reputation for flavor. Like protecting established rights to intangible assets, effective transfer of ideas from the non-appropriable public sphere to the terrain of private appropriability requires a powerful, globally organized legal-administrative apparatus.

Bit-based entrepreneurs have preferences in the realm of norms, culture, and customs, as well as in the realm of legal-administrative apparatuses. Homogenization of consumption preferences across markets and world regions maximizes the extent of the market over which a given idea or image can reap returns. Given that the bulk of the market for most commodities is already located in rich countries, homogenization generally takes the form of trying to spread consumption patterns from rich countries.

The corporate strategies of demand creation that follow from this logic run directly counter to the deliberative model of preference formation advocated by Sen. No matter how carefully individuals reflect on their needs and preferences, they do so within a context of culture and information that is strongly shaped by bit-based "empires" like those of Coca-Cola and MTV.[29] These empires devote immense resources to constructing effective means of diffusing tastes and attributing value to patterns of consumption focused on the ideas and images that they control.

From the point of view of the citizens of the global South, homogenization involves a double loss. First, whatever preferences might emerge out of their own experiences and worldviews are unlikely to be validated by global messages which assign value to particular goods, services, and practices. Second, as Sen points out, "being relatively poor in a rich community can prevent a person from achieving certain elementary 'functionings' (such as taking part in the life of the community)" and may affect the "personal resources needed for the fulfillment of self-respect" (1999a: 71). To the degree that bit-based entrepreneurs succeed in diffusing rich country consumption standards throughout the globe, all but the most affluent citizens of the global South become "relatively poor in a rich community"—much poorer than they would be if they could arrive at consumption standards through open discussion and exchange based on their own experience and resources.

By focusing our attention on the institutional implications of the dominance of global, bit-based entrepreneurship, the institutional turn reveals a key set of challenges to development strategy and policy. This focus also makes it clear that questions of power and politics must take center stage in any response to these challenges. The centrality of questions of power is further reinforced by looking at the implications of Douglass North's version of the new institutionalism.

INERTIA AND LOCK-IN AS PROBLEMS FOR GOVERNANCE INSTITUTIONS

The ambivalent consequences that flow from putting the economic role of ideas at the center of development theory are even more preoccupying when the ideas in question are embodied in basic governance institutions. Institutions depend on mutually shared expectations. Any set of shared expectations has a strong advantage over uncertainty about how other actors will behave. Bardhan (2001:276) summarizes the argument nicely, "there are increasing returns to adoption of a particular institutional form: the more it is adopted, the more it is attractive or convenient for others to conform on account of infrastructural and network externalities, learning and coordination effects and adaptive expectations."

All of this would be fine if there were compelling reasons to believe that the emergence of institutions followed a "functionalist" logic (i.e., that governance institutions could only come to predominate if they were more "efficient" in delivering overall welfare than competing possibilities). North, however, is explicit in rejecting the idea that some kind of automatic functionalist process guarantees the emergence of the most efficient institutional forms. The possibility of institutions that are disadvantageous to long-run development emerging for idiosyncratic reasons that have little to do with any kind of overall "efficiency" or "social return" and then getting "locked-in" (Arthur 1990, 1994) is all too plausible (Bardhan 1989, 2001; Pierson 1997).

Once institutions take hold, they are likely to endure even if they have a long-run negative effect on development, crowding out the possibility for the emergence of more efficacious institutions (cf. Grief 1994).[30] Getting out from under bad institutions is likely to be the most difficult part of trying to develop new ones. This is true even in the unlikely case that the returns from existing institutions are not biased in the sense of favoring one constituency over another. If existing institutions provide differential returns to some portion of society, which consequently has a special vested interest in their maintenance, then the problem gets worse. If that segment is also differentially powerful, which is highly likely if not axiomatic, the problem is even more intractable.

As Robinson (1997) points out, even growth-enhancing institutional transformations that would expand the potential revenues of politically dominant elites are likely to be rejected if such changes imply diminished relative political power. For example, landlords, whose status and political power in agrarian societies depend on their disproportionate control over the principal productive asset (land), are the most obvious illustration. Even if they are promised increased revenues based on the projection of increased productivity from more dispersion of control over agricultural production, this is unlikely to compensate for the likelihood of diminished political power (which must eventually threaten their ability to collect revenues, regardless of whatever guarantees they may be offered) (see Bardhan 2001: 278–79).

The Northian perspective highlights the centrality of the politics underlying effective institutions, both in the positive sense that effective governance institutions require deep political legitimacy and in the negative sense of vested interests creating powerful obstacles to generating the institutional frameworks necessary to enhance either productivity or well-being. The search for social agents and political processes with capacity to generate institutional change becomes even more central to developmental theory and the challenge of building on North begins to look surprisingly similar to the challenge of building on Sen.

INSTITUTIONAL POSSIBILITIES FOR EXPANDING CAPABILITIES

If one of the institutional turn's contributions is to clarify the reasons why institutional change might move in directions that would frustrate development goals, its other function should be to generate new institutional "imaginaries" that expand our definitions of development. Sen's capability approach plays this role. He generates a vision of a counterfactual developmental politics by making a compelling case for the feasibility and necessity of authentic deliberative institutions that will allow choices about allocations and growth strategies to be "democratic" in the thick sense of messy and continuous deliberative involvement of the citizenry in the setting of economic priorities.

The question is, "How can we get from existing institutional configurations to something closer to the deliberative forms of economic governance that Sen proposes?" A full-fledged effort to build a plausible political path lies well beyond the scope of this paper, but some indication of the directions that such efforts might take is in order. I will indicate two. The first might be called "leveling the cultural playing field," the second "creating collective capacity for capability expansion."

The problem of tilt on the cultural playing field has already been discussed. As has been pointed out, the efforts of individuals and communities to make consumption choices consistent with "the kind of lives they value" (Sen 1999a: 18) take place on a culturally tilted playing field, one on which bit-based corporate empires devote immense resources and skill to reshaping preferences. Diversification of sources of information and images should be considered a major public good. Supporting the expansion of opportunities for public discussion and interchange is an equally important investment in leveling the cultural playing field. Both would enhance people's ability to "choose the life that they have reason to value." Currently, the resources and institutional support devoted to this kind of leveling are paltry and unsystematic. Even our theories of what would constitute a level playing field are underdeveloped. Most culturally oriented analysis of development simply combines denunciation of the power of the existing global cultural apparatus (both public and private) with celebration of "local" or "indigenous" culture (cf. Escobar 1995). Plausible institutional strategies that would level the cultural playing field for the bulk of the citizens of the global South who live in market-dominated urban settings are missing.

The importance of enlarging collective capacity for capability expansion is equally obvious. Gaining the freedom to do the things that we have reason to value is rarely something we can accomplish as individuals. Instantiating the social choice exercise that Sen advocates depends on public policy that explicitly acknowledges the importance of collective action. It requires public mores that legitimate contestation and collective struggles. It depends on organizations that transcend primordial and parochial interests. Without organized collectivities—unions, political parties, village councils, women's groups etc.—democracy is too easily hollowed out and the "social capital" created in families and communities too easily turns parochial and exclusionary.

There is, of course, a huge and variegated literature on the development of collective capacities. One strand focuses on collective decision-making at the level of organizations and small communities: studies of participation (e.g., Korten 1980; Uphoff et al.1979; Uphoff 1986, 1992) and collective action (e.g., Ostrom 1990, 1995).[31] A separate but reinforcing strand is the burgeoning literature on "social capital" (e.g., Evans 1996; Putnam 1993, 2000; Woolcock 1997). Perhaps the most intriguing class of institutional forms goes under the rubric of "deliberative democracy," based on a Sen-like premise that collective decision-making can be a process of "joint planning, problem-solving and strategizing" involving ordinary citizens, in which "strategies and solutions will be articulated and forged through deliberation and planning with other participants" (Fung and Wright 2003: 20).[32]

The very size and scope of this variegated literature might be considered an encouraging indicator. Even global development institutions, particularly the World Bank (cf. McNeil 2002), have become intrigued with these ideas, generating an expansive set of empirical work demonstrating the efficacy of both social capital and "participation" at the level of development projects.[33] Kanbur and Squire (2001: 215), for example, argue that "Development practitioners have come to a consensus that participation by the intended beneficiaries improves project performance."[34]

By arguing that choices based on genuine public discussion and interchange are not only feasible but essential to development, Sen sets new goals. Realizing those goals requires finding plausible means of overcoming the obstacles to institutional transformation that are laid out so persuasively in the Northian perspective. There are promising leads to build on but the bulk of the job remains to be done.

BUILDING ON THE INSTITUTIONAL TURN

The institutional turn has taken a firm hold on the future course of development theory. Accumulating capital will remain a key element in economic growth, but the politics of institutional change have become the new point of departure for development theory. Theories of how to build institutions capable of tying the allocation of resources and the organization of production to real "public discussion and interchange" among ordinary citizens are at the heart of the constructive agenda. What makes this constructive agenda challenging is that it contradicts both the current character of economic governance and the likely preferences of the powerful.

The implications of the theories that gave us the institutional turn are fully consistent with observed empirical trends in the contemporary course of development as "globalization." Given the context of existing institutions of economic governance, the new growth theory predicts exactly the kind of increases in inequality, between regions and within countries, that we observe. A Northian nonfunctionalist institutionalism underlines the difficulty of moving beyond the existing matrix of governance to one that would be consistent with either egalitarian growth strategies or the deliberative politics of the capability approach. By arguing that genuine choices based on public interchange and discussion are theoretically feasible and essential to development, the capability approach sets new goals, but does not explicate means of overcoming the Northian obstacles that stand in the way.

This brings us back, finally, to the question of "interdisciplinary opportunities" which has so far been left implicit in the discussion. All of the intellectual developments discussed here have originated within the discipline of economics. Yet the analytical tools and disciplinary presumptions of economics provide little "comparative advantage" in exploring their implications and responding to the challenges that they present. Responding to these challenges demands expertise in the analysis of social organization and culture, the traditional purview of sociologists. Issues of politics, power, and governance, the core expertise of political scientists, are even more central.

Sociologists, political scientists, historians, and others who have fancied themselves spokespersons for institutional approaches to development can no longer hide behind the excuse that the intellectual dominance of economic theories built on atomistic individuals and self-regulating markets leaves other disciplines no viable theoretical space for the exposition of their ideas. Nor can economists interested in institutional analysis claim that marginalization within their discipline hampers their participation in debates on development theory.

Complaints that the sphere of politics and policy continues to be dominated by outmoded theories are still legitimate. Indeed, this is what we would expect given the congruence of those theories with the preferences of the powerful. Nonetheless, such complaints are no excuse for failure to exploit the theoretical space that the institutional turn has made available. Creative advances at the core of the economic analysis of development have created that space by coming up with formulations that are both more theoretically sophisticated and better grounded empirically. Hopefully such efforts will continue apace, but an equally creative complementary response from other disciplines and perspectives is essential.

NOTES

1. Among the important strands of institutionalist thinking that are neglected are organizational and informational approaches (e.g., Stiglitz) and transaction cost approaches (e.g., Williamson). Also neglected is the range of alternative approaches which have been important sources of insights for a long time but never succeeded in generating a "turn" within the economics discipline as a whole—most obviously Marxist, feminist and ecological approaches.

2. For further analysis of some implications for politics and governance policies, see Evans 2003, 2004.

3. See King and Levine, 1994; Easterly 2001a: chap. 3.

4. See Easterly 2001a: 47–53 for a nice summary of what he calls "Solow's surprise."

5. Among the various efforts to defend the idea that capital accumulation is the key to growth, see Jorgenson et al. 1987; DeLong and Summers 1993; Kim and Lau 1994, 1995; Young 1995.

6. King and Levine (1994:286) conclude, "there is little support for the view that capital fundamentalism should guide our research agenda and policy advice. . . . international differences in capital-per-person explain little of the differences in output per person across countries; and growth in capital stocks accounts for little of output growth across countries. Moreover while the ratio of investment to GDP is

strongly and robustly associated with economic growth, there is little reason to believe that this constitutes evidence that increasing investment will cause faster growth. Indeed, recent results indicate the opposite: economic growth Granger-causes investment and savings, not the other way around." Blomstrom, et al. 1996 conclude that "formal and informal tests using only fixed investment ratios as independent variables give evidence that economic growth precedes capital formation, but no evidence that capital formation precedes growth. Thus, causality seems to run in only one direction, from economic growth to capital formation." Barro 1997 agrees as do Lin and Lee 1999. Easterly's (2001a:40) reading of the evidence is that increases in capital accumulation are neither necessary nor sufficient to account for high rates of growth.

7. Chang and Evans (2000:1) offer the following generic definition: "Institutions are systematic patterns of shared expectations, taken-for-granted assumptions, accepted norms and routines of interaction that have robust effects on shaping the motivations and behavior of sets of interconnected social actors."

8. For a review of some other "institutionalisms" within and outside of economics see Hodgson 1988.

9. Again, Hoff and Stiglitz (2001:396) capture the spirit of the transformation involved, when they assert that in "modern economic theory," "the 'deep' fundamentals of neo-classical theory—preferences and technology—are themselves endogenous."

10. See Romer 1986, 1990, 1993a, b, 1994 and Lucas 1988. For recent summaries see Aghion and Howitt 1999 or Easterly 2001a: chap. 3, 8, 9.

11. It still remains important not to extrapolate from the potential for growth generated by the non-rival character of ideas to an assumption of overall increasing returns to capital (broadly defined). As Solow's critique of early endogenous growth modes (1994) points out, in a model in which output is a function of the overall stock of capital and net investment is a roughly constant fraction of output, any departures from the assumption of constant returns to capital produces widely divergent and implausible predictions, making such models "very-unrobust."

12. For a recent analysis of the impressive persistence of the North-South income gap, see Arrighi et al. 2003.

13. Thus, for example, opening up the possibility of Barro (1991) using the rate of assassinations as a variable in a growth equation without fear of being accused of becoming a political scientist.

14. See, among many other earlier efforts, Streeten (1994). See also Stewart and Deneulin (forthcoming) for a comparison of the capability approach with various other efforts to "dethrone GNP."

15. For summaries of the social choice side of Sen's work, see Sen 1995, 1999a, b.

16. For a cogent statement of this point of view, see Srinivasan 1994.

17. The capability position doesn't deny the benefits of income growth. Wealth and income are, as Sen puts it (1999a: 14), "admirably general-purpose means for having more freedom to lead the kind of lives we have reason to value." At the same time, single-minded focus on income growth at the societal level may create trade-offs in which the opportunities of the majority of the population to develop a range of capabilities suffer. In highly unequal societies where growth of GNP primarily reflects the growth of incomes of the richest 20 percent and elites are hostile to public

investment in collective goods like health and education, the translation of increased national income into other things that people "have reason to value" cannot be taken for granted. Brazil has focused (quite successfully) on income growth for the past half century, but poor parents whose greatest goal is keeping their infants alive are still better off living in Kerala than in Brazil (cf. Sen, 1999a: 21–24, 43–49).

18. The prerequisite for these arguments was Sen's ability to move beyond Arrow's (1951, 1963) elegant "impossibility theorems" by showing that even modest additions to the informational base on which social choices are made, for example, even partial interpersonal comparisons of utility, are sufficient to make social choice feasible.

19. The exercise of making social choices is also in itself an opportunity to exercise one of the most important of all capabilities, the capability of making choices. As Sen puts it (1999a:291), "processes of participation have to be understood as constitutive parts of the *ends* of development in themselves."

20. This is not to argue that bureaucracies and markets are irrelevant. Each plays a large role in providing the informational base on which the "social choice exercise" required by the capability approach depends.

21. Sen is, of course, hardly alone in abandoning exogenous preferences. See Hoff and Stiglitz (2001: 396). See also Bowles 1985 for an interesting development of the idea of endogenous preferences.

22. Rodrik argues (1999: 19) that we should "think of participatory political institutions as meta-institutions that elicit and aggregate local knowledge and thereby help build better institutions."

23. Once the number of my friends using MS Word passes a certain point, I have to start using it, too, in order to communicate with them, even if my individual assessment is that it is an inferior product. Bill Gates's returns grow accordingly. Likewise, once enough of my friends decide that *Slate* has the most interesting slant on the news, my views are less valued unless I can place them in relation to the Slate position—whether or not I value that position individually.

24. The examples used here are obviously "ideal typical." The importance of "bit-based" assets extends well beyond "pure cases" like Mickey Mouse and Windows. Most corporations are partially bit-based. Purely "atom-based" commodities (e.g., steel, cotton, soap, or cloth) are increasingly the exception rather than the rule in the modern economy. A wide range of manufactured goods (e.g., Kleenex, Nike shoes) depend on associated images for their profitability and this is even more true of services—whether production or consumption oriented. Thus, the preferences of "bit-based entrepreneurs" play an ever growing role in defining economic rationality.

25. See Easterly (2001a:173–75) for some nice examples.

26. For a more general analysis of the institutional implications of bit-based entrepreneurship, see Varian and Shapiro 1998 and Newman 2002.

27. Goods whose value is based primarily on physical transformation rather than on ideas, the rearrangement of atoms rather than bits can, of course, also be copied. But the potential gains diminish in proportion to the value of the idea content. Unlike pirated copies of Windows, "pirated copies" of a Ford sedan are likely to cost more to produce than the originals.

28. In the conventional political optic, the idea of "free" trade automatically includes intellectual property rights as part of the assumption that "free" obviously

applies only to "legal" trade, but as recent controversies over the inviolability of patent rights in relation to AIDS drugs indicate, definitions of legality are constructions that are always in the process of being reconstructed. Conversely, trade in goods whose production violate labor or environmental law could also be considered trade in "illegal" goods.

29. Cf. Sen (1999: 240), who notes that "The sun does not set on the empire of Coca-Cola or MTV."

30. To the degree that it is possible to imagine that a substantial component of the "institutional framework" governing individual societies are actually generated at the global level (as in John Meyer's 1987 vision of a world dominated by "western scripts") the problem becomes even more difficult. As long as governance institutions inhered in individual societies, it was possible to tell stories in which pressure toward increased institutional "fitness" was generated by Darwinian competition among societies. To the degree that the growing importance of global economic governance rules and institutions compels participants in the globalized political economy to conform to a pattern of "institutional monocropping"—at least as far as major economic and political rules are concerned—the diversity of institutional frames required for selection disappears, heightening North's original skepticism regarding connections between institutional survival and "fitness" (cf. Evans forthcoming; 2003).

31. This work also connects, of course, to work that is not usually considered part of the "development" literature such as work on secondary associations (e.g., Cohen and Rogers 1995) and work on social movements and mobilization (e.g., McAdam et al. 2001).

32. Fung and Wright call it "empowered participatory governance." For other discussions of how "deliberative democracy" might work see Benhabib 1996; Bohman & Rehg 1997; Elster 1998; Gutman and Thompson 1996; Mansbridge 1990.

33. Within this genre, Deepa Narayan's (1994, 2000) work is some of the most compelling.

34. The shift should not be overstated. "Participation" in projects and "ownership" of loans involves limited possibilities for the exercise of choice. The question of how much real "empowerment" is generated remains (cf. Houtzager and Moore 2003). Receptivity among global policy makers is far from universal, as the rejection of the draft version of the 2000–2001 World Development Report, in part on the grounds that it excessively foregrounded the idea of empowerment, illustrates (Wade 2001a, b).

REFERENCES

Adelman, Irma and Cynthia Taft Morris. 1973. *Economic Growth and Social Equity in Developing Countries.* Stanford: Stanford University Press.

Aghion, Philippe and Peter Howitt. 1999. *Endogenous Growth Theory.* Cambridge, Mass.: MIT Press.

Alesina, Alberto and Roberto Perotti. 1994. "Income Distribution, Political Instability, and Investment. NBER Working Paper 4486. Cambridge, Mass.: National Bureau of Economic Research.

Alesina, Alberto and Dani Rodrik. 1994. "Distributive Politics and Economic Growth." *Quarterly Journal of Economics* 109(2): 465–90.

Arrighi, Giovanni, Beverly J. Silver, and Benjamin Brewer. 2003. "Industrial Convergence, Globalization, and the Persistence of the North-South Divide. *Studies in Comparative International Development* 38(1) (Spring): 3–31.

Arrow, Kenneth J. 1951. *Social Choice and Individual Values.* New York: Wiley.

———. 1962. "Economic Welfare and the Allocation of Resources for Invention." In *The Rate and Direction of Inventive Activity: Economic and Social Factors*, ed. Richard R. Nelson. Princeton: Princeton University Press.

———. 1963. *Social Choice and Individual Values.* 2nd ed. New York: Wiley.

Arthur, W. Brian. 1990. "Positive Feedbacks in the Economy." *Scientific American* (February): 92–99.

———. 1994. *Increasing Returns and Path Dependence in the Economy.* Ann Arbor: University of Michigan Press.

Bardhan, Pranab. 1989. "The New Institutional Economic and Development Theory: A Brief Critical Assessment." *World Development* 17(9) (September): 1389–95.

———. 2001. "Deliberative Conflicts, Collective Action, and Institutional Economics." In *Frontiers of Development Economics: The Future in Perspective*, ed. Gerald M. Meier and Joseph E. Stiglitz. New York: Oxford University Press for World Bank. 269–300.

Barro, Robert J. 1991. "Economic Growth in a Cross-Section of Countries." *Quarterly Journal of Economics* 106 (May): 407–44.

———. 1997. *The Determinants of Economic Growth: A Cross-Country Empirical Study.* Cambridge: Cambridge University Press.

Benhabib, Seyla, ed. 1996. *Democracy and Difference: Contesting the Boundaries of the Political.* Princeton: Princeton University Press.

Bertola, Giuseppe. 1993. "Factor Shares and Savings in Endogenous Growth." NBER Working Paper 3851. Cambridge, Mass.: National Bureau of Economic Research.

Biaocchi, Gianpaolo. 2003. "Participation, Activism, and Politics: The Porto Alegre Experiment." In *Deepening Democracy: Institutional Innovations in Empowered Participatory Governance*, ed. Archon Fung and Erik Olin Wright. London: Verso. 47–84.

Birdsall, Nancy and Juan Luis Londoño. 1997. "Asset Inequality Matters: An Assessment of the World Bank's Approach to Poverty Reduction." *American Economic Review* 87(2): 32–37.

Birdsall, Nancy, David Ross, and Richard Sabot. 1995. "Inequality and Growth Reconsidered: Lessons from East Asia." *World Bank Economic Review* 9(3): 477–508.

Blomstrom, Magnus, Robert Lipsey, and Mario Zejan. 1996. "Is Fixed Investment the Key to Economic Growth?" *Quarterly Journal of Economics* 111(1) (February): 269–76.

Bohman, James and William Rehg, eds. 1997. *Deliberative Democracy: Essays on Reason and Politics.* Cambridge, Mass.: MIT Press.

Bourguignon, François. 1995. "Comment on 'Inequality, Poverty and Growth: Where Do We Stand?'" In *Annual World Bank Conference on Development Economics*, ed. Michael Bruno and Boris Pleskovic. Washington, D.C.: World Bank.

Bowles, Sam. 1985. "Endogenous Preferences: The Cultural Consequences of Markets and Other Economic Institutions." *Journal of Economic Literature* 36(1) (March): 75–111.

Branson, William H. and Carl Jayarajah. 1995. "Evaluating the Impacts of Policy Adjustment." *International Monetary Fund Seminar Series* 1 (January).

Bruno, Michael, Martin Ravallion, and Lyn Squire. 1995. "Equity and Growth in Developing Countries: Old and New Perspectives on the Policy Issues." Paper prepared for IMF Conference on Income Distribution and Sustainable Growth, World Bank, Washington, D.C., June 1–2.

Calhoun, Craig, ed. 1992. *Habermas and the Public Sphere*. Cambridge, Mass.: MIT Press.

Chang, Ha-Joon. 2002. *Kicking Away the Ladder: Policies and Institutions for Development in Historical Perspective*. London: Anthem.

Chang, Ha-Joon and Peter Evans. 2000. "The Role of Institutions in Economic Change." Paper presented at the conference The Other Canon and Economic Development, Oslo, August 14–15.

Chenery, Hollis, Montek S. Ahluwalia, Clive L. G. Bell, John H. Duloy, and Richard Jolly. 1979. *Redistribution with Growth: Policies to Improve Income Distribution in Developing Countries in the Context of Economic Growth*. London: Oxford University Press for World Bank.

Chong, Alberto and Jesko Hentschel. 1999. "Bundling of Basic Services, Welfare, and Structural Reform in Peru." Development Research Group and Poverty Reduction and Economic Management Network. Washington, D.C.: World Bank.

Clarke, George. 1996. "More Evidence on Income Distribution and Growth." *Journal of Development Economics* 47(August): 403–27.

Cohen, Joshua and Joel Rogers. 1995. *Associations and Democracy*. London: Verso.

Deininger, Klaus and Lyn Squire. 1996. "A New Data Set Measuring Income Inequality." *World Bank Economic Review* 10(3): 565–91.

———. 1998. "New Ways of Looking at Old Issues: Inequality and Growth." *Journal of Development Economics* 57(2): 259–87.

DeLong, J. Bradford and Lawrence Summers. 1993. "Equipment Investment and Economic Growth." *Quarterly Journal of Economics* 106(2)(May): 445–502.

Domar, Evsey. 1957. *Essays in the Theory of Economic Growth*. Oxford: Oxford University Press.

Easterly, William. 2001a. *The Elusive Quest for Growth: Economists' Adventures and Misadventures in the Tropics*. Cambridge, Mass.: MIT Press.

———. 2001b. "The Failure of Development." *Financial Times*, July 413.

Elster, Jon. 1998. *Deliberative Democracy*. Cambridge: Cambridge University Press

Escobar, Arturo. 1995. *Encountering Development: The Making and Unmaking of the Third World*. Princeton: Princeton University Press.

Evans, Peter. 1995. *Embedded Autonomy: States and Industrial Transformation*. Princeton: Princeton University Press.

———. 1996. "Government Action, Social Capital and Development: Reviewing the Evidence on Synergy." *World Development* 24(6) (June): 1119–32.

———. 2002. "Collective Capitalism, Culture, and Amartya Sen's *Development as Freedom*." *Studies in Comparative International Development* 37(2) (Summer): 54–60.

———. 2003. "Além de 'monocultura institutional': instituições, capacidade e o desenvolvimento deliberativo." *Sociologias* Porto Alegra 5(9) (January–June): 20–63.

———. 2004. "Development as Institutional Change: The Pitfalls of Monocropping and Potentials of Deliberation." *Studies in Comparative International Development* 38(4) (Winter, 2004): 30–53.

Fedozzi, Luciano. 1997. *Orcamento participativo: reflexões sobre a experencia de Porto Alegre*. Porto Alegre: Tomo Editorial.

Ferguson, James. 1994. *The Anti-Politics Machine: Development, Depoliticization, and Bureaucratic Power in Lesotho*. Minneapolis: University of Minnesota Press.

Fishlow, Albert. 1995. "Inequality, Poverty, and Growth: Where Do We Stand?" In *Annual World Bank Conference on Development Economics*, ed. Michael Bruno and Boris Pleskovic. Washington, D.C.: World Bank.

Franke, Richard W. and Barbara H. Chasin. 1989. *Kerala: Radical Reform as Development in an Indian State*. Food First Development Report 6. San Francisco: Institute for Food and Development Policy. October.

Fraser, Nancy. 1997. "Rethinking the Public Sphere: A Contribution to the Critique of Actually Existing Democracy." In Fraser, *Justice Interruptus: Critical Reflections on the "Post-Socialist" Condition*. New York: Routledge.

Fung, Archon and Erik Olin Wright, eds. 2003. *Deepening Democracy: Institutional Innovations in Empowered Participatory Governance*. London: Verso.

Galor, Oded and Josef Zeria. 1993. "Income Distribution and Macroeconomics." *Review of Economic Studies* 60: 35–52.

Genro, Tarso and Ubiratan de Souza. 1997. *Orcamento participativo: a experiencia de Porto Alegre*. Porto Alegre: Fundaçaõ Perseu Abramo.

Goldfrank, Benjamin. 2001. "Deepening Democracy through Citizen Participation? A Comparative Analysis of Three Cities." Paper presented at American Political Science Association Annual Meeting, San Francisco, August 29–September 2.

Greif, Avner. 1994. "Cultural Beliefs and the Organization of Society: Historical and Theoretical Reflection on Collective and Individualist Societies." *Journal of Political Economy* 102(5) (October): 912–50.

Gutmann, Amy and Dennis Thompson. 1996. *Democracy and Disagreement*. Cambridge, Mass.: Belknap Press of Harvard University Press.

Glewwe, Paul, Michele Gragnolati, and Hassan Zaman. 2000. "Who Gained from Vietnam's Boom in the 1990s? An Analysis of Poverty and Inequality Trends." Policy Research Working Paper 2275, Development Research Group, Washington, D.C.

Habermas, Jürgen. 1962. *The Structural Transformation of the Public Sphere*. Translated by Thomas Burger and Frederick Lawrence. Cambridge, Mass.: MIT Press.

———. 1989, 1991. *The Theory of Communicative Action*. 2 vols. Boston: Beacon Press.

———. 1994. *Between Facts and Norms: Contributions to a Discourse Theory of Law and Democracy*. Translated by William Rehg. Cambridge, Mass.: MIT Press.

Heller, Patrick. 1999. *The Labor of Development: Workers and the Transformation of Capitalism in Kerala, India*. Ithaca: Cornell University Press.

———. 2000. "Degrees of Democracy: Some Comparative Lessons from India." *World Politics* 52(July): 484–519.

———. 2001. "Moving the State: The Politics of Democratic Decentralization in Kerala, South Africa, and Porto Alegre." *Politics and Society* 29(1) (March): 131–63.

Hodgson, Geoffrey M. 1988. *Economics and Institutions: A Manifesto for a Modern Institutional Economics.*

Hoff, Karla and Joseph Stiglitz. 2001. "Modern Economic Theory and Development." In *Frontiers of Development Economics: The Future in Perspective*, ed. Gerald M. Meier and Joseph E. Stiglitz. New York: Oxford University Press for World Bank.

Houtzager, Peter and Mick Moore. 2003. *Changing Paths: The New Politics of Inclusion.* Ann Arbor: University of Michigan Press.

Huntington, Samuel P. 1991. *The Third Wave: Democratization in the Late Twentieth Century.* Norman: University of Oklahoma Press.

———. 1997. "After Twenty Years: The Future of the Third Wave." *Journal of Democracy* 8(4) (October): 3–12.

Isaac, Thomas T. M. with Richard Franke. 2000. *Local Democracy and Development: People's Campaign for Decentralized Planning in Kerala.* New Delhi: Left Word Books.

Isaac, Thomas T. M. and Patrick Heller. 2003. "Decentralization, Democracy, and Development: The People's Campaign for Decentralized Planning in Kerala." In *Deepening Democracy: Institutional Innovations in Empowered Participatory Governance*, ed. Archon Fung and Erik Olin Wright. London: Verso. 86–118.

Jorgenson, Dale W., Frank M. Gallop, and Barbara M. Fraumeni. 1987. *Productivity and U.S. Economic Growth.* Cambridge, Mass.: Harvard University Press.

Kanbur, Ravi and Lyn Squire. 2001. "The Evolution of Thinking about Poverty: Exploring the Interactions." In *Frontiers of Development Economics: The Future in Perspective*, ed. Gerald M. Meier and Joseph E. Stiglitz. New York: Oxford University Press for World Bank. 183–226.

Kapur, Devesh. 1997. "The New Conditionalities of the International Financial Institutions." In *International Monetary and Financial Issues for the 1990s: Research Papers.* Vol. 8. New York: United Nations.

———. 2000. "Risk and Reward: Agency, Contracts, and the Expansion of IMF Conditionality." Paper prepared for Workshop on the Political Economy of International Monetary and Financial Institutions, Harvard University, October.

Kapur, Devesh and Richard Webb. 2000. "Governance-Related Conditionalities of the International Financial Institutions." G-24 Discussion Paper 6. Paper presented at the G-24 Technical Meeting, Lima, March 2.

Khoo, Lawrence and Benjamin Dennis. 1999. "Inequality, Fertility Choice, and Economic Growth: Theory and Evidence. Development Discussion Paper 687, Harvard Institute for International Development, Harvard University.

Killick, Tony. 1995. *IMF Programmes in Developing Countries.* London: Routledge

Kim, Jong Il and Lawrence J. Latt. 1994. "The Sources of Economic Growth of the East Asian Newly Industrialized Countries." *Journal of Japanese and International Economies* 8: 235–71.

———. 1995. "The Role of Human Capital in the Economic Growth of the East Asian Newly Industrialized Countries." *Asian Pacific Economic Review* 1: 259–92.

King, Robert G. and Ross Levine. 1994. "Capital Fundamentalism, Economic Development, and Economic Growth." *Carnegie-Rochester Conference Series on Public Policy* 40: 259–92.

Kremer, Michael. 1993. "The O-Ring Theory of Economic Development." *Quarterly Journal of Economics* 108 (August): 551–75.

Landa, Dimitri and Ethan B. Kapstein. 2001. "Review Article: Inequality, Growth and Democracy." *World Politics* 53(1): 264–96.

Larraín B., Felipe and Rodrigo Vergara M. 1997. "Income Distribution, Investment and Growth." Development Discussion Paper 596. Harvard Institute for International Development, Harvard University.

Li, Hongyi and Heng-Fu Zou. 1998. "Income Inequality Is Not Harmful for Growth: Theory and Evidence." *Review of Development Economics* 2(3): 318–24.

Lijphart, Arend. 1999. *Patterns of Democracy: Government Forms and Performance in 36 Countries*. New Haven: Yale University Press.

Lin, Kenneth S. and Hsiu-Yun Lee. 1999. "Can Capital Fundamentalism Be Revived? A General Equilibrium Approach to Growth Accounting." In *The Political Economy of Comparative Development into the 21st Century*, ed. Gustav Ranis, Sheng-Cheng Hu, and Yun-Peng Chu. Northampton, Mass.: Edward Elgard. 77–105.

Lipton, Michael. 1993. "Land Reform as Commenced Business: The Evidence against Stopping." *World Development* 21(4): 641–57.

Lucas, Robert E. 1988. "On the Mechanics of Economic Development." *Journal of Monetary Economics* 22 (July): 3–42.

Mansbridge, Jane. 1990. "Democracy and Common Interests." *Social Alternatives* 8(4): 20–25.

McAdam, Douglas, Sidney Tarrow, and Charles Tilly. 2001. *Dynamics of Contention*. New York: Cambridge University Press.

McNeil, Mary. 2002. "Engaging the Poor." *Development Outreach* (Winter).

Meier, Gerald and James Rauch. 2000. *Leading Issues in Economic Development*. 7th ed. New York: Oxford University Press.

Meier, Gerald M. and Joseph E. Stiglitz, eds. 2001. *Frontiers of Development Economics: The Future in Perspective*. New York: Oxford University Press for World Bank.

Meyer, John W. 1987. "The World Polity and the Authority of the Nation-State." In *Institutional Structure: Constituting State, Society, and the Individual*, ed. John W. Meyer, George . Thomas, Francisco O. Ramirez, and John Boli. Beverly Hills, Calif.: Sage. 41–70.

Narayan, Deepa. 1994. "The Contribution of People's Participation: Evidence from 121 Rural Water Supply Projects." Environmentally Sustainable Development Occasional Paper Series 1. Washington, D.C.: World Bank.

———. 2000. *Can Anyone Hear Us?* New York: Oxford University Press.

Negroponte, Nicholas. 1996. *Being Digital*. New York: Vintage Books.

Newman, Nathan. 2002. *Net Loss: Internet Prophets, Private Profits, and the Costs to Community*. University Park: Pennsylvania State University Press.

North, Douglass C. 1981. *Structure and Change in Economic History*. New York: W.W. Norton.

———. 1986. "The New Institutional Economics." *Journal of Institutional and Theoretical Economics* 142: 230–37.

———. 1990. *Institutions, Institutional Change and Economic Performance*. Cambridge: Cambridge University Press.

O'Donnell, Guillermo. 1993. "On the State, Democratization and Some Conceptual Problems: A Latin American View with Glances at Some Postcommunist Countries." *World Development* 21(8): 1355–69.

Ostrom, Elinor. 1990. *Governing the Commons: The Evolution of Institutions for Collective Action*. Cambridge: Cambridge University Press.

———. 1995. "Incentives, Rules of the Game, and Development. In *Annual World Bank Conference on Development Economics*, ed. Michael Bruno and Boris Pleskovic. Washington, D.C.: World Bank.

Panizza, Ugo G. 1999. "Income Inequality and Economic Growth: Evidence from the American Data." IADB Working Paper 404. Inter-American Development Bank, Washington, D.C.

Persson, Torsten and Guido Tabellini. "Is Inequality Harmful for Growth?" *American Economic Review* 84: 600–621.

Pierson, Paul. 1007. "Path Dependence, Increasing Returns, and the Study of Politics." Working Paper 7. Program for the Study of Germany and Europe, Harvard University.

Pozzobono, Regina. 1998. *Porto Alegre: os desafios da gestaõ democratica*. São Paulo: Instituto Polis.

Pritchett, Lant. 1996. "Where Has All the Education Gone?" Policy Research Working Paper 1581. Policy Research Department, World Bank, Washington, D.C.

Przeworski, Adam, Michael Alvarez, José Antonio Cheibub, and Fernando Limongi. 2000. *Democracy and Development: Political Institutions and Well-Being in the World, 1950–1990*. New York: Cambridge University Press.

Przeworski, Adam and Fernando Limongi. 1993. "Political Regimes and Economic Growth." *Journal of Economic Perspectives* 7(3) (Summer): 51–70.

Przeworski, Adam, Susan C. Stokes, and Bernard Manin, eds. 1999. *Democracy, Accountability and Representation*. Cambridge Studies in the Theory of Democracy. New York: Cambridge University Press.

Putnam, Robert. 1993. *Making Democracy Work: Civic Traditions in Modern Italy*. Princeton: Princeton University Press.

———. *Bowling Alone: The Collapse and Revival of American Community*. New York: Simon and Schuster.

Ravallion, Martin. 1998. "Does Aggregation Hide the Harmful Effects of Inequality on Growth?" *Economic Letters* 61: 73–77.

Robinson, James A. 1997. "Theories of 'Bad' Policy." *Policy Reform* 3: 1–46.

Rodrik, Dani. 1999. "Institutions for High-Quality Growth: What Are They and How to Acquire Them." Paper presented at IMF Conference on Second-Generation Reforms, Washington, D.C., November 8–9.

Romer, Paul M. 1986. "Increasing Returns and Long Run Growth." *Journal of Political Economy* 94 (October): 1002–37.

———. 1990. "Endogenous Technological Change." *Journal of Political Economy* 98(5): S71–S102.

———. 1993a. "Two Strategies of Economic Development: Using Ideas and Producing Ideas." *Proceedings of the 1992 World Bank Annual Conference on Development Economics*, ed. Lawrence H. Summers and Shekhar Shah. Washington, D.C.: World Bank.

———. 1993b. "Idea Gaps and Object Gaps in Economic Development." *Journal of Monetary Economics* 32: 543–73.

———. 1993c. "Economic Growth." In *The Fortune Encyclopedia of Economics*, ed. David R. Henderson. New York: Warner Books.

———. 1994. "The Origins of Endogenous Growth." *Journal of Economic Perspectives* 8(1)(Winter): 3–22.

Rueschemeyer, Dietrich, Evelyne Huber, and John D. Stephens. 1992. *Capitalist Development and Democracy*. Cambridge: Polity Press.

Santos, Boaventura de Sousa. 1998. "Participatory Budgeting in Porto Alegre: Toward a Redistributive Democracy." *Politics and Society* 26(4) (December): 461–510.

Sarel, Michael. 1997. "How Macroeconomic Factors Affect Income Distribution: The Cross-Country Evidence." IMF Working Paper 97/152. Washington, D.C.: International Monetary Fund.

Sen, Amartya. 1995. "Rationality and Social Choice." Presidential Address. *American Economic Review Papers and Proceedings* 85: 1–24.

———. 1999a. *Development as Freedom*. New York: Knopf.

———. 1999b. "The Possibility of Social Choice." Nobel Lecture. *American Economic Review Papers and Proceedings* 89: 349–78.

———. 2001. "What Development Is About." In *Frontiers of Development Economics: The Future in Perspective*, ed. Gerald M. Meier and Joseph E. Stiglitz. New York: Oxford University Press for World Bank.

Solow, Robert. 1957. "Technical Change and the Aggregate Production Function." *Review of Economics and Statistics* 39: 312–20.

———. 1994. "Perspectives on Growth Theory." *Journal of Economic Perspectives* 8(1): 45–54.

Srinivasan, T. N. 1994. "Human Development: A New Paradigm or Reinvention of the Wheel." *American Economic Review, Papers and Proceedings* 84(2): 238–43.

Stewart, Frances. 2000. "Income Distribution and Development." Paper prepared for the UNCTAD X High Level Round Table on Trade and Development: Directions for the Twenty-First Century, Bangkok, February 12.

Stewart, Frances and Severine Deneulin. 2002. "Amartya Sen's Contribution to Development Thinking." *Studies in Comparative International Development* 37(2) (Summer): 61–70.

Streeten, Paul. P. 1994. "Human Development: Means and Ends." *American Economic Review* 84(2): 232–37.

Streeten, Paul P., Shahid Javed Burki, Mahbub Ul Haq, Norman Hicks, and Frances Stewart. *First Things First: Meeting Basic Human Needs in Developing Countries*. New York: Oxford University Press.

Taylor, Charles. 1995. "Irreducible Social Goods." In Taylor, *Philosophical Arguments*. Cambridge, Mass.: Harvard University Press.

Tharamangalam, Joseph. 1998. "The Perils of Development without Economic Growth: The Development Debacle of Kerala, India." *Bulletin of Concerned Asian Scholars* 30(1): 23–34.

UNDP. 1999. *Human Development Report, 1999.* New York: Oxford University Press.

———. 2000. *Human Development Report, 2000.* New York: Oxford University Press.

Uphoff, Norman. 1986. *Local Institutional Development: An Analytical Sourcebook with Cases.* West Hartford, Conn.: Kumarion Press for Cornell University.

Uphoff, Norman, John M. Cohen, and Arthur Goldsmith. 1979. "Feasibility and Application of Rural Development Participation: A State of the Art Paper." Rural Development Committee, Center for International Studies, Cornell University.

Varian, Hal R. and Carl Shapiro. 1998. *Information Rules: A Strategic Guide to the Network Economy.* Boston: Harvard Business School Press.

Wade, Robert. 2001a. "Showdown at the World Bank." *New Left Review* 7 (January–February): 124–37.

———. 2001b. "Making the World Development Report 2000: Attacking Poverty." *World Development* 29(8): 1434–41.

Williamson, Oliver E. 1975. *Markets and Hierarchies: Analysis and Antitrust Implications.* New York: Free Press.

———. 1985. *The Economic Institutions of Capitalism.* New York: Free Press.

Woolcock, Michael. 1998. "Social Capital and Economic Development: Towards a Theoretical Synthesis and Policy Framework." *Theory and Society* 27(2): 151–208.

World Bank (IBRD). 1997. *World Development Report: The State in a Changing World.* New York: Oxford University Press.

———. 2000–2001. *World Development Report: Attacking Poverty.* New York: Oxford University Press.

Young, Alwyn. 1995. "The Tyranny of Numbers: Confronting the Statistical Realities of the East Asian Growth Experience." *Quarterly Journal of Economics* (August): 641–80.

Yusuf, Shahid and Joseph Stiglitz. 2001. "Development Issues: Settled and Open." In *Frontiers of Development Economics: The Future in Perspective,* ed. Gerald M. Meier and Joseph E. Stiglitz. New York: Oxford University Press for World Bank. 227–68.

PART 2

Institutions of American Capitalism

States, Markets, and Economic Growth

Neil Fligstein

THE U.S. ECONOMY IS OFTEN held up as the model of the "free enterprise" system where competition produces firm efficiency and dynamism. It is this dynamism which is supposed to produce economic growth. The role of the state in these processes is viewed in normative terms. States should stay out of the way of market actors, not try to pick firms or technologies as winners and losers, and, if they intervene, do so only to enforce competition and contracts. In reality, understanding this dynamism is more complex. The American state and federal governments have been intimately involved in the functioning of the economy from the very beginning (for discussions of the history of this involvement, see Roy 1998 and Fligstein 1990; for a defense of the role of the state in the economy, see Block 1996; for a theoretical elaboration, see Fligstein 2001). Moreover, the growth and nurturing of new markets are not left entirely to the devices of entrepreneurs. They are helped by a whole array of institutions that are both public and private. My purpose here is not to deny that entrepreneurship and competition matter for the creation of new markets and industry. Instead, it is to supplement our understanding of those activities by demonstrating that they cannot occur without governments and stable social structures to support them.

Two primary forces shape firms' strategic actions: the behavior of their competitors and the actions of the government to define what is competitive and anti-competitive behavior between firms. My key argument is that managers and owners in firms search for stable patterns of interactions with their largest competitors. If firms are able to set up stable patterns of interaction that prove to be both legal and profitable, they work to reproduce those patterns. These patterns are based on a set of strategies about what works to make money. Managers and owners across firms develop expectations of one another's behavior and that increases the reproducibility of their positions in the market (Fligstein 2001: chap. 4). So, for example, in the American market for soft drinks, two firms, Pepsi Cola and Coca

I would like to thank Richard Swedberg and the anonymous reviewers of this paper for helpful comments.

Cola, have dominated since the 1950s. Their basic strategy of competition has been to compete over market share through advertising and taking turns discounting their products every week or two. When challengers have arisen, the firms have frequently bought them out. Their domination of that market has remained stable for almost fifty years.

There are three main ways that the U.S. government has directly affected market activities, in particular markets.[1] First, the government makes laws and rules that determine tax policies, govern the use of equity and debt by corporations, regulate employment relations, enforce patents and property rights, and regulate competition or antitrust policy. Second, the government can act as a buyer of products and a provider of research and development funds to firms. In the U.S., the Defense Department has always played an important role in this regard. Governments fund research in universities and provide support for developing technologies. They also encourage the commercialization of useful products. Third, they also make rules that can directly favor certain firms in particular industries, often at the behest of the most powerful actors in those industries.[2] The main kind of market intervention that the U.S. government has shied away from in the past thirty years is the direct ownership of firms, although even here there has been and continues to be government ownership of utilities. It is useful to show how these types of market interventions by state and federal governments help provide the backdrop for economic growth. Governments build up public and private infrastructure that gave the impetus for the possibility for new firms and industries to emerge.

In this chapter, I consider two major developments in the American economy that have been typically hailed as emblematic of the working out of free markets: the emergence of the "shareholder value" conception of the firm and the rise and growth of Silicon Valley, the home to successive waves of innovation in the computer industry. My purpose is to show how these phenomena were not just caused by entrepreneurial activity. Instead, both were embedded in preexisting social relations, and in both cases the government played a pivotal role in pushing forward the conditions for "entrepreneurial activity."

After considering the role of government in these cases, I discuss more generally why governments sometimes do not figure into either economic or some economic sociological arguments about markets and economic growth. I critique these views by noting that there is ample theory and evidence from both economists and sociologists that governments play important roles in economic development. Finally, I suggest how an economic sociology with a view of embeddedness that includes governments, law, and supporting institutions offers a more complete picture of market evolution. This more complete picture helps us understand why a particular market structure came into existence. It also gives us tools to evaluate how the firms that dominate a particular industry came to occupy that position. So, for example, we would expect to be able to tell if firms have used government connections to help them control competition or if they attain a stable market by virtue of market oriented strategies. This view of economic sociology can be used to analyze when and what kinds of government interventions are likely to produce more or less economic growth.

THE CASE OF SHAREHOLDER VALUE

In order to apply this general understanding about the link between governments and markets to the case of shareholder value, it is important to understand what shareholder value is, the nature of the market order that it implies, what existed before "shareholder value," why the idea of "shareholder value" emerged, and the role of government in aiding the reorganization of firms under the rubric of "maximizing shareholder value." The shareholder value conception of the firm refers to a set of understandings about the relationships between the top managers of publicly held corporations, boards of directors, and the equities markets, where the owners of firms buy and sell shares (Jensen 1989; Fama and Jensen 1983).

The main idea is that the job of top managers is to ensure the highest possible profits for their shareholders. The relationships between managers, boards of directors, and equities markets involve monitoring, rewarding, and sanctioning managers in order to get them to maximize profits. Boards of directors are supposed to monitor managers by tying their pay to performance, and if performance-based incentives fail to produce high profits, to change management teams. If boards of directors fail to monitor managers closely enough, then the equity markets will punish firms when owners begin to sell stock and the share price of the firm drops. If managers and boards of directors continue to ignore taking actions to increase profits, the final source of discipline for recalcitrant firms is the hostile takeover. Here, a new team of owners and managers will take over the assets by buying them at the depressed price and use them more fruitfully in the pursuit of maximizing shareholder value.

The market that the shareholder value conception of the firm describes is the market for corporate control. The market for corporate control concerns how teams of owners and managers seek out opportunities to use assets to make profits. The shareholder value conception of the firm is an idealized version of how this market is supposed to work. Owners and managers who are effective at making profits retain the rights over assets. Other owners will want to purchase the stock of such a firm (which is claims over the profit produced by the assets). The current share price reflects the current and future prospects of the management team in exploiting those assets to produce profits. When managers fail to produce sufficient profit, their share price begins to fall as owners sell stock. If the price falls sufficiently, a new group of owners and managers will appear to take control over those assets and try and raise the profits of the firm.

The shareholder value conception of the firm requires several institutional features. First, of course, there have to be in place the "right" kinds of laws and rules to allow boards of directors and equity markets to function in this way. These include rules about protecting shareholder rights, rules governing accounting practices, and rules allowing hostile takeovers. Second, stock ownership has to be sufficiently defused so that it is possible for teams of owners and managers to be able to make bids for all of the shares of firms. If firms are tightly controlled by a family, a bank, a government, or cross holding of various corporations, it will be difficult if not impossible to make a takeover bid without cooperation from those groups.

The U.S. is unlike most industrialized societies in that ownership of the stock of the largest corporations is highly diffused (Roe 1994; Blair and Roe 1999). The history of the diffusion goes back to the Depression of the 1930s. The banking crisis of the 1930s forced most banks into bankruptcy. Laws were passed to try to restore confidence in banks. Banks were forced to choose which part of the business they wanted to be in and submit to close government scrutiny. Investment banks were separated from commercial and wholesale banks. Commercial and wholesale banks and insurance companies were prevented from holding stock in firms (Roe 1994). After World War II, stocks became available to a wider public and stock ownership became more diffused. As a result, banks, who previously had owned stock and lent money to firms they controlled, were forced only to be in the business of lending money. Firms became less dependent on banks and began to raise money from other sources. This resulted in the expansion of the corporate bond market, in which firms would sell bonds directly to investors. The role of commercial banks, wholesale banks, and insurance companies in directly influencing corporate managers has been decreasing ever since 1950. Now, huge amounts of stock are publicly bought and sold on the equities markets and it is possible, if you have enough money, to buy majority stakes in almost all of the largest corporations.

Societies that might be interested in creating a market for corporate control in order to force firms to maximize shareholder value would have to undertake a series of political reforms for such a market to emerge. This market would not emerge "naturally," but would require active interventions by governments. In Europe and much of the rest of the world, families, banks, and to some degree governments continue to control much of the stock of corporations (see the papers in Blair and Roe 1999). There are also various forms of share crossholding such that firms own shares of their important suppliers or customers. These long term relationships imply that firms' stock is unavailable in the wider market and therefore, cannot be purchased in a hostile takeover. Banks in Germany and Japan, for example, are both owners of equity and often provide loans to their largest customers (Aoki 1988; Alpert 1991). Existing systems of property rights tend to favor currently existing economic elites who certainly would try and prevent governments from undermining their economic power. These elites do not want to give up their control over firms. As a result, it is easy to see why most governments have not put American style corporate governance systems into place. Great Britain, which had laws in place similar to the U.S., is the only major government to have created a market for corporate control in the past twenty years (Blair and Roe 1999).

It is useful to ask how and why the shareholder value conception of the firm came to dominate the market for corporate control in the U.S. Obviously, the managerial elite of large corporations are an entrenched economic interest who would appeal to the state to protect their position. In order to understand the vulnerability of those managers and the rise of shareholder value, one must understand what existed before shareholder value.

The finance conception of the firm emerged during the merger movement of the 1960s to govern the market for corporate control (Fligstein 1990: chap. 7). At this time, the firm was first conceived of as a bundle of assets that managers would deploy and re-deploy by the buying and selling of firms in order to maximize profits. During the 1960s, diversified portfolios of product lines would be manipulated to maximize profits. The idea had three parts. First, firms could smooth out business cycles by investing in businesses that performed differently as the economy expanded and contracted. Second, financially oriented managers would have closer control over assets and thus be able to use them to make more money than they might as passive investors in stock portfolios, or free standing firms. Finally, financially oriented executives would be able to make investments in firms and evaluate the likelihood that their investments would succeed.

There were two conditions that produced the finance conception. First, large firms in the postwar era were already fairly diversified in their product lines. The problem of internally controlling a large number of products opened an opportunity for executives who could claim to evaluate the profit potential of each product line. Finance executives reduced the information problem to the rate of return earned by product lines and thereby made the large diversified corporation manageable. Second, the federal government was strictly enforcing the antitrust laws in the early postwar era and had passed an anti-merger law that made it difficult to merge with direct competitors or suppliers. This had the unintended consequence of encouraging firms to engage in mergers with firms who produced radically different products to produce growth and avoid government intervention. This gave financial executives more legitimacy because they could claim to have the expertise to evaluate the prospects for products outside of a firm's main lines by making those evaluations in financial terms (Fligstein 1990; chap. 6).

The most spectacular organizational examples of the new finance conception came from firms outside the mainstream of American corporate life. The men who pioneered the acquisitive conglomerate (Tex Thornton at Textron, Jim Ling at L-T-V, and Harold Geneen at ITT) showed how financial machinations involving debt could be used to produce rapid growth with little investment of capital. All of the financial forms of reorganization, including hostile takeovers, divestitures, leveraged buyouts, the accumulation of debt, and stock repurchasing, were invented or perfected in this period. The 1960s witnessed a large-scale merger movement whereby many of the largest corporations substantially increased their size and diversification. As a result of this success, finance executives increasingly became CEOs of large corporations. By 1969, the finance conception of control had come to dominate the market for corporate control and, by implication, the strategies and structures of the largest American firms.

The finance conception of control already viewed the firm in primarily financial terms. The shareholder value conception of control is also a financial set of strategies, but it had a particular critique of the finance conception of the firms as it had evolved during the 1960s and 1970s. It viewed the principal failure of the finance conception as the failure to maximize shareholder value by its failure to raise share prices. What caused this critique to evolve?

The large American corporation in the early 1980s was under siege from two exogenous forces: the high inflation and slow economic growth of the 1970s and increased foreign competition. Foreign competition, particularly with the Japanese, heated up, and American firms lost market shares and, in some cases, entire markets, like consumer electronics. The inflation of the 1970s had a set of negative effects on large corporations. Their real assets (land, buildings, and machines) were increasing in value. High interest rates pushed investors toward fixed income securities like government bonds and stock prices drifted downward over the decade. The main reaction for managers during this crisis was to leave assets undervalued on their books. Because of the high inflation and poor economic conditions, profit margins were squeezed. If firms revalued assets, then their financial performance would even look worse as standard measures of performance (like return on assets) would make poor profits stand out even more. Firms avoided borrowing money because of high interest rates. This meant that firms kept large amounts of cash on hand. With low stock prices, undervalued assets, and lots of cash, by the late 1970s, many large American firms had stock prices that valued them as being worth less than their assets and cash (Friedman 1985). There was a crisis of profitability during the 1970s for managers of large firms. The conditions were right for some form of change in the conception of control governing large corporations. There were three problems: what would that analysis of problems looks like, who would spearhead it, and what role would government play in sparking the new conception of the firm?

During the late 1970s in America, the discourse of deregulation was already taking shape in the political arena. The Carter administration embraced the view that one way out of the economic crisis known as "stagflation" (high inflation, low economic growth) was to deregulate product and labor markets. The theory suggested that deregulation would stimulate competition, force down wages, and end inflation. Lower prices would result, and this would stimulate consumption and economic growth. The Carter administration began to experiment by deregulating the airline and trucking industries. The presidential election of 1980 brought Ronald Reagan into power. Reagan embraced a pro-business, antigovernment agenda to combat economic hard times (Block 1996).

Reagan's Administration did several things that directly encouraged the merger movement of the 1980s. William Baxter, Reagan's attorney general in charge of antitrust, had been an active opponent of the antitrust laws while a lawyer and academician. In 1981, he announced new merger guidelines. These guidelines committed the government to approving almost all mergers except those that led to concentration ratios within particular markets of greater than 80 percent. This gave the green light to all forms of mergers, large and small, vertical and horizontal. The Reagan administration also substantially reduced corporate income taxes at the same time. Reagan encouraged firms to use this largesse to make new investments in the economy. The kind of investments that most of them made, were mergers. From this perspective, the 1980s market for corporate control was driven by the crisis in the already existing finance conception of the firm and the changes in the regulatory environment, which encouraged firms to use the market for corporate control to reorganize their assets.

The question of who came up with the shareholder value conception of the firm and how they related to those who were working with the finance conception of control has been studied extensively (Davis and Stout 1992; Fligstein and Markowitz 1993; Useem 1993; Fligstein 2001: chap. 7).

There were a number of important actors involved, mostly in the financial community. These included investment banks, stock brokerages, insurance companies, as well as financially oriented executives in mainstream firms. Davis and Stout (1992) describe what happened as a social movement. These actors came to create the "shareholder value" framing of what corporations should be. The idea of maximizing shareholder value can be traced back to agency theory and financial economics (Jensen and Meckling 1976). Some executives and institutional investors began to realize that some firms had market values that were less than the value of their saleable assets. This caused them to enter the market for corporate control, make hostile takeover bids, and dismantle or absorb existing firms.

Savvy financial analysts began to realize that by breaking firms up, they could make money. Part of the problem for investment bankers and other institutional investors was raising the cash to engage in hostile takeovers. The most important financial invention of the period was the creation of high yield or junk bonds to aid these purchases. These bonds could be used to buy up the shares of the firm, and then the new owners could engage in internal reorganization of the firm to pay the debt down. These reorganizations would involve layoffs and the sale of assets. The shareholder value rhetoric argued that these reorganizations should not worry about workers, consumers, or suppliers, but instead, their aim was to make more money for the owners of the assets.

By touting deregulation as the solution to all economic problems, the American government began the discourse that allowed the "shareholder value conception of the firm" to blossom. Deregulation of product and labor markets was thought to be the tonic to restore the American economy to its former growth. But deregulation did not mean that the government was going to get entirely out of the business of regulating markets, contracts, taxes, labor, and capital. The federal government also provided the institutional infrastructure for the maximization of shareholder value by producing regulation of equity and bond markets. It provided tax incentives and capital for mergers and told corporations that it would not disapprove of any mergers. It refused to consider passing laws to protect anyone's rights but shareholders. State governments did try to intervene to prevent firms who engaged in mergers from decimating local labor markets by closing down plants (Davis 1991). But they were not entirely successful at this effort. The federal government also encouraged firms to rewrite the labor contract to make workers grow more insecure. They refused to protect workers' rights and actively undermined unions. For example, when the Reagan administration came to power, they swiftly decertified the air traffic controllers' union. While the federal government did not invent the idea of "maximizing shareholder value," it continuously worked to advantage the owners of capital in order to increase their profitability.

The shareholder value conception of the firm was touted as the main corporate governance solution to the problem of making corporations more competitive (Jensen 1989). The empirical literature, however, provides mostly negative evidence for this assertion. The people who benefited the most from the 1980s merger movement were those who sold the shares of stock to firms engaging in mergers. But the new owners of the assets made no higher profits on average than the firm had made previously or than firms in their industry were making (Jensen and Ruback 1994). There is an assumption in the theoretical literature that shareholder value style governance will result in the best allocation of a firm's assets and increase profits. But because many of the takeovers involved the use of debt, firms had a hard time showing higher levels of profit given their high levels of debt and elevated equity prices. Of course, there were other beneficiaries of the merger movement: the investment bankers who made the deals and the sellers of equity and debt.

The link between maximizing shareholder value and competitiveness is even more tenuous. The literature on competitiveness shows that the main factors that determine whether or not a firm is competitive have to do with its competencies at organizing production and creating new and useful technologies (Piore and Sabel 1984; Porter 1990, Womack et al. 1991). Having these competencies is strongly related to treating employees fairly or making investments in the future. A narrow focus on shareholders to the exclusion of other constituencies in the firm may result in the exodus of the best people in the firm. It may also result in underinvestment in the future of the firm. This can undermine the competitiveness of the firm. It should not be surprising that American corporations never regained ground in industries where they lost competitive advantage to the Japanese and the Europeans (consumer electronics, automobiles, luxury goods, and high end precision machines) by attempting to maximize "shareholder value." Instead, the general tactic of American managers when they faced aggressive competition would be to exit product lines where they could not dominate. Instead of trying to make better products, they would divest themselves of the assets.

The Case of Silicon Valley and the Computer Industry

The explosion of information technology that occurred at the end of the twentieth century has created a whole new set of markets. Let me tell the story of these markets from the perspective of those who favor the view that this has occurred as a result of the spontaneous actions of entrepreneurs.

Many believe that these new technologies are transforming the world we live in (Castells 1996). This story has captured the attention of journalists, policymakers, and scholars. These markets are supposed to be creating new kinds of firms that are flatter, more networked, and thus quicker to take advantage of opportunities (Castells 1996; Saxenian 1994). The new firms learn and change constantly, because if they stop they die. In doing so, they are creating wealth beyond what anyone has ever imagined. They are also transforming work for the people who run them. People enter and exit firms rapidly, and stock options are a huge part of what attracts work teams to put in extremely long hours to push a new product innovation to market. Silicon Valley and its imitators in Austin, Seattle, Washington, D.C., Boston, New York City (Silicon Alley), and Ann Arbor are living proof that the future belongs to quick, constantly learning, small firms that maintain alliances and networks to keep them alive.

In this new world, firms do not form monopolies because technology will not let it happen. Firms that try to create proprietary processes or products will find others inventing new things in order to go around them. So, Apple (with its proprietary computer operating system) and Sony (with its beta VCR system) found themselves on the losing end of markets as consumers preferred open systems that produced more standard products that were cheaper. Intel and Microsoft with the "open" architecture of their products spawned whole industries of suppliers of hardware and software built on this openness. The lesson of these firms was that fortunes were to be made not by trying to be proprietary, but instead, by being "open." The way to win was to get there first and have your product adopted as the standard because it was the best. To prevent being blown away by the next generation of the technology, one needed to keep one's product developing, and organizational learning was the only answer. Keeping in touch with competitors and customers and using networks to evolve products was the only way to stay in the game. This closed the virtuous circle by which the best technology won out, and the firm that produced the technology only stayed in place if it continued to evolve as other technologies evolved.

In the "old" industrial economics, the bigger a firm got, the less product the market could absorb, the lower the price for the product, and the marginal profit on selling an additional unit of the product would eventually drop to zero. A whole new branch of economics claims that this "law" has been repealed. Information technologies produce "increasing returns to scale" (Arthur 1994). The cost of making a product like software is high at the beginning. But if the product becomes a standard, the market locks-in around the product. This lock-in occurs because consumers get used to a particular product and because other related producers build their products around it. The marginal cost of producing additional products is very low because the cost of the disk, in the case of software, is so small. If the product becomes an industry standard, the profits go up as each additional unit of output is sold because the cost of producing an additional amount of the product is near zero.

If one reads this literature, all of this change in the "new economy" was being done without any input from governments (see Castells 1996; Powell 2001). Governments were not actively regulating these markets, choosing winning and losing technologies, or making investments that promote one set of firms over another. It is the knowledge-based industries, invented in universities, driven by entrepreneurs that learn from each other, that are creating this new community of firms. Indeed, the decentralized nature of the markets and the open standards of products are often characterized as antithetical to the slow moving, unimportant bureaucracies of governments.

It turns out that there are a great many problems with this story. First and most important, it fails to recognize the pivotal role that the government has played as producer of rules that concern issues relevant to hardware and software manufacturers, as funders of research and development, as buyers of products, and as funders of basic and applied research in and around universities. At the beginning of markets, there is always a social movement-like flow of firms to start out. New entrants proliferate and many conceptions of action seem possible (Fligstein 2001). The small, "networked, learning" firm is a strategy for new firms to follow as these markets emerge. Firms face an uncertain market and no one knows which products will be hits. The "networked, learning firm" is a model to deal with these problems. In essence, it makes a virtue out of a vice. If one cannot engage in controlling the competition, one can try to be connected enough to other firms to know what is happening and attempt to anticipate where the market is going.

In this section, I want to consider two issues. First, what has been the role of government in the waves of inventions that have created the computer, software, telecommunications, and internet industries in general, and how did the government help nurture Silicon Valley? Second, I am interested in considering the degree to which the image we have of the industry as small and nimble meshes with the ways in which firms appear to have organized themselves to make money. The question is, will these markets settle on these forms because it will be impossible for bigger firms pursuing more stability-oriented tactics to emerge because of the rapid shifts in technology? Or will some grow large by stabilizing technologies and having control whereby their products lock in a particular market?

There have been four waves of innovation in these industries. World War II and the Cold War stimulated the first by providing backing for innovations in products that were related to radio, microwaves, radar, and guided missile systems. The second came in the late 1950s with the invention and commercial production of the integrated circuit, which became the basis of the semiconductor industry. The first and most important use of these circuits was for guided missile systems. The third wave was personal computers, beginning in the 1970s. Finally, in the 1990s, the Internet was invented and experienced explosive growth. The government played a part in all of these periods of invention, in some a more direct role and in others a more indirect one. I will review some of the literature here in order to make this role more explicit.

Before World War II, there was a small electronics industry in Silicon Valley (Sturgeon 2000). Most of the electronics firms in the U.S. were operated by large corporations and were located in the east. The first real stimulus to the growth of the modern electronics industry in Silicon Valley was World War II, when the electronics industry in Silicon Valley expanded dramatically. Hewlett Packard, the original Silicon Valley firm, expanded from 9 employees and $70,000 in sales in 1939 to over 100 employees and over $1 million in sales by 1943, due entirely to sales to the U.S. military. During the 1950s, the fastest growing firm in Silicon Valley was Varian Associates, which sold over 90 percent of its production to the Defense Department. By the late 1950s, Hewlett Packard, Varian, Lockheed, and other firms were selling the bulk of their computer, electronics, and guided missiles/space vehicles to the government (Henton 2000).

The Defense Department was not just a customer for the region during this period. Leslie (2000) argues that the war effort had pushed along a number of related inventions, in particular advances in tube technology, but also in opening up parts of the electromagnetic spectrum. During the early years of the Cold War, the Defense Department became the most important supplier of money for research and development and the purchaser of many early versions of different technologies. Much of this money poured into firms. But, the government also underwrote research and education at many universities. Bresnahan (1999) estimates that over 70 percent of the research support in engineering, computer science, and related fields came from the federal government. At least half of the graduate students in these fields were supported by federal funds as well. More than half of the papers published in computer science journals cite federal funding as pivotal to their research.

One of the biggest recipients of this largesse was Stanford University. The dean of the Stanford Business School during this period, Frederick Terman, was instrumental in making the Stanford Engineering School the leading research site on the west coast. Terman recognized that the growth of industry in Silicon Valley depended on building research infrastructure in the region. To do this, the Engineering School would need to develop intimate ties to the government (Leslie 2000). He was extremely successful in his efforts. Stanford University set up many programs to exploit the potential linkage between business, government, and students and professors. Terman pioneered the strategy of encouraging professors and students with good ideas to set up shop in the Silicon Valley as private firms. His most successful case was Hewlett Packard. He often worked his connections in government and business to help in these efforts. Stanford University also provided engineers trained in various fields for firms to employ. One of the other features of the Valley that Terman helped promote was the origin of the venture capital industry. He acted as a financial backer of Hewlett-Packard and helped it find funding to expand its activities. During the 1950s, venture capitalists came to Silicon Valley to underwrite both Varian and Associates and Fairchild Semiconductor. All were encouraged to do so because these firms had a natural market for their products in government.

The transistor, semiconductor, and computer industries were all underwritten by the federal government, and in particular by the Defense Department in the years 1945–1965 (Lecuyer 2000). The first of the semiconductor firms was Fairchild Semiconductor, the first company to produce transistors for semiconductors. The major innovations by the firm during the 1950s allowed it to gain a large share of military production. By 1960, it was the leading manufacturer of silicon based components in the U.S., and its main customer was the Defense Department. Ultimately, many of the leaders of Fairchild Semiconductor left the firm and went out on their own. They founded many companies in the Valley, including Intel. It was these products which caused the area to become known as Silicon Valley.

The government continued to support research and development and accounted for a substantial amount of the market for high technology goods until the end of the Cold War. It also continued to underwrite most research and development at universities. During the 1970s and 1980s, the product mix of the Valley began to change. The personal computer and later the Internet meant that consumer markets for goods produced in the Valley were growing very quickly while the markets for goods for the Defense Department were growing less quickly or even contracting.

Most of the stories told about Silicon Valley refer to this period when the government was less in the foreground of development, and more in the background. But it should be noted that the main product innovations that went into these new industries had their origins in the Cold War era. Moreover, the reason that Silicon Valley was poised to be such an important player in these new industries during the 1970s was that thousands of engineers were already working there, mainly for firms supplying goods to the defense industry. There has been an explosion of entrepreneurial activity in the Silicon Valley over the past twenty years and an equally explosive growth of venture capital to support this activity. But both of these activities have their roots in the government-funded activities of the postwar era.

But in spite of the important roles that entrepreneurs have played in the past twenty years, the government has played a part. The last of these new innovations, the Internet, owes many of its key features to the Defense Department. An agency in the Defense Department called the Advanced Research Project Agency (ARPA), founded in the 1960s, funded the "Arpanet," a computer network whose purpose was to create a decentralized network of communication to ensure communication in event of a nuclear war. Scientists and university scholars were given access to the Arpanet, and they used it to send messages and files. In order to make it work better, a series of innovations were necessary to allow for the handling of large amounts of data. This brought forth a number of important software innovations. Most of the basic innovations for these information technologies came from research done in universities where government paid to support the research.

Government support for the computer and electronics industry extends beyond the role of the government as customer and the main organization funding basic research. Congress has written laws that serve the interests of firms. Patent law and property rights issues have favored the holders of patents (Lerner 2000). The state of California, for example, has very well developed intellectual property rights laws which, not surprisingly, favor programmers. The Telecommunications Act of 1996 produced rules of competition that are generally favorable to the current incumbent phone and cable firms. These laws have not forced competition between telecommunications and cable companies, but have reinforced the positions of incumbents. Silicon Valley firms have gotten the government to relax immigration laws to provide a stream of engineers, while these same firms simultaneously moved production offshore. As of 2003, commerce on the Internet is not subject to sales tax, giving electronic retailers a 5-7 percent price advantage over their bricks and mortar competitors. In sum, government is everywhere. It nurtures technologies, allows private exploitation of them, and provides legal and regulatory structures to make it easier for firms to raise and make money. It also allows firms to define the rules of competition.

This brings me to my second question. Is Silicon Valley really dominated by the networks of actors who are in small firms and cooperate extensively with one another, and does this model produce a stable situation for producers? The main scholarly studies (Saxenian 1994; Castells 1996;

Castillo et al. 2000) seem to think that it is this feature of the Silicon Valley which has produced its distinctive competitive advantage. This imagery seems to directly contradict the story I have told about the role of government in supporting innovation and buying products. It also would seem to undermine the idea that large corporations were the primary beneficiary of the government's actions.

I think there are two points of contention here. First, there are many factors that have made Silicon Valley so successful and it is clear that these have changed over time. Thus, it is important to study all of the possible factors and to do it over the whole history of Silicon Valley. So, if one has a sixty-year perspective, one can easily see how the Cold War and active entrepreneurs in universities and firms who took advantage of this opportunity formed the core of the industry. It is also important for scholars who study these processes not to ignore all of the potential social factors in the formation of industrial agglomerations like Silicon Valley even if their interest is in what is going on right now. If scholars ignore government funding of research and training in universities and do not include it as a cause in Silicon Valley's success, they will not see the government as being important to what is going on. If scholars fixate narrowly on the networks of engineers or the venture capitalists as the engines of success, they will see them as the only social groups relevant to study. Second, having said this, I am not denying that entrepreneurs have had the vision to create new and innovative products that created entire new industries. I am only denying that they did this on their own, without the aid of government or other institutions.

But I think that the "network approach" ignores some of the most compelling industrial organization facts about Silicon Valley. There are already high levels of concentration in the main products produced in the information technology revolution. Microsoft (software), Sun (work stations that power the internet), Cisco Systems (the hardware and switches for the internet), Intel (computer chips), Comcast (cable and long distance), and AOL-Time-Warner (internet service provider and cable) control over 60 percent of their relevant markets. While some of these firms are clear technological innovators, they are also using familiar tactics to control competition. Microsoft, Intel, and Cisco have all been targets of antitrust lawsuits based on forms of predatory competition. The Microsoft antitrust case provided ample evidence that Microsoft behaved like a predatory competitor. As each of these new markets has emerged, a single firm has come to dominate.

It is useful to speculate on what kinds of markets are really being built in these new technology industries. The incumbent firms observe the innovators of new technologies and either buy up or incorporate the insights of those technologies into their main products. They stay in the game by aggressively buying up winners in markets connected to these products.

Microsoft, for example, is well known for approaching small software firms and offering to buy them out. If smaller firms refuse, then their products are often re-engineered and made part of the next release of the operating system.

If the incumbents in these industries use their market position to buy out or force out competitors, then what do the challengers do? Challenger firms have a potentially profitable niche strategy available to them. Challenger firms are the innovators who take risks. If they are successful, then they face three potential positive futures (at least from the perspective of their owners): they can go "public" and sell stock, sell out their firm to one of the industry giants, or try to become one of these giants themselves.

This is a conception of control that defines the structure of incumbents and challengers. It means that investors have the ability to reap returns if their products are successful and it provides the largest firms with new innovations to keep their large firms in the center of new technology markets. Challengers and incumbents have a symbiotic relation to one another whereby they are competitors, but they also have created tacit rules that allow all to survive.

The issue of "openness" in computer systems and the related problem of creating technical standards for products are complex (Edstrom 1999). The ability to attach a particular piece of hardware or software to an existing structure makes that structure more valuable. Thus, "openness" benefits the producers of new products and the owners of such standards. The large stable firms update their products and, because of the technological lock-in around their standards, they attain stability. "Openness" is one way to get a stable market. I would argue that "openness" evolved when the attempt to create proprietary systems failed. If firms could not control technology markets through patents, then the second best solution was to get their product to be an open standard. It creates stability because it allows industry leader to form and markets to coalesce around stable standards. The core technologies that form the open standard benefit the incumbent firms that control them. Technical standards can operate in a similar way.

If I am correct, then, as the industry develops, we can expect, consolidation into large firms in many of the major products. We can also expect that firms will pursue one of two tactics in the construction of new markets: either be a small, challenger firm prepared to be bought out, or try to become one of the large diversified firms that offer standards for others to build on and buy up new technology to protect their franchise. This conception of control, if it emerges and stabilizes, is the deep structure by which firms will make money. The incumbents are the large firms. The challengers are the small firms where fortunes can still be made, but only as means to ends. The owners of challenger firms are in the game to cash out. The small, networked firm is a product of the early days of new markets. As time goes on, more familiar structures of industrial organization will continue to emerge.

STATES, MARKETS, AND ECONOMIC GROWTH

This chapter has taken the view that firms and markets are best viewed as deeply dependent on laws, institutions, and governments for their existence. It is unimaginable that firms could find stable solutions to their problems of competition without extensive social relationships. It is equally unimaginable that many of the products and markets that exist could have existed without the active intervention of governments. The "shareholder value" conception of the firm was a solution to a particular problem of American firms. They were financially under-performing circa 1980 due to the high inflation and slow economic growth of the 1970s. This underperformance was blamed on the managers of firms, and financial tools were invented to analyze and transform this condition. The federal government helped this process along by suspending the antitrust laws and cutting corporate taxes. The Carter and Reagan administrations came to evolve the view that the government intervened too much into both product and labor markets and they worked to lessen that role. The Reagan administration worked actively to undermine what was left of unions. These actions had the effect of delivering the message that firms should be reorganized along any lines that owners saw fit.

Ironically, the problem of the lack of competitiveness of American firms did not go away. American firms failed to recapture markets they had lost in the 1970s and early 1980s. Financially reorganized firms did not make higher profits than their counterparts, but instead aided in transferring wealth from workers to managers and owners. The shareholder value conception of the firm is not the fix for industrial competitiveness that some have argued it is (Jensen 1989). Instead, it causes firms to focus more narrowly on financial criteria in their decision-making and less on strategic matters. Because of the shareholder value conception of the firm, managers that are having problems with a particular product will not work to become more competitive in that product, but instead will divest themselves of that product.

The computer revolution led by Silicon Valley during the 1980s and 1990s is emblematic of entrepreneurial American capitalism. Yet close examination of the facts shows that the American government has been intimately involved in funding research, education, and buying the products of the industry for the past fifty years. It has also provided for tax incentives and patent laws that favor producers and investors in risky ventures. But even this has not been enough to stabilize volatile markets for technology products. Firms have found their ways to oligopolies or monopolies whereby innovative firms are selectively absorbed by larger firms. This allows both sides to profit. The founders of small firms are able to take high risks with potentially high returns. The largest firms are able to stabilize their positions by absorbing new technologies.

The lessons typically drawn about the dynamism of the U.S. economy are simple: keep governments and firms apart, make firms compete, and deregulate labor markets. Even sociologists have bought into the view that what happened in Silicon Valley has more to do with the intra-organizational networks between firms than with the whole system of production (Castells 1996; Saxenian 1994; Powell 2001). This chapter should make the reader question this view. Governments and firms are intimately linked. The relative success of capitalist economies in producing wealth, income, goods and services depends on these linkages. Any account of the success or failure of the American economy (or any other economy for that matter) that does not take both into account is likely to be incomplete at best and misleading at worst.

The negative view of state intervention into the economy comes from a strand of thought in economics that focuses on the idea that governments are rent seekers or that firms who seek government help will produce government intervention that promotes rent seeking on their behalf (Buchanan et al. 1990; Noll 1989; the literature is reviewed in Peltzman 1989). This implies that governmental interventions into markets are always at the very least suspiciously likely to undermine the efficient operation of markets or entirely illegitimate (see Block 1996 for the evolution of this argument).

But the idea that all states are predatory is not just a product of rational choice theory. It is related to the scholarly and policy interest in the past fifteen years in trying to assess how nations could attain competitive advantages for their firms in markets. From the point of view of intellectual trends, many scholars became interested in Japan and the "Asian miracle" in the 1980s (Johnson 1982; Dore 1997; Hamilton and Biggart 1988). This caused them to try and decipher why Japan, Taiwan, and Korea were able to develop so quickly and the role of governments were part of the focus of attention.

Others saw the German economy to be admired for its neocorporatist political system, its formal cooperation between labor and capital, and its relatively small firms that were oriented toward exporting high quality manufactured goods (Alpert 1991). Still others viewed the future of manufacturing as being about flexible specialization, where small firms in the industrial districts of Italy, Silicon Valley, or Bavaria existed (Piore and Sabel 1984; Saxenian 1994; Powell 2001). These highly networked firms could respond quickly to changes in market demand. Various scholars became convinced that one of these models held the key to industrial competitiveness among nations.

States played an important part in most of these stories. During the 1990s, the resurgence of the U.S. economy and relative success has propelled scholars to turn back to the U.S. and extol the virtues of American style corporate governance and labor relations as the key to economic success. Given the American view that states should play a minimal role, it is not surprising that governments are now out of favor.

But, these fads in intellectual thought do not do justice to the difficulty of unraveling what causes economic growth. It assumes that all government policies have negative effects on economic growth by consuming economic resources that would otherwise be put to more productive uses by the private sector. This argument is wrong both theoretically and empirically. Even in economics, there can be an argument for the positive role states play in economic growth. The "new institutional economics" suggests several mechanisms by which government spending and policies might positively affect growth. Endogenous growth theory argues that spending on education, health, and communications and transportation infrastructure are thought to have positive effects on growth (Barro 1990; Romer 1990; Aschauer 1990). North (1990) and Maddison (1995) have suggested that states also provide political stability, legal institutions, stable monetary systems, and reliable governments, all of which convince entrepreneurs to invest their money and create new markets.

The approach outlined here agrees with this perspective. Without these social institutions, economic actors will refuse to make investments in economies of scale and scope (for evidence on this point, see the essays in the volume edited by Chandler and Tanaka 1997 that concern why different countries did or did not achieve economic growth). Evans and Rauch have shown recently that the "competence" of bureaucratic officials has a positive effect on economic growth (1999). Some economists are prepared to believe that different forms of industrial policies might be effective by providing investment in research and development, capital for risky ventures, and military spending (Tyson 1992).

At the very least, the choice is not just for or against governments, but for or against policies that might help economic growth (Evans 1996). The comparative capitalisms literature has demonstrated fairly effectively that governments have played positive roles in the development process as well (Evans 1996; Campos and Root 1996; Wade 1990). The literature comparing specific industrial policies and their effectiveness for advanced industrial societies offers both positive and negative evidence for the role of governments (Johnson 1982; Zeigler 1997; Herrigel

1996; Crouch and Streeck 1997; for a recent review see Pauly and Reich 1997).

There are theoretical reasons to believe that states continue to matter in producing economic growth by providing public goods, the stable rule of law, and, under certain conditions, good industrial policy. Investments in research and development, higher education, and the subsidization of technologies in their early stages of development are all policies that have worked to produce economic growth. Property rights and rules governing competition and exchange facilitate stable market relations between firms. These encourage investment and economic growth.

CONCLUSIONS

One task for economic sociology is to theorize what kind of market interventions are more likely to have positive economic consequences and what kind of market interventions are more likely to have negative economic consequences. One of the main contributions economic sociology can make is the careful attempt to empirically analyze particular market situations in order to decide whom economic changes help, whom they hurt, and what effects they have more generally on economic growth. For example, a sober empirical analysis of the positive and negative effects of the rise of shareholder value has never been undertaken. Such an analysis would prove a useful intervention to policymakers engaged in considering how to reform corporate governance practices.

There are many economic sociological analyses that do not situate market structures in larger institutional contexts. Network analysts often ignore factors not associated with conventional network measures in their analyses of firm and market success and failure. This approach works against the grain of most sociology. Sociologists usually work with more multivariate models of social processes because they allow analysts to give weight to various causal factors. Economic sociologists who ignore or avoid other types of social embeddedness will miss key variables that explain positive and negative economic effects. As I have tried to show, firms and states are interrelated and their dynamics over time are pivotal to making sense of the direction of changes in firms and markets. Analyses that do not consider such factors will likely misunderstand many economic processes.

Part of this empirical sensitivity is to not prejudge what effects interventions and changes might have on firms, jobs, inequality, and economic growth. While the problem of rent seeking on the part of different actors, be they managers, firms, the government, or workers, is a theoretical possibility, one has to be cautious in trying to assess whether it really occurs and the degree to which it has bad consequences for other social groups. For example, while Microsoft is a convicted monopolist, the over-all effect of having a single dominant platform for software may be positive on other sectors of the economy. In this case, economic sociology might recommend regulating the monopoly position of Microsoft along the lines of a public utility rather than attempting to create multiple incompatible platforms for the sake of inducing competition.

One of the main purposes of economic sociological analyses could be to present a total picture of what has happened in a certain case. So, for example, government intervention in product and labor markets in Silicon Valley has certainly paid off handsomely for the society. The government's role in training engineers, underwriting innovation, and encouraging the adoption of new technology has created growth and wealth for the entire economy. It is clear that the government is busily trying to reproduce the same effect in the biotechnology industry.

The example of shareholder value is more mixed. Many workers lost jobs and their economic situations suffered for a long time as a result (Bernhardt et al. 2000). Even managers experienced frequent layoffs and those who remained worked longer hours (Fligstein and Shin 2003; Baumol et al. 2003). While a great deal of wealth was created for those who sold stock and those who benefited from that sale, there are less clear results for the overall competitiveness of the American economy. One substantive conclusion that the two cases suggest is that corporate governance is less likely than previously aspected to be a source of competitive advantage and economic growth and more traditional forms of investment (both public and private) are effective ways to attain economic growth.

Economic sociology is uniquely positioned to help us understand how firms and market processes are situated in larger political and legal contexts. It can also be used to understanding the evolution of stable market structures of particular markets. By doing this, economic sociology provides us with theoretical and empirical analyses that can lead to making more sense of the effects of market change on whom in the society gains and who lose.

NOTES

1. Of course, governments do many other things that directly and indirectly help entrepreneurs. They provide for infrastructure like roads, other forms of transportation, utilities, and public safety (including national defense). They also provide for the enforcement of contracts more generally and insure the stability of the financial system. Finally, governments provide social welfare functions.

2. So, for example, the federal government has agreed not to charge sales tax on purchases over the Internet. This policy is supposed to allow the Internet to

"mature" as a medium of exchange. But obviously giving electronic sellers a 5-7 percent price advantage over firms that are "bricks and mortar" is a policy that reflects the interests of one set of sellers over another.

REFERENCES

Albert, Michel. 1991. *Capitalisme contre capitalisme*. Paris: Seuil. English, *Capitalism versus Capitalism*. New York: Four Walls Eight Windows, 1993.

Aoki, Masahiko. 1988. *Information, Incentives and Bargaining in the Japanese Economy*. Cambridge: Cambridge University Press.

Arthur, W. Brian. 1994. *Increasing Returns and Path Dependence in the Economy*. Ann Arbor: University of Michigan Press.

Ashauer, David Alan. 1990. *Public Investment and Private Sector Growth*. Washington, D.C.: Economic Policy Institute.

Barro, Robert J. 1990. "Government Spending in a Simple Model of Endogenous Growth." *Journal of Political Economy* 98(5): 103–25.

Baumol, William J., Alan S. Blinder, and Edward N. Wolff. 2003. *Downsizing in America: Reality, Causes, and Consequences*. New York: Russell Sage.

Bernhardt, Annette D., Martina Morris, Mark S. Handcock, and Marc A. Scott. 2001. *Divergent Paths: Economic Mobility in the New American Labor Market*. New York: Russell Sage.

Blair, Margaret M. and Mark J. Roe, eds. 1999, *Employees and Corporate Governance*. Washington, D.C.: Brookings Institution Press.

Block, Fred L. 1996. *The Vampire State: And Other Myths and Fallacies about the U.S. Economy*. New York: W. W. Norton.

Bresnahan, Timothy F. 1999. "Computing." In *U.S. Industry in 2000: Studies in Comparative Performance*, ed. David C. Mowery. Washington, D.C.: National Academy Press.

Buchanan, James, R. D. Tollison, and Gordon Tulloch, eds. 1980. *Towards a Theory of the Rent-Seeking Society*. College Station: Texas A&M University Press.

Campos, José Edgardo and Hilton R. Root. 1996. *The Key to the Asian Miracle: Making Shared Growth Credible*. Washington, D.C.: Brookings Institution.

Castells, Manuel. 1996. *The Rise of the Network Society*. Information Age 1. Oxford: Blackwell.

Castillo, Emilio J., Hakyu Hwang, Ellen Granovetter, and Mark S. Granovetter. 2000. "Social Networks in Silicon Valley." In *The Silicon Valley Edge: A Habitat for Innovation and Entrepreneurship*, ed. Chong Moon Lee, William F. Miller, Marguerite Gong Hancock, and Henry S. Rowen. Stanford: Stanford University Press.

Chandler, Alfred D., Jr., Franco Amatori, and Takashi Hikino, eds. 1997. *Big Business and the Wealth of Nations*. Cambridge: Cambridge University Press.

Crouch, Colin and Wolfgang Streeck, eds. 1997. *Political Economy of Modern Capitalism: Mapping Convergence and Diversity*. London: Sage.

Davis, Gerald F. 1991. "Agents without Principles." *Administrative Science Quarterly* 36: 583–613.

Davis, Gerald F. and Suzanne K. Stout. 1992. "Organization Theory and the Market for Corporate Control: A Dynamic Analysis of the Characteristics of Large Takeover Targets, 1980-1990." *Administrative Science Quarterly* 37: 605–33.

Dore, Ronald P. 1997. "The Distinctiveness of Japan." In *Political Economy of Modern Capitalism: Mapping Convergence and Diversity*, ed. Colin Crouch and Wolfgang Streeck. London: Sage.

Edstrom, M. 1999. "Controlling Markets in Silicon Valley: A Case Study of Java." M.A. thesis, Department of Sociology, University of California.

Evans, Peter B. 1995. *Embedded Autonomy: States and Industrial Transformation.* Princeton: Princeton University Press.

Evans, Peter B. and James E. Rauch. 1999. "Bureaucracy and Economic Growth." *American Sociological Review* 64: 187–214.

Fama, Eugene F. and Michael C. Jensen. 1983. "Separation of Ownership and Control." *Journal of Law and Economics* 26: 301–25.

Fligstein, Neil. 1990. *The Transformation of Corporate Control.* Cambridge, Mass.: Harvard University Press.

———. 2001. *The Architecture of Markets: An Economic Sociology of Twenty-First-Century Capitalist Societies.* Princeton: Princeton University Press.

Fligstein, Neil and Linda Markowitz. 1993. "Financial Reorganization of American Corporations in the 1980s." In *Sociology and the Public Agenda*, ed. William J. Wilson. Beverly Hills, Calif.: Sage.

Fligstein, Neil and Taek-jin Shin. 2004. "The Shareholder Value Society." In *Social Inequality*, ed. Kathryn Neckerman. New York: Russell Sage.

Friedman, Benjamin N. 1985. "The Substitutability of Equity and Debt Securities." In *Corporate Capital Structures in the United States*, ed. Benjamin N. Friedman. Chicago: University of Chicago Press.

Hamilton, Gary G. and Nicole Woolsey Biggart. 1988. "Market, Culture, and Authority: A Comparative Analysis of Management and Organization in the Far East." *American Journal of Sociology* 94 (Supplement): S52–S94.

Henton, Doug. 2000. "A Profile of the Valley's Evolving Structure." In *The Silicon Valley Edge: A Habitat for Innovation and Entrepreneurship*, ed. Chong Moon Lee, William F. Miller, Marguerite Gong Hancock, and Henry S. Rowen. Stanford: Stanford University Press.

Herrigel, Gary. 1996. *Industrial Constructions: The Sources of German Industrial Power.* Cambridge: Cambridge University Press.

Jensen, Michael C. 1989. "Eclipse of the Public Corporation." *Harvard Business Review* 67: 61–73.

Jensen, Michael C. and William A. Meckling. 1976. "Theory of the Firm: Managerial Behavior, Agency Costs, and Ownership Structure." *Journal of Financial Economics* 3: 305–60.

Jensen, Michael C. and Richard S. Ruback. 1994. "The Market for Corporate Control: The Scientific Evidence." *Journal of Financial Economics* 11: 5–50.

Johnson, Chalmers. 1982. *MITI and the Japanese Miracle: The Growth of Industrial Policy, 1925–1975.* Stanford: Stanford University Press.

Lecuyer, Christopher. 2000. "Fairchild Semiconductor and Its Influence." In *The Silicon Valley Edge: A Habitat for Innovation and Entrepreneurship*, ed. Chong

Moon Lee, William F. Miller, Marguerite Gong Hancock, and Henry S. Rowen. Stanford: Stanford University Press.

Lerner, Josh. 2000. "Small Business, Innovation, and Public Policy in the Information Technology Industry." In *Understanding the Digital Economy: Data, Tools, and Research*, ed. Erik Brynjolfsson and Brian Kahin. Cambridge, Mass. MIT Press.

Leslie, Stuart W. 2000. "The Biggest 'Angel' of Them All: The Military and the Making of Silicon Valley." In *Understanding Silicon Valley: The Anatomy of an Entrepreneurial Region*, ed. Martin Kenney. Stanford: Stanford University Press.

Maddison, Angus. 1995. *Explaining the Economic Performance of Nations: Essays in Time and Space*. Aldershot, Hants: E. Elgar.

Noll, Roger G. 1989. "Economic Perspectives on the Politics of Regulation." In *Handbook of Industrial Organization*, ed. Richard Schmalensee and Robert D. Willig. New York: Elsevier. 1257–87.

North, Douglass C. 1990. *Institutions, Institutional Change and Economic Performance*. Cambridge: Cambridge University Press.

Pauly, Louis and Simon Reich. 1997. "National Structures and Multinational Corporate Behavior. Enduring Differences in the Age of Globalization." *International Organization* 51, 1–30.

Peltzman, Sam, Michael E. Levine, and Roger G. Noll. 1989. "The Economic Theory of Regulation after a Decade of Deregulation." *Brookings Papers on Economic Activity. Microeconomics*, vol. 1989. Washington, D.C.: Brookings Institution. 1–59.

Piore Michael J. and Charles F. Sabel. 1984. *The Second Industrial Divide: Possibilities for Prosperity*. New York: Basic Books.

Porter, Michael E. 1990. *The Competitive Advantage of Nations*. New York: Free Press.

Powell, Walter W. 2001. "The Capitalist Firm in the Twenty-First Century: Emerging Patterns in Western Enterprise." In *The Twenty-First-Century Firm: Changing Economic Organization in International Perspective*, ed. Paul DiMaggio. Princeton: Princeton University Press.

Roe, Mark J. 1994. *Strong Managers, Weak Owners: The Political Roots of American Corporate Finance*. Princeton: Princeton University Press.

Romer, Paul M. 1990. "Endogenous Technological Change." *Journal of Political Economy* 98(5): S71–S102.

Roy, William G. 1998. *Socializing Capital: The Rise of the Large Industrial Corporation in America*. Princeton: Princeton University Press.

Saxenian, AnnaLee. 1994. *Regional Advantage: Culture and Competition in Silicon Valley and Route 128*. Cambridge, Mass.: Harvard University Press.

Sturgeon, Timothy J. "How Silicon Valley Came to Be." In *Understanding Silicon Valley: The Anatomy of an Entrepreneurial Region*, ed. Martin Kenney. Stanford: Stanford University Press.

Tyson, Laura D'Andrea. 1993. *Who's Bashing Whom? Trade Conflicts in High-Technology Industries*. Washington, D.C.: Institute for International Economics.

Useem, Michael. 1993. *Executive Defense: Shareholder Power and Corporate Reorganization*. Cambridge, Mass.: Harvard University Press.

Wade, Robert. 1990. *Governing the Market: Economic Theory and the Role of Government in East Asian Industrialization.* Princeton: Princeton University Press.

Womack, James P., Daniel T. Jones, and Donald Roos. 1991. *The Machine That Changed the World: How Japan's Secret Weapon in the Global Auto Wars Will Revolutionize Western Industry.* New York: HarperPerennial.

Ziegler, J. Nicholas. 1997. *Governing Ideas: Strategies for Innovation in France and Germany.* Ithaca: Cornell University Press.

Venture Capital and Modern Capitalism

John Freeman

OVER THE PAST THIRTY YEARS, organizational ecologists have developed an extensive literature on the founding rates of various organizational forms. In doing so, they have probed the institutional underpinnings of these organization-creation processes. In general, founding rates surge and decline as events in the economy lead to massive reallocation of the "factors of production" (capital, labor, and raw materials), as political upheavals, in which the interests and leadership of nation states and other political units are replaced and waves of scientific discovery and invention produce shifts in technology that provide competitive advantage to some organizations and impose obsolescence on others.

Such societal-level processes do not happen automatically, but reflect a complex pattern of interrelationships between various social institutions that are played out at the population level by competitive and mutualistic relationships among various specialized organizational forms. At the community level these same relationships are manifested in the patterned interactions between individual organizations whose behavioral predilections are engineered into the structures, operating processes and strategic models they employ (Hannan and Freeman 1989; Carroll and Hannan 2000).

Over the past forty years in the United States, some organizational forms proliferate through processes in which various supporting organizations gather and distribute resources used in the organization founding and building processes. Relationships based on ascribed social status have always assisted or impeded organization builders. Being a member of the right kin, ethnic, or social circle has always improved the chances of entrepreneurial success. These factors do so today. In some parts of the world, however, they have been supplemented or even replaced by other, more formal mechanisms as special purpose organizations have emerged that generate their own resources by providing resources to others. Banks and law firms have done so for centuries (see Black and Gilson 1998 for an analysis of the interplay of such institutions). More recently, a community built on relationships among a larger set of actors has emerged. Resources flow through these relationships, whose structure, therefore, defines opportunity for individuals. In addition to commercial banks and law firms, the organizational forms that characterize this community include accounting firms, executive search firms, investment banks, commercial and industrial real estate brokers, and venture capital firms.

All of these specialists provide access to resources that entrepreneurs and other organization-creators routinely use. They also provide access to each other. They develop strong relationships that include personal ties, partly by being involved in various extra-work social networks, but also by "doing deals" together (Bygrave 1988). That is, they cement relationships by stating their willingness to provide resources to organization founders, and then by performing when the time comes. Having done deals together before provides them with the background to trust each other the next time. Similarly, or course, failure to perform establishes a barrier between such actors. These relationships and barriers form the basic social structure through which organization founding occurs (Anderson 1999). When companies succeed or fail on matters of dynamics, when they start a new company and how fast they build it to competitive scale, the efficient interaction of these service providers become especially important. This is, of course, exactly what Richard Swedberg identifies as the core turf of the new economic sociology: amalgamations of interests and social relations (2003: 7).

This paper describes one such organizational form, the venture capital firm. It explains how certain observable behavioral regularities of such organizations can be understood as ordinary outcomes of structural arrangements rather than as the heroic acts of media icons. Venture capital firms participate in a communal system including other kinds of organizations such as commercial banks, investment banks, law firms, accounting firms, and executive search firms. This system is designed to reallocate capital very quickly as new technologies and markets appear. The extraordinarily rapid growth of companies receiving venture capital investment imposes burdens on society, and also creates benefits such as employment. By exploring venture capital as a social institution, the chapter may help add to the understanding of how capitalism works at the start of the twenty-first century.

Venture Capital as a Social Institution

In the nineteenth century, when European and American social scientists were struggling to understand the implications of the Industrial Revolution, capitalism was the frequent subject of analysis. One might even say that early social scientists were preoccupied with it. Political power, social status, and wealth were all bound up in a social system driven by capital formation and the ownership of economic assets (i.e., "the means of production"). In particular, those who financed and organized the areas of economic expansion amassed great fortunes and all that went them.

This is still true today, but two important factors have changed. First, the industrial revolution expanded in areas of infrastructure building (e.g., railroads, bridge and ship building, iron, steel, and lumber mills). It was not until the latter part of the nineteenth century in Europe that science-based entrepreneurship became common. Even then, it was not the principal source of new venture formation, nor was it the principal basis on which great fortunes were built. Today, social change, economic growth, and the creation of great fortunes are driven by the commercialization of science and technology. Second, companies are formed to be sold. Rockefeller and Ford, for instance, did not build their companies in order to sell them. Loss of majority ownership and control of the ventures follow from the speed of the contemporary process and a changed way of thinking. Current financial institutions time-value money, and this makes time to liquidity vitally important for all who invest in the commercialization process. Similarly, the pace of technological change is high in areas of greatest opportunity, and this places a premium on quick injections of capital and rapid growth of new ventures. American venture capital is a device for rapid redirection of the flow of capital, with continuing injections of capital supporting an extraordinarily rapid growth process.

One of the more interesting consequences of modern capitalism is the speed with which new economic entities are formed and the celerity of their growth. Very rapid growth to large size was accomplished in earlier times only out of military necessity. So the firm of Friedrich Krupp A.G., or E. I. DuPont de Nemours & Co., grew very rapidly during World War I, but the conditions generating such growth involved direct governmental mandate and capitalization. More generally, large corporate entities were unknown prior to building the large railroad trunk lines, and such growth occurred through merger and acquisition (Chandler 1977).

VENTURE CAPITALISTS AND VENTURE CAPITAL FIRMS

In this chapter, the term "venture capital" refers to a particular form of organization in its institutional context. A venture capital firm is a management organization that raises money, finds and evaluates entrepreneurial ventures, and participates in their management so as to increase their value as rapidly as possible. The defining characteristics of an American venture capital firm are (see Gompers and Lerner 2000: 17–124):

- *Invest capital provided by others*—they are not principally set up to invest the venture capitalists' own money.

- *Sequential funds organized as limited partnerships*—the venture capital firms raise money in one or more "funds." These funds are commitments by investors to provide capital on request. Investors are partners whose liability is limited to the amounts invested—hence the term "limited partner." The capital provided by the limited partners is invested and managed by general partners, and those general partners are personally liable for the capital invested (i.e., the general partners are fiduciaries). These funds are set up to liquidate on a fixed schedule, usually in ten years. By law, the limited partners may not exercise control over the specific investments or the managers of the portfolio companies that receive them.
- *Carried interest*—when the fund's assets are sold, any profits generated are split between the limited partners and general partners. Usually, 20 percent of this "carried interest" goes to the general partners, the venture capitalists. The rest goes to the limited partners. The original investment of the limited partners is returned before carried interest is calculated. Venture capitalists also charge a yearly management fee. It is 1.5 percent to 3 percent of the fund's capitalization and is intended to reimburse the general partners for the costs of doing business.

Venture capitalists make money by investing when companies are younger, smaller, and less valuable, selling when these companies are older, bigger, and more valuable. As these companies grow, various strategic and managerial problems are solved and risk is mitigated. So investments occurring later in the process are less risky and one would expect the returns to be lower. Carried interest provides a very powerful incentive for venture capitalists to encourage the speed of this process. They make most of their money when they sell their equity in the young company to other investors. To the degree that venture capitalists, other investors, founders, and employees benefit from this growth, their interests are aligned. So they all do most well when the young company grows at a very rapid rate (see Sahlman 1990, for more detail on venture capital firm structure).

Viewed in this structural way, venture capital firms make their money by filling the *structural holes* that exist in the social networks (Burt 1982, 1992) connecting holders of highly aggregated capital (insurance companies, pension funds, endowments) and the entrepreneurs who are trying to start and grow young companies. The venture capitalists, acting as agents of their limited partners, develop specialized skills for identifying and evaluating nascent ventures. On the other hand, the develop strong social relationships with those who manage this highly aggregated capital. They economize on the time it would ordinarily take for an entrepreneur to find and "pitch" the source of financing. The structural hole exists because the money manager does not speak the same language as the entrepreneur and does not have the time to make small investments. So the venture capitalist fills the hole and benefits from the social position.

Liquidity is produced in the capital markets, through an Initial Public Offering of securities (IPO) and subsequently through the sale of stock through the market, or through an acquisition. In the latter scenario, another company buys the young company and pays the investors either in cash or in stock. Since owning stock in the acquiring company entails risks, cash is better. Shares in a publicly traded company are second best, and less desirable if the terms of the deal prohibit the investors from selling those shares for some period of time (during which they are "locked up"). Least attractive of all is an acquisition by a private company, which must itself generate liquidity before the focal company's investors realize a return on their investment. The time between investment and liquidity may be lengthy. Consequently, the venture capitalist assists the managers of the young portfolio company in growing their business as quickly as possible. So creating rapid growth is a means to an end. The end is to produce a return for all the partners in the fund.

Capital Markets. If the capital markets will buy partially formed companies and provide the kinds of rewards they seek, venture capitalists will happily go along. Ordinarily, however, venture capitalists are constrained by the capital markets, which have their own institutionalized practices and standards, and their own economic realities. This means that investment banks will only underwrite an IPO if the portfolio company has characteristics (such as financial performance and stable management) that the analysts working for the purchasers of securities will accept. Investment banks promise to make a market in a new security. This means that they are willing to buy or sell shares if such actions are necessary to support a stable price for the security.

The fixed costs of taking a company public are high. Lawyers, accountants, and other professionals must be hired to generate the documents required by the markets and government agencies. To sustain such fixed costs and justify the risks associated with making a market, the minimum value of the securities sold in an IPO has to be $50–75 million. Since about one-third of a company's stock is sold to the public in an IPO, this means that the company must be worth at least $150 million in order to take it public. This is a typical target set by the venture capitalists. They ask themselves what is the probability that this company will ultimately grow to a valuation of $150 million, and how long will it take?

Successive Funds. Venture capitalists are concerned about both time to liquidity and the return they receive because these issues underlie their carried interest. A second reason for this concern is that the performance of the current fund is the most important issue in raising the next fund. It takes about three years to invest the capital raised in a venture capital fund. Of course, this time period adjusts to the business cycle, lengthening when depressed stock markets make IPOs difficult and shortening when markets are rising. IPOs occur more frequently in a rising market, and entrepreneurs bring more deals to the venture capitalists when they believe that their chances of success are higher. After the fund's capital is invested, venture capitalists continue to work on the portfolio companies in which their capital is invested. After another period of time, they start to have liquidity events and returns can be distributed to the partners. Of course, the venture capitalists do not wait until this happens to raise another fund. They try to time the funds so that they always have funds to invest. So about every three years they raise another fund.

The performance of previous funds is conventionally evaluated in terms of an Internal Rate of Return (IRR). This is time valued against some conservative standard such as returns yielded by government bonds. So current performance fuels future access to capital. Venture capital firms do fail. They disappear when their returns are low by competitive standards. Indeed, sometimes "low" means negative.

So far, we have described what venture capital firms are, but we have not discussed what they actually do. Their activities vary through the cycle of the funds they have organized and the life cycles of the portfolio companies in which they have invested.

INSTITUTIONAL STRUCTURES

The rapid growth that underlies the institution of venture capital requires that resources flow into the new venture at high rates. This, in turn, requires that these resources flow through society in a fluid manner. This depends on a set of legal, financial, and social structures that can be seen as preconditions for the institution to function.

This chapter cannot possibly deal with all of these institutional arrangements, as they constitute the economic underpinnings of a modern state. So it goes almost without saying that contracts have to be enforceable, and there has to be a generally accepted monetary system. More specifically, however, venture capital requires processes for gaining liquidity.

Capital Markets. Initial public offerings are the preferred vehicle for liquidity because they produce higher returns and generate methods of converting large shares of equity into cash. So venture capital tends to work badly without a securities market that has efficient procedures for marketing shares of young companies. This, in turn, requires an underwriting mechanism to reduce risk for the purchasers of IPO stock. That is, someone has to "make a market" in the stock so there is liquidity when the "float" is small (i.e., not much stock is available to be traded). A set of regulations to create and preserve transparency, along with an enforcement structure, is also necessary if human perfidy is to be assumed.

Technology. Protection of intellectual property rights has to be provided if the window of time between the start of the new company and the liquidity event for investors is to stay open long enough for growth to produce the returns venture capital generates. So if patents, trademarks, and the like cannot be defended, new entrants can begin to cut profit margins before early investors can gain liquidity. If this happens, their risks expand substantially.

Labor Markets. Because rapid growth is presumed, venture capital presumes fluidity in labor markets. "Non-compete" clauses in labor contracts keep experienced managers and technical people from moving into rapidly growing young companies. In some countries (e.g., Germany), a presumption of theft of intellectual property is implicit in employment agreements. The burden of proof is on the employee to show that he or she is not taking company trade secrets when employers are changed.

Employee Incentive Stock Options provide an important vehicle for aligning incentives of founders, investors and employees hired during the growth process. These are contracts to purchase common stock in the future at a fixed price, usually the share price paid by the most recent investor at the time the option is granted. These options are not taxed in the U.S. until they are exercised and the stock is sold. So the person receiving the options takes no risk, as the options cost nothing until exercised but permit the option holder to participate in the company's value appreciation. Such options are usually "vested" over time. They cannot be exercised until vesting has occurred. In many parts of the world such options are taxed at the time they are issued, in spite of the fact that they cannot be converted into cash even to pay the tax (Jaffee and Freeman 2002). Furthermore, they are often taxed as ordinary income while in the U.S. they are taxed at a lower capital gains rate. So U.S. tax law discounts such options for the risk associated with the company's future and provides support for the mobility process that underlies rapid growth.

In addition to the legal issues that may lower employment mobility, cultural factors also operate to limit the fluidity of employment. Employees take risks as the economic and social costs of job changes are rarely compensated in full. Much research shows that the probability of failure of young and small companies is much higher (see Carroll and Hannan 2000: 281–312 for a review), so when an employee leaves a big, older company for a younger and smaller one, the risks of subsequent unemployment are higher. One would think this would be accompanied by higher rates of pay, but the reverse is true. Typically, wage rates are lower in the young companies. Social status returns are similarly lower (especially for senior managers and technical people). Compensation usually takes the form of stock options. These options are rights to purchase common stock in the future, and thus fall behind the preferred stock investors of capital receive (what makes such stock "preferred" is principally the liquidation preference in which the proceeds of company liquidation go first to the preferred shareholders). Since the value of these options is a function of company success, this mechanism magnifies the risk. Employees make a bet on the outcome of another bet.

Of course, those making this bet are not just the employees themselves; their families are implicitly doing so as well. So the willingness to take such risks for an employee are in part a function of that employee's family's reactions. If leaving a secure, high status company for an insecure unknown startup is not socially supported, recruiting experienced managers and technical people is made much more difficult. This is the situation in much of the world.

Dilution. So far, we have discussed the growing value of young companies and how venture capitalists profit from that growth. A parallel process is working simultaneously to dampen the returns to all involved. This second process is the distribution of equity to investors and employees as time goes by. The young company's cash requirements rise as it grows. Entrepreneurs and investors conventionally think of this as a "burn rate"; it is evaluated relative to working capital. Simply put, the monthly burn rate and capital resources define the time to failure. Rapid growth ordinarily generates expenses that rise more rapidly than expanding sales can sustain. So successive waves of capital are sought to fuel this rapid growth, and shares in the company are sold in larger and larger quantities. To be sure, the price per share rises. It makes sense for current investors to accept this situation as they own a smaller share of a more valuable entity. When things go well, their absolute interest rises even when their relative position erodes through dilution. When things go badly, of course, this may not be true. In fact, the position of current investors may get worse very fast in hard times as later investors can demand much greater dilution of earlier investors and former employees.

REWARDS FOR SUCCESSFUL VENTURE CAPITALISTS

Depending on competitive conditions, venture capitalists need to return 30 percent or more compounded annually. To meet this target an investment has to double in value in three years. It must increase almost fivefold in six years (see figure 4 below for recent returns of venture capital funds). When venture funds perform at this level, venture capitalists make substantial amounts of money (see Bygrave 1994 for an analysis of venture fund IRR).

A typical fund might have $500 million dollars in commitments from limited partners. Such a fund might have six general partners. Each year, these six partners might charge 2 percent of the fund's value in management fees, $10 million or about $1.7 million each. Of course, expenses such as office rent and salaries of staff come out of this $10 million. If a 30 percent internal rate of return is achieved and results in disbursements according to the indicated return, the original $500 million has grown to a little over $2.4 billion after six years have passed. Of course, some investments produce liquidity earlier and cease to generate returns after the partners have been paid. On the other hand, some of the investments will not produce liquidity until ten or more years have passed. Assuming the process ends in six years, and that the carried interest of the venture capitalists is 20 percent, the six partners will make $380 million, $63.3 million each if they share equally. Their pro rata share of the management fees raises this to about $80 million (although sometimes management fees are treated as an advance against the carry). What do they do to produce such proceeds?

Activities of Venture Capitalists

First, and most obviously, venture capitalists find and evaluate deals. They get paid to pick winning horses. This is difficult to do, as returns are approximately log-normally distributed. A few very successful investments produce the bulk of the fund's returns. The issue is not simply investing in successful companies, but investing in at least a few very successful companies. To do this, venture capitalists need to persuade themselves that there is a billion-dollar market for the new company's products or services, and that the company can take a large share of that market. Such decisions are obviously fraught with uncertainty, which venture capitalists mitigate in part through syndicated investment strategies and in part by tapping into extended information networks (Podolny and Castelucci 1999).

Second, venture capitalists structure deals. They have a great deal of expertise in producing profits for their funds while preserving the incentives the entrepreneurs and other employees require to motivate them in the face of heavy time demands and high levels of risk (Sorenson and Stuart 2001).

Capital is raised for young companies in waves, called "rounds" of investment. Staggering injections of capital this way facilitate monitoring the performance of entrepreneurs as each round provokes a review of the company relative to its plans as stated when previous rounds were raised (Amit et al. 1980; Gompers 1995). Typically, each round is led by one investor who joins the board of directors. Since all investors in the round purchase stock at the same price, this lead investor essentially represents the interests of all investors in the round. The implicit trust constrains the admission of potential investors (Rosenstein et al. 1993). Joining a syndicated round thus involves social acceptance. Some venture capitalists avoid co-investing with others. Leads often help sell the deal to others with whom they prefer to work (Bygrave 1987; Podolny 2001).

Third, venture capitalists add value by drawing on their networks to provide resources the growing company requires (Florida and Kenney 1988). This sometimes takes the form of access to markets. It also involves access to other service providers such as commercial bankers, investment bankers, law firms, accountants, and executive search firms. As Coleman (1988) points out, these various network connections reinforce each other, and they reinforce the value of human capital venture capitalists also bring to their company-building activities. The intense time demands are exacerbates by distance, and this leads venture capitalists, particularly those focusing on the earliest investment in new companies, to confine their activities to areas of close proximity (Sorenson and Stuart 2001).

Fourth, venture capitalists provide management skills—human capital. The earlier they invest, the greater their involvement tends to be. So they advise the entrepreneurs about organizational structure, business strategy, and financial planning, and often participate in negotiations and recruiting (Sapienza and Gupta 1994). Venture capitalists often provoke entrepreneurs to make decisions they would otherwise put off. People tend to magnify the importance of things they know about and trivialize things they do not know intimately. So venture capitalists pressure entrepreneurs to face problems in areas they would prefer to ignore. This often involves hiring managers in fields such as marketing and finance, which technology-oriented entrepreneurs would otherwise leave to much later and tend to fill with less qualified people.

Finally, venture capitalists help prepare the company for a liquidity event. They negotiate with investment banks and help to secure the last rounds of financing that are required to boost performance, making the new issue more attractive to investors. (More details on these activities can be found in Gorman and Sahlman 1989.)

Resources VC Firms Use

Venture capital firms depend on three kinds of resources: capital, deals, and people. Any of these can be scarce or abundant.

Capital. Obviously, when the economy is expanding there is more capital, but there may also be more demand for that capital. Venture capitalists compete well for such capital when IPOs are occurring often and when valuations for those issues are high. They also compete successfully for capital when institutional arrangements favor growth and mitigate risks.

One can think of the dynamics as being represented by a clock that starts ticking the minute some engineer or manager has an idea for a new product or service. This clock keeps ticking as the idea is formed, proposals are made to immediate superiors, and series of revisions and elaborations are demanded followed by new reports and meetings. The more resources the new initiative requires, the higher the proposal must go within the management structure of the corporation. All of this takes time, of course. In a well-managed high technology company this might easily take two years.

Now consider the same clock, ticking since the idea was first generated. This time, however, the person who has the idea takes it to a venture capitalist. A series of conversations commences and a business plan is written. Seed Round funding—$500,000—allows the nascent entrepreneurs to quit their regular jobs and focus on starting the new company. They research existing technology, assess the market and competition, and write a business plan. Perhaps this takes three or four months. They then receive a second round of venture funding, $2 million, which allows them to hire additional engineering help and perhaps a marketing person. They spend another six months and produce a working prototype. A third round of capital finances a marketing effort. After another six months they have customers, sales, and a presence in the marketplace. The time from idea to selling products in this scenario might be twelve to eighteen months.

The difference between the two in this example is about a year. This window of time is the head start the entrepreneurs have to grow the business and build their organization. The challenge is to grow rapidly enough, and well enough, to compete when their larger, slower competitors arrive. Venture capital primarily captures this time advantage. The question for financiers is whether they can gain liquidity before the young company is overtaken. This is why the organizational form is set up to maximize the rate of growth.

History

The venture capital organizational form as described in this chapter dates from 1961, when the venture firm of Davis and Rock was formed. Predecessors were either publicly traded (e.g., American Research and Development), investment banks (e.g., the British company 3i), or firms that lacked the carried interest or fixed liquidation features (e.g., Draper and Johnson). More details are presented in Bygrave and Timmons (1992: 1–30).

In 1979 the so-called "prudent man rule" was changed by the Employee Retirement Security Act (ERISA). This change can be seen as the adoption

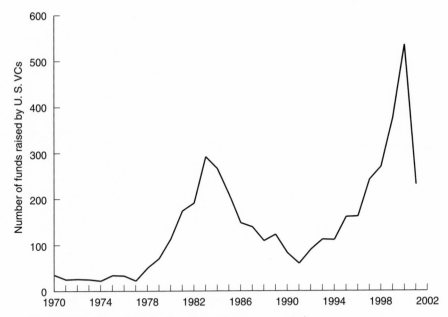

Figure 1 Number of funds raised by U.S. venture capitalists.

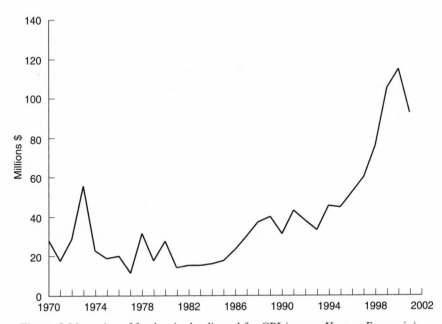

Figure 2 Mean size of funds raised, adjusted for CPI (*source: Venture Economics*).

Figure 3 Percent raised by biggest ten venture capitalists (*source: Venture Economics*).

by regulators of the concept of risk propounded by modern finance theory—risk is to be evaluated at the portfolio level, not at the level of the individual investment. This change in the laws allowed fiduciaries for pension funds, endowments, and financial institutions to allocate portions of their capital to risky investments if they are offset by more conservative investments. Similarly, U.S. tax law in some historical periods favors capital gains with lower tax rates than those that are applied to ordinary income. These and a series of other legal changes led to a very large increase in the capital available for investment in startups and young companies. The earliest venture funds were financed by wealthy individuals and families. In recent times, the bulk of the capital comes from university endowments such as Stanford and Yale, philanthropic foundations, and pension funds. The University of California Retirement System and the California Public Employees Retirement System (CALPERS) are two of the largest investors in venture funds. In 2001, for example, CALPERS had investments in venture funds totaling of $2 billion (*Sacramento Business Journal* 2001).

In this first figure, one can observe the surge in number of funds being formed by venture capital firms in the late 1970s. A few years later there was a drop off, followed by a recovery and another huge surge in the late 1990s. Finally, in 2001 there was a sharp drop in new funds being organized.

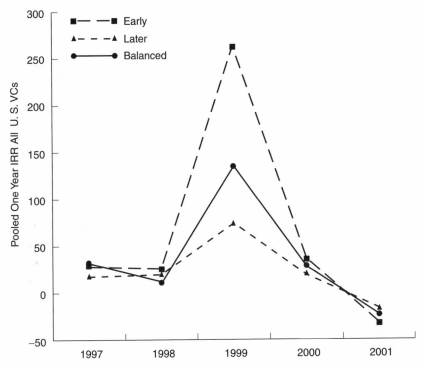

Figure 4 Pooled one-year internal rates of return, all U.S. venture capitalists (*source: Venture Economics*).

The trend toward larger funds is recent. Viewed in constant dollars (adjusted by the base 1984 CPI), funds grew substantially larger only during the surge of the 1990s. A fund with more than $40 million (1984) was not typical until 1994.

While the size of funds rose during the late 1990s, concentration actually fell. The ten largest venture capital firms' share of the total capital raised from limited partners fell during this period.

One can see what was driving this surge in venture capital fund raising and investment in startups. The capital markets were absorbing IPOs as an economic bubble drove the price of securities upward. Of course, this also meant that public companies could easily raise large amounts of cash with which to purchase private companies. So acquisitions also surged. Software companies, fiber optic infrastructure companies, and internet companies were valued at higher levels than companies like Boeing and General Motors. So both IPOs and acquisitions produced great returns for venture capital firms holding equity in the companies being sold. This is reflected in their internal rates of return (which are conventionally updated as the values of portfolio companies, in which they have invested, are adjusted to reflect the price paid per share by the most recent investors).

A "good" IRR of 30 percent in the 1980s looked pale when evaluated by the typical returns on 1999. In an expanding economy, the riskier early stage investments performed the best, producing an *average* of 150 percent in 1999. By 2001, when the returns were typically negative, later round specialists did slightly less worse then those investing in earlier and middle stage deals.

ORGANIZATION OF THE VENTURE CAPITAL FIRM

We have described venture capital funds and the limited partnership structure they employ, but we have not dealt with how the firm is organized. Venture capitalists often talk about their partners and, indeed, being a general partner in the latest fund the firm has raised defines membership in the elite who run the firm. Only general partners have a say in the decision to invest; only they share in the carried interest generated by the most recent fund. Not all partners carry over from one fund to the next, but even when they do not participate as general partners in the most recent fund, they may still be involved in the firm as they discharge their fiduciary responsibilities to previous funds and the partners of those funds. The venture capital firm may still be drawing management fees from those previous funds and portfolio companies may still be producing disbursements as liquidity is achieved by those companies.

Mortality Events. This partial overlap in the groups of general partners between funds creates some interesting organizational properties. Venture capital firms rarely disband suddenly. Rather, they die a lingering death. Generally, the end of a firm is signaled when it fails to raise another fund. This may happen because of poor performance, or because economic times have gotten more difficult, or simply because the general partners decide to pursue other interests and opportunities. After it becomes clear that there will not be another fund, people still come to work. The phones are answered. Portfolio companies that have received funding are still supported with various services. As long as there are assets to be managed, the funds raised by that venture capital firm still impose duties on the venture capitalists. They will keep their offices going so long as the workload requires a place of business. On the other hand, venture capitalists peel off when their firm falls on hard times. As the prospect of substantial carried interest dissipates, they simply spend less time at the venture firm.

The Division of Labor. Venture capital firms are rather small organizations. Many have only one or two partners and a single salaried staff person. The bigger firms have a more elaborate division of labor.

Most venture capital firms seem to have a differentiated status structure among *general partners.* While all have the same legal status with regard to the current fund whose capital is being invested, some are more senior than others. Some firms have a title like "Founding Partner" or "Managing Partner" to signify such differences in status. Status appears to be linked rather directly to the ability to attract resources and to recent investing successes. So partners whose presence is a lure for limited partners and the capital they bring, or deal flow, speak with a louder voice than partners who make less many for the others. Like most professional services organizations, the partners who bring in the most business and generate the profits always have the option of going elsewhere and taking their business with them. This translates into power and differential status.

While most of the attention is rightly placed on the general partners, venture capital firms have other kinds of employees. They have *associates* who are usually younger than the general partners. They are venture capitalists in training and, like most apprentices, do much of the routine work. When the general partners are not available, associates often serve to meet and greet entrepreneurs whose companies might receive funding. They perform due diligence investigations on companies that are candidates for funding. This means calling the entrepreneurs' references, talking with customers and employees, and analyzing the business plans and financial statements provided by the entrepreneurs. Associates generally hope to be promoted to general partner status; they cannot be formally involved in investment decisions or take a share of carried interest until that happens.

Venture partners are generally either entering or leaving the venture capital firm. Sometimes senior managers who are transitioning from other careers into venture capital are given an office and a lofty sounding title while they prove that they can add value to the venture capital firm. They do this by bringing deals to the firm and helping to evaluate those deals. They are usually given some portion of the carried interest generated by the deals they bring to the firm, but do not share in carried interest generated by other deals.

The venture partner job title is often given to general partners who are not participating in the next fund to be raised. This generally signifies a part-time status. They may move to this status voluntarily, when, for example, they plan to retire before the next fund's expected liquidation arrives. Sometimes, however, their performance is deemed unsatisfactory and they are not invited to join the next fund. They still may be managing investments from previous funds, however, and retain the venture partner title to provide a legitimate position in the firm while they continue to be active with these earlier investments and to provide a bridge as they move to another employment situation.

An *entrepreneur in residence* is someone who the venture capitalists think has potential to lead a startup team, but who lacks a company or concept that is an attractive investment. Sometimes he or she had a company that received funding but failed. Such a person is provided with an office and frequently receives a salary or some minimal seed financing with the opportunity to attend presentations by other entrepreneurs who visit the venture capital firm seeking funding. Such a person sometimes offers to take over leadership of the new venture with the promise that the venture capital firm will invest if he or she is the Chief Executive Officer. Sometimes, this amounts to stealing the entrepreneur's idea. Other times such a person adds management skills that are badly needed.

Venture capital firms also employ clerical *staff*. One of their principal jobs is to buffer the venture capitalists from those seeking their attention. Venture capitalists generally want to be available to those with whom they are doing or intend to do business, and they want to be kept free from social contacts with others.

Decision Processes. The general partners in the most recent fund meet weekly. They bring each other up to date on deals they have recently done, are closing, or are contemplating. At some point, they propose an investment to their partners and a vote is taken. Each venture capital firm has a set of norms about the percent ownership they seek in a company in return for their investment. They will insist on sufficient equity to be reserved for employees in order to attract additional talent to the company and to provide sufficient incentive for the employees. They want to know how their investment will move the company forward and how risk will be mitigated. For example, they might expect the proceeds to be used in part of generate working prototype. They are interested in how much additional capital will be required.

Usually, venture capitalists are investing after others have already invested. The treatment these earlier investors receive is very much contingent on market conditions. The stronger the position of the current round investors, the more dilution they can force previous investors to accept. The same is true of former employees who have left the company. The venture capitalists investing in the current round are principally concerned with maximizing value creation going forward. So employee incentive stock options are structured to provide incentive for future efforts, not to reward past good deeds. An employee or investor will be treated well to the degree that his or her future efforts and cooperation are expected to accelerate or retard the company's growth and appreciation in value.

The details of these decision processes are not well known outside the firms themselves. All general partners have a say in such decisions, but some obviously speak with a louder voice than others. In the end, people who make money for their partners receive social status for doing so, and their judgment is weighted more heavily based on their demonstrated ability to do this.

Limited Partners. are partners in the funds, not in the venture capital firms. When they invest repeatedly over a long period of time, the venture capitalists know that they will be patient when economic times are perilous.

COSTS TO THE ENTREPRENEURS

We have described how venture capital works, what the institution does, and what venture capitalists do for those who start young companies. The next issue is the cost. We have already discussed how venture capitalists make their money. It might be tempting to assume that their management fees and carried interest are subtracted from the founders' equity, or from the limited partners' capital. If the venture capitalists were not adding value, this would be true. To the degree that their activities do, in fact, identify new companies with high potential (or they do it better than others would do without them), and if their contacts and advice result in more rapid growth, then all parties share in the success. It is an open question how often and to what extent these propositions are true.

There are other costs associated with venture capital investing. These have to do with the organizational dynamics accompanying growth. As the new company proceeds, a series of rounds of financing is often required. As one proceeds from "early" to "late" rounds, amounts of capital raised in the round increase, periods of illiquidity are shorter and, generally, risk is lower. Returns are usually lower as well. Loss of control by the entrepreneurs is one kind of price paid at each round. The investors as a group take seats on the company's board of directors with each round. Depending on the state in which the company is incorporated, boards have a minimum number of members. In many states, they start out with three members, and one seat is given up in the first round. Usually, one member of the original board drops off the board. When a second round is raised, the lead investor takes a seat, and it is common for the deal to stipulate that a fifth member is added from "outside." That is, someone joins the board who is neither an investor nor an employee (although such a person usually purchases stock on joining the board). If the venture capitalists nominate this fifth member, control of the board (i.e., the ability to command a majority of votes on the board) is lost at this point. If another (third) round occurs, control will most likely be lost then if not previously.

So as the capitalization rises, the investors gain power. Since this is normally occurring as a concomitant of growth and increasing complexity, management requires increasing levels of expertise. When the company has ten employees, weak financial controls can be tolerated. A year or two later the company may employ two hundred people, and such sloppiness can produce large losses. Similarly, when the company has no products, marketing is more a matter of strategic planning than operation. Once the company is selling products, its relationships with customers must be managed if repeated sales are valued. Similar points can be made for human resource management, production, and other business functions.

Entrepreneurs who have little or no prior management experience generally surrender control as problem complexity exceeds their skill level. If the founders do a very good job early on, the company grows more rapidly. The faster it grows, the more likely its complexity will increase faster than founders can learn. So they surrender managerial control either voluntarily, when they realize that they are out of their depth, or involuntarily, when investors exercise their governance rights. Either way, it is common for founders to exit, or to assume jobs with less demanding managerial tasks. They become chairs of boards, giving up the Chief Executive's title; they become Chief Technology Officers. The nineteenth-century model of Andrew Carnegie or Henry Ford is obsolete as waves of new management replace founders. The venture capital model rewards such new managers with equity through direct grants of stock and with Employee Incentive Stock Options. So while the rise of professional, salaried managers was the hallmark of capitalism at the turn of the twentieth century, the rise of owners with equity interests is the hallmark of capitalism at the end of the century.

The ability of venture capitalists to seize control as their capital investment rises depends in part on their community of interest as reflected in the common terms of investment for each round. Employees almost always receive common stock, while equity investors receive preferred stock. The preference most at issue is a liquidity preference that puts them first in line to recoup their original investment should the company be liquidated on terms that produce little or no returns. The important point is that all investors in a round receive the same preference and purchase their stock at the same price. So when a "lead" investor joins the board, this person can represent the interests of all those who co-invest.

Just as corporate governance shifts over time, so does equity interest in the company. The percent founders and early investors own declines over time—their positions are diluted. Of course, if all goes well the value of the company rises, so they have a small share of a much more valuable entity. If things do not go so well, however, later investors can successfully demand greater rewards for the capital they invest. The principal constraint on them is that rapacious behavior may rob the employees of the incentive that rapid growth generally requires. So later round investors can demand that the equity holdings of various previous investors, employees who are no longer with the company, and current employees are adjusted as a condition of investment. Even when things go well, and an IPO is planned, the investment banks underwriting the process may insist on a "reverse stock split" in which a quantity of "old" shares is replaced by a smaller number of "new" shares. This process is driven by demand for shares in the newly traded company relative to its value. Investment bankers want to bring an issue to the public at around $15 per share. If too many shares have been granted or sold, and investors balk at paying the prices the underwriters expect, they will require a reverse stock split. Sometimes, they ask current owners of stock to sell some of their holdings as part of the IPO in order to increase the number of shares trading (i.e., "the float"). So after the IPO, founders may own even or smaller share of the company and their ability to maintain control drops.

All of this is contingent on the founders' (perceived) importance to the company's future success. If the founder remains a key leader, and has expertise that is difficult to replace, additional grants of equity in the form of options can be demanded. Some founder-CEOs receive large shares of new shares created by the board to replenish the employee option pool. This is all a matter of bargaining and the power they wield based on their supposed contributions to the company going forward.

The venture capitalists generally sell their interests in the new company when they can. Liquidity for them is ordinarily not achieved at the IPO, but in a subsequent Secondary Offering. The IPO process requires a six-month lockup period during which the underwriter guarantees to make a market in the stock, and will not tolerate investors selling into that market. They usually own too much stock to sell it on the open market, so a Secondary Offering is organized to provide liquidity. Employees and founders may gain some liquidity at this point but generally have to wait until the drop in the stock price that accompanies the large sales of investors has passed. So holders of common stock must wait their turn and this usually requires at least a year after the IPO.

CONCLUSION

The analysis presented above should make it clear that venture capital is an intensely social business. Venture capital is embedded in networks of social relationships in exactly the ways identified by Granovetter (1985). Venture capitalists build trust through their social connections and track records.

The former magnify the latter. They mitigate risk by pooling capital and taking many small positions in ventures that are themselves connected by ties with other service providers (e.g., accountants, bankers). And they find deals through their networks.

Population ecologists of organizations have devoted much effort to theorizing about how resource and institutional environments produce circumstances under which founding rates surge and failure rates drop (Hannan and Freeman 1989; Carroll and Hannan 2000; Hannan 1998). It is generally held that founders of organizations have an easier time of it when they can borrow existing solutions to problems of organizing, and when access to resources is facilitated by resource providers who interact with new organizations through well-established routines and modes of transaction. Venture capitalists assist entrepreneurs precisely by instructing them on how to access such resources, providing social connection and legitimacy through which such resources are provided, and helping entrepreneurs learn what problems need to be solved and what established solutions are available. In short, all of the factors that increase founding rates and lower the risk of mortality in organizational populations are enhanced when venture capitalists do what they are supposed to do. The principal cost is that their services are not cheap. They often receive huge fees for providing such services. Whether the theorist focuses on age-dependence, size-dependence, or dependence of organizational populations on density (population size), venture capitalists play a role that generally increases the growth of business organizational populations. A secondary cost of their services is that they sometimes overshoot the optimal mark, creating too many organizations of a given form that grow too quickly given the realistic prospects of success (Lomi et al. 2001). Within one year, for example, at least five venture-backed pet food Internet companies were financed. They all failed.

Venture capital firms provide very powerful incentives to increase founding rates where opportunities are thought to exist, and to accelerate the growth of the resulting young companies. These incentives may fail, of course, and do so when the capital markets will not absorb the young companies that have grown to a size that would ordinarily suffice for an IPO, or when an early acquisition provides the returns that venture capitalists seek but forecloses future opportunities for founders and employees. This is especially likely when the founders and employees are motivated by other, nonpecuniary factors, such as the desire to avoid direct supervision or the desire to make some technology broadly available. For the venture capitalists, starting and growing young companies is about the money, and this may not be so true of others involved in the process.

This process depends on the continuing stream of technology that underlies commercial innovation. Venture capitalists do not drive such innovation—they derive economic rewards from applying it economically.

Their rewards depend on their ability to gain liquidity in a time horizon that fits the partnership structure they employ. This does not always map onto the technology-development time horizon. For example, biotechnology firms once received large amounts of venture capital financing. This stream had almost disappeared by the late 1990s in the U.S. because experience showed that the time to develop and market applications of biotechnology has been much longer than venture capital can tolerate.

The venture capital model as described here does not scale very well. Venture capital firms are never really large organizations, with thousands of employees, because their partnership structure breaks down when there are large numbers of people involved. There is so much subjective judgment involved in deciding what companies and people to back, and in nurturing the young companies, that formal organizational mechanisms stifle rather assist the process. So the large funds that appeared at the end of the 1990s drove firms to make larger investments because they could not simply add legions of partners.

Venture capital does not transport geographically very well either, for much the same reason. Venture capital firms periodically attempt to set up offices in remote locations such as Europe or Asia, and typically do not succeed. The capital they bring is not sufficient to support the returns they seek. The other things they do are somewhat societally specific as they depend on the functioning of other social institutions. Their network contacts are usually local as well, so the value they can add is principally in introducing young ventures to the resource providers and customers located in the U.S. These relationships are difficult to maintain when one spends much of one's time outside the area. And indirect connections through U.S. partners are difficult to manage.

This venture capital organizational form can be copied by private equity investors in other countries, sometimes with the cooperation of U.S. venture capitalists. This works well if the political and economic elites in those countries are willing to adjust laws and financial structures to mimic comparable models in the U.S. So tax laws are sometimes changed to provide the same favorable treatment for employee incentive stock options as found in the U.S. Stock markets may make it easier for young companies to do IPOs. Such changes can be seen in Britain, Singapore, and Taiwan, for example.

The venture capital organizational form is a highly specialized mechanism that facilitates the founding processes of other highly specialized business organizations. It is adapted to restructuring economic circumstances, where there is a premium to be paid for very rapid reallocation of capital and very rapid company growth. Of course, such situations are not evident everywhere or even in the United States at all times. When venture capital is functioning best, however, many other changes are under way that have long-lasting consequences.

REFERENCES

Amit, Raphael, Lawrence Glosten, and Eitan Muller. 1990. "Entrepreneurial Ability, Venture Investments, and Risk Sharing." *Management Science* 36: 1232–45.

Anderson, Philip. 1999. "Venture Capital Dynamics and the Creation of Variation through Entrepreneurship. In *Variations in Organization Science: In Honor of Donald T. Campbell*, ed. Joel A. C. Baum and Bill McKelvey. Thousand Oaks, Calif.: Sage. 137–53.

Black, Bernard S. and Ronald J. Gilson. 1998. "Venture Capital and the Structure of Capital Markets." *Journal of Financial Economics* 47: 237–77.

Burt, Ronald S. 1982. *Toward a Structural Theory of Action: Network Models of Social Structure*. New York: Academic Press.

———. 1992. *Structural Holes: The Social Structure of Competition*. Cambridge, Mass.: Harvard University Press.

Bygrave, William D. 1987. "Syndicated Investments by Venture Capital Firms: A Networking Perspective." *Journal of Business Venturing* 2: 139–54.

———. 1988. "The Structure of Investment Networks of Venture Capital Firms." *Journal of Business Venturing* 3: 137–57.

———. 1994. "Rates of Return from Venture Capital." In *Realizing Investment Value*, ed. William D. Bygrave, Michael Hay, and Jos B. Peeters. London: Pitman.

Bygrave, William D. and Jeffrey A. Timmons. 1992. *Venture Capital at the Crossroads*. Boston: Harvard Business School Press.

Carroll, Glenn R. and Michael T. Hannan. 2000. *The Demography of Corporations and Industries*. Princeton: Princeton University Press.

Case, Daniel H. and Standish H. O'Grady. 2001. "An Overview of Venture Capital." In *Start-Up and Emerging Companies*, ed. Richard D. Harroch. New York: Lay Journal Press.

Chandler, Alfred D., Jr. 1977. *The Visible Hand: The Managerial Revolution in American Business*. Cambridge, Mass.: Harvard University Press.

Coleman, James S. 1988. "Social Capital in the Creation of Human Capital." *American Journal of Sociology*. Supplement 94: S95–S120.

Cyert, Richard M. and James G. March. 1963. *A Behavioral Theory of the Firm*. Englewood Cliffs, N.J.: Prentice-Hall.

Fenwick and West LLP. 2003. Panel, 2003 Venture Capital Report: A Savvy Assessment of Current Financing Trends. Berkeley Entrepreneurs Forum, Lester Center for Entrepreneurship and Innovation, Haas School of Business, University of California, September 25.

Freeman, John. 1999. "Venture Capital as an Economy of Time." In *Corporate Social Capital and Liability*, ed. Roger Leenders and Shaul M. Gabbay. Boston: Kluwer. 460–82.

Gompers, Paul A. 1995. "Optimal Investment, Monitoring, and the Staging of Venture Capital." *Journal of Finance* 50: 1461–89.

Gompers, Paul A. and Josh Lerner. *The Venture Capital Cycle*. Cambridge, Mass.: MIT Press.

Gorman, Michael and William Sahlman. 1989. "What Do Venture Capitalists Do?" *Journal of Business Venturing* 4: 231–48.

Granovetter, Mark S. 1985. "Economic Action and Social Structure: The Problem of Embeddedness." *American Journal of Sociology* 91(3): 481–510.

Hannan, Michael T. 1998. "Rethinking Age Dependence in Organizational Morality: Logical Formalizations." *American Journal of Sociology* 104: 85–123.

Hannan, Michael T. and John Freeman. 1977. "The Population Ecology of Organizations." *American Journal of Sociology* 82: 929–64.

———. 1989. *Organizational Ecology.* Cambridge, Mass.: Harvard University Press.

Jaffee, Jonathan and John Freeman. 2002. "Institutional Change in 'Real Time': The Development of Employee Stock Options in German Venture Capital Contracts, 1994 to 1999." In *Advances in Strategic Management*, ed. Paul Ingram and Brian Silverman. Stamford, Conn.: Elsevier.

Lomi, Alessandro, Erik R. Larsen, and John Freeman. 1991. "Decline, Resurgence, and Extinction in Organizational Populations: Mechanisms and Hypotheses." Paper presented at American Sociological Association Annual Meeting, Cincinnati, August 23–27.

March, James G. and Herbert A. Simon. 1958. *Organizations.* New York: John Wiley.

Podolny, Joel M. 2001. "Networks as the Pipes and Prisms of the Market." *American Journal of Sociology* 107: 33–66.

Podolny, Joel M. and Fabrizio Castellucci. 1999. "Choosing Ties from the Inside of a Prism: Status and Egocentric Uncertainty in the Venture Capital Markets." In *Corporate Social Capital and Liability*, ed. Roger Leenders and Shaul M. Gabbay. Boston: Kluwer.

Rosenstein, Joseph, Albert V. Bruno, William D. Bygrave, and Natalie T. Taylor. 1993. "The CEO, Venture Capitalists, and the Board." *Journal of Business Venturing* 8: 99–113.

Sacramento Business Journal. 2001. "CalPERS Ups Its Ante in Venture Capital." March 26.

Salzman, Alan E. and L. John Doerr. 2001. "The Venture Financing Process." In *Start-Up and Emerging Companies*, ed. Richard D. Harroch. New York: Lay Journal Press. Chapter 7.

Sahlman, William A. 1990. "The Structure and Governance of Venture-Capital Organizations." *Journal of Financial Economics* 27: 473–521.

Sapienza, Harry J. 1992. "When Do Venture Capitalists Add Value." *Journal of Business Venturing* 7: 9–27.

Sapienza, Harry J. and Allen C. Amason. 1993. "Effects of Innovativeness and Venture Stage on Venture Capitalist-Entrepreneur Relations." *Interfaces* 23: 38–51.

Sapienza, Harry J. and Anil K. Gupta. 1994. "Impact of Agency Risks and Task Uncertainty on Venture Capitalist-CEO Interaction." *Academy of Management Journal* 37: 1618–32.

Sorenson, Olav and Toby E. Stuart. 2001. "Syndication Networks and the Spatial Distribution of Venture Capital Investments." *American Journal of Sociology* 106: 1546–88.

The Economic Sociology of Organizational Entrepreneurship: Lessons from the Stanford Project on Emerging Companies

James N. Baron and Michael T. Hannan

DISCUSSIONS OF THE PATH of contemporary capitalism routinely focus on California's Silicon Valley, which is often viewed not only as the launching pad for technological breakthroughs, but also as the point of origin for major social trends and transformations in markets, economic institutions, organizational designs, and work arrangements. Over the last decade, our research group—the Stanford Project on Emerging Companies (SPEC)—has tracked a large sample of Silicon Valley high-technology start-ups. The project aimed to examine how founders approached key organizational and human resource challenges in the early days of building their enterprises and to learn whether these activities have had enduring effects on the companies. Through interviews with founders, chief executives, and human resource (HR) directors—supplemented by quantitative information on strategy, HR practices, business partners, financing, and the like, obtained from public and private sources—we constructed a detailed record of the evolution of nearly 200 young technology start-ups.[1]

Based on a paper prepared for the conference on The Economic Sociology of Capitalism, Cornell University, September 28–29, 2001. We acknowledge generous support from the Stanford Graduate School of Business, particularly the Center for Entrepreneurial Studies, the Human Resources Initiative, and the Stanford Graduate School of Business Trust, which enabled us to carry out the research described here. We are also very grateful to Diane Burton, Greta Hsu, Özgecan Koçak, Daniel Stewart, Aimee Noelle-Swanson, and the many other past and current students who have assisted in the SPEC project. In conducting this research, we have also received a great deal of helpful advice, input, and support from former and current colleagues at Stanford, particularly Glenn Carroll, Irv Grousbeck, Charles Holloway, David Kreps, Charles O'Reilly, Joel Podolny, and Garth Saloner. We have also benefited from conversations with numerous entrepreneurs, human resources professionals, and venture capitalists about these results; we wish in particular to acknowledge and thank Debra Engel, Kathryn Gould, Felda Hardymon, Mike Levinthal, Burt McMurtry, and William Unger.

Without realizing it when we launched our study in 1994–1995, we assembled the most comprehensive database to date on the histories, structures, and HR practices of high-tech companies in Silicon Valley, just as the region was about to witness an economic and technological boom of historic proportions. We returned to the field on several occasions, updating information on how the firms were faring; and, in 1997–1998, we supplemented our study by adding a group of "new economy" companies to the sample, founded as part of the "dot.com" explosion. Having tracked this sample of companies during the ups and downs of the recent high-technology roller coaster, we have learned some valuable substantive and methodological lessons for economic and organizational sociology. In this chapter, we summarize some conclusions that have emerged from our ongoing research on these companies and sketch some implications for those interested in understanding contemporary organizational entrepreneurship.

FOUNDERS' BLUEPRINTS FOR HIGH-TECH START-UPS

Neo-institutionalists have emphasized the importance of normative blueprints in shaping organization-building and organizational evolution (e.g., Meyer and Rowan 1977; Guillén 1994; Fligstein and Byrkjeflot 1996). They argue that those who design and manage organizations draw on culturally appropriate templates and conceptions of control in crafting structures, work roles, and employment relations, because this increases organizational legitimacy and because their own prior socialization presumably precludes doing otherwise (Fligstein 1987, 1990).

Organizational ecologists also have argued that legitimation is crucial in the early days of building and sustaining new kinds of organizations (Hannan and Carroll 1992). However, ecologists tend to view the imprint of founding conditions as being more indelible than is implied by many neo-institutional accounts, which stress the protean character of organizational arrangements. For instance, Hannan and Freeman (1984, p. 153) argue that survival prospects are enhanced by organizational features that promote reliability and accountability, including a coherent system for managing employees: "Testing for accountability is especially intense during organization building. . . . When membership involves an employment relation, potential members often want guarantees that careers within the organization are managed in some rational way." Among the most important factors in generating reliability and accountability, according to this account, are clearly specified forms of authority and well-understood bases of exchange between members and the organization. Hence, organizations stand to benefit by developing and institutionalizing coherent blueprints for employment relations that can generate reliability and accountability; once such a blueprint gets adopted, it is risky and costly for an organization to try to alter it.

A major goal of the SPEC research was to obtain fine-grained information suitable for testing this argument. Accordingly, the first stage of our project sought to understand the organizational models or blueprints that entrepreneurs brought to bear, explicitly or implicitly, in designing and launching their new ventures. One of our more intriguing initial findings was that founders espoused quite different mental models of the ideal organizational form for a technology start-up. This diversity is striking, given that we were looking at companies that are all concentrated in high technology industries, located in the same part of the country, and founded within a brief historical period by a set of people who are tightly connected by virtue of the abundant labor mobility, dense social networks, and powerful brokers (venture capitalists, lawyers, and the like) that characterize Silicon Valley.

When we first visited each enterprise (hereafter referred to as the "time of sampling"), we asked founders what ideas they had when they were launching their company about how it might "look and feel" organizationally. (We also asked the then-current CEO in each firm parallel questions about the period corresponding to the date of the interview.) We probed by asking these leaders whether they had specific models in mind that they sought to emulate or avoid in building their companies. We tried to get at the premises that guided their thinking about how to organize employment relations and manage personnel.

In poring over the transcripts of interviews with founders and CEOs, we found that their notions about how to structure work and employment varied along three main dimensions—attachment, coordination/control, and selection—each characterized by a small number of distinct approaches from which organizational architects seemed to be choosing. Figure 1 summarizes the three dimensions and the main variants along each dimension, which capture the primary differences we unearthed among founders' (and, later, CEOs') notions of how to organize employment relations in high-tech start-ups.

Attachment. Founders articulated three different bases of employee attachment, which we label *love*, *work*, and *money*. Some founders envisioned creating a family-like feeling and strong emotional bonds between the firm and its workforce to inspire motivation and help retain valuable knowledge workers. In this model, employees are bound to the firm by a strong sense of personal belonging to the company—in a sense, *love*. Within many other SPEC firms, the primary motivator for employees is the desire to work at the technological cutting-edge. Recognizing this, many founders anticipated

Basis of Attachment & Retention	• Compensation ("money") • Qualities of the work ("work") • Work group as community ("love")
Criterion for Selection	• Skills • Exceptional talent/potential • Fit with the team or organization
Means of Control & Coordination	• Direct monitoring • Peer and/or cultural control • Reliance on professional standards • Formal processes and procedures

Figure 1 Dimensions of employment blueprints.

providing opportunities for *interesting and challenging work* to attract and motivate retain personnel. Here, employees were not expected to be loyal to the company, supervisor, or even co-workers per se, but instead to a project. Finally, other founders stated that they regarded the employment relationship as a simple exchange of labor for *money*.

Basis of Coordination and Control. A second dimension concerned the principal means of coordinating and controlling work. The most common conception involved reliance on *informal control through peers* or *organizational culture*. Other founders intended to rely on *professional control*; they implicitly assumed that workers were committed and could do outstanding work because they had been professionally socialized to do so. (Not surprisingly, this approach tends to be accompanied by an emphasis on hiring high-potential individuals from elite institutions.) Professional control emphasizes autonomy and independence, rather than enculturation. A third group of founders envisioned achieving control via *formal procedures and systems*. Finally, some founders indicated that they planned to control and coordinate work by *direct oversight*, somewhat reminiscent of small capitalist firms in the late nineteenth and early twentieth centuries.

Selection. The third dimension concerns the primary basis for selecting employees. Some founders conceived of the firm as a bundle of tasks, seeking employees to carry out particular tasks effectively. Because time and money tended to be their paramount concerns, the focus was on selecting employees who could be brought up to speed quickly and cheaply. In these cases, founders envisioned selecting employees having the *skills and experience needed to accomplish some immediate task(s)*. Other founders focused less on immediate and well-defined tasks than on a series of projects—often

DIMENSIONS			EMPLOYMENT MODEL
Attachment	Selection	Coordination/ Control	
Work	Potential	Professional	**STAR**
Work	Skills	Peer/cultural	**ENGINEERING**
Love	Fit	Peer/cultural	**COMMITMENT**
Work	Skills	Formal	**BUREAUCRACY**
Money	Skills	Direct	**AUTOCRACY OR DIRECT CONTROL**

Figure 2 Typology of employment blueprints, based on three dimensions.

not yet even envisioned—through which employees would transition over time. Accordingly, they focused on *long-term potential*. Finally, some founders focused primarily on *values and cultural fit*, emphasizing how a prospective hire would relate with others in the organization.

Relationships among the Three Dimensions. These blueprints can be classified into three types of attachment and selection and four types of control, yielding $3 \times 3 \times 4 = 36$ possible combinations. However, we found that the observations cluster into a few cells, which we call the five basic model types for employment relations, summarized in figure 2.[2]

The *Engineering* model involves attachment through challenging work, peer group control, and selection based on specific task abilities. This model parallels standard descriptions of the default culture among high-tech Silicon Valley start-ups, such as the account provided by Saxenian (1994), and it is the modal employment blueprint among founders of SPEC firms. The *Star* model refers to attachment based on challenging work, reliance on autonomy and professional control, and selecting elite personnel based on their long-term potential. The *Commitment* model emphasizes emotional or familial ties of employees to the organization, selection based on cultural fit, and peer group control. The *Bureaucracy* model involves attachment based on challenging work and/or opportunities for development, selecting individuals based on their qualifications for a particular role, and formalized control. Finally, the *Autocracy* model refers to attachment premised on monetary motivations, control through personal oversight, and selection of employees to perform prespecified tasks.

What does it mean to refer to these types as "models" or "blueprints"? We are not claiming that these specific types are universal, exhaustive, or generalizable outside the population we studied. But the specific types we identified have several important properties that are suggestive of what it means to describe organizations as adhering to culturally delineated templates. First, each of the model types exhibits a high degree of *coherence* or *internal consistency* among the three dimensions, suggesting that they complement one another to form an overarching system. For instance, consider a founder intending to control and coordinate via organizational norms and seeking to promote emotional bonds to the company itself (rather than attachment based on the specific work assignment), perhaps in order to create overarching goals among differentiated subunits. Here there would be a clear technical complementarity with selection mechanisms that screen for values and cultural fit, as in the Commitment model.

Second, these types display *cultural resonance* and *salience* within this population. When we have described these archetypes to Silicon Valley employers, employees, and other knowledgeable parties, they understand the distinctions and frequently begin classifying organizations with which they have experience in these terms.

Third, the types reflect different logics of organizing within other institutions that actors in this organizational field have experienced; indeed, the labels for the types are fairly evocative of the logics. For instance, the Star blueprint, especially prevalent among firms developing medical technology or pursuing research,[3] resonates closely with the model that underlies academic science, from which many of the founders and key scientific personnel sought for these start-ups are recruited. The Commitment model draws instead on familial imagery and the revered legend of Hewlett-Packard within Silicon Valley, encouraging employees to view their associations with the firm in similar terms. The Engineering model resonates with the socialization that engineers receive in professional school and suits the Valley's highly mobile labor force. The Bureaucratic model is readily familiar to most employees from encounters with bureaucracies in numerous contexts. And the Autocracy model communicates a powerful and consistent message that employees are likely to have encountered elsewhere: as one SPEC founder put it, "You work (for me, the founder), you get paid (by me)."

Table 1 classifies SPEC companies according to the type of employment model coded from the interview responses provided by founders and by CEOs at the time of sampling.[4] Note that in labeling the cases that do not fit into any of the five primary categories as "non-type," we are not claiming that their employment models are necessarily incoherent or detrimental. For instance, consider a firm whose founder held a model of attachment based

TABLE 1
Founder and CEO Blueprints of Employment Relations in SPEC Firms*

Founder's Blueprint	CEO's Blueprint						
	Commitment	Star	Engineering	Bureaucratic	Autocratic	Non-type	Total
Commitment	7 (17)	0 (1)	0 (0)	0 (0)	0 (2)	4 (2)	11 (22)
Star	0 (0)	6 (6)	1 (1)	1 (1)	0 (0)	5 (5)	13 (13)
Engineering	0 (1)	0 (0)	25 (25)	12 (13)	1 (1)	11 (9)	49 (49)
Bureaucratic	0 (2)	0 (1)	2 (2)	5 (6)	0 (0)	1 (0)	8 (11)
Autocratic	0 (1)	0 (0)	0 (0)	0 (1)	3 (5)	2 (3)	5 (10)
Non-type	3 (2)	1 (0)	9 (9)	8 (10)	1 (1)	48 (29)	70 (51)
Total	10 (23)	7 (8)	37 (37)	26 (31)	5 (9)	71 (48)	156

*Note: Results (in parentheses) group "near-type" cases with their pure-type counterparts; see fn. 2 in text for explanation.

on challenging work, selection based on skills, and professional control. This blueprint falls, in a sense, midway between the Star and Bureaucracy models: changing the selection dimension from *skills* to *potential* would place it in the Star category; changing the coordination dimension from *professional* to *formal control* would place it in the Bureaucracy category. This kind of hybrid blueprint might represent a reasonable "compromise" for firms that anticipate undergoing future transitions that will necessitate a more rationalized management approach. (This conjecture is not borne out, however, by the evidence we report below concerning organizational performance.)

Several aspects of table 1 are interesting. First, note the diversity of organization-building templates among the SPEC companies. A number of perspectives on organizations and environments—particularly neoinstitutional approaches—imply that we should not expect to find much diversity within this population. After all, the SPEC companies are all young, founded in the same period, quite small, concentrated in a single locale, in a narrow set of technology-based industries, and founded by a set of individuals (entrepreneurs, venture capitalists, etc.) who are tightly connected through social networks, patterns of career mobility, and other ties. To be sure, some of the variation in initial blueprints reflected in table 1 reflects differences in industry and strategy among the companies in our sample. For instance, as noted above, the Star model predominates among medical and biotechnology firms. Yet, even *within* industries and among firms whose founders articulated similar competitive strategies, we observe quite striking differences in the organizational blueprints.

These intra-industry differences also do not square with some scholarly accounts of organizational forms. For instance, neo-institutionalists (e.g., Suchman 1994, 2000) have argued that venture capitalists and high-tech lawyers promote the diffusion of specific corporate structures and practices. Although we found a slight tendency for VC-backed companies to bureaucratize more and earlier (Baron 1999), organizational blueprints vary considerably even among venture-backed companies. We attribute this variation, at least in part, to the fact that venture capitalists and law firms, like start-ups, operate in a competitive marketplace that encourages differentiation in their strategies and structures. Some VC companies, for instance, proudly trumpet their fondness for building enduring companies based on strong, long-lasting emotional ties that transcend money, along the lines of our Commitment model.[5] Others are known for valuing technologies and products largely in isolation from considerations of organizational capability or quality of management. Still others are attracted to "star" cultures or, in some cases, have even been known to oppose efforts by founders to create any kind of distinctive culture at all during the start-up phase. Aspiring entrepreneurs in Silicon Valley no doubt recognize these differences, which enables a sorting process that matches entrepreneurs and venture capitalists with compatible perspectives and philosophies. For that reason, we see no reason to expect any simple monolithic pattern of imprinting on initial organizational blueprints by VCs, high-tech lawyers, HR professionals, or others.

In the same vein, we cannot find any simple mapping between employment models on the one hand, and founders' background characteristics on the other hand. One might expect, for instance, that founders who launched entrepreneurial ventures after working in older, more bureaucratic organizations would be more likely to adopt a bureaucratic template. Yet, for every founder in our sample whose thinking appeared to be consistent with that conjecture (based on interview transcripts), another reported a desire to escape what he or she had experienced in the past as dysfunctional bureaucratic pathologies, by building a new enterprise with a radically different culture and operating style.

For example, one founder, with a doctorate and more than sixty published papers on fluid dynamics and laser techniques, explained his impetus to create a new company:

Interviewer: What was the impetus and the catalyst for founding [company name], and how did the company get started?
Founder: I always had an idea that I wanted to be independent and even as an engineer I wanted to hang out my shingle and operate as a professional rather than working for some company. I also felt that I didn't fit into the requirement that a person climbing the corporate ladder would fit into. I tend to be

someone . . . [who doesn't] follow structure, I'm not able to do what I think is necessary to rise in a big company or to do government laboratory work.

I: What would that be?

F: I think you have to do certain bureaucratic things, you have to follow someone else's rules in the corporation, you have to kiss ass . . . the internal politics, you have to play the political game, and I could never bring myself to do that. I realized that not wanting (or maybe [not] being able) to do that, I'd be better off working independently. When you have a Ph.D. in engineering or in science, you're really kind of stuck going into a big corporation or government lab and not that many people start companies and go out on their own. So there was a dilemma there and I did work at NASA for a while as a post-doc and [then] I went to a small company where I again had that experience and eventually I did run afoul of the management. I felt that my need for independence was conflicting with that company's President's idea of what was on the agenda. Eventually getting that urge to get out on my own was pretty strong. (Founder interview, firm #47, 8/9/94)

In a company manufacturing composite materials, one executive described how he and his colleagues on the founding team explicitly sought from the inception to create an organizational culture different from that of the large missile and defense contractor where all the founders had worked previously. Another firm's founder, with a Ph.D. in information technology and considerable experience working in the research laboratory of a large corporation, described her impetus similarly:

Interviewer: Did you . . . have an idea what type of company you wanted to have—what type of culture or atmosphere?

Founder: One of the things we did not like in a large company was bureaucracy, where things don't get decided or you can't do something because there is some policy that says you can't. Policies are guidelines, they're what the legal world bonds to—everything looks right. But if you need to go for something, you need to go for it. . . . I remember they had an administrator at [former employer, a large research lab] as you said farewell [to start your own company], telling us . . . "enjoy building your own bureaucracy." And of course the minute you get three people in a room, you've got a bureaucracy. [But] I hope we're not as inflexible as very, very large companies grow to be. And that was certainly in our minds. In those early days we were small enough we had a monthly potluck and we specifically did that so family members would get to know each other, so they would know who their husband and wife or whoever was spending time with at work, so there would be a little more familiarity in the real sense of coming and going and that was a lot of fun. (Founder interview, firm #68, 9/16/94)

One factor did seem to bear directly on initial employment blueprints: the founder's intended business strategy. In particular, companies whose founders reported that they had intended to compete principally by superior marketing, service, or customer relationships were significantly more likely to choose the Commitment model at founding.[6] We believe this association reflects a complementarity between relational contracting with both customers and employees: that is, when enduring relations with customers are vital to the strategy, enduring employment relations become critical because employees represent the ties to key customers.

Also noteworthy in table 1 are the patterns of movement observed among firms whose blueprint changed, based on the responses provided to us by the founder and by the CEO at the time of sampling. Only 23 of the 156 firms in table 1 (14.7 percent) changed from one of the five pure model types to another; of these, 17 moved between Engineering and Bureaucracy, the two closest pure model types (i.e., they differ only along one of the three dimensions shown in figure 2). We do not observe firms routinely shifting among models that, on their face, appear highly distinctive (e.g., Commitment and Bureaucracy). Moreover, 79 of the 156 companies (50.6 percent) did not change their blueprint at all.[7] Another 47 (30.1 percent) changed on only one dimension.[8] The fact that we do not see firms frequently changing their blueprints on multiple dimensions or moving between very disparate blueprints bolsters our confidence in the validity of our typology of organizational blueprints.

EFFECTS OF BLUEPRINTS ON ORGANIZATIONAL EVOLUTION

As noted above, founding premises about employment relations ought to be among the most difficult and contentious organizational features to alter. Changing these premises can erode skills, alter bases of power and status, call cherished belief systems into question, confuse outsiders about the organization's identity, and cloud a firm's reputation. Hence, another way of gauging whether our inductively derived typology captures meaningful distinctions in the "genetic material" of start-up firms is to examine whether a firm's founding model affects organizational evolution and whether efforts to alter the blueprint destabilize organizations.

In a series of recent papers, we have provided evidence in the affirmative on both counts. For instance, we have documented that firms whose founders initially championed a Commitment model subsequently developed less administrative overhead, especially relative to firms with Bureaucracy model founders (Baron, Hannan, and Burton 1999). Moreover, administrative intensity at the time of sampling was a function of the employment model initially espoused by the founder, not the model being espoused by the CEO at the time of sampling. In other words, the propensity for (or against) self-management appears to have been preprogrammed into SPEC companies from their inception.

Moreover, we have documented that changing the HR blueprint has a strong net positive effect on labor turnover, particularly among the most senior employees (Baron, Hannan, and Burton 2001). Labor turnover, in turn, has a profound negative effect on subsequent revenue growth, a crucial dimension of organizational performance for young technology companies seeking to demonstrate their commercial viability. Hence, this evidence is consistent with the population ecologists' view that efforts to change the organizational blueprint destabilize enterprises in ways that harm performance, at least in the near-to-moderate term.

Though suggestive, these analyses suffer from some ambiguity about the temporal connection between blueprint change and the outcomes being analyzed. After all, we do not know precisely *when* the organizational model changed; rather, we infer blueprint change by comparing how founders and then-current CEOs responded to our questions about organization-building, based on interviews conducted at the time of sampling. In the analyses of labor turnover and administrative intensity, we also measured outcomes at or near the time of sampling, so one cannot be certain that the blueprint changes were temporally prior. More compelling evidence of path dependence and of the destabilizing effects of change comes from our recent work, which examines how founders' employment models and changes in models up through the time of sampling have affected organizational performance *after* sampling. (Specifically, we examine performance outcomes through June 2001, which provides observations during the great boom of the late 1990s as well as during the bust of 2000–01.)

We focused on three performance outcomes: (1) time to initial public offering (IPO); (2) survival vs. failure; and (3) for companies that have gone public, growth in market capitalization following the IPO (Hannan, Baron, Hsu, and Kocak 2005). We find that organization-building and high commitment HRM seem to pay, even in the turbulent "built to flip" environment of Silicon Valley. In particular, firms founded on a Commitment model were the fastest to go public, relative to otherwise comparable companies with different founding models. Companies with Star or Non-type founder blueprints were the least likely to go public, controlling for age, industry, revenues, venture capital financing, and macroeconomic conditions (the prime interest rate and IPO activity in the company's industry). To gain an appreciation of the magnitude of the difference, consider two companies that were identical in every respect except that Firm A was founded on a Commitment blueprint (and did not change model) and Firm B was founded on a Star blueprint (and also did not change model). Firm A's hazard of going public after the time of sampling was more than four times that for Firm B, a sizable difference indeed.[9] Companies with nontype blueprints (i.e., not fitting into any of our five pure types) were also relatively unlikely to go public, with a hazard that was only 15 percent of the hazard for otherwise comparable firms founded on a Commitment model.

Firms founded on a Commitment model were not only the most likely to go public but also the least likely to fail (i.e., go bankrupt, get acquired on very unfavorable terms, or disappear). Indeed, none of the firms with Commitment model founders failed during our observation period. Among founder models, the Star blueprint fared second best insofar as failure is concerned, and Autocracy fared the worst.[10]

Companies founded along Star model lines fared the best by far in terms of stock market performance following the IPO; the worst performers were companies founded on an Autocracy blueprint. For a company with a Star model founder, the predicted rate of growth per month in (logged) market capitalization following the IPO is 11.6 percent higher than for a comparable company founded on an Autocracy model.

As we noted above, the main focus of this research was to learn whether *changing* initial blueprints destabilized the SPEC companies. The answer is unambiguous. Companies that had changed their blueprint by the time of sampling subsequently were significantly more likely to fail; indeed, changing the HR blueprint raises the failure rate by more than 220 percent (Hannan et al. 2005: table 4). And, if they went public, firms that had previously changed employment models saw their market values following the IPO fall substantially (and significantly) behind otherwise comparable firms whose models remained unchanged.[11] Only for the hazard of IPO do we fail to find a significant overall negative net effect of model change.[12]

Several things are worth noting about these results. First, these findings regarding the enduring imprint of founders' blueprints and the disruptive effects of blueprint change on performance come from longitudinal analyses that control for numerous other factors that might affect the success of young technology ventures, such as company age, size, access to venture capital, changes in senior leadership, revenue growth, and the economic environment (e.g., the state of the stock market, interest rates and inflation, the IPO market). As best we can tell, neither initial blueprint choices nor changes in blueprints are simply proxies for some unmeasured determinants of performance.

Second, the enduring imprint of initial conditions on organizational performance is particularly striking given the *milieu* we examined: high technology start-ups in California's Silicon Valley in the late 1990s. It is hard to imagine a context in which constant flux and change is a more routine fact of life than in our research setting. The modal SPEC founder described the business strategy for his or her new venture as involving pathbreaking technological innovation—being the first to generate a new product or service. In such a technological race, fast development of superior technologies and agile response to changes in technologies and markets might outweigh organizational capabilities in generating success. Furthermore, the geographical proximity, frequent labor mobility, and dense network ties among Silicon Valley firms are generally thought to provide founders with timely information about the activities of other enterprises, which should encourage the diffusion of managerial approaches and lower the difficulty and cost of changing organizational blueprints. Finally, the benefits of having a consistent, reproducible organizational structure might not loom as large in Silicon Valley: the fluid labor market, the rapid pace of technical, market, and social change, and the abundance of relative newcomers in the regional economy might make consistency less of a virtue than in some other venues. In short, we cannot imagine a setting where companies are *less* constrained by their origins or *less* destabilized by organizational change than Silicon Valley's high-tech sector in the mid- to late 1990s.

Although the Commitment and Star models appear to have contributed to success over the period we have studied, one could easily imagine it having turned out otherwise. For instance, some observers might be inclined to agree with a founder whom we interviewed for our study, a prominent and highly successful Silicon Valley entrepreneur who argued that founders make a grave error if they articulate a particular cultural model in the early days of an enterprise:

> Organization models and culture are a source of failure for start-ups. . . . In order to have a successful company organization, one must first have a successful company. Companies that strive to put in place organizational norms and models, cultures from the outset, are working on the wrong thing. HP's written document of seven corporate objectives got written almost 20 years after the company was started, after more than 20 years of practice building a successful company. . . . We in Silicon Valley have forgotten this and have become too enamored with "Gosh, I've started a company, now I have to have a culture." One of the first mistakes I made when I got involved with [prior company] was at one company meeting I got up and outlined what the company culture was. . . . After the meeting one of the other founders came up to me and said, "You've only been here 3 months, the company is only a year old. . . . Why don't we come back in five years and do this?" (CEO interview, firm #45, 7/13/94)

Alternatively, institutional theory presumably implies that adopting the Engineering model (the Silicon Valley default) might prove especially beneficial in the years spanned by our study. Or, one could have speculated that—given the inevitable need for more bureaucratic managerial approaches as start-ups grow and mature, and given the perils of organizational change—firms would have profited from embracing a Bureaucracy blueprint from the outset. Although these conjectures are eminently plausible, each is inconsistent with our findings.

The payoff that SPEC firms seem to have reaped from high commit- ment cultures deserves particular emphasis. Interestingly, "commitment" was widely pronounced dead in Silicon Valley not long after we first visited the SPEC companies in the mid-1990s. Loyalty, long-term employment, well-defined careers, and similar notions generally came to be viewed as quaint but outdated constructs for a new economy that thrives on con- stant mobility, "employability," flexibility, and an incoming generation of employees with shorter attention spans and a heartier appetite for personal fulfillment outside of work. At the first conference we organized for the CEOs and HR executives of the SPEC companies, in 1995, almost every- one in the audience professed unabashed support for the Commitment model.[13] A little over a year later, at a second conference, virtually nobody in the auditorium wanted to be associated with that moniker.

Yet, ironically, the minority of firms with Commitment model founders actually outperformed the rest of the SPEC sample in terms of survival and speed to IPO. The field of competitive strategy teaches that for something to be a source of competitive advantage, it must be relatively scarce and difficult for competitors to emulate. This appears to be no less true in the arena of *human resources strategy*. Perhaps the relatively strong performance of the Commitment firms stems precisely from the fact that the model ran counter to the conventional wisdom, which pronounced it unworkable in Silicon Valley in the late 1990s. Moreover, the signals a company sends by championing the Commitment model are especially powerful in a world in which relatively few companies are sending these signals. In emphasizing the organizational benefits of conforming to prevalent and accepted models, neoinstitutional theorists should not lose sight of the potential benefits of *differentiation* and *distinctiveness*, espe- cially for those aspects of organizational structure and practice that might activate gift exchange when organizations deviate from what is customary or convenient.[14]

One other pattern of results in our analyses supports our assertion that founders' employment models get indelibly imprinted on their new ven- tures. In the analyses of organizational performance discussed above, we estimated specifications in which each of the outcome measures depends on the founder's blueprint *and* on the blueprint of the CEO at the time of sampling. Given that the CEO's model is more proximate to the out- comes, one might expect it to have stronger and more systematic effects on performance outcomes than does the employment model associated with the founder. This does not turn out to be the case in our analyses. In terms of model fit, specifications that use founders' blueprints (and change in blueprint) do as well as those that use CEOs' blueprints (and change in blueprint).[15]

The Process of Launching Companies: Evidence on the Sequencing of Entrepreneurial Activity

Entrepreneurship has not been a particularly vibrant or high-status focus of research in most scholarly fields, including organizational and economic sociology (for a useful overview, see Thornton 1999). Yet, quite apart from the obvious relevance of entrepreneurship to public policy and economic development, many of our theories about organizations and environments differ most pointedly in their claims about the processes of organization-building and organizational evolution. This observation suggests that studying samples of nascent enterprises is likely to prove especially informative in adjudicating among rival theoretical accounts.

Our ongoing study of the SPEC companies has generated some insights that might have broader conceptual and methodological implications for students of organizations and entrepreneurship. First, any study that seeks to examine "start-ups" confronts an ambiguity that is both vexing from a methodological standpoint and intriguing from a theoretical standpoint: it is often difficult to specify precisely when (and how) an organization has come into (or out of) existence. We originally conceived the SPEC project as a corrective to the acute survivor bias characterizing most research on organizational design and human resource practices, which looks at the structures and practices of large, long-lived enterprises. We soon recognized that a significant selection process confronts any effort to construct a large representative sample of entrepreneurial companies. This occurs because any feasible sampling frame must utilize listings of firms (industry or business press publications, lists of venture-funded enterprises, marketing directories, etc.) that, by definition, only include enterprises that have completed enough organization-building activity to capture the attention of whoever is responsible for compiling the lists. Whereas population demographers have access to comprehensive data on abortions and neonatal mortality, researchers interested in *organizational* births, for the most part, do not. We do know that mortality rates for small organizations are very high (Carroll and Hannan 2000: chap. 13).[16] So it should not be altogether surprising that mail we sent to sampled SPEC companies was frequently returned to us, marked "Addressee Unknown" or "No Forwarding Address."

Moreover, we discovered that the sequence of steps involved in starting a new company varied markedly among the SPEC firms, making it difficult to identify a set of generic stages or characteristics that depict the formation of an organization (also see Hannan and Freeman 1989: 147–94). As part of our efforts to understand the company formation process, we asked informants the questions reproduced below. To summarize the diversity of company-formation sequences observed among SPEC companies, we constructed measures of the earliest date reported by the firm for each of the following events:

- Organization- or identity-building (earliest of: mission or values statement,[17] organization chart, personnel manual or handbook, or hiring of first full-time personnel specialist)
- Product (first product announcement or sale[18])
- Financing (receipt of external financing or venture capital)
- Patent issued
- Hiring first employee(s)
- Preparing business plan
- Legal incorporation

Organization-Building Information Gathered from SPEC Respondents

Questions A and B were directed to founders as part of a questionnaire they were asked to complete prior to our interviews. Question C was asked of the HR informant on a questionnaire filled out prior to that interview.

A. When would you date the beginning of normal business operations?

B. When, in relation to the above date, did you accomplish the following activities?

Legally establish the company
Prepare a business plan
Retain an attorney
Establish an accounting system
Obtain first external financing
Write a mission or values statement
Hire an employee
Develop a marketing plan
Announce a product
Have a working prototype
File a patent application
Sell first product
Hire a full-time sales/marketing specialist
Hire a full-time financial officer
Hire a full-time personnel specialist

C. Listed below are various types of human resources documents, practices, and systems which an organization might have. For each item that your organization currently has, please indicate when it was created and the last time it was significantly modified. *(Check the "Not Applicable" column if your firm does not have the item.)*

Documents	Not Applicable	Month/Year Developed	Month/Year Last Modified
Mission or values statement	❑		
Organization chart	❑		
Standardized employment application	❑		
Written job descriptions	❑		
Personnel manual or handbook	❑		
Written employment tests	❑		
Written performance evaluations	❑		
Standard performance evaluation form	❑		
Written affirmative action plans	❑		
Standard employment contract for exempt employees	❑		
Employee grievance or complaint form	❑		
Legal agreements about intellectual property/non-competition	❑		
Regular employee morale survey	❑		
Newsletter or other regular company-wide correspondence	❑		
Systems and Practices			
Human resources information system	❑		
Company-wide electronic mail	❑		
Employee suggestion system	❑		
Employee involvement programs (e.g. quality circles)	❑		
Background checks of prospective employees	❑		
Employee orientation program	❑		
Job rotation program	❑		
In-house training	❑		
Regular company-wide meetings	❑		
Regular company-sponsored social events	❑		

TABLE 2.
Differences Among SPEC Companies In Timing of Key Events (N = 143)*

Event[§]	Firms in which Event Occurred First	%	Firms in which Event Occurred First or Second	%
Organization- or identity-building	12	8.4	30	21.0
Product	13	9.1	31	21.7
External financing	23	16.1	42	29.4
Patent	5	3.5	10	7.0
Hired first employee(s)	24	16.8	57	39.9
Business plan	48	33.6	65	45.5
Legal incorporation	67	46.9	109	76.2

[§]See text for definitions of events.

*Note: Percentages in third column do not sum to 100% (or to 200% in fifth column) because multiple events co-occurred in some firms and are therefore double-counted.

Table 2 summarizes differences in the start-up sequences.[19] We believe there is considerable noise in the information we obtained about the precise timing of specific events, and we are currently attempting to resolve some ambiguities in the information that respondents provided to us regarding the sequencing of various events. Accordingly, our intent in summarizing these data in this chapter is merely exploratory; we view these results as suggestive, but by no means as definitive.

Not surprisingly, legal incorporation and/or drafting a business plan was most likely to rank among the earliest company-building activities. For more than three-quarters of the companies, legal incorporation was one of the first two events observed among the set of company-building activities we examined, and nearly half drafted a business plan as one of the first two steps in launching the new enterprise. Yet, consistent with other studies of entrepreneurship (Carter et al. 1996), we find remarkable variation in the sequence of events that characterize the start-up phase of these young technology-based companies.

Indeed, in more than one-fifth of the companies, early entrepreneurial activities were directed toward formalizing a distinctive identity and/or organizational configuration for the new enterprise, either through employment-related policies and activities (drawing an organization chart, drafting a personnel manual, or hiring a full-time HR director) or by promulgating a statement of organizational mission and vision. We view these as different ways in which entrepreneurs sought from the inception to create a distinctive identity and organizational ethos for their nascent enterprises. Various excerpts from our interviews illustrate these intentions and efforts:

Interviewer: Was it a pretty quick decision [to start your own firm] or had you been kind of discussing it [with the other founders] for a while?

Founder: It was a pretty quick decision.

I: You just saw an opportunity and just wanted to—

F: Well, actually we knew that we didn't like working at [former employer]. There was a fundamental distaste for what was going on there in any number of areas. But one could say that we felt like leaving because we actually didn't have a business plan or know even what industry we were going to get into. We just knew that as a collection of bright people that we would eventually settle on something that would be very good. We were right. We dedicated the first six months of our time to just researching what the opportunities were in front of us. We knew we wanted to do client–server tools. What we didn't know was what industry we wanted to go into. Was it hospital, was it finance, was it this, was it that? Eventually we settled into finance because of the problems that were there and there was less of a price point when solving that industry's problems. But, we didn't sit around and talk about how we were going to compete with our then current employer. That [was] just not in the cards. We actively— from, say, maybe June 1, 1989, something like that, clearly by April or May— the disenchantment had settled into a fairly deep degree where one had emotionally bowed out of certain processes that were happening at [former employer]. It was a rapid move to make a decision to leave from that point on.

I: How soon after you did start researching the possibilities did you decide on heading into the financial area?

F: About the three-month mark.

I: Did you have a formal business plan at some point? When would that have been?

F: In the September through November time frame of '89. From the three to six-month mark, we wrote our business plan. Our first document that we ever wrote actually was the Employee Handbook.

I: Is that right?

F: We were so disenchanted with the way employees were treated at [our former employer] that we said, "Let's build something on a rock solid foundation where we take care of our people, [decide] what our culture is, [what we] cared about." That took us about three months to put together.

I: That was the first thing you did?

F: The first thing we did. (Financial trading and risk management software company, Founder/CEO interview, firm #130, 7/18/95)

Interviewer: I'm curious to know how you've seen the corporate culture develop and change over time. You've been with [Company] since Day One. I know in the fourth month after founding you got together to put together the company tenets. Although they've grown and expanded, they are still with the company today. [Is this correct?]

Founder: [They were] actually discussed before then. We had discussed those before and during the founding. I think they officially were written on paper about that time. I think the main tenets are the same. The basic ideas of what makes [our company] different . . . we have a bit different focus than a lot of companies. Things like saying that everyone is "sales and support." This is not just something to say. If you are talking to a customer, you own that customer's problem. You don't necessarily have to solve that, but it's your job to make sure that customer gets the person needed if you can't solve the problem. We're serious about being serious about that. . . .

The idea is to set down a set of guidelines and ideas and say, "You can make a difference. You can have an impact on the company and you can do the right thing and move that forward." That was the idea. You come in from Day One knowing that's where you're headed. (Business process automation software company, Founder interview, firm #134, 8/95)

Interviewer: Did you have a model or blueprint of what the company would become?

Founder: In a sense it was modeled to be totally unlike [my prior employer]. As [different] as I could possibly get it. They are extremely autocratic. The president is king. He pretended he made all the decisions.

I wanted a company with ground up participation of management. Not only from the management team but people on the floor. I genuinely believe we achieved that. Our employee turnover is extremely low even with our stock price having been creamed by a bad quarter. Our employees are very happy and I think they enjoy working here. They think they are listened to and paid attention to. [My co-founder] is particularly good at a participative management style. That's helped set the tone. Sometimes we are criticized by employees who say, "You should just quit listening and do something." So in some people's opinion there is almost too much participation. I suppose you could find one employee who says, "They never listen to me." But not very many. (Biotechnology instrumentation company, Founder interview, firm #23, 7/14/94)

Interviewer: Was there a particular kind of culture you wanted to create in the company?

Founder: Absolutely. Given our backgrounds at Sun and SGI [Silicon Graphics]— which are fairly similar in the way the companies are run—I think we certainly wanted to create the whole regular flex time and sort of very loose model, hiring very qualified people but delegating responsibility out to them as opposed to running it as a traditional, non-Silicon Valley company.

For instance, most of our hires are extremely experienced people who [have] even managed projects at larger companies. They require very little supervision. When you are a start-up you don't have time to sort of waste on teaching people, getting them up to speed, or micromanaging them. (E-business infrastructure software company, Founder interview, firm #206, 11/17/97)

Interviewer: Can you briefly describe how you got involved with Dr. XXX [founder] and YYY [company]?

HR Consultant: Very early in their growth, I believe at the time they had three employees, I was contacted by their VP of Finance. We were referred to him by someone who had worked with us. YYY is a very unique company in that most of our clients come to us when they have 50–100 employees and they are embroiled in some problems and issues. They say, "Come in and save us. Fix these problems for us." YYY approached us when they had three employees and said they wanted a HR consultant very early on. They wanted to do things right from the very beginning. It's very unique. We met with them and set up an initial relationship where we provided one day a week service, 8 hours a week on-site doing HR work. Eventually they grew beyond that. They are up to three days now. Now they are actually growing beyond that where they need a full-time HR professional. We're working with them to identify and get one hired for them. (Biomedical research company, HR interview, firm #108, 8/4/95)

Other entrepreneurs voiced sentiments similar to those of a founder who left a large semiconductor company to create a company producing ATM networking products. He argued that many technology companies stumble by focusing principally on one nifty technological idea or by chasing immediate market opportunities. In his view, the key sustainable advantage for a company such as his is the ability to *execute*, which in turn requires organizational excellence, built by focusing tirelessly on employees and culture from the inception:

Founder: The next ten years are going to be dictated by companies who have the ability to execute in the time to market manner. That's the name of the game.

Interviewer: So what are ways that you are making sure you have the best in that area?

F: Complete infrastructure, complete understanding and respect for all the different disciplines from concept to delivery, the follow-through, support, after sales maintenance, you name it. The whole thing. The demeanor. How you are received at the front desk. How people talk within/without the company. It's the culture. You have to have a culture. . . .

I: Did the founders have a model in mind for how the employment relationship should be managed?

F: Absolutely. We basically believe that every employee is the most [important] employee to the company. We decided long ago to do what it takes to keep the employees happy. (Founder/CEO interview, firm #154, 7/31/95)

As the data in table 2 indicate, however, these particular founders were somewhat atypical in their early attention to building organizational excellence and/or a distinctive cultural vision or mission. SPEC companies were a bit more likely to have announced or sold a product and considerably more likely to have secured financing as the first step in company formation than to have engaged in organization- or identity-building. And table 2 suggests that many more entrepreneurs were hiring employees in the earliest stages of launching their new enterprises than were focusing on issues of long-term organization- or identity-building. Indeed, there appears to have been a trade-off between early hiring of employees versus focusing initially on organization- and identity-building: among founders who hired employees as one of their first two company-building activities, 49 percent embraced one of our five pure-type employment models, compared to 64 percent of the remaining founders ($\chi^2 = 3.10$, $df = 1$, $p = .078$). Those entrepreneurs who envisioned the most enduring attachments to their employees—those who chose the Commitment model at founding— were particularly slow to hire their first employees: only 9 percent of founders whose firms were built along Commitment model lines reported hiring their first employee(s) as one of the first two events among our list of company formation activities, compared to 42 percent of the remaining founders ($\chi^2 = 4.71$, $df = 1$, $p = .030$). Presumably, founders who embraced the Commitment model were more selective and devoted more effort up front to architecting their culture and employment practices.

An exploratory examination of the event sequence data suggests some other interesting differences in the sequences by which founders launched their new enterprises as a function of the initial employment blueprints they embraced. For instance, those companies that were initially product-driven were a bit less likely to exhibit one of the five coherent (pure-type) HR blueprints at the inception.[20] More important, the product-driven companies were considerably more likely to *alter* their initial employment model over time.[21] This suggests that the early-mover advantages technology-based companies might garner by being quick to launch products are counterbalanced by at least two potential disadvantages: (1) failing to embrace a coherent organizational blueprint initially; or (2) having to modify the blueprint significantly at a later date. Both of these have adverse effects on subsequent performance according to the analyses we summarized above.

Not surprisingly, an early focus on organization/identity building is related to the specific employment blueprint that founders selected. Among the firms classified as being founded on an Engineering model (nearly a third of the sample), *not a single founder* reported that the first activity in launching the company was related to organization- or identity-building.[22] In contrast, firms founded along Star, Bureaucracy, or Commitment model lines are over-represented among the companies in which the first event was related to organization- or identity-building.[23] Moreover, there is a strong association between having legally incorporated the firm as one of the first two company-building activities (clearly the default approach to company building; see table 2) and adopting the default HR model (namely, Engineering): 38 percent of the firms that were early to incorporate were founded along Engineering model lines, compared to only 18 percent of the remaining companies ($\chi^2=4.68$, $df=1$, $p=.030$). These results are consistent with our characterization of the Engineering model as the Silicon Valley default, constituting a simple, "out of the box" approach to building a high-technology start-up that eschews explicit organization- or identity-building.

Predictably, companies that focused early on organization- or identity-building were also more likely to *retain* their initial employment blueprint. Among SPEC firms in which the first event reported related to organization- or identity-building, 75 percent did not change the HR blueprint, compared to 47 percent of the other enterprises ($p=.059$).[24] Interestingly, firms that obtained early external financing were also somewhat more likely to retain the founder's initial employment blueprint: among companies that secured external financing as one of the first two company-building activities, 60 percent retained their initial employment blueprint, compared to 45 percent of the remaining enterprises ($p=.103$).[25] These results suggest that securing funding early in the firm's history might have given entrepreneurs an external mandate and time cushion to plan for the future by mapping out a scalable identity and organizational design.

These variations in company-building sequences suggest some interesting avenues for theoretical and empirical investigation, particularly given the path-dependent development we have documented. Table 2 shows that ties to outside stakeholders (e.g., financiers, customers) provide the initial catalyst for some start-ups, whereas other companies focus inward in their formative period (e.g., developing mission statements, policy handbooks). Such initial differences might plausibly affect how firms evolve. Moreover, the payoffs from focusing externally rather than internally might vary across types of environments.

It would also be invaluable to examine how receiving financing and/or having a clearly defined product early in a firm's history affects its firm's life chances, subsequent evolution, and performance. On the one hand, one might expect that quickly surmounting those milestones improves an organization's likelihood of gaining external acceptance and weathering the challenges facing young, small, high-tech enterprises. On the other hand, Barnett and his collaborators (Barnett and Hansen 1996; Barnett and Sorenson 2000) have argued that survival prospects are enhanced when firms face more formidable competition in their early years. If so, then the experience of confronting a series of early challenges might actually prove *beneficial* to (surviving) organizations in the long run.[26] One founder whom we interviewed invoked similar reasoning in justifying his decision to decline abundant venture capital in the middle of 1990, just as he was launching his new endeavor:

Founder: I had the interest and support of the two VCs that I was working for. . . . Of course, they and many other groups like [Kleiner Perkins and Institutional Venture Partners] were interested in doing a large amount of money to get started. I think $3.5 million was the last deal on the table for incorporating or before anything more than a presentation [about] starting the company. We rejected that idea.

Interviewer: Why did you reject the venture capital?

F: We rejected *that much* venture capital. Maybe it's because I was working for two VCs. Adding up the numbers of ownership and that kind of stuff [is] the way to do two negative things. First, you give up control of the company. Second, it makes you feel like you are spending important money. There is only one source of important money and that's from customers. Very poor cultures get created when you start spending large amounts of venture capital. It's the unusual organization that can recover and ramp straight up and go from a culture where it's OK to think of venture money as good money.

I: You felt bringing in venture capital would create a culture that might not look as closely at the customer as you would if you . . .

F: . . . [T]he real reason for the business . . . is to make profits and to serve and create great products and services. As many smart people as there are in the Valley, it's amazing how many people think it's a good thing to show up on the Money Tree[27] with big numbers next to your name. Our goal was to show up on the Money Tree with as little numbers as possible next to our name.

We took a couple hundred thousand from these guys and $100K from me and that was our seed money and we were going to try to go as far as possible with that. We didn't have a product decision at that time. This presentation proposed characteristics of products and a portfolio of applications in the system network management area. We didn't actually make the final selection of our first product until January '91. (Founder interview, firm #134, 7/28/95)

Some commentators, such as Collins and Porras (1994), have also claimed that products or technologies provide an unstable foundation on which to build enduring organizations. In their view, early attention to organization- and culture-building promotes long-term adaptation and performance, insulating firms from the uncertainties associated with technologies, products, and markets. It would be very interesting to examine whether the types and magnitude of "lock-in" that firms experience—in technology, customer relationships, culture, and so on—depend on the domain(s) given earliest priority by founders.

FUTURE DIRECTIONS

The findings that have emerged to date from the SPEC study suggest some profitable directions for future theory development and empirical research on the economic and organizational sociology of entrepreneurship.

Theory Development. The SPEC project sought to operationalize the menu of employment blueprints from which entrepreneurs were selecting (explicitly or implicitly) in shaping their enterprises. We hope that future studies will gauge the degree to which our findings generalize to other kinds of organizations and other environments.

A particularly interesting question about generalizability concerns whether our conclusions regarding the relative performance among blueprints apply to periods of marked economic contraction. For the most part we tracked the SPEC companies during the course of an unprecedented technological and market boom. Since early in 2000, however, conditions have deteriorated markedly in Silicon Valley, raising intriguing questions about whether the same organizational factors that were advantageous during good times have served firms well in tougher times. In supplementary analyses, we have explored whether our conclusions are altered by including the recent period of economic decline or, more generally, by allowing the effects of blueprints and of model change to vary across periods of boom and bust (see Hannan et al. 2004). Those analyses are by no means conclusive—for instance, relatively few additional IPOs have occurred since 2000—but in general they suggest that our broad conclusions about the relative performance of different blueprints and the adverse effects of blueprint change apply equally to periods of expansion *and* contraction.

The diversity in start-up sequences summarized in the previous section raises interesting questions about the essential ingredients of "organization." Some SPEC companies were financed before having either products, employees, a business plan, or a legal identity; other ventures had products or customers before being endowed with any other resources; still others had crafted mission statements before having any employees, products, customers, or funding. Our research also makes clear that start-ups are not simply younger, smaller versions of the more established organizations that have been commonplace subjects of scholarly research on organizations. For instance, a number of SPEC firms did not have a CEO for a considerable period of time after their founding (see Baron, Hannan, and Burton 2001).

Sometimes, there was little clear delineation among the roles of founders until external constituents (customers, financiers, etc.) demanded it. Indeed, popular accounts of some now-prominent technology companies emphasize that the initial entrepreneurial catalyst or impulse was frequently not even clearly commercial—for example, the efforts of two Stanford Ph.D. students to catalog their favorite web sites, which ultimately spawned Yahoo!; or the tinkering by (husband and wife) IT managers at Stanford's Business and Engineering schools who wished to network their respective systems, which eventually became Cisco Systems. In short, one of the most fascinating and distinctive features of high-tech entrepreneurship in Silicon Valley—the absence of any clear company-building steps, sequences, structural characteristics, or even commercial intentions that provide a workable definition of what constitutes a "start-up"—represents a significant conceptual and methodological challenge to organizational scholars.

More broadly, given the importance of the "form" construct to organizational ecology[28] and the emphasis that neo-institutionalists have placed on cultural templates, we have remarkably little theory to guide us in identifying *ex ante* the set of possible models or blueprints from which entrepreneurs might select in crafting new organizations. We need stronger theoretical grounds for predicting which kinds of models emerge within given settings and what determines the diversity of the menu of acceptable models. Neo-institutionalists have argued that the specific kinds of cultural prescriptions for organizing that are promulgated, as well as the consequences for organizational success, depend on the measurability of output (Meyer and Scott 1983), the role played by various professional groups, and processes of imitation and regulation (DiMaggio and Powell 1983). We speculate that some other factors also affect the type and diversity of organization-building models observed in a specific setting:

Social and Occupational Heterogeneity among Founders and Key External Stakeholders (e.g. Venture Capitalists). If entrepreneurs import models from their cultural or vocational backgrounds, then the range of backgrounds represented among the architects of organizations in any field is likely to influence the types and diversity of models that are considered. For instance, as the focus of internet companies has shifted from technology to content, it is likely that the entrepreneurs drawn to new ventures in this sphere import models that have developed in advertising, journalism, education, and other domains, supplanting more engineering- or technology-driven models that predominated at the inception of the industry.

It has been asserted that increased access to venture capital for female entrepreneurs might help redress women's under-representation in high technology. This argument seems to presume that female entrepreneurs would embrace organizational models that are more attractive to female scientists, technicians, and engineers than the dominant models in existence. In the same vein, Fligstein (1987, 1990) has argued that the ascendance of chief executive officers with particular occupational backgrounds (finance, law, etc.) within large organizations has altered the dominant "conception of control" brought to bear in running those companies.

Social and Demographic Heterogeneity among the Prospective Labor Force. Hannan (1988) argued that diversity in career outcomes depends in large measure on the diversity of organizational forms within a sector. He suggests that a more diverse menu of organizational forms reduces ascriptive inequalities by providing a more varied set of employment opportunities that can be matched to differences in worker abilities, experiences, and preferences. This line of reasoning suggests that we might observe a more varied menu of organizational models in those locales and industries having the most diverse prospective labor force in terms of socioeconomic and cultural background.

Stage of Industry Evolution. Work by organizational ecologists on density-dependent evolution suggests that industries tend to experience characteristic stages of early legitimation, followed by more intensive competition (Hannan and Carroll 1992). It seems reasonable to conjecture that conformity to a small number of culturally acceptable organizational models will be greater when legitimation concerns are paramount: in the early stages of industry evolution and for the sorts of entrepreneurial ventures for which legitimacy is most problematic (e.g., for-profit child care centers versus for-profit laser-tag parlors). In contrast, intensification of competition might encourage differentiation, particularly as enterprises seek to distinguish themselves in the labor market by embracing distinctive human resource blueprints.

If organizations adopt prescribed models to gain legitimacy and to develop coherent identities, then we also might expect to observe the emergence of clear cultural templates only after an industry or sector has achieved a certain scale. By analogy, nametags are seldom worn by guests at an intimate dinner party or by academics at a small research conference, because the small number of invitees and their connectedness through social networks reduces the need for that sort of external identifier. In the same vein, we expect that a culturally prescribed model is most likely to emerge and be relied on within organizational fields containing numerous enterprises, all of which share certain latent characteristics (that serve as viable bases for a common external identity) but lack direct linkages so that socially constructed identity markers are valuable (see Pólos et al. 2002). McKendrick and Carroll (2001; McKendrick et al. 2003) have presented some evidence on the emergence of organizational forms within the disk-array industry that is broadly consistent with this speculation. They find that organizational forms were slow to arise in this large and rapidly growing industry because entrants lacked common initial identities: they came from many diverse industries and did not concentrate geographically. However, the rise of a large number of new firms in the population (with no identity in another industry) sparked the common pattern of density-dependent legitimation, which McKendrick and Carroll interpret as indicating that a coherent form had coalesced.

Interfirm Ties. Finally, descriptions of Silicon Valley invariably emphasize the fluidity of its labor markets, the density of social and professional networks, and the prevalence of other prominent intermediaries (such as venture capital and law firms) that promote wide and rapid diffusion of information. Such an environment would seem likely to contain a relatively small menu of cultural blueprints, which diffuse quickly throughout the relevant population. In contrast, when labor markets are not so fluid, or networks so dense, or informational intermediaries so prevalent, it seems reasonable to expect a somewhat larger menu of models emerging and less conformity to that menu being observed.

We noted above that entrepreneurs' origins are likely to influence the types and diversity of organizational models that they consider. Various studies (e.g., Burton et al. 2002; Dobrev and Barnett 2002) have suggested that a great deal of entrepreneurial activity emanates from well-established organizations, either overtly (spin-offs and carve outs, joint ventures, etc.) or covertly (by employees who are unable to pursue specific opportunities in their current place of employment and hence leave to form new ventures). The role of established organizations (corporations, banks, government agencies, etc.) in fostering entrepreneurial ventures deserves additional study. Involvement of such organizations might reduce the diversity of organizational models pursued, as mature organizations superimpose relatively bureaucratic blueprints on the nascent endeavors. Alternatively, if well-established organizations stimulate entrepreneurship *unintentionally* or *unwillingly*—for instance, through oppressive policies or limits on pay and promotion that encourage "brain drain"—then we might expect entrepreneurship to resemble social movement activity, with decidedly anti-bureaucratic overtones, as we observed in several of the SPEC founder transcripts quoted above.

More broadly, a useful focus of inquiry would examine how insider versus outsider status with respect to the region, culture, and industry in which entrepreneurs' new ventures are located affects the organizational models that emerge within a given field. Ruef (2002) has recently demonstrated that entrepreneurs are more likely to leverage weak ties than strong ties when the new ventures they are launching are highly innovative and depart from their prior endeavors. If those results generalize to innovations in organizational forms, we should observe more novel and diverse models when entrepreneurs are either themselves outsiders or else draw heavily on network ties that link them to outsiders.

We offer one additional speculation, based less on our SPEC project than on our casual observations of entrepreneurship in Silicon Valley versus other regions. At a Silicon Valley conference on electronic commerce, which occurred before the current dot.com shakeout, a high-tech CEO discussing entrepreneurial opportunities told his audience: "You have to remember, this is not the PC era." He meant that unlike the era of entrepreneurship that yielded the personal computer—when individuals were mortgaging their homes, running up huge credit card debt, and the like— would-be entrepreneurs riding the dot-com wave believed that they confronted relatively little financial risk. After all, a buoyant labor market, generous VC funding, and in some cases ample personal resources (stock option payouts, home equity, etc.) served to minimize the apparent downside financial risk from pursuing ventures in the "new economy." This might have been somewhat more pronounced in Silicon Valley, but one suspects it was also the case along Route 128 and elsewhere.

Suppose, then, that the salient risks to entrepreneurs are primarily *social*: fear of the reputational consequences of failing in their new ventures. What seems to be distinctive about Silicon Valley in this respect is the almost complete absence of any social stigma attached to failure. Indeed, it has been sometimes suggested that the next best outcome to an audacious success is an audacious failure (or, perhaps, a well-managed and dignified failure). More generally, we suspect that the traditional sources of status in a community affect the perceived reputational risks associated with entrepreneurship. For instance, status has historically been tied more closely to employment in large, long-lived bureaucracies—such as universities, government bureaus, hospitals, or financial services companies—in the Boston area (and in other locales, such as Japan and Europe) than in Silicon Valley. Hence, we contend that would-be entrepreneurs along Route 128, in the Randstat, or in Oxbridge face not only the same challenges of procuring resources as their colleagues in Silicon Valley, but also a greater risk to their reputations and a more formidable challenge in fashioning plausible and legitimate social accounts of their careers.

This line of argument implies that we should see more entrepreneurial activity in regions where status has not historically been associated with long-term employment in large, old, bureaucratic organizations.[29] And, this argument suggests that entrepreneurship will flourish most in those industries and locales within which the Schumpeterian gale of creative destruction is most forceful—that is, where pre-existing sources of status have been weakened due to economic, technological, and social changes (plant closings, downsizings, etc.) that have altered the organizational landscape, obsolesced traditional routes to status, and thereby reduced the perceived social risks to entrepreneurship.

Finally, our results have potential implications for broad issues concerning the contours of contemporary capitalism addressed by several papers in this volume. Some neoinstitutionalists (e.g., Davis and Marquis, this volume) posit a convergence toward generic forms of capitalism. Such convergence may indeed be occurring; indeed, there are indications within the SPEC sample of a tendency for firms to evolve toward more bureaucratic, professionalized managerial structures. Nonetheless, we have found quite disparate templates for organizing being adopted by high-tech Silicon Valley entrepreneurs, with persistent effects on the evolution and performance of their companies, despite numerous forces that would ostensibly promote convergence. The existence of so much organizational diversity and path dependence among the SPEC companies—all young enterprises that were founded in one locale, industrial sector, and time period—leaves us skeptical about theories suggesting a common destination state for the structure or form of capitalist firms.

Our results suggest that high-tech companies are not all created alike. Yet neither are they entirely unique. Both scholarly and popular discussions of entrepreneurship commonly put enormous weight on the role of the founder(s) in molding the culture, structure, and evolution of the firms they launch. Notwithstanding founders' idiosyncrasies, we can characterize their implicit organizational blueprints along a small number of dimensions and into a small number of distinct types, which our research shows differ significantly in their evolutionary trajectories and performance outcomes. In short, even if entrepreneurs formulate unique visions for their nascent enterprises and leave their personal mark in many ways during the formative stages of organization building, technology entrepreneurs seem to be choosing implicitly from a relatively small menu of distinct recipes in launching their companies. Founders may indeed embed their distinctive visions and values on the enterprises they create, or they may simply be conduits through which economic, social, or cultural forces systematically shape organizational blueprints. Our results here demonstrate that those blueprints are consequential for the pace of bureaucratization, but they do not resolve the thorny issue of the distinctive contribution made by founders and other actors in building and changing organizations.

Countless other interesting questions could be asked about the origins of new firms in capitalist economies, and numerous useful data sources and research approaches should be marshaled besides the ones we have discussed here. Nonetheless, we believe the theoretical issues and research approaches sketched here will ultimately prove invaluable not only in augmenting our understanding of entrepreneurship in capitalist economies, but also in strengthening economic and organizational sociology.

NOTES

1. These companies were concentrated in computer hardware and software, medical devices and biotechnology, semiconductors, telecommunications and networking, and computer-related manufacturing or research. The typical SPEC company was born around 1989 (though the range is from 1980 through 1996). On average, the firms were just under six years old and employed roughly 70 people when we began to study them. For additional details, see the various publications from our research program cited in the References, as well as recent manuscripts posted on the SPEC website (http://www-gsb.stanford.edu/SPEC).

2. A significant number of companies differed from one (and only one) of the basic model types on only one dimension. We refer to these as *near-model* types. For instance, about 3 percent of founders envisioned basing attachment on love, selecting based on fit, and utilizing direct control. This combination represents a near-Commitment blueprint: it differs from the basic Commitment model firm in terms of control (only), and differs substantially (i.e., on two or more dimensions) from the other four model types. Such an organization suggests an autocratic cult variant on the Commitment model. We use the term *non-type* to refer to all other blueprints—firms in which the blueprint either: (a) differs from two or more basic model types on one dimension (and doesn't fall into any of the basic types); or (b) differs along two or more dimensions from every basic model type.

3. Among SPEC firms in the medical technology or research sectors (including biotechnology), 42 percent were founded on a star model, compared to only 2 percent of firms in other industry sectors ($p < .001$).

4. Of the 183 companies in the SPEC sample, we were able to code the founder's and CEO's HR blueprint reliably from completed interview transcripts for only 165. The tabulation in table 1 eliminates another 9 firms that were not directly comparable for one reason or another. (For example, a handful were linked to some other organization, either as a subsidiary or through a joint venture, and a few were created as not-for-profit research enterprises.)

5. For examples, see the perspectives expressed by two prominent venture capitalists: Kathryn Gould of Foundation Capital and Dave Marquardt of August Capital (see http://www.forbes.com/asap/2001/0528/057.html and http://www.augustcap.com/about/index.shtml).

6. Among the companies in table 1, 36.4 percent of firms that intended to compete principally through marketing or customer relations adopted a Commitment or near-Commitment blueprint at their inception, compared to 10.4 percent of firms pursuing other strategies (technological innovation, technological enhancement, and/or cost); $\chi^2(1) = 10.48$; $p = .001$.

7. Of the 48 companies that were classified in table 1 as "non-type" at both time points, 15 (31.2 percent) had changed the blueprint in some respect.

8. As one might imagine, the control-coordination dimension was the likeliest to have changed: 36.5 percent of the companies in table 1 modified their HR blueprint along that dimension, compared to 19.2 percent and 17.3 percent on the attachment and selection dimensions, respectively.

9. The situation is actually a bit more complicated than this. For the hazard of IPOs—but not the hazard of failure or the rate of growth in market capitalization—adding CEOs' blueprints to the specification with the effects of founders' blueprints improves the fit significantly. And, it turns out that firms that changed from a Star blueprint to some other model had a hazard of IPO about as high as that of firms with the Commitment model at the start.

10. The differences among models (aside from the contrast vis-à-vis Commitment) are not jointly significant.

11. Change in model did not affect speed to IPO or market valuation at the time of IPO.

12. There is, however, an interesting pattern of interactions, with firms founded along Star lines benefiting most from blueprint change in terms of the odds of going public and firms founded along Engineering and Commitment lines benefiting the least (for details, see Hannan et al. 2004, table 6). There is also an indirect link between blueprint change and the odds of going public. Model change is associated with labor turnover, which in turn diminishes subsequent revenue growth (Baron, Hannan, and Burton 2001). Revenue growth, in turn, is a very strong predictor of the odds of going public (Hannan et al. 2004, table 5).

13. It is important to stress that we coded blueprints from the three underlying dimensions, based on how founders and CEOs talked about their companies, not from choices among a menu of alternative labels. There was often little relationship between the model that a given founder or CEO publicly endorsed at one of our conferences on the one hand and the interview responses that we coded for their firm on the other hand. In hindsight, it was a good design decision not to provide our respondents with a checklist of blueprints from which to choose.

14. Some venture capitalists with whom we have shared our findings also tell us that the resilience of the Commitment model resonates with their experience. They note that the technological and economic uncertainties inherent in high-tech entrepreneurship, combined with the interpersonal stresses involved, put a premium on employees and organizational designs that can cope and adapt. In their judgment, blueprints that manage to capture the hearts and minds of employees up front can better achieve this adaptation.

15. We do not have enough power to make finer discriminations in most cases. In particular, for failure and growth in market capitalization, specifications with both founders' and CEOs' employment blueprints and change in blueprint do not improve significantly over more constrained specifications that drop either the founder blueprint effects or the CEO blueprint effects.

16. It is less clear whether mortality rates are also elevated for young organizations. Much, but not all, recent research shows that the apparent liability of newness is actually a liability of smallness (Carroll and Hannan 2000).

17. Both the founder and HR informant surveys asked about the timing of the company's first mission/values statement. If the founder provided a response, we used that information; otherwise, we relied on the date provided by the HR informant.

18. Information on the timing of a product prototype was only available for companies sampled in 1995 or later; fewer than half of those companies listed a date for a prototype, and only 12 companies indicated having a prototype before their first product announcement and/or sale. The results are generally comparable if we include the product prototype variable in our definition of the timing of product-related events.

19. In some firms that did not fill out the event grid, informants provided dates for particular company-building activities during the course of our interviews. Table 2 analyzes a subset of 143 SPEC companies (among those in table 1) for which we had reliable and complete information on the timing of two or more company-building activities from the event grid and/or interview responses.

20. Among companies in which a product-related event occurred first on our list of activities, 38.5 percent displayed one of our five pure employment model types; among the rest of the sample, the fraction was 60.0 percent ($\chi^2=2.25$, $df=1$, $p=.134$). (The pattern is somewhat different if we define product-driven foundings as those in which either the *first or second* company-building activity was product-related. Here, we find that companies that developed products early were somewhat more likely than others to adopt a Commitment model and less likely to adopt any of the four other pure model types: if we trichotomize founders' HR model into non-type, Commitment, and all other pure types, $\chi^2=4.82$, $df=2$, $p=.090$). Some founders and venture capitalists we have interviewed suggest that the Commitment model might be particularly well suited to firms that need to hire, mobilize, and retain a loyal captive sales force to gain momentum for early generation products, which might explain this observed association among companies that were relatively quick to launch products.

21. Among the product-driven companies, 35.5 percent retained their founder's model and 19.4% changed on all three dimensions, whereas corresponding percentages for the rest of the sample are 52.7 percent and 0.9 percent, respectively ($\chi^2=18.84$, $df=3$, $p=.001$).

22. Nor did any of the 10 companies classified as Autocracies or near-Autocracies report an organization- or identity-building activity as their first milestone event.

23. For the cross-tabulation of founders' HR model with a dummy variable for whether the first event was related to organization-building, $\chi^2=9.57$, $df=5$, $p=.088$. (If near-type cases (see note 2) are grouped with their corresponding pure model type, $\chi^2=9.93$, $df=5$, $p=.077$.)

24. The results are very similar if we use a measure of whether either of the *first two* activities in launching the company was related to organization- or identity-building.

25. The firms that first lined up external financing were also a bit more likely to adopt a Bureaucracy or near-Bureaucracy model at founding—12 percent, versus 4 percent for the rest of the sample ($\chi^2=3.18$, $df=1$, $p=.075$).

26. A different stream of work in organizational ecology, labeled density delay

theory, finds a robust pattern that runs counter to this argument. To wit, organizations founded in periods of high density within the relevant organizational population experience elevated mortality rates in infancy and throughout their lifetimes. Carroll and Hannan (2000: chap. 1) review the evidence.

27. A reference to the "Money Tree™" survey of venture-capital corporate investments conducted by PricewaterhouseCoopers, published quarterly in the *San Jose Mercury News.*

28. See Ruef (2000); Pólos, Hannan, and Carroll (2002); McKendrik and Carroll (2001); McKendrik, Carroll, Jaffee, and Khessina (2001).

29. Given the current dot.com shake out, it is also interesting to speculate whether the reabsorption of unsuccessful entrepreneurs might prove more challenging in contexts where status has had more traditional origins. For instance, relative to Silicon Valley entrepreneurs, we predict much tougher sledding for the Oxbridge crowd that, in search of "e-wealth," abandoned the investment banks, consulting firms, university positions, and British civil service posts to which their compatriots have traditionally flocked.

REFERENCES

Barnett, William P. and Morten Hansen. 1996. "The Red Queen in Organizational Evolution." *Strategic Management Journal* 17: 139–57.
Barnett, William P. and Olav Sorenson. 2002. "The Red Queen in Organizational Creation and Development." *Industrial and Corporate Change* 5(2): 289–325.
Baron, James N., M. Diane Burton, and Michael T. Hannan. 1996. "The Road Taken: Origins and Early Evolution of Employment Systems in Emerging Countries." *Industrial and Corporate Change* 5(2): 239–75.
———. 1999. "Engineering Bureaucracy: The Genesis of Formal Policies, Positions, and Structures in High-Technology Firms." *Journal of Law, Economics, and Organization* 15: 1–41.
Baron, James N., Michael T. Hannan., and M. Diane Burton. 1999. "Building the Iron Cage: Determinants of Managerial Intensity in the Early Years of Organizations." *American Sociological Review* 64: 527–47.
———. 2001. "Labor Pains: Organizational Change and Employee Turnover in Young, High-Tech Firms." *American Journal of Sociology* 106: 960–1012.
Burton, M. Diane, Jesper B. Sørensen, and Christine Beckman. 2002. "Coming from Good Stock: Career Histories and New Venture Formation." In *Research in the Sociology of Organizations*, vol. 19, ed. Michael Lounsbury and Marc J. Ventresca. Oxford: JAI/Elsevier Science. 229–62.
Carroll, Glenn R. and Michael T. Hannan. 2000. *The Demography of Corporations and Industries.* Princeton: Princeton University Press.
Carroll, Glenn R. and Anand Swaninathan. 2000. "Why the Microbrewery Movement? Organizational Dynamics of Resource Partitioning in the U.S. Brewing Industry." *American Journal of Sociology* 106: 715–62.
Carter, Nancy M., William B. Gartner, and Paul D. Reynolds. 1996. "Exploring Start-Up Event Sequences." *Journal of Business Venturing* 11: 151–66.

Collins, James C. and Jerry I. Porras. 1994. *Built to Last: Successful Habits of Visionary Companies*. New York: HarperCollins.

DiMaggio, Paul J. and Walter W. Powell. 1983. "The Iron Cage Revisited: Institutional Isomorphism and Collective Rationality in Organizational Fields." *American Sociological Review* 48: 147–60.

Dobrev, Stanislav D. and William P. Barnett. 2002. "Organizational Roles and Transitions to Entrepreneurship." *Academy of Management Journal* (forthcoming).

Fligstein, Neil. 1987. "The Intraorganizational Power Struggle: The Rise of Finance Presidents in Large Corporations." *American Sociological Review* 52: 44–58.

———. 1990. *The Transformation of Corporate Control*. Cambridge, Mass.: Harvard University Press.

Fligstein, Neil and Haldor Byrkjeflot. 1996. "The Logic of Employment Systems." In *Social Differentiation and Social Inequality*, ed. James N. Baron, David B. Grusky, and Donald J. Treiman. Boulder, Colo.: Westview Press. 11–35.

Guillén, Mauro F. 1994. *Models of Management: Work, Authority, and Organization in a Comparative Perspective*. Chicago: University of Chicago Press.

Hannan, Michael T. 1988. "Social Change, Organizational Diversity, and Individual Careers." In *Social Structures and Human Lives*, ed. Matilda White Riley. Newbury Park, Calif.: Sage and American Sociological Association. 161–74.

Hannan, Michael T., James M. Baron, Greta Hsu, and Özgecan Koçak. 2005. "Organizational Identities and the Hazard of Change." Working paper, Graduate School of Business, Stanford University, January.

Hannan, Michael T. and Glenn R. Carroll. 1992. *Dynamics of Organizational Populations: Density, Legitimation and Competition*. Oxford: Oxford University Press.

Hannan, Michael T. and John H. Freeman.1984. "Structural Inertia and Organizational Change." *American Sociological Review* 49: 149–64.

———. 1989. *Organizational Ecology*. Cambridge, Mass.: Harvard University Press.

McKendrick, David G. and Glenn R. Carroll. 2001. "On the Genesis of Organizational Forms: Evidence from the Market for Disk Drive Arrays." *Organization Science* 12: 661–82.

McKendrick, David G., Glenn R. Carroll, Jonathan Jaffee, and Olga M. Khessina. 2003. "In the Bud? Analysis of Disk Array Producers as a (Possibly) Emergent Organizational Form." *Administrative Science Quarterly* 48: 60–93.

Meyer, John W. and Brian Rowan. 1977. "Institutionalized Organizations: Formal Structure as Myth and Ceremony." *American Journal of Sociology* 83: 340–63.

Meyer, John W. and W. Richard Scott. 1983. *Organizational Environments: Ritual and Rationality*. Beverly Hills, Calif.: Sage.

Pólos, László, Michael T. Hannan, and Glenn R. Carroll. 2002. "Foundations of a Theory of Social Forms." *Industrial and Corporate Change* 11: 85–115.

Ruef, Martin. 2000. "The Emergence of Organizational Forms: A Community Ecology Approach." *American Journal of Sociology* 106: 658–714.

———. 2002. "Strong Ties, Weak Ties, and Islands: Structural and Cultural Predictors of Organizational Innovation." *Industrial and Corporate Change* 11: 427–49.

Saxenian, AnnaLee. 1994. *Regional Advantage: Culture and Competition in Silicon Valley and Route 128*. Cambridge, Mass.: Harvard University Press.

Suchman, Mark C. 1994. "On Advice of Counsel: Law Firms and Venture Capital Funds as Information Intermediaries in the Structuration of Silicon Valley." Ph.D. dissertation, Department of Sociology, Stanford University.

———. 2000. "Dealmakers and Counselors: Law Firms as Intermediaries in the Development of Silicon Valley." In *Understanding Silicon Valley: The Anatomy of an Entrepreneurial Region*, ed. Martin Kenney. Stanford: Stanford University Press. 71–97.

Thornton, Patricia H. 1999. "The Sociology of Entrepreneurship." *Annual Review of Sociology* 25: 19–46.

Making Sense of Recession: Toward an Interpretive Theory of Economic Action

Mitchel Y. Abolafia

> *"When it comes to action, economic theory is only one input among many. It has to be combined with a grasp of political and administrative feasibility and above all has to take advantage of experience and observation, not rely wholly on logic."*
>
> Sir Alec Cairncross

THE CAIRNCROSS QUOTE ABOVE (quoted in McCloskey 1994: 50) suggests that a theory of action adequate to understanding major economic institutions must go beyond the simple idea that individual beliefs, values, and motives predict action. Cairncross's insight about economic action challenges economic sociology to craft a theory of action that takes account of the interpretive process that guides action. Such a theory would illustrate how economic actors place diverse bits of information (economic, political, administrative, experiential, etc.) into frameworks. The frameworks are not unique to individuals, but rather social products. Moreover, such a theory would show that as economic actors respond to their changing environment they continually reframe the past. They use this reframing to make sense of the present and shape their actions in the future. The ambiguous and often unpredictable nature of information finds actors shifting between economic, political, social, and psychological decision criteria, weaving complex narratives to rationalize their actions and negotiating these narratives with others. It is this interpretive/pragmatic theory of action that motivates the analysis below.

This paper examines action in a major economic institution of capitalism, the U.S. Federal Reserve. It explores the process by which the Federal Reserve decides whether to buy or sell government securities to stabilize the economy. It demonstrates how economic elites, such as those at the Federal Reserve, apply a fluctuating stream of decision criteria to make sense of the changing situations they face. An important part of this sensemaking includes crafting strategies to convince both the market and political arenas of the plausibility and the efficacy of their actions.

The chapter will explore the efforts of the twelve voting members of the Federal Open Market Committee, the Federal Reserve's chief policymaking unit, to respond to indicators of a downturn in the domestic and world economies. The analysis is based on verbatim transcripts of the regular meetings at which monetary policy is set. These meetings are held behind closed doors and a norm of secrecy prevails among their participants. One result of this secrecy is that the Federal Reserve chairman, currently Alan Greenspan, is alternately portrayed in the media as guru, Delphic oracle, demigod, and wizard. Another is that the policymaking process has remained mysterious. The transcripts, obtained through a Freedom of Information Act request, suggest that monetary policymaking involves a less enigmatic interpretive process.

THE SENSEMAKING MODEL

There is no lack of effort to explain Federal Reserve (Fed) monetary policy. For a representative sample see the edited volumes by Mayer (1990) and Persson and Tabellini (1994). These volumes consist of efforts by economists to correlate historic Fed policy with such variables as congressional and presidential pressures, the business cycle, reputational effects, and its own stated goals. The papers reflect an effort either to infer a model of what drives Fed policymaking or to prescribe one. The secrecy of the Fed's policymaking proceedings has inhibited understanding of which factors policy elites actually examine and talk about when making policy. An exception to this is the work by Karamouzis and Lombra (1989) and Lombra and Moran (1980). These authors analyzed the summary Memoranda of Discussion written after Federal Open Market Committee (FOMC) meetings. Their findings reflect a decided consternation at the "ad hoc" nature of Fed policymaking and its distance from their ideal notion of decision-making. Lombra and Moran expressed concern that "the FOMC appeared to have neither ultimate goals nor a consensus view (model?) of the effects of monetary policy" (1980: 42). Their disdain for the absence of a model is expressed in the following summary.

> In short, without the guidance or discipline offered by an analytic model and formal targets for nonfinancial variables, the formulation of monetary policy often seemed to be a seat-of-the-pants operation. Moreover, it would appear that new members of the Committee rather quickly assimilated into the world of ad hoc theorizing and policymaking. . . . The ad hoc approach of the FOMC certainly did not produce superior policy. (1980: 43)

This same sense of dismay is found in one of the few discussions of FOMC proceedings by a former member.

Before my appointment to the Board of Governors of the Federal Reserve System in 1965, I had spent nearly twenty years studying and teaching monetary economics. I thought I understood what the Fed did and how it affected the economy. I soon discovered how little I knew. I also found that the Fed itself, while it had a definite philosophy, had no clear concept of how monetary policy worked. (Maisel 1973: ix)

My own assessment of policymaking at the FOMC, based on review of transcripts from 1982 to 1992, is in substantial agreement these descriptions. But I do not share their dismay. Rather, my skepticism about the capacity or wisdom of any group to use preexisting models to analyze such a complex and shifting environment leaves me unsurprised at the ad hoc and indeterminate nature of Fed policymaking. I want to argue, following Knorr-Cetina (1981), that where no determinate model exists, the oscillation of decision criteria is preferable to misplaced concreteness for the progressive understanding of complex processes.[1] Decision criteria oscillate because the salience of concerns and interests is contingent on the details of the situation being considered. Each successive decision by the Committee is considered contextually specific to the problem confronting them at the moment. It is a reflective intelligence responding to the moment's contingencies and its unique combination of concerns and interests. Although individual decisions may seem ad hoc, they are part of an ongoing effort to progressively clarify, discover, and shape the nature of the U.S. economy. I prefer to replace the disdainful and vague "ad hoc theorizing" with Weick's more positive and proactive "sensemaking" (Weick 1995). This concept will help us develop a more accurate and meaningful picture of the process by which elite policy makers interpret and construct U.S. monetary policy. It also provides the basis for a rich theory of action for economic sociology.

Sensemaking refers to the ongoing effort actors make to interpret their environment. For example, Daft and Weick remark "Managers . . . must wade into the ocean of events that surround the organization and actively try to make sense of them" (1984: 286). According to Starbuck and Milliken, this includes "comprehending, understanding, explaining, attributing, extrapolating, and predicting, at least (1988: 51)." What these processes have in common is that "they involve placing stimuli into frameworks . . . that make sense of the stimuli" (Starbuck and Milliken 1988: 51). Sensemaking, then, is about placing diverse bits of often ambiguous information into frameworks. These frameworks are filters that allow actors to organize and interpret this information as cues or guides to action. The purpose of this chapter is to examine how such frameworks shape what matters to Fed policymakers and to show how the group collectively uses these frameworks to create policy that reflects a diverse and shifting set of political, economic, social, and psychological concerns.

The policymaking process at the FOMC is an exemplar of collective sensemaking. Meetings, which are scheduled every fifth or sixth week and last for one to two days, are designed to facilitate the ongoing interpretive process. Each meeting begins with short reports from Fed staff members. These offer a selection of economic and organizational frames for making sense of the current situation. This framing phase is followed by open discussion of existing conditions. Members of the Committee add their own frames and begin to negotiate a consensual interpretation. Contrary to media hype, the chairman is neither guru nor Svengali. The chairman works to build a consensus, cajoling as well as compromising as coalitions form. Although his position as chair provides considerable influence, the benefits of a strong majority make him responsive to competing interests. The negotiation continues into the final strategic phase of the meeting where members debate alternative strategies, ultimately crafting one that is designed to elicit a majority vote.

Despite the apparent rationality of this process, we must be careful not to over-rationalize what happens. The mandate of this group is to produce a directive, that is, instructions for the open market desk at the Federal Reserve Bank in New York where traders will buy or sell Treasury securities to expand or contract the money supply. The creation of the policy directive should not be taken as evidence of consensus on a single interpretation of the strategy or agreement on the causal thinking behind it. Sensemaking is neither so linear nor so tightly coupled. Sherman Maisel, a former member of the FOMC, explained this well.

> The fact that instructions must be issued forces the Committee to come to some agreement on operating policy, even though individual members may have various estimates as to what effect the purchase or sale of more securities may have. . . . For example, the Committee may vote to make no change in a directive. It would not be unusual to find two members voting not to change policy because they fear a balance of payments effect; two others who are concerned over a possible slowdown in the economy; another who desires lower interest rates; and still another who feels that the policy would lead to higher interest rates but welcomes them. (Maisel 1973: 51)

What then is the nature of rationality in the sensemaking process at the FOMC? The monetary economists previously quoted share the complaint that the members of the FOMC subscribe to no model, no clear concept of how monetary policy works. Rather than assume ignorance on the part of these policy elites, most of whom have considerable economic training and practical experience, I find that they have developed a pragmatic response to high stakes decision-making under conditions of ambiguity. This response is grounded in a healthy skepticism about what it is possible to know. The quote below, questioning a forecast, is a typical example of FOMC members' skepticism about predictive models.

> This is by no means a criticism of the staff's efforts to forecast because I think the staff is among the best in terms of that job, but it's a very difficult job. The third quarter served as a reminder to me of the questionability, if you will, of short-run fine-tuning of monetary policy based on economic forecasts. As good as that process may be, it's a very, very difficult thing to do. We essentially are looking at a rate of growth in GDP that is probably twice what we thought a couple of FOMC meetings ago.

Their skepticism about indicators and predictions suggests a conviction that such knowledge does not rest on firm foundations. There is, in fact, a cultural understanding that there is no certainty and that "interpretations are always and necessarily open to further interpretation, determination, and critical question" (Bernstein 1997:386). Lombra and Moran (1980) express surprise that new members, many of them with years of academic experience, are "quickly assimilated" into the group culture. Rather, this assimilation suggests that in the world of highly consequential and ambiguous decisions, the skeptical caste of sensemaking easily supercedes academic models.

The FOMC culture is that of a continuous inductive exploration. For them, knowledge is tentative and subject to correction. There is no beginning or end and no absolute truth when it comes to knowledge about the workings of the monetary system. The fundamental epistemological assumption of the FOMC is at odds with the deductive theorizing of academic economics. This assumption, about the nature of what is knowable, was described well by Charles Sanders Peirce, the pragmatic philosopher, when he wrote generally of scientific knowledge, "trust rather to the multitude and variety of its arguments than to the conclusiveness of any one. Its reasoning should not form a chain which is no stronger than its weakest link, but a cable whose fibers may be ever so slender, provided they are sufficiently numerous and intimately connected" (quoted in Bernstein 1997: 387). It is with this sense of fallibility that FOMC meetings weave together a variety of frames, not trusting in the conclusiveness of any one.

Frames are among the most important tools for sensemaking. They are narrative abstractions used to structure ambiguous reality. A frame, then, is a narrative or prescriptive story line that guides both analysis and action (Rein and Schon 1996). Organizations generate a variety of frames that shape sensemaking by their members. Among the most important are budgets, strategic plans, hurdles, and targets that define the premises of subsequent decision making (Simon 1997; Perrow 1986). At a less obtrusive level are the vocabularies found in every organization that constrain the thinking of its members and serve as generators of action (Mills 1940;

Starbuck 1983; Weick 1995). The FOMC has both targets and a special-ized vocabulary as well as more general competing ideologies.

Frames are not straitjackets that determine policymakers' behavior, and frames alone cannot determine policy. They are tools that actors use to interpret complex situations. Even these tools are used with flexibility and some skepticism. In the case of monetary policy, neither academic economists nor policymakers can agree on the right model or the right econometric techniques. As Alan Blinder, a recent vice chairman of the Federal Reserve Board, has written, "We do not know the model, and we do not know the objective function, so we cannot compute the optimal policy rule" (Blinder 1998: 6). The result of this uncertainty is a negoti-ation over similar and competing frames, some of which will coexist in the final policy. Borrowing Peirce's metaphor, the FOMC's policy analy-sis is less a chain of logical arguments than it is a cable with many fibers. The cable is woven together using three elements of sensemaking: an-choring, negotiating, and signaling. This chapter will illustrate how these three elements are intertwined throughout the sensemaking process, though one may be dominant at any particular moment.

Our analysis of sensemaking at the FOMC is based on verbatim tran-scripts (310 pages) from three consecutive meetings during the recession of 1982. These meetings reflect the moment at which the Fed decided that it was time to recognize the severity of economic conditions and re-verse its tight hold on the money supply. Economic growth had slowed, unemployment had risen, and inflation was in rapid decline. In the first of the three meetings members began to express the view that it was time to let the money supply grow. Growth required that they either raise their earlier monetary growth targets or deliberately tolerate an overshoot of the stated target. Much of the discussion involved building a consensus interpretation of the situation and a strategy for growth of the money supply.

ANCHORING

Anchoring is the process of embedding an interpretation in data. Data are necessarily retrospective. Policymakers use indicators of the past (anchors) to make sense of the future. One important kind of anchor in monetary policy is a target. Targeting refers to the effort to control the amount of money in the U.S. economy based on economic indicators, for example, aggregate measures of the existing U.S. money stock (M1, M2, M3) or short-term interest rates (the Fed funds rate). It is the interpretation of the past movement of indicators that guides a substantial portion of the an-choring at the FOMC. Decisions to buy or sell government securities are based on the movement of the target. Although policymakers are hoping to shape the future performance of the target, it is the recent past of the anchor that is the basis for their thinking. Anchors, then, are data-based tools that guide members' analysis and action.

By the summer of 1982 the FOMC had spent almost three years targeting M1 and its cousins in a forceful effort to bring down the inflation rate. Following monetarist theory, Fed policy focused on maintaining a consistent level of growth in the money supply as measured by M1. But in the summer of 1982, the volatility in M1 began to make its meaning ambiguous and its use as an anchor for policy making questionable. The result was a framing contest. The opposing positions on the FOMC are represented below by Mr. Black and Ms. Teeters. The former, a monetarist, favored strict adherence to M1, the latter called for flexibility and renewed attention to the Fed funds rate as a preferable target.

> *Mr. Black:* Well, Mr. Chairman, now that we're back inside the target range for M1, I think we ought to concentrate a little on trying to keep it there. . . . I would hate for the record to show that we were aiming at something above the range.
>
> *Ms. Teeters:* I'm really very reluctant to see (interest) rates go back up because I think people need the relief all of us have been talking about. . . . It seems to me, as I mentioned earlier, that we have to be extremely flexible and look at all of our indicators to make sure that we don't bounce the funds rate down to zero or accidentally bounce it back up to 15 percent. . . . So, a little change in our focus from reserve provisions and money supply growth to a smooth constant rate on federal funds seems to me more important at the present time. (FOMC 1982B: 25)

But the criticism of M1 really went beyond flexibility in targeting to a feeling that this particular indicator, which shaped much of their policy-making, couldn't be interpreted, that is, it had lost its usefulness for sense-making.

> *Mr. Morris:* Well, Mr. Chairman, we've been describing the M1 box into which we have woven ourselves rather tightly here. I've heard a number of people say that they think our policy is too tight but we can't do anything about it. And it seems to me that that is indeed an unfortunate situation to be in. It has cleared my mind considerably to have arrived at a conclusion that M1 is no longer a reliable guide to policy and I would recommend that view to all of you or recommend that you at least contemplate it. It clears one's mind on such issues as contemporaneous reserve requirements and many other things. If you look at the situation, last year M1 ran low relative to the other aggregates and low relative to expectations. We didn't understand why it ran low

last year. Although I don't recall debating it very much, we didn't decide to rebase our M1 guidelines for 1982.

Mr. Partee: But we did discuss it at length.

Mr. Morris: We did? Well, we came up with the wrong conclusion, obviously. (FOMC 1982A: 15)

From October 1979 until the summer of 1982, monetary policy had been guided by "practical monetarism," a philosophical framework in which targeting was focused on a single goal: achieving a steady stable rate of growth in the stock of money through strict adherence to a monetary target. This frame, concentrating on M1 as its anchor, had been useful for bringing down inflation without blaming the Fed for high interest rates. The discussion above reflects the recognition that this anchor is beginning to be seen as highly fallible and perhaps misleading. When a policy group treats such anchors as determinative, it becomes highly invested in their accuracy. The identity of the group, its sense of self, and its external credibility are tied to the highly visible anchor. M1 had become an anchor that shaped how members talked about the economy and what they should do about it. By the third meeting, on October 6, 1982, the Committee, with some resistance, was ready to abandon the anchor, although not necessarily the larger frame. In the two quotes below, the first speaker is still reluctant; the second speaker is already strategizing about how to spin the change.

> *Mr. Roos:* . . . I believe that what we're about to do today will unquestionably be viewed by those who watch what we do as a major change. I don't think it will be possible to explain away the fact that, albeit temporarily, we are moving away from targeting a narrow aggregate that has predicted prices and output better than other variables. It will be apparent, in spite of any disclaimers we may or may not make, that we are moving toward placing greater emphasis on controlling the fed funds rate. And I think it will be misconstrued by the markets. It will be associated with the forthcoming election; I think it will give comfort to those who, rightly or wrongly, have sat on the sidelines and implied that somewhere along the line we would cave in on our present policy posture.
>
> *Vice Chairman Solomon:* I think this is a rather momentous FOMC meeting. I had thought that we had until maybe 1986 before the pace of deregulation and innovation would bring us to this point. . . . I recognize that there will be a good deal of questioning, not only in monetarist circles but more generally. I don't think there will be an avalanche of criticism given our credibility, but there will be major questioning as to what this means in terms of longer-run anti-inflationary policy. And it seems to me that there ought to be some words to convey our longer-run commitment and our expectations that inflation will continue to come down. (FOMC 1982c: 48–49)

Anchors, like other aspects of organizational culture, are fundamentally conservative and inertial. Once in place they are hard to change. Nevertheless, the highly pragmatic members of the FOMC were not wedded to the monetarist frame. Beyond a few ideologically committed monetarists who feared that failure to adhere to the target reflected in M1 would reignite inflation, most seemed to care more about the effect of high interest rates on economic recovery. In fact, as the following quote suggests, some of those who defended M1 in the first meeting, justified it as a shelter from public criticism over high interest rates, rather than its efficacy as an instrument for controlling the money supply.

> *Mr. Morris:* I think it would be a big mistake for us to announce that we were willing to peg interest rates again. One thing we've learned in the last few years is that the presence of an intermediate target for monetary policy has sheltered the central banks—not only ourselves but the Germans said the same thing at that meeting in New York as did the British and the Canadians and others—from a direct sense of responsibility for interest rates, and I think that has contributed to a stronger policy posture. To begin, even in a little way, to back away from that would be a serious mistake strategically. (FOMC 1982a: 56)

As the quote suggests, anchors have a political as well as an economic logic. They are used not only for facilitating the analysis of a complex system and for guiding action, but also, and maybe most importantly, for shaping the expectations of stakeholders in the group's environment. In this case, the FOMC deflected criticism for the continuing high interest rates in the seventies by focusing on M1. They were able to coopt their critics and mobilize support for the frame. These stakeholders, primarily participants in the bond markets but also Congress and the administration, expend substantial resources in making sense of the Fed's actions, predicting and interpreting behavior based on the Fed's own espoused anchors. This has a recursive effect in that the Fed is closely watching how its stakeholders make sense of Fed actions. This makes the anchor far more than an analytic tool. It has a life of its own. Its efficacy is based on the fact that the stakeholders believe in it, a self-fulfilling prophecy effect. This makes anchors hard to abandon.

Negotiating

Most of the economic literature on monetary policy is premised on the theoretical fiction that Fed policy "is made by a single individual maximizing a well defined preference function" (Blinder 1998: 22). Contrary to this, the transcript data used here suggest that decisions are made by a committee of opinionated elites with ambiguous and shifting preferences who frequently compromise in order to reach consensus. Blinder, who was a member of the FOMC in the mid-1990s, describes the collective nature of its decision-making.

> While serving on the FOMC, I was vividly reminded of a few things all of us probably know about committees: that they laboriously aggregate individual preferences; that they need to be led; that they tend to adopt compromise positions on difficult questions; and—perhaps because of all of the above—that they tend to be inertial. (Blinder 1998: 20)

The sensemaking approach taken in this paper substitutes group negotiating for individual maximizing and focuses on the dynamics of compromise needed for consensus. The shifting nature of opinion within each meeting suggests an absence of fixed preferences. Committee members debate the merits of various arguments, identifying theoretical as well as practical issues, political, administrative, as well as economic ones. It is less a process of aggregating individual preferences than negotiating an ambiguous reality.

The process of negotiating begins at the inception of each meeting and continues until the vote is taken. It connects framing to the eventual strategic action mandated for each meeting. This is accomplished through talk. It is in talking that collective sensemaking occurs. It is through talk that the meaning of frames is established and a direction for action is agreed upon. Weick (1995) calls this "sensemaking as arguing." The negotiating both reduces ambiguity and, more importantly, establishes which interpretation(s) will shape policy and which of these will be made public. Since members entertain a variety of arguments, negotiation is used to select, combine, and connect them. It is a question not of finding the right one, but of weaving enough threads together to produce a consensus.

It is important to note that this negotiating process is somewhat ritualized. Negotiations follow rules, understandings, and procedures for interaction—a negotiated order (Strauss 1978; Maines 1977; Fine 1984). At the FOMC, the chair sets the agenda, everyone who raises a hand gets a turn to speak, all members are invited and expected to participate, and the vote is not taken until a majority compromise has emerged. These rules and understandings are shaped by the structural characteristics of the setting. The Federal Reserve Act mandates twelve voting members, including the chair. Creating a majority out of this large a number of participants evokes negotiation. The relative status equality of the members (one person, one vote) evokes turn taking. The high stakes of the decisions, the visibility of their consequence, and the complexity of the issues elicits extensive discussion taking most of a day and occasionally a second day.

Also shaping negotiation is the diversity or lack of it among the participants. The mix of opinions on the Committee is shaped by a combination of the rotation of presidential appointees, changing fashions in monetary economics, and changes in the real economy. Nevertheless, diversity is limited by the fact that most participants have either worked at the Fed, taught monetary economics, or both before joining the committee. The only interest group with formal representation on the FOMC is banking, with five of the twelve votes going to the regional Federal Reserve Bank presidents.[2] In the summer of 1982, the Committee had a small group of committed monetarists, a larger group of pragmatic monetarists in the midst of disenchantment, and another small group of Keynesians more focused on economic growth than inflation. Despite these labels, all are pragmatists to the extent that they seem willing to compromise in order to reach agreement. As Lombra and Moran pointed out in an earlier quote, "new members of the Committee rather quickly assimilated into the world of ad hoc theorizing."

Each meeting begins with short reports from staff economists and the managers for foreign and domestic operations. Following these reports, the chair sets the tone by calling for open discussion. "Well, who would like to make some comments or ask questions, particularly about the economic situation, but even general questions or comments on the strategic decisions facing us?" (FOMC 1982a: 2). The chair recognizes hands and the discussion proceeds. Participants angle to build a baseline majority position. They often "piggyback" their opinion onto others or begin to define others as being in their camp.

> *Mr. Rice:* Well, Mr. Chairman, much of what I had in mind was very well stated by Jerry Corrigan. I do think the main difficulty and the main thing that puts us into the dilemma we are in is the current level of interest rates. I agree with Chuck Partee that our main objective ought to be to find a monetary policy strategy that would minimize the likelihood of shocks to the economy caused by monetary policy. . . . So, I'm in a position of trying to choose the least bad of the alternatives before us, and I think the least bad is the one that Tony (Solomon) proposed: That is, that we stick with the current targets but allow ourselves the flexibility to come in above these targets—and in my judgment, considerably above these targets—if necessary. I want to say that I'm very gratified to see so much flexibility around the table, and flexibility in unexpected quarters in some cases. (FOMC 1982s: 21)

In that short statement Mr. Rice is working hard to suggest as large a coalition as possible for his position without actually counting names. Despite the effort to piggyback, the abandonment of a tight money policy will not come without some conflict. In the following exchange, Nancy Teeters makes clear that her concern with economic growth is greater than her concern for inflation. She denotes the strength of her conviction using words like "intolerable" and "catastrophe."

Ms. Teeters: Well, I want to get interest rates down. I'm not worrying about them going up, because I think that's intolerable. Therefore, I would move toward what Pres and Chuck have said but a little more strongly. If we do get some increase in velocity, we should let it carry through and take the drop in interest rates that I think we need to keep this economy going and to avoid, really, almost a catastrophe. (FOMC 1982a: 46)

Bill Ford, a monetarist, disagrees and responds strongly to the growing interest rate concern. Finding himself in a newly emerging minority he combines humility with criticism. He gently mocks the pessimists who think that it is time to focus on economic growth, but leaves his strongest disagreement for setting interest rate caps, which would be tantamount to setting controls on the price of money. Mr. Ford's and other members' strong antagonism puts them outside of any possible compromise policy.

Mr. Ford: Well, I sense a rather interesting shift in the perspective of the Committee. I will talk about the things I agree with first. I was happy to hear you, Mr. Chairman, indicate that there is some chance that the economy may be getting better. I guess I'm a hopeless optimist, but I always notice that economists have a penchant for gloom and tend to acknowledge that a recovery his happened after it has happened. I hold onto and cherish this ray of hope that the economy may actually be turning around now; with three upward-ticks in the leading indicators and all the other positive things that one can-point to if one wants to be a little optimistic. It may be improving right now. There is, of course, the downside risk that everybody has expressed. That can't be discounted or ignored. I certainly am not a fan of high interest rates, but I very strongly oppose any shift in policy toward putting on a maximum rate cap, particularly the notion that a number of people who have already spoken have expressed of setting a rate cap at or below the present level. (FOMC 1982a: 47)

As the majority and minority positions become clear the chair assumes a more assertive role in nailing down the specifics of an agreement. In the following exchange the participants are negotiating the upper range of an interest rate target. Mr. Ford and Mr. Black, in the minority, have been pushing for 16 percent. Mr. Gramley offers a compromise where the chairman will consult with the committee through a conference call if the Fed funds rate goes above 15 percent before the next meeting. Those favoring the compromise climb on the bandwagon. When the chair senses a significant majority, he calls for a vote.

Mr. Gramley: If we have an understanding that the Chairman is going to consult if the funds rate is over 15 percent, that ought to be the upper end of our range. We ought not to say one thing and have an understanding on something else. If you're going to wait to consult until the Fed funds rate gets up to 16 percent, I'm not happy with that.

Chairman Volcker: Well, I must confess that I'm not either. In the end we might well have to, in some sense, let it go to 16 percent. But I feel strongly enough about it that that is a point where I would want to take a look at it.
Mr. Martin: I think consulting if it's over 15 percent softens the rigidity, and I would go along with it.
Ms. Teeters: All we've ever done when it hits the ceiling is let it go through. Consulting hasn't triggered any action to keep it below that level.
Chairman Volcker: . . . So, how many would find 10 to 15 percent acceptable?

In this exchange Mr. Volcker works with Mr. Gramley to build the acceptable compromise. The efforts at compromise are engendered by the requirement that the committee issue a policy directive to the open market desk to guide its purchase or sale of Treasury securities over the next six weeks. It is at this stage in the meeting that Mr. Volcker, the chair, begins to use his positional power. He asserts that he would not want the rate to go to 16 percent, softening his disagreement with the minority by using the phrase "I must confess . . ." It is the chair's prerogative to assert his position more strongly than others given both his status and public visibility. In the June and August meetings, Mr. Volcker held back and asserted a compromise position toward the end of the meeting. In the October meeting, he was out front from the beginning, pushing for the abandonment of M1 (Abolafia 2002).

SIGNALING

As the negotiating continues and a consensus policy begins to emerge, discussion focuses on externalizing the interpretation, that is, creating a plausible account for public consumption. Members of the FOMC are acutely aware that every word and action issuing from their committee are closely watched and interpreted. There is a small industry of Fed watchers at banks, brokerage firms, and the media that will parse every suspected signal. Corporations, governments, and private investors will make major investment decisions based on FOMC actions. If the Committee is to enact the environment it intends, it must control the signals it sends to whatever extent possible. As much as a third of each meeting is dedicated to shaping the sense that others will make of their work. Most of this "sensegiving" (Gioia and Chittipeddi 1991) is done through crafting the directive that that the Committee sends to the open market desk. The following quote illustrates the kinds of concerns that FOMC members express about how they will be interpreted. It is typical of the discussion that went on as the FOMC tried to change its direction toward a looser monetary policy in the summer of 1982.

Mr. Roos: I don't think it's necessary to repeat that everybody around this table would like to see lower interest rates. But these interest rates are quite obviously affected by how the financial markets view the signals that we send or the signals that we are imagined to send. And I think any change of wording in the directive that could be interpreted as signaling, even temporarily, a return to placing primary emphasis on controlling interest rates—placing a cap on interest rates or anything like that would be disastrous because people would say, after they've seen the effect on inflation of our 1979 change of emphasis, that we're going back to the old way of doing things. In an historical perspective I think the last thing the markets want to see—and this goes for this business of flexibility—is a return to a fine-tuning, interest-rate-control-oriented method of conducting policy. (FOMC 1982a: 48)

One aspect of signaling involves "psyching out" the market, that is, predicting the response of the financial community to the FOMC's action for the purpose of influencing that response. This is a major preoccupation of the members of the committee. It is very much a game of strategy in which the members try to predict the expectations and probable actions of market participants. Unlike the earlier negotiations over policy, there is no resort to data. Signaling is the most intuitive aspect of sensemaking, one in which the members rely on their experience. In the following example Mr. Balles is talking about the acceptable range for M1 and whether to announce that the Committee expects to overshoot it. His concern is with the potential unintended consequences of such an announcement.

Mr. Balles: I am in favor either of announcing an increase in the 1982 range or permitting a modest overshoot, maybe up to a point. The difficulty with not announcing it or at least saying that we're going to tolerate an overshoot is that if we have an overshoot and the market doesn't hear us say anything about not correcting it, they are going to assume that we will correct it. And that sets up expectations of a tighter policy in the weeks and months immediately ahead. They will be anticipating some action by us to tighten up again. So, we're in somewhat of a box on that score, Mr. Chairman. (FOMC 1982a: 49)

FOMC members do not settle for just predicting market response. Another aspect of psyching out the market involves controlling market expectations. Mr. Balles is pointing out that if FOMC doesn't explain that they expect an overshoot and the money supply does indeed grow faster than expected then, under the old regime, the market will expect them to tighten. Thus they must control market expectations by announcing some tolerance of an overshoot, thereby reversing three years of policy. Under monetarism, M1 targets were sacred and inflation was the foremost concern. Abandoning a once-sacred frame disturbs the stable expectations of stakeholders and creates new tensions in the signaling mechanism. This tension is a reflection of the fact that the Fed balances competing demands for economic growth and price stability. Mr. Balles is predicting that the market will expect the old equilibrium to be reestablished.

Members try to control market expectations by clarifying the signal. A frequent concern in the FOMC is that that the intention behind any signal that is sent may easily be misinterpreted or misunderstood. Whereas, in the paragraph above, members were concerned that the market would expect tightening because of adherence to monetarist rules, in the following example the concern is that the market may expect loosening. The members are concerned that a focus on interest rates will mistakenly be interpreted as a return to discredited policies.

> *Mr. Wallich:* Maybe a signal that we care about rates—a signal that we're not going to tolerate an increase in rates—would be favorable, but the market could just as well react in the opposite direction if people think we are pegging rates again. They will think we are going to flood the economy with liquidity as we've done in the past: and we may be shooting ourselves in the foot. (FOMC 1982a: 50)

> *Mr. Martin:* The consumer does not understand the technical matters. If you start talking to him about velocity, he becomes very glassy-eyed. I think the consumer understands that if we raise the targets, we may be liberalizing policy, and he may feel that's a bad thing. I don't think he will ever understand our explanations, however well expressed by anybody—excuse me, Chairman—about the overshooting phenomenon. (FOMC 1982a: 17)

The FOMC members are concerned that their explanations are too complex and that observers will assume new policy trends that aren't really there. These quotes suggest that the process of sensegiving and signaling is extremely delicate. The fear of misinterpretation constrains both the Committee's words and its actions. Members expect that there will be some misinterpretation. As a result their statements are often oblique, reducing the interpreters' certainty and making their intentions difficult to discern. Actions are probably more conservative than they would be if over-reaction on the part of the market were not a concern.

Underlying the tactics involved in psyching out lies the deeper purpose of signaling: maintaining the Fed's reputation. Not only does the Fed need to maintain its legitimacy with Congress, its creator; it also wants to keep various stakeholders in the market convinced of its serious intentions about controlling inflation. As a result of its adoption of monetarism in October 1979, the FOMC had spent nearly three years establishing that it was serious about bringing down inflation. It had taken a long time to convince the markets that the Fed would stick to a tight money policy even when under political pressure to ease up. Members were understandably reluctant to lose the credibility they had built up by raising the monetary targets. Mr. Roos went so far as to poll visitors to his regional Reserve bank including "our board of directors, twelve corporate treasurers of our largest companies who were in for lunch, and most recently the five heads of our major banks." He asked them whether the Fed should tolerate an overshoot of its monetary target or adjust the ranges upward.

> *They said:* For heavens sake, don't adjust your ranges upward because if you do that, it will be interpreted as a dramatic indication that you are softening up on your anti-inflationary effort. This was just the judgment of a bunch of people, but they felt that the danger to our credibility would be significantly less if we were to allow a minor overshoot of our stated targets rather than announce an upward adjustment of those targets. So, that's where I stand.

This position was echoed by Mr. Corrigan.

> *Mr. Corrigan:* I would stay where we are. I think changing them, particularly in the context of the fiscal situation, does entail a very high risk of some significant loss in credibility when all that has been achieved so far is so fragile. I don't want to lose that.

This reluctance is based on a desire not to squander the goodwill the Fed has worked so hard to build. The efficacy of Fed actions is tied to the market's belief that the Fed will behave consistently. This faith can become a self-fulfilling prophecy in which economic actors will restrain or increase their spending because of expectations about the Fed's commitment to a policy. Members take the credibility of the Committee very seriously. Reputation is experienced not just as an organizational characteristic but as a personal identity. Members of the FOMC are very visible in the financial community and their commitment to anti-inflation policy was frequently questioned. In the following quote, Mr. Roos refers to Chairman Volcker's heroic persona. Volcker replies modestly, but the importance of personal identity should not be minimized.

> *Mr. Roos:* Isn't it desirable, with things at least presently going our way, in effect, to word this directive much like previous directives? In other words, isn't it desirable to avoid anything that might imply any move away from such a directive? I think the world today thinks that you have done a great job since '79 in getting us where we are right now and I just—
> *Chairman Volcker:* A small part of the world?
> *Mr. Roos:* My side of the world.
> *Mr. Black:* People in St. Louis!

A final aspect of signaling involves wordcrafting: carefully constructing the signal to be sent with an eye to its interpretation(s). Members of the committee try to imagine how market participants will read specific words. Words are used to further specific goals of flexibility, clarity or even intentional ambiguity. Keeping its preferences hidden is the safest way to prevent misinterpretation. In the following example Chairman Volcker favors a wait and see policy that would give him maximum flexibility to tighten or loosen. He wants to replace specification of an interest rate range with an assurance that the committee will respond to extreme swings in the market. He proposes new wording for the directive that would serve this purpose.

> *Chairman Volcker:* I don't know how to word all this, frankly, but what I would be inclined to do—let me experiment here a bit—is to take out that last sentence entirely and replace it with something like this: "The Chairman may call for Committee consultation if it appears that pursuit of the monetary objectives and related reserve paths during the period before the next meeting is likely to be associated with unusually volatile conditions in credit markets." That covers a multitude of sins. The reason I'm reluctant to put a federal funds rate range in there is that I don't think it's realistic. (FOMC1982b: 29)

Members of the committee focus in on Volcker's use of the term "unusually volatile." The fear is that these words may be taken as a signal of extreme fragility in the financial markets.

> *Vice Chairman Solomon:* Well, if we choose the wording "unusual volatility," we haven't any range. Some of you are—
> *Mr. Partee:* It's just a question of the definition of "unusual volatility."
> *Mr. Martin:* We have a very [unintelligible] word in here.
> *Mr. Black:* Yes, all volatility is unusual but some is more unusual than others.
> *Chairman Volcker:* It has to be pretty darn unusual to be unusual compared to what we've had!
> *Mr. Wallich:* Well, they probably will think when they read this seven weeks from now that we thought the banking system was even more delicate than it had appeared to the market. I'm not sure that that is a good signal to give them ex post. (FOMC 1982b: 33)

A few minutes later the discussion clarifies that the use of this term depends on how bad you think things really are. The use of such a term can become a self-fulfilling prophecy. Volatility may increase as economic actors lose faith in financial institutions and the broader markets. Only the most liberal member of the Committee, Nancy Teeters, seems willing to send the strong signal that Volcker advocates. Mr. Volcker finds himself in the minority.

> *Mr. Corrigan:* I'm getting more and more nervous about this wording. Again. I have no problems with any of this, but this language or prospective language

about unusual volatility or instability or whatever we put in there runs at least some risk, it seems to me, of a self-fulfilling prophecy down the road.

Mr. Ford: The market will wonder why we said that.

Mr. Corrigan: I started out liking it, but I'm getting more and more gun-shy about it. I'm not sure it's the right way to go.

Chairman Volcker: I'm not sure I understand the point.

Mr. Corrigan: What I'm suggesting is that when that language is published, even though it will be some time from now, it entails some risk—and I didn't think it was much until I listened to this discussion—that we are telling the world that things are a lot worse than the world thinks they are.

Ms. Teeters: I think they're pretty bad.

Chairman Volcker: Oh, boy.

Mr. Corrigan: That's precisely what worries me. As I listen to the discussion, I'm beginning to think it's a bit too much of a red flag.

In the end, Mr. Volcker did not get his way. The Committee ended up specifying a range of 7 to 11 percent for the Fed funds rate. Volcker's response was "Well, I don't like it much, but if that's what you want to do, let's do it. Let's have a vote" (FOMC 1982b: 41). As is evident, the chair cannot dictate policy and must accept the direction in which the consensus is moving. At the next meeting, in October 1982, Mr. Volcker takes the initiative required for a major institutional change (Abolafia 2002). His aggressive sensegiving from the beginning of this meeting suggests that he is attempting to engineer a major policy change. In this meeting, which finally enacted a major change on monetary aggregates, more than half the meeting was spent discussing the wording of the directive.

DISCUSSION

Sensemaking does not occur in a vacuum. There is always a wider context shaping the frames that sensemakers employ. The Fed is both a part of the federal government of the United States and a part of the financial community. As part of the government, the FOMC regulates the money supply and is responsible for maintaining price stability and economic growth. Both Congress and the president have a strong interest in this policy domain. Several studies have tried to establish a relationship between Fed policy and institutional pressures (e.g., Woolley 1984; Havrilesky 1988; Willett 1990; Beck 1990a, b). Despite suspicion by journalists, especially during the Nixon administration, there seems to be little evidence that the Fed manipulates the money supply in support of presidential elections (Hibbs 1987; Beck 1990a). The evidence for such a "political monetary cycle" suggests that it is a product more of fiscal than of monetary policy (Beck 1990a).

Looking more specifically at the loosening of monetary policy in the summer of 1982, I found only one mention of the elections amid a variety of other causal arguments for easing up on the targets in the transcripts. In that instance a member expressed concern that the FOMC's action to ease up on the targets might be interpreted as politically motivated. This was given as reason not to ease. FOMC members seem to be more concerned with the Committee's reputation than with electoral politics. While this is not definitive evidence of member' motives, I find myself in agreement with Beck (1990a: 121) who wrote that given all the reasons to ease in the summer and fall of 1982, it would have been foolish not to take the politically expedient course.

In the case of Congress, there has never been much evidence of congressional influence on the Fed. Since Congress created the Fed in 1913 it has done very little to rein it in. It does not even have budgetary control over the Fed, allowing the Fed to fund itself out of the substantial profits it makes on its own portfolio. Attempts to correlate changes in the interest rates with measures of congressional liberalism over time show no association (Beck 1990b). Some have pointed out that the relative autonomy of the Fed allows Congress to use the Fed as a scapegoat, blaming the Fed for bad times (Kane 1980). The three meetings reviewed here suggest that blaming goes both ways. At the July meeting the members expressed considerable skepticism that Congress will get its fiscal policy under control, thereby leaving it up to the Fed to control growth.

The somewhat indignant discussion of congressional fiscal policy at the July meeting had been elicited by a budget resolution. "It is the sense of the Congress that if Congress acts to restore fiscal responsibility and reduces projected budget deficits in a substantial and permanent way, then the Federal Reserve's Open Market Committee shall reevaluate its monetary targets in order to assure that they are fully complementary to a new and more restrained fiscal policy" (FOMC 1982a: 89). The ensuing discussion suggests that the Committee hardly felt pressured.

Vice Chairman Solomon: Do you feel under an obligation to respond?

Chairman Volcker: Oh, I don't know if we have an obligation to volunteer a response. . . . Let me just say that I think what we were saying implicitly earlier was that there was great skepticism. We can say we welcome any restraint that that resolution signifies or will result in and we encourage the action in that respect, but we have a good deal of skepticism or questioning at this point. It could be put more strongly. Or put more politely there was no assurance, if I may put it that way, that the budgetary figure was going to come in at $104 billion or thereabouts next year. . . . But certainly there was some concern over the net result of the resolution. It is constructive in the right direction but a concern was expressed by a number of people about the budgetary outlook . . .

Mr. Roos: Do you think the Congress is serious? . . . They didn't really expect us to do more than put together some verbiage that would be respectful and dismiss it, did they? (FOMC 1982a: 92)

There seems little predisposition in the Committee to shape policy based on congressional pressure. At this point in Fed history, the agency enjoyed high public approval, the kind of approval that would be likely to expand its sense of autonomy. It seems more likely to be responsive to congressional pressure in periods of broad disapproval, when its legitimacy and survival are threatened. The last major reform of the Fed was in the 1930s. Since that time the Fed has grown both more influential and more autonomous.

The Fed is not just a government regulatory agency. It is a central bank, and as such it is part of a wider financial community. It is this community that is its major constituency. Members of the FOMC freely discuss the expected reaction of markets to their actions, arguing for policies based on their likely credibility with those markets. Since the events of 1982, the Fed has worked hard to maintain its reputation as a tight money inflation hawk, a position strongly favored by the financial community. On the other hand, the transcripts reflect little concern with unemployment and there is no representation of labor. It is not so much that the Fed is captured by the money and credit markets as it is part of them. The Fed is part of a larger system of sensemaking in the financial markets that is going on continuously. All participants in the credit and money markets are anchoring, negotiating, and signaling in keeping with their place in the market system. The Fed, in its position as smoother and guarantor of the system, is the master sensemaker, but each unit in the system takes part. As White (1981) explains, actors in the market are looking at each other, trying to judge the other's intentions. The Fed is simply the largest, most important of these actors in the network.

CONCLUSION

This paper has focused on the social processes of policy elites who are also economic actors participating in and shaping markets. This focus on economic action argues for an interpretivist/pragmatist approach to economic sociology. Such an approach brings attention back to the economic actors themselves, focusing on their efforts to construct the market. It challenges economic sociologists to remember that structures are the product of action and that this action is constructed in complex political, economic, administrative, and experiential contexts. Using an interpretivist approach we may hear the voices of these pragmatic actors coping with ambiguity, complexity, and responsibility. This approach also draws attention to the tentative nature of knowledge in economic decision making. Not only do policy elites not consider all alternatives nor apply the best available models, they intuit from ambiguous data, they argue over interpretations, they compromise, and they knit together solutions. The actors consider their decisions tentative and subject to iterative correction. Ultimately, they are compelled to act by the mandate of their role, but the action itself has significant improvised characteristics.

The ambiguous and limited nature of the information available for policymaking precipitates sensemaking: placing available stimuli into frameworks. The assumption that neatly packaged statistics and projections are adequate for strategic thinking is fallacious. Such data lack richness, are overly aggregated, and are often in need of revision at the time they are used. Policymakers prefer to weave complex narratives that are used retrospectively and prospectively. The oscillation in decision criteria found in this study reflects efforts to create a richer, more pertinent narrative. As such this constant reframing is a rational response to the situation, presumably more rational then applying models that aren't trusted. Monetary policy then is a consequence of an ongoing process of sensemaking and sensegiving. There is no inherent truth to be discovered. Rather, Committee members use their sensemaking craft to arrive at a plausible interpretation of reality that they expect will maintain market stability and their own legitimacy.

NOTES

1. It is not that models of monetary policy do not exist, but rather that the members of the FOMC, viewing them as inadequate, do not choose to base their discussion on them. Economist and former FOMC member Alan Blinder has written, "We do not know the model, and we do not know the objective function, so we cannot compute the optimal policy rule" (1998: 6).

2. Seven of the twelve members are appointed by the president of the United States. Each serves for fourteen years, well beyond the term of the president. The other five members are presidents of regional Federal Reserve banks. These five positions rotate among the twelve bank presidents. The strongest inflation hawks in 1982 came from among the regional bank presidents.

REFERENCES

Abolafia, Mitchel Y. 2002. "Framing Moves: The Micropolitics of Institutional Change." Working paper, Rockefeller College of Public Affairs and Policy, State University of New York at Albany.

Beck, Nathaniel. 1990a. "Political Monetary Cycles." In *The Political Economy of American Monetary Policy*, ed. Thomas Mayer. Cambridge: Cambridge University Press. 115–30.

——. 1990b. "Congress and the Fed." In *The Political Economy of American Monetary Policy*, ed. Thomas Mayer. Cambridge: Cambridge University Press. 131–50.

Bernstein, Richard J. 1997. "Pragmatism, Pluralism, and the Healing of Wounds." In *Pragmatism: A Reader*, ed. Louis Menand. New York: Vintage. 382–401.

Blinder, Alan S. 1998. *Central Banking in Theory and Practice*. Cambridge, Mass.: MIT Press.

Daft, Richard and Karl E. Weick. 1984. "Toward a Model of Organizations and Interpretation Systems." *Academy of Management Review* 9: 284–95.

Fine, Gary Alan. 1984. "Negotiated Orders and Organizational Cultures." *Annual Review of Sociology* 10: 239–62.

FOMC. 1982a. "Transcript—Federal Open Market Committee Meeting June 30–July 1, 1982." Board of Governors of the Federal Reserve.

——. 1982b. "Transcript—Federal Open Market Committee Meeting August 24, 1982." Board of Governors of the Federal Reserve.

——. 1982c. "Transcript—Federal Open Market Committee Meeting October 6, 1982." Board of Governors of the Federal Reserve.

Gioia, Dennis and Kumar Chittipeddi. 1991. "Sensemaking and Sensegiving in Strategic Change Initiation." *Strategic Management Journal* 12: 433–48.

Havrilesky, Thomas. 1988. "Monetary Policy Signaling from the Administration to the Federal Reserve." *Journal of Money Credit, and Banking* 20: 83–101.

Hibbs, Douglas. 1987. *The American Political Economy*. Cambridge, Mass.: Harvard University Press.

Kane, Edward. 1980. "Politics and Fed Policy-Making." *Journal of Monetary Economics* 6: 199–212.

Karamouzis, Nicholas and Raymond Lombra. 1989. "Federal Reserve Policymaking: An Overview and Analysis of the Policy Process." In *International Debt Federal Reserve Operations and Other Essays*, ed. Karl Brunner and Allan Meltzer. Amsterdam: North-Holland. 7–62.

Knorr-Cetina, Karin D. 1981. *The Manufacture of Knowledge*. Oxford: Pergamon.

Lombra, Raymond and Michael Moran. 1980. "Policy Advice and Policymaking at the Federal Reserve." In *Monetary Institutions and Policy Processes*, ed. Karl Brunner and Allan Meltzer. Amsterdam: North-Holland. 9–68.

Maines, David R. 1977. "Social Organization and Social Structure in Symbolic Interactionist Thought." *Annual Review of Sociology* 3: 235–59.

Maines, David. 1982. "In Search of Mesostructure: Studies in Negotiated Order." *Urban Life* 11: 267–79.

Maisel, Sherman J. 1973. *Managing the Dollar*. New York: W.W. Norton.

Mayer, Thomas, ed. *The Political Economy of American Monetary Policy*. Cambridge: Cambridge University Press.

Mills, C. Wright. 1940. "Situated Actions and Culture." *American Sociological Review* 5: 904–13.

Perrow, Charles. 1986. *Complex Organizations: A Critical Essay*. New York: Random House.

Persson, Torsten and Guido Tabellini, eds. *Monetary and Fiscal Policy.* Cambridge, Mass.: MIT Press.

Rein, Martin and Donald Schon. 1996. "Frame Critical Policy Analysis and Frame Reflective Policy Practice." *Knowledge and Policy: The International Journal of Knowledge Transfer and Utilization* 9: 85–104.

Simon, Herbert A. 1997. *Administrative Behavior.* 4th ed. New York: Free Press.

Starbuck, William H. 1983. "Organizations as Action Generators." *American Sociological Review* 48: 91–102.

Starbuck, William H. and Frances Milliken. 1988. "Executives' Perceptual Filters: What They Notice and How They Make Sense." In *The Executive Effect: Concepts and Methods for Studying Top Managers,* ed. Donald Hambrick. Greenwich, Conn.: JAI Press.

Strauss, Anselm L. 1978. *Negotiations: Varieties, Contexts, Processes, and Social Order.*

Weick, Karl E. 1995. *Sensemaking in Organizations.* Thousand Oaks, Calif.: Sage.

White, Harrison C. 1981. "Where Do Markets Come From?" *American Journal of Sociology* 87: 517–47.

Willett, Thomas. 1990. "Studying the Fed: Toward a Broader Public-Choice Perspective." In *The Political Economy of American Monetary Policy,* ed. Thomas Mayer. Cambridge: Cambridge University Press.

Woolley, John. 1984. *Monetary Politics: The Federal Reserve and the Politics of Monetary Policy.* Cambridge: Cambridge University Press.

Information Inequality and Network Externalities: A Comparative Study of the Diffusion of Television and the Internet

Paul DiMaggio and Joseph Cohen

THE TERM "NETWORK" HAS become a dominant trope in studies of contemporary capitalism, used to explain what distinguishes advanced capitalism from its industrial predecessors (DiMaggio 2002). Capitalist workplaces are alleged to be more egalitarian with more lateral and fewer hierarchical ties than their more bureaucratic ancestors. Companies are said to collaborate to a greater degree, their ties characterized more by the fluidity and give-and-take of social relationships than by the fixity and formality of arms-length contractual agreements. Consumers purchase goods as much for their ego-congruence as for their instrumental utility, bolstering identities negotiated in social interaction rather than through fixed and formal statuses. The global economy itself is portrayed as a vast network of exchanges that crisscross national boundaries, leaving states powerless to control them. It is clear that students of capitalism have found networks "good to think with," in Mary Douglas's phrase (1979: 40), a powerful metaphor for capturing the fluidity and reach of economic relations. Indeed, in the most ambitious effort to characterize contemporary capitalism, Manuel Castells (1996) characterizes the dominant contemporary social formation as "the network society."

In this chapter, we focus on two more concrete and specific ways in which networks figure into the practice and study of contemporary capitalism. The first is as concrete technology. Communications networks are the vehicles through which information flows, and for the past century, information and the services used to communicate it have become ever larger components of capitalist production and distribution, roughly doubling (with nontrivial disagreements resting on definitional issues) in the

The authors thank the editors for wise and helpful editorial suggestions. Research support from the Russell Sage Foundation and from the National Science Foundation, Office of Science and Technology through grants NSF01523184 and NSF0086143 is gratefully acknowledged.

advanced economies during the last half of the twentieth century (Machlup 1962; Porat 1977; Rubin and Huber 1986; Castells 1996). Global telecommunications networks did not *cause* the changes in capitalist workplaces noted above, but they clearly facilitated them (Castells 2001). Mobile telecommunications increase both the ease with which employees can share information and solve problems across departmental lines and the costs to firms that insist on maintaining hierarchical lines of communication. New kinds of management information systems permit firms to coordinate their activities in real time by making data on production schedules and inventories immediately accessible to both partners. The Internet places an immense range of products within the grasp of anyone with sufficient income, facilitating new levels of stylistic differentiation and enabling middle-class consumers to reinvent themselves with props from around the world. And global communications networks undergird the transborder flows of money and data upon which the world economy has come to depend. In this sense, then, "network" as trope rests on "network" as literal technology.

Second, we employ "network" as a theoretical construct, drawing on economic theories of "network goods" and services. Network goods and services are those that exhibit "network externalities": that is, their value to adopters increases as a function of the number of other people who use them. Such technologies have increased in number and importance over the past century, as people's consumption decisions and opportunities have become more interdependent. We draw on the work of economists to understand patterns of technology diffusion, and expand upon it by suggesting that the concept should be understood more broadly to include social, as well as individually instrumental, utilities.

Our interest in these topics was stimulated by the senior author's research on inequality in access to and use of the Internet in the United States, and therefore we focus on that technology in much of this chapter. Once one documents inequality in access to a relatively new technology, it becomes imperative to understand the trajectory along which that technology is diffusing. Without a model of the diffusion process, one has no way of knowing whether a given level of inequality represents a long-term policy challenge or a temporary inconvenience. Thinking about the Internet leads one to ask what general factors account for group-specific patterns of technology adoption. This line of questioning that led us both to the notion of "network externalities" *and* to the exploratory analysis, comparing the early diffusion trajectories of television and the Internet, with which we conclude this chapter.

We have three goals here. First, we want to bring the economic construct of network externalities into sociological analysis of technological inequality, while at the same time inflecting it sociologically. Second, we sketch a comparative model explaining variation in the diffusion patterns of different communications technologies, in order to place the Internet case in a broader theoretical and empirical context. Third, we present findings from a comparative analysis of household adoption of television from 1948 to 1957 and the Internet from 1994 to 2002 that cast light on the extent to which intergroup inequality in Internet access is likely to persist as the diffusion process continues.

SOCIAL INEQUALITY AND INTERNET ACCESS, 1994–2003

Social scientists recognize that information plays a crucial role in processes that generate social inequality. Measures of "aptitude" or "achievement" (which serve as proxies for generalized information or for the capacity to acquire information) are staples of work in educational attainment. Studies of the impact of networks on career advancement (Granovetter 1974; Burt 1992) and consumer purchases (DiMaggio and Louch 1996) emphasize the role that interpersonal relationships play in the acquisition of market information. It stands to reason that if information is important, then command of technologies that provide access to information or facilitate communication (telephones, fax machines, television sets, computer modems) must help people get ahead. Yet with few exceptions (Attewell 2001; Autor et al. 1998), neither sociologists nor economists have studied systematically the relationship between life chances, on the one hand, and access to information technology and the ability to use it, on the other.

The Internet, which occupied such a large space in America's consciousness during the technology boom of the 1990s, began to change this situation. By appearing to reduce the marginal cost of information and communications nearly to zero, the Internet and World Wide Web inspired extravagant claims that a new age of information equality was dawning. Now everyone, the Web's advocates claimed, could have access to the best information about health, the means to participate fully in the polity, wide-ranging information about job opportunities, and other advantages formerly restricted to the well to do or well educated. Because people can benefit from the Internet's offerings only if they can go on-line, it was natural for policymakers to worry about, and social scientists to study, the "digital divide," as inequality in access to this new technology came to be called.

The basic dimensions of the digital divide are well known (DiMaggio et al. 2004). In the United States, having a college education, a high income, "white" racial identification, and youth all raise the odds of having Internet access. In 2001, among Americans aged eighteen or older, just 26 percent of African-Americans compared to 47 percent of everyone else could go on-line from home. So could more than two of three college graduates, but just 43 percent of high school graduates who had not gone on to college. Americans with family incomes greater than $67,500 were twice as likely to live in homes with Internet service as those with incomes from $20,000 to $30,0000, and people aged eighteen to twenty-five were twice as likely to have such service as persons older than fifty-five (DiMaggio et al. 2004, table 1).

Policy analysts and communications experts agree that these differences exist but quarrel over what they mean. The problem is this: At any point in a diffusion process, intergroup inequalities reflect distinctive diffusion processes for particular population subgroups. If groups are traveling along the same path, but have started at different points and are proceeding at different speeds, different adoption rates simply reflect the shape of the diffusion curve and the groups' relative progress toward a common destination. If their trajectories are radically different, disadvantages may persist indefinitely.

Most diffusion processes are roughly S-shaped, with a long and gradual build-up period followed by a rapid ascent after which growth levels off. For technologies that are eventually adopted universally (or nearly so), absolute differences in penetration rates between more and less advantaged groups tend to be modest during the build-up phase, spiral upward during the early takeoff phase, and diminish rapidly once the less advantaged group has also entered take-off and the rate of increase of the more advantaged group has slowed. The global diffusion rate for a given society, of course, represents the aggregate of these different group-specific trajectories.

Between 1994 and 2001 (the last year of Current Population Survey data available to us), different intergroup disparities followed differing paths. Gender inequality in Internet access, significant in the mid-1990s, largely disappeared, and place of residence likewise became less important. By contrast, inequality in access on the basis of race, educational attainment, and income remained substantial (DiMaggio et al. 2004).

There are many reasons for the persistence of intergroup differences, not the least of which is their mutually reinforcing character due to correlations among education, income, and race. The underlying process generating these differences is one of individual choice under institutional constraint. Institutional factors loom large because of unequal access to schools and jobs that provide access to and training in new technologies, unequal investments in neighborhood libraries or community technology centers, and unequal access to high-speed Internet service based on place of residence. Many, although not all, of these institutional factors tend to raise the effective cost of Internet access (in time or money) to precisely those people—low-income persons with relatively little education—who have fewer resources to invest in information technology in the first place. Individual choice is also crucial, especially for household Internet service, because, except in those rare cases where a resident's employer provides it, at least one household member must invest in a service contract.

Individual choices to invest in communications technologies and related goods and services are systematically different from choices to purchase many other kinds of goods and services. Most goods are "rival": if I consume them there will be fewer left for you. Consumption of many other services is competitive: purchasing more or better education offers advantages to me only if you decline to do the same. By contrast, comunications technologies tend to have what economists refer to as "network properties," whereby my purchase of a good or service may *increase* its value to you. Indeed, one can argue that an important feature of contemporary capitalism is the increasing economic and social prevalence and importance of goods and services with "network externalities" relative to earlier market economies. In order to understand the factors influencing inequality in access to the Internet, then, it is necessary to understand a little about goods and services of this kind.

NETWORK EXTERNALITIES, TECHNICAL AND SOCIAL

A product or service possesses network externalities if the utility one derives from it is a positive function of the number of other people who consume it.[1] For example, a telephone is of little value if no one else is using it; of moderate value if only a few of one's potential contacts use it; and indispensable if everyone uses it. Most communications technologies are network goods in this sense: They literally constitute a network, and the value of the network depends on the number of persons (or organizations or other entities) connected to it (Shy 2001; Varian 2000).

Earlier communications technologies typically came in the form of goods (newspapers, books, magazines) or services (performing-arts events, the conveyance of telegraph messages). By contrast, modern communications technologies typically combine a product (radio, telephone, fax machine, television set, computer, or piece of software) *and* a service (broadcast programming, telephone service, fax transmission, or Internet access). Also typically, the real money is in selling the service (which produces an ongoing revenue stream) rather than the product (which is usually a one-shot purchase), and the value of the service derives from the number of persons on-line, which is to say the positive network externalities. Often these externalities are *direct*: The value of e-mail to me depends on how many of my friends I can reach through it. The value of Kazaa to its users depends on how many other users make their own MP3 collections accessible through it. The more people participate in eBay auctions, the more attractive the merchandise and the more spirited the bidding. Positive network externalities may also be *indirect*, based on role complementarity. The more people who watch a network television program, the more advertisers will compete to buy commercial time on it; the more people who put Acrobat Reader on their computer, the more likely are people who want to share documents to buy the full software package; the more consumers join Pay Pal, the more merchants will give Pay Pal a cut of their revenue for mediating transactions. Such complementary network externalities often redound to the benefit of nonpaying consumers (in the form, for example, of more lavishly produced television shows, more accessible manuscripts, or easier on-line shopping).

This feature of information technologies (that they simultaneously comprise products and services, and that these services entail significant network externalities) produces a distinctive form of business strategy: subsidization of some forms of consumption in order to build networks large enough to sustain particularly profitable revenue streams. Thus IBM shared its operating system with software makers in the 1980s, telephone companies practically give away cell phones to new subscribers, and you can download Netscape or Acrobat Reader software for free. (Where producers are unable to charge continuing fees for services, they may take the opposite approach. Thus in the 1920s, producers of radio equipment subsidized radio programming in order to sell more radio sets [Douglas 1987: 299–300].)

Social Network Externalities

So far we have been talking about material or market externalities, where the rewards to network expansion are of tangible utility to consumers, service providers, or advertisers. From a sociological perspective, there are other, equally important, forms of network externalities, both negative and positive, which may also play a role in the diffusion of new technologies. We define an externality as *social* when the size or composition of the market for a good or service influences the value of consumption of that good or service *as an input into an individual production function, the output of which is social identity*. We discuss briefly three simple and familiar kinds of social network externality.

Societal Membership as a Network Externality. People need certain goods or services to be full-fledged members of their community (Rainwater 1974). Within any community, there are reasonably well-established expectations about what bona fide members owe one another in terms of both availability and knowledgeability. The spread of communications and information technologies extended the scope and changed the nature of such claims. With respect to availability, Americans, for example, are expected to be reachable by telephone. Individuals without telephone service occupy a kind of social and labor-market limbo. (Within the academic community, failure to use e-mail came to be perceived as a lamentable abdication of citizenship obligations at some point during the early 1990s.)

With respect to information, the emergence of mass communications placed a premium on certain kinds of baseline knowledge, which became the stuff of everyday conversation. In the contemporary United States, knowledge of this kind is occasionally political—Americans expect one another to have opinions about presidential candidates, and to be able to identify such figures as Arnold Schwarzenegger and Osama Bin Ladin. More often, however, such information concerns popular forms of entertainment like *The Simpsons, Seinfeld, South Park,* or *Sesame Street.* As Horace Newcomb and Paul Hirsch (1983) and W. Russell Neuman (1991) have noted, television has played a key role as a source of such socially expected information since the 1950s, a role to which it was well suited during the network era but which the proliferation of cable channels and satellite services has undermined. Goods and services that provide such socially expected information are an integral medium through which groups convey basic elements of their shared construction of reality, making connectivity essential if one wants to participate in communal discussion and comprehension of the world.

Information and communications technologies that are sources of socially mandated forms of availability and knowledgeability become effectively indispensable. To achieve such social indispensability, technologies must have two properties. First, they must be reasonably attractive and effective. (The advantages of telephone communication became quickly apparent, although economic factors slowed its spread, and television beguiled audiences from the start.) Second, they must be economically affordable (either because they require one-shot purchases like television sets, or because minimal service is kept relatively cheap as a matter of public policy, as is the case for telephone and basic cable service in the United States). If these conditions are present, social-membership externalities eventually reach a tipping point at which only the very poor or very eccentric will do without them. Indeed, near universal diffusion is probably only achieved by technologies for which such social-membership externalities are present.

Status-Group Affiliation as a Network Externality. By "status group," I refer to a social group united by a shared sense of identity, a common status culture, and practices that produce internal cohesion and clear boundaries. Certain forms of communication and information technologies are useful in the production of group identities, with their utility increasing with the proportion of group members employing the technology. (Goods with this type of externality are similar to what economists have called "club" goods.) In some cases, as when Islamic militants in pre-revolutionary Iran used sound cassettes as a means of spreading their beliefs because other media were closed to them (Manuel 1993), a technology is put to practical use.

This is also the case for virtual groups (for example, isolated persons with low-incidence medical conditions or political extremists with low-incidence ideologies) that the Internet has brought together and given voice. In other cases, consumption may be more strictly symbolic (e.g., the ubiquitous use of transistor radios by U.S. teenagers in the 1960s, of pagers by their urban counterparts in the 1980s, or of Internet-equipped cellular devices among contemporary Japanese adolescents).

Prestige and Negative Externalities. Since Veblen (1899), economists have noted that consumers pursue certain goods because they bestow social distinction upon their possessors. For consumers of such goods, the diffusion of a technology or product to additional strata represents a negative externality because it reduces the prestige value of consumption. This can occur when the price falls, when the technology becomes simpler, or when producers alter the contents to make it more appealing to a mass audience. Negative externalities are relatively rare in information and communications technologies, although they can be discerned in the negative response of some techies to the commercialization of the Internet or to the rise of mass portals like AOL; in cases in which original participants in interactive spaces withdraw when the number of less committed or less sophisticated users multiplies; or, as we shall see, in the aversion of college graduates to television during the 1950s. Other things equal, prestige hierarchies moderate the slope of adoption curves, as early adopters flee in the face of new entrants.

Note that we use the term "network good" more broadly and loosely than do economists, who restrict it to what we refer to in figure 1 as "pure network goods." We broaden the term in three ways. First, we identify "social" as well as "instrumental" externalities, and suggest that the former may be as important as the latter. Second, we regard the extent to which a good or service possesses network externalities as a continuous variable, rather than viewing network goods and other goods as clearly separable classes. Third, we identify two analytically independent dimensions of "networkness," the degree to which goods' use entails social interaction and the extent to which users care about the specific identities of other consumers.[2]

Network Externalities, Social Networks, and Technology Diffusion

Think of diffusion curves as the precipitate of millions of individual choices. Such choice processes can be modeled in the following way (Granovetter and Soong 1983). Each potential adopter places a value on the technology, such that she or he will purchase it when its cost falls to her or his reservation price. Where reservation prices are normally distributed and scale economies apply, we get the familiar S-curve. Each new wave of adoption reduces the cost a little bit, so that it reaches the level at which new consumers will sign on. (Because reservation prices are normally distributed it does this at an increasing rate, generating a slow uptake followed by a rapid ascent.) Where reservation prices are clumpy or scale economies weak, the process may be arrested early on, so that only a small proportion of the potential market ever adopts.

We expect network externalities to generate the S-curve in a similar, but exaggerated way, due to the interaction of two mutually reinforcing processes. First, prices decline due to economies of scale. Second, at the same time, the *value* that potential consumers place on the good—and therefore their reservation prices—rises at the same time, as more people adopt. This combination of scale-economy dynamics and ascending reservation prices can yield explosive patterns of growth, similar to the increase in Internet usage in the U.S. between 1995 and 2000.

Not all network externalities have the same implications for diffusion processes, however. Although all network externalities lead users to benefit as a function of the overall size of the user population, they vary along two key, correlated dimensions (see figure 1). First, to what extent does use of the technology entail direct interaction with other users? Second, to what extent do users care who else is using the technology? The two are correlated: In general, we care about the identities of technology users more if we use the technology to interact with them. We sign on to an instant messaging service not because lots of other people do but because *our friends or family members* use it. We download Adobe Acrobat Reader because we believe that the particular people who use Acrobat Writer will produce .pdf files that we will want to read. In these cases, adoption by many users raises our reservation price only slightly, but adoption by a few particular users may increase it significantly. So network externalities are strongest, and the dynamics associated with them particularly intense, in the bottom right region of figure 1, where both identity specificity and intensity of interaction are high.

When we neither care about the identities of other technology users nor interact with them, network externalities are weak—so weak that economists do not even consider such technologies to be network goods. Rather, they use the term "scale economies" to refer to benefits conferred upon producers by third parties (for example, vendors who reduce prices or advertisers who pay more for airtime), some fraction of which are passed on to consumers in the form of lower prices or higher quality (in response to which potential adopters may raise their reservation prices).

The correlation is not perfect, however. The mass media have social-membership externalities that enable us to refer to media content in interaction with many other people. But we do not care (or at least not very much) *who* else is watching Seinfeld reruns, the Emmy Awards show, or

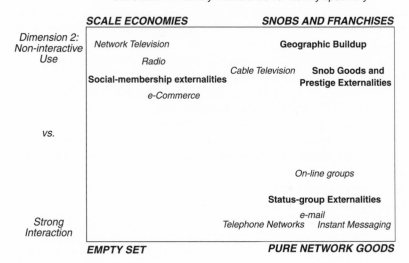

Figure 1 Types of network externalities.

the Olympics. Rather we value the fact that we can make conversation about such media content with almost anyone we happen to meet.

On the other hand, people who use commodities for status display may care deeply that the right kind of people have adopted a given product (e.g., a Movado watch or an expensive brand of Scotch) even though it is only rarely a focus of interaction. Technologies like cable television that require local infrastructure also inhabit the upper right quadrant, but for a quite different reason: because of physical constraints, distribution markets are localized, and other people's adoption will only enhance the availability and quality of my service if those other adopters occupy the same service area as I do.

Why Network Externalities Make a Difference to Technology Adoption. Network externalities are important for technology diffusion because they make adoption decisions interdependent. This in turn means that the structure of social networks—in particular, density, homophily, and the location and availability of "bridges" connecting networks comprising people of different kinds (Rogers 2003: 306; Watt 1999)—will have important implications for adoption rates in general, and for intergroup inequalities in particular. Network structures interact with the types of externalities illustrated in figure 1. Each location in figure 1 mandates a characteristic pattern of diffusion, other things equal. The further to the right on the *x*-axis (identity specificity), the more adoption will be bound by the contours of social networks, and tend to occur one network region at a time. (This is because my reservation price becomes lower not when *anyone* adopts, but only when someone in my own social circle comes on board.) The further to the left on the *x*-axis, the more adoption will be driven by individual convenience and exposure to marketing. The *y*-axis refers primarily to the rate at which adoption information circulates—quickly at the bottom, where the technology is a focus of interaction, more slowly at the top—and therefore largely influences the rate at which the process proceeds.

True network goods—that is, those that are high in interactivity and identity specificity—are likely to have distinctive growth profiles, based on the island-like quality of group-specific diffusion processes (where "group" refers to a relatively highly bounded social network). Adoption proceeds slowly within each network region until reaching a tipping point after which network members find the new technology indispensable. Depending upon the number and shape of bridges across network regions, adoption will cascade from one network region to another, as "bridges" (persons connected to others in each network area) act as seeds for new adoption processes.

What does this have to do with intergroup inequality in access to the Internet? First, the Internet is a network service par excellence—or rather it is a technology that includes a range of network services (e-mail, instant messaging, interactive discussion groups, file-sharing software), in addition to some services with weaker network externalities (e.g., on-line shopping, downloading IRS forms). It seems likely that most adoption to this point has been driven more by the former than by the latter.

Second, due to *social homophily* (the tendency of people to interact most heavily with people like themselves) the network regions in which adoption gestates and across which diffusion cascades are often characterized by substantial homogeneity with respect to such things as educational attainment, income, and race. Although a formal development of these ideas is beyond this chapter's scope, intuitively it seems likely that, other things equal, the rate at which initially disadvantaged groups catch up with initially advantaged groups will depend not simply on the economic resources they command, but also on the homogeneity of the social networks in which they participate. Where social isolation of outgroups is high, members of initially low-adopting social categories may have little reason to adopt a network technology. Where interaction across categorical boundaries is high, one would expect intergroup disparities to be only temporary. The fact that differences in Internet access related to race and educational attainment, for example, have shown little sign of abating is consistent with research demonstrating high levels of network homophily with respect to these very characteristics (Marsden 1987).

Toward a Comparative Model of Technology Diffusion

The strength and nature of network externalities is only one of the factors that influence patterns of technology diffusion and the extent and tenacity of intergroup inequality in adoption. In this section we take an inventory of consequential conditions.

One set of influences is technological. Diffusion rates are shaped by the development and location of infrastructure necessary to sustain individual or household use (e.g., local broadcasters for television, broadband connections for streaming video). In the early years of television, the major constraint on adoption was whether one lived close enough to a broadcast station to receive the signal. In the early years of high-speed Internet service, major constraints have included the distance of one's home from one's ISP and the age of the local cable system (for DSL and cable, respectively).

Purely economic influences also come into play. Cost significantly constrains adoption, especially early in the diffusion process before significant scale economies have been achieved. Equally important is the distinction between one-time purchases (like television sets) and services (like telecommunications) that require monthly fees. Even expensive consumer items often become widely available at low prices once scale economies are reached and secondary markets develop. By contrast, monthly service fees place ongoing pressure on household budgets.

A third set of influences reflect the technology's fit with existing knowledge and practice, and the extent to which potential consumers can assimilate it to routines of everyday life. Historians have demonstrated that new technologies ordinarily shape themselves to the contours of existing practices, affording opportunities more than affecting behavior (Agre 1998). In the short run, at least, technologies that are simple to use and reinforce familiar behavior patterns will diffuse more quickly than those that are difficult to use or require users to change their habits.

A fourth set of influences reflects the versatility of the technology. By versatility, we refer, first, to the number of uses to which the technology can be put, and, second, for information technologies, to the diversity of content that one can find on it. Other things equal, there will be greater demand for technologies that can be put to many uses. The greater the content diversity, the more similarly will members of different identity groups value the technology.

A final set of influences are institutional: first, strategies of the business enterprises that develop and distribute the technology, and, second, policies of government. Business strategies enhance diffusion rates and reduce intergroup differences when firms subsidize initial adoption. They are likely to do this when programming is paid for by third parties (for example, when audience size augments advertising revenue) or when adopters must make recurrent purchases (for example, ink cartridges for printers). Businesses are more likely to cultivate small, segmented markets insofar as consumption entails negative externalities (for example, snob appeal or information of competitive value, for which a few purchasers will pay a great deal). Government may stimulate a technology's development by subsidizing capital costs (which increases diffusion rates, but does not reduce intergroup differences). Or government may seek to reduce intergroup inequality by subsidizing (or mandating the subsidization) of adoption for groups based on income (e.g., policies that aim to keep the cost of local basic telephone or cable service low) or life-cycle stage (e.g., technology grants to public schools or senior centers).

Each of these sources of variation has different implications for inequality in access (see table 1). Cost shapes inequality with respect to income (and characteristics or identities that are correlated with income). Infrastructure availability shapes inequality by place of residence (rural areas ordinarily have less well-developed communications infrastructures than urban places) and may make income more important (e.g., if the well-off can compensate for locational disadvantage through spending, as when prosperous rural dwellers purchase high-speed, high-cost Internet connections using satellite dishes). When users require knowledge or skill to make a technology useful, we are likely to see more inequality with respect to formal education (with more educated people better able to learn how to use the technology) and age (with younger people more likely to receive training in school or at work). Versatility should dampen intergroup differences and (other things equal) increase the rate of adoption. Versatility may also shape the competitive challenges facing innovators, with versatile technologies capable of competing on a number of fronts and avoiding direct competition with powerful existing media. Business strategies or government policies that affect the costs and benefits of different consumer groups differentially may exacerbate or moderate inequality.

It follows from the heterogeneity of factors affecting adoption, and the differing position of groups with respect to these factors, that inequality based on different individual characteristics may vary sharply over the course of the diffusion process, with some groups attaining advantages early on that they lose thereafter (Bonus 1973; Van den Bulte and Lilien 2001: 1411). We have already described the influence of network externalities on diffusion processes, and their dependence on the structure of subcommunity networks and the prevalence of bridges among them. The impact of residence often declines over time as technical infrastructure is built out or delivery technologies become more sophisticated and powerful.

Table 1
Factors Influencing the Rate of and Intergroup Inequality in Information
Technology Diffusion

Influencing factor	Implication if high
Extent of network externalities Instrumental Social (Membership, Identity, Prestige)	Exaggerates nonlinearity in adoption pattern; the more that externalities are identity- specific, the more persistent will intergroup differences be, in proportion to the lack of intergroup interaction, and the more network structure will matter.
Location-specificity of *distribution technology*	Increases urban-rural/ metropolitan- nonmetropolitan inequality; often income inequality.
Cost One-time purchase price Is there an ongoing cost?	The higher the price, the greater the impact of income on adoption. Income especially strong predictor of adoption of technologies that require subscriptions or other ongoing expense.
Complexity Skill requirements Fit to existing routines	High complexity (in both senses) leads to high educational inequality in adoption, and advantages younger adopters.
Versatility Functional versatility (variety of affordances) Content diversity	Increases rate of adoption and reduces intergroup differences in adoption. Implications for competition (none, head-on, multiple fronts).
Institutional policies Business strategies Government policies	Third-party payments and ongoing expenses lead businesses to subsidize adoption. Government subsidies to disadvantaged groups reduce inequality.

The impact of income declines insofar as diffusion is accompanied by producers' exploitation of scale economies. The effects of education and age are likely to decline if technical interfaces become simpler and if new practices associated with new technologies become institutionalized and taken for granted.

These observations constitute an analytic framework and nothing more. It remains to develop these hypotheses through simulation modeling of adoption processes and to test such refined hypotheses through appropriate comparisons among individuals, technologies, and national societies. In the remainder of this chapter, we illustrate the possibilities with a primitive comparison between diffusion patterns in the United States for two influential communication technologies: television and the Internet.

Television and the Internet: An Heuristic Comparison

Recall that this inquiry began with the following question: Does inequality in access to the Internet reflect the differing rates at which different groups are proceeding along a single trajectory, or does it represent intractable patterns of disadvantage such that different groups will follow fundamentally different trajectories with different outcomes? Our goal, then, is to develop a comparative framework to explain variation in the trajectories of different information and communications technologies, including the extent of intergroup inequality during and at the end of the diffusion process. In this section, we apply the framework developed in the previous sections of this paper to a comparison of television and the Internet, focusing on the first decade or so of the market for each.

Comparing Television to the Internet

How do television and the Internet compare on the salient dimensions identified earlier in this chapter? Table 2 summarizes key differences that are posited to influence the rate and trajectory of diffusion and the degree and persistence of socioeconomic inequality.

Externalities. One important difference is that the Internet possesses much stronger network externalities than television. Many of the most popular Internet-based programs (electronic mail, instant messaging, peer-to-peer networks, auction sites, and various kinds of interactive spaces) are valuable in proportion to the number of people who participate. Moreover, many of these network externalities have high levels of specificity with respect to the particular persons who participate. In addition to the pure economic externalities, there are also important social-identity externalities, as the Internet generates new areas of expertise and new materials for the construction and maintenance of distinctive identities and status cultures. The strength of these network externalities would lead us to anticipate (other things equal) a slow takeoff and then a rapid diffusion. (The strong network character would suggest a very steep upward trajectory, but the fact that the affordances that possess strong externalities are relatively loosely coupled—likely to appeal to somewhat different sets of users—would tend to moderate the explosive character of growth.) The high level of network specificity (i.e., the fact that people care for many purposes who the other users are) leads us to expect a diffusion process characterized by considerable lumpiness (as different networks join up more or less en masse when local tipping points are reached) and persistent intergroup inequality (especially among groups with relatively low rates of social interaction).

TABLE 2
Television vs. Internet: Relevant Similarities and Differences

	Television	*Internet*
Economic Externalities	*Indirect*: TV ownership (and viewership) provides basis for advertising which encourages more expensive programming and investment in new transmitters and local stations	*Direct*: many uses including e-mail, auctions, peer-to-peer file-sharing, and some software *Indirect*: patronage produces advertiser support of sites (in theory)
Social externalities	Strong societal-membership externalities	Group identity *and* societal membership
Location-specificity	Strong regional specificity, weak within-metropolitan specificity	Moderate within-region specificity; weak regional specificity
Cost	*Product*: Television sets— declining price over time (starting at c. $3000 in year 2000 dollars in 1948), comparable to computers but higher relative median income in earliest years (although cheaper by 1960s) *Service*: Free	*Product*: Computer—declining price over time (although price rises quickly with quality, which keeps increasing) *Service*: Continuing fee, rising with connection quality, some reduction with scale
Complexity	Simple technology/ Relatively easy fit to radio routines	Relatively complex technology/ less easily adapted to existing routines
Versatility	Low: Single use, mass programming	Very high: Multiple uses, very diverse programming
Competition	Head on with radio, cinema	Modest niche overlap with many media, head on with none
Institutional Policies	Powerful business and content model from radio; controlled by established radio networks	Few business models; no clear content models; programming highly competitive with few barriers to entry, especially in early years

By contrast, television was characterized by a lower-specificity societal-membership externality, based on the importance to most people of being able to exhibit familiarity with "what everyone is talking about," as the latter increasingly was defined by what appeared on the television screen. Note that, although the strength of this factor may have declined with the growth of cable channels and the increasing segmentation of the audience after the mid-1980s (Turow 1997), we are here concerned with the period of network dominance during the 1950s. Television also has indirect and nonspecific externalities in the form of scale economies, as increased viewership led to higher advertising rates and higher production budgets. Such externalities should have been adequate to produce an S-shaped diffusion curve with a steep trajectory, but (other things equal) their lack of specificity would tend to encourage relative intergroup equality.

Technological Infrastructure. Different communications media distribute information in different ways, and the technology of distribution places constraints on both overall adoption levels and the opportunities of members of different groups. Early television depended upon broadcasting by stations whose signals were largely confined within metropolitan limits. In the early years, then, the effective ceiling on the U.S. television adoption rate was the percentage of Americans living within range of a broadcast station, which was just over half in 1950. By 1954, with 95 percent of the population with broadcast range, space was no longer a significant constraint (Bogart 1972).

It is less easy to generalize about the Internet because of the variety of means through which it can be accessed. Most Americans with telephones can access the Internet through telephone hook-ups, an arrangement that puts service within reach of the vast majority, but penalizes certain groups (Native Americans on rural reservations, persons in low-income urban communities) (Mueller and Schement 1996). And cell phone users can access the Internet wirelessly (if slowly) in most of the U.S. (Wireless is even more available and considerably more popular in East Asia and Europe.) Access to high-speed Internet, on the other hand, has been more vulnerable to technological limitations: DSL service, for example, is available only to consumers whose homes are relatively close to originating servers, and effective cable service has been available only in communities with relatively modern cable infrastructures. Complicating matters even further, wealthy consumers can turn to more expensive solutions (e.g., satellite dishes in rural communities) unavailable to their less well-off neighbors. Considering all this, *we anticipate that region had a large effect on television adoption in the early years but that its effect became negligible by 1957; and that rural areas experienced a significant but declining disadvantage in Internet adoption.*

Cost. Early television and Internet service were both expensive, albeit in different ways. The average retail price for a television set was around $400 in 1948 and fell to $308 by 1951 (Machlup 1962: 253; Spigel 1992: 32). Taking account of inflation, these prices were roughly the equivalent in 2000 dollars of $3000 and $2200 respectively. This price was similar to the cost of name-brand personal computers in the early 1990s. Both costs declined, though television prices fell a little more quickly than those for computers.[3] For both television sets and computers, bargain-hunters or shoppers willing to take a chance on the resale market could purchase units for well under the median, and consumers wanting state-of-the-art devices could pay considerably more.

There is an important difference, however, in the cost structure of television in the 1950s and the Internet in the 1990s. Television involved a one-time purchase: Once one bought a television receiver, programming was free. By contrast, Internet service required an ongoing service charge, the price of which declined, but only modestly, in the early 2000s. Moreover as the Internet developed commercially in the late 1990s, site designs came to rely more heavily on detailed graphics and java applications and more uses emerged that entailed downloading large files. By the end of our time series, users would find it difficult to access many services without high-speed DSL or cable connections that cost between $20 and $60 per month.

Data on the diffusion of communications devices suggest that the presence of ongoing expense is a greater economic impediment to diffusion than one-time purchase costs, even when prices are high. Compare, for example, the rapid diffusion of radio to the slow and uneven progress of telephone service, which, despite a federal policy of universal service, took half a century to reach 90 percent penetration; or compare the glacial progress of cable television service to the nearly instantaneous acceptance of VCRs (DiMaggio et al. 2004). *Consequently, we anticipate that while income would represent a significant predictor of adoption for both television and the Internet in the earliest years, in the longer run low incomes would remain a more obdurate barrier to Internet access.*

Complexity. Of the two media, the Internet is by far the more complex, requiring greater skill, experience, and assistance to use effectively than television (Hargittai 2002). Moreover, the returns to skill in utility—that is, the difference between what an experienced and an inexperienced user can obtain—is far greater for the Internet than for television. To be sure, the Internet has become more user-friendly over the years, and many Internet users restrict themselves to relatively easy-to-use services (for example, e-mail). Nonetheless, the difference is still very significant. Consequently, *we anticipate that educational attainment will be associated with Internet adoption and not with television, and that its influence will remain strong over time.* Moreover, although the young tend to be among the first to adopt most new technologies, we anticipate that *the advantage of the young will persist longer for Internet adoption than for use of television.*

Versatility. The Internet provides many affordances, television only one, that of entertainment. The Internet serves as an instrument of two-way communication, as well as a source of entertainment, news and information, and a means of shopping and acquiring education. One might, for this reason, expect it to be widely attractive, its utility perhaps outweighing its complexity.

Internet programming is also far more diverse in content and perspective than television (though television in the early days featured more highbrow programming that it would in later years). Television's mass appeal enabled it to serve as a primary source of common knowledge and social membership (Neuman 1991). By contrast, the Internet can sustain the identities of small, spatially dispersed communities. Although critics have noted that relatively few sites specialize in offering information or services to Americans of color (Kolko et al. 2000), the Internet certainly features more culturally specific "programming" than did early television. *Thus one might expect weaker effects of race and ethnicity on Internet than on television adoptions.*

Institutional Context. Television competed directly with radio and film. Because the same networks that had dominated radio broadcasting also controlled television broadcasting, the succession was relatively smooth. (Radio listenership declined as radio's function changed, and radio programming evolved accordingly, shifting from dramatic series and spectaculars to demographically specialized musical formats.) Television's effect on film is ordinarily held to have been more devastating, with a dramatic decline in cinema attendance attributed to television's rise. Baumann (2001), however, contends that the film audience had already started to decline before the expansion of the television audience, due to the postwar baby boom, which restricted the mobility of young adults newly burdened with parental duties. The Internet, by contrast, competed obliquely with many sources of information and communications at once, without entirely supplanting any, initially at least. The Internet's rise has eaten into, but not yet devoured, the markets for postal delivery, long-distance telephone service, television, recorded music, and, increasingly, film. Because of its versatility, it has not needed to dominate any of these niches in order to succeed.

Government regulation of broadcasting primarily addressed the broadcast spectrum and the number and distribution of broadcast stations (Owen 1999). It shaped the structure of the television industry, the nature of competition (and therefore of programming), and the pace at which the television audience expanded. Government policy toward the Internet was more facilitative, fostering the commercialization of the medium after 1995 and investing in programs to ensure that schools and libraries offered Internet access. Efforts to use public schools to provide Internet competency, if successful, will in the long run have egalitarian effects. In the short run, however, they reinforce the advantage of the young.

Television was supported by advertisers, who first sponsored entire programs and later paid rates based on the number of viewers that particular shows could command. Viewership research in the early years was relatively primitive, treating all viewers as equivalent, regardless of the economic resources at their disposal. Consequently, incentives for television producers rewarded audience expansion over niche marketing. By contrast, commercial development of the Internet has concentrated on high-end consumers, while noncommercial development has been driven by institutions of higher education. *On balance, then, television's institutional context militated toward a declining effect of socioeconomic status on adoption, whereas the Internet's institutional context, despite competing influences, has tended to reinforce the importance of education, income, and youth.*

Predictions. Given the preliminary nature of the theoretical framework and the inadequacy of our data, it would be premature to generate formal hypotheses. At the same time, our theoretical framework facilitates an analysis that does lead to some general expectations about the difference we would expect in the diffusion of the television and the Internet. The least controversial (and most banal) prediction is that the diffusion of each would follow the usual S-pattern of slow start-up, rapid ascent, and eventual leveling off. The Internet's progress might be expected to be more explosive because of the strong network externalities associated with its use; at the same time, adoption would be smoothed by the variety of groups attracted by the medium's versatility and impeded by the cost of Internet service.

At the same time, we would anticipate that the Internet's diffusion would level off at a lower rate of penetration, due to the constraining effect of subscription service, and that the effects of income would remain significant longer than was the case for television. Because of the Internet's complexity, we would anticipate that educational attainment would remain a strong predictor for Internet adoption but not for television adoption, and that the advantage of the young would also persist longer for the Internet. By contrast, we would anticipate a swifter effacement of the net effects of race and ethnicity on Internet than on television adoption, due to the more varied content on the former.

Data

We sought data that could capture the first few years during which television and the Internet were commercialized. We required micro-data in order to be able to plot group-specific diffusion rates and to analyze adoption in a series of repeated cross-sections for each medium. We would have preferred data that were fully comparable, but we could not find them. Incomparability between data for the Internet and for television, and within each over time, renders our results less precise than we would like. Nonetheless, the analyses, crude as they are, suffice to illustrate our theoretical argument and to reveal interesting features of the two cases.

Data on Internet access are from supplements to the Census Bureau's Current Population Survey (CPS) fielded in 1994, 1997, 1998, 2000, and 2001. These supplements were sponsored by the National Telecommunications and Information Agency (NTIA), a bureau of the federal Commerce Department that has taken the lead in policies aimed at achieving universal telephone service and, during the Clinton years, expanding access to the Internet.[4] The CPS provides data for individuals and for households. In this chapter we report analyses at the individual level. Internet users are those respondents and household members who used the Internet *either* at home *or* outside the home.

Data on television are from the 1949 to 1951 Surveys of Consumer Finances (SCF) (Economic Behavior Program [1949], [1950], [1951] 1999), and from the News Media Study (NMS) of 1957 (Withey and Davis [1957] 1999).[5] SCF respondents were asked as part of a series of questions about purchases: "How about such large items as furniture, a refrigerator, radio, television set, household appliance and so on—Did you buy anything of this nature during the past year, [calendar year before year of survey]? If Yes, what did you buy?" Thus SCF data indicate whether respondents had *purchased* television sets during the previous twelve months, not whether they owned them. They therefore underestimate television ownership insofar as respondents owned television sets purchased in previous years or given them by others, and overstate it insofar as respondents report purchases of television sets for others (for example, parents buying units for adult children). Thus these data provided suitable proxies for in-home access only in the earliest years of television's diffusion, when one could assume that the vast majority of people who had not purchased a TV set during the year of the survey were unlikely to have purchased one in the past. We concluded our analyses with the 1951 SCF (which recorded purchases made in 1950), because by that point too many households— 3.875 million as opposed to just 940,000 the year before (Rubin and Huber 1986: 142)—owned television sets for that assumption to remain tenable.

To examine the correlates of television adoption at a latter stage in its diffusion, we used data from the NMS, a 1957 survey on behavior and attitudes related to news media, which asked respondents "Do you ever watch television?" These data overestimate household access by including respondents who watched television at the homes of relatives, friends, and neighbors but did not own sets themselves. The effect is slight: a survey of Kansans in 1953, when television service was new to much of the state, reported that 14 percent of viewers watched television only outside the home (Bogart 1972), a figure that would have been much lower for the national population four years later.

Our decision to treat the years 1948 and 1994 as starting points reflects a combination of convenience and conviction. Although the FCC authorized commercial television broadcasting in 1941, the war effectively halted the medium's development. Television began to take off in 1948: whereas 6500 sets were manufactured in 1946 and 179,000 in 1947, nearly one million were produced in 1948. Although aggregate penetration was low (in part because there were so few stations outside of the New York area), adoption rose quickly thereafter, with new stations opening throughout the U.S. (slowly at first, and more rapidly once the FCC lifted regulatory restrictions in 1952), until 95 percent of Americans were within broadcast receiving range by 1954 (Bogart 1972). By 1957, when the News Media Study was undertaken, television's penetration rate had reached nearly 80 percent.

The Internet was unleashed by a combination of the gradual development of graphical interfaces (browsers), which first became widely available in 1993, and regulatory change encouraging commercialization in 1996. In 1994, the first year from which CPS modem-ownership data are available, penetration was still under 4 percent. Internet use began to spiral upward in 1997, with adoption leveling off between 2000 and 2001 at approximately 60 percent of households.[6]

In other words, the periods 1948 to 1957 and 1994 to 2001 represent comparable eras in the histories of the two media. Each medium had existed as a technical possibility with specialized noncommercial uses for more than a decade before the starting point. In each case, the proportion of adopters at the onset of the series was in the very low single digits. For each, diffusion grew rapidly approximately three years after our starting date and continued throughout the period under investigation.

Results

Figure 2 compares the diffusion of the Internet to that of television. In 1948, less than one out of every hundred households possessed a television receiver. In 1994, 3.4 percent of households used e-mail from a home computer. Data for the Internet are from the Current Population Surveys. Television data for 1950 through 1957 were assembled by Leo Bogart (1972) from research by A.C. Nielsen, NBC, and CBS; 1948 and 1949 data are from Kurian (1994).

The two media followed rather similar paths, but television diffused more quickly did the Internet, pulling ahead by year four (even before television signals became available in many parts of the United States, and while prices were still high), with the gap increasing in years five through eight. Television's entry into 80 percent of U.S. households by

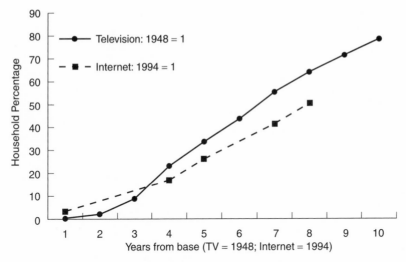

Figure 2 Television and internet diffusion in the United States (*source*: TV: Bogart, 1972; Internet: NTIA, 1994 (modem), 1997, 1998, 2000, 2001).

1958—a degree of penetration substantially greater than that of radio during its first decade—reflected not only the appeal of its programming, but also its relatively easy assimilation into the lifestyles of viewers who had for years followed many of the same programs on radio, its simplicity of use, the fact that its operation was effectively free, and the powerful social-membership externalities that it quickly came to generate (Butsch 2000). By contrast, for all of its utility and appeal, the Internet diffused more slowly due to its novelty and strangeness (especially to older Americans), its complexity, and the ongoing service charge. Whether the strength and specificity of network externalities contributed to the rapidity of the Internet's rise (by creating a series of little tipping points for separate user publics) or slowed the rise (due to the absence of network bridges between different user publics) cannot be discerned from these data.

What about diffusion trajectories for different subgroups? Figure 3 reports Internet adoption rates for subgroups based on analysis of individual-level CPS data; and reports constructed pseudo-adoption rates for television, based on SCF data for 1948 through 1950, with rates for 1957 calculated from the News Media Survey. We constructed the SCF rates by adding the percentage purchasing television sets each year to the percentage in each subgroup that had purchased them in the previous years. The assumption that television purchasers in this era did not already own a set is reasonable: as late as 1957, only 6 percent of households owned more than one television set (Bogart 1972: 13). This procedure exaggerates

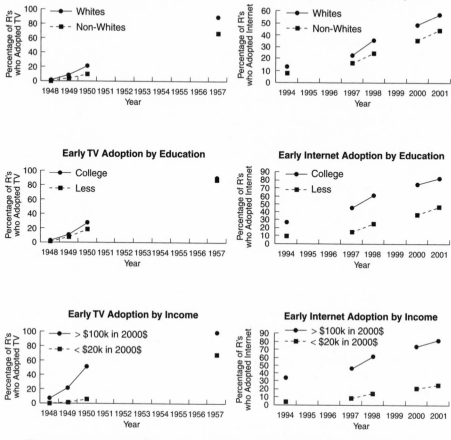

Figure 3 Television and internet household adoption curves for selected household-head/respondent subgroups (*source:* Data on television are from 1949, 1950, and 1951 Surveys of Consumer Finance (SCF) and 1957 News Media Survey. SCF data refer to purchases of television sets in the previous year and penetration rates for 1950 and 1951 are derived by summing previous years in the series. NMS data refer to television viewing, not ownership. Data on Internet are from Current Population Surveys of 1994, 1997, 1998, 2000, and 2001 and refer to Internet use. The 1994 survey referred to ownership of "modems" rather than use of Internet, so also include connections to dedicated networks).

the slope of the increase from 1950 to 1957 (more people watched television than bought television sets), but intergroup comparisons in each year are probably sound. As anticipated, initial differences in television adoption were driven primarily by income, reflecting the high cost of television receivers in the early years. By 1958, income differences had moderated, although well-to-do families were still surprisingly (given the lack of an on-going service charge) more likely to own television sets than were the poor. Differences between whites and nonwhites in television set ownership were modest in the early years, but grew somewhat over the course of the 1950s. By contrast, college graduates were only slightly more likely to purchase television sets than persons without college training, and this difference evaporated entirely by 1957.

By contrast, and consistent with expectations, differences in Internet adoption between college graduates and persons without education beyond high school were notable in 1994 and remained substantial through 2001. Similarly, income inequality in Internet adoption remained strong, with penetration rates starting higher and growing more quickly among prosperous than among poor Americans throughout the 1990s. Racial differences, by contrast, were somewhat smaller, but still substantial and persistent. (For review of a wider range of evidence indicating the persistence of racial, educational, and income inequality in Internet use see DiMaggio et al. 2004.)

Figure 4 explores Internet diffusion rates in more depth by providing exponentiated results (odds ratios) from logistic regressions of Internet use against selected independent variables (income and dummy variables for college, postsecondary and high school education, male gender, white-collar occupation, student status, African-American racial identification, and Hispanic ethnic identification). By using controls, we are able to isolate more effectively the continuing effects of particular factors over this period.

We emphasized that the complexity of a technology is likely to exacerbate differences in adoption rates based on education and, indeed, the advantage accruing to education increased throughout this period. College graduates were almost ten times as likely to be on-line as persons without high school degrees in 1997 and nearly nine times as likely through 2001. The advantages of high school graduates and persons with less than four years of college were considerably less but still substantial, and constant throughout this period.

We also argued that the existence of continuing service costs would render income inequality persistent. The impact of income was less in the 1997 than in the 1994 model (probably because income has less of an effect on Internet use than on owning a modem), but increased monotonically from that point on. The advantages of white-collar workers and students as opposed to persons with other employment statuses fluctuated during this period, but remained substantial.

Gender inequality in Internet use disappeared (by 2001 women were more likely to be on-line than comparable men). By contrast the disadvantages associated with being African-American remained constant and those associated with being Hispanic increased. These results probably reflect the specificity of Internet externalities and the degree of social separation

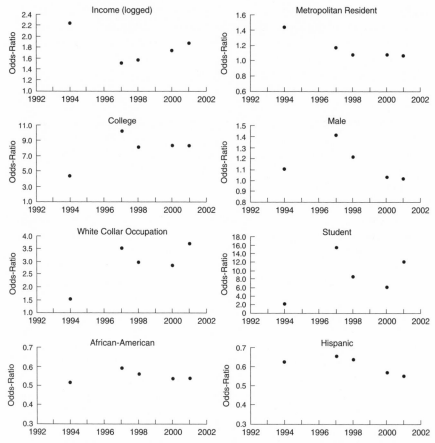

Figure 10.4 Odds-ratio estimates from CPS Logit Models, 1994 to 2001 *source:* Current Population Survey. Coefficients generated from regression of Internet connectivity on log income and dummy variables for college graduation, some postsecondary, and high school education, male gender, white-collar occupation, student status, African-American racial and Hispanic ethnic identification, and metropolitan residence.

between networks of English-speaking whites and those of African-Americans and Hispanic Americans, respectively.

It may be useful to focus in greater depth on the impact of various factors on adoption at different points in the diffusion process. Rather than exaggerate the degree to which our data sets are comparable by using the same models throughout, we acknowledge the exploratory nature of this enterprise and use different predictors based on their availability in different data sets. (This means that our results are only loosely comparable, but

TABLE 3
Logistic Regression Models of TV Purchase, 1948 to 1950 (Survey of
Consumer Finances)

Year	1948			1949			1950		
Metropolitan	4.7369	***	1.6356	5.6576	***	0.9737	3.6123	***	0.4125
Male	3.1528		3.2611	1.8933		0.8129	2.5791	**	0.8142
White	0.8084		0.6230	2.2661		1.2050	1.5105		0.4507
Married	NA			1.8350		0.5899	1.8900	**	0.4445
Age	0.9900		0.0167	0.9947		0.0072	0.9998		0.0050
Income (logged)	2.5070	***	0.5738	1.9535	***	0.2707	1.6903	***	0.1580
White Collar	1.9051		0.7518	0.9577		0.1701	1.1879		0.1526
Unemployed	ELIM			0.5545		0.2952	0.6593		0.4011
Retired	ELIM			0.2818	**	0.1348	1.1097		0.3385
Number of Children	1.7889	**	0.3686	1.3384	**	0.1377	1.2051	**	0.0851
Children^{squared}	0.8439	*	0.0727	0.9401		0.0359	0.9398	*	0.0250
High School	0.5729		0.2439	1.0822		0.2156	1.2885		0.1864
College	0.6744		0.3063	0.7395		0.1841	1.0121		0.1817
N	2,733			3,408			3,315		
Pseudo R-Squared	18.78%			19.11%			14.72%		

Coefficients reported in odds-ratios; standard errors in italics.
***p<0.001, **p<0.01, *p<0.05.
Individual characteristics pertain to household head, not respondent; ELIM=Eliminated from analysis because predicts outcome perfectly; NA=Not Available

given differences in measurement of the dependent variables, this would be the case even if we *had* used the same models.)

Table 3 reports predictors of television purchase in surveys from 1948, 1949, and 1950, in which years 1.5, 6.3, and 15.0 percent of respondents (respectively) reported buying a set. Table 4 reports predictors of television viewing in 1957, when penetration was close to 80 percent. In the early period, the importance of infrastructure was paramount, with metropolitan residence a highly significant predictor of television ownership. By 1957, with 519 television stations operating (compared to just over 100 in 1951), metropolitan residence mattered much less.

Income was also an important predictor of television purchases between 1949 and 1951, not surprisingly given the high cost relative to median income. More surprisingly, income remained an important predictor of

TABLE 4
Logistic Regression Models of TV Viewership, 1957 (News Media Study)

Metropolitan	1.7241	**	0.3092
Male	0.9346		0.1653
White	2.8462	***	0.6686
Age	0.9780	**	0.0069
Married	1.4000		0.2828
Income (logged)	2.1017	***	0.2378
White Collar	0.8895		0.2169
Unemployed	0.9185		0.4302
Student	0.3804		0.4628
Retired	0.8962		0.2576
Number of Children	0.9391		0.0502
Number of Group Affiliations	1.5286	***	0.1563
Church Attendance	0.8667		0.1519
High School	1.9219	*	0.5836
Some College	0.7917		0.2581
College	0.5413		0.2168
N	1,688		
Pseudo R-Squared	21.56%		

Coefficients reported in odds-ratios; standard errors in italics.
***p<0.001, **p<0.01, *p<0.05.

ownership in 1957 (by which time television had reached majorities of all but the poorest Americans). Families with children were particularly likely to purchase television sets (although the effect of additional children turned negative as families grew in size). This may reflect some combination of three factors: the role of older children as lobbyists for the new technology; the utility of television as a babysitter; and the desire of parents of small children for substitute entertainment given their inability to seek entertainment outside the home as frequently as when they were childless. (Baughman 1992 and Baumann 2001 note that movie attendance began to plummet at the start of the postwar baby boom, before the rise of television.)

By 1957 television was firmly established in American households, with or without children. Television in the early years was an intensely social medium. In the 1940s, it was primarily watched in bars, which used television sets as a means to attract patrons. Once it moved into the home, the living rooms of early adopters often attracted neighbors and friends to showings of favorite programs (Butsch 2000). Consistent with the notion that television viewing represented a form of social membership, television ownership was significantly associated by 1957 with memberships in lodges and clubs. (Interestingly, this did not apply to membership in churches, which may have discouraged television viewing.)

Our analysis of the NMS data suggests that in 1957 no one was excluded from the circle of television but the poor (who still could not afford sets), the elderly (who may have rejected the new technology), and African-Americans (who possessed little wealth and who appeared rarely and unflatteringly in TV programming; Baughmann 1992: 56). Many college graduates excluded themselves, as the negative coefficient indicates, perhaps viewing television's embrace by the mass public as a kind of negative externality (Steiner 1963: 33–34, 57–58). (The proportion of college graduates who watched television was high, just not as high as one would have expected given the fact that they earned high incomes, were disproportionately white, and joined lots of associations.)

Table 5 provides a more detailed view of factors predicting Internet adoption from 1994 through 2001, adding additional covariates to the simpler model that generated the exponentiated coefficients reported in figure 4. The exponentiated logit coefficients represent net differences in odds of adoption associated with particular characteristics or identities. Values greater than 1 indicate a positive impact on adoption, whereas values lower than 1 indicate the opposite.

College graduates maintained a very strong advantage (and one that grew relative to high-school graduates) over this period. Similarly, the impact of income increased between 1997 and 2000. White-collar employees and students maintained a sizable advantage over other groups (with blue-collar workers the omitted category).[7]

Perhaps reflecting the importance of local networks, modest regional disparities have persisted, with the midwest and southeast falling behind as the northeast has caught up with the west. The development of technological infrastructure reduced the initial advantage of center-city residents, which disappeared by 2000. Suburbanites maintained a small edge over people living outside metropolitan areas, perhaps reflecting network externalities in the use of the Internet by schools and community organizations, or increasing use of superior suburban cable infrastructure for high-speed Internet access.

As was the case for television in 1957, youth was associated with Internet use throughout this period with little change from year to year, a difference that reflected the greater openness of the young to new technology, their greater familiarity with computers, and the premium placed upon the Internet by high schools (especially in the informal student culture) and, even more so, institutions of higher education. Indeed, the reliance of

TABLE 5
Logistic Regression Models of Internet Adoption, 1994 to 2001 (Current Population Survey)

Year	1994		1997		1998		2000		2001	
Dependent Variable	Modem Ownership		Internet Use		Internet Use		Internet Use		Internet Use	
Metro Central	1.4159 ***	0.0510	1.2573 ***	0.0395	1.1785 ***	0.0332	1.0861 **	0.0307	1.0350	0.0279
Metro Other	1.5232 ***	0.0472	1.1536 ***	0.0319	1.0599 *	0.0260	1.1031 ***	0.0269	1.1108 ***	0.0257
Income (logged)	1.9187 ***	0.0444	1.4507 ***	0.0259	1.4692 ***	0.0242	1.6189 ***	0.0261	1.6773 ***	0.0250
Income (top code)	1.2542 ***	0.0418	1.1711 ***	0.0348	1.2385 ***	0.0346	1.1693 ***	0.0332	1.1789 ***	0.0330
White Collar	1.3608 ***	0.0373	2.8091 ***	0.0709	2.3336 ***	0.0503	2.2500 ***	0.0483	2.9188 ***	0.0620
Student	1.8504 ***	0.0996	7.8607 ***	0.3695	3.7431 ***	0.1702	2.6677 ***	0.1610	4.9673 ***	0.2794
Unemployed	1.2392 **	0.0927	1.1291	0.0875	1.3784 ***	0.0816	1.4895 ***	0.0812	1.4086 ***	0.0684
Retired	0.7617 ***	0.0437	0.6563 ***	0.0394	0.7683 ***	0.0344	0.8767 **	0.0345	0.8853 **	0.0313
Disabled	0.9386	0.0921	0.5846 ***	0.0615	0.8037 **	0.0546	0.7904 ***	0.0444	0.7098 ***	0.0346
Number of Children	NA		NA		NA		1.0301 **	0.0101	1.0423 ***	0.0100
Age	0.9860 ***	0.0010	0.9744 ***	0.0009	0.9686 ***	0.0008	0.9631 ***	0.0008	0.9633 ***	0.0008

	(1)			(2)			(3)			(4)			(5)		
High School	1.6845	***	0.0951	2.5561	***	0.1494	2.2518	***	0.0907	2.3250	***	0.0818	2.3295	***	0.0713
Post-Secondary	2.7585	***	0.1541	5.5152	***	0.3151	4.5249	***	0.1807	4.8582	***	0.1745	4.7952	***	0.1524
College or More	4.2000	***	0.2404	9.9811	***	0.5856	8.6454	***	0.3647	9.5477	***	0.3725	9.6163	***	0.3446
Married	1.3674	***	0.0363	1.1211	***	0.0263	1.0669	*	0.0224	1.1438	***	0.0252	1.2714	***	0.0264
Male	1.1006	***	0.0238	1.4144	***	0.0284	1.1965	***	0.0218	0.9756		0.0180	0.9329	***	0.0166
African-American	0.5360	***	0.0281	0.5617	***	0.0237	0.5058	***	0.0182	0.4737	***	0.0158	0.4768	***	0.0151
Asian-American	0.9955		0.0543	0.7231	***	0.0367	0.5851	***	0.0275	0.5356	***	0.0250	0.5576	***	0.0256
Hispanic	0.5378	***	0.0321	0.5181	***	0.0245	0.4544	***	0.0176	0.3833	***	0.0132	0.3592	***	0.0117
Mid-West	1.0975	**	0.0347	1.0390		0.0310	1.0196		0.0276	0.9786		0.0269	0.9360	*	0.0244
South	1.1047	**	0.0335	1.1103	***	0.0321	0.9839		0.0256	0.9407	*	0.0249	0.8691	***	0.0221
West	1.3737	***	0.0427	1.3381	***	0.0397	1.2982	***	0.0351	1.2188	***	0.0337	1.0632	*	0.0281
N	88,662			79,202			77,583			75,380			88,426		
Pseudo R-Squared	16.03%			25.94%			25.54%			28.64%			32.40%		

Coefficients reported in odds-ratios, standard errors in italics.

***p<0.001, **p<0.01, *p<0.05; NA=variable not available in set.

Coefficient estimates for variable demarcating unidentified metropolitan region omitted.

high-school and college students on instant messaging represents as pure a network-externality effect as one can find.[8] Even controlling for age, full-time students maintained a substantial advantage over other labor-force-status categories.

Finally, as was the case for television in the early years, married people and parents were significantly more likely to use the Internet than were people without children. (Moreover, results not reported here demonstrate that, as was also the case for television, the positive impact of children declines as the number of children grows.) The attractiveness of the medium to older children, its perceived educational value, and its usefulness in managing children's school and social lives probably share responsibility for this finding.

The relative position of Hispanics appears to have deteriorated over time, and African-Americans remain only about half as likely as similar whites to use the Internet throughout this period. Surprisingly, despite high absolute rates of Internet use, Asian-Americans used the Internet less than sociodemographically similar Euro-Americans.[9]

Note that the Internet's relative content diversity would lead one to expect that Internet usage patterns for members of racial and ethnic minority groups would differ less from those of whites compared to television in the 1950s. At the same time, however, insofar as members of these groups are socially isolated as well as (in the case of Hispanics and African-Americans) economically disadvantaged, the networks in which they participate may be expected to have adopted the Internet *more* slowly than television due to the greater role of pure network effects in the diffusion of the former. Insofar as network effects matter, we would expect that members of minority groups with characteristics like high levels of formal education or white-collar employment that are associated with lower levels of social isolation will adopt at a higher rate, relative whites, than people with less education or lower-status occupations.

We explored this possibility by adding two sets of interaction effects to the models reported in table 5.[10] In one set of models we included interactions of the three educational levels with the three racial and ethnic identities. In a second set of models we included interactions of the latter with white-collar employment. The exponentiated logistic regression coefficients in table 6 represent the extent to which adoption rates differ less (for values greater than 1) or more (for values less than 1) from the white rates for group members with the indicated characteristic than for other group members.

For African-American and Hispanic respondents, the results are consistent with the proposition, based on the network-externalities framework, that group-specific adoption rates are retarded by social isolation. For Blacks, white-collar employment appears to be especially important,

TABLE 6
Race/Ethnicity Interaction Effects on Internet Use

Interactions	1994	1997	1998	2000	2001
BlackXHS	1.018	1.071	1.350	1.053	0.846
BlackX some college	0.983	1.607*	1.603**	1.167	0.953
Black X college	1.442	1.914**	2.004***	1.412**	1.129
Asian-American XHS	0.396***	0.959	0.912	1.260	0.802
Asian-Am. X some col.	0.492**	0.920	1.194	1.585*	0.869
Asian-Am. X college	0.557**	1.205	1.328	1.408	0.946
Hispanic X HS	1.331	1.680*	2.221***	1.858***	1.327***
Hispanic X some college	1.823**	2.466***	2.658***	2.138***	1.458***
Hispanic X college	2.438***	2.518***	2.522***	2.166***	1.471***
Black X white-collar	1.270*	1.528***	1.506***	1.296***	1.281***
Asian-Am. X white-collar	0.811*	0.880	1.034	1.223*	0.948
Hispanic X white-collar	1.620***	1.428***	1.421***	1.544***	1.384***

***p<0.001; ** p<0.01; * p<0.05; two tailed.

Education interactions and occupation interactions added (in separate models) to basic model predicting use of the Internet at any location from Table 5. Figures are exponentiated logistic regression coefficients, with values >1 representing smaller differences from white rates for group members with the indicated trait than for the group as a whole. 1994 data are for modem in the home.

although in most years African-American college graduates differ less from their white counterparts than do less educated African-Americans. For Hispanics, occupational status *and* educational attainment both have large effects, with higher education substantially reducing inequality, and even high school graduation having a strongly beneficial effect. Educational effects for both African-Americans and Hispanics, and occupational effects for Blacks, have tended to decline over time, perhaps reflecting within-group diffusion to less elite networks.

By contrast, neither education nor occupation has a consistent impact on net differences between Asian-American and Euro-American rates of use. We have no way of knowing whether this reflects the relatively small size of the Asian-American samples (especially given the heterogeneity of this population) or something distinctive about patterns of Internet diffusion in Asian-American communities. Although the results certainly do not support a network-externalities interpretation, neither do they in themselves disconfirm it. (From a network perspective, we would expect such results if Internet use had been high enough within homophilous Asian-American networks that contact with outsiders was unnecessary to stimulate diffusion, or if white-collar employment and higher education had less of an impact on outgroup contact for Asian-Americans than for African-Americans or Americans of Hispanic descent due to strong enclave economies.)

For the most part these findings are consistent with the six predictions that emerged from our comparison of television and the Internet in the light of our analytic framework. First, as predicted, Internet and television diffusion both roughly fit the expected logistic pattern, with the former leveling of earlier than the latter. Second, also as predicted, regional effects on television were stronger than on the Internet, whereas rural/ metropolitan differences were important for the Internet, and both declined in importance over time. Third, as predicted, income had a significant effect on the adoption of both television and the Internet and persisted in its effects on Internet adoption, but its effects on television adoption declined less quickly than we anticipated. Fourth, as anticipated, both age and, especially, educational attainment were more strongly associated with Internet than with television adoption, especially after the first few years. Fifth, contrary to expectations based on content versatility, but consistent with rough intuitions about social homophily and network effects on adoption, racial and ethnic effects on Internet adoption remained strong. Finally, as noted and with some exceptions, sociodemographic factors have tended to have more persistent effects on Internet adoption than on television adoption, a finding also consistent with the framework developed earlier.

Conclusion

The development of capitalism over the past two centuries has been marked by growing interdependence of markets and consumption. From the autarchy of agricultural communities through the small-scale production of early capitalism; from the emergence of the factory system, which ushered in mass production, economies of scale and, ultimately, mass consumption, to the rise of flexible production and the use of consumption as a means of defining shared identities as well as satisfying needs, goods and services with network externalities have played an increasingly important role in both economy and society. When the economist Fritz Machlup (1962) first called attention to the growing importance of the U.S. information economy, with its strong network properties, almost half a century ago, he could not have imagined the extent to which the Internet revolution of the 1990 (in combination with the loss of most of the traditional manufacturing sector) would bring his vision to fruition.

In this chapter we have tried to accomplish three things. First, like the other authors in this volume, we have exploited insights from the field of economics, specifically the notion of "network externalities." And, like others, we have prodded and stretched as we have borrowed, rendering the concept more sociological in three ways: calling explicit attention to *social*-network externalities that are as real in their consequences as purely instrumental effects; making a case for treating "network-ness" as a continuous variable rather than a binary classification; and distinguishing between two correlated but analytically independent dimensions of variation in network goods (the degree to which their use entails social interaction and the extent to which users care about the specific identities of other consumers).

Second, we have developed a systematic analytic framework for understanding differences in the diffusion patterns of new technologies, especially new technologies of information and communications with at least some of the properties of network goods. In particular, we are interested in explaining the rate of diffusion, the extent of diffusion, and the degree of socioeconomic inequality in adoption over the course of the diffusion process. The framework described in this chapter should be useful both for comparing the trajectories of different technologies within societies and for comparing the trajectories of similar technologies across different societies.

Third, we have illustrated the utility of this framework in the context of a comparison between the diffusion of television between 1948 and 1957 and the diffusion of the Internet between 1994 and 2001, both in the United States. Each of these media was enormously successful in its first years; each was initially constrained by spatial factors that became less important as the technological infrastructure developed; and each appealed especially to young people and their parents. Yet there were also significant differences that are explicable with reference to the analytic framework presented here, especially the lower level at which Internet penetration began to plateau and the persistence of socioeconomic inequality in its distribution. This analysis also demonstrates the utility of our framework for policy-analytic purposes by answering a question that has been a source of much contestation in the communications-policy field: The "digital divide" is *not* simply developmental, but is likely to persist indefinitely, at least in the absence of concerted public action.

The analyses presented here, both theoretical and empirical, are preliminary and crude. The theoretical framework needs further development, ideally with the use of computational models to illuminate the less intuitively obvious implications of different forms of social-network externalities. And the empirical analyses would benefit from the application of better data to more technologies in cross-national perspective. Joining with this volume's other authors in the attempt to integrate insights from economics and sociology in order to better understand the capitalist economies of the twenty-first century, we hope that we have provided a start to the comparative analysis of goods and services depending on technical systems with network externalities, on which others can improve.

NOTES

1. Economists use the term "externality" to refer to positive or negative consequences of the production or consumption of a good or service that are not captured by or charged to the producer or consumer. The particular class of externality upon which we focus in this paper comprises cases in which one person's consumption of a service generates utilities from which other consumers benefit.

2. Some economists have modeled the influence of social relations on consumer decision-making (e.g., Leibenstein 1950; Akerlof 1997), but of the ones we have seen, only Shy (2001: chap. 10) does so in the context of network externalities.

3. The SCF asked respondents the price they paid for their television set by dollar ranges. Taking the median of these ranges for each year yields estimates ($425 for 1948 and 1949; $325 for 1950 for the median categories) similar to estimates based on retail surveys.

4. In this paper we report analyses at the individual level, although the dependent variable in 1994 (modem ownership) can be interpreted as household connectivity. In 1994, respondents were asked if their household owned a modem attached to a telephone line, whereas from 1997 on the question referred to Internet service. Therefore, the 1994 data underestimate Internet use insofar as some respondents may have used a modem they did not own, and overestimates insofar as some respondents used modems to connect to dedicated networks that were not part of the Internet. Individual-level and household-level results for Internet penetration differ because some members of households with Internet connections do not use the Internet and because many people without household connections go on-line at school or work (DiMaggio et al. 2004). Coding Notes for Current Population Survey. *Metropolitan Status.* The distinction between central and non-central areas of metropolitan areas is crucial to studies on Internet access inequality. However, the CPS variable that delineates central versus non-central areas of metropolitan regions (gtmsast) often has many missing values. The difficulty with this identification problem affects a large proportion of the data set (around 15% of respondents or more). To avoid losing too much data, the following strategy was used. First, within descriptive statistics, graphs and tables depicting metropolitan respondents do not differentiate between central and non-central residents (which allows us to use the gemetsta variable, for which there are substantially fewer missing values). However, within the regressions, members of unidentified groups were placed in a residual category, the coefficient of which is not reported in the tables of coefficients. *Occupational Groupings.* Occupational groupings (students, white- and blue-collar workers, unemployed, disabled, and retired individuals) were placed

into mutually exclusive categories. *White-collar* and *blue-collar* workers were categorized as such only if they were in the labor force at the time of the survey *and* did not claim to be full-time students or retirees. Disabled people in the labor force were included in the white- and blue-collar categories. *Students* are restricted to respondents who either (1) reported being full-time students who were not in summer vacation in the week prior to the survey, *or* (2) claimed to not be in the labor force because they were students. The use of these criteria is an artifact of the way the CPS assesses student status. Full-time students who claimed to have full-time jobs were placed in the student category, while part-time students were all placed within other occupational categories. *Disabled* individuals only include those who were not in the labor force during the survey. Respondents are categorized as *retired* if they simultaneously report being not in the labor force as a result of being retired and report having a profession. *Education*. Education is grouped into four categories: (1) less than a high school degree, (2) completed a high school degree (including GED), (3) some postsecondary schooling, and (4) completion of a college degree or more. *Children*. People who were coded as having missing values for number of children are described as not being parents, and thus were assigned zero children for this variable. This variable was only available after 1999. *Age*. Respondents who were top coded at age 90 were represented as being 90 in the data set. *Income*. Respondents who were top coded at an annual income of $75,000 or more were coded as having incomes of $100,000 in the data set. *Modem Ownership*. Many observations in the modem ownership variable (hesq2) were coded as blank. Those who were coded as having a computer (from hesq1) and were left blank in hesq2 were classified as *not* having a modem.

5. Coding Notes for Survey of Consumer Finances. Survey years correspond to responses given one year earlier. The number-of-children variable was top coded at 7 and recorded as 7.5 children for the1949 and 1950 surveys, and top coded and coded at 9 in 1951. Age was top coded at 65 and recorded at 70. In the 1949 survey, income was top coded at $99,995 and recorded as $100,000. In all years, one dollar was added to the income to define its log when income equaled zero. In 1950, the top code was $200,000 and coded as such. The incidence of income top coding was extremely rare. The 1949 survey lacked information on marital status. Occupational categories refer to the household head. *White-collar* workers include professionals, technical workers, self-employed, artisans, managers, clerical, and sales workers. For the 1950 and 1951 surveys, the *high school* and *college* variables appear to include those who completed some high school or college, respectively. The codebook is not completely clear. The 1949 survey explicitly refers to completion of high school and college. Documentation does not specify whether the *race* variable refers to the respondent or to the household head in the 1950 and 1951 surveys, but it was assumed to refer to the household head.

Coding Notes for News Media Survey. Respondents top coded at 65 years of age or over were assigned an age of 70. Those who were top coded as having 9 or more children were coded as having 9 children, and those who reported having 9 or more group affiliations were coded as having 9 group affiliations. Respondents were coded as attending religious services if they reported going to services more than "two or three times per month" or "regularly." This data set top coded income at "$20,000 or over" which was converted into $32,000 (which corresponds to

$200,000 in 2000 dollars). Occupational codes are similar to those in the Survey of Consumer Finances. *High School* only includes those who completed high school.

6. Hannemyr (2003) places the inception dates at 1945 (when commercial development resumed after being suspended during the Second World War) for television and at 1989 (when the first commercial ISPs opened their virtual doors) for the Internet. This approach is reasonable, but given our focus on long-term diffusion trends, little is lost by setting the date later. Despite the differing chronology, we concur with Hannemyr's main conclusion—that television and the Internet diffused at similar rates.

7. The results for the unemployed appear anomalous but are explicable as follows: On average, the unemployed are less likely to connect to the Internet. But they also have a high incidence of other factors associated with low rates of connectivity—low incomes, non-white race, Hispanic ethnicity, rural residence, lower educational attainment, residence in the south. Detailed analyses found that unemployment coefficient estimates were sensitive to the inclusion of white-collar workers and students, and income in most years. The unemployed tend to have very low incomes, but may go online more than others with equally low incomes because they have more free time and special incentive to seek work on the Internet. The effect of unemployment also showed some sensitivity to educational levels, but not to race or ethnicity.

8. A fall 2002 study revealed that well over 90 percent of Princeton University freshman used instant messaging and most preferred it to e-mail or telephones for coordinating activities, as well as for staying in touch with old friends (Schrader 2003).

9. Because previous studies have shown such high rates of Internet use for Asian-Americans, we subjected this finding to particularly close scrutiny. In every year, Asian-Americans had higher absolute rates of connectivity than Euro-Americans, African-Americans, or Hispanics. But Asian-American CPS respondents also had very high average levels of the strongest predictors of Internet use, including income, white-collar employment, full-time student status, college-degree attainment, non-central metropolitan and western regional residence. Including these variables in the models reduced Asian-Americans' zero-order advantage to the negative coefficients visible in table 5.

10. We thank Victor Nee for suggesting this strategy.

REFERENCES

Agre, Philip E. "The Internet and Public Discourse." *First Monday* 3. http://www.Firstmonday/dk/issue3_3/agre/index.html.
Akerlof, George. 1997. "Social Distance and Social Decisions." *Econometrica* 65: 1005–27.
Attewell, Paul. 2001. "The First and Second Digital Divides." *Sociology of Education* 74: 252–59.
Autor, David H., Lawrence F. Katz, and Alan B. Krueger. 1998. "Computing Inequality: Have Computers Changed the Labor Market?" *Quarterly Journal of Economics* 113: 1169–213.

Baughman, James. 1992. *The Republic of Mass Culture: Journalism, Filmmaking, and Broadcasting in America since 1941.* Baltimore: Johns Hopkins University Press.

Baumann, Shyon. 2001. "Intellectualization and Art World Development: Film in the United States." *American Sociological Review* 66: 404–26.

Bogart, Leo. 1972. *The Age of Television: A Study of Viewing Habits and the Impact of Television on American Life.* 3rd ed. New York: Frederick Ungar.

Bonus, Holger. 1973. "Quasi-Engel Curves, Diffusion, and the Ownership of Major Consumer Durables." *Journal of Political Economics* 81: 655–77.

Brinton, Mary C. and Victor Nee, eds. 1998. *The New Institutionalism in Sociology.* New York: Russell Sage.

Burt, Ronald S. 1992. *Structural Holes: The Social Structure of Competition.* Cambridge, Mass.: Harvard University Press.

Butsch, Richard. 2000. *The Making of American Audiences: From Stage to Television, 1750–1990.* New York: Cambridge University Press.

Castells, Manuel. 1996. *The Rise of the Network Society.* Information Age 1. Oxford: Blackwell.

———. 2001. *The Internet Galaxy: Reflections on the Internet, Business and Society.* New York: Oxford University Press.

DiMaggio, Paul. 2001. "Conclusion: The Futures of Business Organization and Paradoxes of Change." In *The Twenty-First-Century Firm: Changing Economic Organization in International Perspective,* ed. Paul DiMaggio. Princeton: Princeton University Press. 210–43.

DiMaggio, Paul, Eszter Hargittai, Coral E. Celeste, and Steven Shafer. 2004. "From the Digital Divide to Digital Inequality: A Literature Review and Research Agenda." In *Social Inequality,* ed. Kathryn Neckerman. New York: Russell Sage.

DiMaggio, Paul, Eszter Hargittai, W. Russell Neuman, and John Robinson. 2001. "Social Implications of the Internet." *Annual Review of Sociology* 27: 307–36.

DiMaggio, Paul and Hugh Louch. 1996. "Socially Embedded consumer Transactions: For What Kinds of Purchases Do People Most Often Use Networks?" *American Sociological Review* 63: 619–37.

Douglas, Mary and Baron Isherwood. 1979. *The World of Goods.* New York: Basic Books.

Douglas, Susan J. 1987. *Inventing American Broadcasting: 1899–1922.* Baltimore: Johns Hopkins University Press.

Economic Behavior Program, Survey Research Center, University of Michigan. [1949]1999. SURVEY OF CONSUMER FINANCES, 1949. Computer file, ICPSR version. Ann Arbor, Mich.: Survey Research Center.

———. [1950]1999. SURVEY OF CONSUMER FINANCES, 1950. Computer file, ICPSR version. Ann Arbor, Mich.: Survey Research Center.

———. [1951]1999. SURVEY OF CONSUMER FINANCES, 1951. Computer file, ICPSR version. Ann Arbor, Mich.: Survey Research Center.

Granovetter, Mark S. 1974. *Getting a Job: A Study of Contacts and Careers.* Cambridge, Mass.: Harvard University Press.

Granovetter, Mark S. and Roland Soong. 1983. "Threshold Models of Diffusion and Collective Behavior." *Journal of Mathematical Sociology* 9: 165–79.

Hannemyr, Gisle. 2003. "The Internet as Hyperbole: A Critical Examination of Adoption Rates." *Information Society* 19: 111–21.

Hargittai, Eszter. 2002. "Second Level Digital Divide: Differences in People's Online Skills." *First Monday* 7: Issue 4 (no pagination). Last accessed October 30, 2003 at http://www/firstmonday.dk/issues/issue7_4/hargittai/index.html.

Kolko, Beth E., Lisa Nakamura, and Gilbert B. Rodman, eds. 2000. *Race in Cyberspace*. New York: Routledge.

Kurian, George Thomas. 1994. *Datapedia of the United States, 1790–2000: America Year by Year*. Lanham, Md.: Bernan Associates.

Leibenstein, Harvey. 1950."Bandwagon, Snob, and Veblen Effects in the Theory of Consumers' Demand." *Quarterly Journal of Economics* 64: 183–207.

Leigh, Andrew and Robert D. Atkinson. 2001. "Clear Thinking on the Digital Divide." PPI Policy Report, Progressive Policy Institute, June.

Machlup, Fritz. 1962. *The Production and Distribution of Knowledge in the United States*. Princeton: Princeton University Press.

Manuel, Peter L. 1993. *Cassette Culture: Popular Music and Technology in North India*. Chicago: University of Chicago Press.

Marsden, Peter. 1987. "Core Discussion Networks of Americans." *American Sociological Review* 52: 122–31.

Mueller, Milton and Jorge Schement. 1996. "Universal Service from the Bottom Up: A Study of Telephone Penetration in Camden, New Jersey." *Information Society* 12: 273–91.

Neuman, W. Russell. 1991. *The Future of the Mass Audience*. New York: Cambridge University Press.

Newcomb, Horace M. and Paul M. Hirsch. 1983. "Television as a Cultural Forum: Implications for Research." *Quarterly Review of Film Studies* 8: 45–55.

Owen, Bruce. 1999. *The Internet Challenge to Television*. Cambridge, Mass.: Harvard University Press.

Porat, Marc. 1977. *The Information Economy: Definition and Measurement*. OT Special Publication 77–12. Washington, D.C.: U.S. Department of Commerce, Office of Telecommunications.

Rainwater, Lee. 1974. *What Money Buys: Inequality and the Social Meanings of Income*. New York: Basic Books.

Rogers, Everett M. 2003. *Diffusion of Innovations*. 5th ed. New York: Free Press.

Rubin, Michael Rogers and Mary Taylor Huber. 1986. *The Knowledge Industry in the United States, 1960–1980*. Princeton: Princeton University Press.

Schrader, James. 2003. "Instant Messaging at Princeton." Term paper prepared for Princeton University course, FRS129.

Shampine, Allan L. "Determinants of the Diffusion of U.S. Digital Telecommunications." *Journal of Evolutionary Economics* 11: 249–61.

Shapiro, Carl and Hal R. Varian. 1998. *Information Rules: A Strategic Guide to the Network Economy*. Boston: Harvard Business School Press.

Shy, Oz. 2001. *The Economics of Network Industries*. New York: Cambridge University Press.

Spigel, Lynn. 1992. *Make Room for TV: Television and the Family Ideal in Postwar America*. Chicago: University of Chicago Press.

Steiner, Gary A. 1963. *The People Look at Television: A Study of Audience Attitudes.* New York: Knopf.

Turow, Joseph. 1997. *Breaking Up America: Advertisers and the New Media World.* Chicago: University of Chicago Press.

Van den Bulte, Christophe and Gary L. Lilien. 2001. "*Medical Innovation* Revisited: Social Contagion vs. Marketing Effort." *American Journal of Sociology* 106: 1409–35.

Varian, Hal R. 2000. "Market Structures in the Network Age." In *Understanding the Digital Economy: Data, Tools, and Research,* ed. Erik Brynjolfsson and Brian Kahin. 137–51.

Veblen, Thorstein. 1899. *The Theory of the Leisure Class: An Economic Study of the Evolution of Institutions.* New York: Macmillan.

Watt, Duncan. 1999. "Networks, Dynamics, and the Small-World Phenomenon." *American Journal of Sociology* 105: 493–527.

Withey, Stephen B. and Robert C. Davis. [1957]1999. NEWS MEDIA STUDY. Computer file, ICPSR version. Ann Arbor, Mich.: Institute for Social Research, Social Science Archive.

Affective Attachment in Electronic Markets
A Sociological Study of eBay

Ko Kuwabara

ONLINE MARKETS IN THE NEW ECONOMY

THE INTERNET HAS BECOME a major institution in today's capitalist economy. More money is spent on the Web than ever, and e-businesses have grown rapidly in size and diversity over the past few years. Indeed, the promise of digital technology has variously inspired many commentators to assert that perfect competition will finally prevail in the New Economy: "[The] Internet cuts costs, increases competition and improves the functioning of the price mechanism. It thus moves the economy closer to the textbook model of perfect competition" (*Economist* 2000). Echoing a similar sentiment, Bill Gates (1999) proclaimed a "friction-free economy" driven by information technology.

Surely, the Internet has dramatically transformed the nature of markets. On the Internet, exchange processes are increasingly automated, communication across geographical distance is instant, and information is stored, searched, distributed, and updated far more efficiently than is generally possible offline. Moreover, bits and bytes provide cheap and readily available raw material for the infrastructure of online markets. A storefront can be created overnight on the Net for a fraction of what a brick-and-mortar store might cost on Main Street, U.S.A. Whereas offline markets often emerge spontaneously through local, informal exchanges, then, online markets can be designed much more formally and systematically from the top down. Regarding the eBay auction market, for example, *Business Week* (1999: 33) notes: "eBay has single-handedly created a new market." Similarly, Amazon, Half.com, and other online markets have made vast fortunes engineering hyper-rational flea markets

I thank Victor Nee, Richard Swedberg, Paul Resnick, Michael W. Macy, Edward Lawler, and Mihir Mahajan for useful comments. This research was partially supported by Paul Resnick under NSF 9977999 while the author was a graduate student at the University of Michigan.

that deliver efficient and reliable services to tens of millions of people worldwide, day after day.

These success stories notwithstanding, the Internet also poses serious challenges for the New Economy. For many, the fundamental appeal of the Net is the vast opportunities for meeting new people, whether for sharing esoteric trivia in newsgroups, finding romantic partners, or collecting rare Australian coins. For others, however, the Internet remains a world of anonymity, pervasive automation, and disembodied strangers. Embedded relationships are notably absent and institutions are partial. In communities as vast and decentralized as those online, intimate ties and third-party enforcers no longer ensure safety and comfort against crime and predation. At the same time that the Internet helps us reach wider and deeper across social ties, it also threatens to dislodge us from familiar, local relationships.

The issue of trust is particularly pervasive in online markets. In contrast to businesses that offer business-to-customer (B2C) or business-to-business (B2B) services, online markets provide meeting places for customer-to-customer (C2C) exchanges of goods and services. Online auctions, such as eBay, are primary examples. Half.com and Amazon Marketplace offer alternative forms of exchanges for customers to purchase goods from registered sellers without bidding. Either way, transactions in these markets are significantly riskier than face-to-face exchanges in the offline world, for at least two reasons. First, buyers usually cannot inspect what they are receiving before committing themselves to the transaction. Second, buyers are generally required to make their payment before the seller delivers the product or service. But what motivates sellers to actually deliver goods and services once they receive payments from buyers?

Game theorists formalize this problem as the Trust Game (Dasgupta 1988; Kreps 1990), a sequential and one-sided version of the well-known Prisoner's Dilemma. Facing a transaction, the truster decides to trust the trustee or not. Once trust is placed, the trustee decides whether to honor the trust or exploit the truster. Unlike the players in the Prisoner's Dilemma, the trustee has perfect information about the truster's decision, because the Trust Game is played sequentially, not simultaneously. On the other hand, if the truster decides not to trust the trustee, the game ends without an exchange.

The Trust Game is characterized by the same payoff inequalities that describe the basic dilemma in the prisoner's dilemma: $T > R > P > S$, where T is the "temptation" payoff from exploitation, R is the "reward" payoff from mutual cooperation, P is the "punishment" payoff from mutual defection, and S is the "sucker" payoff from unilateral cooperation against a defector. While it is collectively rational to cooperate and exchange honestly (since $R > P = 0$), defection dominates cooperation for individual actors. In

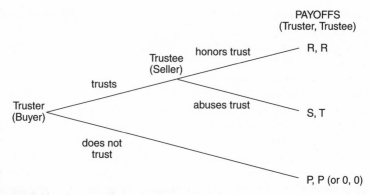

Figure 1 Trust Game in extended form.

the Trust Game, however, these payoffs are distributed asymmetrically. As shown in figure 1, the dilemma for the trustee is that $T>R>P$, in which greed $(T>R)$ motivates dishonesty, whereas the dilemma for the truster is that $R>P>S$, in which fear $(P>S)$ prevents risk-taking. More specifically, if the truster places trust, the trustee's best option is to exploit the truster. Knowing this, however, the truster should never enter the transaction in the first place. In this way, mutual defection prevails as the unique Nash equilibrium.

As Coleman (1990) noted, transactions that occur across time and space require much more trust than those without physical distance or time delays. If so, and if the model of a perfect market assumes costless and instantaneous transactions, the challenge for online markets is to provide institutional mechanisms to reduce uncertainty and information asymmetries in these transactions. One solution is to encourage repeated transactions. It is well known that cooperation can emerge naturally between selfish actors through reciprocity in iterated exchanges (Axelrod 1984; Molm 1994). Given the sheer size of online markets, however, repeated transactions are both unlikely and impractical for most buyers and sellers.

EBay suggests another curious solution to the problem of trust. Pierre Omidyar founded eBay in 1995 for online traders and auctioneers. Online trading through newsgroups and public bulletin boards already existed before eBay, to be sure, but the genius of Omidyar was to create a formal reputation system that allowed people to post and view feedback on each other on public space after each transaction. Reputation facilitates cooperation in at least two important ways (Yamagishi and Yamagishi 1994). On the one hand, it supplies valuable information about the past history of potential partners and hence mediates the problem of adverse selection. On the other hand, it provides means of sanctioning the partner after the interaction, inasmuch as a good reputation is an asset for the signaler, thereby moderating the problem of moral hazard. More generally, to the extent that sellers in a formal reputation system are dependent on feedback from buyers to attract future partners, the reputation system moderates the asymmetry of dependence and risk that threatens honest exchanges in Trust Games.

In the offline world, reputations are created and communicated through the word of mouth. Hence, the trust relationships among the Maghribi traders that Greif (1989:881) studied did not depend on central policing systems or internalized norms, but on informal reputation systems that linked "past conduct and future economic reward" in close-knit communities of merchants. In contrast, eBay harnesses the power of digital technology to provide an institutional mechanism for creating, maintaining, organizing, and disseminating reputations more systematically (Resnick et al. 2000).

Nee and Swedberg (this volume; also see Nee and Ingram 1998) define an institution as an interrelated web of formal and informal norms that govern social relationships. The effectiveness of institutional mechanisms in organizational performance depends crucially on the "coupling" of informal and formal norms. Informal norms can complement or oppose formal norms, just as formal norms can facilitate or undermine informal norms. While institutions are undoubtedly important, then, they are not sufficient to ensure socially desired outcomes or explain the rich complexities of economic action without the support of informal norms.

The case of eBay illustrates this point clearly. Feedback provision in eBay is strictly voluntary, and eBay does virtually nothing to ensure that people give honest and fair feedback. Given the cost of posting feedback in time and Internet connection, how do we explain buyers and sellers with hundreds and sometimes thousands of feedback points? How do we understand the success of eBay in terms of its institutional design? In this global electronic market, how are informal norms regulated and sustained? These are the questions that motivate this chapter.

In the following sections, I consider the affective basis of economic and social exchanges to account for the provision of feedback in eBay. Emotions have been largely neglected in sociology and economics alike (Frank 1988, 1993; Massey 2002; Pixley 2002). Weber, in *Economy and Society* (1968), considered markets devoid of emotions. But the growing literature on emotions in recent years has cast much suspicion on such statements. It is in this vein that I explore how the expression and the attribution of emotions might play an important role in online exchanges. A global electronic market may be an unlikely arena for rich emotional experiences. But if emotions can be found in online auctions, the case for a more integrated approach to the emotional basis of economic behavior, online or offline, is compelling.

EBAY AUCTIONS

> *"I think the first challenge that always confronts an online merchant is the idea of creating trust and confidence among users. There are still a large number of people who do not use the Internet on a regular basis, and there are, of course, a large number of people who have no interest in the Internet at all."*
>
> —Pierre Omidyar, Founder of eBay

THE SUCCESS OF eBay has been phenomenal. In its short history since 1995, it has become the largest person-to-person online auction site, boasting more than ten million auctions on any given day and 95 million registered users worldwide.[1] By total minutes spent browsing by users, it is the most popular shopping site on the Internet today—and all this for a marketplace so "ripe with the possibility of large-scale fraud and deceit" (Kollock 1999). Surprisingly, eBay offers no warranty. Instead, it serves only as a listing service while the buyers and the sellers assume all the risks associated with transactions between faceless strangers. Reports of fraud and complaints are not rare. Nonetheless, the overall rate of successful transactions remains remarkably high.

EBay attributes its success to the so-called Feedback Forum. After a transaction is completed, the buyer and the seller are given an opportunity to rate each other (+1, 0, or −1) and leave comments (e.g., "Nice person to do business with! Would highly recommend.") reflecting on their satisfaction with each other. EBay, in turn, posts their running net total of feedback points next to their screen names for others to view in the course of future transactions. Only registered users can participate in the reputation system. Each user can receive only one feedback point from a given partner, and they are not retractable once posted.

EBay's reputation system is far from perfect. It is hardly likely, for example, that a 3-point system can adequately capture the character and the motivations of so many sellers. Another issue is whether simply aggregating feedback points into net totals is meaningful. Malaga (2001) and Dellarocas (2000) have suggested more sophisticated algorithms to improve the accuracy of reputation systems. On the other hand, for what it is worth, the reputation system seems to be working remarkably well for eBay. In this virtual marketplace, where familiar faces are replaced by unmemorable pseudonyms, good reputations are indeed valuable assets, both as signals and as a basis of social control. Led by eBay's example, similar reputation systems have appeared in a number of other sites, including e-Businesses (e.g., Amazon.com), expert sites (e.g., ePinion.com, AllRecipes.com), and "meta-systems" (e.g., RepCheck.com).[2]

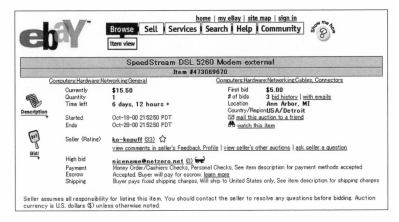

Figure 2 A screenshot of an eBay auction.

In this paper I consider an alternative interpretation of feedback exchange. In this view, based on Lawler's (Lawler and Yoon 1996; Lawler et al. 2000) theory of relational cohesion, feedback provision is motivated not by expectations of personal efficacy in exercising social control or by a sense of moral obligation to serve the eBay community at large, but by the expressive utility of affirming affective attachment to the other through symbolic gift-giving. These motivations are not mutually exclusive, of course, but their relative salience directly informs decisions to give feedback. I formalize this proposition in a model that proposes structural determinants of motivational salience.

The Problem of Feedback Provision

A growing body of empirical research has documented the significance of reputation effects on purchasing decisions in online auctions. Reputation has been found to have important economic values to sellers in particular. In a study of coin markets in eBay, Lucking-Reiley (2000) reports positive effects of seller reputation on final winning prices. Similarly, Ba and Pavlou (2002), Houser and Wooders (2001), and others (see Resnick et al. 2002) have variously found positive effects of reputation that increase with the market value of items sold. Bajari (2000) shows that sellers' reputation affects buyers' probability of entry into their auctions, and that negative feedback points in a seller's reputation profile are weighed more heavily than positive feedback in entry decisions.

In comparison to the growing interest in reputation effects, relatively little attention has been given to the problem of feedback provision. On the one hand, we needn't look far to see that high volumes of feedback are in fact exchanged between sellers and buyers on a daily basis in eBay. On the other hand, however, to assume that feedback provision is automatic is hardly warranted. As one eBayer complains:

> I was just wondering how much feedback other people get. . . . I've had 142 transactions as a seller this year, but I've received feedback for only 84 of them. 84! That's less than 60 percent. None of them are negative, so I must be a decent seller, and I always give feedback. . . . This is just ridiculous.
>
> (message posted on a public bulletin board)

Even if people decide to leave feedback, their choice of feedback may be biased by threats of retaliation (returning a negative for a negative) or the norm of reciprocity (returning a positive for a positive). "Negging" undeserving people, for example, is a recurrent problem in eBay:

> one of my bidders wasn't responding to emails from me regarding a payment that was owed to me for a won auction. I let about 30 days pass before I filed a NPB warning, then another 10 pass after that (at least) before I requested the refund. Days after I did that, he filed a negative comment towards me. I upheld my end—and did my best to contact him. However, now I have this negative comment on my rating. Isn't there anything I can do about this? I am an honest ebayer doing my best. Note, I never got an email from him—just a negative remark on my record.

> I know that an awful lot of eBayers do not leave feedback because they fear retaliation, and as a result the feedback system doesn't work as well as it could.

> I recently had the misfortune of being the high bidder on two auctions that were for fake Aubrey Beardsley prints. Images of authentic prints were used on the auction that had been taken from the web site of a reputable art dealer in Washington DC. The seller refused to answer my e-mails about the images having been taken from another site. I stated in my communication to her that my bid was based on the authenticity of the prints, but it was only after the auction closed that she admitted the fraud, and of course I did not pay for the fakes. A month later the same seller has the same fakes back up on eBay again. This time with new pix's, but the same fake prints. When I informed the seller that I would report her for fraud if she continued trying to sell the fake art, she used negative feedback to take revenge on me. Since I buy and sell art on eBay, this is a clear case of abuse of the feedback system.

Given possibilities of abusive and dishonest feedback exchanges, what is at stake is the very integrity of eBay as a whole, for the feedback system rests on two obvious yet critical assumptions. First, feedback must be given, and second, feedback must be given honestly (Resnick et al. 2000). The problem, of course, is that neither assumption seems to hold entirely in practice, as the messages from the online bulletin boards suggest. Some

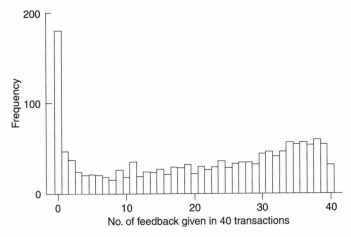

Figure 3 Distribution of buyers by the level of feedback provision in 40 transactions.

people may be more given to complaining than to praising, others to praising than to complaining. Still others might not bother leaving feedback at all. Surely, there are certain norms and codes of conduct regarding feedback exchanges, and new members can refer to written rules and guidelines provided on eBay's website.[3] Nevertheless, eBay does very little in the way of formally enforcing feedback provision.

Perhaps because reputations emerge in the offline world as natural byproducts of everyday interaction, how reputations are created has been generally overlooked in both empirical and theoretical research. In the online feedback system, however, feedback provision presents a compelling case of collective action (Avery et al. 1999). From the perspective of narrow rationality, it is surprising that anyone actually bothers to give feedback, particularly to people with hundreds and thousands of feedback points already—so many that another point hardly seems to matter. Considering the small but nontrivial cost of personal time and connection time on the Internet expended in each feedback exchange, as well as the absence of serious consequences for not giving feedback, it may be in the best rational interest of the individual simply to default on feedback provision. If so, feedback is likely to be underprovided.

Empirical findings suggest a more complex picture, however. The histogram in figure 3 shows the distribution of buyers by the number of feedback points given over their first 40 transactions.[4] Rational free-riders are well represented, to be sure. Those who gave fewer than 10 feedback points in 40 transactions constitute as much as 27 percent (N=408) of the buyer sample, including those gave who gave no feedback at all (N=181,

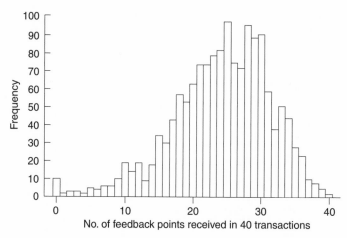

Figure 4 Distribution of buyers by the number of feedback points received in 40 transactions.

12 percent of the buyers). At the other end of the distribution, however, those who gave more than 30 feedback points (that is, in more than 75 percent of the transactions) make up 33 percent (N=496) of the buyers. Plausibly, then, many buyers are also motivated by normative concerns to provide feedback after every transaction.

But equally prominent in the distribution is the broad distribution of buyers across the middle ranges of feedback provision. What accounts for this heterogeneity in feedback provision levels? One possibility is that people have different threshold levels for participating in the reputation system. While everyone tends to drop out and become a free-rider sooner or later, some drop out after 10 transactions while others perhaps drop out after 30 transactions. Although this is a plausible explanation, actual feedback exchanges seem to be much more sporadic; a cursory look at individual feedback exchange patterns shows people giving feedback after one transaction, not giving feedback for sometime, then giving feedback a few more times. Moreover, it does not explain why some buyers receive more feedback than others, as shown below.

Figure 4 shows how much the same buyers received feedback from their sellers. While the shape of the distribution is quite different, what is to be noted here, again, is the large variance in feedback provision levels. While acknowledging certain differences across individuals in their propensity to exchange feedback, it seems difficult to account for the range of provision rates adequately on the basis of individual types alone. The aim of this study, then, is to explore an alternative explanation that accounts for situational variables in the exchange structures of online auctions.

Feedback provision in online reputation systems has been rarely considered at length so far. A notable exception is Resnick and Zeckhauser (2002; see also Avery et al. Zeckhauser 1999 and Dellarocas 2000). Using 1999 eBay transaction records as their data source, Resnick and Zeckhauser report feedback provision rates by buyers and sellers, the composition of feedback exchanges, and other vital statistics. Their findings, however, are primarily descriptive in nature. More broadly, then, the goal of this chapter is to complement their findings with a broader theoretical framework that suggests causal explanations and to make better sense of the feedback exchange patterns at the level of individual transactions.

Although the consequences of embeddedness have inspired much research, the causes of embeddedness have received much less attention (Uzzi 1996, 1997). Exceptions include studies by Kollock (1994) and Molm (1994). Their studies show that the formation of commitment relationships is facilitated by conditions of uncertainty in social and economic exchanges. The standard interpretation of this process is the reduction of uncertainty afforded by repeated interactions (Kollock 1994; Yamagishi and Yamagishi 1994; Axelrod 1984). Through repeated interactions, actors learn more about each other, invest in future profits from mutual cooperation, and generally become more committed to the relationship in which they have already expended so much time and other resources.

Lawler's theory of relational cohesion proposes an alternative avenue towards commitment in dyadic relationships and groups involved in joint projects. The fundamental premise of the theory is simple:

> [Social] exchange has emotional effects on actors, and if these are attributed to social units, the social unit takes on expressive value or intrinsic worth. Persons develop stronger ties to groups that are perceived as a source of positive feeling or emotion and weaker ties to those perceived as a source of negative feelings or emotion. (Lawler 2001: 625)

Successful exchanges produce an emotional "buzz" while unsuccessful exchanges produce mild negative feelings (Lawler and Yoon 1996; Lawler 2001). Actors are motivated to repeat transactions to the extent that they enjoy the experience of positive emotions. In other words, what underlies the formation of commitment under conditions of uncertainty in Lawler's theory is not uncertainty reduction, but affective attachment mediated by emotions generated in exchanges.

AFFECT ON THE INTERNET

But why do exchanges produce emotions? Surely, we seek in exchanges outcomes that are inherently valuable and desirable to various degrees.

But our emotional experiences are also conditioned by the level of risk and uncertainty in exchanges. We are more likely to feel stronger emotions— whether joy, relief, or anger and frustration—during and after risky exchanges than routine transactions.

Uncertainty is a significant aspect of eBay transactions as well. In online transactions between strangers, information asymmetry is inherent. Buyers in particular must be wary of dishonest sellers who misrepresent their auction items, never send their items after receiving payment, or send defective items. In contrast, sellers are relatively immune from exploitation, since they can withhold their items until they receive their payment. Still, they incur the cost of paying service charges to eBay for each completed auction (an auction that receives at least one bid before closing), even if the buyer backs out of the transaction. In fact, a majority of complaints associated with negative feedback points are from sellers to buyers who default on transactions (Mahajan and Lockwood 2001). More generally, sellers effectively have no control over who decides to buy from them; as a rule, they are obligated to honor any customers who win the auction, however high or low their reputations are. Some are responsible buyers, while many others do not care to send in their money promptly or communicate clearly, much to the annoyance of sellers. In all, these elements of risk and uncertainty create likely conditions for emotional experiences in online exchanges.

As operationalized in Lawler's studies (Lawler and Yoon 1996; Lawler 2001), gifts are token (has no or little monetary value), unilateral (given without an explicit expectation of reciprocity) and noncontingent (given voluntarily). Gift-giving occurs after the first-order exchange as an expression of gratitude or approval for a satisfactory exchange. Feedback provision in eBay can also be construed as a form of gift-giving: a feedback point is token to the extent that each point is worth very little, unilateral to the extent that nothing assures that the other gives feedback in return, and noncontingent to the extent that it does not obligate the other to reciprocate. According to Lawler, expressions of gratitude directed at the exchange partner after the first-order exchange "affirms a common definition of the situation and generates a measure of pride on the part of the giver. . . . Thus, giving behavior becomes important, not just because of future receiving, but because giving itself produces an internal reward (pride) mediated by the other's immediate reaction" (2001: 23). It may be an overstatement to speak of pride as such in simple online auctions between nameless strangers. Then again, it seems reasonable to assume that a successful transaction in a risky auction market can conjure some sort of emotional buzz, whether in the form of relief, a reaffirmed faith in the goodness of people, or—for that matter—a genuine sense of pride for having taken the risk to obtain a rare collector's item.

An interesting implication of an affective model of feedback provision is that giving feedback is assumed to be inherently gratifying or expressive rather than obligatory. From this perspective, actors are fundamentally willing to give feedback, although whether they do so depends on the outcome of exchange mediated by the structure of online exchange. Failure to give feedback therefore signifies not so much free-riding but a transaction, neither positive nor negative, that fails to induce feedback exchange as a means of expressing affective attachment or gratitude.

FEEDBACK PROVISION: AN AFFECTIVE-ATTACHMENT MODEL

I conceptualize an eBay transaction as consisting of the first-order economic exchange of material goods and the second-order social exchange of feedback. As illustrated in figure 5, the first-order exchange generates emotions that condition the process of evaluation, which determines the eventual decision to give or withhold feedback based on one's satisfaction with the outcomes of the first-order exchange.

Two structural variables constitute the main causal mechanism in my model. On the one hand, the effect of asymmetric risk in the first-order exchange is to mediate the emotional experience, such that a risky transaction generates higher levels of satisfaction or dissatisfaction compared to a less risky transaction. It follows that buyers, who assume greater risk in making their payment before receiving their items, are generally more likely to experience strong emotions than sellers are. On the other hand, the effect of asymmetric power in the second-order exchange is to orient the motivational basis of evaluation toward an expression of affective-symbolic attachment or rational-normative assertion of social control. Following Emerson (1976) I define the power to apply sanctions in second-order exchanges as inversely proportional to the receiver's dependence on the feedback. The implication for my model is that feedback to sellers, because of their greater dependence on feedback for reputation, is more likely to be given as social control on the basis of normative-rational evaluation, while feedback to buyers, by virtue of their relative immunity from reputation effects, is given on the basis of affective attachment. Thus, depending on the structure of exchange, the resulting feedback expresses the affective utility of gift giving or the normative-instrumental utility of social control in varying degrees.

While the main determinants of feedback provision in this model are situational—the structure and the outcome of exchanges—it does not preclude individual differences in sensitivity to power asymmetries, risk-aversion, etc, that similarly affect the evaluative process, as illustrated. Construed as personality types or behavioral orientations, these differences remain relatively stable across exchanges with different partners. Decisions to give feedback are therefore informed for each individual and

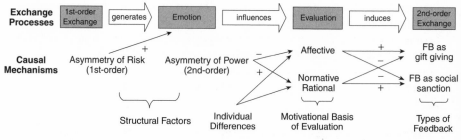

Figure 5 Exchange processes and causal mechanisms of feedback provision.

each transaction by the relative salience of the motivational bases of evaluation that varies according to both personal and situational factors.

SOME TESTABLE HYPOTHESES OF THE THEORY

My hypotheses concern the main structural variables of my model, risk asymmetry in first-order exchange of economic goods and power asymmetry in second-order exchange of feedback. The model predicts greater emotional experience in more risky transactions. For buyers, then, risk increases monotonically with the final bid. It follows that buyers should be more likely to give feedback after winning more expensive items. The effect of price on sellers is similar. While sellers assume comparatively less risk, they should experience greater affective attachment as buyers place greater trust in them.

> H1a: Price has a positive effect on feedback provision by buyers.
> H1b: Price has a positive effect on feedback provision by sellers.

Various price determinants in eBay have been studied in some detail, including bidding behavior (Roth and Ockenfels 2000), reputations of sellers (Lucking-Reiley 1998; Kollock 1999), and the presentation of items (Wood and Kauffman 2001). No study, however, has yet explored price effects on feedback provision.

Feedback provision, by hypothesis, is also affected by the asymmetry of power in the second-order exchange of feedback. To the extent that sellers are more dependent than buyers on building and maintaining good reputations, buyers are more likely to use feedback exchanges as social control. The implication is that buyers should be less likely to give feedback to sellers who have good reputations already. In comparison, for sellers, feedback exchanges remain primarily symbolic and affective in the sense of gift giving, in which the value of feedback is unaffected by the reputational profile of the receiver. Therefore:

H2a: Buyers are less likely to give feedback to sellers with many feedback points than those with few feedback points.

H2b: Sellers are equally likely to give feedback to buyers with many feedback points as to those with few feedback points.

These four hypotheses were tested using original data from eBay. Specifically, the dataset consisted of 282 auctions on collectible American penny coins, each receiving at least one bid. The final prices ranged from $6.50 to $750. The overall feedback provision rate was 48.3 percent by buyers and 57.2 percent by sellers. Repeated transactions—those occurring between buyers and sellers who have had at least one transaction before—comprise 9 percent of the buyer dataset and 18 percent of the seller dataset.

PRELIMINARY RESULTS

The results of logistic regression on feedback provision from buyers and from sellers are given below. Each exchange in the dataset was coded as 1 if feedback was given to the partner, 0 if otherwise. Two independent variables tested the hypotheses: final price and partner reputation. Two control variables were also included: own reputation and the number of previous exchanges with the same partner (repeats). But reputation measures were operationalized as the net of positive and negative feedback points. Two equivalent models were considered for two dependent variables, feedback provision from buyers to sellers and feedback provision from sellers to buyers. To control for within-subject heterogeneity in repeated measures across transactions, subjects were clustered in a random-effects model.

As shown in table 1, final price has a marginally significant effect for buyers $(0.018, p < 0.1)$ in the predicted direction, but its effect on sellers was not significant $(0.241, p = 0.36)$. Partner reputation is also marginally significant for buyers with a negative effect on feedback provision $(-0.025, p < 0.1)$, while—as predicted—it has no effect on feedback provision by sellers $(0.063, p = 0.74)$. Overall, the results seem to show moderate support for three of the four hypotheses, failing to support H1b.

While my model is agnostic about the control variables, their statistical significance is worth noting. The negative effects of own reputation suggest that both buyers and sellers are increasingly less likely to give feedback as they accumulate feedback points. One likely explanation, as already mentioned, is that they simply begin to free-ride after engaging in more and more transactions. Whatever motivates feedback exchanges—be it

TABLE 1
Predictors of Feedback Provision by Buyers

Predictors	Model 1	Model 2
Constant	0.391	0.405
Time	−0.015**	−0.015**
Repeats	0.023**	0.020**
Final Price ($)		0.018*
Seller Reputation		0.025*
Goodness of Fit[1]	0.19	0.48
% Correct Predictions	53.9%	56.4%

Note. 1: p values from Pearson goodness of fit test
*=$p<0.1$; **=$p<0.05$.

reciprocity, a sense of obligation, or affective attachment—the motivation probably wears off over time.

In repeated transactions, on the other hand, both buyers and sellers seem to exchange more feedback. Statistically, the effect of repeated exchanges is marginally significant for buyers (0.02, $p<0.1$) and strongly significant for sellers (0.012, $p<0.05$). If the natural tendency is to give less feedback over time, what sustains feedback exchanges in repeated transactions? It is well known that cooperation can emerge naturally in repeated interactions. Similarly, actors are more likely to experience affective attachment when successful interactions are repeated. More to the point, then, the positive effects of repeated exchanges are consistent with the predictions of the affective-attachment theory that gift-giving behavior increases across repeated interactions (Lawler and Yoon 1996; Lawler and Thye 1999).

Of course, these results must be qualified within their proper context. There are several outstanding issues with the data and analyses. First, the data include transactions in many categories in eBay, ranging widely in quality, quantity, and market price. My analyses do not control for these market conditions. Second, as already mentioned, the sellers in the data are neither random nor fixed, but selected by both the buyers and the larger market forces. It therefore remains to be seen how representative these sellers are. Finally, my analyses do not fully consider the implications of reciprocity and retaliation in feedback exchanges. The theory of affective-attachment assumes that gifts are given without expectations of reciprocity. Whether this assumption can be qualified in the context of feedback exchanges, and to what extent reciprocity (and not gift-giving) actually motivates feedback provision, are important questions for future research.

Conclusion

In large online markets, where monitoring and sanctioning by third parties are ineffective and costly, ensuring trust and honesty between anonymous strangers is a difficult issue. EBay's solution is to harness informal exchanges of feedback into a formal market for reputations. And for what it is worth, the system has worked out remarkably well so far. EBay provides no formal means of enforcing feedback provision. Nevertheless, large portions of the user community appear to participate in the reputation system. At a minimum, eBay's own success as well as similar adaptations by a number of other sites testify to the viability of formal reputation systems in the competitive and insecure world of emerging online markets.

This chapter has sought to make sense of feedback exchanges in eBay, focusing particularly on possible motivations for feedback provision. To this end, a model of feedback provision was proposed, in which affective attachment induces feedback exchange as gift-giving while rational-normative evaluation induces feedback exchange as social control. The initial analysis using a large but incomplete dataset confirmed the hypothesized effects of price and seller reputation on feedback provision by buyers. In the light of these findings, a more complete test of my hypotheses seems due for future research.

Overall, the contributions of this chapter are threefold. First, it draws heavily on Lawler's theory of relational cohesion and suggests its external validity in the context of online trading. More broadly, it calls for greater attention to the importance of affective behavior that shapes transactions in markets as seemingly impersonal as online auctions. In *Economy and Society* (1968), Weber referred variously to the market community as "the most impersonal relationship of practical life into which humans can enter with one another" and "fundamentally alien to any type of fraternal relationship" (636–37). Since Weber, few sociologists (e.g., Hochschild 1983; Katz 1999; see also Heckathorn 1993) have focused extensively on emotions. Sociologists are not alone in neglecting emotions, however. Elster (1998) has noted the overwhelming absence of attention to emotions in economic theory. Similar views have been expressed by Frank (1988, 1993), Etzioni (1988), and others. To be sure, of course, we need to look no farther than our own actions to see that we do care about how we feel and how we feel profoundly affects even our most impersonal or unconscious decisions, as numerous studies have also shown (see Goleman 1995; Claxton 1997). Similarly, Massey (2002:1) claims in his recent presidential address to the American Sociological Association that the emotional brain "operates independently of and strongly influences the rational brain." Lawler's theory of relational cohesion suggests one way in which emotions might help cement social bonds and provide a basis for commitment in online exchanges.

Second, this chapter has preliminary policy implications for eBay and online communities in general. My findings suggest that people may be reasonably willing to provide feedback, whether in the form of social sanctions or gift-giving, but whether they actually do depend critically on situational determinants. Crucial for the future of online markets, then, is to understand the actual motivations and intentions of their users and provide institutional mechanisms that structures their exchanges in ways that are most transparent and natural to them.

More to the point, institutional infrastructures must complement user experiences more broadly, not just their narrow rational interests but their broader social and personal needs as well. While game theory remains a powerful tool for guiding analyses of strategic interactions, it also tends to overstate the problem of cooperation. Heckathorn (1996), for example, has formally shown that not all social dilemmas are zero-sum games. Thus, in the type of dilemmas knows as Stag Hunt, the main issue is not trust, as in Prisoner's Dilemmas, but coordination. Likewise, if people are indeed motivated to cooperate for whatever reason, the important question may not be why they cooperate but how. In various interviews, Omidyar has repeatedly affirmed his view that "people are generally honest and trustworthy" (*Business Week* 2001). The critical function of the feedback system, from this perspective, may be not so much to induce cooperation and eradicate malfeasance, but simply to provide an institutional framework that organizes and structures the way people communicate their intentions to cooperate. This is one sense in which institutions serve as "focal points" of cooperation and coordination outside dyadic exchanges (Schelling 1960).

Finally, this paper suggests online markets as an important and intriguing avenue of social research, both methodologically and substantively. By their very nature, informal processes are difficult to observe in large scales, but successful implementations of information technologies help capture precious "e-trails" of social exchanges that constitute the fabric of growing online markets. As the case of eBay shows, the Internet affords us rich sources of data that allow us to study many fundamental social processes such as reputation effects that have eluded empirical research until now. Yet, in and of itself, the Internet has also become an important subject of social research. For better or worse, online markets have become permanent fixtures of today's capitalist economy. In many important ways, the Internet has borne more fluid, more dynamic, and more rational markets than we have ever seen offline. In other ways, however, online markets have also departed in many crucial ways from fundamental assumptions of the neoclassical model of markets (DeLong and Froomkin 2000). If so, studying online markets—from their emergence to their core processes—may prove a fruitful and fresh approach to understanding the logic of capitalism. Time seems ripe for an economic sociology of the Internet.

Notes

1. Source: *CNN Money*, January 2004. http://money.cnn.com/2004/01/21/news/companies/ebay

2. For a general discussion of online auction sites, see Lucking-Reiley (1999). For a general discussion of online reputation sytems, see Resnick et al. (2000) and Kollock (1998). For a review of empirical studies on online auctions, see Bajari and Hortaçsu (2004).

3. See eBay's SafeHarbor: Rules and Safety Overview. http://pages.ebay.com/help/community/index.html.

4. The dataset consisted of the first 40 transactions of 1,508 buyers in which they were the winning bidders. All the buyers in the sample were extracted randomly from a larger pool of people who joined eBay after February 20, 1999, and won 40 or mor auctions by June 1, 1991. I thank Paul Resnick for sharing these data.

References

Arrow, Kenneth J. 1962. "Economic Welfare and the Allocation of Resources for Invention." In *The Rate and Direction of Inventive Activity: Economic and Social Factors*, ed. Richard R. Nelson. Princeton: Princeton University Press.

Avery, Christopher, Paul Resnick, and Richard Zeckhauser. 1999. "The Market for Evaluations." *American Economic Review* 89(3): 564–84.

Axelrod, Robert. 1984. *The Evolution of Cooperation*. New York: Basic Books.

Ba, Sulin and Paul A. Pavlous. 2002. "Evidence of the Effect of Trust Building Technology in Electronic Markets: Price Premiums and Buyer Behavior." *MIS Quarterly* 26(3): 243–86.

Bajari, Patrick L. and Ali Hortaçsu. 2003. "The Winner's Curse, Reserve Prices and Endogenous Entry: Empirical Insights from EBay Auctions." *Rand Journal of Economics* 3(2): 329–55.

Business Week. 1999. "Going, Going, Gone: Online Haggling Is the Hottest Thing Happening in E-Commerce." Issue 3624, April 12.

———. 2001. "The People's Company." Issue 3760, December 2.

Claxton, Guy. 1997. *Hare Brain, Tortoise Mind: Why Intelligence Increases When You Think Less*. New York: HarperCollins.

Coleman, James S. 1990. *Foundations of Social Theory*. Cambridge, Mass.: Belknap Press of Harvard University Press.

Dasgupta, Partha. 1988. "Trust as a Commodity." In *Trust: Making and Breaking cooperative Relations*, ed. Diego Gambetta. Oxford: Blackwell.

Dellarocas, Chrysanthos. 2000. "Immunizing Online Reputation Reporting Systems against Unfair Ratings and Discriminatory Behavior." Paper presented at ACM Conference on Electronic Commerce, Minneapolis, October 17–20.

DeLong, J. Bradford and A. Michael Froomkin. 2000. "Speculative Microeconomics for Tomorrow's Economy." In *Internet Publishing and Beyond: The Ecomomics of Digital Information and Intellectual Property*, ed. Brian Kahin and Hal. R. Varian. Cambridge, Mass.: MIT Press.

Economist. 2000. "Internet Economics: A Thinker's Guide." March 30.

———. 2001. "Doing eBay's Bidding." November 9.

Elster, Jon. 1998. "Emotions and Economic Theory." *Journal of Economic Literature* 36: 47–74.

Emerson, Richard. 1962. "Power-Dependence Relations." *American Sociological Review* 27: 31–40.

———. 1976. "Social Exchange Theory." *Annual Review of Sociology* 2: 335–62.

Etzioni, Amitai. 1988. *The Moral Dimension: Toward a New Economics.* New York: Free Press.

Flache, Andreas and Michael W. Macy. 1996. "The Weakness of Strong Ties: Collective Action Failure in a Highly Cohesive Group." *Journal of Mathematical Sociology* 21: 3–28.

Frank, Robert H. 1988. *Passions within Reason: The Strategic Role of the Emotions.* New York: W.W. Norton.

———. 1993. "The Strategic Role of the Emotions." *Rationality and Society* 5(2): 160–84.

Gambetta, Diego. 1988. *Trust: Making and Breaking Cooperative Relations.* New York: Blackwell.

Gates, Bill. 1999. *Business @ the Speed of Light: Using a Digital Nervous System.* New York: Warner Books.

Goleman, Daniel. 1995. *Emotional Intelligence.* New York: Bantam Books.

Granovetter, Mark S. 1985. "Economic Action and Social Structure: The Problem of Embeddedness." *American Journal of Sociology* 91(3): 481–510.

Greif, Avner. 1989. "Reputation and Coalitions in Medieval Trade: Evidence on the Maghribi Traders." *Journal of Economic History* 49(4): 857–82.

Hardin, Russell. 2001. "Conceptions and Explanations of Trust." In *Trust in Society*, ed. Karen S. Cook. New York: Russell Sage.

Heckathorn, Douglas D. 1993. "Emotions and Rational Choice." *Rationality and Society* 5(2): 157–59.

Hochschild, Arlie Russell. 1983. *The Managed Heart: Commercialization of Human Feeling.* Berkeley: University of California Press.

Houser, Daniel E. and John Wooders. 2001. "Reputation in Auctions: Theory and Evidence from eBay." Working paper, Department of Economics, University of Arizona.

Katz, Jack. 1999. *How Emotions Work.* Chicago: University of Chicago Press.

Kollock, Peter. 1994. The Emergence of Exchange Structures: An Experimental Study of Uncertainty, Commitment, and Trust. *American Journal of Sociology* 100: 313–45.

———. 1999. "The Production of Trust in Online Markets." In *Advances in Group Processes*, vol. 16, ed. Shane R. Thye, Edward J. Lawler, Michael W. Macy, and Henry Walker. Geeenwich, Conn.: JAI Press.

Kreps, David M. 1990. "Corporate Culture and Economic Theory." In *Perspectives on Positive Political Economy*, ed. James E. Alt and Kenneth A. Shepsle. Cambridge: Cambridge University Press.

Lawler, Edward J. 2001. "An Affect Theory of Social Exchange." *American Journal of Sociology* 107(2): 321–52.

Lawler, Edward J. and Shane R. Thye. 1999. "Bringing Emotions into Social Exchange Theory." *Annual Review of Sociology* 25: 217–44.

Lawler, Edward J., Shane R. Thye, and Jeongkoo Yoon. 2000. "Emotion and Group Cohesion in Productive Exchange." *American Journal of Sociology* 106: 616–57.

Lawler, Edward J. and Jeongkoo Yoon. 1996. "Commitment in Exchange Relations: Test of a Theory of Relational Cohesion." *American Sociological Review* 61: 89–108.

Lucking-Reiley, David. 2000. "Auctions on the Internet: What's Being Auctioned and How?" *Journal of Industrial Economics* 48: 227–52.

Lucking-Reiley, David H., Doug Bryan, Naghi Prasad, and Daniel Reeves. 2000. "Pennies from eBay: The Determinants of Price in Online Auctions." Working paper, Department of Economics, Vanderbilt University, January.

Luhmann, Niklas. 1979. *Trust and Power.* London: John Wiley.

Mahajan, Mihir and Kate Lockwood. 2001. "An Analysis of eBay Feedback Comments." Working paper, School of Information, University of Michigan.

Malaga, Ross. 2001. "Web-Based Reputation Management Systems: Problems and Suggested Solutions." *Electronic Commerce Research* 1:403–17.

Massey, Douglas S. 2002. "A Brief History of Human Society: The Origin and Role of Emotion in Social Life." *American Sociological Review* 67: 1–29.

Molm, Linda. 1994. "Dependence and Risk: Transforming the Structure of Social Exchange." *Social Psychology Quarterly* 57: 163–89.

Nee, Victor and Paul Ingram. 1998. "Embeddedness and Beyond: Institutions, Exchange, and Social Structure." In *The New Institutionalism in Sociology*, ed. Mary C. Brinton and Victor Nee. New York: Russell Sage. 19–45.

Nowak, Martin A. and Karl Sigmund. 1992. "Tit for Tat in Heterogeneous Populations." *Nature* 355: 250–52.

———. 1993. "A Strategy of Win-Stay, Lose-Shift That Outperforms Tit-for-Tat in the Prisoner's Dilemma Game." *Nature* 364: 56–58.

———. 1998. "Evolution of Indirect Reciprocity by Image Scoring." *Nature* 393: 235–39.

Oliver, Pamela. 1980. "Rewards and Punishments as Selective Incentives for Collective Action: Theoretical Investigations." *American Journal of Sociology* 85: 1356–75.

Pixley, Jocelyn. 2002. "Finance Organization, Decisions and Emotions. *British Journal of Sociology* 53(1): 41–65.

Resnick, Paul and Richard Zeckhauser. 2002. "Trust among Strangers in Internet Transactions: Empirical Analysis of eBay's Reputation System." In *The Economics of the Internet and E-Commerce*, ed. Michael R. Baye. Advances in Applied Microeconomics 2. Amsterdam: Elsevier.

Resnick, Paul, Richard Zeckhauser, Eric Friedman, and Ko Kuwabara. 2000. "Reputation Systems." *Communications of the ACM* 43: 45–48.

Resnick, Paul, Richard Zeckhauser, John Swanson, and Kate Lockwood. 2002. "The Value of Reputation on eBay: A Controlled Experiment." Paper presented at the Economic Science Association Conference, Boston. http://www.si.umich.edu/~presnick/papers/postcards/

Roth, Alvin E. and Axel Ockenfels. 2000. "Last Minute Bidding and Rules for Ending Second-Price Auctions: Theory and Evidence from a Natural Experiment on the Internet." NBER Working Paper 7729, June. National Bureau of Economic Research online.

Schelling, Thomas C. 1960. *The Strategy of Conflict.* Cambridge, Mass.: Harvard University Press.

Sztompka, Piotr. 1999. *Trust: A Sociological Theory.* Cambridge: Cambridge University Press.

Wood, Charles A. and Robert J. Kauffman 2001. "What Factors Drive Final Price in Internet Auctions? An Empirical Assessment of Coin Transactions on eBay." Paper presented at Institute for Operations Research and the Management Sciences annual meeting, Boca Raton, Florida, November 6.

Uzzi, Brian. 1996. "The Sources and Consequences of Embeddedness for the Economic Performance of Organizations: The Network Effect." *American Sociological Review* 61: 674–98.

———. 1997. "Social Structure and Competition in Interfirm Networks: The Paradox of Embeddedness." *Administrative Science Quarterly* 42: 35–67.

Weber, Max. [1922]1968. *Economy and Society: An Outline of Interpretive Sociology.* 3 vols. New York: Bedminster Press.

Yamagishi, Toshio. 1998. *The Structure of Trust: The Evolutionary Games of Mind and Society.* Tokyo: University of Tokyo Press.

Yamagishi, Toshio and Midori Yamagishi. 1994. "Trust and Commitment in the United States and Japan." *Motivation and Emotion* 18: 9–66.

Yin, Pai-Ling. 2003. "Information Dispersion and Auction Prices." Working paper, Harvard Business School.

Circuits within Capitalism

Viviana A. Zelizer

IN RECENT YEARS, economic prophets have frequently warned us against global commodification and the loss of moral-emotional fiber it brings. From Robert Kuttner's (1997) *Everything for Sale*, Robert Lane's (2000) *The Loss of Happiness in Market Democracies*, to Jeremy Rifkin's (2000) *The Age of Access: The New Culture of Hypercapitalism Where All of Life is a Paid-For Experience*, social critics fret incessantly over what Rifkin calls the "clash of culture and commerce." "When most relationships become commercial relationships," Rifkin (2000: 112) worries, "what is left for relationships of a noncommercial nature . . . when one's life becomes little more than an ongoing series of commercial transactions held together by contracts and financial instruments, what happens to the kinds of traditional reciprocal relationships that are born of affection, love, and devotion?" Rifkin's implied answer: nothing is left but cold instrumental rationality. Jean Bethke Elshtain (2000: 47) agrees: while "it used to be that some things, whole areas of life, were not up for grabs as part of the world of buying and selling," today, she laments, "nothing is holy, sacred, or off-limits in a world in which everything is for sale."

Worries about the incompatibility, incommensurability, or contradiction between intimate and impersonal relations follow a longstanding tradition. Since the nineteenth century social analysts have repeatedly assumed that the social world organizes around competing, incompatible principles: Gemeinschaft and Gesellschaft, ascription and achievement, sentiment and rationality, solidarity and self-interest. Their mixing, goes the theory, contaminates both; invasion of the sentimental world by instrumental rationality desiccates that world, while introduction of sentiment into rational transactions produces inefficiency, favoritism, cronyism, and other forms of corruption.

The theory gained force with reactions to nineteenth-century industrial capitalism. We can usefully follow Chris and Charles Tilly in defining

I have adapted a few passages each from Zelizer 2000a, b, 2001, and 2002a, plus substantial portions of Zelizer 2002b and 2004. I thank Nina Bandelj, Bernard Barber, Jérôme Blanc, Randall Collins, Eric Helleiner, Alexandra Kalev, Andrew Leyshon, Gary T. Marx, Victor Nee, Alex Preda, Arthur Stinchcombe, Richard Swedberg, Nao Terai, and Charles Tilly for their advice, suggestions, and assistance on different versions.

capitalism as "the system of production in which holders of capital, backed by law and state power, make the crucial decisions concerning the character and allocation of work" (Tilly and Tilly 1998:24). Although markets for commodities, labor, land, and capital itself thrive under a wide variety of economic systems, capitalism stands out from the rest in the extent to which holders of capital shape those markets by means of their investments, transfers, and organizational interventions. For advocates of the system, it benefits from the tight interaction of capitalist rationality with the rationality of markets. For critics of the system, that is precisely the problem: capitalism serves capital all too well, while neglecting or exploiting other worthy contributors to collective welfare.

Although earlier theorists had often allowed for the coexistence of solidarity and self-interest, both advocates and critics of industrial capitalism therefore adopted a sweeping, risky assumption: that capitalist rationality was driving solidarity, sentiment, and intimacy from markets, firms, and national economies (Hirschman 1977; Tilly 1984). Whether they deplored capitalism's advance, celebrated it, or treated it as a necessary evil, they commonly agreed on an idea of contamination: sentiment within the economic sphere generates favoritism and inefficiency, while rationality within the sentimental sphere destroys solidarity. Thus strong segregation of the spheres served both of them.

The theory of separate spheres had a perverse consequence. It provided a justification for giving lesser economic rewards, or none at all, to efforts supporting solidarity, sentiment, and intimacy. Parents, spouses, friends, and providers of care, ran the argument, acted out of duty and love that would dissolve if exposed to the acid of markets. Public policy, the argument continued, should actually reinforce the barrier between the two spheres by such devices as assuring male breadwinners of sufficient wages to support their (nonworking) families, banning the underpaid work of women and children, encouraging charity for the worthy unemployed, and (more daringly) paying family allowances from public funds.

The theory reappeared in camouflage as organizational analysts noticed new forms of capitalism emerging after World War II. Where firms, markets, friendships, families, governments, and associations had seemed to be differentiating ever more sharply as capitalism advanced, now new organizational forms called forth such terms as flexible production, hybrid firm, and network forms. As Paul DiMaggio puts it,

> For all their diversity, the firms to which researchers called attention shared several notable features: greater suppleness than their more traditionally bureaucratic counterparts, a greater willingness to trust employees and business partners, a preference for long-term "relational contracting" over short-term market exchange for many transactions, a commitment to ongoing technological improvement—and

an apparent renunciation of central features of Weber's model [of bureaucratization]. (DiMaggio 2001: 19)

Given dichotomous theories of sentiment and rationality, the new organizational forms raised an acute puzzle: would such new ways of doing business eventually suffer inefficiency, cronyism, and corruption precisely because they breached boundaries between Gemeinschaft and Gesellschaft? For the most part, analysts of economic change clung to the idea of incompatible separate spheres.

Economic sociologists and other professional students of economic processes have commonly incorporated more sophisticated versions of the same doctrine into their analyses of globalization, commodification, and rationalization. They have thought that market expansion inexorably eroded intimate social ties and narrowed the number of settings in which intimacy could prosper, while increasing contrasts between such settings and the cold world of economic rationality. They have therefore often joined social critics in supposing that twenty-first-century globalization will undercut caring activity, deplete the richness of social life, and thus threaten social solidarity.

The twenty-first century may well bring terrifying changes in social life, but they will not occur because commodification in itself generally destroys intimacy. This paper challenges the widespread assumption that markets ipso facto undercut solidarity-sustaining personal relations. It offers an alternative to the conventional account of interplay between market transactions and personal relations. The analysis brings together seven elements:

- a sustained critique of radical dichotomies between intimate and impersonal social ties;
- identification of commercial circuits as bridging structures that facilitate the coexistence of intimate and impersonal social ties;
- reminders that anthropologists have frequently encountered commercial circuits in supposedly noncapitalist social settings;
- After a quick glance at capitalist firms, a review of two areas of economic activity commonly thought to demonstrate (and suffer from) the incompatibility of intimate and impersonal social ties—local monetary systems, and caring labor—for evidence of stable coexistence between commercial transactions and interpersonal intimacy;
- identification of parallels in the formation and operation of commercial circuits within those two areas;
- arguments that in each area those circuits facilitate the coexistence of commercial transactions and interpersonal intimacy, but also generate exclusion and inequality in relation to outsiders;
- proposals for further inquiry into relations between commercial circuits (which form widely outside of capitalism) and capitalism as such.

Interweaving these themes, the paper takes up in order the general critique, the presentation of circuits, the anthropological literature, circuits of local money, caring connections, proposals, and conclusions.

How Analysts Go Wrong

Explicitly or implicitly, most analysts of intimate social relations join ordinary people in assuming that the entry of instrumental means such as monetization and cost accounting into the worlds of caring, friendship, sexuality, and parent-child relations depletes them of their richness, hence that zones of intimacy only thrive if people erect effective barriers around them. Thus emerges a view of *Hostile Worlds*: of properly segregated domains whose sanitary management requires well maintained boundaries.

Uncomfortable with such dualisms and eager to forward single-principle accounts of social life, opponents of Hostile Worlds views have now and then countered with reductionist *Nothing But* arguments: the ostensibly separate world of intimate social relations, they argue, is nothing but a special case of some general principle. Nothing But advocates divide among three principles: nothing but economic rationality, nothing but culture, and nothing but politics. Thus for economic reductionists caring, friendship, sexuality, and parent-child relations become special cases of advantage-seeking individual choice under conditions of constraint—in short, of economic rationality. For cultural reductionists, such phenomena become expressions of distinct beliefs. Others insist on the political, coercive, and exploitative bases of the same phenomena.

Neither Hostile Worlds formulations nor Nothing But reductions deal adequately with the intersection of intimate social ties and ordering institutions such as money, markets, bureaucracies, and specialized associations. Careful observers of such institutions always report the presence, and often the wild profusion, of intimate ties in their midst.

In order to describe and explain what actually goes on in these regards, we must move beyond Hostile Worlds and Nothing But ideas. Let me propose an alternative third way: the analysis of *Bridges*. We can bridge the analytical gap between intimacy and impersonality by recognizing the existence of differentiated ties that cut across particular social settings. In all sorts of settings, from predominantly intimate to predominantly impersonal, people differentiate strongly among various kinds of interpersonal relations, marking them with distinctive names, symbols, practices, and media of exchange. Ties themselves do vary from intimate to impersonal and from durable to fleeting. But almost all social settings contain mixtures of ties that differ in these regards.

Interpersonal ties typically connect people within the setting to different arrays of others both within and outside the setting. Such differentiated ties often ramify into what Randall Collins (2000, 2004) calls "Zelizer circuits." Each distinctive social circuit incorporates somewhat different understandings, practices, information, obligations, rights, symbols, and media of exchange. I call these *circuits of commerce* in an old sense of the word, where commerce meant conversation, interchange, intercourse, and mutual shaping. They range from the most intimate to quite impersonal social transactions.[1]

By definition, every circuit involves a network, a bounded set of relations among social sites. "Circuit," however, is neither simply a fancy new name for "network" nor a sanitized version of "community." Two features distinguish circuits from networks as usually conceived. First, they consist of dynamic, meaningful, incessantly negotiated interactions among the sites—be those sites individuals, households, organizations, or other social entities. Second, in addition to dynamic relations, they include distinctive media (for example, legal tender or localized tokens) and an array of organized, differentiated transfers (for example, gifts or compensation) between sites. Commercial circuits also differ from communities as conceived of in the Gemeinschaft-Gesellschaft tradition. They do not consist of spatially and socially segregated rounds of life; although circuits sometimes exist *within* encompassing communities, they ordinarily cut across multiple social settings, coordinating only certain kinds of activities and social relations within each setting.

More specifically, any commercial circuit includes four elements:

- it has a well-defined boundary with some control over transactions crossing the boundary;
- a distinctive set of transfers of goods, services, or claims upon them occurs within its interpersonal ties;
- those transfers employ distinctive media;
- ties among participants have shared meaning.

In combination, these four elements imply the presence of an institutional structure that reinforces credit, trust, and reciprocity within its perimeter, but organizes exclusion and inequality in relation to outsiders.

Social relations vary in the extent to which they convey information and attention that is (or is not) widely available to third parties. We call *impersonal* those relations conveying only widely available information and attention, *intimate* those that convey information and attention not widely available to third parties. Since media and transfers always attach to specific sets of meaningful social relations and since to choose a medium is also to commit oneself to a corresponding set of transfers and relations, Hostile Worlds doctrines express wariness of conflicting commitments between impersonal and intimate relations to the same or closely connected persons.

Earmarking practices and creation of circuits reduce that risk, especially because (almost by definition) intimate relations generate circuits of smaller scope—particularized information and attention depends heavily on shared local knowledge and does not easily sustain uniform institutions like those that underlie standardized large-scale exchange systems. The fragility of disciplined sects that do impose intimacy, and their reliance on extensive institutional controls, indicate that the point is not tautological; intimate circuits only work on the large scale under exceptional institutional conditions. Hence the interest of trade diasporas, migrant remittances, underground sects, rotating credit associations, and credit in the absence of authoritative central institutions.

Circuits, then, do not comprise communities in the sense of closed-off, all-encompassing social relations. Circuits do not differentiate whole social settings or organizations. In fact, the same people participate in different circuits simultaneously. Contrary to the views of such social critics as Michael Walzer (1983), that is why there are no specific "spheres" that can be contaminated by money. Despite the ideologies of their proponents, as we shall see, local monies do not form closed communities; the same people who participate in local currency systems ordinarily use nationally sanctioned legal tender for a wide variety of transactions outside of those systems.

Nevertheless, circuits do not exhaust all cross-cutting social structures. Legally established categories such as Social Security recipient or registered Republican do not in themselves constitute circuits. Nor do organizations, neighborhoods, kinship groups, religious congregations, or networks defined by diffusion of certain objects or information (e.g., disease or rumor)—*unless* they also create bounded sets of media and transfers. The pressing theoretical and empirical tasks are therefore (1) to specify the mechanisms and processes that generate bounded media and transfers and (2) to describe and explain how and why those mechanisms and processes operate differently across the range from impersonal to intimate transactions.

How does thinking about circuits improve on straightforward thinking about networks? If you only have a set of relations which are not bounded and have no distinctive content, no circuit exists. Every circuit includes a boundary, distinctive cultural materials, and particular forms of transfer and media. It of course also includes a network—particular ties and relations. But thinking about circuits raises questions that remain invisible to strict network analysis.

ANTHROPOLOGISTS CONFRONT CIRCUITS

Without using the term "circuits," anthropologists have frequently noticed the phenomenon. Nearly half a century ago, Paul Bohannan (1955, 1959) discerned what he called spheres of exchange among the Tiv. Each sphere, according to Bohannan, specialized in a restricted set of commodities which people could not exchange across spheres. In this analysis, modern money supplanted such spheres by making a medium of universal exchange available. Subsequent anthropologists followed Bohannan's error in supposing that restricted spheres of exchange disappeared with the onset of modern society or the integration of nonliterate people into the metropolitan world.

Frederick Pryor (1977) formalized the idea, identifying "exchange spheres" as social arrangements in which valuables of one delimited set cannot be exchanged for valuables of another such set without the breaking of a prohibition or one of the parties' losing prestige if the transaction becomes widely known. For Pryor an "exchange circuit" is the special case of an exchange sphere in which goods within the set cannot be traded symmetrically—for example, one can get B for A, C for B, and A for C, but not A for B, B for C, or C for A. Pryor actually recognizes that money in complex societies shares some characteristics of exchange spheres and circuits, by excluding certain goods and services, but fails to pursue that insight into the contemporary world (see also Barth 1967).

Recent ethnography has moved one step beyond Pryor, noting how the integration of previously distinct economies has refuted the widespread expectation that state-backed currencies would obliterate those economies' differentiated monetary spheres. For Melanesia, Joel Robbins and David Akin remark that:

> Widespread social scientific expectations that global capitalist expansion would quickly overwhelm traditional Melanesian economies have been confounded by the latter's dynamism and resilience. Indeed, many local systems of exchange appear to have flourished rather than withered from linkage with the world economy, and state currencies and imported goods mingle within formal exchange systems fundamental to social reproduction. Far from the advent of money having consigned indigenous currencies to irrelevance, the two instruments of exchange are clearly in dialogue throughout Melanesia. (Akin and Robbins 1999: 1; see also Crump 1981; Parry and Bloch 1989; Guyer 1995)

Thus, anthropologists have recognized most elements of commercial circuits in nonliterate as well as in developing social settings, and even occasionally in advanced capitalist countries (see Bloch 1994). They have not, however, assembled those elements into a working model, or traced their variations within contemporary capitalist economies. Similarly, economists are increasingly paying attention to the phenomenon that Jérôme Blanc (2000) calls "parallel monies." Pointing to the vibrant presence of multiple monies in contemporary economies—ranging among foreign currencies circulating alongside national legal tender, merchandise coupons, school vouchers, local currencies, and commodities such as cigarettes used as media of exchange—Blanc contends that such parallel currencies

> are not a residual and archaic phenomenon, which would imply their disappearance with the increasing rationalization of money in westernizing societies; it concerns as well, and especially so, developed and financially stable economies. As witnessed by the emergence of a vast number of parallel monies in the last quarter of the 20th century, we cannot conclude that social modernity will destroy these instruments. (Blanc 2000: 321)

Still, neither anthropologists nor economists have specified the social processes through which people create, sustain, and change distinctive configurations of media, transfers, and social relations.

We can gain theoretically and empirically by picking up where the anthropologists and economists have left off. Many apparently disparate social phenomena incorporate circuits of commerce. Sensitized by the concept, we can detect interesting parallels among the worlds of professional boxers, the art trade, sales of electronic components; financial traders, favor-trading networks maintained by Russian households, French amateur gardeners, American garment manufacturers, Australian hotel managers, rotating credit associations, direct sales organizations, migrants' use of remittances, ties among venture capitalists, and concentration camps (see, e.g., Wacquant 1998, 2000; Velthuis 2003; Darr 2003; Knorr Cetina and Bruegger 2002; Ledeneva 1998; Weber 1998; Uzzi 1997; Ingram and Roberts 2000; Biggart 1989, 2001; Durand et al. 1996; Indergaard 2002; Narotzky and Moreno 2002).

Circuits of commerce, then, clearly play significant parts in economic transactions. Economists, sociologists, and anthropologists who have seen them in operation have commonly treated them as imperfect markets, as institutional contexts for market transactions, or as nonmarket systems of exchange, but not as distinctive social structures with dynamics of their own. Nevertheless, close observers of capitalist corporations have regularly detected circuits operating *within* those presumably rationalized hierarchies—not only internal labor markets and patron-client networks with their own distinctive media and understandings, but also faction-defined circuits, gender-segregated circuits, and circuits separating major "cultures" within the firm (see, e.g., Anteby 2003; Dalton 1959; Kanter 1977; Morrill 1995; Tilly 1998).

Instead of following such important but relatively well documented instances of corporate circuits, let us examine their operation in two spheres that people have usually considered to be extra-economic: local currencies and the provision of personal care.

LOCAL CURRENCIES

An intriguing instance of circuit-building comes from a recent proliferating movement in Europe and the Americas: the local money movement. In a partial reconstitution of the multiple monetary circuits that existed before governments imposed national legal tenders, many communities around the world have over the past two decades been creating their own distinctive currencies. During the nineteenth century, American stores, businesses, and other organizations often produced their own currency, mostly as a way to counter the scarcity of small change. Even company towns, labor exchanges, churches, and brothels sometimes issued their own monies. Similarly, during the United States Depression of the 1930s, many schemes of barter and scrip grew up in economically hard-pressed areas (for a more general review of labor exchanges dating from the Depression, see Diehl 1937).

Creating a medium to mark a circuit, then, is not a new strategy. Plenty of current practices include one version or another of specialized media. Discount coupons in grocery chains, frequent flier miles on airlines, and credit purchasing within local communities involve formation of distinctive circuits. Food stamps likewise establish their own configurations of media, transfers, and interpersonal ties. Or consider the case of affinity credit cards, issued by a given community or organization and having proceeds earmarked for that group. Local currencies, however, are uniquely situated within distinct spatial territories. The recent deliberate creation of local monies simply dramatizes the significant place of interpersonal circuits in the organization of ostensibly impersonal economic life. Unlike their predecessors, however, many of the new local currencies come out of a broader movement seeking to escape what participants commonly regard as the corrupting effects of national and global economies.

From the Australian "green dollars" and the French "grain de sel" to the Italian "Misthòs," the German Talent, the Mexican Tlaloc, the Argentine "créditos," the Japanese "ecomoney," or the "Seeds" of Mendocino, California, local currencies mark geographically circumscribed circuits of commerce (see Helleiner 1999, 2000; Powell 2002; Rizzo 1999; Schroeder 2002; Servet 1999; *Trends in Japan* 2001). These currencies belong to well-organized local groups that go by names such as local exchange and trading schemes (LETS), systèmes d'échange local (SEL), Banca del Tempo

(Bdt), SRI (Sistema di Reciprocità Indiretta), Club del Trueque, Tauschring, and HOURS.

In the year 2000, an obviously incomplete listing by the Schumacher Society, specialists in promoting local currencies, included 33 such groups in the U.S. alone.[2] Observers of Germany, France, and Italy report some 300 such circuits in each country, including such currencies as grain de sel (Ariège), Piaf (Paris), Cocagne (Toulouse), or Talent (Germany) (see, e.g., Laacher 1999; Pierret 1999). In the U.S., along with the Mendocino SEEDS, we find such fetching currency names as Kansas City's Barter Bucks, Prescott, Arizona's High Desert Dollars, New Orleans's Mo Money, and Berkeley's BREAD. Although some enthusiasts for these local arrangements imagine they are doing away with money entirely, in fact they are creating new forms of money devoted to distinctive circuits.

Discussions of local money often mention, and sometimes confuse, four rather different phenomena: pegged currencies, time exchanges, commodity-based systems, and barter. *Pegged currencies* establish a distinct local medium whose value corresponds to that of legal tender. *Time exchanges* take their value from hours of effort contributed by their members. *Commodity-based systems* involve coupons, vouchers, and credits that are ultimately redeemable only in certain earmarked goods or services. *Barter* includes direct exchange of goods and services for each other without intervention of a currency. Although combinations of all four systems appear here and there, the overwhelming majority of deliberately organized local monetary systems fall in the range of the first two, from pegged currencies to time exchanges.

To see the actual working of local currency circuits, we can focus on one example each of those two types; first, pegged systems and then, time exchanges. In neither case is the local currency convertible into national legal tender. In Local Exchange and Trading Schemes (LETS) members transfer goods and services using a locally circumscribed medium, usually pegged to a national currency. At least two major variants of LETS exist. Some create tokens to represent their currency, while others rely on telephone-linked or computer-based central accounts without physical tokens. How do LETS work? Participants generally pay an entrance fee and subscribe to a service listing available goods and services provided by members of a circuit. Buyers and sellers contact each other and negotiate a price; their transaction is then recorded by the local LETS office.

These local monetary systems range from half a dozen members to several thousand. Observers report a total of some 20,000 LETS members in England and 30,000 in France, a figure suggesting an average of about 100 members per circuit (see Williams 1996; Laacher 1999). In his excellent survey of local currencies, Jérôme Blanc estimates 250,000 members of LETS across the world at the beginning of the year 2000 (Blanc 2000: 243). The systems vary with respect to each of the elements of circuits identified earlier: a well-defined boundary with some control over transactions crossing the boundary; a distinctive set of transfers of goods, services, or claims upon them occurring within the ties; those transfers employing distinctive media; and ties among participants having some shared meaning.

The hundreds of French SEL for example, vary in the networks on which they build; local memberships range among engineers, ecological enthusiasts, city people who have fled to the country, and low-income populations. In the French town of Pont-de-Montvert, of the local SEL's 130 members, 15 are children who exchange toys, books, and musical instruments (Servet 1999: 45).

Although no one has looked comparatively at the composition of local monetary systems in detail, available descriptions leave the impression that they tend to be socially homogeneous and, on balance, relatively high in status. Internal differences in participation by age and gender (see, e.g., Raddon 2003) do not significantly qualify that impression. All such systems restrict participation in some regards. In Germany some *Tauschring* circuits restrict their membership to the elderly, the handicapped, foreigners, or women. Others expand their circuit to include whole communities or firms (Pierret 1999). Even those, however, remain radically delimited as compared to the scope of legal tender.

Accordingly, local trading systems also specialize in different arrays of goods and services. In France, for example, exchanges in urban SEL concentrate on transportation, administrative service, education, bodily care, and counseling (Laacher 1999). In rural areas, on the other hand, participants are more likely to trade in food products, clothing, construction, and machine repair. As a French commentator observes, "Courses in analytic philosophy offered in Ariège are less likely to find takers than food or transportation. In Paris, a laying hen or farm tools would most likely be less in demand than administrative services computing" (Laacher 1998: 251).

Significantly, many SEL circuits ban transfers of certain goods and services as morally, ecologically, or politically off-limits. Banned commodities include firearms, animals, goods manufactured by third-world exploitation, and in one case a member's book on "how to get rich quick" (Bayon 1999: 73–74). Denis Bayon, an investigator at the University of Lyon, reports:

> One of the SEL made an interesting specification concerning "massages." An internal document distinguishes erotic massages (growing out of members' personal relations), therapeutic massages (that require the intervention of qualified professionals, eligible for social security reimbursement and exchanges in national currency) and massages designed for general well-being and relaxation. (Bayon 1999: 73–74)

The first two kinds of massage, according to Bayon, are forbidden, the third acceptable. More generally, this circuit favors treatment by means of alternative medicines.

At first, the list of exchanges at Italy's Ferrara's Bdt seems enormous: it ranges across *lavori e servizi vari* (for example, animal sitting, assistance with school papers, making ice cream, proofreading, company for the elderly, reading aloud), *consulenze* (for example, assistance with computers, social activities, organizing a library), and *lezioni* (for example, lessons in martial arts, dance, German, Tai Chi, photography).[3] Nevertheless the list concentrates very heavily on small and personal services, excluding a wide range of consumer goods and commercially available services.

When it comes to pricing goods and services they exchange, local trading systems commonly reject existing market prices for their own negotiated tariffs. Often the local price reflects the circuit's greater evaluation of services that, in the members' estimation, the national market undervalues. What is more, apparently equivalent goods and services fetch different prices depending on the parties' evaluation of the relationship. In a report from the Centre Walras, Étienne Perrot (1999:386) notes: "The personality of the *provider* and the affective dimension of SEL relationships lead the 'client' to pay a friend's price (*prix d'ami*) independent from strict economic calculation." Similarly, Bayon observes:

> We do not set against each other the hours of baby-sitting, or the hours of reading stories to children. . . . It's Jean-Paul my neighbor who watched my child yesterday, it's Hélène who came to read "scary stories" to my young children, etc. At the core of SELs . . . we find chains of exchange and solidarity mixing and interweaving with each other as invisible threads designing the common good. It's Jacques who tells Françoise he needs someone to help him with housework, or precisely Françoise knows Pierre who was helped by Luc, etc. It's people who join in to share chores. (Bayon 1999:80–81)

As a result, Bayon continues,

> The structure of "prices" in SEL currency would make an ordinary economist scream. The "same" (but precisely it is not the same) hour of ironing gives us here 50 grains, there, 60 grains, here 40 grains, etc. An oversized new pair of shoes bought by mistake will be given here for 100 grains, there 150 grains. (Bayon 1999: 81)

By the same token SEL members, according to Bayon, reject prices that seem morally excessive to them, regardless of the amount that the good or service would bring in national currency outside the circuit (see also Raddon 2003).

Even the best managed SEL however, eventually discover that they cannot insulate their circuit entirely from the rest of the world. In 1998, a
landmark lawsuit in France, for instance, found external labor unions trying to control exchanges of goods and services that they themselves have
an exclusive right to produce.[4] It also shows courts re-translating SEL's
own unit of currency into its national equivalent and interpreting it in
terms of market value. Thus, SEL circuits' boundary becomes something
each SEL must not simply draw but also defend.

Time exchanges attempt to reinforce that boundary by insulating themselves more firmly from national currencies. While pegged systems have
become much more common in Europe and Canada, time-based systems
prevail in the United States. Ithaca, New York's HOURS, the community
currency pioneer, is the best known of the more than thirty American local
monetary circuits. Each prints its own, fully legal, local currency. The U.S.
government, however, regulates the physical dimension of notes—smaller
than dollar bills—and requires their issue in denominations valued at a
minimum of $1.

Since the currency's creation in 1991, over 7,000 Ithaca HOURS have
been issued. Each HOUR, which must be spent in local transactions, is valued at $10. The organization estimates that through multiplier effects the
$70,000 equivalent has added several million dollars to the local economy.
HOURS have gained strong local legitimacy: grants of Ithaca HOURS
have been awarded to 35 community organizations, political candidates so-
licit Hours, the town's Chamber of Commerce accepts them, the Department of Social Services distributes HOURS to its clients, while the local
credit union offers HOUR-denominated accounts.[5] During the summer of
2000, in what it hailed as "the world's largest local currency loan," the
Ithaca HOUR system issued 3,000 HOURS ($30,000) to the Alternatives
Federal Credit Union; the loan covered 5 percent of contract work involved in building the credit union's new headquarters (*HOUR Town*,
Summer 2000). Like their European counterparts, American authorities
take Ithaca HOURS seriously enough to impose income and sales tax on
transactions taking place within the system.[6]

To join Ithaca HOURS, participants pay a small fee in exchange for their
first 2 HOURS; the goods or services they offer as well as those they request, are then printed in the bi-monthly *HOUR Town* newspaper.[7] Three
categories of HOURS members participate in the Ithaca circuit: individuals with listings in the group directory, employees of participating
businesses who collect part of their wages in HOURS, and other HOURS
supporters. In Ithaca and elsewhere, HOURS exchanges range across auto
repair, carpentry, counseling, errand running, editing, grant writing, Internet
training, notarizing, trucking, weddings, and yoga. Generally, price-setting

reflects hours of work, but is still subject to bargaining over the relative value of different kinds of labor.

Concretely, this system produces extensive rounds of life for some participants: as Elson, a retired Ithaca craftsman who earns HOURS doing heating and air conditioning consulting, reports:

> My wife and I spend HOURS at the Farmer's Market, where we browse and chat with old friends. We dine at restaurants, buy apples for mother's homemade apple pie and applesauce. I had my hearing aid repaired and get periodic massages for my failing back. Also I was very pleased last winter to hire two girls with HOURS to shovel heavy snow. They used the HOURS for rent (Glover n.d.).

Other HOURS circuits place greater restrictions on relations and transfers. Kansas City's Barter Bucks, for instance, are earned by city volunteers as payment for one day's work in a farm, and are then spent back in the city to buy produce from the farmer at the Farmer's Market. In Toronto, Dollars are awarded as grants to community organizations; while the group's "Spirit at Work" project fosters caring services by offering honoraria or Toronto Dollars Gift certificates to needy volunteers.

IDEOLOGIES IN LOCAL CURRENCIES

Zealots among local currency advocates commonly reject compromises built in by systems like Ithaca HOURS or LETS that permit variable valuation of members' times. Purists insist on strong insulation from anything that resembles a commercial market and on strict equivalents of hourly inputs. They often justify this strictness with an appeal to moral values of equality and community. Consider the notable case of Time Dollars, a system of chits use to regulate exchange of services such as elderly care, tutoring, phone companionship, house cleaning, or reading to the blind. A central coordinator keeps a record of time spent and received: exchange rates are fixed. Unlike the negotiated HOURS pricing system, here all hours of service have identical value.[8] And, in contrast to the expansiveness of Ithaca HOURS, Time Dollars organizers deliberately restrict the range of services and the participants within their circuit.

One of its earliest and most successful projects, Brooklyn's Member to Member Elderplan is a social HMO which allows seniors to pay 25 percent of their premiums in Time Dollars, earned by providing social support for other seniors. For each hour they serve, members get a credit which they "bank" in Elderplan's computer, to be spent when they need help. Services exchanged include shopping, transportation, bereavement counseling, or telephone visiting among housebound members (Binker 2000; Rowe n.d.). Meanwhile, in Suffolk County, Long Island, welfare mothers earn enough Time Dollars to make a down payment toward a computer by bringing their children to the public library for computer lessons, and in Washington, D.C., teenagers earn Time Dollars by serving on youth juries sentencing first-time juvenile offenders (Cahn 2001).

These systems have a remarkable feature: instead of simply facilitating short-term exchanges, they allow people to accumulate credits over a long period, against a day of need. As a result, beyond their immediate payoff, Time Dollar systems require greater guarantees of continuity in availability of services than other sorts of local monies. Authorities recognize the difference of Time Dollars transactions by refraining from taxing them.

Indeed, one subset of currency systems concentrates on the transfers of caring personal services among people with strong commitments to each other. Time Dollars and some of the LETS circuits have already shown these principles in operation; they often restrict the range of services that members may exchange, setting an ethical standard for those services. What is more, they commonly assure that restriction by limiting membership as well. Advocates of Time Dollars, in fact, often call them the "currency of caring."

A distinctive time exchange variant appears in New York City's Womanshare, a women-only group restricted to 100 members exchanging their skills; members receive "credits" from the Womanshare "bank" to be spent on other members' services. Devoted to "honor what is traditionally called 'women's work'—work that has been denigrated in our culture,"[9] participants, as the *New York Times* describes it, "have planted one another's gardens, cooked for the weddings of one another's daughters, seen one another through illnesses and grief, vacationed together, counseled one another on changing careers or wardrobes" (Kaufman 1993).

In both systems—pegged currencies and time exchanges—the very creation and coordination of local monies establishes distinctive circuits of interpersonal relations. To manage their currencies, for instance, participants regularly create standards, institutions, and practices, such as local meetings to decide the issue of new notes, newsletters, websites, catalogues of available goods and services, monthly potluck dinners, and trading fairs. In Ithaca, the organizers of Ithaca HOURS have created a formal organization that elects officers and holds regular public meetings. An instructional Hometown Money Starter Kit and video, produced by the Ithaca HOURS inventor, Paul Glover, has sold briskly to over 600 communities, instructing other local money organizers on step-by-step how-to's of creating currencies.

Participants often reinforce their community by incorporating locally meaningful symbols into their monetary tokens. Ithaca HOURS, for example, feature native flowers, waterfalls, crafts, and farms, while LETS networks, which do not rely on physically distinct monies, use symbolically charged names. In Britain, for instance, Greenwich uses "anchors," Canterbury "tales," and Totnes "acorns" (Helleiner 2000:46–47). Here, as elsewhere, the choice of a medium actually involves commitment to a particular network of social relations, localized symbol system, and set of transfers.

What *meanings* do organizers of local currencies attribute to ties among members? In fact, competing positions have arisen within the local currency movement. Time Dollars creator Edgar Cahn (2001) claims moral and political superiority for the strict hour system, as compared to others, in these terms:

> LETS is expressly a currency designed to create an *alternative* economy, one that sees to offer much that the global market economy offers but on a more decent, human, sustainable basis. . . . Time Dollars . . . are designed to rebuild a fundamentally different economy, the economy of home, family, neighborhood and community. . . . Home, family, and neighborhood are not an alternative economy. They are the CORE Economy.

With Kahn's position at one ideological extreme, local monetary circuits also vary greatly in the meaning that they attribute to relations within them. While some of their advocates mean them to protect local commercial interests, others insist that local monies build community ties, forging social along with monetary bonds Local currencies often serve as potent ideological symbols of what Nigel Thrift and Andrew Leyshon (1999) see as alternative moral economies, countering global financial markets. At times, organizers' ideologies dip into the wells of communitarian cooperativism and even anarchist thinking.

In the latter vein, savor the tone of a French pronouncement:

> The resurgence of parallel or alternative experiences goes beyond its microscopic dimensions representing the health of civil society. . . . Social cleavage is the chasm into which the state, having forsaken its duties as guardian of the public interest, will now collapse. By rejecting its role as an actor, the state reveals its failure and its self-contradiction. Civil society had made the state responsible, but its ethical treason and its political withdrawal are now on the way to forcing it to give up its function, without glory or honor. (Latour 1999: 83)

As this pronouncement suggests, communitarian advocates of local currencies easily slip over into radical libertarianism, a program for the dismantling of governmental controls on behalf of individual freedom.[10]

Others take on a missionary tone. For example, from Argentina's Club de Trueque we get the following pronouncement:

> Our system has extended to Spain (the Basque Country), Uruguay, Brazil, Bolivia and now Ecuador and Colombia. The web page has also allowed us to advise faraway countries, such as Russia and Finland. . . . We are not building

barriers to protect our domestic economies, but the foundations and walls for the great cathedral our millenium demands. (Primavera 1999; see also DeMeulenaere 2000; Guerriero 1996)

Such ideological and moral resolutions result in a paradox: while local money practices directly challenge Hostile Worlds ideas, their ideologies often reinforce those very same ideas by postulating a frontier between the impure external world of legal tender and the purity of local money. Indeed, the effort of Manchester LETS organizers to integrate their exchanges extensively into the national economy outrages other British LETS organizers. Critics of the Manchester plan, Keith Hart (1999:283) reports, prefer "sealing off a more wholesome kind of circuit from the contamination of capitalism."

Although most enthusiasts for local currency are practical activists rather than high-flying social critics and theorists, the movement has attracted attention from critics and theorists (e.g., Williams 1996; Lee 1996; Thorne 1996; Neary and Taylor 1998; Hart 1999; Thrift and Leyshon 1999; Boyle 2000; Helleiner 2000; 2003). In their *Beyond Employment* (1992), for example, Claus Offe and Rolf Heinze lay out a program of reform clearly influenced by the local money movement. Their Cooperation Circle program has the following components:

- It centers on exchange of services among households.
- It employs a principle of equivalence represented by media deliberately insulated from legal tender.
- The accounting system depends on time expended, with the implication that every member's time is equivalent.
- The currency and the membership network form as a function of potential service exchanges.
- They exclude services that are widely available in markets mediated by legal tender.
- They are designed to operate in milieux-especially urban milieux- where participants do not all know each other, and were trust-maintaining institutions must be built into the design.
- They depend on "supportive, promotional initiatives by provincial or municipal authorities or other sponsors" (Offe and Heinze 1992: 52–55).
- In short, Offe and Heinze are specifying boundary, transfers, media, and ties among participants.

As local currency systems create their particular forms of commercial circuits, we can expect more social thinkers to treat them as promising alternatives to the prevailing organization of work and exchange. That worries practitioners such as Paul Glover, Ithaca HOURS founder. The self-regarding academic, he predicts, is going to dissect this like a living cadaver. . . . Part of my aggravation with the academics is that they pile on this as a phenomenon, a novelty, something they can study, write papers about, pass the papers back and forth to each other, getting comfortable salaries. And I'm out here up to my neck in it day to day, translating what I learn into actual programmes. (Boyle 2000: 114; see also Savdié and Cohen-Mitchell 1997)

Glover is certainly right to think that local monies are attracting widespread attention among scholars. But scholars and activists can benefit each other: activists gain by knowing where their particular practices fit into the range of possible practices, while scholars gain from drawing on the practical experience of activists.

As we might reasonably expect, it turns out that local currencies overlap with our second sort of circuit, the circuit of intimacy.

CARING CONNECTIONS

What about intimate circuits of commerce? Monetized intimate ties loom as the ultimate nightmare for Hostile Worlds analysts and the strongest challenge for Nothing But reductionists. Many observers assume that when money enters relations between spouses, parents and children, or caregivers and care recipients, intimacy inevitably vanishes. Nothing But opponents, on the other hand, typically argue that monetized intimate relations reduce to another indistinguishable market exchange, exercise in coercion, or expression of general cultural values. Thus they deny effectively any special features of intimacy as such.

Let us think of relations as intimate to the extent that transactions within them depend on particularized knowledge and attention deployed by at least one person, knowledge and attention that are not widely available to third parties. Intimacy thus defined connects not only family members, but also friends, sexual partners, healer-patient pairs, and many servant-employer pairs as well. Although Hostile Worlds doctrines lead to the expectation that commercial transactions will corrupt such relations and eventually transform them into impersonal mutual exploitation, close studies of such relations invariably yield a contrary conclusion: across a wide range of intimate relations, people manage to integrate monetary transfers into larger webs of mutual obligations without destroying the social ties involved. As Carol Heimer (1992: 145) puts it, "universalistic norms generate responsibilities to particular others as named nodes in a functioning network" (see also Zelizer 2000a). People do so precisely by constructing differentiated circuits of commerce.

As examination of local currencies has already shown us, the existence of differentiated circuits challenges two cherished and oddly complementary myths: of the universal, unifying, all-pervasive market on one side, and of incompatibility between rationality and intimacy on the other. Instead of either one, we discover multiple partly independent circuits, each one incorporating a distinctive system of valuation into its bounded media, transfers, and social relations.

My survey of local currencies has only hinted at two further features of commercial circuits that observers regularly misconstrue through failure to recognize those circuits' existence. The first is their production and maintenance of inequality through what Charles Tilly (1998) calls "opportunity hoarding," the second, fortification of differences among circuits through legal distinctions cast in other terms but corresponding precisely to the boundaries of their media, transfers, and social relations. Just as we see French labor unions seeking the aid of courts in declaring local labor exchanges "clandestine labor," we find generations of male American workers using legal means to contest any claim of equality for women's work, caring or otherwise. In effect, legal distinctions back the opportunity hoarding of those who already maintain and benefit from advantaged circuits. Feminists and advocates of rewards for caring labor—who overlap, but sometimes disagree furiously with each other—have sensed the existence of circuit-based inequality without quite recognizing what it was or how it worked.

Consider the debate over paid care, which has emerged as a crucial issue on the national political agenda. With the aging of the baby-boom generation, and as most mothers in the U.S. participate in paid work, the care of children, the elderly, and the sick is being seriously reconsidered. Would the generalization of payment for such care destroy caring itself? Would its subjection to calculation in terms of legal tender rationalize away its essential intimacy?

Increasingly impatient with standard Hostile World and Nothing But answers, feminist analysts—sociologists, economists, philosophers, and legal scholars—are rethinking the economics of intimacy generally, and of care in particular. Some argue that care should acquire full market value, while others defend new conceptions of rewards for caring, and still others carry out empirical studies that document what actually takes place in paid systems of care. In the process they are discovering how interpersonal circuits of intimacy shape monetary media.

Take for instance Deborah Stone's (1999) study of home care workers in New England, which documents two points of great importance for my argument:

A highly bureaucratized monetary payment system for intimate personal care does not by any means produce a cold, dehumanized relationship between caregiver and recipient.

Caregivers actually manipulate the payment system to make sure they can provide care appropriate to the relationship. Although they do not usually create new currencies, they actually redefine the media of payment.

Deeply concerned with the effects of turning care into a profit-making business, Stone investigated how changes in Medicare and managed care financing restructured caring practices. Interviewing home care workers, she discovered a payment system that compensated caregivers exclusively for patients' bodily care, not for conversation or other forms of personal attention or assistance. She also discovered, however, that home care workers did not transform themselves into unfeeling bureaucratic agents. They remained, Stone reports, "keenly aware that home health care is very intimate and very personal" (Stone 1999:64).

The care providers she interviewed included nurses, physical therapists, occupational therapists, and home care aides. Almost without exception, they reported visiting clients on their days off, often bringing some groceries or helping out in other ways. The agency's warnings against becoming emotionally attached to their clients, aides and nurses told Stone, were unrealistic: "If you're human," or "if you have any human compassion, you just do" (Stone 1999:66). To circumvent an inadequate payment system, home care workers define their additional assistance as friendship or neighborliness. Or they simply manipulate the rules, for instance by treating other than the officially approved problems and sometimes even attending to a patient's spouse's health. To be sure, as Stone remarks, inadequate payment structures exploit paid caregivers' concerns for patients. Her interviews conclusively demonstrate, however, that monetary payment systems do not obliterate caring relations.

In short, Stone is observing the creation of interpersonal caregiving circuits with their own representations of values, symbols, and practices (see also, e.g., Hondagneu-Sotelo 2001; Menjívar 2002; Nelson 2002; Salazar Parreñas 2001; Ungerson 1997; Uttal 2002). Caregiving circuits are not unique. Similar circuits involving their own monetary practices arise in networks of kinship, friendship, and neighborhood, not to mention within households.

The Politics of Care

While analysts such as Stone document and explain caring circuits, others have focused on the politics and morality of caring labor. They raise pointed questions about the equity and propriety surrounding the reward and recognition of care as a critical contribution to social well-being. A significant part of the debate focuses on the economics of care: proper compensation for paid care workers, adequate provision for care of children, the sick, and the elderly, and economic security for unpaid caregivers.

As the normative questions gain focus, the debate encounters the same difficulties that come up each time people try to think through the relationships between market activity and social obligations. What will happen, they worry, if paid care substitutes for informal assistance? Will recognizing the economic contributions of housewives turn households into impersonal mini-markets? How can we possibly arrive at an appropriate financial evaluation of caretakers' contributions? Will subsidies to housewives increase the ghetto barriers separating them from other workers?

Rejecting both Nothing But and Hostile World formulations, a group of imaginative thinkers are moving toward a contrasting approach very much in the spirit of bridging. They identify multiple forms of connection between interpersonal relations and different spheres of economic life. In the process, they are building a new economics of care. Consider for instance, the challenge laid down by economists Nancy Folbre and Julie Nelson:

> An a priori judgment that markets must improve caregiving by increasing efficiency puts the brakes on intelligent research, rather than encourages it. Likewise, an a priori judgment that markets must severely degrade caring work by replacing motivations of altruism with self-interest is also a research stopper.

Instead, they insist, "the increasing intertwining of 'love' and 'money' brings us the necessity—and the opportunity—for innovative research and action" (Folbre and Nelson 2000:123–24).

What's more, Bridges advocates note that Hostile Worlds assumptions portraying love and care as demeaned by monetization may in fact lead to economic discrimination against those allegedly intangible caring activities. As Paula England and Nancy Folbre (1999: 46) point out "the principle that money cannot buy love may have the unintended and perverse consequence of perpetuating low pay for face-to-face service work."

Books by Joan Williams, Ann Crittenden, and Nancy Folbre advance this line of thought. Williams's *Unbending Gender* boldly sets out to transform outdated and unjust American gender arrangements. Invoking the tradition of Latin America feminists, legal theorist Williams (2000: 243) intends "to spark a movement within feminist theory that is theoretically sophisticated, yet committed to talking in language capable of reaching audiences outside of academics."

Williams's diagnosis is forthright: our inherited system of domesticity, she argues, binds us to a deeply flawed organization of market work and household labor. On the one hand, an ideal-worker norm demands fulltime workplace involvement leaving little space for child bearing or child rearing. Occupational excellence and caregiving are thereby inexorably pitted against each other. On the other hand, and as a direct result of traditional ideal-worker norms and practices, our system of caregiving routinely marginalizes caregivers—typically women—making them economically vulnerable.

Williams focuses on the liabilities of mothering. Our economy, she asserts, "is divided into mothers and others" (Williams 2000: 2). Yet mothers are not the only victims of current domesticity structures: so are men obliged to perform as ideal-workers and children raised in flawed caring arrangements. When their mothers are economically marginalized, children are also more likely to be poor.

There is a way out. *Unbending Gender* works as a manual in what Williams calls "reconstructive feminism." Its goal is to restructure current family and work arrangements that routinely marginalize caregivers, instituting a norm of parental care to replace mother care. Its three-step method consists of (1) eliminating the ideal (male) worker norm in market work; (2) eliminating it also in family entitlements; and (3) introducing a new gender discourse. Williams offers us more than passionate rhetoric: she provides a set of specific policies to restructure both work and family, most notably legal action. She makes a sustained, knowledgeable case for treating the lower rewards given to the kinds of work women do as a violation of equal rights. She also points out the blatant and perhaps legally remediable differences between women's market and nonmarket work, between men's and women's sides of divorce settlements, and between evaluations of men's and women contributions to household wealth. In all these cases, a sentimentalized conception of women's caring labor justifies discrimination.

Determined to undo such prejudicial sentimentality, Williams puts forth remedial policies to achieve just compensation for women. For instance, her joint property proposal would recognize family work as economically valuable, justifying income sharing by spouses after divorce. It would thereby undermine courts and legislatures' assumption that "men's claims give rise to entitlements while women's claims are treated as charity" (Williams 2000: 131).

At times, Williams's hard-nosed critique of Hostile Worlds edges toward Nothing But economistic reductionism. Nevertheless, she is careful to distinguish her income sharing proposals from others which rely on what she sees as "strained analogies to commercial partnership law" (Williams 2000: 126). In so doing she begins to recognize differentiation of social ties among such settings as families, firms, markets, and organizations. At the same time, however, she wants a reading of the law in which such relations cast legal shadows that are financially equivalent. In short, Williams rejects both Hostile Worlds and Nothing But arguments in favor of building bridges by legal means. She does not quite say that her analysis gains plausibility from its implicit identification of distinctive caring circuits with their own media, transfers, and social relations.

Explicit recognition of caring circuits would actually advance Williams's program by specifying the new institutional forms whose legal standing she seeks to fortify.

CRITTENDEN'S CRITIQUE

In *The Price of Motherhood* (2001), investigative journalist Ann Crittenden deploys a line of argument overlapping with that of Williams. The result is a compelling exposé of current misunderstandings on the subject of caring. In 15 crisp chapters, sprinkled with pointed vignettes, Crittenden dissects the current U.S. domestic economy, unmasking its relentless marginalization of careworkers generally, mothers in particular.

Her catalogue of unjust treatment ranges across

- the "mommy tax" exacted by workplaces discriminating against workers who adapt their working schedules to care for their children;
- divorce courts which disregard the economic contributions of caregivers;
- child support arrangements which shift the bulk of child-raising costs to divorced and single mothers;
- a Social Security system which protects only paid labor;
- unemployment and workmen's compensation policies which exclude mothers;
- internal domestic economies which perpetuate mothers' financial dependency on husbands.

True, Crittenden agrees, women's recent progress in the labor market has indeed been remarkable, but that success stops short when it comes to mothers. Despite media images of career-driven working mothers, and the relative increase in father-care, mothers, insists Crittenden, continue to provide the bulk of child care. Like Williams, Crittenden punctures the illusory goal of achieving women's full-time labor market participation while retaining their second unpaid job as primary housekeeper and child-carer.

Crittenden writes after more than five years of research, wide-ranging reading of the relevant literature, plus hundreds of interviews with mothers and fathers in the U.S. and Europe, as well as with leading experts—including Joan Williams and Nancy Folbre themselves. Crittenden (2001: 9) concludes that fairness can only be achieved by redefining caregiving as work, thereby putting a stop to our collective "free riding on women's labor." It's time to break down, she contends, the "artificial distinction" between wageearners and providers of unpaid care (Crittenden 2001: 263).

Inspired by the more enlightened European model, Crittenden (2001: 259) concludes with a wide-ranging blueprint for change: "adding care to our pantheon of national values, along with liberty, justice and the pursuit of happiness through the pursuit of money." Her proposals include workplace reforms (e.g., parental one year's paid leave); government policies (e.g., equalizing Social Security for spouses); new marital financial arrangements (e.g., after a child is born or adopted, both parents' income becomes the joint property of the new family unit); and increased community support. Even adopting a few such measures, Crittenden reasons, would transfer significant income to women. "Female caregivers," she repeatedly reminds us, "have been the world's cheap labor for too long" (Crittenden 2001: 274). Once again, Crittenden's analysis would gain strength from recognition that she is simultaneously discovering the existence of distinctive care circuits and advocating their fortification by legal and economic means.

FOLBRE CARES

Economist Nancy Folbre adds important new notes to the discussion. In *The Invisible Heart* (2001), she embraces both Williams's and Crittenden's challenges to our current economics of caring. Like Williams and Crittenden, she implicitly recognizes the distinctive character of care circuits, takes them as models for economic reform, and advocates injecting new resources into them. Unlike Williams and Crittenden, however, Folbre calls for fundamental revisions of the economy, the state, and kinship in order to accomplish their shared goals. Along with Julie Nelson and other colleagues, Folbre has pioneered the feminist critique of standard economic models.

For too long, Folbre argues, our confidence in the self-regulating powers of the invisible hand to coordinate market transactions has concealed the crucial economic and moral significance of the invisible heart. True, economists from Adam Smith's theory of moral sentiments onward have recognized the crucial place of honesty and trust as underpinnings of market transactions. They saw, as Folbre puts it, how the "invisible handshake" helps the invisible hand. They failed, however, to examine the equally fundamental invisible heart: those "feelings of affection, respect and care for others that reinforce honesty and trust" (Folbre 2001: xiv).

Indifference to caring labor was possible, Folbre explains, so long as patriarchal arrangements kept women involved in attending to children, the elderly, and the sick. Not any more: since competitive labor markets upset traditional separate spheres worlds by opening up better paid employment for women, the caring problem has become an urgent economic, social, and political concern.

Yet caring remains marginalized, exacting an economic and emotional "care penalty" from its providers. One of Folbre's few flickers of ambivalence appears in her treatment of markets for care. She worries about two possible consequences of the market's extension: first, that inferior care providers will enter the market and second, that the market will form in such a way as to undervalue proper care. On the other hand, she wants proper compensation for caring labor, recognizing that payment does not necessarily erode love. Folbre dismisses conventional economic reasoning that poorly paid caring jobs assure properly altruistic motivations. Perhaps a better formulation of her argument would have been to say that every market transaction has a moral penumbra and that beneficial market transactions must have the right penumbra. In my terms, she is emphasizing the distinctive systems of valuation built into caring circuits.

Even more emphatically than Williams and Crittenden, Folbre challenges two common feminist lines of argument. The first is that full integration of women into markets will in itself produce equity and efficiency. The second, rather different, challenge denies that recognizing the special contributions of caretakers and their empirical association with women will undermine demands for gender justice and equality. Folbre (2001: 20) is certainly not yearning for a return to romantic visions of traditional families, where "Big Daddy was usually in control." Nor is raw selfish individualism the only answer. The alternative? A social feminist agenda fashioned to "distribute responsibilities for care more equally and reward caring more generously" (Folbre 2001: 18).

Folbre relies on a folksy, breezy tone to deliver a set of profoundly insurrectionary proposals. If carried out, her agenda amounts to a social revolution. Its three key elements are market socialism, participatory democracy, and shared care. More concretely, Folbre includes reformed ownership, a highly progressive income tax, an expanded welfare state, restructuring capital mobility, revamping definitions of kinship to strengthen caring obligations to children and the elderly, and expanding recognition of caring ties to include friends.

To accomplish such change, Folbre notes, we need to revise economic theory fundamentally, incorporating the economic value of nonmarket work:

> we can't continue to visualize the economy as a man's world of cars and trucks and steel, things that can be easily counted and weighed. The economy now encompasses many and varied activities that once took place within families, activities whose quality is defined by personal contact, responsiveness to individual needs, respect, and affection. (Folbre 2001: 79)

Williams and Folbre are marvelously complementary. While Williams confronts the legal apparatus that maintains inequality and inhibits care, Folbre addresses the economic theories, practices, and institutions that do the same. Williams makes proposals in sympathy with Folbre but concretely tell us how to carry out change: identifying features of existing laws that produce inequality and suggesting remedies based on existing laws.

Williams, Crittenden, and Folbre join efforts in breaking down the traditional Hostile Worlds dichotomies that erroneously split economic transactions and intimate personal relations into separate spheres. To bring caring labor out of its economically marginal ghetto, they forcefully establish its fundamental economic significance and its variable economic content. The three authors mostly stay away from alternative economic, cultural, or political reductionisms, working their way to a fuller understanding of multiple, variable interactions between intimate ties and economic transactions. Only after we recognize that caring labor has always involved economic transfers can we construct democratic, compassionate caring economies.

Awareness of care's economic contribution leads quickly to a further discovery: that caregivers create and operate distinctive circuits of commerce, with their own bounded media, transfers, and meaningful social relations. The new economic feminist agenda rests on a half-articulated recognition that existing circuits of care organize around distinctive media, transfers, and social relations without somehow suffering the disabilities feared by Hostile Worlds theorists. Economic feminists call, in essence, not only for recognizing those circuits as distinctive but also for supplying them with greater resources, legal standing, and respect than they have previously enjoyed.

PROPOSALS AND CONCLUSIONS

This chapter has by no means developed a full theory of circuits, much less explained their variability across local monies and caring connections. It has elaborated on an important but poorly recognized phenomenon: formation of differentiated ties crossing organizational or household boundaries, involving organizational and household members in distinct circuits of commerce. It has not provided a coherent, comprehensive answer to the larger question it raises: how do new forms of differentiation and integration, such as commercial circuits, arise and change? The analysis merely suggests that culturally embedded, problem-solving people devise solutions to pressing new social challenges by inventing novel commercial circuits.

Nevertheless, concrete observation of these commercial circuits raises some more general questions and conjectures concerning their relationship to capitalism as an economic system. Without quite articulating the concept, after all, anthropologists and historians have long since documented the activity of commercial circuits in a wide variety of economic systems, including not only non-industrial economies but also those of state socialism.

What, if anything, distinguishes the operation of commercial circuits under capitalism? Let me propose three ideas for further investigation:

First, precisely because capital-dominated markets serve the interests of capital, they fail to solve a wide range of problems that matter greatly to concrete economic actors: creating solidarity, providing security, maintaining self-esteem, caring for dependents, and more. Solutions to those problems require economic resources: labor, land, and capital. People create or adapt commercial circuits at exactly those intersections between capitalist markets and pressing problems.

Second, capitalists and their political allies commonly act to contain or suppress those commercial circuits that threaten their own power to control markets and the disposition of capital, for example, by subordinating local monies to legal tender and by driving unlicensed but paid providers of care underground. Since capitalists and their political allies also employ commercial circuits to solve their own problems, however, they never suppress circuits entirely.

Third, participants in commercial circuits regularly invoke Hostile Worlds doctrines as they distinguish those circuits from other social relations and defend the circuits' boundaries against complicating interference from other social relations, including those of wide-ranging capitalist markets. They thereby hide from themselves and others the extensive economic activity and the mingling of economic with intimate transactions that occur incessantly within commercial circuits.

Obviously my investigations of local monies and caring relations do not provide nearly enough evidence to validate these conjectures. But proliferation of the two sorts of circuits under capitalism does suggest that the people involved are, among other things, solving problems posed by capitalism itself.

Local monies and caring connections obviously differ in their settings and contents. We should resist, however, the ever-present temptation to array them along a standard continuum from genuine, general, impersonal markets at one end to nonmarket intimacy at the other. To do so would reconstruct the very Gesellschaft-Gemeinschaft dichotomies a clear recognition of circuits helps us escape. In all three types of circuits—corporate, monetary, caring—mentioned in this chapter, we find intense interpersonal ties commingling with regularized media and transfers. In all three, for that matter, we find ties that vary greatly in their intensity, scope, and durability. Differences among the three types of circuits depend not on overall extent of rationalization or solidarity but on variable configurations of media, transfers, interpersonal ties, and shared meanings attached to their intersection.

How then should we generalize the cases of local monies and caring connections? Here is a rapid summary.

- Neither Hostile Worlds nor Nothing But accounts adequately describe, much less explain, the interplay of monetary transfers and social ties, whether relatively impersonal or very intimate.
- Analysts of that interplay clearly need theoretical Bridges—ways of explaining the mostly peaceful coexistence of impersonality and intimacy within the same social settings.
- Both intimate and impersonal transactions work through differentiated ties, which participants mark off from each other through well established practices, understandings, and representations.
- Such differentiated ties compound into distinctive circuits, each incorporating somewhat different understandings, practices, information, obligations, rights, symbols, idioms, and media of exchange.
- Far from determining the nature of interpersonal relationships, media of exchange (including legal tenders) incorporated into such circuits take on particular connections with the understandings, practices, information, obligations, rights, symbols, and idioms embedded in those circuits.
- Indeed, participants in such circuits characteristically reshape exchange media to mark distinctions among different kinds of social relations.

These are the means by which people bridge the apparently unbridgeable gap between social solidarity and commercialized transactions.

NOTES

1. For a clear statement of the assertion that such circuits emerge from small scale social interactions, see Collins 2000. In fact, as we shall see, they can also form through borrowing of organizational models across social settings.
2. www.schumachersociety.org/cur_grps.html. The E.F. Schumacher Society. June 2001. Local Currency Groups. 25 June 2001.
3. http://www.comune.fe.it/bancadeltempo/listaispir.htm. Banca Del Tempo di Ferrara. February 1999. La Lista di Ispirazione. June 25, 2001.
4. The appeals court finally decided to support the exemption, recognizing that the SEL members involved in the dispute were not guilty of "clandestine labor"; see Laacher 1999.
5. www.schumachersociety.org/cur_grps.html.
6. On the legal aspects of local currencies, see Solomon 1996.
7. http://www.ithacahours.org. Ithaca Hours Local Currency. June 2001. Ithaca Hours Local Currency Home Page. 25 June 2001. In 2001, to manage the growing volume of participants and transactions, organizers began issuing a yearly HOUR Directory.
8. For a contrasting way of negotiating time's monetary value, see Yakura 2001.
9. http://www.angelfire.com/ar2/womanshare/principl.html Womanshare: A Cooperative Skill Bank. 1999. Statement of Principles. June 25, 2001.

10. For an illuminating discussion of local currencies as a political movement challenging neoliberal ideologies by changing consumption patterns, see Helleiner 2000.

REFERENCES

Akin, David and Joel Robbins, eds. *Money and Modernity: State and Local Currencies in Melanesia*. Pittsburgh: University of Pittsburgh Press.
Anteby, Michel. 2003. "The 'Moralities' of Poaching: Manufacturing Personal Artifacts on Factory Floors." *Ethnography* 4: 217–39.
Barth, Fredrik. 1967. "Economic Spheres in Darfur." In *Themes in Economic Anthropology*, ed. Raymond Firth. London: Tavistock.
Bayon, Denis. 1999. *Les S.E.L., systèmes d'échanges locaux, pour un vrai débat*. Levallois-Perret: Yves Michel.
Biggart, Nicole Woolsey. 1989. *Charismatic Capitalism: Direct Selling Organizations in America*. Chicago: University of Chicago Press.
———. 2001. "Banking on Each Other: The Situational Logic of Rotating Savings and Credit Associations." *Advances in Qualitative Organization Research* 3: 129–53.
Binker, MaryJo. 2000. "Volunteers Use Time dollars to Help Others." http://www.timedollar.org/Articles/Articles2000/Points_of_light.htm. Timedollar Institute, January 21. June 25, 2001.
Blanc, Jérôme. 2000. *Les monnaies parallèles*. Paris: L'Harmattan.
Bloch, Maurice. 1994. "Les usages de l'argent." *Terrain* 23: 5–10.
Bohannan, Paul. 1955. "Some Principles of Exchange and Investment among the Tiv." *American Anthropologist* 57: 60–70.
———. 1959. "The Impact of Money on an African Subsistence Economy." *Journal of Economic History* 19: 491–503.
Boyle, David. 2000. *Funny Money: In Search of Alternative Cash*. London: Flamingo.
Cahn, Edgar S. 2001. "On LETS and Time Dollars." *International Journal of Community Currency Research* 5; http://www.geog.le.ac.uk/ijccr/5no2.html.
Collins, Randall. 2000. "Situational Stratification: A Micro-Macro Level of Inequality." *Sociological Theory* 18: 17–43.
———. 2004. *Interaction Ritual Chains*. Princeton: Princeton University Press.
Crittenden, Ann. 2001. *The Price of Motherhood: Why the Most Important Job in the World Is Still the Least Valued*. New York: Metropolitan Books.
Crump, Thomas. 1981. *The Phenomenon of Money*. London: Routledge and Kegan Paul.
Dalton, Melville. 1959. *Men Who Manage: Fusions of Feeling and Theory in Administration*. New York: Wiley.
Darr, Asaf. 2003. "Gifting Practices and Interorganizational Relations: Constructing Obligation Networks in the Electronics Sector." *Sociological Forum* 18: 31–51.
DeMeulenaere, Stephen. 2000. "Reinventing the Market: Alternative Currencies and Community Development in Argentina." *International Journal of Community Currency Research* 4; http://www.geog.le.ac.uk/ijccr/4no3.html.

Diehl, Karl. [1930–35]1937. "Labor Exchange Banks." In *Encyclopaedia of the Social Sciences*, ed. Edwin R. A. Seligman. New York: Macmillan. 7: 737–44.

DiMaggio, Paul. 2001. "Introduction: Making Sense of the Contemporary Firm and Prefiguring Its Future." In *The Twenty-First-Century Firm: Changing Economic Organization in International Perspective*, ed. Paul DiMaggio. Princeton: Princeton University Press. 3–30.

Durand, Jorge, Emilio A. Parrado, and Douglas S. Massey. 1996. "Migradollars and Development: A Reconsideration of the Mexican Case." *International Migration Review* 30: 423–44.

Elshtain, Jean Bethke. 2000. *Who Are We?* Grand Rapids, Mich.: William B. Eerdmans.

England, Paula and Nancy Folbre. 1999. "The Cost of Caring." In *Emotional Labor in the Service Economy*, ed. Ronnie J. Steinberg and Deborah M. Figart. Special Issue, *Annals of the American Academy of Political and Social Science* 561: 39–51.

Folbre, Nancy. 2001. *The Invisible Heart: Economics and Family Values*. New York: New Press.

Glover, Paul. n.d. *Hometown Money: How to Enrich Your Community with Local Currency*. Ithaca: Ithaca Money.

Guerriero, Leila. 1996. "Siglo XXI: la vuelta al trueque." *Revista la Nación*, November 3: 44–49.

Guyer, Jane I., ed. 1995. *Money Matters: Instability, Values, and Social Payments in the Modern History of West African Communities*. Portsmouth, N.H.: Heinemann.

Hart, Keith. 1999. *The Memory Bank: Money in an Unequal World*. London: Profile Books.

Heimer, Carol A. 1992. "Doing Your Job and Helping Your Friends: Universalistic Norms about Obligations to Particular Others in Networks." In *Networks and Organizations: Structure, Form, and Action*, ed. Nitin Nohria and Robert C. Eccles. Boston: Harvard Business School Press. 143–64.

Helleiner, Eric. 1999. "Conclusions—The Future of National Currencies." In *Nation-States and Money: The Past, Present and Future of National Currencies*, ed. Emily Gilbert and Eric Helleiner. London: Routledge. 215–29.

———. 2000. "Think globally, Transact Locally: Green Political Economy and the Local Currency Movement." *Global Society* 14: 35–51.

———. 2003. *The Making of National Money: Territorial Currencies in Historical Perspective*. Ithaca: Cornell University Press.

Hirschman, Albert O. 1977. *The Passions and the Interests: Political Arguments for Capitalism before Its Triumph*. Princeton: Princeton University Press.

Hondagneu-Sotelo, Pierrette. 2001. *Doméstica: Immigrant Workers Cleaning and Caring in the Shadows of Affluence*. Berkeley: University of California Press.

Indergaard, Michael. 2002. "The Bullriders of Silicon Alley: New Media Circuits of Innovation, Speculation, and Urban Development." In *Understanding the City: Contemporary and Future Perspectives*, ed. John Eade and Christopher Mele. Malden, Mass.: Blackwell. 339–62.

Ingram, Paul and Peter W. Roberts. 2000. "Friendships among Competitors in the Sydney Hotel Industry." *American Journal of Sociology* 106: 387–423.

Kanter, Rosabeth Moss. 1977. *Men and Women of the Corporation*. New York: Basic Books.

Kaufman, Michael T. 1993. "Trading Therapy for Art to Forge a Community." *New York Times*, May 19.

Knorr Cetina, Karin D. and Urs Bruegger. 2002. "Global Microstructures: The Virtual Societies of Financial Markets." *American Journal of Sociology* 107: 905–50.

Kuttner, Robert. 1997. *Everything for Sale: The Virtues and Limitations of Markets*. New York: Knopf.

Lane, Robert E. 2000. *The Loss of Happiness in Market Democracies*. New Haven: Yale University Press.

Laacher, Smaïn. 1998. "Économie informelle officielle et monnaie franche: l'exemple des systèmes d'échange locaux." *Ethnologie française* 28: 247–56.

———. Nouvelles formes de sociabilités ou les limites d'une utopie politique: l'exemple des systèmes d'échange locale (SEL)." *International Journal of Community Currency Research* 3; http://www.geog.le.ac.uk/ijccr/3no2.html.

Latour, Germain. 1999. "Crépuscule de l'État ou l'écomomie au péril de la république." In *Exclusion et liens financiers*, ed. Jean-Michel Servet. Paris: Économica. 380–33.

Ledeneva, Alena V. 1998. *Russia's Economy of Favours: Blat, Networking and Informal Exchange*. New York: Cambridge University Press.

Lee, Roger. 1996. "Moral Money? LETS and the Social Construction of Local Economic Geographies in Southern England." *Environment and Planning* A28: 1377–94.

Menjívar, Cecilia. 2002. "The Ties That Heal: Guatemalan Immigrant Women's Networks and Medical Treatment." *International Migration Review* 36: 437–66.

Morrill, Calvin. 1995. *The Executive Way: Conflict Management in Corporations*. Chicago: University of Chicago Press.

Narotzky, Susana and Paz Moreno. 2002. "Reciprocity's Dark Side: Negative Reciprocity, Morality, and Social Reproduction." *Anthropological Theory* 2: 281–305.

Neary, Michael and Graham Taylor. 1998. *Money and the Human Condition*. New York: St. Martin's Press.

Nelson, Julie A. 1999. "Of Markets and Martyrs: Is It OK to Pay Well for Care?" *Feminist Economics* 5: 43–59.

Nelson, Margaret K. 2002. "Single Mothers and Social Support: The Commitment to, and Retreat form, Reciprocity." In *Families at Work: Expanding the Boundaries*, ed. Naomi Gerstel, Dan Clawson, and Robert Zussman. Nashville: Vanderbilt University Press. 225–50.

Offe, Claus and Rolf G. Heinze. 1992. *Beyond Employment: Time, Work, and the Informal Economy*. Cambridge: Polity Press.

Parry, Jonathan and Maurice Bloch, eds. 1989. *Money and the Morality of Exchange*. New York: Cambridge University Press.

Perrot, Étienne. 1999. "La compensation des dettes de SEL." In *Exclusion et liens financiers*, ed. Jean-Michel Servet. Paris: Économica. 384–91.

Pierret, Dorothée. 1999. "Cercles d'échanges, cercles verteux de la solidarité: le cas de l'Allemagne." *International Journal of Community Currency Research* 3; http://www.geog.le.ac.uk/ijccr/3no2.html.

Powell, Jeff. 2002. "Petty Capitalism, Perfecting Capitalism or Post-Capitalism? Lessons from the Argentinian Barter Network." Working Paper 357. Institution of Social Studies, The Hague.

Primavera, Heloísa. 1999. "Como formar un primer club de truecque pensando en la economica global." http://www3.plala.or.jp/mig/howto-es.html.

Pryor, Frederick L. 1977. *The Origins of the Economy: Comparative Study of Distribution in Primitive and Peasant Economies*. New York: Academic Press.

Raddon, Mary-Beth. 2003. *Community and Money: Caring, gift-Giving, and Women in a Social Economy*. Montreal: Black Rose Books.

Rifkin, Jeremy. 2000. *The Age of Access: The New Culture of Hypercapitalism Where All of Life Is a Paid-For Experience*. New York: Tarcher/Putnam.

Rizzo, Pantaleo. 1999. "Réciprocité indirecte et symétrie: l'émergence d'une nouvelle forme de solidarité." In *Exclusion et liens financiers*, ed. Jean-Michel Servet. Paris: Économica. 401–8.

Rowe, Jonathan. n.d. "Life-Enhancing social Networks for the Elderly." http://www.timedollar.org/Applications/Elderly_article.htm. Timedollar Institute, January 2001. June 25, 2001.

Savdié, Tony and Tim Cohen-Mitchell. 1997. *Local Currencies in Community Development*. Amherst, Mass.: Center for International Education.

Salazar Parreñas, Rhacel. 2001. *Servants of Globalization: Women, Migration, and Domestic Work*. Stanford: Stanford University Press.

Schroeder, Rolf F. H. 2002. "Talente Tauschring Hannover (TTH): Experiences of a German LETS and the Relevance of Theoretical Reflections." *International Journal of Community Currency Research* 6; http://www.geog.le.ac.uk/ijccr/vol4-6/6toc.htm. July 25, 2003.

Servet, Jean-Michel, ed. 1999. *Une économie sans argent: les systèmes d'échange local*. Paris: Seuil.

Solomon, Lewis D. 1996. *Rethinking Our Centralized Monetary System: The Case for a System of Local Currencies*. Westport, Conn.: Praeger.

Stone, Deborah. 1999. "Care and Trembling." *American Prospect* 43: 61–67.

Thorne, Lorraine. 1996. "Local Exchange Trading Systems in the United Kingdom: A Case of Re-embedding?" *Environment and Planning* A 28(8): 1361–76.

Thrift, Nigel and Andrew Layshon. 1999. "Moral Geographies of Money." In *Nation-States and Money: The Past, Present and Future of National Currencies*, ed. Emily Gilbert and Eric Helleiner. London: Routledge. 159–81.

Tilly, Charles. 1984. *Big Structures, Large Processes: Huge Comparisons*. New York: Russell Sage.

———. 1998. *Durable Inequality*. Berkeley: University of California Press.

Tilly, Chris and Charles Tilly. 1998. *Work Under Capitalism*. Boulder, Colo.: Westview.

Trends in Japan. 2001. "Yen Rivals: The Rising Popularity of Local Currencies." January 15; http://www.jinjapan.org/trends00/honbun/tj010115.html. July 25, 2003.

Ungerson, Clare. 1997. "Social Politics and the Commodification of Care." *Social Politics* 4: 362–81.

Uttal, Lynet. 2002. "Using Kin for Childcare: Embedment in the Socioeconomic Networks of Extended Families." In *Families at Work: Expanding the Boundaries*, ed. Naomi Gerstel, Dan Clawson, and Robert Zussman. Nashville: Vanderbilt University Press. 162–80.

Uzzi, Brian. 1997. "Social Structure and Competition in Interfirm Networks: The Paradox of Embeddedness." *Administrative Science Quarterly* 42: 35–67.

Velthius, Olav. 2003. "Symbolic Meaning of Prices: Constructing the Value of Contemporary Art in Amsterdam and New York Galleries." *Theory and Society* 32: 181–215.

Wacquant, Loïc. 1998. "A Fleshpeddler at Work: Power, Pain, and Profit in the Prize Fighting Economy." *Theory and Society* 27: 1–42.

———. 2000. *Corps et âme.* Marseilles: Agone.

Walzer, Michael. 1983. *Spheres of Justice: A Defense of Pluralism and Equality.* New York: Basic Books.

Weber, Florence. 1998. *L'honneur des jardiniers.* Paris: Belin.

Williams, Colin C. 1996. "The New Barter Economy: An Appraisal of Local Exchange and Trading Systems (LETS)." *Journal of Public Policy* 16: 85–101.

Williams, Joan. 2000. *Unbending Gender: Why Family and Work Conflict and What to Do about It.* New York: Oxford University Press.

Yakura, Elaine K. 2001. "Billables: The Valorization of Time in Consulting." *American Behavioral Scientist* 44: 1076–95.

Zelizer, Viviana. 2000a. "The Purchase of Intimacy." *Law and Social Inquiry* 25: 817–48.

———. 2000b. "How and Why Do We Care about Circuits?" *Accounts* (Newsletter of the Economic Sociology Section of the American Sociology Association) 1:3–5.

———. 2001. "Transactions intimes." *Genèses* 42: 121–44.

———. 2002a. "Intimate Transactions." In *The New Economic Sociology: Developments in an Emerging Field,* ed. Mauro F. Guillén, Randall Collins, Paula England, and Marshall Meyer. New York: Russell Sage. 274–300.

———. 2002b. "How Care Counts." *Contemporary Sociology* 31: 115–19.

———. 2004. "Circuits of Commerce." In *Self, Social Structure, and Beliefs: Explorations in Sociology,* ed. Jeffrey Alexander, Gary T. Marx, and Christine Williams. Berkeley: University of California Press. 122–44.

Znoj, Heinzpeter. 1998. "Hot Money and War Debpts: Transactional Regimes in Southwestern Sumatra." *Comparative Studies in Society and History* 40: 193–222.

PART 3

Global Transformation and Institutional Change

Brain Circulation and Capitalist Dynamics: Chinese Chipmaking and the Silicon Valley-Hsinchu-Shanghai Triangle

AnnaLee Saxenian

Howard Yang was among the first "returnees" to China in 1994. Yang was from Beijing but had spent more than a dozen years in the U.S., first obtaining a doctorate in electrical engineering from Oregon State University and then working for Silicon Valley companies like National Semiconductor, Chips & Technologies, and start-up Pericom Semiconductor. He returned in part to contribute to the growth of the Chinese IC industry.

After working for two years at Shanghai Beiling, China's leading state-owned semiconductor company, Yang joined two colleagues to start a firm to design ICs for telecommunications. One of the co-founders, Hau Ming, was from Taiwan and the other, Ying Shum, from Hong Kong. Both also had graduate degrees from the U.S. and many years of work experience in Silicon Valley. This common background informed their decision to create a private Silicon Valley style company with venture capital funding and stock options for workers—rather than the following the Chinese model of state ownership or a joint venture.

Yang and his co-founders tapped their professional networks in the U.S. and Taiwan as well as China to start the company. NeWave Semiconductor Corp. began operations in 1997 with venture financing of $5.4 m. from Silicon Valley and Taiwanese investors, Hua Hong Microelectronics (a state-owned enterprise in Shanghai), and several individual investors. The firm's headquarters is in Silicon Valley but most of the company's employment, including R&D and design as well as marketing, sales and administration, are in Shanghai. Taiwan's leading chipmaker, Taiwan Semiconductor Manufacturing Co. serves as its foundry. In short, NeWave was a global company from the start—leveraging the distinctive resources of three different, and distant, regional economies.

THE ECONOMIC IMPACT of increased international trade and capital flows dominates most contemporary discussions of globalization. However, the growing mobility of labor—particularly highly skilled workers—promises to be at least as significant a force in transforming the organization of the world economy in coming decades. As the costs of international travel and communications continue to fall, what in the past was a one-way "brain drain," the loss of the best and brightest youth from developing to developed economies, is giving way to a more complex, two-way process of "brain circulation" that is transforming the developmental opportunities for formerly peripheral economies by accelerating long-distance transfers of knowledge and information and facilitating access to leading-edge customers and partners.

While some U.S.-educated engineers like Howard Yang return to their home countries to start new technology businesses, others start companies in the U.S. and take advantage of their linguistic and cultural knowledge to gain access to low cost technical skill or to build partnerships in their home countries, and still others establish themselves as professional "bridge-builders" whose networks allow them to link specialized enterprises and entrepreneurs in distant regions. These returnees, entrepreneurs, and "astronauts" (so called by the Chinese because they appear to live in airplanes) are part of a transnational technical community that is transferring knowhow and skill between distant regional economies faster and more flexibly than most corporations.

This chapter explores the role of transnational communities in transforming the global organization of semiconductor production over the past two decades. Semiconductor manufacturing is a technically complex and demanding process that requires sophisticated technological and managerial knowhow as well as exacting environmental conditions. This makes it particularly difficult to transfer manufacturing to a new location, particularly in less developed economies. Nevertheless production has shifted from advanced to developing economies in a very short period. In less than twenty-five years the balance of semiconductor manufacturing and design shifted from the U.S. and Japan to formerly peripheral regions in the Asia-Pacific region, Taiwan and the urbanized east coast of China, in particular.

In 1985 a handful of large integrated producers from the U.S. and Japan accounted for 87 percent of world semiconductor output. When Taiwan Semiconductor Manufacturing Co. (TSMC) pioneered the stand-alone foundry in 1985 it triggered a process of vertical fragmentation and innovation in the industry. By 1995 Taiwan's leading manufacturers had reached the world technological frontier and dominated the global foundry market. And in the first years of the twenty-first century the leading semiconductor producers in China gained technological capability faster than their predecessors. Industry analysts predict that by 2010 firms from the Asia-Pacific region will account for 35 percent of world semiconductor production (double their share in 2000), with China alone accounting for 7 percent. The U.S. and Japanese share is forecast to fall to 50 percent of the global market.

This chapter suggests that transnational technical communities—foreign-born, U.S.-educated engineers and scientists who establish long distance professional and economic networks linking regions in their home countries to Silicon Valley—have become important actors in the global economy.[1] Theories of capitalist development focus almost entirely on the role of the firm and the state in economic change. However, the main actors driving the changing location of semiconductor production are transnational entrepreneurs and their communities—not multinational corporations or nation-states, although both play a role. These skilled immigrants boast the technical capabilities and know how as well as the professional networks to affect far-reaching transformations of their home countries, even if a majority never return permanently.

Transnational communities have the potential to change the dynamics as well as the spatial organization of capitalist development. As transnational entrepreneurs seed new centers of entrepreneurship and innovation in distant regions, they undermine traditional relationship between core and periphery. The one-way flows of capital from the U.S. to developing countries in Asia to take advantage of low-cost skill during the 1970s and 1980s, for example, were replaced in the 1990s by complex two-way flows of capital, skill, and technology between these differently specialized regions. A similar process is now underway linking Silicon Valley and the urban centers of eastern China. And transnational communities have played a central role in the emergence and upgrading of software capabilities in India, Ireland, and Israel (Autler 2000; Bresnahan and Gambardella 2004).

The contributions of a transnational community—seeding domestic technology entrepreneurship and innovation—should not be confused with the broader impacts of a diaspora on the home country. The aggregate remittances, investments, or demonstration effects of a diaspora can affect an economy in a variety of different, but largely limited, ways. The transnational networks described here, by contrast, are created by a very small subset of highly educated technical professionals whose impacts on development can be disproportionately significant. The community of engineers and entrepreneurs described in this chapter, for example, is distinguished from the broader Chinese diaspora or "overseas Chinese business networks" by shared professional as well as ethnic identities and by their deep integration into the Silicon Valley technical community.[2]

The next section argues that the modularization of production in the information technology (IT) industry has created new opportunities for highly skilled immigrant engineers who are ideally positioned to seed new centers of entrepreneurship in formerly peripheral regions of the world. The subsequent section summarizes briefly how overseas Chinese engineers in Silicon Valley created the cross-Pacific collaborations that fueled Taiwan's emergence in the 1990s as a global center of technology production. The balance of the chapter suggests that regions of China are now poised to repeat Taiwan's experience a decade later, albeit under significantly different conditions. Taiwanese IT investments in the Mainland are exploding (in spite of political tensions across the straits) at the same time that returning entrepreneurs like Howard Yang are using their experience and connections in the U.S. to accelerate the upgrading of China's semiconductor industry. The Shanghai region has already become an important global center of semiconductor production and design. This is not to suggest that China will technologically surpass industry leaders like the U.S. and Japan soon. However, the circulation of world-class engineering and entrepreneurial talent between regions in the U.S., Taiwan, and China is altering the trajectories of all three economies.

TECHNICAL COMMUNITIES AND INDUSTRIAL FRAGMENTATION

The emergence of new centers of technology, like Taiwan, in locations outside of the advanced economies has been possible because of transformations in the structure of the information technology sector. The dominant competitors in the computer industry in the 1960s and 1970s were vertically integrated corporations that controlled all aspects of hardware and software production. Countries sought to build a domestic IBM or "national champion" from the bottom up. The rise of the Silicon Valley industrial model spurred the introduction of the personal computer and initiated a radical shift to a more fragmented industrial structure organized around networks of increasingly specialized producers (Bresnahan 1998).

Today, independent enterprises produce all of the components that were once internalized within a single large corporation—from application software, operating systems, and computers to microprocessors and other components. The final systems are in turn marketed and distributed by still other enterprises. Within each of these horizontal segments there is, in turn, increasing specialization of production and a deepening social division of labor. In the semiconductor industry today, independent producers specialize in chip design, fabrication, packaging, testing, marketing, and distribution as well as in the multiple segments of the semiconductor equipment manufacturing and materials sectors. A new generation of firms emerged in the late 1990s that specializes in providing intellectual property in the form of design modules rather than the entire chip design. For example, there are over 200 independent specialist companies in Taiwan's integrated circuit (IC) industry (figure 1).

This change in industry structure appears as a shift to market relations. The number of actors in the industry has increased dramatically, and competition within many (but not all) horizontal layers has increased as well. Yet this is far from the classic auction market mediated by price signals alone; the

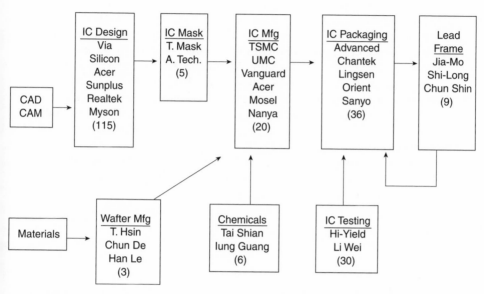

Figure 1 The structure of Taiwan's integrated circuit (IC) industry (# of establishments).

decentralized system depends heavily on the coordination provided by cross-cutting social structures and institutions. While Silicon Valley's entrepreneurs innovate in increasingly specialized niche markets, intense communication in turn ensures the speedy, often unanticipated, recombination of these specialized components into changing end products. This decentralized system provides significant advantages over a more integrated model in a volatile environment because of the speed and flexibility as well as the conceptual advances associated with the process of specialization and recombination.[3]

The deepening social division of labor in the industry creates opportunities for innovation in formerly peripheral regions—opportunities that did not exist in an era of highly integrated producers. The vertical specialization associated with the new system continually generates entrepreneurial opportunities. By exploiting these opportunities in their home countries, transnational entrepreneurs can build independent centers of specialization and innovation, while simultaneously maintaining ties to Silicon Valley to monitor and respond to fast-changing and uncertain markets and technologies. They are also well positioned to establish cross-regional partnerships that facilitate the integration of their specialized components into end products.

The social structure of a technical community thus appears essential to the organization of production at the global as well as the local level. In the old industrial model, the technical community was primarily inside the corporation. The firm was seen as the privileged organizational form for the creation and internal transfer of knowledge, particularly technological knowhow that is difficult to codify (Kogut and Zander 1993).

In regions like Silicon Valley, however, where the technical community transcends firm boundaries, such tacit knowledge is often transferred through informal communications or the inter-firm movement of individuals (Saxenian 1994). This suggests that the multinational corporation may no longer be the advantaged or preferred organizational vehicle for transferring knowledge or personnel across national borders. An international technological community provides an alternative and potentially more flexible and responsive mechanism for long distance transfers of skill and know-how—particularly between very different business cultures or environments.

THE SILICON VALLEY-HSINCHU CONNECTION

Thousands of U.S.-educated Chinese engineers returned from Silicon Valley to Taiwan annually in the early 1990s. Some went to start technology companies, others to set up branches of U.S.-based companies, and still others to work for local companies or to provide professional services to Taiwan's growing technology community. Most were lured by the promise of greater economic opportunities, particularly after the lifting of martial law, and the U.S. recession of the early 1990s undoubtedly served as a significant push factor. This "reversal" of the brain drain provided the skill, knowhow and business connections that facilitated the accelerated development of Taiwan's semiconductor and personal computer (PC) manufacturing capabilities in the 1980s and 1990s (figure 2).

The development of a transnational community—a community that spans borders and boasts as its key assets shared information, trust, and contacts (Portes 1996)—has been largely overlooked in accounts of Taiwan's accelerated development. However, the contributions of this technical community have been key to the successes of more commonly recognized actors: government policymakers and global corporations. Both rely heavily on the dense professional and social networks that keep them close to state-of-the-art technical knowledge and leading edge markets in the U.S. The close connections to Silicon Valley, in particular, help to explain how Taiwan's producers innovated technologically in the 1980s and 1990s independent of their OEM customers.

The development of an international technical community transformed the relationship between the Silicon Valley and Taiwan economies as well. In the 1960s and 1970s capital and technology resided mainly in the U.S.

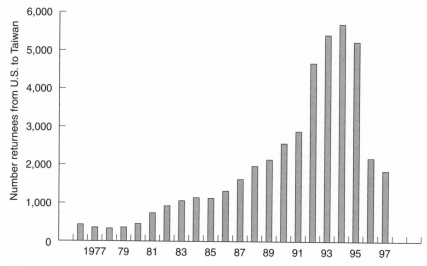

Figure 2 Returnees from the United States to Taiwan, 1976–1996 (*Source:* National Youth Council, Taiwan Ministry of Education, 1999).

and Japan and were transferred to Taiwan by multinational corporations seeking cheap labor. This one-way flow gave way in the 1990s to more decentralized two-way flows of skill, technology, and capital. The Silicon Valley-Hsinchu relationship today consists of formal and informal collaborations between individual investors and entrepreneurs, small and medium-sized firms, and divisions of larger companies located on both sides of the Pacific. A new generation of venture capital providers and professional associations serve as intermediaries linking the decentralized infrastructures of the two regions. As a result, Taiwan is no longer a low-cost location, yet local producers continue to gain growing shares in global technology markets. (Saxenian 2001; Saxenian and Hsu 2001)

Taiwan is now home to the world's most sophisticated PC manufacturers and their networks of small and medium-sized suppliers of components ranging from scanners and keyboards to motherboards and video cards—along with a world class semiconductor design and manufacturing infrastructure. As one observer notes:

Taiwan claims an advantage as a one-stop shop for every link in the technology production chain, headed by executives with leading edge US tech firms on their CVs and client lists. Chip designer VIA Technologies can have its blueprints etched into silicon by Taiwan Semiconductor Manufacturing and then have the naked wafers packaged by Advanced Semiconductor Engineering (ASE), placed on a motherboard by Asustek Computer, then sold to PC maker Acer—all without ever leaving Taiwan. (*South China Morning Post* May 23, 2001)

Taiwan's advantage over the U.S. and Japan lies in its achievements in technology logistics and management as well as process technologies: "No one beats TSMC with logistics of managing 8 fabs with 10 billion dollars of investment and 140,000 SKUs moving through on a given day to 500 customers globally all ordering different kinds of chips; and no one beats ASE in bringing package and test costs down" (Ho 2001).

Taiwan's total IT revenues exceeded $20 billion in 2000, with the semiconductor industry reaching $16 billion, from less than half a million a decade earlier. And instead of competing directly with Silicon Valley, Taiwan's IT sector has defined and excelled in a distinctive niche. As a result, the Silicon Valley and Taiwan economies remain closely linked, with Taiwan's PC and chip manufacturing expertise complementing Silicon Valley's leading edge product development, design, and marketing capabilities.

CROSS-STRAITS TECHNOLOGY TRANSFERS

The transfer of technology and skill from Silicon Valley to Taiwan that occurred in the 1980s and 1990s is now being replicated across the Taiwan straits as well as between Silicon Valley and the Mainland. In the early 1990s Taiwan's PC firms, driven by intensifying competition, began locating their most labor-intensive activities like the assembly of power supplies, keyboards, and scanners in China to exploit the lower cost labor and land. Following an earlier generation of Taiwanese footwear, toy, and light consumer goods manufacturers, they relocated to the south of China, particularly Fujian and Guangdong provinces (figure 3).

By 1999 over one-third of Taiwanese PC manufacturing was located in China, and a majority of these investments were clustered in the city of Dongguan, located between Shenzhen and Guangzhou in the Pearl River Delta, and one of the five Special Economic Zones in China. While manufacturers moved to exploit lower costs in China, the superiority of Taiwanese managerial and technological capabilities means that they continue to maintain control over the production process.

This geography shifted significantly after 2000. Faced with intensifying cost competition, the leading Taiwanese PC firms such as Compal, Mitac, Twinhead, and Acer began to move even their highest value-added activities such as motherboards, video cards, scanners, and even laptop PC manufacturing to China. However, rather than continuing to invest in South China, they are locating further north in Shanghai and Zhejiang province and the nearby cities of Suzhou and Kunshan in Jiangsu province. For

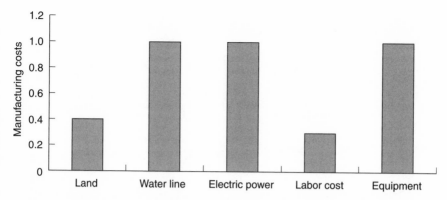

Figure 3 Manufacturing costs in Mainland China v. Taiwan (*Source:* Nikkei Business Times, 2001).

example, Quanta, the world's largest laptop manufacturer, is building a "manufacturing city" in Shanghai that has the capacity to produce 5 million laptops a year (figure 4).

Most of these investments are not officially permitted under Taiwanese regulations, which until very recently prohibited investments of over U.S. $50 million per project and in strategic sectors like advanced chip manufacturing.[4] However the channels for doing so through foreign subsidiaries are well established. This means that the official figures substantially understate total cross-straits investments. A 2001 poll by the Taipei Computer Association found that 90 percent of Taiwan-based high tech companies have invested or plan to invest in the Mainland (Naughton 2003). And China has replaced Taiwan as the third largest IT manufacturing center in the world, following only by the U.S. and Japan.

In another break from the past, teams of managers have moved from Taiwan to oversee these sophisticated operations, and they have encouraged their networks of suppliers to move as well. A manager from component-maker Logitech reports that the firm has encouraged its entire production chain, from ICs to cable wire and plastic mouse cases, to move to Suzhou with it because of the cost advantages of having an integrated local supply base from which to serve international customers. (A typical Taiwanese PC manufacturer relies on approximately 100 different component and part suppliers.) By 2001 there were an estimated 8,000 Taiwanese companies located in the Shanghai area and between 250,000 and 400,000 Taiwanese, including the families of plant managers and engineers, living in the region. However these are far from self-contained operations: the expatriate managers and engineers typically travel back across the straits quarterly, suggesting that these firms continue to rely on their Taiwanese headquarters for strategic decision-making and direction.

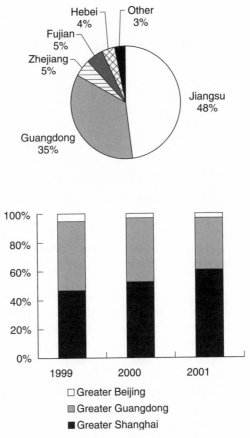

Figure 4 Officially approved Taiwanese investments in China, by region (*Note:* Great Shanghai includes Zhejiang and Jiangsu provinces. Greater Guangdong includes Guandong and Fujian Provinces, Greater Beijing includes Hebei province) (*Source*: http://www.chinabiz.org.tw/maz/Eco-Month, 1999, 2000, 2001).

SHANGHAI'S ZHANGJIANG SCIENCE PARK

The Chinese government designated Shanghai as the capital of the country's semiconductor industry in 2001, which should deepen as well as diversify the technology base in the region. As in Taiwan a decade earlier, this creates opportunities for mutually beneficial collaborations between local PC and systems producers and IC designers and manufacturers. The Zhangjiang High Tech Park in the Shanghai's Pudong New Area is emerging as the locus of new investments in the semiconductor industry. The Park was established in 1992 by the Ministry of Science and Technology as

TABLE 1
China's Tax Cuts for Semiconductor Industry

	Pre-July 2000	Post-July 2000
Value-added tax	17%	6% (3% for chip design)
Regular tax		
• First two years of profitability	33%	0
• Next three years of profitability	33%	15%
Depreciation		
• Mechanical equipment	10 years	3 years
• Electronic equipment	5 years	3 years
Materials		
• General	24–30%	0
• Selected	6–10%	0
• Value-added tax	17%	0
Equipment		
• Import	8–13%	0
• Value-added tax	17%	0

Source: Chen and Woetzel (2002).

a national center for development of new and high technology. By 2001, with 4.4 sq km developed area (approximately three times the size of Taiwan's Hsinchu Science Park) the Park was home to 267 establishments, mostly IT-related, and reported output of close to US $1 billion.

Both the Shanghai government and the Park Administration have aggressively pursued investment by offering subsidized loans, generous tax exemptions and a 50% discount on land rent in the Park. Zhangjiang's developers have also carefully planned the area's development. The Master Plan includes not only areas for high-tech research, incubation and manufacturing, but also residential, commercial, and education facilities, green space (40 percent), and mass transit links. Zhangjiang Park has emerged as a center of foreign investment, which reached U.S. $3.4 billion in 2000, or triple the average in previous years. This contrasts with joint ventures, which invested US $659,000, and domestic ventures, which invested only U.S. $451,000. Motorola, Lam Research, and Sun Microsystems are among the U.S. firms with operations in the Park. However the majority (80 percent) of the foreign investments come from Hong Kong and Taiwan.

The semiconductor industry in Shanghai took off following the Chinese government's announcement, in July 2000, of substantial tax reductions for the industry (see table 1). Later that year, three major manufacturers announced plans to build chip fabrication facilities in Zhangjiang Park:

TABLE 2
The IC Industry in Shanghai Zhangjiang High-Tech Park, 2001

- **3 IC Manufacturers:** SMIC, GSMC, Shanghai Beilin
- **5 IC Research & Development Units:** Fudan Micro-analysis Center, Hua Hong R&D Center, Fudan Micro-electronics Research Institute, Research Institute of Xi'an Jiaotong University, Fudan Information College
- **19 IC Design Companies:** Huahong, Fudan Micro-electronics, Haulong, Hongsheng, Avanti!, Synopsys, SST, ISSI, and others.
- **6 IC Packaging and Testing Companies:** Alphatec, Hongyi, Tailong, Hongsheng, Qingyi and others
- **15 IC Equipment Manufacturers and Supporting Companies:** PaxAir, SAES, Lam Research, Novellus, Applied Materials, TOWA, TIC, DiAi, and more

Source: Shanghai Zhiangjiang Hi-Tech Park (2001).

Shanghai Beilin Microelectronics Co., the leading Chinese semiconductor company, and two new joint ventures: Shanghai Grace Semiconductor Manufacturing Corp. (GSMC) and Semiconductor Manufacturing International Corp. (SMIC). Even Taiwan's leading foundry, TSMC, recently announced plans to invest in China in the future. According to CEO Morris Chang:

> when the Mainland authorities provide such incentives like tax breaks as well as sufficient supplies of high tech personnel and water and electricity, and our competitors have started to use these advantages, we would lose our competitive edge if we did not follow suit. (SCMP, 8/27/01)

These investments have in turn attracted downstream and upstream producers, making Zhangjiang Park home to over 100 IC-related firms representing all stages of the IC production chain, from wafer manufacturing, IC design, and fabrication to packaging and assembly-and-test. Taiwanese design house VIA Technologies and assembly firms ASE and Siliconware Precision Industries have also located facilities near the park (table 2).

The joint ventures, GSMC and SMIC, represent a mix of resources and talent from Silicon Valley, Taiwan and China. GSMC is a high profile venture founded by Mianheng Jiang, the son of China's President Jiang Zemin, and Winston Wong, son of the chairman of Formosa Plastics and head of Taiwan's most powerful business family. Wong is chairman and Jiang is vice chairman of the Board and principal shareholder of GSMC, which raised U.S. $1.6 billion for its first foundry.

The senior executives and managers in both firms have extensive experience in the semiconductor industry in the U.S. and/or Taiwan. SMIC,

TABLE 3
Semiconductor Manufacturing International Corporation (SMIC)

- Established: April 2002
- Incorporation: Cayman Islands
- Location of IC Production: Shanghai Zhangjiang Park
- Equity raised: US $1.5 billion
- President & CEO: Richard Chang, former CEO World Semiconductor of Taiwan
- Products: SRAM, Standard Logic, Analog IC, Flash Memory & LCD Driver ICs
- Technology: 8" wafers, sub-0.25 micron (2002), LT goal 12" wafers, 0.11 micron
- Production Capacity: 30,000/month by end of 2002, 85,000/month by end 2004
- Employees: Approximately 1600
- First Round Investors: Shanghai Industrial Holdings Limited, Walden International, Goldman Sachs, H&Q Asia Pacific Limited, and a Singapore consortium led by Vertex Management
- Future Plans: Total of 6 fabs in Shanghai Zhangjiang Park

Source: http://www.smics.com

for example, recruited 300 engineers away from Taiwan's leading IC manufacturing firm, TSMC, and another 50 directly from leading Silicon Valley companies. According to one of these recruits: "The salaries here [in China] are lower than they are in the U.S.—but there is a greater upside. Things are moving very fast here. SMIC built its fab in one year, which may be record time. There is tremendous room for growth in China" (interview, January 2001).

The financing for these deals typically comes from U.S. and foreign investors with experience in either Taiwan or China, as well as from local partners. Both are financed from abroad to avoid Taiwan's investment limits and the complex regulatory system in China. SMIC, for example, is incorporated in the Cayman Islands, and is structured as a U.S. Delaware-style corporation so it will follow U.S. corporate and securities law and governance, which preserves the option of raising capital in the public markets in the U.S. or Asia. And following Silicon Valley practice, employees of SMIC receive stock options as part of their compensation.

SMIC had also relied almost exclusively on legal and financial advice from Silicon Valley professionals. Carmen Chang, a partner from Silicon Valley's leading law firm, Wilson Sonsini, managed the legal details of the SMIC financing and incorporation. She has also played an active role in

Table 4
Salaries of IC Design Employees, US $thousand

	China	United States
Senior design engineer (5 years experience)	14–30	80–150
Junior design engineer (<5 years experience)	9–20	50–100
Other design employees	9–20	50–100

Source: Chen and Woetzel (2002).

related business details, from lobbying the U.S. government to open to leading edge chip making equipment to advising the Chinese policymakers on opening a second board in Shenzhen. Her main clientele in the 1990s were Taiwanese entrepreneurs starting firms in either the U.S. or Taiwan. Today she says that business is overwhelmingly from Mainland Chinese—both returnees and Chinese firms setting up operations in the U.S.—and there are far more requests than she can accept. Experienced industry observers report that the clustering of the IC industry in Shanghai and the market, technology, talent pool, government support, and capital supply in China today resembles that of Taiwan's Hsinchu region ten or fifteen years ago. Some predict the industry will grow faster than it did in Taiwan because it has a large base of experience from the U.S. and Taiwan to tap and an existing model to follow. The Chinese market is also a key factor in these predictions: China's accounts for 6 percent (U.S. $13 billion in 2000) of worldwide demand for semiconductors, following only the U.S., Japan, and Taiwan. This market is predicted to grow at a compound annual rate of 17 percent in the next five years as domestic output of electronics goods grows. Yet domestic companies currently supply only 5% of the total Chinese demand.

While there is tremendous room for growth of the domestic semiconductor industry, it is likely that China will continue producing relatively low-end chips (the type used in watches, radios, cell phone, and other consumer electronics products) for the next 5–10 years. The IC manufacturing technology in China remains two or three generations behind Taiwan, and U.S. regulations on export of the most advanced manufacturing equipment to China will slow the adoption of leading edge process technologies.

McKinsey & Co. consultants in Shanghai predict that the large supply of low-cost engineering talent will allow China to grow more quickly as a center for semiconductor design than for advanced manufacturing, which requires sophisticated technology and management skills. Salaries for chip designers in China are about 20 percent of those in the U.S., and the domestic market for IC design in China will reach an estimated $10 billion in 2010 (figure 4).

This suggests the possibility that the relationship between China and Taiwan, like that between the U.S. and Taiwan, will be complementary rather than competitive, with Taiwan moving up the value chain to provide leading-edge manufacturing services and high-value-added design while China becoming a center of low-end, labor-intensive design and assembly-and-testing as well as non–leading-edge manufacturing.

CHINA AND SILICON VALLEY: FROM BRAIN DRAIN TO BRAIN CIRCULATION

At the same time that networks of Taiwanese PC and semiconductor makers were moving their low-end manufacturing to the Chinese Mainland, the "best and brightest" of China's youth were leaving to pursue their education abroad. The brain drain, which increased significantly after 1989 and the Tianamen Square events, has been so great that Mainland Chinese are now the largest and fastest growing group of foreign-born students in U.S. universities, with 54,466 students (or 10.5 percent of the total) enrolled in 1999-2000. Moreover, they have not returned to China in large numbers. One source reports that while approximately 320,000 Chinese students have studied abroad since 1978 only one-third have returned (*Science* 2000).

The loss of talent is especially acute in technical fields. Chinese students in the U.S. are concentrated at the graduate level and in science and engineering fields: about 2,500 Chinese students per year received doctoral degrees in science and engineering from the U.S. in the 1990s—for a total of 28,000 S&E doctorates between 1985 and 2000 (NSF 2001). This is more than double those from the next largest groups of foreign students in the U.S., from Taiwan and India (figure 5). Mainlanders also have historically had the highest stay rates of all of these groups. An NSF study found that 88 percent of Chinese who earned doctorates in science and engineering in 1990-91 were still working in the U.S. in 1995. This is consistent with the data on visas issued by the U.S. for workers with exceptional skills: Mainland Chinese received 20,885 H-1B visas between 1990 and 1999, second only to immigrants from India.

Chinese policymakers have recognized the opportunity to tap this pool of foreign-educated technology professionals for domestic development purposes. Over the past decade, governments at both local and central levels have pursued two strategies in their efforts to counteract the brain drain. Following Taiwan's model, Chinese agencies have sought to increase professional connections and communications with the overseas community by sponsoring study tours, conferences, joint research projects, and short-term work and teaching opportunities. The Ministry of

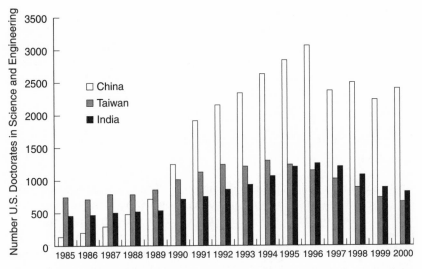

Figure 5 U.S. doctorates in science & engineering to foreign-born students (*Source:* National Science Foundation, 2001).

Education, for example, established the Chun Hui Program to finance trips to China by technologists trained abroad to participate in conferences and academic research (table 5). Other programs provide opportunities for short term lecturing, teaching, and postdoctoral appointments in China. Participants from the U.S. report that these programs have succeeded in increasing technical exchange between Chinese scholars based in China and the U.S.

The other approach to the brain drain is to directly recruit engineers and scientists with business experience to return to work or to start companies. Representatives of cabinet-level ministries as well as municipal governments from large cities such as Shanghai and Beijing paid regular visits to the U.S. throughout the 1990s to recruit Chinese professionals. These visiting officials typically hold dinners or meetings to publicize the favorable incentives and business environment in China.

Competition between municipal and provincial governments for returnees has increased significantly in recent years. There is now an almost continuous flow of delegations of company and government representatives recruiting in Silicon Valley, and they come from all over China—not just coastal urban areas, but central and western provinces as well.

Many municipal governments have also established Returning Students Venture Parks (or Overseas Student Parks) within the new and high tech development zones. These parks are reserved exclusively for companies started by returnees. They offer not only low rent, tax relief, shared infrastructure

TABLE 5
Policies on Technical Exchange with Overseas Chinese

- Ministry of Education: policies for overseas talent to return for conferences or short-term academic programs (Chun Hui program); policies for overseas talent to participate in scientific education and research (Chang Jiang Scholar project); start-up funds for research by Chinese overseas talent.

- Ministry of Personnel: financial aid for short-term work in non-educational departments for overseas talent and financial support for overseas talent to return for science activities in non-educational fields

- National Natural Sciences Foundation: funds for overseas talents to do short term research or teaching in China; control of use of funds for international cooperation and communications

- Chinese Academy of Science: one hundred talents project; high level program for visiting scholars; funds for overseas talent to return to work in China

Source: Dahlman and Aubert (2001).

and financial benefits like other science parks in China, but they also address the special needs of returnees, such as accelerating the bureaucratic process involved with establishing residency to insuring access to housing and prestigious, often bilingual, schools for their children (table 6).

By 2000 there were 23 Returning Students Science Parks across China, and many other municipalities had policies to attract returning students but no park. The Overseas Students Science Park in the Zhongguancun (Haidian) district of Beijing, the largest and oldest of the three overseas student parks located in Beijing, housed 48 companies and 68 returning students in 1998. There are no aggregate data on how many returnees these policies have attracted overall, and now way to determine the extent to which they have succeeded in producing successful companies. However, some Silicon Valley returnees who have started companies in China say that they would never locate their companies in such a facility, primarily because it would involve closer government ties and scrutiny.

Silicon Valley's Mainland Chinese immigrants, like their Taiwanese predecessors, have built extensive professional and social networks both in Silicon Valley and back in China. These ties are often coordinated through the alumni associations of the elite technical universities such as Beijing University, Tsinghua University, and Shanghai Jaiotong University. These alumni ties appear to gain importance when living abroad. In addition, there are close to a dozen specialized Chinese professional and technical associations in Silicon Valley ranging in size from 200 to over 2000 members. These organizations breed shared understandings and worldviews among their members while providing forums for mentoring and the exchange of contacts, capital, know how, and information within the community. While Taiwanese

TABLE 6
Distributed Electronically to Bay Area China Network (8/11/98) with Subject
Heading: A Great Business Opportunity for You

A Briefing on China Suzhou Pioneering Park for Overseas Chinese Scholars	
Sponsors	Chinese Scholarly Exchange Service Center, Ministry of Education Torch Program Office, Ministry of Science and Technology Jiangsu Service Center for the Shift of Qualified Personnel Jiancsu Science and Technology Commission The Administrative Committee of the Suzhou New Technology District Suzhou Science and Technology Commission
Location	The Park is located in the Suzhou New District (Suzhou National New & High Technology Industrial Development Zone) to the west of the old city proper of Suzhou. The district is only 80 km away from Shanghai and 1.5 hour drive from Shanghai Hongqiao Airport.
Mission	To create a favorable environment for exploitation of research results and development of small and medium-sized technology based enterprises by providing all around service and quality facilities
Target clients	Technology-based companies and research institutes run by students and scholars studying or working or returned from abroad
Incentives for tenants	• Three year refund of business tax starting the first day of operation • Three year-refund of the local part of VAT • Exemption from income tax in the first two profit-making years, six-year reduction of the rate by 50% that and then levied at a special rate of 15% for the next three years • Minimum registered capital of US$10,000 provided for technology consultancy or service provider, US$60,000 for manufacturing enterprises • Application priority for different-level grants and funds • Application priority for certificate of new & high technology product/enterprise • Building management and business services • Free provision of registration formalities • Provision of advice on policy and technical issues • Business promotion • Assistance in obtaining financing and refunds of duties • Provision of training programs
Progress to date	A news conference was held in Beijing this February to declare the establishment of the Park. The six sponsors have jointly set up the Torch New & High Technology Investment and

TABLE 6 (*continued*)

A Briefing on China Suzhou Pioneering Park for Overseas Chinese Scholars	
	Guarantee Company and registration is now underway. The company is not-for-profit and will specialize in venture capital and credit guarantees for tenants of the park.
Building	The park owns one four-story building with floor space of 10,000 square meters. It hosts 88 units ranging from 20 to 100 sq meters. Services and facilities include the following:
	–Conference room with conferencing facilities –Seminar room –Product display chamber –Internet access, central air conditioning –Reception –Fax, typing, word-processing, and photocopying services –Air ticket booking, hotel room reservations –24-hour security services
Applicants and companies	Till now, the Park has received more than 50 applications and 30 of them are in operation. Business of theses companies mainly covers electronics, biotech, mechanics (sic), computer software, and environmental protection. Presidents or managing directors of these companies have studied in U.S.A., Japan, France, and U.K.

China Suzhou Pioneering Park for Overseas Chinese Scholars invites you to apply today.

immigrants started, and historically dominated some of the associations, and Mainland Chinese in turn started parallel associations, largely because of distrust bred by lack of familiarity, the two communities are increasingly drawn together by the shared goal of building business links to China.

The Hua Yuan Science & Technology Association was formed in Silicon Valley in 2000 to "promote the technological, professional and scientific development of the Chinese business community." Its membership has grown very fast: over 1000 Chinese engineers attended the 2002 Hua Yuan Annual Conference entitled "Opportunities and Challenges: Riding the China Wave." Their website describes the association's mission: "Hua Yuan assists and encourages professional development and entrepreneurship of our members, facilitates exchange between Chinese and other business communities in the United States, and strengthens cross-border business relationships between Silicon Valley and China" (http://www.huayuan. org/). Hua Yuan maintains a Chinese office in Beijing and describes its role as a "bridge between Chinese and US high tech industries":

Hua Yuan has established strong associations with Chinese business community, and has built up a close working relationship with the Chinese regulatory authorities. Members of Hua Yuan exploring business opportunities in China are backed by our strong networks in China. Such supports include concrete administrative helps (sic) from Hua Yuan's Chinese office located in the center of high-tech development in Beijing. Hua Yuan continues to engage in high-level exchanges between business executives from Silicon Valley and China.

A recent Hua Yuan meeting featured a keynote address by Dr. Char-pin Yeh, president of Macronix Electronics IC design operation in Suzhou, China. Macronix was started by a Taiwanese engineer who studied and worked in Silicon Valley for fifteen years before returning to start one of the first companies in the Hsinchu Science Park. Dr. Yeh, also Taiwan-born, earned a Ph.D. in electrical engineering from Georgia Institute of Technology, holds 26 U.S. patents in microelectronics-related fields, and worked in the U.S. semiconductor industry for almost fifteen years. His speech was a technical analysis of the "Strengths and Weakness Analysis of Cross-Straits IC Design Industries." He also participated in a forum on the trade-offs between a corporate career and entrepreneurship, the business environment in China, and steps to "start the wheel of business in China."

Hua Yuan and other Chinese professional associations also sponsor regular business tours to China, receive government delegations, and serve as conduits for Chinese firms recruiting in the U.S. The delegation from the 2001 Back to China trip sponsored by the Chinese Internet and Networking Association (CINA) gave a series of public presentations on the topic of "The China Wave—A Reality Check" soon after their return. The speakers provided detailed information on the challenges as well as opportunities facing those considering returning to the Mainland, with individuals addressing issues relevant to the telecommunications, wireless, software, and IC sectors.

These associations also provide multiple forums for information exchange and technology transfer between Chinese engineers in the U.S., Taiwan, and China. The Chinese Institute of Engineers (CIE), which has branches in all three places, has sponsored technical conferences that have attracted practicing engineers as well as scholars for decades. Business-oriented organizations are also starting to play this role. In 1998 the Chinese American Semiconductor Association (CASPA) sponsored a delegation of local technologists for a two-week study tour of the Shanghai semiconductor industry. After returning the group produced a technical report assessing the status of the Chinese microelectronics industry that was widely circulated among in the Valley.

Equally important, according to one of the group's leaders, Peter Yin of ICT Inc: "we were instrumental in helping our Shanghai counterparts solve current technical problems, [but] we also served as vehicles of

knowledge transfer and new modes of thinking." He described an exchange with sessions organized according to detailed technical specializa-
tions of the semiconductor engineers and commented:

> They benefited a great deal from exposure to advanced technologies and novel
> analytical methodologies during the sessions, as much as their Silicon Valley col-
> leagues gained first-hand knowledge of China's determination to develop its in-
> digenous IC base and challenges that lie ahead. (CASPA press release, 1998)

These exchanges also help pave the way for returnees. Four of the former
heads of CASPA were among those successfully recruited in 2001 to become
senior executives in SMIC's newly announced in Shanghai's Zhangjiang
Park.

The impetus for these technology transfers is not just one-sided. The
Zhangjiang High Tech Park Administration has been quite entrepreneurial in creating opportunities for exchange. One of its recent activities is the
institutionalization of a two-hour monthly video conference allowing
about fifty Chinese engineers—some based in the Park and others in Silicon Valley—to communicate face-to-face on areas of shared interest. In
recent months they have sponsored forums focusing on the software industry, recent trends in the IC industry, and the development of telecommunications technologies.

The first notable wave of high technology returnees from the U.S. to
China began in the late 1990s, triggered by a combination of Internet en-
thusiasm, the lure of the large China market, and various government incentives. This group located their businesses primarily in Beijing to be part
of the fast-growing Internet and dot.com industries. While accurate data
are not available, it appears that these returnees came from all over the
U.S., many were young (recent graduates) with little or no work experience in the U.S., and many had business rather than technology backgrounds. Two of the high profile firms of this era are AsiaInfo, started by
returnees from Texas and now China's largest systems integrator for the
telecommunications and Internet industries, and Sina.com, the leading
Internet portal in China. Both firms are now publicly listed on NASDAQ,
although their future remains uncertain. Most of these Internet start-ups
failed within a couple of years and this flow of returnees ended abruptly
with the collapse of the dot.com bubble.

A distinct, and apparently larger, wave of returnees began in 2001 with
the acceleration of foreign investment in China's semiconductor industry.
The recruits to these ventures were typically older engineers with substantial
experience in the semiconductor industry in Silicon Valley and/or Taiwan.
Many returned to work the fast growing IC industry cluster in Shanghai,
lured by stock options and the promise of professional opportunities not
available to Chinese in the U.S. The recession in the U.S. economy served

as a push factor as well, with layoffs growing and new jobs hard to find. By one count, returnees to China started 166 firms specializing in semiconductor and software development during 2001 and 2002 (Naughton 2003).

The Shanghai Pudong District High Tech Delegation that visited the U.S. in late 2001, for example, attracted close to 4,000 Chinese students to recruitment sessions in New York, Chicago, and San Francisco (including over 1,000 at the Silicon Valley session). The delegation, which included executives from 35 Shanghai businesses along with political officials, reportedly received over 2,500 applications for the 238 positions available. While these numbers must be treated with a grain of salt because they are from China's Xinhua News Agency, individuals who attended the meeting in the Bay Area report being amazed at the turnout and the interest in the employment opportunities.

The return rate among U.S.-educated Mainland Chinese has historically been low, below 30 percent according to most estimates and as low as 10 percent among engineers and scientists. However, the Taiwanese case suggests that such trends can reverse quickly and then accelerate because of the networked nature of these communities: news of successes and opportunities travels quickly. In Taiwan the recession of the early 1990s triggered a tripling of returnees within three or four years. The events of 9/11 appear to have had a similar impact on Mainlanders. One career search Web site in China reports a dramatic increase in resumes in early 2002: "In the past couple of months we have about 10,000 to 15,000 interested in returning to China to work. Six months ago we would get only 10 to 100 resumes in the same period" (SFC January 2, 2002). Another Chinese observer describes the growth of the B2C trend, or "Back to China."

As professional opportunities in places like Shanghai grow, strengthened by the cross-straits transfers of manufacturing operations and skill, it is likely that more Mainland engineers and managers will return from the U.S. According to Lu Chunwei, a software developer who recently returned from a job at Microsoft to start his own B2Bcompany, "it's a big trend now, people just want to return to China. Its like the Gold Rush. They're successful in the US, but in their hearts they still feel like immigrants. They feel welcome here in China. . . . There are not many new opportunities in the U.S." He added that that cheaper labor, lower rents, and better business opportunities in the Mainland were important factors in his decision (SCMP, January 12, 2002).

Chris Xie returned from Silicon Valley to China to start a peer-to-peer computing company after failing to find funding in the Bay Area. He built a partnership with a Shanghai-based biotech company that has provided seed funding and is allowing the start-up to share its office space. Xie reports that the environment for his start-ups was more attractive in China because of government incentives that include $36,000 in cash grants and 390 square feet of free office space, as well as substantially lower cost labor. He reports that he hired a staff of 10 in Shanghai for what it would have cost to hire a single comparable employee in Silicon Valley (SFC, January 2, 2002).

Of course this does not amount to a reversal of the brain drain. It is likely that the net loss of talent from China will continue for a long time. However, the acceleration of the brain circulation and the growing interest in returning to China among US-educated engineers and scientists (particularly those with experience in Silicon Valley) could have a lasting impact on the economy of the centers of IT production along China's coast. There are many broader political, regulatory and institutional factors that will shape the precise trajectory of the economy and the impact of returnees and the circulation of brains on the IT industry. But there have already been important technology and know how transfers from both Silicon Valley and Taiwan and they show not sign of slowing.

The emergence of successful role models—either successful start-ups or large firms that provide sizable economic returns for employees with stock options—is likely to be an important turning point in this process. UTStarcom is one such model. The firm, which provides telecommunications network products for the Chinese market, was founded in 1991 by a group of U.S.-educated Chinese engineers. Most of the original founders are classmates from a Ministry of Posts and Telecommunications-run university, and almost of the senior management team worked at Bell Labs in the U.S.

UTStarcom is headquartered in Silicon Valley, but 99 percent of its 1,800 employees as well as its primary market focus are at manufacturing and R&D facilities in China. According to founder Hong Lu, UTStarcom has leveraged its "many connections in China," including its access to Chinese officials, intimate knowledge of the China market, and ability to combine modern business structures from the U.S. with this ethnic and cultural knowhow. The firm went public on NASDAQ in 2000 and is currently valued at $1.4 billion.

Successes like UTStarcom remain limited so far. While Mainland entrepreneurs have done well in Silicon Valley, success in China has been more elusive thus far. The growing interest of U.S. venture capitalists in funding returning Chinese entrepreneurs from Silicon Valley suggests, however, that the opportunities are there. The Walden International Investment Group (WIIG), for example, was one of the original investors in NeWave Semiconductor. The firm was sold in 2002 to a Silicon Valley semiconductor company for $80 million—making money for both WIIG and Chinese government-owned Hua Hong Microelectronics that entity that had invested $1.5 million.

According to WIIG chairman Lip-Bu Tan, the NeWave experience has taught him that the best strategy in China is to invest in U.S.-educated students who want to return home to start firms. He tried in the early 1990s to invest in Chinese state-owned enterprises, but learned that there was no way to get his money out. Then he tried to create joint ventures between U.S.-based and local Chinese companies, but the challenge of bridging the two management cultures was insurmountable. The key, says Tan, is to find graduates of U.S. universities who have stayed and worked in companies in a place like Silicon Valley for many years. "You have to be reasonably brainwashed in the U.S." As the Mainland Chinese community in the U.S. matures, such seasoned start-ups seem increasingly plausible.

The Acorn Campus was established in Silicon Valley by a team of experienced (and unusually successful) Overseas Chinese engineers. They serve as angel investors and provide mentoring and connections, as well as space, for promising new local ventures with Chinese founders. One of their portfolio firms, Newtone Communications, a telecom software firm, realized that its seed money of $500,000 would go much further in China, where it could to hire five of the nation's best engineers for the price of one engineer in the Bay Area. By moving to Shanghai, Netwone doubled its employment without increasing the budget. This experience spurred the creation of a new Acorn Campus in Shanghai. The founders' mission, according to their website, is to "leverage the highest level of Silicon Valley entrepreneurial experiences to create, invest, and incubate high technology startups in China . . . and promote global leadership through Silicon Valley-Asia value chain partnerships." They have targeted Chinese entrepreneurs returning from Silicon Valley, and they seek to access the best resources from three different locations: R&D, new product development, and marketing in the U.S., high end logistics, design and manufacturing in Taiwan, and low cost engineering and manufacturing talent in China.

THE SILICON VALLEY-TAIWAN-CHINA CONNECTION

This case underscores suggests the importance of space and geography to understanding the developmental dynamics of capitalism. The transnational networks linking Silicon Valley and China parallel those established a decade earlier between Taiwan and Silicon Valley—and are creating the third leg in a triangle of social, professional, and business ties between Silicon Valley, Hsinchu, and Shanghai. As Overseas Chinese technologists extend their professional and technical networks to the Mainland, they are contributing to the growth of an important new global center of technology entrepreneurship as well as deepening the division of labor between these increasingly specialized—and mutually interdependent—regional economies.

And they are doing so from the bottom up, through the networks of entrepreneurs and enterprises that make up a transnational technical community, rather than as individuals or through the activities of multinational corporations or the direction of state policymakers. The state and multinationals have facilitated the development of the semiconductor industry in both Taiwan and China, to be sure, but it is the networks of Chinese entrepreneurs and managers with ties to Silicon Valley who have contributed the critical transfers of know how as well as the business connections that are essential to technological learning in the current era.

In short, neither the state nor the multinationals, either individually or jointly, could have achieved the rapid technological upgrading that occurred in Taiwan in the 1980s and 1990s and that is underway today in China. This is clear from the experience of Singapore and Malaysia. Both have benefited from extensive foreign direct investment by Silicon Valley semiconductor and computer corporations—investments that began in the 1960s and continue today. And in both, policymakers have developed explicit and aggressive strategies for encouraging the development of technology production. Yet neither has achieved the technological level or responsiveness of Taiwan's semiconductor design and manufacturing enterprises—capabilities that have growth through two decades of transnational entrepreneurship linking Hsinchu and Silicon Valley.

This is not to suggest that returnees are creating replicas of Silicon Valley in their home countries. These regions differ from the original Silicon Valley in a multiplicity of small and large ways. Different economic and political institutions, the product of varied histories and cultures, ensure that each region will pursue its own distinctive trajectories. It is more appropriate to see these new regions as hybrids that merge elements of the Silicon Valley industrial system with indigenous institutions and resources.

The power of the transnational community is most evident in the case of the semiconductor industry, which originated in Silicon Valley and has been transferred by Chinese entrepreneurs first to Taiwan and then from Taiwan as well as from Silicon Valley to China. However a similar process is occurring in linked sectors as well. Of course these are not one-way flows. While the Taiwanese IC industry initially grew out of talent and technology from the U.S., producers like TSMC contributed indigenous innovations that in turn benefited the entire industry. Likewise, while China remains at a lower technological level that both Taiwan and the U.S., it has all of the resources (skill, capital, knowhow, connections) to innovate, and there is evidence that the large Chinese telecommunications market will provide local producers with the opportunity to experiment with, and ultimately innovate, in the field of wireless communication.

NOTES

1. Alejandro Portes (1996) describes the growing importance of transnational entrepreneurs and communities, but his focus is exclusively on low-skill immigrants.

2. Taiwanese and Mainland-born engineers speak different native languages and grew up in very different political and economic systems. They have developed collective identities based on common educational and work experiences: many have attended the same elite universities in their home countries and have worked for the same or related companies in Silicon Valley. Many also participate in activities of the numerous Chinese professional and technical organizations in Silicon Valley.

3. It is possible to specialize without innovating, and it is possible to innovate without changing the division of labor. However it seems that the deepening social division of labor enhances the innovative capacity of a community: expanding opportunities for experimentation generate ideas, these ideas are in turn combined to make new ideas, and so forth in a dynamic and self-generating process. This suggests that specialization increases innovation and ultimately economic growth.

4. This ban was ended in late 2001 and replaced by case-by-case evaluation in a policy called "active opening, effective management."

REFERENCES

Autler, Gerald. 2000. "Global Networks in High Technology: The Silicon Valley-Israel Connection." Master's thesis, Department of City and Regional Planning, University of California, Berkeley.

Bresnahan, Timothy F. 1998. "New Modes of Competition: Implications for the Future Structure of the Computer Industry." Paper presented at the Progress and Freedom Conference on Competition, Convergence, and the Microsoft Monopoly. Progrress and Freedom Foundation. Washington, D.C., February 5.

Bresnahan, Timothy F. and Alfonso Gambardella, eds. 2004. *Building High Tech Clusters: Silicon Valley and Beyond.* Cambridge: Cambridge University Press.

Chang, Shirley L. 1992. "Causes of Brain Drain and Solutions: The Taiwan Experience." *Studies in Comparative International Development* 27(1)(Spring): 27–43.

Chen, Andrew Chun and Jonathan R. Woetzel. 2002. "Chinese Chips." *McKinsey Quarterly* 2.

Dahlman, Carl J. and Jean-Eric Aubert. 2001. *China and the Knowledge Economy: Seizing the 21st Century.* Washington, D.C.: World Bank.

Dedrick, Jason and Kenneth Kraemer. 1998. *Asia's Computer Challenge: Threat or Opportunity for the United States and the World?* New York: Oxford University Press.

Granovetter, Mark S. 1995. "The Economic Sociology of Firms and Entrepreneurs." In *The Economic Sociology of Immigration: Esays on Networks, Ethnicity, and Entrepreneurship,* ed. Alejandro Portes. New York: Russell Sage.

Hamilton, Gary G. 1997. "Organization and Market Processes in Taiwan's Capitalist Economy." In *The Economic Organization of East Asian Capitalism,* ed. Marco Orru, Nicole Woolsey Biggart, and Gary G. Hamilton. Thousand Oaks, Calif.: Sage.

Ho, John Paul. 2001. Speech, Asian American Manufacturers Association annual conference.

Hsu, Jinn-Yuh. 1997. "A Late Industrial District? Learning Networks in the Hsincu Science-Based Industrial Park." Ph.D. dissertation, Department of Geography, University of California, Berkeley.

Industrial Technology Research Institute, Electronics Research, and Service Organization. 1991. What You Wish to Know about the Taiwan Semiconductor Industry. 1991 ed. ERSO-ITRIS; http://www.itri.org.tw.

Kogut, Bruce and Udo Zander. 1993. "Knowledge of the Firm and the Evolutionary Theory of the Multinational Corporation." Journal of International Business Studies 24(4): 625–45.

Lu, Qiwen. 2000. China's Leap in the Information Age: Innovation and Organization in the Computer Industry. London: Oxford University Press.

Meany, Connie Squires. 1994. "State Policy and the Development of Taiwan's Semiconductor Industry." In The Role of the State in Taiwan's Development, ed. Joel D. Abarbach, David Dollar, and Kenneth Lee Sokoloff. London: M.E. Sharpe.

National Science Board. 2001. "Higher Education in Science and Engineering." In Science and Engineering Indicators. NSB-00-01. Arlington, Va.: National Science Foundation.

Naughton, Barry, ed. 1997. The China Circle: Economics and Technology in the PRC, Taiwan, and Hong Kong. Washington, D.C.: Brookings Institution Press.

———. 2003. "The Information Technology Industry and Economic Interactions between China and Taiwan." Paper presented at the conference New Information Technologies and the Reshaping of Power Relations. CERI, Paris, December 16–17.

Portes, Alejandro. 1996. "Global Villagers: The Rise of Transnational Communities." American Prospect (March–April): 74–77.

Saxenian, AnnaLee. 1994. Regional Advantage: Culture and Competition in Silicon Valley and Route 128. Cambridge, Mass.: Harvard University Press.

———. 2001. "Taiwan's Hsinchu Region: Imitator and Partner for Silicon Valley." Policy Paper 00-44. Stanford Institute for Economic Policy Research, June.

Saxenian, AnnaLee and Chuen-Yueh Li. 2003. "Bay-to-Bay Strategic Alliances: The Network Linkages between Taiwan and the U.S. Venture Capital Industries." International Journal of Technology Management 25(1/2): 136–50.

Saxenian, AnnaLee and Jinn-yuh Hsu. 2001. "The Silicon Valley-Hsinchu Connection: Technical Communities and Industrial Upgrading." Industrial and Corporate Change 10(4).

Shanghai Zhangjiang Hi-Tech Park. 2001. Annual Report 2000. Shanghai: Shanghai Z. J. Hi-Tech Park Development Co.

Science. 2000. "China's Leader Commits to Basic Research, Global Science." 288 (5473) (June 16): 1950–53.

Zweig, David and Chen Changgui. 1995. "China's Brain Drain to the United States: Views of Overseas Chinese Students and Scholars in the 1990s." China Research Monograph 47. Institute of East Asian Studies, University of California, Berkeley.

The Globalization of Stock Markets and Convergence in Corporate Governance

Gerald F. Davis and Christopher Marquis

THE INTERNATIONAL INTEGRATION of financial markets is a central dynamic of the globalization process and a potent force for driving changes in the institutions of corporate governance. During the late 1980s and 1990s, cross-border portfolio investment expanded dramatically. The number of regional and global investment funds focused on emerging markets increased from nine in 1986 to nearly 800 in 1995, and the combined assets of emerging market funds grew from $1.9 billion to $132 billion during this time (World Bank 1997: 16). Conversely, the number of foreign companies listed on the two major U.S. stock markets (Nasdaq and the New York Stock Exchange) increased from roughly 170 in 1990 to over 750 in 2000.[1] There are now more non-U.S. companies traded on Nasdaq and NYSE than there are German corporations traded on the Deutsche Boerse. Some theorists have taken these trends to indicate a coming convergence in the institutions of corporate governance around the world, at either the national or the firm level (see Davis and Useem 2002 for a review). At the national level, states may adapt their system of corporate governance to the American model in order to achieve the growth benefits of "shareholder capitalism" (e.g., Levine and Zervos 1998). As Larry Summers put it, "Financial markets don't just oil the wheels of economic growth—they *are* the wheels" (Murray 1997). Thus, forty-three nations opened their first postwar local stock exchange during the 1980s and 1990s, often as a means to attract foreign portfolio investment in local companies (Weber and Davis 2000). At the firm level, managers of companies seeking to attract equity investors have strong incentives to follow the standards of American institutional investors for appropriate governance structures. The ultimate impact, according to enthusiasts, will be the worldwide dominance of the American model of how to finance and govern a corporation.

Discussions of the "American model" portray it as a blueprint for an institutional matrix oriented toward dispersed investors, from the proper way to compose a board of directors to how to generate shareholder-friendly bodies of corporate and securities law (Easterbrook and Fischel

1991; cf. North 1990). But to the extent that the "American model" is a coherent construct at the national level, there are substantial legal and cultural barriers to its spread across nations (Guillen 2001), and many of the relevant institutions of corporate governance—such as stock markets—are not strictly contained within nation-states. It is largely the choices of decision-makers within firms that determine how corporations will be structured, from what stock market they list on and how they compose the board of directors to the strategy and goals of the firm. Law and culture provide some constraints at the firm level, of course, but these constraints are arguably more negotiable now than at any time in history.

We argue in this chapter that the appropriate level of analysis to address the issue of convergence in corporate governance is the individual firm, and that organization theory provides a useful toolkit for linking the macro aspects of economic globalization to the micro processes of business decision making. In their introduction, the editors of this volume argue that "economic sociologists need to . . . specify the mechanisms that account for continuity and discontinuity in institutional structures." Organization theory provides an extensive suite of theoretical mechanisms to understand processes of corporate change, including selection, diffusion, and the birth of new entrants to organizational fields. By examining how national context conditions the choices available to corporate decision-makers, and specifying the organizational processes underlying field-level change in the institutions of corporate governance, we hope to contribute to the project of explaining institutional continuity and discontinuity at the macro level.

Moreover, while institutions constrain firms, decision-makers within firms can choose their institutional jurisdiction. U.S. corporations have long experience with this notion: while securities law is national in scope, corporate law is made by states, and companies choose their state of incorporation, thereby creating competition among state legislatures to provide corporate law that appeals to corporate decision-makers (Romano 1993). To an increasing extent such institutional competition now takes place at a global level, as choices about where a firm incorporates (corporate law) and what market its securities trade on (securities law) are decoupled from where a firm is headquartered and where production takes place. By some accounts, just as Delaware won the competition to be the preferred state of incorporation, U.S. stock markets are likely to emerge as the preferred trading locale through voluntary "institutional migration" by global firms.

In this chapter, we examine the consequences of listing on a U.S. stock market for the governance practices of non-U.S. firms. Our general questions are: Do U.S.-listed foreign firms adopt the governance practices typical of American firms, and what effect does this have on their patterns of ownership and control? We study the network ties, governance structures, disclosure patterns, and investor recognition of 209 firms listed on Nasdaq and the New York Stock Exchange from the UK, France, Germany, Japan, Chile, and Israel in 2000. Each of these nations represents a divergent tradition of corporate governance and thus a different starting place for convergence. To the extent that stock markets are a device for homogenizing the practice of corporate governance around the world, it should be most visible among these firms.

Listing on a U.S. stock market is a compelling way for foreign firms to signal their shareholder orientation because it requires them to meet the relatively stringent standards of American securities markets (see Licht 1998 for a review of the empirical evidence on foreign listings). Indeed, Coffee (1999) argues that the dominant multinationals of the future—those whose higher valuations allow them to survive global industry consolidation—will tend to be listed on U.S. stock markets, and thereby subject to American securities laws, accounting standards, and the listing criteria of their chosen market. This is not trivial: when Daimler-Benz (Germany's largest industrial corporation) chose to list on the New York Stock Exchange in 1993, its 1992 earnings of DM 615 million under German accounting standards had to be restated as a loss of DM 1,839 million under U.S. standards. Moreover, disclosure requirements under U.S. securities law extend to transparency of corporate ownership. In principle, a Russian citizen or group that accumulates 5 percent of the shares of an Italian firm that lists ADRs on the NYSE is required to disclose its stake and intentions to the Securities and Exchange Commission, which makes such information publicly available (Coffee 1999). More recently, the SEC announced that foreign private issuers would be required to disclose activities in countries facing U.S. government sanctions, such as Cuba (*Economist* 2001).

But listing on a U.S. market falls short of adopting "shareholder capitalism" *tout ensemble*. Shareholder capitalism is more a genre of corporate capitalism than a prescription for specific governance practices. As such, its spread is akin to acculturation, for which listing on a U.S. market is only a first step. Organization theory suggests several possible pathways to convergence that may imply divergent patterns in the spread of governance practices among U.S.-listed firms, from institutional inertia—in which foreign firms retain the structures they had at their founding (Stinchcombe 1965)—to complete isomorphism (DiMaggio and Powell 1983). Examining the discretionary governance practices of U.S.-listed corporations from the perspective of organization theory gives some sense of the prospects for convergence going forward.

The Globalization of Stock Markets and Governance Convergence

The international expansion of financial markets in the late 1980s and 1990s generated a vigorous interdisciplinary analysis of the institutions of corporate governance around the world. The study of corporate governance expanded from evaluations of specific governance mechanisms in large U.S. corporations (e.g., boards of directors, capital structures, and takeovers) to cross-country comparisons of national systems for channeling capital and their impact on economic growth. The very definition of the object of study expanded correspondingly, from "the ways in which suppliers of finance to corporations assure themselves of getting a return on their investment" (Shleifer and Vishny 1997:737) to "the whole set of legal, cultural, and institutional arrangements that determine what publicly traded corporations can do, who controls them, how that control is exercised, and how the risks and returns from the activities they undertake are allocated" (Blair 1995:3). By hypothesis, some institutional configurations are better than others for generating economic growth (cf. North 1990), and institutional analysis can guide public policy by locating the best-performing model of economic organization and transplanting relevant elements (e.g., to transitional economies).

Some enthusiasts concluded that the American model, in which corporations are financed primarily by financial markets and governance institutions compel managerial attention to share price, was destined to emerge as the global standard in a world of internationally mobile capital (see, e.g., Friedman's [1999] distillation of the current received view). At the national level, the vibrancy of financial markets is empirically associated with subsequent economic growth (e.g., Levine and Zervos 1998), giving policy makers an incentive to create an institutional infrastructure conducive to vibrant financial markets. At the firm level, the ability to raise capital at low cost is a competitive advantage, and those firms that have structured themselves to be attractive to arms-length investors are the ones most likely to survive and grow. Because a disproportionate amount of investment capital is controlled by American institutional investors and others sharing their models of appropriate corporate governance, managers of firms—especially those with global aspirations—have incentives to structure themselves according to their templates (see a review and critique in Davis and Useem 2001). In effect, this means adopting the practices typical of U.S. firms: much as Toyotaism became the world's standard for manufacturing, American-style shareholder capitalism is en route to becoming the world's standard for corporate governance (Useem 1998). Thus, Bradley et al. (1999) argue that "The Anglo-American governance system . . . notwithstanding its idiosyncratic historical origins and its limitations, it is clearly emerging as the world's standard."

While this exuberance around the financial market-based model may be premature, one salutary outcome has been a resurgence of interdisciplinary research on the links among law, finance, social structure, and economic growth in the late 1990s. By the end of the decade, claiming that "institutions matter" had gone from apostasy to received wisdom, even within financial economics. Yet there is little agreement even within the relatively circumscribed realm of law and economics as to *how* institutions matter. Some see nations as rigidly constrained by events and choices made long ago, and the prospects for the spread of the American model as quite limited. Mark Roe (1994) argued that nineteenth-century populism was ultimately responsible for the American system of corporate governance, in which banks are weak, financial markets expansive, and corporate ownership dispersed. In contrast, nations that inherit French civil law rather than English common law typically have poorly developed financial markets and concentrated corporate ownership because of their relatively weak protection of minority investors (LaPorta et al. 1999). Factors ranging from the power of those with inherited wealth (Morck et al. 1999; Rajan and Zingales 2000) to the proportion of Roman Catholics in the population (LaPorta et al. 1999) all limited the likelihood of institutional change in the direction of shareholder capitalism at the national level. The U.S. was like the institutional equivalent of the Galapagos Islands, having evolved an intricately interdependent ecosystem in which managerialist corporations with dispersed ownership could thrive and contribute to national economic growth. Removed from this ecosystem, however, their prospects were dim; in particular, under code law (shared by most former French colonies or protectorates), managerialist firms find few investors.

The alternative view argues that corporate decision-makers face an array of choices among suppliers of legal and regulatory institutions that do not necessarily limit them to domestic providers. In this "issuer choice" view, law is a product and decision-makers in public corporations are consumers that shop among different vendors to find the best product to maximize shareholder wealth. Their concern with shareholder wealth is not driven by altruism but by the fact that the company's securities are products that must be sold in a competitive marketplace. Managers of firms competing for investment voluntarily adopt internal structures and practices that limit their own discretion and align their interests with those of investors because these structures make the company's securities more highly valued (Easterbrook and Fischel 1991). By the same token, managers in the U.S. choose their state of incorporation in part to certify that they are being governed by rules that are best for shareholders. Firms can easily re-incorporate if an alternative legal regime proves superior for investors, and thus state legislatures compete to provide investor-friendly regimes of corporate law in order to capture corporate franchise revenues (Romano 1993). Stock markets also compete to provide listing standards and regulations valued by corporate managers and investors, and firms can change their listing market to appeal to investors (Rao et al. 2000). And more recently, nation-states in effect compete to provide securities regulation valued by stock markets, corporations, and investors (Licht 2001). There are several devices available for corporations to circumvent domestic institutions and choose a new institutional jurisdiction for corporate governance (e.g., creating a separate corporation in the preferred locale which then merges with the old entity; see Gilson 2001).

It is possible, of course, that both accounts are correct: national institutions may be relatively inert, and issuers may choose to migrate to new institutional jurisdictions, so that a lack of convergence at the national level does not eliminate the prospect for convergence at the firm level. What seems clear is that this institutional migration is far more prevalent now than it was even ten years ago. Just as multinational corporations may choose among low-cost locales for production around the world, they are increasingly able to make delicately calibrated choices of their place of incorporation and stock market listing. For example, several Chinese firms are headquartered in Hong Kong, incorporated in the British Virgin Islands, and trade in the U.S. on Nasdaq. In matters of corporate governance, institutions constrain firms, but managers of firms elect which institutions they choose to be constrained by. Thus, to understand globalization in corporate governance, one must unpack the organizational processes involved in issuer choice.

In this context, the recent upsurge of foreign firms listing shares on U.S. markets merits attention. By 1998, upward of 1000 companies were traded on U.S. markets (Geiger 1998), and the number traded on the New York Stock exchange had tripled over a five-year period. As figure 1 shows, several foreign firms have been listed for decades: a few British firms listed in the late 1950s and 1960s, and a handful of large Japanese firms listed during the 1970s. But the 1990s witnessed the range of nationalities with substantial U.S. listings expand to include Chile, France, Germany, Hong Kong, Israel, and Mexico (see figure 2).

Why are these firms listing in the U.S.? The empirical literature indicates that when U.S. firms list securities abroad, they suffer share price declines, while foreign companies listing in the U.S. experience increases (see Licht 1998 for a review). This might reflect several factors: firms listing in the U.S. might be those in industries in which U.S. markets provide a higher valuation, and the U.S. capital markets are far larger and more liquid than those in other countries (Velli 1994). But a more intriguing interpretation

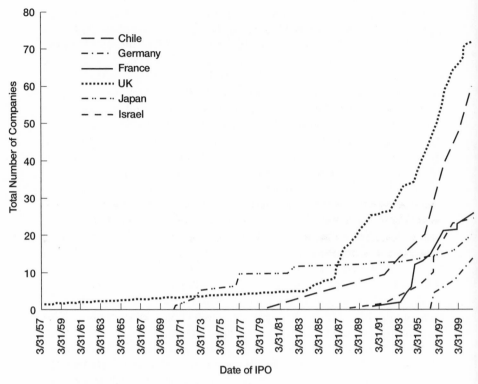

Figure 1 Growth in U.S. listings among six countries.

of these findings is that U.S. markets provide a more rigorous regulatory regime that favors investors: "the United States boasts a strict set of mandatory disclosure rules and a vast industry of securities houses and securities analysts. Taken together, the American market operates as a powerful monitoring and pricing system" (Licht 1998: 582). Thus, a U.S. listing may be seen as a bonding mechanism and a signal of the firm's proposed adherence to shareholder-oriented corporate governance. Moreover, American markets actively court foreign issuers, with substantial success (see figures 1 and 2). More than 60 firms from Israel trade on U.S. markets, for example, and several are incorporated in the U.S. and funded by American venture capitalists (Rock 2001).

Most firms that list on U.S. markets do so by sponsoring American Depository Receipts (ADRs). ADRs are certificates representing foreign shares held by a custodian bank in the issuer's home country that trade like other U.S. securities and are denominated in dollars. ADRs were invented in the 1920s as a way for U.S. investors to buy foreign securities without the transaction costs and risks of buying them on local markets in local

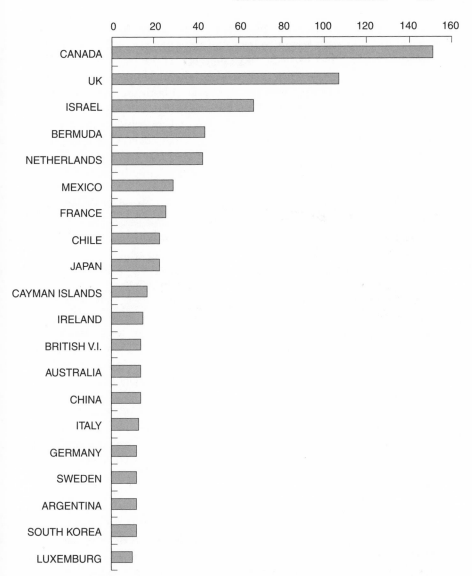

Figure 2 Largest sources of U.S. listings (by nation of incorporation).

currency. They also provide a relatively easy way for foreign issuers to access the U.S. capital markets (see Velli 1994 for an overview). The primary cost for a foreign issuer is that it must file audited annual financial statements with the SEC that conform to GAAP (or equivalent) accounting standards and must furnish reports of information provided to security holders or domestic regulators (see Coopers & Lybrand 1999). It also becomes subject to other U.S. securities laws, including the ownership disclosure and takeover regulations of the Williams Act. Those owning more than 5 percent of a U.S.-listed firm's shares, or those seeking to take over such a firm, are required to file with the SEC even if both they and the target firm are domiciled outside the U.S. Potential acquirers of foreign issuers are bound by the procedural rules governing takeover bids, which are intended to ensure fair treatment of minority shareholders. U.S.-listed firms are also bound by the Foreign Corrupt Practices Act and by Rule 10b-5, allowing shareholders to sue for losses based on fraudulent statements made by management (see Coffee 1999).

The demands imposed by a U.S. listing suggest a plausible firm-level argument for convergence. Corporations that voluntarily list on a U.S. market are opting into a strict set of laws and regulations designed to protect the interests of (American) investors. As a result, they generally get higher valuations than comparable firms that are not subject to these laws do (Licht 1998). Coffee (1999) argues that such firms are more likely to survive imminent global industry consolidations because their higher valuations make them more costly to acquire and give them a valuable currency to make acquisitions. Owners of acquisition targets are more likely to accept payment in shares of U.S.-listed firms than in shares of firms listed only in France or Japan, and therefore foreign corporations intending to make substantial global acquisitions have incentives to list in the U.S. Daimler Benz represents one possible case of this process, listing on the NYSE in 1993 and acquiring Chrysler in 1998. At present, U.S.-listed firms include Vodafone, Deutsche Telecom, France Telecom, British Telecomm, and Nippon Telegraph & Telephone—among the world's largest telecom firms—as well as many of the largest global auto, pharmaceutical, oil, and electronics companies. These firms have, in effect, opted in to American securities laws without having either to reincorporate in the U.S. (which is impractical for many established firms) or to change domestic laws to conform. Thus, nations need not seek to become "more American" for their indigenous firms to converge on American-style governance. This suggests that *if firm-level convergence is happening anywhere, it should be among U.S.-listed foreign firms.* By contrast, if U.S.-listed firms are *not* adopting American governance practices, we should be able to falsify (at least tentatively) the strong account for convergence.

There are two difficulties with an approach that assumes that corporate managers unproblematically recognize and act on the incentives for institutional migration, and that a U.S. listing represents opting in to the larger system of shareholder capitalism. First, the relevant actors are relatively large corporations for whom choice processes at the board level are subject to a number of influences that may stand in the way of voluntary conformity. If demonstrating fitness to investors were the motivation for listing in the U.S., then firms from nations with a French civil law tradition have much greater incentives to do so because of the relatively poor investor protections encoded in their domestic laws (Reese and Weisbach 2000). Yet by far the largest number of foreign firms on U.S. markets come from Canada, Great Britain, and Israel (accounting for nearly 40 percent of foreign listings)—each of which has investor-friendly common law (see figure 2). Second, shareholder capitalism as a style or genre of corporate governance entails a set of shared understandings of how business is done that go beyond disclosure requirements, and as such it is "as American as a Faulkner or Hemingway novel" (Davis and Useem 2002). Such shared understandings are not part of securities regulations or the NYSE listing agreement but underlie the governance practices of the U.S. corporation. Both these elements were exemplified by German steelmaker Krupp-Hoesch's takeover bid for rival Thyssen in March 1997. The hostile bid was decried as American-style "cowboy capitalism" and prompted massive street protests and high-level political intervention. Krupp's CEO Cromme was pelted with eggs and tomatoes by laborers fearing job cuts, and the bid was ultimately withdrawn in favor of a negotiated joint operating agreement. At the time, Gerhard Schroeder (then premier of Lower Saxony and a board member of Volkswagen) publicly welcomed the prospect of Cromme's joining VW's supervisory board so he could be "re-socialized" (Shroeder's term) into the German way of doing business (*Deutsche Presse-Agentur* 1997). "Issuer choice" is evidently not the autonomous process that law and economics scholars portray.

An Organizational Theory Approach to Studying Governance Convergence

As the Krupp-Thyssen case shows, issuer choice is "embedded and enmeshed" in larger social processes that shape the evolution of governance structures and institutions. Individual firms may not be as institutionally footloose as the imagery of issuer choice implies, and even firms that elect to list shares in the U.S. may not be willing or able to adapt the full slate of governance reforms associated with shareholder capitalism. At the center of this question is the board of directors—it is both the locus of top-level corporate decision making about governance reform and its object. Codes of good corporate governance have proliferated during the past few years (see http://www.ecgn.ulb.ac.be/ecgn/codes.htm for several), and behind all these codes are the assumptions that (1) boards of directors are ultimately responsible for the direction of the corporation and (2) the appropriate guiding principle for board decision making is attentiveness to shareholder value as an ultimate criterion.

The first assumption is only moderately controversial, the second one wildly so. Indeed, by law and custom, corporate boards around the world reflect very different notions of the role of the corporation in society and the range of constituencies whose interests ought to be reflected in the board's makeup (see Charkham 1994). Possibilities range from the communitarian view, in which corporations are social entities with obligations to labor, capital, and broader communities, to the contractarian view, in which corporate decision making should be entirely driven by what is best for residual claimants (see Davis and Useem 2001). Activist institutional investors take the latter view (unsurprisingly) and argue that boards should be as small as is practical (because large boards promote passivity among directors) and there should be large majority of "independent" directors (not executives of the firm or others with potential conflicts that might impede their shareholder orientation). U.S. boards are relatively small (about nine members) and contain few executives (two on average), and the CEO is also Chair in more than three out of four firms. The small size and numerical dominance of outside directors in the boards of large firms is consistent with the preferences of the institutional investors that hold most of their equity. Very similar size and composition figures hold for French corporate boards; however, French boards are also densely connected by a network of shared directors who were often "old boys" of the Ecole Nationale d'Administration (Kadushin 1995), perhaps reflecting a cultural view of the necessary background for corporate oversight (Dobbin 1994).

The size of German supervisory boards (*Aufsichtsrat*) is keyed by statute to the number of employees (ranging from 12 to 20 for large firms), and half the directors represent labor, while by tradition banks are represented among the "shareholder" directors—in contrast to the U.S., banks traditionally held substantial ownership blocks of the largest public firms in Germany. Thus, both capital (banks) and labor are traditionally represented in the governance of German public corporations. Japanese boards are huge (averaging 19 for all public companies, and from 30 to 40 for the largest firms) and dominated by executives of the firm (roughly 80% insiders on average), arguably reflecting the notion that a broad sampling of the firm's managers best represent the interests of the organization qua organization. And British boards have similar sizes but very different structures than U.S. boards, with half the directors being "insiders" and the Chair generally being separate from the CEO (see Charkham 1994 and Hopt et al. 1998 for broad overviews of each of these systems).

In each of these cases, the governance structure of the typical firm reflects a view of the corporation's place in society, and to whom it is responsible. Thus, signs of governance convergence at the organizational level would be reflected in moves from traditional patterns of board structure toward the American pattern: relatively small boards numerically dominated by outsiders. But as Stinchcombe (1965: 161) put it long ago, for an organizational form such as the public corporation to survive, it "must have an elite structure of such a form and character that those people in the society who control resources essential to the organization's success will be satisfied that their interests are represented in the goal-setting apparatus of the enterprise." Moreover, the processes used to legitimize these authority structures tend to institutionalize them in a particular form that reflects the social conditions at the time and place of their founding: they become "infused with value . . . an institution rather than a dispensable technical device" (167). The Krupp-Thyssen case illustrates some of the social and political forces at work in maintaining institutionalized governance practices. Thus, we may consider Stinchcombe's account to suggest a null hypothesis: governance structures will typically follow well-established traditions reflecting the interests of power-holders; firms listing shares in the U.S. will not come to look appreciably different than their domestic peers. To the extent that U.S.-listed foreign firms adopt American-style corporate governance, it will be among new firms, not established ones.

Yet while the case for inertia in corporate governance is suggestive, there are other plausible theoretical accounts that suggest devices militating toward homogeneity in organizational practices. Each account suggests empirical traces that we can investigate.

Anticipatory Socialization. The simplest account would be that non-U.S. corporations already have U.S.-style governance structures upon entry to the U.S. system. Such firms would adopt a package of governance reforms as a group in response to the incentives residing in financial markets. This can take two forms: either the kinds of firms that list on Nasdaq or NYSE are those that already have U.S.-style governance structures (and thus a U.S. listing is not causal), or firms that expect to list in the U.S. adopt such structures in anticipation. This is the strongest version of the convergence hypothesis, and suggests that foreign firms would be effectively indistinguishable from U.S. firms, at least structurally. Firms listing in the U.S. range from former state-owned phone companies, to venerable auto manufacturers (including DaimlerChrysler, Honda, Toyota, Volvo, Fiat, and Brilliance China Automotive Holdings), to newly-minted software and biotech firms. While the time-stamping hypothesis would lead us to expect such types of firms to retain the governance structures they had upon founding, the strong convergence thesis sees them as moving swiftly to the American standard. This is most consistent with the process described by Useem (1998) and Coffee (1999).

Networks and Corporate Governance. In between these all-or-nothing hypotheses are approaches that point to the specific cogs and wheels responsible for governance change (cf. Hedstrom and Swedberg, 1998). Neo-institutional theory highlights the role of networks in the spread of practices and in processes of homogenization (DiMaggio and Powell 1983). Thus, for instance, within-nation networks among businesses such as the keiretsu in Japan and the *grupos economicos* in Latin America reinforce local models of governance (Granovetter 1994). Perhaps the most important network for understanding corporate governance is the interlock network created by shared directors. Interlock networks within nations have been studied in the U.S., Canada, France, the UK, Germany, the Netherlands, and elsewhere (see Stokman et al. 1985 for a collection). In the U.S., the vast majority of large corporations are tied into a single network created by overlapping board memberships. This network has "small world" properties, in the sense that the shortest path between any two firms created by shared directors is quite small, averaging about 3.5 "degrees of separation" among the 1000 largest U.S. firms, and about 4.5 degrees of separation among their 7000+ directors (Davis et al. 2003). There is now a large literature documenting the role of board interlocks in the spread of governance practices such as adopting a poison pill (Davis and Greve 1997), creating an investor relations office (Rao and Sivakumar 1999), making particular types of acquisitions (Haunschild 1993), and others. In each case, directors who have experience with the practice under consideration are especially influential in board discussions of its merits. Rao et al. (2000), for instance, show that Nasdaq-listed firms are particularly likely to re-list on the New York Stock Exchange when they share directors with other Nasdaq firms that re-list, a sort of "chain migration" process familiar to Nasdaq officials. To the extent that there is a "culture of the boardroom," shared directors serve a crucial role in transmitting it across firms, and the network they create is an ideal substrate for contagion processes.

Although the internationalization of U.S. and European firms was well underway by the 1970s, their boards were still remarkably domestic in orientation—particularly those of American corporations. Fennema and Schijf (1985) studied interlocks among the 40 most central corporations in the U.S. and each of several Western European nations in 1976 and found only six ties between American and European businesses. (There was modestly more overlap among the boards of European companies.) There were, in short, few channels for the sort of cultural understanding of corporate governance we have described; each nation's network was relatively self-contained, reinforcing local practices. But the explosion of U.S. listings in the 1990s opens up the prospect for a more expanded cross-national network, and with it a mechanism for the spread of governance practices among firms across borders. To the extent that foreign firms are tied to U.S. firms, we might expect their governance practices to converge toward the American model.

Convergence over Time. Finally, governance change may be more evolutionary and occur over time through exposure. This suggests that foreign firms would continue to reflect their country of origin upon listing, but would come to look more American the longer they were listed on U.S. markets.

As indicated by figure 1, it is still quite early in the process, and we cannot expect much settlement. At best we might be able to falsify the hypothesis of strong convergence and give some sense of what to expect going forward. Thus, we ask: (1) What distinguishes U.S.-listed foreign firms that share directors with American firms? (2) What effect do size, country of origin, listing time, and U.S. ties have on discretionary choices (the size of the board, the proportion of insiders, whether the CEO holds the Chairman title, and disclosure)? and (3) What impact do U.S. ties and national origin have on investor and analyst recognition and the degree of ownership concentration?

METHODS

Sample

We gathered data on every corporation listed on the New York Stock Exchange and Nasdaq in August 2000 that had filings available through *Disclosure*, which contracts with the SEC to make filings publicly available. The population included 2040 firms on NYSE (1658 U.S. firms) and 3841 Nasdaq firms (3466 U.S.). The most relevant information for our purposes was the composition of the board of directors, which U.S. firms report annually on their 10K and proxy statement and which foreign firms report annually on form 20F. We assembled information on 47,349 directors serving on 5,627 boards, and from this derived a number of other measures (board size, proportion of "insiders," separation of the positions of CEO and board chair, and the other boards the directors served on). The minimum criterion for inclusion in our final sample was the availability of data on the board of directors. Our sub-samples included 72 firms from the United Kingdom, 24 firms from France, 12 from Germany, 59 from Israel, 23 from Chile, and 20 from Japan. *Disclosure* is the most comprehensive source of data from current SEC filings; thus, availability of board data from this source is an appropriate criterion for defining the study population of "U.S.-listed firms at risk of adopting American-style governance practices."

We selected firms from these countries for several reasons. First, excellent data on patterns of domestic corporate governance structures and board of director networks are available on the UK, France, Germany, and Japan (e.g., Charkham 1994; Wymeersch 1998; Stokman et al. 1985). This provides a baseline against which to compare the governance of U.S.-listed firms from those nations. Corporations from these nations and the U.S. are also those that are most prevalent in the global economy. Second, Chile and Israel each provide interesting but less-studied cases. Chile has undergone a series of free-market economic reforms, including a significant overhaul of its pension system (see Khanna and Palepu 2000). This has resulted in a partial unwinding of traditional business networks and the listing of nearly two dozen domestic corporations on the New York Stock Exchange. Israel now provides the third-largest number of foreign firms listed on U.S. markets (after Canada and the UK), and listing on Nasdaq (rather than the Tel Aviv Stock Exchange) has become the exit strategy of choice for high-tech firms in Israel (Rock 2001). Moreover, as our results indicate, Israeli firms are largely indistinguishable in their governance structures from U.S. firms listed on Nasdaq—an informative anomaly, as it turns out.

Data

Measuring convergence in corporate governance is problematic at the national level but somewhat more tractable at the firm level. We sought multiple indicators of two constructs: "governance practices" and "investor recognition." The size and composition of the board are relatively discretionary choices that show great variation across national systems (see Charkham 1994). By world standards, American boards are small relative to the size of the companies they represent: the board of the median NYSE-listed U.S. firm had nine directors, while Nasdaq boards had seven members on average. Convergence in board size would be represented by a relatively small board. The boards of U.S. firms also typically have a large proportion of outside (non-executive) directors. We measured the percentage of insiders as the proportion of directors that were currently officers of the corporation; convergence would be indicated by having a relatively small proportion of insiders. (Practically speaking, it was not possible to determine the proportion of "affiliated" outside directors on a large and multinational sample using public data.) We created an indicator variable for whether the CEO also held the position of Chairman of the Board. In the large majority of major U.S. firms, one person holds both positions; thus, convergence would be indicated by one person holding both slots.

Our final board measure is the number of board ties to U.S. corporations created by shared directors. We again started with the directors of all firms traded on Nasdaq and NYSE in Fall 2000, a group of over 38,000 directors occupying over 47,000 directorships. We used both computerized routines and hand-checks to verify that directors were identified unambiguously (i.e., different directors sharing the same name were identified separately, using data on their ages) and correctly (i.e., directors' names were rendered consistent across the different boards on which they served). Our primary variable of interest from this dataset is simply the number of boards of U.S. firms that each of our sample firms shared directors with. For example, Peter Magowen, a DaimlerChrysler director, also served on the boards of Safeway and Caterpillar, thus creating two "U.S. ties" for DaimlerChrysler. We also turned the board network data into a matrix to calculate a number of other network measures.

In addition to the board-based measures of conformity, we used another indicator of a discretionary choice, namely, does the firm make its 20F SEC filings available via EDGAR (the SEC's Electronic Data Gathering and Retrieval system). Under Regulation S-T, all domestic filers are required to submit all documents electronically, and most (including proxy statements and annual reports) are subsequently made available publicly via the Web. Foreign private issuers and foreign governments are not subject to this requirement, but they may choose to file electronically as well. We take electronic filing of the 20F to be an indicator of attentiveness to investors. Among our 209 sample firms, only 46 (22 percent) filed 20Fs electronically.

We also counted the number of 6K filings by each firm per year as an indication of the expansiveness of the firm's disclosure. Although all foreign private issuers are required to file 20Fs annually, they have some discretion over the other information they file with the SEC. Other items are filed with form 6K, including information "(i) required to be made public in the country of its domicile; (ii) filed with and made public by a foreign stock exchange on which its securities are traded; or (iii) distributed to security holders" (Securities and Exchange Commission). Typically these filings are press releases made by the company to announce events that are material to investors, such as mergers, changes in executives, and so on. What is "material," however, is not exhaustively defined by the SEC. For example, Arel Communications and Software (an Israeli firm) includes among its 6Ks the following press releases: "France Telecom's FCR subsidiary launches hyperfax service with Arelnet's I-Tone"; "Arel to provide interactive distance learning system for Good Samaritan Society", "Volkswagen of America selects interactive distance learning system from Arel"; "Arel raises $4 million from exercise of Series A warrants"; "Bob Jones University selects interactive distance learning system from Arel"; and so on. We take the number of 6Ks to indicate a firm's approach to disclosure, with more extensive disclosure indicating a more American approach.

Other variables included in the models are size (measured as the market value of common equity in August 2000, and alternatively as the number of employees worldwide and annual sales volume); country of origin (we include dummy variables for Chile, Germany, France, Israel, and Japan; United Kingdom was the omitted category); time listed on a U.S. stock market (in days); and the stock market on which the firm was listed (a dummy variable for NYSE). Based on Stinchcombe's (1965) arguments, we also took account of the age of the firms' primary industry by including a set of dummy variables (for computers, communications equipment, electronic components, software and information processing, and biotech). In our sample of 209 firms, 63 were in these industries, with software accounting for 37 of them.

We were also interested in the degree to which foreign issuers received recognition from investors. Investor recognition is both an outcome of shareholder-oriented governance and an additional source of scrutiny and influence with respect to governance practices. Securities analysts and institutional investors (such as public pension funds) form a sort of Greek chorus for corporate management, examining their management and governance practices and offering (often unbidden) advice (Useem 1996). Firms that attract more analysts subsequently achieve higher average valuations, and firms with more extensive disclosures attract more analysts and more institutional ownership (see Davis and Useem 2002 for a review). To the extent that non-U.S. firms list on American stock markets as part of a program oriented toward shareholder value, then larger analyst followings and more extensive interest from institutional investors are indications of success. We included two measures of investor recognition. First, the number of analysts following a firm was the count of those issuing earnings estimates reported by I/B/E/S in 2000. I/B/E/S gathers information from over 7000 securities analysts working at more than 1000 investment houses (and covering 18,000 companies) around the world. (Although purportedly global in scope, I/B/E/S analysts disproportionately represent North American financial institutions.) The more analysts following a firm, the more it is on the radar screen of significant investors (Rao et al. 2001). Second, data on institutional ownership (as a proportion of a firm's outstanding shares) came from 13F disclosures, which the SEC requires of any entity owning more than $100 million in equity capital. These are overwhelmingly American (and to a lesser extent British) financial institutions, mutual funds, and pension funds. The magnitude of a firm's 13F ownership is a direct measure of success at attracting investor interest.

Finally, we examined the size of the firm's single largest ownership block. While the original discovery of the separation of ownership and control lamented the consequences of dispersed ownership (Berle and Means 1932), more recent research has emphasized that dispersed ownership is a positive achievement for a national system of corporate governance. By hypothesis, dispersed ownership only arises when a nation's law and institutions of corporate governance are well developed for protecting the interests of minority shareholders. When legal protections for minority shareholders are weak (or not well-enforced) and monitoring devices are not well developed, businesses tend to be privately held, and those corporations that are publicly traded tend to have highly concentrated ownership, with the single largest ownership block often passing 50 percent (LaPorta et al. 1999). Around the world, ownership of the largest firms tends to be dispersed in common law countries with strong investor protections and concentrated in countries with civil law. If a U.S. listing is sufficient to bring a broad array of investor protections via American securities laws (Coffee 1999), then we should expect levels of ownership concentration to be lower among U.S.-listed firms than those not listed in the U.S. The size of the largest ownership block was calculated using 13D and 13G filings, which are required of all owners of 5 percent or more of a U.S.-listed corporation's voting securities (regardless of their nationality).

We note several limitations at this point. First, because all the measures were contemporaneous, it is impossible to draw strong causal inferences. About 60 percent of the firms we studied first listed on U.S. markets in 1995 or later, and only about 20% listed prior to 1990 (see figure 1). Thus, because the events we study are so recent, a time-series study that might partial out the temporal ordering of them was effectively impossible. Second, our ultimate outcomes (investor recognition and ownership concentration) are of course endogenous: there is a cycle between the quality of disclosure, level of analyst following, ownership by institutions, and governance reform. Better-run firms with higher-quality disclosure may attract more institutional investors, while institutional investors and analysts exert pressure for better governance and disclosure. Although we cannot verify a causal account, it is nonetheless possible in principle to falsify the strongest account of convergence and to document which factors move together.

Models

We used a variety of statistical methods, according to the question being asked. For modeling the number of board ties to U.S. firms, the size of the board, number of 6K filings, and the size of analyst following, we used negative binomial regression. This model is appropriate for count data where dispersion is likely to be too large to be consistent with the assumptions of the Poisson model. For modeling whether the firm split the positions of CEO and board chair, and whether the firm's filings were available via EDGAR, we used logistic regression. For examining the size of the largest known ownership block, we used Tobit. This model is appropriate when the outcome variable is censored (i.e., the value is unobserved above or below a certain level); in this case, owners are only required to report their stake if it exceeds 5 percent, and we thus used 5 percent as a cut-off level.

Finally, for institutional ownership, we used ordinary least squares regression. (Although, strictly speaking, percentages are bounded and thus violate the assumptions of OLS, we believe this violation is harmless in this case.)

RESULTS

Table 1 shows a correlation matrix for the primary variables studied. Several things are notable. Larger firms (as measured by sales or market capitalization) tend to have larger boards and are more likely to be listed on the NYSE, as one would expect. There are substantial correlations among national origin and the various measures of governance. And we find significant intercorrelations among board ties to U.S. firms, market capitalization, size of analyst following, volume of disclosures (as indicated by the number of 6Ks), and accessibility of disclosures (filing via EDGAR). In contrast to market capitalization, size measured by sales has a small or negative correlation with disclosures, analyst following, and U.S. board ties.

Table 2 compares U.S. firms listed on NYSE and Nasdaq with their counterparts in the UK, France, Germany, Japan, Israel, and Chile. The averages are quite consistent with the reported averages for domestic companies in each of these places. Tricker (1998), for instance, reports that among UK corporations, the average board size is 12, of whom 50 percent are insiders; in 90 percent of firms, the CEO and the Chair are different persons. Wymeersch (1998: 1107, 1113) reports an average board size of 10 and 84 percent with a split CEO/Chair. We find an average board size of 10, 50 percent insiders, and 92 percent with a CEO/Chair split. U.S. firms listed on NYSE average 9 persons on the board, 22 percent insiders, and only 35 percent with a split CEO/Chair. In short, the average U.S.-listed British firm is much more similar to its domestic counterparts than to American firms.

French boards average 13 members, of whom 18 percent are insiders, and the Chair is almost universally the CEO (Tricker, 1998; Wymeersch, 1998). We find an average size of 10, 20 percent insiders, and in 76 percent a unified CEO/Chair. As shown in figure 3, we also find dense interlocks among large French corporations listed on U.S. stock markets. Indeed, French firms on NYSE—which tend to be relatively large and well established—interlock almost exclusively with other French firms or U.S.-based French subsidiaries. In contrast, high tech French firms, usually listed in Nasdaq, are well connected to other high tech firms—often through venture capitalists on their boards.

German boards are somewhat more difficult to classify by the standards applied to U.S. corporate governance, as their size and composition have traditionally been regulated rather than left to the discretion of the board itself. The average board size of U.S.-listed German firms (12) is comparable to domestic firms (13). By our calculations, 17 percent of the average supervisory board members are current executives of the firm, and on 92 percent of boards separate persons hold the titles of CEO and Chair (see Hopt 1998; Prigge 1998 for comparable figures). Several German firms share directors with U.S. firms, as well as with firms from France, Japan, Norway, Israel, and Canada. As figure 4 shows, DaimlerChrysler accounts for about half the German firms' ties to U.S. boards, largely from former Chrysler directors who were retained on the board after Daimler acquired Chrysler in 1998.

Several Japanese firms have been listed on NYSE since the 1970s, and the figures in table 2 indicate that there has been little movement on average toward U.S. governance norms. The average U.S.-listed firm from Japan has 18 directors on the board (compared to 19 for all listed firms in Japan), of which 70 percent are insiders (vs. 77 percent in Japan), and 90 percent of boards are led by a Chairman other than the CEO—usually the prior CEO (see Kanda 1998 for descriptive data on Japanese boards). U.S.-listed Japanese firms rarely share directors with other U.S.-listed firms, from Japan or elsewhere, except in the case of subsidiaries—see figure 5.

Chilean corporations present an interesting case. The median Chilean firm has no interlocks with any other U.S.-listed firms, and none of the nearly two dozen Chilean firms listed on the New York Stock Exchange shares directors with a U.S. firm (see figure 6). Given the historical significance of elite networks for the Chilean economy, it is surprising that U.S.-listed firms are as disconnected as they are (Khanna and Palepu 2000). Chilean firms also attract very little interest from analysts or institutional investors.

Contrast this with Israeli firms. Nearly half the Israeli firms listed in the U.S. share directors with at least one U.S. firm, they have substantial analyst followings, and they attract significant interest from institutional investors. Most are listed on Nasdaq, most are in high-tech industries—particularly software—and a large number are funded by Silicon Valley venture capitalists, who typically serve on their boards (see Rock 2001). Many Israeli firm bypass the relatively anemic Tel Aviv Stock Exchange in favor of a primary listing on Nasdaq. Indeed, listing in the U.S. is the predominant exit strategy of venture capitalists funding Israeli firms; put another way, Nasdaq is largely accountable for the proliferation of new business starts in high-tech industries in Israel. By most measures, these firms are effectively indistinguishable in the governance practices from American firms listed on Nasdaq. (The number of firms and density of ties makes graphs of the Israeli interlock network rather uninformative.)

In the aggregate, compared to U.S. firms, foreign firms listed on U.S. markets have significantly larger boards (mean of 10 vs. 8.3); more insiders

TABLE 1
Correlation Matrix Among Variables

		1	2	3	4	5	6	7	8	9
1	U.S. ties									
2	Board size	0.16								
3	Insider %	0.01	0.09							
4	CEO = chair	0.05	−0.13	−0.16						
5	EDGAR filer	0.22	0.00	0.13	0.02					
6	6Ks filed	0.34	0.15	0.13	−0.09	−0.02				
7	Analysts	0.58	0.16	−0.07	0.15	0.10	0.29			
8	Institutional ownership	0.01	−0.21	0.06	0.09	0.16	−0.13	0.14		
9	Market capitalization	0.48	0.51	0.03	−0.01	0.02	0.42	0.50	−0.09	
10	Sales	−0.08	0.55	0.20	−0.14	0.07	−0.01	−0.08	0.03	0.38
11	NYSE listed	0.08	0.32	−0.03	−0.13	−0.14	0.23	0.12	−0.32	0.32
12	Chile	−0.16	−0.13	−0.18	−0.16	−0.15	−0.09	−0.05	−0.16	−0.15
13	France	−0.05	0.04	−0.25	0.47	−0.02	−0.03	0.06	0.09	0.05
14	Germany	0.04	0.14	−0.16	0.00	0.08	−0.09	0.04	−0.06	0.08
15	Israel	−0.09	−0.31	−0.25	0.11	−0.02	−0.16	−0.03	0.27	−0.27
16	Japan	0.10	0.55	0.41	−0.14	0.11	−0.07	−0.16	0.07	0.22
17	Time listed	0.26	0.43	0.17	−0.14	−0.07	0.11	0.22	−0.08	0.31
18	Computers	−0.06	−0.07	0.05	−0.12	0.10	−0.06	−0.01	0.23	−0.02
19	Communications equipment	−0.06	0.03	0.00	0.15	−0.02	0.00	0.14	0.10	−0.02
20	Electronic components	−0.04	−0.02	−0.05	0.09	0.01	−0.06	0.05	0.01	−0.01
21	Software and info processing	−0.03	−0.29	0.02	0.16	0.18	−0.11	−0.09	0.04	−0.18
22	Biotech	0.05	−0.02	0.09	−0.04	−0.04	0.01	−0.06	−0.04	−0.03

10	11	12	13	14	15	16	17	18	19	20	21
0.15											
0.00	0.35										
−0.09	0.06	−0.13									
−0.05	0.16	−0.08	−0.08								
−0.17	−0.57	−0.24	−0.24	−0.14							
0.68	0.03	−0.12	−0.12	−0.07	−0.21						
0.21	0.13	−0.10	−0.11	−0.15	−0.14	0.30					
0.15	−0.15	−0.07	−0.07	−0.05	0.19	0.14	−0.01				
0.02	−0.16	−0.09	−0.01	−0.05	0.27	0.01	0.00	−0.05			
−0.04	−0.01	−0.06	−0.06	0.33	−0.02	−0.05	−0.11	−0.03	−0.04		
−0.13	−0.51	−0.18	−0.04	−0.04	0.32	−0.11	−0.18	−0.10	−0.12	−0.08	
−0.02	−0.08	−0.03	−0.03	−0.02	−0.05	−0.02	0.01	−0.02	−0.02	−0.01	−0.04

TABLE 2

Comparative Statistics on Corporations Listed on Nasdaq and the New York Exchange, Fall 2000

	NYSE U.S.	Nasdaq U.S.	UK	France	Germany	Japan	Israel	Chile
Number of firms covered	1695	3533	72	24	12	20	59	23
Market value	1018	139	5194	2565	5175	26800	184	421
Employees	5200	384	5178	3800	20450	35472	367	2626
% on NYSE			61	60	83	57	8	100
% owned by largest shareholder	13	15	15	28	20	19	27	47
# of analysts	5	2	2	4	1	1	2	2
% owned by 13F filers	55	23	1	5	4	1	10	0.3
Board size	9	7	10	10	12	18	7	9
% insiders	22	33	50	20	17	70	29	25
% of firms with split CEO/Chair	35	49	92	24	92	90	67	96
Number of interlocks	6	2	2.5	3	2	1	2	0
Board ties to U.S. firms	6	2	1	0	1	0	0	0
Mean # of outside execs	0.13	0.14	0.18	0.08	0.33	0.19	0.1	0.13

Note: All figures are medians unless otherwise noted. Reported figures represent the largest sub-sample for which relevant data were available; thus, for example, if a firm had no 13D or 13G filings associated with it, it is not included in the calculation of "% owned by largest shareholder."

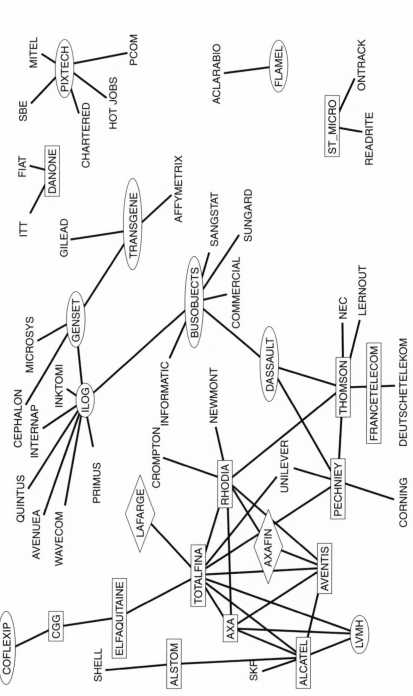

Figure 3 Shared directors among French firms listed on U.S. stock markets (Rectangles are French firms listed on NYSE; ovals are French NASDAQ firms; diamonds are U.S. subsidiaries of French parents; other firms are non-French).

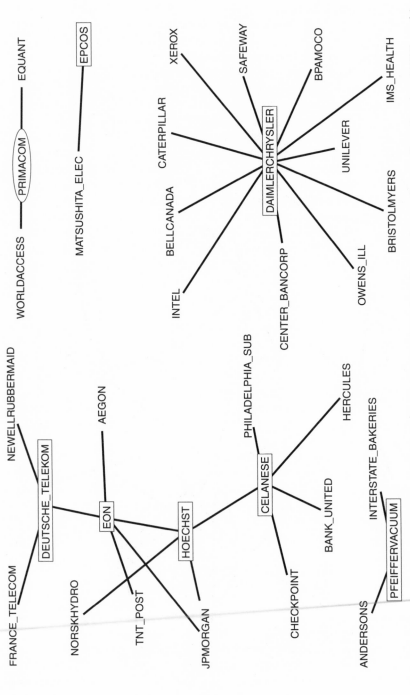

Figure 4 Shared directors among German firms listed on U.S. stock markets (Rectangles are German firms listed on NYSE; oval is German NASDAQ firm; other firms are non-German).

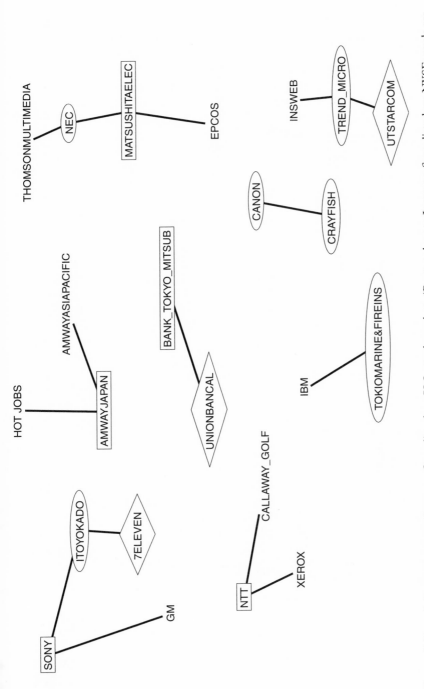

Figure 5 Shared directors among Japanese firms listed on U.S. stock markets (Rectangles are Japanese firms listed on NYSE; ovals are Japanese NASDAQ firms; diamonds are U.S. subsidiaries of Japanese parents; other firms are non-Japanese).

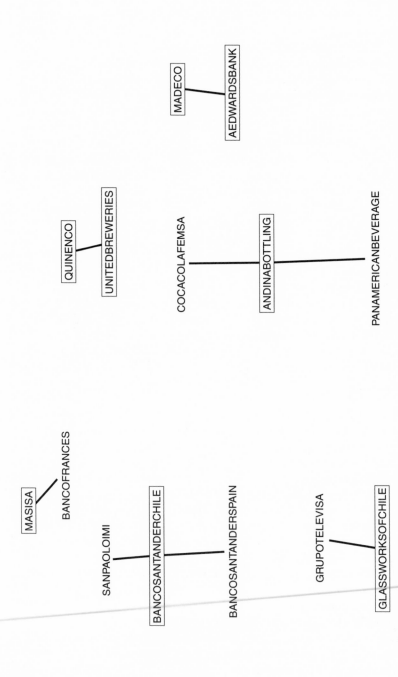

Figure 6 Shared directors among Chilean firms listed on U.S. stock markets (Rectangles are Chilean firms listed on NYSE; other firms are non-Chilean).

(34 percent vs. 31 percent), fewer analysts (3.3 vs. 4.8), lower institutional ownership (14 percent vs. 38 percent), and more concentrated ownership (23 percent vs. 19 percent, when the largest block is reported). (All these results hold when controlling for the market value of the firm's equity and the market on which it is listed). These results hold fairly broadly, with the notable exception of Israeli firms. Based on these findings, we can tentatively rule out the strongest convergence hypothesis—that firms listing on U.S. markets are indistinguishable from U.S. firms.

We next consider distinctions among firms listed on U.S. markets according to their level of network embeddedness. There is little doubt that there has been a substantial increase in cross-national interlock ties among boards of directors, albeit relative to a very small base among U.S. firms. Among the boards of the 40 most central (well-connected) American firms in the mid-1970s, Fennema and Schijf (1985) found only *six* international interlocks. In our data, we find 49 ties between the 40 most central U.S. firms and non-U.S. firms listed on U.S. markets; presumably there are even more ties to non-U.S. listed foreign firms. By far the largest number of ties are to British firms. BP Amoco, for instance, shared directors with 21 U.S. firms; most of these were legacies of the Amoco board retained after its acquisition by BP. Smithkline Beecham shared directors with 19 U.S. firms. These were exceptions, however: 58 percent of the non-U.S. firms in our sample had no board ties to U.S. firms, and 18 percent had only one. Yet foreign firms outside the Anglo-American system have incentives to appoint U.S. or UK directors. Randey and Oxelheim (2001) find that Norwegian and Swedish firms achieve higher valuations (as measured by Tobin's q) when they have British or American directors, above and beyond the effect achievable by listing on a foreign exchange. Whether American directors function simply as signals, or as conduits for governance norms and practices, it appears that they are perceived favorably by the stock market.

Table 3 examines the factors influencing the degree to which sampled firms shared directors with U.S. companies. The results show that, not surprisingly, large firms are more likely to share directors than small firms. Relative to firms from the United Kingdom (the omitted category in the models), firms from Japan and Chile were significantly less likely to have U.S. directors, while French and German corporations were no less likely to have U.S. directors. These differences are likely to reflect both the relative ease of travel between Europe and the U.S. (at least for directors of firms headquartered on the East Coast) and language ability (Conference Board 1999). Yet there are also substantial cross-national differences in the board network patterns that are not as easily explained by geography.

There is clearly a great deal of cross-national variation among U.S.-listed firms, both in their governance structures and in their degree of network

380 • Davis and Marquis

TABLE 3
Correlates of Board Ties to U.S. Companies (Negative Binomial Regression)

	Coef.	Z
Market value (millions)	0.0130	3.26
Listed on NYSE	−0.2752	−0.83
Chile	−3.1296	−2.96
Germany	0.0147	0.03
France	−0.3541	−0.94
Israel	−0.3438	−0.97
Japan	−1.5740	−3.01
Time listed in U.S.	0.0001	1.35
Computers	−0.7882	−1.00
Communications equipment	−0.4636	−0.76
Electronic components	−0.2391	−0.35
Software/info processing	−0.0132	−0.04
Biotech	0.7175	0.74
Constant	0.2326	0.74
$n = 193, \chi^2 = 55.6$		

embeddedness. To what extent are these things related, and what is their impact on investor recognition? Table 4 reports analyses of the factors influencing governance choices. The first model analyzes the factors influencing board size among firms listed on Nasdaq and NYSE. Most firms had larger boards than U.S. firms listed on the same markets, and this is reflected in the results: larger firms and firms that had been listed on the U.S. market for longer tended to have larger boards on average, and French, German, and particularly Japanese firms had significantly larger boards than UK firms, even after controlling for firm size (sales, employment, and market capitalization). Chilean, German, French, and Israeli firms had proportionally fewer insiders on the boards than UK firms, while Japanese firms had significantly more (70 percent on average). French and Israeli firms were more likely than UK firms to have a CEO who was also Chairman of the Board. None of these three outcomes was affected by board ties to U.S. companies. In contrast, the firm's likelihood of filing documents with EDGAR, thus making them more readily accessible to investors, was significantly higher to the extent that its board shared directors with U.S. firms, and significantly lower the longer it had been listed in the U.S.. Interestingly, Japanese firms were more prone than other firms

TABLE 4
Influences on Governance Structure and Disclosure

	Board Size		% Insiders		CEO is Chair		EDGAR Filer		6Ks Last Year	
	Coef.	t	Coef.	t	Coef.	z	Coef.	z	Coef.	z
Market value (millions)	0.0035	3.87	-0.0943	-1.66	0.0013	0.16	-0.0177	-1.78	0.0051	2.57
Listed on NYSE	0.2154	2.89	-2.8258	-0.72	0.3761	0.59	-0.2969	-0.55	0.4080	2.70
Chile	-0.1273	-1.24	-20.2893	-3.99	-0.3557	-0.30	-1.3183	-1.18	-0.6529	-3.50
Germany	0.4394	3.92	-24.1270	-3.78	1.2465	1.41	0.3255	0.40	-1.0409	-3.75
France	0.2288	2.66	-27.0799	-5.94	3.7644	5.23	-0.2515	-0.38	-0.3536	-1.98
Israel	0.0713	0.83	-26.7553	-6.37	1.4395	2.19	-1.0984	-1.88	-0.2571	-1.60
Japan	0.6600	7.00	23.4440	4.05	0.0765	0.06	1.7934	2.23	-0.6455	-3.08
Time listed in U.S.	0.0000	3.86	-0.0003	-0.43	-0.0001	-0.67	-0.0002	-2.33	0.0000	-0.71
Board ties to U.S. companies	0.0016	0.16	0.1789	0.30	0.1149	1.38	0.3666	3.64	0.0445	1.87
Computers	-0.2932	-1.86	7.3547	0.94			1.6173	1.68	-0.0929	-0.32
Communications equipment	0.0328	0.26	11.7506	1.75	1.4094	1.67	0.8552	0.90	0.3476	1.45
Electronic components	-0.1471	-0.90	0.9116	0.11	0.3929	0.36	0.6830	0.70	-0.3545	-0.92
Software/info processing	-0.1929	-2.11	6.7101	1.54	1.2270	1.96	1.0703	1.85	0.0825	0.49
Biotech	0.0863	0.32	0.0314	0.00					0.1254	0.19
Constant	1.9650	24.78	51.9348	13.06	-2.8747	-3.90	-0.9525	-1.82	2.1873	13.22
	n=193, Chi²=160		n=193, Chi²=95.7		n=184, Chi²=59.5		n=191, Chi²=38.3		n=170, Chi²=78.6	

to filing electronically. Finally, the sheer volume of disclosures increased with firm size and a NYSE listing. Firms from the UK (the omitted category) filed substantially more disclosures than firms from the other nations, and ties to U.S. firms had a borderline significant positive relation with the volume of disclosures. Overall, these results are consistent with the argument that cross-national variation in governance persists even among U.S.-listed firms.

We also considered three aspects of investor recognition, reported in table 5. Analyst following is positively associated with a firm's size, as one would expect. Controlling for size, Israeli firms have significantly larger analyst following than UK firms, while Japanese firms have substantially smaller analyst followings. We also find that analyst following increases with the number of board ties to U.S. firms. Firms get roughly one more analyst for every two U.S. firms with which they share directors. We also find that analyst following is the only outcome for which our set of industry indicators had a significant collective effect—in other words, technology firms attracted greater analyst attention than firms in other industries from these six countries, as indicated by a likelihood ratio test. Institutional ownership is higher among French, Israeli, and Japanese firms than comparably-sized UK firms. Finally, we find that the size of the largest ownership block is larger among firms from Chile, France, and Israel relative to firms from the UK, and that the size of this block declines with the amount of time the firm has been listed in the U.S.. We note that this result should be treated with considerable caution. The Tobit model we report assumes that values below 5 percent (the reporting threshold under section 13d) are censored, or—put another way—if we do not have data on the largest ownership block, then its true value is below 5 percent. But while in principle foreign owners of foreign issuers may be required to disclose their ownership stakes to the SEC (see Coffee 1999), in practice we suspect that compliance outside the U.S. is low. Of these firms 32 percent had no data available on large blockholders, and 45 percent of those entities reporting a large holding were American firms or individuals, which is rather implausible. Put another way, it appears unlikely that one can use U.S. securities disclosures to ferret out the true ownership structures of foreign issuers.

Discussion

Our findings show substantial variation across nations in the propensity to appoint U.S.-based directors, in patterns of corporate governance and disclosure, and in the level of investor recognition, even among U.S.-listed foreign firms. The interlock networks among firms from Chile, France,

TABLE 5
Influences on Investor Recognition

	Analyst Following		Institutional %		Largest Owner %	
	Coef.	z	Coef.	t	Coef.	t
Market value (millions)	0.0086	2.81	−0.0384	−0.72	−0.2404	−1.70
Listed on NYSE	0.2206	1.01	−8.9474	−2.33	13.0790	1.70
Chile	0.2980	1.12	−0.6884	−0.14	10.3976	1.11
Germany	0.1259	0.39	2.3024	0.37	12.1291	1.08
France	0.4368	1.88	8.4485	1.96	13.0224	1.48
Israel	0.1980	0.84	7.3303	1.83	34.3074	4.39
Japan	−1.0868	−3.13	9.4064	1.76	21.4069	1.82
Time listed in U.S.	0.0000	1.36	−0.0007	−1.29	−0.0030	−2.07
Board ties to U.S. companies	0.0857	2.95	0.8414	1.51	−0.7903	−0.48
Computers	0.5903	1.44	11.7725	1.64	−18.4736	−1.21
Communications equipment	0.9078	2.75	−0.0807	−0.01	−7.7560	−0.66
Electronic components	0.5350	1.33	−3.9108	−0.52	19.1267	1.47
Software/info processing	0.1040	0.43	−6.9773	−1.69	7.4063	0.95
Biotech	−19.0807	0.00	−4.2250	−0.33		
Constant	0.3946	1.77	12.4934	3.14	−15.9941	−1.83
	n=193, χ^2=74.1		n=185, R^2=.18		n=193, χ^2=46.1	

Germany, Israel, Japan, and the UK varied widely. Most Chilean and Japanese firms were isolates; older French firms were densely connected among themselves but not to firms from other nations, while new economy French firms had varied ties; and Israeli firms were well-connected among themselves and to high-tech U.S. firms, typically through venture capitalists on their boards. German and British firms often inherited American directors in the wake of their acquisitions. Overall, the patterns of governance among U.S.-listed firms mirrored the patterns of their domestic counterparts.

We were particularly interested in whether sharing directors with U.S. corporations acted to spread norms of corporate governance among non-U.S.

firms. As it happens, most foreign corporations do not avail themselves of this channel. Firms with a large market capitalization were more likely to share directors with U.S. firms, but national origin had a larger impact on U.S. interlocks. *No* Chilean firms shared directors with a U.S. firm and very few Japanese firms did so, while most British firms interlocked with at least one American firm, and U.S. ties were quite common among Israeli firms. These ties were also associated with patterns of disclosure and with the size of analyst following. Because our data are contemporaneous, we cannot demonstrate that the U.S. ties led the disclosure practices and analyst interest; it is also possible that disclosure and board composition are jointly decided upon, and that the size of analyst following is a result. But prior research finds that interlock ties play an important role in reinforcing normative standards among directors (e.g., Davis and Greve 1997), and U.S. ties in particular are valued by the stock market (Randey and Oxelheim 2001). Time will tell if these ties have an ongoing impact on firm governance.

We find no support for the notion that firms move in the direction of U.S. practice simply as a result of their time listed on a U.S. market—the long-tenured firms had large boards and had less accessible disclosures, which are the opposite of what we would have expected. (The negative relation between time listed and size of the largest ownership block is most likely due to failures of disclosure, not a positive impact of U.S. listing on governance.) Indeed, it is the most recently listed firms—particularly those from Israel—that appeared closest to the U.S. standard.

We considered several possible trajectories for U.S.-listed firms with respect to their governance practices. We can reject two of them: foreign firms do not adopt U.S. governance practices prior to listing in the U.S., nor do they gravitate in that direction with time. There is a modest association between appointing U.S. directors and making more (and more accessible) disclosures, and these firms attract more analysts. But most foreign firms do not appoint U.S. directors, adopt U.S. governance practices, or receive much investor recognition. Indeed, institutional investors owned just 0.3 percent of the median Chilean firm, compared to 49 percent for all NYSE-listed firms. It appears that core aspects of governance, such as the size and structure of the board of directors, are not malleable and maintain their distinctive national structure even after a U.S. listing, whereas a firm's investor interface—how it portrays itself to the investor world, and how many analysts it attracts—are influenced by ties to U.S. companies. U.S.-listed firms may wear American fashions, but they continue to speak in their native tongue.

The major exception to these generalizations is Israeli firms. As we remarked previously, these firms are often funded by American venture capitalists who then serve on their boards, and their exit strategy is to go public in the U.S., typically bypassing their domestic stock exchange. Many Israeli firms have headquarters or representative offices in the U.S., and some are incorporated in an American state (see Rock 2001 for details). These new economy firms are largely indistinguishable in their corporate governance practices from U.S. firms in the same industries (mostly software and electronics); indeed, they were created in their image. In contrast, Chilean firms are primarily in financial services, utilities, and beverages, and the median firm was roughly eighty years old.

This suggests an interpretation of our findings that accords with Stinchcombe's "organizational archeology": because the governance structures of firms reflect the balance of power in society, they are likely to be highly institutionalized and resistant to substantial change. Firms founded in earlier eras will have governance structures that reflect the priorities of their time and place, and a U.S. listing will have minimal impact. But new firms, particularly those founded under the influence of "shareholder capitalism" (such as start-ups in Israel), will be structured to reflect the expectations about good governance embedded in financial markets. Put another way, the engine of convergence in corporate governance is likely to be the creation of new firms, not the transformation of old ones (much less societal-level transformation).

CONCLUSION

We have argued that the contemporary debate about convergence in corporate governance is most usefully framed at the level of the firm and its decision-makers. Over the past decade, public corporations around the world have faced a range of choices of institutional jurisdiction; in particular, for many firms the place of incorporation and the market on which securities are traded are no longer dictated by geography. Changes on the demand side for corporate and securities laws most likely will not lead to convergence in legal regimes, but there is a plausible case to be made for firm-level convergence in governance structures. By hypothesis, public corporations gravitate toward the institutions that are perceived to be best for investors, creating a "race to the top" among institutional regimes in a process that ultimately favors U.S. securities markets (Easterbrook and Fischel 1991; Romano 1993; Coffee 1999). Also by hypothesis, public firms will voluntarily adopt the structures that best reflect the interests of investors.

We have explored the argument that foreign firms listing on U.S. stock markets may come to adopt the American shareholder capitalist approach to their discretionary corporate governance practices. Such firms are subject to U.S. securities regulations, and are required to file financial statements and other disclosures consistent with relatively stringent requirements (GAAP or similar). On average, they are rewarded with higher stock market valuations, and thus U.S. markets could be part of a race to the top in corporate governance practices, as global corporations converge in their practices in order to gain the benefits of a U.S. listing. But while there are a handful of highly visible examples of this—and the story appears broadly applicable to Israeli firms listed in the U.S.—we found little evidence for it as a general account. On average, the foreign firms we studied organize their boards in the same ways as their domestic counterparts. Few make their financial statements available electronically to (potential) investors. They typically attract few equity analysts and receive very little interest from institutional investors (a median of under 2 percent). And the lack of transparency of their ownership structures suggests that the SEC's enforcement does not extend beyond U.S. borders. In short, while "the United States boasts a . . . vast industry of securities houses and securities analysts [and] the American market operates as a powerful monitoring and pricing system" (Licht 1998:582), foreign issuers are not especially well integrated into this system as of yet. At this time, the choice to list on a U.S. securities market may be intended as a signal of shareholder-friendly governance, but it is evidently not followed by other substantial structural changes.

There are, of course, exceptions. Firms that recruit American directors also have more accessible disclosure and attract more analysts. Even one tie to an American firm is sufficient to place a firm within "six degrees of separation" from JP Morgan Chase—the best-connected board in corporate America (Davis et al. 2003). And some foreign firms—particularly those that retained directors after acquiring a major U.S. corporation—are well acquainted with the American corporate governance genre. Moreover, the required disclosures that accompany a U.S. listing are not trivial and may in themselves induce changes in some aspects of corporate governance over time (cf. Fox 1998). But our findings suggest that issuer choice will not extend to core questions about the governance structure of the firm. New firms founded with the explicit intention of listing on U.S. markets will easily adapt to the standards of American investors, but old and large firms are unlikely to do so because their governance is more "institutionalized" (in Stinchcombe's 1965 sense). Based on the evidence currently available, the vision of the dominant multinationals around the world converging on American practice appears remote.

We see two theoretical implications of our findings for the economic sociology of capitalism. First, recent discussions of law, culture, and financial markets have taken a turn toward highly stylized depictions of relatively frictionless institutional change. With the right nudge from the IMF or other international advisors, nations might install American-style shareholder capitalism, with a realignment of other national institutions to follow. Yet if foreign firms that voluntarily list on the New York Stock Exchange continue to be imprinted by their home institutions, we have little reason to expect that those institutions themselves will easily shift directions. As James Scott pointed out in *Seeing like a State* (1998), there is often a substantial gulf between the simple institutional blueprints of policymakers and how institutional change happens on the ground. Second, our approach has been to take the corporation as the relevant unit of analysis and to consider alternative mechanisms by which institutional change—in this case, convergence in corporate governance—is accomplished. Firms might converge in their practices via contagion through social networks linking their decisionmakers, or through voluntary adoption of the practices of exemplars, or through differential failure rates of firms with and without those practices, or through simple drift over time. In our case, we found that it was new entrants most prone toward convergence on the American model, while incumbents generally maintained their traditional governance practices over time. But it was organizational processes that were the cogs and wheels underlying (dis)continuity in institutional structures. This is the distinctive contribution that organization theory can make to the economic sociology of capitalist institutions.

NOTE

1. By "listed" we include firms that trade only on a U.S. market and those that trade on both a local market and a U.S. market, typically by sponsoring American Depository Receipts (ADRs).

REFERENCES

Berle, Adolph, Jr. and Gardiner C. Means. 1932. *The Modern Corporation and Private Property.* New York: Macmillan.
Blair, Margaret M. 1995. *Ownership and Control: Re-Thinking Corporate Governance for the Twenty-First Century.* Washington, D.C.: Brookings Institution Press.
Bradley, Michael, Cindy Schipani, Anant K. Sundaram, and James P. Walsh. 1999. "The Purposes and Accountability of the Corporation in Contemporary Society: Corporate Governance at a Crossroads." *Law and Contemporary Problems* 62(3): 9–85.
Charkham, Jonathan. 1994. *Keeping Good Company: A Study of Corporate Governance in Five Countries.* Oxford: Oxford University Press.

Coffee, John C., Jr. 1999. "The Future as History: The Prospects for Global Convergence in Corporate Governance and Its Implications." *Northwestern University Law Review* 93: 641–720.

Conference Board. 1999. *Globalizing the Board of Directors: Trends and Strategies.* New York: Conference Board.

Coopers & Lybrand. 2000. *The Coopers & Lybrand SEC Manual.* 7th ed. New York: Wiley.

Davis, Gerald F. and Henrich R. Greve. 1997. "Corporate Elite Networks and Governance Changes in the 1980s." *American Journal of Sociology* 103: 1–37.

Davis, Gerald F. and Michael Useem. 2002. "Top Management, Company Directors, and Corporate Control." In *Handbook of Strategy and Management,* ed. Andrew Pettigrew, Howard Thomas, and Richard Whittington. London: Sage.

Davis, Gerald F., Mina Yoo, and Wayne Baker. 2003. "The Small World of the American Corporate Elite, 1982–2001." *Strategic Organization* 1: 301–26.

Deutsche Presse-Agentur. 1997. "Krupp-Hoesch Takeover of Thyssen Already Mapped Out." March 22.

DiMaggio, Paul and Walter W. Powell. 1983. "The Iron Cage Revisited: Institutional Isomorphism and Collective Rationality in Organizational Fields." *American Sociological Review* 48: 147–60.

Easterbrook, Frank H. and Daniel R. Fischel. 1991. *The Economic Structure of Corporate Law.* Cambridge, Mass.: Harvard University Press.

Economist. 2001. "A Long Arm for Securities Law: Foreign Listings in America." May 19, 65.

Fennema, Meindert and Huibert Schijf. 1985. "The Transnational Network." In *Networks of Corporate Power: A Comparative Analysis of Ten Countries,* ed. Frans N. Stokman, Rolf Ziegler, and John Scott. Oxford: Polity Press.

Fox, Merritt B. 1998. "Required Disclosure and Corporate Governance." In *Comparative Corporate Governance: The State of the Art and Emerging Research,* ed. Klaus J. Hopf, Hideki Kanda, Mark J. Roe, Eddy Wymeersch, and Stefan Prigge. Oxford: Oxford University Press.

Friedman, Thomas L. 1999. *The Lexus and the Olive Tree: Understanding Globalization.* New York: Farrar, Straus, Giroux.

Geiger, Uri. 1998. "Harmonization of Securities Disclosure Rules in the Global Market: A Proposal." *Fordham Law Review* 66: 1785–1836.

Gilson, Ronald J. 2000. "Globalizing Corporate Governance: Convergence of Form or Function." Columbia Law School.

Granovetter, Mark S. 1994. "Business Groups." In *The Handbook of Economic Sociology,* ed. Neil J. Smelser and Richard Swedberg. Princeton: Princeton University Press.

Guillen, Mauro F. 2001. "Corporate Governance and Globalization: Is There Convergence across Countries?" *Advances in International Comparative Management* 13: 175–204.

Haunschild, Pamela. 1993. "Interorganizational Imitation: The Impact of Interlocks on Corporate Acquisition Activity." *Administrative Law Quarterly* 38: 546–92.

Hedstrom, Peter and Richard Swedberg, eds. 1998. *Social Mechanisms: An Analytical Approach to Social Theory.* Cambridge: Cambridge University Press.

Hopt, Klaus J. 1998. "The German Two-Tier Board: Experience, Theories, Reforms." In *Comparative Corporate Governance: The State of the Art and Emerging Research*, ed. Klaus J. Hopt, Hideki Kanda, Mark J. Roe, Eddy Wymeersch, and Stefan Prigge. Oxford: Oxford University Press.

Kadushin, Charles. 1995. "Friendship among the French Financial Elite." *American Sociological Review* 60: 202–21.

Kanda, Hideki. 1998. "Comparative Corporate Governance—Country Report: Japan." In *Comparative Corporate Governance: The State of the Art and Emerging Research*, ed. Klaus J. Hopt, Hideki Kanda, Mark J. Roe, Eddy Wymeersch, and Stefan Prigge. Oxford: Oxford University Press.

Khanna, Tarun and Krishna Palepu. 2000. "The Future of Business Groups in Emerging Markets: Long-Run Evidence from Chile." *Academy of Management Journal* 43: 268–85.

LaPorta, Rafael, Florencio López-de-Silanes, Andrei Shleifer, and Robert Vishny. 1999. "The Quality of Government." *Journal of Law, Economics, and Organization* 14: 222–82.

Levine, Ross and Sara Zervos. 1998. "Stock Markets, Banks, and Economic Growth." *American Economic Review* 88: 537–54.

Licht, Amir N. 1998. "Regulatory Arbitrage for Real: International Securities Regulation in a World of Interacting Securities Markets." *Virginia Journal of International Law* 38: 563–638.

———. 2001. "Stock Exchange Mobility, Unilateral Regulation, and the Privatization of Securities Regulation." *Virginia Journal of International Law* 41(3): 583–628.

Modigliani, Franco and Enrico C. Perotti. 2000. "Security Markets versus Bank Finance: Legal Enforcement and Investor Protection." *International Review of Finance* 1: 81–96.

Morck, Randall K., David A. Stangeland, and Bernard Young. 1998. "Inherited Wealth, Corporate Control, and Economic Growth: The Canadian Disease." NBER Working Paper 6814. National Bureau of Economic Research online.

Murray, Alan. 1997. "Super Model: Asia's Financial Foibles Make American Way Look like a Winner." *Wall Street Journal*, December 8, A1.

North, Douglass C. 1990. *Institutions, Institutional Change and Economic Performance*. Cambridge: Cambridge University Press.

Prigge, Stefan. 1998. "A Survey of German Corporate Governance." In *Comparative Corporate Governance: The State of the Art and Emerging Research*, ed. Klaus J. Hopt, Hideki Kanda, Mark J. Roe, Eddy Wymeersch, and Stefan Prigge. Oxford: Oxford University Press.

Rajan, Raghuram G. and Luigi Zingales. 2001. "The Great Reversals: The Politics of Financial Development in the 20th Century." CRSP Working Paper 6. University of Chicago Graduate School.

Randøy, Trond and Lars Oxelheim. 2001. "The Impact of Foreign Board Membership on Firm Value." IUI Working Paper 567, Agder University College, Norway.

Rao, Hayagreeva, Gerald F. Davis, and Andrew Ward. 2000. "Embeddedness, Social Identity, and Mobility: Why Firms Leave the NASDAQ and Join the New York Stock Exchange." *Administrative Science Quarterly* 45: 268–92.

Rao, Hayagreeva, Henrich R. Greve, and Gerald F. Davis. 2001. "Fool's Gold: So-cial Proof in the Initiation and Discontinuation of Coverage by Wall Street An-alysts." *Administrative Science Quarterly* 46: 502–26.

Rao, Hayagreeva and Kumar Sivakumar. 1999. "Institutional Sources of Boundary-Spanning Structures: The Establishment of Investor Relations Departments in the Fortune 500 Industrials." *Organization Science* 10: 27–42.

Reese, William A., Jr. and Michael Weisbach. 2000. "Protection of Minority Shareholder Interests, Cross-Listings in the United States, and Subsequent Eq-uity Offerings." Paper presented at Sixth Annual Meeting of the Latin American Research Consortium, Tulane University, March.

Rock, Edward B. 2001. "Greenhorns, Yankees, and Cosmopolitans: Venture Capi-tal, IPOs, Foreign Firms, and U.S. Markets." *Theoretical Inquiries in Law* 2: 711.

Roe, Mark J. 1994. *Strong Managers, Weak Owners: The Political Roots of Ameri-can Corporate Finance*. Princeton: Princeton University Press.

Romano, Roberta. 1993. *The Genius of American Corporate Law*. Washington, D.C.: American Enterprise Institute.

Scott, James C. 1998. *Seeing like a State: How Certain Schemes to Improve the Human Condition Have Failed*. New Haven: Yale University Press.

Scott, W. Richard. 1995. *Institutions and Organizations*. Thousand Oaks, Calif.: Sage.

Shleifer, Andrei and Robert W. Vishny. 1997. "A Survey of Corporate Gover-nance." *Journal of Finance* 52: 737–83.

Stinchcombe, Arthur I. 1965. "Social Structure and Organization." In *Handbook of Organizations*, ed. James G. March. Chicago: Rand McNally.

Stokman, Frans N., Rolf Ziegler, and John Scott, eds. 1985. *Networks of Corporate Power: A Comparative Analysis of Ten Countries*. Oxford: Polity Press.

Useem, Michael. 1996. *Investor Capitalism: How Money Managers Are Changing the Face of Corporate America*. New York: Basic Books.

———. 1998. "Corporate Leadership in a Globalizing Equity Market." *Academy of Management Executive* 12: 43–59.

Velli, Joseph. 1994. "American Depository Receipts: An Overview." *Fordham In-ternational Law Journal* 17: 38–50.

Weber, Klaus and Gerald F. Davis. 2000. "The Global Spread of Stock Exchanges, 1980–1998." William Davidson Institute Working Paper 341, University of Michigan Business School.

World Bank. 1997. *Private Capital Flows to Developing Countries: The Road to Fi-nancial Integration*. Oxford: Oxford University Press.

Wymeersch, Eddy. 1998. "A Status Report on Corporate Governance in Some Continental European States." In *Comparative Corporate Governance: The State of the Art and Emerging Research*, ed. Klaus J. Hopt, Hideki Kanda, Mark J. Roe, Eddy Wymeersch, and Stefan Prigge. Oxford: Oxford University Press.

Fiscal Sociology in an Age of Globalization: Comparing Tax Regimes in Advanced Capitalist Countries

John L. Campbell

IN ORDER TO ADVANCE the enterprise of economic sociology, the editors of this volume call for a comparative analysis of the institutions of capitalism, including its political institutions. This chapter does this by examining one form of property rights in the advanced capitalist economies. Property rights are the backbone of capitalist economies and of utmost importance to economic sociology. They consist of rules that define not only who owns the means of production, but also who uses them and who appropriates the benefits from their use (Bromley 1989: 187–206; Barzel 1989: 2). They constitute an essential part of the institutional membrane that connects the state and economy and are among the most important institutions in which capitalist economic activity is embedded. Economic sociologists and others have argued that through the control of property rights states influence both the behavior and organization of firms within national economies (Campbell and Lindberg 1990; Fligstein 1990; North 1990).

Taxation is one of the most important forms of property rights. States manipulate tax policy in ways that have far-reaching consequences for private property and the economy. Because tax policy determines the degree to which states take profits from firms and earnings from individuals, it impinges directly on rights of private property ownership and appropriation. Tax policy also affects firm and individual investment strategies and, thus, how people use their property. For example, shifts in tax policy, such as the provision of investment tax credits or individual retirement accounts, can influence capital investment, which affects the distribution of capital across firms and sectors and, in turn, production. It also affects savings, which

A much extended version of this paper appears in my Institutional Change and Globalization *(Princeton University Press, 2004). Thanks for comments on the ideas in this paper go to Michael Allen, Peter Evans, Doug Hechathorn, Joel Levine, Michael Macy, Victor Nee, Kathy Sherrieb, Richard Swedberg, and Ivan Szelenyi. Jessica Houston provided research support.*

influences consumption. As a result, cross-national and historical variation in taxation helps explain differences in national economic performance and income and capital redistribution (Martin 1991; North 1990,
1981; Steinmo 1993). In sum, taxation can facilitate or inhibit the release
of economic energy and, therefore, enable or constrain capitalist activity
because it influences the distribution, production, consumption, and productivity of capital—four processes that are central to an economic sociology of capitalism (Swedberg, this volume). It follows that variation in
taxation should be a significant explanatory variable for economic sociology (Campbell 1993).

But capitalism is changing in ways that may reduce the international
variation among tax regimes. By *tax regime* I mean a combination of taxes
and tax rates that policy makers adjust in order to achieve their policy
goals. Scholars have argued that the increased globalization of economic
activity during the late twentieth and early twenty-first century is resulting
in the homogenization of national political systems, including tax regimes,
throughout the advanced capitalist world (e.g., Cerny 1997; Guéhenno
1995; Strange 1997). Why?

According to globalization theory, improvements in transportation and
telecommunication technologies have vastly improved firms' knowledge of
profitable international economic opportunities and have increased the
speed with which these opportunities can be pursued and achieved. This is
especially true for financial transactions, which now can be conducted almost instantaneously between parties around the globe. All of this has been
exacerbated by increased trade liberalization and decontrol of capital flows
both unilaterally and through international agreements. In short, economic
activity has become far more integrated on a worldwide basis than it was
thirty years ago and capital moves much more freely across borders. In turn,
because capital has become so mobile internationally the threat of capital
flight has become pervasive and, as a result, states must now compete more
than ever to attract and retain capital investment within their borders.

Of course, globalization theorists recognize that capital investment decisions are based on a variety of considerations and that there are several
ways states can seek to attract or retain capital, including further lowering
tariffs, easing the regulatory burden on business, and so on. But they are
clear that one of the most important competitive strategies available to
states is to reduce the tax burden on individuals and corporations (McKenzie and Lee 1991). As such, "many economists argue that the competition
for a mobile tax base will lead to a fiscally ruinous 'race to the bottom,'
where the competing states interactively cut their taxes on capital and
other mobile factors to ever lower levels" (Dehejia and Genschel 1999:
403–4). Over the long term this will lead to an eventual convergence on
low tax rates and a depletion in the ability of national governments to

control the making of tax policy (Hallerberg 1996: 324; see also Crafts 2000: 42–43; Kurzer 1993; Steinmo 1993: 29; Tanzi 1995: xxi). The OECD is so concerned about this that it warned recently that tax competition will undermine the ability of national governments to maintain their tax bases and, therefore, urged international cooperation to eliminate such harmful tax practices (OECD 2000b). In some cases, this was tried but failed. Notably, despite several attempts, members of the European Union have been unable to harmonize their tax systems (Dehejia and Genschel 1999; Hallerberg 1996).[1]

The implication of this argument for economic sociology is disturbing. If globalization theory is right, then an important explanatory variable for economic sociology is becoming irrelevant in the age of global capitalism. After all, if tax regimes (and other forms of property rights) converge cross-nationally as predicted, then differences among these regimes disappear and we lose what has proven to be a powerful analytic approach for explaining variation in national economic organization and performance.

Contrary to globalization theory, this chapter argues that there is little cause for alarm insofar as taxation is concerned. Tax regimes in the advanced capitalist countries are not converging and there is little evidence of a race to the bottom. Instead, I will suggest that nationally specific politics and political institutions limit the degree to which states reduce tax levels and the degree to which national tax regimes converge. This is ironic. Globalization theory maintains that increased capital mobility undermines the national political institutions through which states regulate economic activity within their borders (Giddens 2000; Sassen 1996). Yet these political institutions are largely responsible for the persistent differences among tax regimes and are, therefore, quite useful for demonstrating why the globalization thesis is misguided in the first place. More important, evidence that contradicts the race to the bottom hypothesis represents a major challenge to the empirical validity of globalization theory.

More specifically, I suggest that the manner in which labor and business are organized affects how they perceive their tax-related interests and thus the sorts of tax policies they are willing to support. Where labor is well organized and politically influential, unions and their political supporters are willing to support relatively high taxes because they expect that these will help finance programs from which they benefit. Similarly, where business is well organized, such as through business associations, it tends to see that relatively high taxes support programs, including health insurance, education, and research and development, that ensure social peace and help firms remain competitive internationally. Moreover, the manner in which politics is arranged institutionally affects tax policymaking. Countries with inclusive policymaking institutions, such as corporatism or electoral systems that yield coalition governments, tend to be less inclined to race toward the bottom than others because these institutional arrangements encourage compromises that mitigate such behavior. This line of argument is consistent with those who maintain that national political and economic institutions mediate how states manage globalization pressures (e.g., Berger and Dore 1996; Campbell and Pedersen 2001: 269–73; Garrett 1998a; Weiss 1998).

What follows, then, is an exercise in fiscal sociology—an analysis of tax regimes. It proceeds as follows. First, I present evidence that contradicts globalization theory by showing that the overall *level* of taxation among the advanced capitalist countries has not converged on lower rates of revenue extraction since 1970. Nor has there been much convergence in the *structure* of tax regimes, that is, the proportion of revenues collected through different types of taxes, in these countries. After globalization accelerated in the mid-1980s, the proportion of revenues collected through different types of taxes did not change very much. There has been surprisingly little empirical research on the interaction between globalization and taxation, especially on the period of the 1990s (Schulze and Ursprung 1999: 312, 321), so this paper helps to fill that gap. Second, I suggest that unique configurations of national politics and political institutions mediate how states cope with the pressures of globalization. As a result, cross-national variation in politics and institutions goes a long way to explain why there is not a convergent race to the bottom. Third, I address more specifically the situation in the United States, a country that at first blush seems to provide evidence in support of globalization theory to the extent that it has experienced increased trade and international capital flows as well as several big tax cuts since 1980. Finally, I discuss why the globalization thesis may also not be well suited for understanding tax reforms in countries outside the advanced capitalist world, notably postcommunist Europe.

Have There Been Convergence and a Race to the Bottom in Taxation?

Globalization theorists argue that several aspects of economic activity have taken on increasingly international proportions. To begin with, international trade expanded dramatically among the advanced capitalist countries during the last few decades. Between 1960 and 1990 the ratio of merchandise exports to Gross Domestic Product (GDP) increased worldwide from 8 to 13 percent, a significant if not dramatic rise (Crafts 2000: 20). The ratios were nearly twice as large for many advanced capitalist countries. More notable increases occurred in foreign direct investment (FDI), the investments firms make in foreign firms and production facilities, which jumped from 6.4 to 56.8 percent of GDP between 1960 and 1995, with almost all of this growth occurring after 1985 (Crafts 2000: 21; Hirst and Thompson

1996: 55). Even more impressive was the increase in international portfolio investment, that is, investment by financial and fiduciary institutions in foreign stocks, bonds, and the like, which grew among OECD countries at rates two and sometimes three times faster than those of FDI between the mid-1980s and mid-1990s (Simmons 1999: 46). Finally, and perhaps most spectacular of all, foreign exchange turnover skyrocketed from $18 trillion in 1979 to $297 trillion in 1995 (Held et al. 1999: 209).

There is much debate about whether current levels of global economic activity are really so different from those seen in the early twentieth century prior to the contraction of international trade and investment associated with the two world wars and the Great Depression. The term "globalization" is also contested insofar as most of the change described above has been restricted primarily to the so-called triad region of North America, Western Europe, and Japan (e.g., Fligstein 2001: chap. 9; Hirst and Thompson 1996). Nevertheless, few scholars dispute the fact that economic activity has become increasingly globalized, or at least internationalized, since 1970, thanks in part to the advent of revolutionary changes in transportation and communication technologies. There is also agreement that some aspects of economic activity have become globalized more extensively and rapidly than others.

The Level of Taxation

But has the globalization of economic activity triggered a race to the bottom and convergence on generally lower levels of taxation? Apparently not. Table 1 presents total government tax revenues as a percentage of GDP between 1970 and 1998 for 18 advanced capitalist countries. An examination of the means and medians shows that over this period the average tax burden actually *increased*. The means rose from about 32 percent of GDP to nearly 40 percent of GDP. The medians rose from 33 percent of GDP to 39 percent of GDP. Furthermore, the corresponding measures of dispersion *increased*. The standard deviation, associated with the mean, rose during this period from about 6.1 to 7.2, and the interquartile range, associated with the median, increased from 8.1 to 9.9.[2] In this case, the measures of dispersion indicate how close countries tend to cluster around the average tax burden for the group as a whole. Smaller measures of dispersion indicate tighter clustering (i.e., convergence) than larger ones. Thus, not only did the tax burden increase rather than decrease, but there was no convergence toward a common level of taxation among these countries. On both counts the evidence contradicts globalization theory.

One argument that might rescue globalization theory from this evidence is that there may be convergent tendencies within smaller groups of countries. Understand that there are different types of capitalism, each with

Table 1
Total Tax Revenues in 18 OECD Countries (as a percentage of GDP)

	1970	1980	1990	1998
Australia	22.9	27.4	29.3	29.9
Austria	34.9	39.5	40.2	44.4
Belgium	35.7	43.1	43.1	45.9
Canada	31.2	32.0	36.1	37.4
Denmark	40.4	43.9	47.1	49.8
Finland	32.5	36.2	44.7	46.2
France	35.1	40.6	43.0	45.2
Germany	32.9	33.1	32.6	37.0
Ireland	29.9	31.5	33.6	32.2
Italy	26.1	30.3	38.9	42.7
Japan	19.7	25.4	30.9	28.4
Netherlands	37.1	43.4	42.8	41.0
New Zealand	27.4	33.0	38.1	35.2
Norway	34.9	42.7	41.8	43.6
Sweden	39.8	47.1	53.7	52.0
Switzerland	22.5	28.9	30.9	35.1
United Kingdom	37.0	35.3	36.0	37.2
USA	27.7	27.0	26.7	28.9
Mean	31.54	35.58	38.31	39.56
Median	32.70	34.20	38.50	39.20
Standard deviation	6.06	6.73	6.97	7.15
Interquartile Range	8.08	11.58	10.10	9.88

Data are from OECD (2000a: Table 3, 67–68).

unique political, economic, and institutional arrangements (Hollingsworth et al. 1994; Hollingsworth and Boyer 1997). Countries of a particular type tend to share common features, such as similar tax regimes. It follows that different types of countries may tend to cope with globalization pressures in different ways. Thus, although convergent tendencies in taxation might not be apparent when all the advanced capitalist countries are examined as a single group, there may be convergent, race to the bottom effects among countries that share important features (e.g., Kitschelt et al. 1999). In other words, multiple equilibria are possible (Shepsle 1986).

One useful distinction is that made between coordinated and liberal market economies (Soskice 1999). *Coordinated market economies,* such as

Germany and the Northern European countries, are those whose institutions facilitate strong labor unions and business associations, cooperative industrial relations between unions and managers both within and across firms, long-term corporate investment and profit horizons, inter-firm cooperation in areas like research and development, and extensive vocational training systems. In contrast, *liberal market economies*, such as the Anglo-Saxon countries, have weaker unions and business associations, deregulated labor markets and firm-level rather than sectoral or industrial bargaining between labor and management, short-term corporate investment and profit horizons, strong competition requirements that limit possible cooperation among firms, and educational systems that emphasize general rather than vocational training. Furthermore, states in coordinated market economies tend to pursue developmental and distributive goals much more vigorously and directly than their counterparts in liberal market economies, such as by providing financial support to firms or sectors for economic development projects, active labor market policies, and hefty welfare state programs to maintain a comparatively high social wage (Albert 1993; Best 1990; Hicks and Kenworthy 1998; Weiss 1998). Of course, these are policies that are expensive and require relatively high levels of taxation.

Table 2 compares the tax burdens in coordinated and liberal market economies from 1970 to 1998. Countries were classified as either coordinated or liberal market economies according to the index developed by Western (2001: 78). An analysis of the means and medians reveals, as expected, that tax burdens are consistently lower in the liberal market economies. An inspection of the means shows that in the liberal market economies the average tax burden increased from 30 to 36 percent of GDP, and in the coordinated market economies it increased from 33 to 42 percent of GDP. The medians show similar trends, rising from 29 to 36 percent of GDP in the liberal market economies and from 35 to 44 percent in the coordinated market economies. Furthermore, in the liberal market economies the standard deviations increased from 4.7 to 5.8, and in the coordinated market economies they increased from 6.8 to 7.1. The interquartile ranges rose, from 5.1 to 7.1 in the liberal economies and from 4.2 to 8.1 in the coordinated economies. So average tax burdens in both types of societies *increased* during this period, and measures of dispersion showed no tendency toward convergence. There is little support within these country types for globalization theory.

Another way that scholars often group advanced capitalist countries is according to their type of welfare state (e.g., Esping-Andersen 1999). The *social democratic* welfare states of Northern Europe have typically been the most generous to their citizens and, thus, ought to be associated with the highest tax burdens insofar as these states utilize tax revenue to finance welfare spending. In contrast, *residual* welfare states, like those in the Anglo-Saxon countries, have been more stingy historically and so should

TABLE 2

Total Tax Revenues in Liberal and Coordinated Market Economies (as a percentage of GDP)

	1970	1980	1990	1998
Liberal Economies				
Australia	22.9	27.4	29.3	29.9
Canada	31.2	32.0	36.1	37.4
France	35.1	40.6	43.0	45.2
Ireland	29.9	31.5	33.6	32.2
Italy	26.1	30.3	38.9	42.7
New Zealand	27.4	33.0	38.1	35.2
United Kingdom	37.0	35.3	36.0	37.2
United States	27.7	27.0	26.7	28.9
Mean	29.66	32.14	35.21	36.09
Median	28.80	31.75	36.05	36.20
Standard deviation	4.68	4.39	5.26	5.80
Interquartile range	5.10	4.00	5.78	7.10
Coordinated Economies				
Austria	34.9	39.5	40.2	44.4
Belgium	35.7	43.1	43.1	45.9
Denmark	40.4	43.9	47.1	49.8
Finland	32.5	36.2	44.7	46.2
Germany	32.9	33.1	32.6	37.0
Japan	19.7	25.4	30.9	28.4
Netherlands	37.1	43.4	42.8	41.0
Norway	34.9	42.7	41.8	43.6
Sweden	39.8	47.1	53.7	52.0
Switzerland	22.5	28.9	30.9	35.1
Mean	33.04	38.33	40.78	42.34
Median	34.90	41.10	42.30	44.00
Standard deviation	6.83	7.19	7.42	7.14
Interquartile range	4.15	9.45	9.80	8.13

Data are from OECD (2000a: Table 3, 67–68).

be associated with lower tax burdens. Finally, because *Christian democratic* welfare states fall between these extremes, so should their tax burdens (Esping-Andersen 1999; Stephens et al. 1999).

Table 3 shows changes in total tax revenues as a percentage of GDP from 1970 to 1998 for these three types of welfare states. Countries were classified as residual, Christian democratic, or social democratic welfare states according to the index developed by Kitschelt et al. (1999: 436).

TABLE 3
Total Tax Revenues in Residual, Christian Democratic, and Social Democratic
Welfare States (as a percentage of GDP)

	1970	1980	1990	1998
Residual				
Australia	22.9	27.4	29.3	29.9
Canada	31.2	32.0	36.1	37.4
Ireland	29.9	31.5	33.6	32.2
Japan	19.7	25.4	30.9	28.4
New Zealand	27.4	33.0	38.1	35.2
United Kingdom	37.0	35.3	36.0	37.2
United States	27.7	27.0	26.7	28.9
Mean	27.97	30.23	32.96	32.74
Median	27.70	31.50	33.60	32.20
Standard deviation	5.63	3.65	4.14	3.86
Interquartile range	5.40	5.30	5.95	6.80
Christian Democratic				
Austria	34.9	39.5	40.2	44.4
Belgium	35.7	43.1	43.1	45.9
France	35.1	40.6	43.0	45.2
Germany	32.9	33.1	32.6	37.0
Italy	26.1	30.3	38.9	42.7
Netherlands	37.1	43.4	42.8	41.0
Switzerland	22.5	28.9	30.9	35.1
Mean	32.04	36.99	38.79	41.61
Median	34.90	39.50	40.20	42.70
Standard deviation	5.53	6.10	5.08	4.17
Interquartile range	5.90	10.15	7.15	5.80
Social Democratic				
Denmark	40.4	43.9	47.1	49.8
Finland	32.5	36.2	44.7	46.2
Norway	34.9	42.7	41.8	43.6
Sweden	39.8	47.1	53.7	52.0
Mean	36.90	42.48	46.83	47.90
Median	37.35	43.30	45.90	48.00
Standard deviation	3.83	4.58	5.07	3.73
Interquartile range	5.65	3.63	4.78	4.80

Data are from OECD (2000a: Table 3, 67–68).

Table 3 confirms that average tax burdens are lowest in residual welfare states, followed by Christian democratic welfare states, and then social democratic welfare states, which have the highest tax burdens. Furthermore, within each group of countries tax burdens increased over time. In residual welfare states the means and medians rose from 28 to 33 percent and from 28 to 32 percent of GDP, respectively. In Christian democratic welfare states the means and medians rose from 32 to 42 percent of GDP and from 35 to 43 percent of GDP, respectively. In social democratic welfare states the means and medians both rose from about 37 to 48 percent of GDP. These upward trends do not support globalization theory. However, in all three sets of countries the standard deviations declined slightly, from 5.6 to 3.9 in residual welfare states, from 5.5 to 4.2 in Christian democratic welfare states, and from 3.8 to 3.7 in social democratic welfare states. The interquartile ranges declined from 5.9 to 5.8 in Christian democratic welfare states and from 5.7 to 4.8 in social democratic welfare states. However, they rose from 5.4 to 6.8 in the residual welfare states. Overall, this suggests a modest tendency for all three types of welfare states to adopt *higher* tax burdens, not lower ones as globalization theory predicts, and at least for Christian democratic and social democratic welfare states to converge modestly within their groups toward these higher burdens.

In sum, analyses of tax levels in the advanced capitalist countries provide no support for the notion that globalization is causing states to converge on lower tax burdens. However, there may still be a way to redeem globalization theory. It is possible that globalization may have caused changes in the *structure* of national tax regimes without affecting the overall *level* of tax burdens. After all, states may implement significant changes in their tax regimes by shifting where the tax burden falls without altering the level of taxation per se (e.g., Allen and Campbell 1994; Campbell and Allen 2001; Przeworski and Wallerstein 1988). For example, shifting from progressive income taxes to flat social consumption taxes, such as sales or value-added taxes, may move the burden of taxation from one income group to another without affecting the total amount of revenue the government collects. So it is possible that if states did not converge toward lower levels of taxation due to globalization, perhaps they tended at least to alter the structure of their tax regimes by shifting the tax burden off investors and on to others.

The Structure of Taxation

In order to investigate this possibility, Table 4 examines for 17 advanced capitalist countries the percentage of total central government revenues collected through three major taxes: income and profit taxes, social security taxes, and taxes on goods and services.[3] Together these three types of taxes comprise the vast majority of government revenues and constitute the foundation of modern tax regimes. They provided on average between

TABLE 4

Central Government Revenues for 17 OECD Countries by Tax Type (as a percentage of Total Government Revenues)

	Income & Profit Taxes		Social Security Taxes		Taxes on Goods & Services	
	1990	1998	1990	1998	1990	1998
Australia	65	68	0	0	21	21
Austria	19	26	37	40	25	25
Belgium	35	37	35	33	24	25
Canada	51	54	16	19	17	17
Denmark	37	36	4	4	41	42
Finland	31	29	9	10	47	44
France	17	20	44	42	28	29
Germany	16	15	53	48	24	20
Ireland	37	42	15	13	38	37
Italy	37	33	29	31	29	26
Netherlands	31	25	35	41	22	23
New Zealand	53	62	0	0	27	28
Norway	16	21	24	23	34	38
Sweden	18	14	31	34	29	28
Switzerland	15	15	51	51	23	23
United Kingdom	39	39	17	17	28	31
United States	52	57	35	32	3	3
Mean	33.47	34.88	25.59	25.77	27.06	27.06
Median	35.00	33.00	29.00	31.00	27.00	26.00
Standard Deviation	15.37	16.98	16.78	16.50	9.85	9.87
Interquartile Range	21	21	20	27	6	8

Data are from World Bank (2001: Table 4.13, 242–44).

86 and 88 percent of all the revenue these governments collected during the 1990s. The rest came from taxes on international trade, miscellaneous taxes, and non-tax revenue (World Bank 2001: 242–44). The table presents data from 1990 and 1998, a relatively short period, but one that is appropriate because the sharp increases in foreign direct investment, international portfolio investment, and foreign exchange transactions with which globalization theory is so concerned occurred after 1985 so their effects, if any, would not likely begin to appear until the 1990s.

Table 4 shows that there was very little change in the percentage of revenues received from each type of tax during the 1990s. In particular, we might expect that taxes on income, which include individual and corporate income taxes, profit taxes, and capital gains taxes, would be the form of taxation most likely to be affected by globalization pressures if states want to shift taxes off individual and corporate investors. Yet the evidence is inconclusive. An examination of the means shows that the percentage of revenues collected through income and profit taxes increased from 34 to 35 percent of total government revenues. However, the median declined from 35 to 33 percent of total government revenues. Neither the standard deviation nor interquartile range of income taxes declined at all. The mean of the percentage of revenues collected through social security taxes was essentially stable and the median increased slightly from 29 to 31 percent of total revenues. The standard deviation declined slightly from 16.8 to 16.5, but the interquartile range increased from 20 to 27. The mean of the percentage of revenues collected through taxes on goods and services was unchanged while the median declined from 27 to 26 percent of total revenues. The standard deviation was virtually unchanged and the interquartile range increased from 6 to 8. There is little evidence here that the structure of tax regimes changed in ways that are consistent with globalization theory.

In order to determine whether there might be different results within types of countries, the liberal and coordinated market economies again were examined separately. Contrary to globalization theory, Table 5 shows that within the liberal market economies there was a slight *increase* in the amount of revenue collected through income and profit taxes between 1990 and 1998. The mean and median rose from 44 to 47 percent of total revenues collected and from 45 to 48 percent of total revenues collected, respectively. The measures of dispersion increased as well. Indeed, the increase in income and profit taxation is surprising insofar as these are the countries that tend to be most likely to favor lower income taxes, at least judging by the rhetoric of ruling politicians like Ronald Reagan, Margaret Thatcher, and other conservatives in power who have called frequently since 1980 for lower taxes on individuals and corporations. The mean for social security taxes in liberal market economies was virtually stable and the median increased from about 17 to 18 percent of total revenues collected. The standard deviation declined slightly from 15.7 to 15.1 and the interquartile range rose from 19.3 to 21.5. For taxes on goods and services, the mean, median, and standard deviation remained quite stable, but the interquartile range increased slightly from 8.3 to 9.5. Insofar as the liberal market economies are concerned, these results provide no support for globalization theory.

For the coordinated market economies Table 5 reveals that the percentage of revenues collected through income and profit taxes did not decline. The mean remained unchanged and the median rose from 19 to 25 percent of total revenues collected. Furthermore, the standard deviation and

TABLE 5

Central Government Revenues by Tax Type in Liberal and Coordinated Market Economies (as a percentage of Total Government Revenues)

	Income & Profit Taxes		Social Security Taxes		Taxes on Goods & Services	
	1990	1998	1990	1998	1990	1998
Liberal Economies						
Australia	65	68	0	0	21	21
Canada	51	54	16	19	17	17
France	17	20	44	42	28	29
Ireland	37	42	15	13	38	37
Italy	37	33	29	31	29	26
New Zealand	53	62	0	0	27	28
United Kingdom	39	39	17	17	28	31
United States	52	57	35	32	3	3
Mean	43.88	46.88	19.50	19.25	23.88	24.00
Median	45.00	48.00	16.50	18.00	27.50	27.00
Standard deviation	14.57	16.16	15.72	15.13	10.43	10.43
Interquartile range	15.25	20.75	19.25	21.5	8.25	9.50
Coordinated Economies						
Austria	19	26	37	40	25	25
Belgium	35	37	35	33	24	25
Denmark	37	36	4	4	41	42
Finland	31	29	9	10	47	44
Germany	16	15	53	48	24	20
Netherlands	31	25	35	41	22	23
Norway	16	21	24	23	34	38
Sweden	18	14	31	34	29	28
Switzerland	15	15	51	51	23	23
Mean	24.22	24.22	31.00	31.56	29.89	29.78
Median	19.00	25.00	35.00	34.00	25.00	25.00
Standard deviation	9.07	8.76	16.64	16.26	8.92	9.05
Interquartile range	15.00	14.00	13.00	18.00	10.00	15.00

Data are from World Bank (2001: Table 4.13, 242–44).

interquartile range declined very slightly from 9.1 to 8.8 and from 15 to 14, respectively. There was virtually no change in the proportion of revenues collected either through social security taxes or taxes on goods and services. Nor did the standard deviations change much. However, the interquartile range increased from 13 to 18 for social security taxes and from

Table 6

Central Government Revenues by Tax Type in Residual, Christian Democratic, and Social Democratic Welfare States (as a percentage of Total Government Revenues)

	Income & Profit Taxes		Social Security Taxes		Taxes on Goods & Services	
	1990	1998	1990	1998	1990	1998
Residual						
Australia	65	68	0	0	21	21
Canada	51	54	16	19	17	17
Ireland	37	42	15	13	38	37
New Zealand	53	62	0	0	27	28
United Kingdom	39	39	17	17	28	31
United States	52	57	35	32	3	3
Mean	49.50	53.67	13.84	13.50	22.33	22.83
Median	51.50	55.50	15.50	15.00	24.00	24.50
Standard deviation	10.27	11.29	13.01	12.24	11.86	12.04
Interquartile range	10.75	15.75	12.99	15.24	9.75	12.25
Christian Democratic						
Austria	19	26	37	40	25	25
Belgium	35	37	35	33	24	25
France	17	20	44	42	28	29
Germany	16	15	53	48	24	20
Italy	37	33	29	31	29	26
Netherlands	31	25	35	41	22	23
Switzerland	15	15	51	51	23	23
Mean	24.29	24.43	40.57	40.86	25.00	24.43
Median	19.00	25.00	37.00	41.00	24.00	25.00
Standard deviation	9.64	8.48	8.98	7.24	2.58	2.82
Interquartile range	16.50	12.00	12.50	8.50	3.00	2.50
Social Democratic						
Denmark	37	36	4	4	41	42
Finland	31	29	9	10	47	44
Norway	16	21	24	23	34	38
Sweden	18	14	31	34	29	28
Mean	25.50	25.00	17.00	17.75	37.75	38.00
Median	24.50	25.00	16.50	16.50	37.50	40.00
Standard deviation	10.15	9.56	12.62	13.43	7.89	7.12
Interquartile range	15.00	11.50	18.00	17.25	9.75	7.00

Data are from World Bank (2001: Table 4.13, 242–44).

10 to 15 for taxes on goods and services. Again, these results offer virtually no support for globalization theory.

Table 6 examines tax shifting in different types of welfare states between 1990 and 1998. Residual welfare states experienced little tax shifting other than an *increase* in the amount of revenue generated through income and profit taxes. Contrary to globalization theory, the corresponding means and medians climbed from about 50 to 54 percent of total revenue and from 52 to 56 percent of total revenue, respectively. Both measures of dispersion increased. The mean, median, and standard deviation for social security taxes declined very slightly, but the interquartile range increased from about 13 to 15. Mean and median taxes on goods and services increased marginally as did the measures of dispersion.

Christian democratic welfare states also encountered little tax shifting in line with globalization theory. For income and profit taxes the mean was essentially unchanged and the median increased from 19 to 25 percent of total revenues collected. The standard deviation declined from 9.6 to 8.5 and the interquartile range decreased from 16.5 to 12. For social security taxes the mean and median values also increased while the measures of dispersion decreased. So for both types of taxation to the extent that any trend is evident it is one of convergence toward a *greater* reliance on income and profit taxes and social security taxes, evidence that does not square well with globalization theory. The results for taxes on goods and services are inconclusive. The mean declined slightly and the standard deviation increased. Conversely, the median increased slightly and the interquartile range decreased.

Finally, the results regarding social democratic welfare states are largely inconclusive. For income and profit taxes an examination of the means reveals a very slight decrease from 25.5 to 25 percent in the amount of total revenue collected. An examination of the medians shows a similarly small increase from 24.5 to 25 percent of total revenue collected. Both measures of dispersion declined. For social security taxes the mean increased modestly and the median remained unchanged while the standard deviation increased and the interquartile range decreased. For taxes on goods and services the mean was basically stable and the median rose from 37.5 to 40 percent of total revenue collected. The standard deviation declined from 7.9 to 7.1 and the interquartile range declined from 9.8 to 7. Thus, in the social democratic welfare states there is no consistent evidence to support globalization theory.

To summarize briefly, there is no support for the notion that globalization precipitated a convergent race to the bottom in levels of taxation. This was true for both the full group of advanced capitalist countries and the various subgroups. Nor was there much tax shifting in the direction that globalization theory would predict. Moreover, why liberal market economies and residual welfare states shifted their tax burdens toward *higher* levels of taxation and a *greater* reliance on income and profit taxes is unclear and very much at odds with globalization theory. Because these

tend to be countries with more conservative governments and because they tend to collect a considerably larger percentage of their revenues from income and profit taxes than do others, globalization theory would imply a shift away from these taxes, not a shift toward them.

To the extent that we have been interested in how globalization affects different varieties of capitalism, it is also worth noting that within country types there was only very limited evidence of convergence as reflected by the fact that *both* measures of dispersion declined over time. For changes in tax levels (see tables 2 and 3), comparing 1970 and 1998 reveals that only the Christian democratic and social democratic welfare states experienced any convergence toward the average level of taxation for their groups. Even so, these trends were not linear. In both cases there were times between these years when these countries diverged from their average levels of taxation. For changes in the structure of tax regimes (see tables 5 and 6), comparing 1990 and 1998 shows that coordinated market economies converged toward the average for their group in terms of the percentage of total revenues collected from income and profit taxes. Christian democratic welfare states did the same for both income and profit taxes and social security taxes. Finally, social democratic welfare states converged toward the averages for their group in terms of the percentage of total revenues collected from income and profit taxes and from taxes on goods and services. As noted above, these shifts were generally modest and none involved convergence toward lower levels of taxation or away from a reliance on income and profit taxes, as globalization theory predicts. All of this suggests that in only a few instances has there been any congealing of tax regimes within types of capitalist countries. Mostly, there was no evidence for convergence and in several instances the evidence pointed toward divergence. As a result, these findings do not lend much support to those who have argued that globalization will produce further homogenization within country types and the hardening of multiple, country specific equilibria (e.g., Kitschelt et al. 1999).

One caveat is in order. Some might suspect that the evidence for convergence is likely to be greatest for countries outside of the OECD, particularly because it is in these developing countries that the influence of international organizations, such as the International Monetary Fund and World Bank, have had the most influence in pushing a neoliberal set of economic policies, including low tax rates (Wade and Veneroso 1998a, b). This is an issue that requires further analysis. However, the vast majority of international capital and trade flows are within the so-called triad region of advanced industrial economies upon which I have focused here: Japan, North America, and Western Europe (Hirst and Thompson 1996: 63–67). Thus, it is still surprising how little evidence we have seen of convergence among these countries. Indeed, given the high concentration of world trade and capital flows within this region, one would expect, following globalization theory, that if there should be evidence of convergence anywhere, then it should be among these countries.

In any case, the big picture remains one in which there is precious little empirical support for globalization theory (see also Swank and Steinmo forthcoming). But what accounts for the fact that states did not reduce tax levels or change their tax regimes much despite a sharp increase in the globalization of economic activity?

NATIONAL POLITICS AND INSTITUTIONS

The answer seems to have much to do with national politics and political institutions. Two things are important. First, the manner in which social actors, particularly representatives of labor and business, are organized affects how they perceive their interests around issues of taxation in the first place. Second, the manner in which electoral politics are organized affects the degree to which politicians and organizations are willing to compromise on issues of taxation. Let me explain.

To begin with, countries where the labor movement is centralized and strong politically tend to have higher tax rates than countries where labor is more decentralized and weak politically. In coordinated market economies collective bargaining is often organized at the sectoral or industrial level rather than at the level of the firm, which is typically the case in liberal market economies. Additionally, workers in coordinated economies as well as social democratic welfare states tend to enjoy the benefits of works councils, state employment services, active labor market policies, and various employment guarantees (Hicks and Kenworthy 1998; Western 2001). Insofar as the state pays for these benefits, labor has an interest in supporting relatively high taxes and does so in the expectation that this will lead to a higher social wage. Labor's capacity to support these policies is often enhanced in these countries because it is integrated into the policymaking process through corporatist institutions that provide it with an important voice in policy making (Steinmo and Tolbert 1998). Moreover, when strong centralized labor unions are coupled with strong labor or social democratic governments, as is often the case in these countries, the tax burden on everyone, including business, tends to be higher than elsewhere. This is not to say, however, that leftist governments allied with well-organized labor movements have free rein to do as they please. They still exercise self-restraint recognizing that excessive demands for a very high social wage could drive away capital and, therefore, hurt the labor movement as a whole (Garrett 1998a).

However, business and investors also seem willing to bear heavier tax burdens in countries with coordinated market economies and social democratic welfare states. This is because they recognize that it actually may be in their own interests to do so. Corporatist countries with strong centralized business associations have higher tax rates than elsewhere because capital is willing to pay for social expenditures that protect workers from the risks associated with an increasingly global economy, thereby ensuring the social peace that business needs (Garrett 1998a). Indeed, a top priority of business is to reduce uncertainty and stabilize the business environment (Fligstein 2001; Kolko 1963). Business may also support higher taxes insofar as this enables the state to provide public goods that directly benefit firms, such as a more educated and, therefore, flexible workforce, universal pension and health benefits that reduce job shifting, and the like (Kiser and Laing 2001). In many cases, business had to learn that there were long-term benefits to be gained from this sort of social investment (Martin 2000: chap. 3, 2002; Streeck 1997). But once this lesson was learned, even in a rapidly globalizing environment where the pressure for institutional convergence may be greater than ever before, the business community's perception of its interests are still shaped by the legacies with which they have lived for decades. This is one reason, for example, why German business associations have defended co-determination practices (Thelen 2000) and why Scandinavian business associations continue to educate their members to the benefits of substantial welfare spending (Swank and Martin 2001). The point is that for institutional reasons business may be less averse to high taxes in some countries than globalization theory recognizes. Thus, perhaps surprisingly, in some cases, depending on its institutional configuration, business and labor may have common interests when it comes at least to the broad contours of taxation.

In addition to the institutional capacities of important economic organizations, electoral institutions exert important effects on tax policy. In majoritarian systems, like Britain and Japan, single parties tend to control the government. The party in power wants to keep taxes low in order not to lose voters and the next election, which would result in its removal from power. In systems that tend to result in coalition governments where one party dominates the coalition, as the Social Democratic Party has done in Sweden, the dominant party strikes long-term compromises with its coalition partners in order to keep the coalition in tack. Taxes tend to be higher in order to pay for the expenditures required to keep coalition members happy. Finally, in systems that tend to produce shifting coalition governments in which no single party dominates the coalition, all parties have incentives to defect and try to gain control of new coalition governments, so there is little incentive for long-term compromise and, thus, spending and taxes tend to be low (Steinmo and Tolbert 1998).

Overall, the point is that the institutional configuration of national politics shapes people's perceptions of their interests and political strategies when it comes to tax policy. Because these institutions are rather constant, they sustain and perpetuate tax regimes despite global pressures for a convergent race to the bottom. As a result, the tax regimes of the advanced capitalist countries have remained remarkably stable in the age of globalization.

WHAT ABOUT THE UNITED STATES?

At first glance it seems that if any country supports the globalization thesis, it is the United States. After the Second World War, trade as a percentage of GDP increased in the United States and was associated with significant declines in effective corporate income tax rates (Campbell and Allen 1994: 660). Moreover, the outflow of FDI from the United States increased sharply after 1975 and by 1994 was the largest of any country in the world, accounting for 25 percent of total world FDI (Held et al. 1999: 247). There were also two very big globalization era tax cuts through 2000: the 1981 Economic Recovery Tax Act and the 1986 Tax Reform Act. By the end of the 1980s, the United States had some of the lowest corporate and overall tax rates in the OECD (Steinmo 1993: chap. 6).

However, despite this evidence, it would be wrong to conclude that the U.S. case supports globalization theory. To begin with, corporate income tax rates actually began declining steadily in 1954. This was long before the 1970s when globalization is said to have begun, so the U.S. trend toward lower corporate tax rates must have resulted at least in part from things unrelated to globalization. In fact, time-series analysis reveals that several other factors have been associated with declining corporate tax rates in the United States. Among the most important, the declining strength of organized labor tracks very closely with declining corporate taxes. As the organizational and political strength of labor deteriorated after the Second World War it became less able to defend against cuts in corporate tax rates. This, of course, supports my earlier claim that, globalization pressures not withstanding, national politics and political institutions have significant effects on tax policy. Furthermore, higher levels of unemployment have been associated with lower corporate tax rates while larger federal budget deficits have been associated with higher corporate tax rates. These are clear indications that tax policy has been used frequently to cope with domestic economic and fiscal problems (Campbell and Allen 1994).

I am not claiming that globalization has had no relation to tax cuts in the United States. Rather its effects have been more subtle and less determinant than globalization theory predicts. To be sure, tax reform in the 1980s was motivated in part by concerns about U.S. international competitiveness, trade deficits, and capital flight (Steinmo 1993: 165). But these reforms were also motivated in large part by domestic politics in ways that had little to do with globalization.

For example, the Reagan administration's 1981 Economic Recovery Tax Act, the largest tax cut in U.S. history up to that point, was driven partly by concerns with trade deficits and flagging international competitiveness—problems that were viewed as contributing to the stagflation malaise then gripping the country (Martin 1991, chap. 5). These were supply-side tax cuts that were focused on wealthy individuals and business and intended to stimulate investment in a non-inflationary way (Roberts 1984). However, other factors were also at work. First, some of the administration's most ardent supporters for the tax cuts, notably David Stockman, director of the Office of Management and Budget, advocated deep tax cuts in order to force Congress to reduce spending and, therefore, reduce the size and influence of the federal government in the economy (Makin and Ornstein 1994: 30–31). This, of course, had long been a central part of the Republican Party's domestic political agenda and had nothing to do with globalization. Second, the depth of the cuts was exacerbated by a bidding war that broke out between the administration and members of Congress. Each side repeatedly sought to increase the size of the cuts in order to win political points with its constituents. Again, domestic politics rather than globalization was at work. Finally, and perhaps most important, a year later the 1982 Tax Equity and Fiscal Responsibility Act was enacted, which reduced many of the cuts associated with the 1981 legislation. This was done to counteract a skyrocketing budget deficit that the 1981 Act helped to trigger (Martin 1991, chap. 6). If globalization pressures were so powerful, then it is hard to understand how a year after the 1981 tax cuts were implemented they were suddenly rolled back. As noted above, fiscal pressures have often precipitated U.S. tax reform.

The 1986 Tax Reform Act was also initiated in part due to concerns over capital flight. However, equally if not more important were concerns about the increasing complexity of the tax code and the need to make it neutral with respect to the investment incentives it offered to different sectors of the business community. This was another effort to reduce the federal government's influence in the economy. Indeed, the legislation cut corporate and individual income tax rates and simplified the tax code. Nevertheless, because the bill also reduced or eliminated a variety of tax loopholes, such as those regarding accelerated depreciation and investment tax credits, it actually led to a $120 billion *increase* in corporate taxes paid to the federal government over the next five years (Martin 1991: chap. 7; Steinmo 1993: 165). Once again, this evidence defies globalization theory, especially to the extent that by 1986 the forces of globalization were in full swing, but corporate taxes were increased, not decreased.

In the end, evidence from the United States does not lend much support to globalization theory. The *timing* in the decline of corporate income tax rates is not consistent with globalization theory because that decline began nearly two decades before the onset of globalization. More-over, the *motivation* for important tax reforms stemmed at least as much from domestic fiscal and political concerns as it did from concerns about international capital mobility. Domestic political interests were of para-mount importance again early in 2001 when the Bush administration won a $1.6 trillion multiyear tax cut package and later that year sought an ad-ditional $60 billion tax cut. These initiatives were not offered in response to capital mobility problems. Instead, they were intended ostensibly to re-turn a hefty budget surplus to the public and to stimulate an economy that was mired in recession (Pearlstein 2001). Some have speculated that they were also aimed at fulfilling promises made during the presidential cam-paign, including those made to influential supporters (Allen and Kessler 2001), and to restrain government spending, as occurred twenty years ear-lier in the Reagan administration (Toner 2001).

A BRIEF NOTE ABOUT SOME OTHER COUNTRIES

If well-established politics and institutions mediate the effects of global pressures on national tax regimes, as I have suggested, then the effects of globalization should be strongest in countries without such well-established traditions. Arguably, postcommunist Europe is such a case. After all, since the collapse of their communist regimes these countries have been dis-mantling their old political institutions and creating new ones, which re-main relatively fragile (Elster et al. 1998: 17) and, thus, unlikely to provide an effective buffer against global pressures. Although I do not have good comparative and historical data on tax rates per se for these countries, there is at least some evidence that tax reform in these countries has not conformed with globalization theory.

After the old regimes collapsed in 1989 most of these countries re-formed their tax systems along western lines. They adopted value added taxes and individual and corporate income taxes; lowered tax rates; re-duced the number of tax rates on business; and generally made the system of taxation more transparent. In part, this was done to attract capital in-vestment (Campbell 1996). However, this was motivated largely by other considerations. First, powerful international lending agencies, notably the International Monetary Fund, demanded such reform as a quid pro quo for the release of vitally important financial aid packages to these govern-ments. Second, the IMF, World Bank, OECD, top Western universities, and other institutions convened many conferences designed to familiarize postcommunist officials with normatively appropriate western fiscal policy. Some especially influential East European reformers, including Czecho-slovakia's Vaclav Klaus, who became that country's first postcommunist finance minister, and Leszek Balcerowicz, chief architect of Poland's initial reform program, were exposed to these ideas both before and after 1989 during economic studies in the United States, Britain, and West Germany. Finally, these governments were eager to join western organizations, such as the OECD, GATT, and NATO, and so were quick to mimic Western practices in order to do so. In particular, immediately after the old regimes collapsed, Poland, Hungary, and Czechoslovakia aspired to European Union membership and began to harmonize their fiscal systems with those in the EU in order to accomplish this goal (Campbell 2001).

Furthermore, once tax rates had been lowered, some countries actually raised them again in order to stop the budgetary hemorrhaging and fiscal deficits that emerged as a result of revenues lost through tax evasion and the inability of new governments to reduce spending—a story that has much to do with the organization of national politics and electoral institutions (Campbell 2001). The point is that a variety of factors beside concerns with international capital mobility led to the lowering of tax rates and other transformations of postcommunist tax regimes. International considerations were important, but not so much the kind that are central to globalization theory. Rather than being driven by concerns with international capital mobility, these reforms seem to have been designed more to curry favor with the international political community and stemmed more from coercive, normative, and mimetic pressures, as some sociologists would predict (e.g., Meyer 1987), than market pressures exerted by investors.

Conclusion

Nearly a century ago, Joseph Schumpeter (1991: 101) wrote that, "public finances are one of the best starting points for an investigation of society, especially though not exclusively of its political life." The arguments presented here show that Schumpeter's claim is as relevant today as it was then. In this case, by exploring changes in tax regimes we learn much about the dynamics of global capitalism in the late twentieth century.

The analysis reported here offers very little evidence that tax regimes, a critical element of the institution of capitalist property rights, are converging in the broad set of advanced capitalist countries through some sort of race to the bottom inspired by increasing levels of international capital mobility. Nor is there much evidence that convergence in tax regimes is occurring within institutionally specific subsets of these countries. As a result, contrary to those who maintain that globalization is undermining the capacity of nation states to regulate economic activity within their borders (e.g., Giddens 2000; Guéhenno 1995; Sassen 1996), little seems to have changed insofar as taxation is concerned in the advanced capitalist world. Thus, globalization does not appear to be threatening the ability of economic sociologists to account for variation in national economic organization and performance by focusing on the effects of tax regimes.

But what if we wait a little longer? After all, it has only been about twenty-five years since the forces of globalization are said to have been unleashed. Perhaps convergence will still occur eventually. There are good reasons apart from those already discussed to doubt that this will happen. As suggested earlier, the behavior of firms and investors is not necessarily defined solely, or even primarily, by an interest in seeking geographical locations with the lowest production costs, including the lowest costs of taxation (Doremus et al. 1998). Of course, some firms do compete by minimizing costs, but others compete by being fast innovators, producing high quality goods, and pursuing other strategies that depend less on cost reduction than other things. The ability to innovate and compete on the basis of quality rather than price and cost is affected by the institutional environment in which firms and investors operate. For instance, liberal market economies are good for firms that want to compete by keeping costs low and moving capital quickly from sector to sector and region to region. However, organized market economies are good for firms that want to compete on the basis of high quality or the capacity for flexible specialization because they provide, for example, especially well trained workers. In other words, firms compete on the basis of *comparative institutional advantage* as well as *comparative cost advantage*. Firms and investors often understand this and this understanding affects their interests when it comes to making decisions about where to invest (Hall 1998; Soskice 1999). That is, firms may be willing to endure higher taxes in exchange for a particularly favorable institutional environment. As a result, the threat of capital flight itself may be less pronounced than globalization theory assumes (Garrett 1998b). If so, then the essential dynamic underlying globalization theory's prediction about a race to the bottom is wrong and there is no reason to expect convergence in the future, no matter how long we wait.

To be sure, I am not arguing that interests are unimportant. I agree with the editors of this volume that interests matter. But interests are more complex or multidimensional than globalization theory recognizes. They are not simply an automatic reaction to, for example, prices or transaction costs. This complexity stems from the fact that institutions shape the perception of interests. Hence, cross-national variation in the institutions of capitalism, like property rights in general and taxation in particular, leads to cross-national variation in the perception of interests. And, as I have argued, this variation of interests is one reason why we have not witnessed a convergence among tax regimes. Of course, this does not imply that globalization has had no transformative affects on other capitalist institutions or that economic sociology should assume that these institutions are always in equilibria. Whether they are or not is something that economic sociologists need to scrutinize much more carefully.

NOTES

1. When I have discussed globalization theory with colleagues, some of them have dismissed it out of hand and argued that we should not take it seriously. I disagree. First, globalization theory is not so naive as to predict that tax rates will eventually drop to zero. Proponents of this theory recognize that states require at least some minimal level of revenues in order to survive. Second, as will become clear later in this chapter, while I believe that there has not been a race to the bottom in taxation, I believe that the argument itself is important and needs to be taken seriously. It continues to enjoy a respectable place in academic debate (e.g., Genschel 2002). Politicians frequently invoke the argument to justify a variety of policy moves (e.g., Schmidt 2002, part III). And international agencies, such as the OECD (2000b), continue to lament the threat of capital flight and urge countries to collectively address it. In short, the argument still carries weight in academic and policy-making circles.

2. I report median as well as mean values of central tendency because the median is not affected by countries with extreme values as is the mean. Similarly, I report the interquartile range because, in contrast to the standard deviation, it is a measure of dispersion that is not influenced as much by extreme values in the data. It represents the range of dispersion around the median. It is calculated by subtracting the twenty-fifth percentile of the data from the seventy-fifth percentile and, therefore, encompasses the middle 50 percent of the observations (Pagano and Gauvreau 1993: 41–43).

3. Although included in tables 1–3, Japan is omitted in the remaining tables due to missing data for some years.

REFERENCES

Albert, Michel. 1993. *Capitalism versus Capitalism*. New York: Four Walls Eight Windows.

Allen, Michael P. and John L. Campbell. 1994. "State Revenue Extraction from Different Income Groups: Variations in Tax Progressivity in the United States, 1916–1986." *American Sociological Review* 59(2): 169–86.

Allen, Mike and Glenn Kessler. 2001. "Bush's Tax Cut Proposal Renews Party Differences." *Washington Post*, October 7, A16.

Barzel, Yoram. 1989. *The Economic Analysis of Property Rights*. Cambridge: Cambridge University Press.

Berger, Suzanne and Ronald P. Dore, eds. 1996. *National Diversity and Global Capitalism*. Ithaca: Cornell University Press.

Best, Michael H. 1990. *The New Competition: Institutions of Industrial Restructuring*. Cambridge, Mass.: Harvard University Press.

Bromley, Daniel W. 1989. *Economic Interests and Institutions: The Conceptual Foundations of Public Policy*. New York: Blackwell.

Campbell, John L. 1993. "The State and Fiscal Sociology." *Annual Review of Sociology* 19: 163–85.

———. 1996. "An Institutional Analysis of Fiscal Reform in Postcommunist Europe." *Theory and Society* 25: 45–84.

———. 2001. "Convergence or Divergence? Globalization, Neoliberalism, and Fiscal Policy in Postcommunist Europe." In *Globalization and the European Political Economy*, ed. Steven Weber. New York: Columbia University Press.

Campbell, John L. and Michael P. Allen. 1994. "The Political Economy of Revenue Extraction in the Modern State: A Time-Series Analysis of U.S. Income Taxes, 1916–1986." *Social Forces* 72: 643–69.

———. 2001. "Identifying Shifts in Policy Regimes: Cluster and Interrupted Time-Series Analyses of U.S. Income Taxes." *Social Science History* 25(2): 37–65.

Campbell, John L. and Leon N. Lindberg. 1990. "Property Rights and the Organization of Economic Activity by the State." *American Sociological Review* 55(5): 634–77.

Campbell, John L. and Ove K. Pedersen. 2001. "The Second Movement in Institutional Analysis." In *The Rise of Neoliberalism and Institutional Analysis*, ed. John L. Campbell and Ove K. Pedersen. Princeton: Princeton University Press.

Cerny, Philip G. 1997. "International Finance and the Erosion of Capitalist Diversity." In *Political Economy of Modern Capitalism: Mapping Convergence and Diversity*, ed. Colin Crouch and Wolfgang Streeck. London: Sage.

Crafts, Nicholas. 2000. "Globalization and Growth in the Twentieth Century." In *World Economic Outlook: Supporting Studies*. Washington, D.C.: International Monetary Fund.

Dehejia, Vivek H. and Philipp Genschel. 1999. "Tax Competition in Europe." *Politics and Society* 27(3): 403–30.

Doremus, Paul, William Keller, Louis Pauly, and Simon Reich. 1998. *The Myth of the Global Corporation*. Princeton: Princeton University Press.

Elster, Jon, Claus Offe, and Ulrich K. Preuss. 1998. *Institutional Design in Post-Communist Societies*. New York: Oxford University Press.

Esping-Anderson, Gosta. 1999. *Social Foundations of Postindustrial Economies*. New York: Oxford University Press.

Fligstein, Neil. 1990. *The Transformation of Corporate Control*. Cambridge, Mass.: Harvard University Press.

———. 2001. *The Architecture of Markets: An Economic Sociology of Twenty-First-Century Capitalist Societies*. Princeton: Princeton University Press.

Garrett, Geoffrey. 1998a. *Partisan Politics in the Global Economy*. New York: Cambridge University Press.

———. 1998b. "Global Markets and National Politics: Collison Course or Virtuous Circle?" *International Organization* 2(4): 787–824.

Genschel, Philipp. 2002. "Globalization, Tax Competition, and the Welfare State." *Politics and Society* 30(2): 245–77.

Giddens, Anthony. 2000. *Runaway World: How Globalization Is Reshaping Our Lives.* New York: Routledge.

Guéhenno, Jean-Marie. 1995. *The End of the Nation-State.* Minneapolis: University of Minnesota Press.

Hall, Peter A. 1998. "Orthodox Market Economies and Unemployment in Europe: Is It Finally Time to Accept Liberal Orthodoxy?" Paper presented at the Eleventh International Conference of Europeanists, Baltimore.

Held, David, Anthony McGrew, David Goldblatt, and Jonathan Perraton. 1999. *Global Transformations: Politics, Economics, and Culture.* Stanford: Stanford University Press.

Hicks, Alexander and Lane Kenworthy. 1998. "Cooperation and Political Economic Performance in Affluent Democratic Capitalism." *American Journal of Sociology* 103: 1631–72.

Hirst, Paul and Grahame Thompson. 1996. *Globalization in Question: The International Economy and the Possibilities of Governance.* London: Polity Press.

Hollingsworth, J. Rogers and Robert Boyer, eds. 1997. *Contemporary Capitalism: The Embeddedness of Institutions.* Cambridge: Cambridge University Press.

Hollingsworth, J. Rogers, Philippe C. Schmitter, and Wolfgang Streeck, eds. 1994. *Governing Capitalist Economies: Performance and Control of Economic Sectors.* New York: Oxford University Press.

Kiser, Edgar and Aaron Laing. 2001. "Have We Overestimated the Effects of Neoliberalism and Globalization?" In *The Rise of Neoliberalism and Institutional Analysis,* ed. John L. Campbell and Ove K. Pedersen. Princeton: Princeton University Press. 51–68.

Kitschelt, Herbert, Peter Lange, Gary Marks, and John D. Stephens. 1999. "Convergence and Divergence in Advanced Capitalist Democracies." In *Continuity and Change in Contemporary Capitalism,* ed. Herbert Kitschelt, Peter Lange, Gary Marks, and John D. Stephens. New York: Cambridge University Press. 427–60.

Kolko, Gabriel. 1963. *The Triumph of Conservatism: A Re-interpretation of American History, 1900–1916.* Chicago: Quadrangle.

Kurzer, Paulette. 1993. *Business and Banking: Political Change and Economic Integration in Western Europe.* Ithaca: Cornell University Press.

Makin, John H. and Norman J. Ornstein. 1994. *Debt and Taxes.* New York: Random House.

Martin, Cathie Jo. 1991. *Shifting the Burden: The Struggle over Growth and Corporate Taxation.* Chicago: University of Chicago Press.

———. 2000. *Stuck in Neutral: Business and the Politics of Human Capital Investment Policy.* Princeton: Princeton University Press.

———. 2002. "Activating Employers." Manuscript, Department of Political Science, Boston University.

McKenzie, Richard and Dwight R. Lee. 1991. *Quicksilver Capital: How the Rapid Movement of Wealth Has Changed the World.* New York: Free Press.

Meyer, John W. 1987. "The World Polity and the Authority of the Nation-State." In *Institutional Structure: Constituting State, Society, and the Individual,* ed. John W. Meyer, George Thomas, Francisco O. Ramirez, and John Boli. Beverly Hills, Calif.: Sage. 41–70.

North, Douglass C. 1990. *Institutions, Institutional Change and Economic Performance.* Cambridge: Cambridge University Press.

North, Douglass C. 1990. *Institutions, Institutional Change and Economic Performance.* Cambridge: Cambridge University Press.

OECD. 2000a. *Revenue Statistics, 1965–1999.* Paris: OECD.

———. 2000b. *Toward Global Tax Cooperation: Report to the 2000 Ministerial Council Meeting and Recommendations by the Committee on Fiscal Affairs.* Paris: OECD.

Pagano, Marcello and Kimberlee Gauvreau. 1993. *Principles of Biostatistics.* Belmont, Calif.: Duxbury.

Pearlstein, Steven. 2001. "Should the Tax System Redistribute the Wealth?" *Washington Post,* March 11, H01.

Przeworski, Adam and Michael Wallerstein. 1988. "Structural Dependence of the State on Capital." *American Political Science Review* 82(1): 11–29.

Roberts, Paul Craig. 1984. *The Supply-Side Revolution: An Insider's Account of Policymaking in Washington.* Cambridge, Mass.: Harvard University Press.

Sassen, Saskia. 1996. *Losing Control? Sovereignty in an Age of Globalization.* New York: Columbia University Press.

Schmidt, Vivien A. 2002. *The Futures of European Capitalism.* New York: Oxford University Press.

Schulze, Günther B. and Heinrich W. Ursprung. 1999. "Globalization of the Economy and the Nation State." *World Economy* 22(3): 295–352.

Schumpeter, Joseph A. [1918]1991. "The Crisis of the Tax State." In Schumpeter, *The Economics and Sociology of Capitalism,* ed. Richard Swedberg. Princeton: Princeton University Press. 99–140.

Shepsle, Kenneth A. 1986. "Institutional Equilibrium and Equilibrium Institutions." In *Political Science: The Science of Politics,* ed. Herbert F. Weisberg. New York: Agathon. 51–81.

Simmons, Beth. 1999. "The Internationalizition of Capital." In *Continuity and Change in Contemporary Capitalism,* ed. Herbert Kitschelt, Peter Lange, Gary Marks, and John D. Stephens. New York: Cambridge University Press. 36–69.

Soskice, David. 1999. "Divergent Production Regimes: Co-ordinated and Uncoordinated Market Economies in the 1980s and 1990s." In *Continuity and Change in Contemporary Capitalism,* ed. Herbert Kitschelt, Peter Lange, Gary Marks, and John D. Stephens. New York: Cambridge University Press. 101–34.

Steinmo, Sven. 1993. *Taxation and Democracy: Swedish, British, and American Approaches to Funding the Modern State.* New Haven: Yale University Press.

Steinmo, Sven and Caroline J. Tolbert. 1998. "Do Institutions Really Matter? Taxation in Industrialized Democracies." *Comparative Political Studies* 31(2): 165–87.

Stephens, John D., Evelyne Huber, and Leonard Ray. 1999. "The Welfare State in Hard Times." In *Continuity and Change in Contemporary Capitalism,* ed. Herbert Kitschelt, Peter Lange, Gary Marks, and John D. Stephens. New York: Cambridge University Press. 164–93.

Strange, Susan, 1997. "The Future of Global Capitalism; Or, Will Divergence Persist Forever?" In *Political Economy of Modern Capitalism: Mapping Convergence and Diversity,* ed. Colin Crouch and Wolfgang Streeck. London: Sage. 182–92.

Streeck, Wolfgang. 1997. "Beneficial Constraints: On the Economic Limits of Rational Voluntarism." In *Contemporary Capitalism: The Embeddedness of Institutions,* ed. J. Rogers Hollingsworth and Robert Boyer. Cambridge: Cambridge University Press. 197–219.

Swank, Duane and Cathie Jo Martin. 2001. "Employers and the Welfare State: The Political Economic Organization of Firms and Social Policy in Contemporary Capitalist Democracies." *Comparative Political Studies* 34 (October): 889–923.

Swank, Duane and Sven Steinmo. 2002. "The New Political Economy of Taxation in Advanced Capitalist Democracies." *American Journal of Political Science* 46 (3): 477–89.

Tanzi, Vito. 1995. *Taxation in an Integrating World.* Washington, D.C. Brookings Institution.

Thelen, Kathleen. 2000. "Why German Employers Cannot Bring Themselves to Dismantle the German Model." In *Unions, Employers and Central Banks,* ed. Torben Iverson, Jonas Pontousson, and David Soskice. *New York: Cambridge University Press.* 138–69.

Toner, Robin. 2001. "Now, Government Is the Solution, Not the Problem." *New York Times,* September 30, 14.

Wade, Robert and Frank Veneroso. 1998a. "The Asian Crisis: The High Debt Model versus the Wall Street-Treasure-IMF Complex." *New Left Review* 228: 3–24.

———. 1998b. "The Gathering World Slump and the Battle over Capital Controls." *New Left Review* 231: 13–42.

Western, Bruce. 2001. "Institutions, Investment, and the Rise in Unemployment." In *The Rise of Neoliberalism and Institutional Analysis,* ed. John L. Campbell and Ove K. Pedersen. Princeton: Princeton University Press. 71–94.

Weiss, Linda. 1998. *The Myth of the Powerless State.* Ithaca: Cornell University Press.

World Bank. 2001. *World Development Indicators.* Washington, D.C.: World Bank.

Trouble in Paradise: Institutions in the Japanese Economy and the Youth Labor Market

Mary C. Brinton

THE ECONOMIC AND SOCIAL organization of capitalist societies is one of the most classical of sociological subjects, as the editors of this volume point out. Pioneers of economic sociology such as Weber were fundamentally comparative, but the comparative analysis of the institutions governing capitalism in different cultural contexts has unfortunately received relatively short shrift within the new economic sociology of the late twentieth and early twenty-first century (Swedberg, this volume). Instead, much of this terrain has been implicitly ceded to political economists working in the newly-developed "varieties of capitalism" framework (see discussions in Brinton 2005, and Swedberg this volume). The geographical center of attention in this line of analysis has been Europe and the principal analytical focus has been the complementarity between a country's "production regime" and the system of social protection (e.g., employment, unemployment, and wage protection) offered by employers and the state (Hall and Soskice 2001; Hollingsworth and Boyer 1997).

The varieties of capitalism agenda is ambitious. But it leaves many areas of interest to economic sociologists wide open. As Swedberg's chapter notes, the way labor is organized in capitalist societies and the implications for social stratification patterns is a field to which economic sociologists should be able to make major contributions through their expertise in social network and institutional analysis. Likewise, Fligstein (2001) cites the comparative study of countries' "systems of employment relations"—labor market rules and practices and the educational institutions that feed into them—as central to economic sociology but as a relatively untouched field. As he notes, employment relations have a logic derived from the configuration of state, employer, and worker interests at the time of industrialization, a logic that is not set in stone but that nevertheless sets the

I would like to thank Victor Nee, Richard Swedberg, Wubiao Zhou, and Dong-Il Jung for their insightful comments on an earlier draft of this chapter. The research assistance and input of Zun Tang are gratefully acknowledged.

parameters for future change in labor market practices. The importance of such path dependence for institutional change is consistent with other work in the new institutional economic sociology (Nee 2003).

The present chapter takes as its point of departure the recognition that employment systems are embedded within the context of particular capitalist societies and, by the same token, that changes in these circumstances create pressures for institutional change. In keeping with this volume's emphasis on the impact of globalization on the institutions of capitalism, I ask how employment institutions are being affected in an economy that was one of the most productive and vibrant of the late twentieth century: Japan. The employment institutions I consider are among the most resilient and purportedly effective ones in the Japanese labor market, dealing with the recruitment and allocation of new graduates into the economy. The system of school-firm relations that orchestrates the training and recruitment of labor in Japan has been regarded as a hallmark of effective labor market policy by a number of Japanese as well as Western scholars in economics and sociology (Freeman and Katz 1994; Kariya 1998; Rosenbaum and Kariya 1989; Ryan 2001). In this chapter I focus less on the origins of the particular institutions governing school to work and more on the way these institutions operate and the pressures they currently experience in the wake of global pressures for Japanese industry to restructure and for Japanese firms to downsize.

The first section of this chapter puts the study of Japanese labor market institutions in the context of Japanese economic institutions writ large, suggesting that prior analyses have generally assumed a correlation between the particularities of these institutions and Japan's phenomenal economic growth throughout most of the post–World War II era. In the rest of the chapter I evaluate the performance of school-work institutions across changed economic circumstances.

Institutions and Markets in Japan

The institutions governing economic transactions in Japanese society have been of special interest to many sociologists, with the general perception being that they are quite different (perhaps qualitatively so) from those in other capitalist economies. Scholars both Japanese and foreign have frequently pointed out that economic life in Japan seems unusually governed by social relations and long-term implicit contracts.[1] The literatures on *keiretsu* (intercorporate groups), *shitauke* (subcontracting relationships between manufacturers and suppliers), and *shūshin koyō seido* (the so-called "permanent employment system") are cases in point (Cole 1979; Dore 1983, 1987; Fruin 1998; Gerlach 1992; Gerlach and Lincoln 1998; Lincoln 1990; Lincoln et al. 1996; Murakami and Rohlen 1992; Sako 1991, 1992).

Research on the social embeddedness of market exchange in Japan has generally focused on one of two theoretical questions: (1) the *historical origins* of the institutions that seem particularly distinctive in the Japanese economy, and (2) the *effect* of these institutions, especially their supposed contributions to economic efficiency, growth, and productivity, as well as to a relatively high level of economic equality among social groups.[2]

The literature on the first question—institutional origins—is very extensive, and includes comparative institutional analysis within East Asia and vis-à-vis Western capitalist economies (Fruin 1998b; Gerlach and Lincoln 1998; Hamilton 1998; Hamilton and Biggart 1988; Murakami and Rohlen 1992; Schwartz 1992). Meanwhile, decades of strong economic growth and relative income equality coupled with seemingly stable institutional arrangements in Japan have often seemed to make the answer to the second question—on institutional effects—self-evident.[3] For example, a scholar of subcontracting relationships in Japanese manufacturing wrote in the early 1990s, "It has become an accepted view that long-term continuous transactions which characterize such buyer-supplier relationships account for the international competitiveness of manufactured goods in Japan" (Sako 1991: 449). Similarly, a recent book on network organization in East Asia opened with the strong assertion, "Indeed, network forms of organization are part of the reason why Japan, South Korea, Taiwan, and other high-performing Asian economies have done so well in the past" (Fruin 1998a: v).

But times have changed. Japan scholars as well as those who track the global economy know the situation of Japan's economy well by now. Between 1955 and 1992, the Japanese economy and real GDP grew at a robust and consistent rate; the average growth rate from 1955 to the early 1970s was 10 percent per annum. The labor force also expanded at a relatively stable rate of 1 percent per year until 1992. But when the "bubble economy" of the late 1980s–early 1990s burst, the economy entered a period of crisis from which it has yet to emerge. In 1998 the Japanese economy recorded *negative* growth; the growth rate recovered only slightly in 1999, to ½ of one percent. The record has improved little since the beginning of the present century.

The advent of the deepest economic recession in Japan since World War II during the past decade is now forcing academics, social pundits, and policymakers to take a new look at the oft-assumed stability of Japanese institutions as well as the assumed correlation between those institutions and economic growth, efficiency, and equity. Granted, there have always been some naysayers, and there has often been considerable muddiness in the level of analysis at which analysts are dealing. If Japanese *keiretsu* are an efficient form of organization, are they efficient for individual member companies, for the *keiretsu* as a group, or for the economy as a whole? If, as one prominent Japanese economist (Aoki 2001) has claimed, there is an isomorphism between financial markets and labor markets, has Japan's supposedly distinctive main-bank financing system resulted in the most efficient management of human resources in the labor market and in firms, or instead, one that is inefficient (leading to lower productivity)? More baldly stated, is there *any* causal relationship between Japanese-style corporate governance—purportedly involving implicit long-term contracts among firms, between firms and their "main bank," and between employers and workers—and the positive economic outcomes of Japan in the three decades preceding the recession of the 1990s?[4]

In this chapter I join a growing number of Japanese and foreign scholars who argue that it is time we abandon the presumed ironclad causal relationship between Japanese institutional arrangements in the economy on the one hand and positive economic consequences on the other hand. Rather than asking, and indeed often *assuming*, how particular Japanese institutional arrangements have contributed to economic efficiency, growth, and equality, I propose instead that we use the natural experiment produced by the recent economic recession in order to evaluate institutional performance under radically changed conditions. In the process, I consider the social and economic pressures for institutional change that have accompanied the slowdown and reversal of Japanese economic growth over the past decade.

INSTITUTIONS IN THE JAPANESE LABOR MARKET

My analysis centers on a set of Japanese labor market institutions that reflect an unusual degree of government regulation and encouragement of implicit contracting. The institutions governing the youth labor market, especially the transition of high school graduates into work, have been especially strong, especially "unique" compared to other capitalist industrial societies, and, many have argued, especially effective (Kariya 1998; Lynch 1994; National Research Council 1994; Okano 1993; Rosenbaum and Kariya 1989; Rosenbaum et al. 1990; Ryan 2001).

I begin by outlining the nature of the institutional arrangements governing the transition from school to work for Japan's youth, and discuss claims made in the late 1980s and 1990s for the efficiency and fairness of school-employer networks in allocating jobs to new high school graduates in the second half of the twentieth century. I then turn to the aggregate economic outcomes—the levels of youth unemployment and job turnover—that have been used as evidence that the system works well. I argue that Japan does not look nearly as good on these indicators in a comparative context as many have assumed. More importantly, I suggest that only one of these two measures—turnover rates—is substantively related to the job-matching mechanisms inherent in Japan's school-work system. A third measure—the rate of youth idleness (defined as the proportion of young people who are neither employed nor enrolled in school) captures the inability of either schools or the labor market to engage youth. I demonstrate that not only has this measure been ignored by foreign admirers of the Japanese high school-work system, but it has been underestimated by the Japanese government.

I look more closely at the issue of idleness by drawing on data from my current empirical research on urban Japanese labor markets. Calculations from school-level data produce high rates of idleness for youth currently graduating from public high schools, particularly those in the lower tier of the highly delineated school hierarchy. I suggest that high idleness rates were not evident during Japan's high-growth period of the 1970s and 1980s, *not necessarily because of Japanese institutional arrangements but because economic growth and labor demand were so high.* The concurrence of these two phenomena in the earlier period—persistently high labor demand for high school graduates, and a set of institutional arrangements that match youth to jobs—perhaps made it natural for observers to claim a major role for Japanese labor market institutions and to downplay the role of the economy in facilitating a smoothly functioning youth labor market. But Japan's recent economic woes make it possible to see how its labor market institutions fare under radically altered circumstances. These include economic circumstances that more closely resemble those endured by other OECD countries one decade earlier as well as cultural changes that reflect the increasing absorption of global youth lifestyle ideals into Japanese society.[5]

THE YOUTH LABOR MARKET IN COMPARATIVE PERSPECTIVE

The youth labor market is a particularly appropriate site for the study of how labor market institutions differ across capitalist economies. The transition from school to work is an area of great concern for labor economists and sociologists interested in the large wage gap between high school and college graduates and the high rates of unemployment and idleness among less-educated youth; both are problems that have increasingly afflicted postindustrial economies (Neumark 1998; Ryan 2001). Youth labor markets in industrial and postindustrial societies were arguably in disarray at the start of the twenty-first century. In most member countries of the OECD (Organization for Economic Cooperation and Development), the employment and earnings prospects for young workers were considerably worse than they had been two decades earlier. For example, the average unemployment rate for the male population aged fifteen to nineteen in OECD countries rose from just under 14 percent in 1979 to nearly 19 percent in 1997, and was over 30 percent in a number of countries.

Some commentators, and reports by the OECD as well, have consistently suggested that social institutions can play a significant role in dampening youth unemployment. Notably, countries with institutionalized school-work programs had some of the lowest unemployment rates for new school-leavers in the late 1990s (OECD 1998; Ryan 2001). These included countries with apprenticeship or "modified apprenticeship" systems (identified by the OECD as Austria, Denmark, Germany, Luxembourg, and Switzerland) and one country with a strikingly different school-work system, Japan.

School-Work in Japan: Comparisons with Other Systems. The high school-work transition system in Japan is one of the most coordinated and highly structured set of labor market institutions in any highly industrialized country. While scholars of Japan have often labeled as "unique" various institutional arrangements that comparativists find ready analogies to in other countries, this is not the case for the high school-work system in Japan; it is indeed unusual in comparative perspective. Its principal uniqueness stems from the fact that it does not encompass a vocational training component but rather, it is at root a system of screening and matching prospective graduates to firms seeking young, full-time workers. Apprenticeship systems such as the German one prepare students for particular occupations (Kerckhoff 2000; Mortimer and Krüger 2000). In Germany, Austria, and Switzerland, training is jointly organized by schools, firms, and employer organizations, and is clearly geared toward the provision of occupationally oriented skills (Allmendinger 1989; Maurice et al. 1986; Shavit and Müller 2000). The Japanese system has no apprenticeships, and a large proportion of high school graduates who enter the labor market do so from general academic high schools rather than vocational ones (typically industrial or commercial). Currently, just under 20 percent of all high school students intend in their senior year of schooling to enter the labor market in a full-time capacity when they graduate. Secondary schooling is principally geared toward the acquisition of general human capital rather than human capital geared to a particular occupation, although vocational high schools do impart skills that equip graduates to work in particular industries.

If Japanese high schools are not connected to employers through the conceptual link of the occupation, then what is the content of their connection? The recruitment linkages between Japanese schools and firms purportedly are an example of the "relational contracting" typical in Japanese businesses, where partners engage in repeated exchanges over an extended period of time. As outlined above, throughout the extended period of high economic growth in Japan, such relational contracting was heralded as contributing to the smooth functioning of the economy (Dore

1987). In a similar vein, the high level of involvement by Japanese high schools in the labor market placement of their graduates has been cited as a highly effective way to organize the youth labor market (Rosenbaum and Kariya 1989; Rosenbaum et al. 1990; Hansen 1994; Lynch 1994).

To recruit new high school graduates, Japanese employers are legally required to provide a detailed description of their job openings (*kyujinhyô*) to the local public employment security office.[6] The average jurisdiction of such offices is about 800 square kilometers; Japan has a total of 480 such local offices spread throughout the country (OECD 1996).[7] Job listing forms are standardized nationally and can be submitted by employers any time after June 20 each year for openings available to students graduating and entering the labor market the following spring. The Japanese school year typically ends in early February, and new graduates begin employment in April.

The local public employment security office must approve the job description and working conditions listed on each employment form. Employers are then permitted from early in the school year to personally deliver or send the notices of job openings to high schools from which they are interested in recruiting graduating seniors. Teachers in the career guidance section of each school counsel workbound students as to the appropriateness of the specific companies and the jobs they are offering to potential applicants from the school. Students are not permitted to contact employers or apply directly for jobs; rather, they must receive their school's recommendation before being invited for an interview by the employer (Okano 1993; U.S. Department of Education 1996). The selection of students for jobs is based on the student's own preference, parents' preferences, and the homeroom teacher's and guidance section's knowledge and opinion of the student. Most schools traditionally have selected only one student to recommend for a given job in order to forestall direct competition between multiple students for the most desirable jobs. Competition occurs between students from different schools only if the employer has submitted copies of the job opening notice to multiple schools. The school recommendations are forwarded to firms beginning in early September, at which point the interviewing and selection process begins. Informal employment commitments (*naitei*) can legally be announced only after October 1; they more or less guarantee employment as of the following April, the traditional starting date for new employees in Japanese companies.[8]

To an outside observer it may seem puzzling how employers select schools from which to attempt labor recruitment. But unlike students in American public schools, students in Japan are extensively sorted through ability-testing at the point of high school entrance (LeTendre 1996; Rohlen 1983). In this sense the Japanese educational system bears more similarity to the systems in a number of European countries than to the U.S. system. Student ability at individual high schools is considerably more homogeneous than is the case in the United States. Compulsory education in Japan ends with junior high school, and admission to public high school is governed largely by one's score on the prefectural standardized entrance examination and, to a lesser extent, by junior high school grades. As I will show shortly, within each school district there is a finely graded hierarchy of public, general academic high schools and vocational high schools.[9]

Assessments of the Japanese school-work system in the English-language literature in the social sciences are almost uniformly positive, stressing the effectiveness of long-term implicit recruitment contracts (*jisseki kankei*) between high schools and employers. Rosenbaum and Kariya, the most widely cited and positive of the advocates, claim that the reliance of employers on particular schools continues unabated through economic downturns because firms prefer stable and reliable sources of labor rather than shopping around for workers. Rosenbaum and Kariya suggest that employers' attempts to minimize transaction costs lead them to "try to maintain their hiring relationships with contract schools [schools with whom they have implicit contracts] *even if they do not need new workers.* Although they may try to reduce the numbers they recruit from contract schools, they try to maintain their contracts by hiring some graduates from these schools" (1989: 1346; italics mine). Further, Rosenbaum and Kariya laud the meritocratic nature of the system, arguing that teachers allocate the most high-performing students into the most desirable jobs. I consider the structure of competition and the degree of meritocracy more closely elsewhere (Brinton and Tang 2005). In the following, I examine the performance of the system based on the aggregate economic indicators Rosenbaum and Kariya and other observers have used.

THE HIGH SCHOOL–WORK SYSTEM IN JAPAN:
    INDICATORS OF PERFORMANCE

Discussions of school-work systems in the social science literature often are placed in the context of two aggregate economic outcomes: youth unemployment rates and turnover rates. For better or worse, research referring to the Japanese system is quite consistent with this emphasis; Rosenbaum and Kariya (1989) point to Japan's good showing on both of these measures relative to the United States. They cite statistics demonstrating that Japan had a lower youth unemployment rate relative to adult unemployment than the U.S. in the 1980s, and the same for youth turnover rates in the 1960s. While they comment on the difficulties of controlling for differences in the economic environments of the two countries during these periods, they nevertheless come out strongly supporting Japan's institutional mechanisms vs. the more open, spot-market situation faced by young workers in the United States. Yet leaving the macroeconomic context out of the discussion of comparative youth unemployment rates is clearly problematic, as I detail below.

Youth Unemployment. Employment growth in Japan in the 1960s, 1970s, and 1980s lay between the very strong growth in North America and the weaker growth in the nations of the European community. But job growth in Japan during those three decades was in sectors that traditionally have welcomed high school graduates, whereas this was not true in the U.S. Japan was one of only two OECD countries (the other being Greece) that experienced growth in manufacturing jobs in the 1980s. As is well known, the U.S. experienced a large loss in this sector. Japan also experienced greater growth than the U.S. in those parts of the service sector for which a high school education was sufficient, whereas service sector growth in the U.S. was much stronger in the areas of finance, insurance, real estate, and business services, where a university credential is typically required (OECD 1994).

Given such an economic context, if one wished to use the youth unemployment rate as a rough indicator of the performance of a school-work system, Japan had every reason to look good relative to the U.S. and most other industrial economies in the late 1980s to the mid-1990s *with or without a system of institutionalized job matching.* Was this borne out?

Figure 1 shows the youth unemployment rate in Japan in 1990 compared to that in other industrialized countries. This figure shows the unemployment rate for males age fifteen through nineteen in 29 OECD countries, with countries coded "1" if they have an institutionalized school-work system and "0" otherwise.[10] As indicated, Japan had a low male youth unemployment rate relative to countries without an institutionalized school-work system. But it did not have the lowest rate, even during the "bubble economy" and the high labor demand conditions of the late 1980s to early 1990s. Figure 2 shows the ratio of youth unemployment to adult unemployment in 1990; notably, Japan had the *highest* figure among the group of countries with institutionalized school-work systems, and one of the highest figures among all industrialized nations.

Given that Japan's school-work system does not involve job creation, I would argue that the level of youth unemployment (either absolute or relative to adult unemployment) is not a very appropriate indicator of the system's effectiveness in any case. The prevalence of internal labor markets in large Japanese firms and the emphasis on external hiring at the entry level mean that young people are disproportionately affected by economic

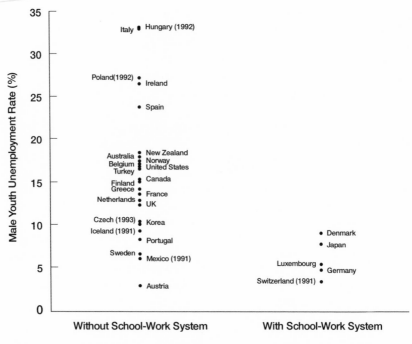

Figure 1 Unemployment rate for males age 15–19 (1990). Switzerland data are for males age 15–24. (*source*: OECD Labor Force Statistics 1982–2002).

stagnation; it is *their* jobs that are cut. Despite the absence of written contracts between large Japanese employers and their "core" male workers, employers exerted considerable efforts in the 1990s (as in prior, less severe economic slowdowns) to avoid laying off mid-career full-time male employees. The implications of this implicit job protection are particularly severe for female workers of all ages (the vast majority of whom are not promised implicit permanent employment) and entry-level workers, both male and female.

Appropriateness of Job Matches. A more appropriate measure of a school-work system like Japan's that consists primarily of a set of job-matching mechanisms is the turnover rate. Comparative Japan-U.S. statistics cited by Rosenbaum and Kariya for the 1960s indicate that youth job turnover rates were lower in Japan, both in absolute terms and as a ratio of total turnover across age groups. However, Japanese Labor Ministry estimates, based on employment insurance data, consistently indicate that about 50 percent of new high school graduates separate from their jobs within the first 3 years of employment (Ministry of Labor, November 1999).[11] This is hardly a low level of labor market "churning." Labor

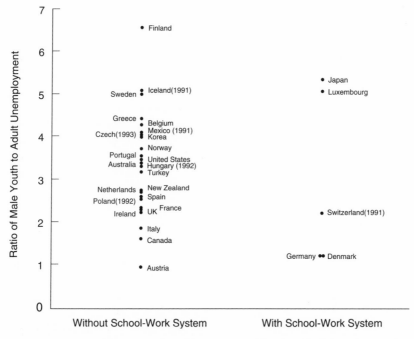

Figure 2 Ratio of male youth (15–19) to adult (25–54) unemployment (1990) (*source*: OECD Labor Force Statistics 1982–2002).

economists stress that voluntary turnover may be regarded in either a negative or a positive light. On the negative side, it represents labor market friction. But on the positive side, it may result in better job matches. Whichever viewpoint one adopts, it is certainly not the case that the Japanese high school-work system can boast placing the majority of graduates into anything resembling "permanent employment" or a situation involving a long-term implicit contract that both the employer and the worker consider satisfactory. This is reinforced in a recent comprehensive article on school-work systems. In his otherwise positive review of the Japanese system, Ryan argues that "The comparative evidence is however less than conclusive about the merits of school-to-work institutions. Although the Japanese system has been praised for reducing the need for job search by young workers, its qualitative efficiency is questionable" (2001: 60). Ryan goes on to point out that over 80 percent of unemployed workers aged fifteen to twenty-four in Japan in 1998 who had previously been employed had quit their last job (citing Mitani 1999). As he eloquently puts it, "At its worst, it [the Japanese school-work system] simply bangs square pegs into round holes. Japan's need for more search and matching in the youth market appears to be making its mark, as youth turnover rises" (2001: 61).

In sum, long-term implicit contracts between Japanese high schools and local employers have been claimed to effect both *more* and *better* job matches than would occur under conventional market mechanisms (Rosenbaum and Kariya 1989; Rosenbaum et al. 1990). But the youth unemployment rate is but a crude measure of the effectiveness of school-work institutions such as Japan's that do not involve job creation; moreover, Japan does not appear to be exceptional in terms of low youth unemployment. The job turnover rate for young workers, arguably a better indicator of the effectiveness of the school-work system, does not paint an unequivocally good picture of Japan either. How well, then, do the educational system and the labor market perform in terms of keeping Japanese youth from idleness?

POSTINDUSTRIAL DIFFICULTIES

Japan's worsening economic environment during the last decade of the twentieth century had three fundamental impacts on youth employment: employers became less likely to offer long-term employment guarantees to young full-time workers, especially the less-skilled; the skill mix of available jobs underwent modification, with those jobs that were traditionally occupied by high school graduates suffering a severe numerical decline; and the proportion of all employees who were part-time showed a significant increase.

Job Openings.   The ratio of job applicants to job openings for Japanese high school graduates entering the labor market has fallen dramatically during the past decade. As a result, in September 2001 the *naiteiritsu* (rate of promised employment) to high school seniors due to graduate in spring 2002 was only 37 percent, 5.5 percentage points lower than the previous year. By November, by which time the majority of companies have traditionally completed their hiring decisions for the following spring, the rate had risen to 63.4 percent. But this was still the lowest rate of promised employment since 1987, when the government first collected such data (Japan Institute of Labor 2002a). The *naitei* rates were lower than the prior year for every region of the country, and in some regions had dropped by more than 20 percent in just one year (Japan Institute of Labor 2002b). Particularly hard hit were regions of the country that had previously been able to attract manufacturing industries to local areas. This reflected in part the accelerated rate of manufacturing plants' relocation to China, where hourly wages are as low as one-twentieth the rate for Japanese workers. The rate of youth unemployment reflects the dramatic decline in job openings. Figure 3 shows unemployment figures by sex and

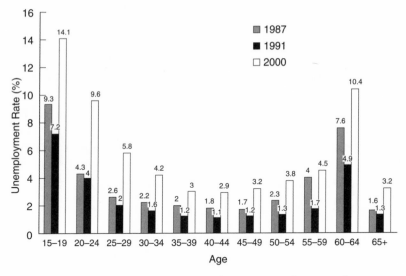

Figure 3 Changes in the Japanese unemployment rate, by sex and age group (*source*: Japan Institute of Labor, *Monthly Labor Bulletin*, 2001).

age group since the late 1980s. The figure for males age fifteen to nineteen had risen to 14 percent by 2000, and the rate for this age group continued to remain high throughout 2001.[12]

Changes in Skill Mix. In tandem with the economic recession of the past decade, important structural changes in the Japanese economy have radically altered the mix of jobs available to high school students—both full-time post-graduation jobs and part-time jobs while they are still in school. With the shift to a postindustrial economy, the old "good" jobs such as those in large automobile firms and other manufacturing firms are many fewer than in previous years. Figure 4 shows yearly changes in the numbers of Japanese employed in each of the major industries. Only the highly heterogeneous service industry has shown any substantial net increase in employment levels over the past decade. Manufacturing and construction, the two industries that traditionally have been the most likely to hire high school graduates, suffered major employment losses over the past decade.

Increase in Part-Time Employment. As the stock of industrial jobs traditionally earmarked for high school graduates has dwindled, a variety of low-paying, part-time jobs in the service sector have been created. Prior to 1997, part-time and "nonregular" workers (the latter a euphemism for workers without implicitly guaranteed lifetime employment) had been the

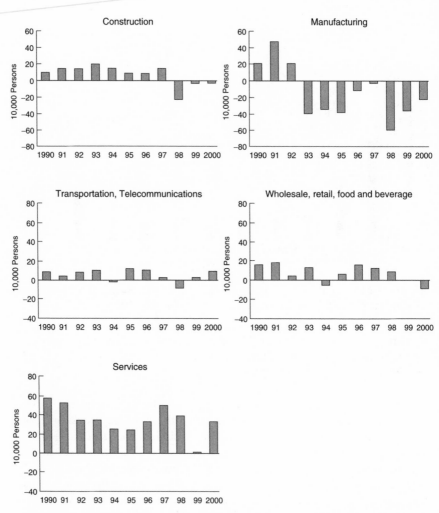

Figure 4 Yearly increases and decreases in Japanese employment, by industry (*source: Report on the Labor Force Survey,* Management and Coordination Agency of Japan, 2000).

first to be cut during recessions. But between 1997 and 2001, the number of "regular" employees declined by 1.71 million and the number of "non-regular" workers, including temporary and part-time workers, increased by 2.06 million. While the trend toward part-time or temporary work was particularly marked among female workers, it was by no means restricted to them. As one commentator noted, "The implication of such analyses is that part-time and other nonregular employees are not being used to adjust employment levels nor as a buffer, but as substitutes for regular employees;

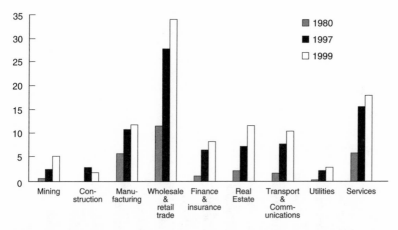

Figure 5 Change in percentage of all employees that are part-time, by industry (1980–1999) (*source*: Management and Coordination Agency of Japan, 2000).

that is, enterprises are beginning to replace the former kind of workers with the latter" (Wakisaka 2002).

Figure 5 documents the rapid growth in the share of all employees who are part-time, by industry, since 1980. Particularly notable is the increase in the service sector and, even more so, the wholesale and retail trade sector. While this part-time employment is comprised of both married women and young single men and women, the willingness of small retail outlets in urban Japanese centers to hire high school students on a part-time basis *while they are still in school* is readily apparent to any observer. Large numbers of high school students engage in *arubeito* (the Japanese term for a part-time job for students, coined from the German word *arbeiter*). High school teachers I interviewed in the mid-1990s at low-level public general high schools in Yokohama-Kawasaki shrugged their shoulders when I asked about school policies prohibiting *arubeito*, commenting that their school had either given up the policy altogether or still had the policy but found it to be unenforceable. Students desiring to have spending money could quite easily find jobs as gasoline station attendants, dishwashers, cash register clerks at convenience stores, or in the illicit economy (for young women, prostitution and its variants). While job benefits are nonexistent in part-time, temporary positions in the service sector, the hourly wage is large enough to be appealing to high school students living with their parents and desiring spending money for the luxuries of adolescence (which in Japan, as elsewhere in the postindustrial world at the beginning of the twenty-first century, included cell phones, baggy jeans, cigarettes, and the newest CDs).

But amidst the worried pronouncements of the Japanese government concerning the dismal employment situation of the early twenty-first century,

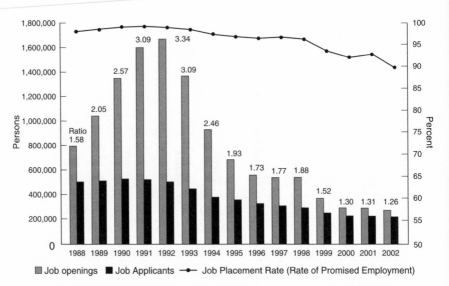

Figure 6 Job opening–applicant ratio and job placement rate for new high school graduates in Japan, 1988–2002 (*source*: Kanagawa-ken Public Employment Security Office, 2002).

a surprising number of young people remain missing from official statistics. Figure 6 shows data I obtained in June 2002 from officials at the *shokugyô anteijo* (public employment security office) for Kawasaki, one of the major cities in Kanagawa prefecture. The *kyujin bairitsu*, or ratio of job openings to applicants, for high school graduates soared as high as 3.34 in 1992, then plummeted to its current level of 1.26. The graph also shows the job placement rate for graduating high school seniors throughout Japan in March (just prior to employment commencement on April 1), across the years 1988–2002. As indicated, during the "bubble years" of the early 1990s, the placement rate was over 99 percent. Even in the dire current economic environment, the government reports that 89.7 percent of all high school graduates who sought jobs obtained a commitment from an employer by the end of their senior year. This economic outcome seems oddly rosy compared with the unemployment and turnover rates cited earlier in this paper. Why is this the case?

Uncertain Destinations: The Hidden Rate of Idleness. I argue that when we look beyond unemployment statistics and consider the proportion of Japanese graduating high school seniors who have made no concrete employment or enrollment plans, nor plan to spend the ensuing year as *rônin*, the picture is sobering. (In Japan's case the state of being a *rônin*, defined as sitting out of school for a full year or more to prepare for the following year's university entrance exams, is an additional category of post-graduation activity.) Youth who do not fall into any of these groups fall into the category of having an "uncertain" destination. It is worth re-iterating that in Japan it is standard for students to graduate and begin work at only one time point during the year, unlike in the U.S. Therefore, if one does not secure a commitment from an employer for a full-time job that will start immediately after graduation, one is likely to encounter es-pecially severe difficulty securing full-time work. This adds increased sig-nificance to the state of being "idle" in the Japanese economy.

The idle population does not appear in unemployment or job turnover statistics and has not been systematically studied by the advocates of Japan's institutionalized job-matching mechanisms. Indeed, the impres-sion one gets from the English-language literature on the Japanese school-work system is that virtually all graduating seniors who desire jobs are matched with employers. Research reports that are otherwise highly so-phisticated cite without question Japanese Ministry of Labor statistics such as those in Figure 6 indicating that, even in the depths of the recent eco-nomic downturn, 90 percent of workbound high school seniors had se-cured a job at the time of graduation (Ryan 2001). Similarly, I found that Japanese high schools typically reported in the mid-1990s either very high or perfect placement rates for graduating workbound seniors by the end of the school year. This perfection struck me as an impossibility for even the most effective school-work system, and it was something I inquired about in long, semi-structured interviews I conducted with teachers at public high schools in the Yokohama-Kawasaki area southwest of Tokyo in the mid-1990s. The next section reports those findings.

EVIDENCE FROM AN URBAN JAPANESE LABOR MARKET

Data from an urban Japanese labor market in the mid-1990s demonstrate graphically the problems in the youth labor market that began to appear early in the Japanese economic recession, problems that were not pre-dicted by Western advocates of Japan's unique school-work institutions.

The research site from which I draw data is the densely urban Yokohama-Kawasaki area of Kanagawa prefecture, directly southwest of Tokyo and contiguous to it. I chose this area as a research site in the mid-1990s because of its comparability with major metropolitan areas in the American Midwest and Northeast in terms of industrial composition. Kanagawa prefecture has been a typical manufacturing region in Japan, producing in the past decades a large quantity of durable goods such as electrical machinery, transportation-related machinery, and general ma-chinery. Yokohama and Kawasaki, the two largest cities in the prefecture, are connected to Tokyo by a dense network of public and private railway and subway lines. The prefecture had 243 public high schools in the mid-1990s, academic and vocational, distributed across 14 school districts. About 50 percent of graduating high school seniors in Kanagawa prefecture proceed directly to university, a rate that is comparable to other prefectures in Japan with major cities.

Estimating the "True" Rates of Idleness. In the interviews I conducted in 1996 at 16 public high schools sampled from three school districts in the Yokohama-Kawasaki area, teachers were helpful in demystifying the oddly perfect job placement rates I had encountered in published statistics. They frankly informed me that high school seniors who become discouraged in their job search are often taken out of the denominator when school-level statistics are calculated. Why? As the senior year wears on, if a student has been recommended by the school for a job but has failed the interview with the employer, teachers in the school's placement office must start over again and locate another suitable job opening for him or her. But once again the student may fail the interview. With several of these failures in hand, some students will ultimately give up and drop out of the discouraging placement process altogether. They may decide instead to go to *senmon gakkō.* This is the most likely educational alternative, as many *senmon gakkō* have low entrance requirements (sometimes matched unfortunately by very high tuition fees). In such cases, students are put into the tabulation of matriculants to *senmon gakkō.* If they drop out of the placement process orchestrated by schools and firms and do not decide to go on for further education, their post-graduation destination is listed as being "unknown." (Yet another alternative for some students is to find a job through a relative; in these cases, they are included in the workbound tabulation.) If all of the "non-successes" are artificially subtracted from the denominator of the job placement rate, the obvious result is a 100 percent success rate.

Pursuing this line further, I realized that it is possible to examine the proportion of graduating high school seniors in the category of "uncertain" destinations. I use school-level data from all school districts in Kanagawa prefecture. Data are drawn from the *Kanagawa-ken Jūken Annai,* a yearly publication from a private publishing company that gives school-level data on the outcomes for graduating seniors from each high school in Kanagawa prefecture. I use data from the 1998 publication, reflecting the destinations of the 1997 graduating class. This publication groups graduating seniors in each high school into the following categories: entrants to 4-year universities, entrants to 2-year junior colleges, entrants to 2-year training schools (*senmon gakkō*), job market entrants, and a residual "uncertain" category. The latter category is highly heterogeneous across school ranks, as it includes *rônin* and students who are neither continuing on directly to higher education nor have been hired by an employer to begin a post-graduation job. This latter group includes students for whom the highly structured school-work system has failed, for they were not placed into either a job or a higher educational institution by the time of graduation.

Data for the nearly 250 public high schools in Kanagawa prefecture indicate that 23 percent of graduating seniors go directly on to university, 34 percent go either to junior college or to 2-year training schools, 18 percent go into the labor market (having secured jobs), and 25 percent have "uncertain destinations." As pointed out above, this last category includes both those who will eventually go to university and those who are truly "idle," with no definitive employment or educational plan. In order to estimate the "true" percent going to university and the "true" percent idle, I performed the following calculations:

True university = university + [university / (100 − uncertain)] * uncertain   (1)
True uncertain = uncertain − [university / (100 − uncertain)] * uncertain   (2)

where "university" is the reported (observed) percent directly entering university and "uncertain" represents the reported percent uncertain in the data set. These calculations result in an upward revision of the percent going to university, as *rônin* are now incorporated into that figure; likewise, the percent uncertain declines but now more accurately reflects the "true" percent idle.

Based on this estimation procedure, the mean "true" percent idle per school is over 16 percent; the figure varies between 10 and 48 percent across the 14 school districts of Kanagawa prefecture. Fully half the districts have true idleness rates for new high school graduates of 19 percent or higher. As we might expect, the true rates of idleness are significantly higher for the lowest-ranked high schools. The thumbnail way to measure a high school's quality in Japan is by its *hensachi* (exam cutpoint), the minimum score on the prefectural high school entrance exam that a student needed in order to enter that school the prior year. The Pearson correlation coefficient between exam cutpoint and true percent idle across the schools in Kanagawa prefecture is a whopping $-.83$ ($p<.001$), indicating that a higher proportion of students from lower-ranked schools are indeed "floating" or idle. The graduating class of one school in Kanagawa prefecture had an astounding 48 percent idle; in the Kawasaki school district that I have studied the most intensively, two of the twelve schools had rates above 30 percent.

Consistent with these troubling statistics, the Japan Institute of Labor began to pay increasing attention to "freeters" (a combination of the English word "free" and the German word "arbeiter," or part-time worker) by the late 1990s, making frequent reference to the increasing numbers of young people who were in neither full-time education or employment. Government concern over the apparent ineffectiveness of high school–work institutions has continued to grow, and in 2001 the Ministry of Health, Labor, and Welfare and the Ministry of Education, Culture, Sports, Science and Technology set up a joint study group to consider how the system might be modified to be less rigid. Their report, issued in March 2002, recommended that schools relax the provision that a student be recommended for one and only one job at a time. This represented an attempt to reduce the tendency of students to become discouraged in their job search after sequential failures at job interviews. Instead, the report suggested that students either be allowed to apply for more than one job at a time or be restricted to applying to one employer until October 1, then be allowed to apply to more than one employer at one time if they were not accepted on their first try. By the end of 2002, twelve prefectures had changed the *hitori isshasei* (policy of one company per applicant) and adopted the recommended policy that allowed students to apply to more than one company at a time. Such changes are indicative of the growing recognition that the system is no longer working as smoothly as it once did.

CONCLUSION

Japan's institutionalized mechanisms of matching high school graduates to jobs may have functioned quite well under the favorable economic conditions that lasted into the early 1990s, marked by continued economic expansion coupled with growth in the manufacturing sector. But I have argued in this chapter that omitting these aspects of the economic environment from the analysis of the system's performance led to an overemphasis on Japan's unique institutional structure and the advantages of the embeddedness of labor recruitment in long-term ties between schools and firms. Simply put, it is difficult to measure the effectiveness of labor market practices under economic conditions that keep labor demand high. In the context of low or even negative economic growth, a different mix of jobs in the economy (fewer manufacturing jobs and a bifurcation of the service sector into low-skill and high-skill jobs) and changes in employers' preferences for hiring long-term workers, the system appears in a different light. As I have shown from disaggregated school-level data, rates of idleness among Japanese high school graduates are high and are disproportionately concentrated among schools at the lower end of the academic spectrum, where rates of higher education attendance are low and rates of labor market entrance have traditionally been high. Unemployment statistics do not completely reflect this, as young people who find part-time or temporary jobs do not appear in these statistics, nor do those who become so disenchanted with the job search process orchestrated by their high schools that they become "discouraged workers."

This research raises critical questions about the efficacy of a set of institutional arrangements in the Japanese labor market that have been in place since shortly after the creation of the Labor Ministry, a half-century ago. More broadly, this case from Japan illustrates how crucial it is for social scientists to place their analysis of particular institutions—and especially their analysis of the *outcomes* or *effects* of those institutions—in the context of economic conditions and the broad institutional landscape. I have argued that in the analysis of institutions governing how new graduates move into the labor market, youth unemployment may not be an appropriate measure of institutional effectiveness; youth turnover in jobs may be a better measure, and rates of idleness (lack of attachment to either school or work) may be even better. Once economic sociologists better specify the outcomes that can be produced by the institutions they are studying, they are in a better position to theorize how these outcomes and ultimately the institutions themselves may change under new economic circumstances. Speaking to fellow economists, the labor economist Richard Freeman has made the point that "Analyses that examine how particular institutions work invariably consider those institutions in isolation, rather than as part of broader labor relations and economic systems" (Freeman 1994: 233). Economic sociologists have a comparative advantage in this respect, especially given that like other sociologists, they are often driven as much or more by deep knowledge of the phenomena and contexts they are studying as by abstract theory.

The last decade of the twentieth century sadly reminded us that Japanese social and economic institutions, from *keiretsu* to permanent employment to school-work institutions, operated in the enviable environment of high economic growth rates for nearly three decades and did not face the challenge of low or negative growth rates until the past few years. The "natural experiment" for the performance of these institutions is now truly underway and presents an excellent opportunity for research by economic sociologists.

NOTES

1. Gerlach, for example, describes as follows the relationship between financial institutions and large industrial firms in Japan: "Unlike the relatively fragmented, loosely organized ties typically discerned in the American corporate network, the reality in Japan appears far closer to one of coherent and enduring cliques among affiliated financial institutions and industrial firms" (1992: 135).

2. I use the standard economic definition of institutions, which includes the formal rules and informal constraints that structure interaction by defining the choice set and the incentives for actors (North 1991).

3. As Hein writes, "Finding the 'secrets' of Japanese economic success has driven nearly all work done on the economy since the 1960s" (1993: 99). This focus "has obscured all those aspects of Japanese economic history that have not directly contributed to Japanese success" (1993: 99–100).

4. Ramseyer and Miwa (2002a) pose an even starker question: whether implicit contracts exist at all in the Japanese economy. In a related paper, they make the similarly provocative argument that Japanese *keiretsu* "neither shape the Japanese economy nor illustrate anything about relational contracting or social embeddedness" (2002b: 170).

5. In related work I devote more attention to changes in Japanese youth culture that are at least partially traceable to globalization and that are leading to a rejection of traditional patterns of full-time employment (Brinton 2005; Tang and Brinton 2005).

6. The original legal framework, developed shortly after WWII, also applied to junior high school graduates. But given that Japan has achieved near-universal rates of advancement to high school, the legal guidelines are mainly relevant for workbound high school seniors.

7. In Kanagawa, the main prefecture I have studied, there are 15 of these offices.

8. Data from a cross-national survey conducted by the Japan Institute of Labor in 1989 throw into sharp relief the differences in the amount of help American and Japanese high schools provide to graduating seniors entering the job market. Nearly two-thirds of Japanese workbound high school seniors reported that they relied on their school to help them find their first full-time post-graduation job, compared to about one-seventh of American students. The latter were much more likely to report relying on friends and acquaintances and reading job advertisements. Moreover, Japanese high school students' job search was much more focused than Americans'. Over three-quarters of Japanese students said that they searched for jobs in only one field or industry, compared to just a third of American students who reported this. In short, Japanese high school students' job search is focused on specific fields and is carried out mainly with the assistance of their school. The job search process in the United States, as well-documented in many studies, is heavily reliant on whom one knows.

9. There are also private academic high schools and public vocational high schools. Consideration for admission to these is not governed by residence in the local school district as is the case for the public, general academic high schools.

10. I used OECD discussions of school-work transition systems as a basis for the categorization of countries. As mentioned earlier, those with apprenticeship or "semi-apprenticeship" systems are Austria, Denmark, Germany, Luxembourg, and Switzerland.

11. The Ministry of Health and Welfare and the Ministry of Labor merged in 2001. Since many of the statistics cited in this chapter come from pre-2001 Ministry of Labor publications, for consistency I simply refer to the Ministry of Labor throughout.

12. Comparing Japan to the U.S in the late 1980s, the youth unemployment rate had changed in opposite directions, reflecting economic growth rates that had

changed sharply in the two countries. Unemployment for high school graduates in the U.S. had fallen to 9.6 percent in 1995 and has since dropped lower (OECD 1998). It is not that the school-work system (or lack thereof) had changed in either country during the mid- to late 1990s; the economy had.

REFERENCES

Allmendinger, Jutta. 1989. "Educational Systems and Labor Market Outcomes." *European Sociological Review* 5: 231–50.
Aoki, Masahiko. 2001. *Toward a Comparative Institutional Analysis.* Cambridge, Mass.: MIT Press.
Brinton, Mary C. *Out of School, Out of Work: Youth and Jobs in Postindustrial Japan.* Book manuscript.
———. 2005. "Education and the Economy." In *The Handbook of Economic Sociology,* ed. Neil J. Smelser and Richard Swedberg. 2nd ed. Princeton: Princeton University Press.
Brinton, Mary C. and Zun Tang. 2005. "Networks of Competition: Hidden Stratification in the Japanese Youth Labor Market." Working Paper, Department of Sociology, Harvard University.
Cole, Robert E. 1979. *Work, Mobility, and Participation: A Comparative Study of American and Japanese Industry.* Berkeley: University of California Press.
Dore, Ronald P. 1983. "Goodwill and the Spirit of Market Capitalism." *British Journal of Sociology* 34: 459–82.
———. 1987. *Taking Japan Seriously: A Confucian Perspective on Leading Economic Issues.* Stanford: Stanford University Press.
Fligstein, Neil. 2001. *The Architecture of Markets: An Economic Sociology of Twenty-First-Century Capitalist Societies.* Princeton: Princeton University Press.
Freeman, Richard B. 1994. "Lessons for the United States." In *Working under Different Rules,* ed. Richard B. Freeman. New York: Russell Sage. 223–39.
Freeman, Richard B. and Lawrence F. Katz. 1994. "Rising Wage Inequality: The United States versus Other Advanced Countries." In *Working under Different Rules,* ed. Richard B. Freeman. New York: Russell Sage. 29–62.
Fruin, W. Mark. 1992. *The Japanese Enterprise System: Competitive Strategies and Cooperative Structures.* Oxford: Oxford University Press.
———. 1998a. Preface. In *Networks, Markets, and the Pacific Rim: Studies in Strategy,* ed. W. Mark Fruin. New York: Oxford University Press. v–vi.
———. 1998b. "Analyzing Pacific Rim Networks and Markets: An Introduction." In *Networks, Markets, and the Pacific Rim: Studies in Strategy,* ed. W. Mark Fruin. New York: Oxford University Press. 3–31.
———. 1998c. "Governance, Managed Competition, and Network Organization at a Toshiba Factory." In *Networks, Markets, and the Pacific Rim: Studies in Strategy,* ed. W. Mark Fruin. New York: Oxford University Press. 255–72.
Gerlach, Michael L. 1992. "The Japanese Corporate Network: A Blockmodel Analysis." *Administrative Science Quarterly* 37: 106–39.
Hall, Peter A. and David Soskice, eds. 2001. *Varieties of Capitalism: The Institutional Foundations of Comparative Advantage.* Oxford: Oxford University Press.

Hamilton, Gary G. 1998. "Patterns of Asian Network Capitalism: The Cases of Taiwan and South Korea." In *Networks, Markets, and the Pacific Rim: Studies in Strategy*, ed. W. Mark Fruin. New York: Oxford University Press. 181–99.

Hamilton, Gary G. and Nicole Woolsey Biggart. 1988. "Market, Culture, and Authority: A Comparative Analysis of Management and Organization in the Far East." *American Journal of Sociology* 94 (Supplement): S52–S94.

Hansen, Janet S. 1994. *Preparing for the Workplace: Charting a Course for Federal Postsecondary Training Policy*. National Research Council. Washington, D.C.: National Academy Press.

Hollingsworth, J. Rogers and Robert Boyer, eds. 1997. *Contemporary Capitalism: The Embeddedness of Institutions*. Cambridge: Cambridge University Press.

Japan Institute of Labor. 1989. *Seinen no shokugyô tekiyô ni kansuru kokusai hikaku kenkyû* (A comparative study of youth's work adjustment). Tokyo: Koyô shokugyô sôgô kenkyûjo.

———. 2002a. "Local Governments Tackle Job Creation for High School Graduates." *Japan Labour Bulletin* (April): 5–6.

———. 2002b. "Regional Employment Situation and Government Measures." *Japan Labour Bulletin* (March): 6–8.

Kariya, Takehiko. 1998. "From High School and College to Work in Japan: Meritocracy through Institutional and Semi-Institutional Linkages." In *From School to Work: A Comparative Study of Educational Qualifications and Occupational Destinations*, ed. Walter Müller and Yossi Shavit. Oxford: Oxford University Press.

Kerckhoff, Alan C. 2000. "Transition from School to Work in Comparative Perspective." In *Handbook of the Sociology of Education*, ed. Maureen T. Hallinan. New York: Kluwer Academic/Plenum. 453–74.

Kumon, Shumpei. 1992. "Japan as a Network Society." In *The Political Economy of Japan*, vol. 3, *Cultural and Social Dynamics*, ed. Shumpei Kumon and Henry Rosovsky. Stanford: Stanford University Press. 109–42.

LeTendre, Gerald. 1996. "Constructed Aspirations: Decision-Making Processes in Japanese Educational Selection." *Sociology of Education* 69: 193–216.

Lincoln, James R. 1990. "Japanese Organization and Organization Theory." In *Research in Organizational Behavior*, vol. 12, ed. Barry M. Staw and Larry L. Cummings. Greenwich, Conn.: JAI Press. 225–94.

Lincoln, James R., Michael L. Gerlach, and Christina L. Ahmadjian. 1996. "Keiretsu Networks and Corporate Performance in Japan." *American Sociological Review* 61: 67–88.

———. 1998. "Evolving Patterns of Keiretsu Organization and Action in Japan." In *Research in Organizational Behavior*, vol. 20, ed. Barry M. Staw and Larry L. Cummings. Greenwich, Conn.: JAI Press. 303–45.

Lynch, Lisa M. 1994. "Payoffs to Alternative Training Strategies at Work." In *Working under Different Rules*, ed. Richard B. Freeman. New York: Russell Sage. 63–95.

Maurice, Marc, François Sellier, and Jean-Jacques Silvestre. 1986. *The Social Foundations of Industrial Power: A Comparison of France and Germany*. Cambridge, Mass.: MIT Press.

Mitani, Naoki. 1999. "The Japanese Employment System and the Youth Labour Market." In *Preparing Youth for the 21st Century: The Transition from Education to the Labour Market*. Paris: OECD. 305–28.

Miwa, Yoshiro and J. Mark Ramseyer. 2002a. "The Myth of the Main Bank: Japan and Comparative Corporate Governance. *Law and Social Inquiry* 27: 401–24.
———. 2002b. "The Fable of the Keiretsu." *Journal of Economics and Management Strategy* 11: 169–224.
Mortimer, Jaylan and Helga Krüger. 2000. "Pathways from School to Work in Germany and the United States." In *Handbook of the Sociology of Education*, ed. Maureen T. Hallinan. New York: Kluwer Academic/Plenum. 475–98.
Murakami, Yasusuke and Thomas P. Rohlen. 1992. "Social-Exchange Aspects of the Japanese Political Economy: Culture, Efficiency, and Change." In *The Political Economy of Japan*, vol. 3, *Cultural and Social Dynamics*, ed. Shumpei Kumon and Henry Rosovsky. Stanford: Stanford University Press. 63–105.
Nee, Victor. 2005. "The New Institutional Approach to Economic Sociology." In *The Handbook of Economic Sociology*, ed. Neil J. Smelser and Richard Swedberg. 2nd ed. Princeton: Princeton University Press.
Neumark, David. 1998. "Youth Labor Markets: Shopping Around vs. Staying Put." NBER Working Paper 6581. Cambridge, Mass.: National Bureau of Economic Research.
North, Douglass C. 1991. "Institutions." *Journal of Economic Perspectives* 5(1)(Winter): 97–112.
OECD. 1994. *OECD Employment Outlook*. Paris: OECD.
———. 1996. *The OECD Jobs Strategy: Enhancing the Effectiveness of Labour Market Policies*. Paris: OECD.
———. 1999. *OECD Employment Outlook*. Paris: OECD.
Okano, Kaori. 1993. *School to Work Transition in Japan*. Clevedon, Avon: Multilingual Matters.
Rohlen, Thomas P. 1983. *Japan's High Schools*. Berkeley: University of California Press.
Rosenbaum, James E. and Takehito Kariya. 1989. "From High School to Work: Market and Institutional Mechanisms in Japan." *American Journal of Sociology* 94: 1334–65.
Rosenbaum, James E., Takehito Kariya, Rick Settersten, and Tony Maier. 1990. "Market and Network Theories of the Transition from High School to Work: Their Applications to Industrial Societies." *Annual Review of Sociology* 16: 263–99.
Ryan, Paul. 2001. "The School-to-Work Transition: A Cross-National Perspective." *Journal of Economic Literature* 39: 34–92.
Sako, Mari. 1991."The Role of 'Trust' in Japanese Buyer-Seller Relationships." *Richerche Economiche* 45: 449–74.
———. 1992. *Prices, Quality and Trust: Inter-Firm Relations in Britain and Japan*. Cambridge: Cambridge University Press.
Schwartz, Michael. 1992. "Japanese Enterprise Groups: Some American Parallels." *Shoken Keizai* 180: 1–10.
Shavit, Yossi and Walter Müller. 2001. "Vocational Secondary Education, Tracking, and Social Stratification." In *Handbook of the Sociology of Education*, ed. Maureen T. Hallinan. New York: Kluwer Academic/Plenum. 437–52.
Tang, Zun and Mary C. Brinton. 2004. "From Implicit Contracts to Spot Markets: The Transformation of Japan's Youth Labor Market." Working Paper, Department of Sociology, Harvard University.

U.S. Department of Education. 1996. *Education Indicators: An International Perspective.* Washington, D.C.: U.S. Department of Education, Office of Educational Research and Improvement.

Uzzi, Brian. 1996. "The Sources and Consequences of Embeddedness for the Economic Performance of Organizations: The Network Effect." *American Sociological Review* 61: 674–98.

Wakisaka, Akira. 2002. "Work-Sharing in Japan." *Japan Labour Bulletin* (June): 7–13.

Mitchel Y. Abolafia,
Rockefeller College of Public Affairs, University at Albany
James N. Baron,
Walter Kenneth Kilpatrick Professor of Organizational Behavior and
Human Resources, Graduate School of Business, Stanford University
Mary C. Brinton,
Reischauer Institute Professor of Sociology, Department of Sociology,
Harvard University
John L. Campbell,
Department of Sociology, Dartmouth College
Joseph Cohen
Ph.D. Candidate, Department of Sociology, Princeton University
Gerald F. Davis
Sparks Whirlpool Corporation Research Professor; Professor of Organiz-
ational Behavior and Human Resource Management; Department
Chair, Organizational Behavior and Human Resource Management,
Stephen M. Ross School of Business, University of Michigan
Paul DiMaggio
Department of Sociology, Princeton University
Peter Evans
Department of Sociology, University of California at Berkeley
Neil Fligstein
Class of 1939 Chancellor's Professor, Department of Sociology, Univer-
sity of California at Berkeley
John Freeman
Helzel Professor of Entrepreneurship and Innovation, Haas Organiz-
ational Behavior and Industrial Relations Group, Haas School of Busi-
ness, University of California at Berkeley
Francis Fukuyama
Bernard L. Schwartz Professor in International Political Economy, The
Paul H. Nitze School of Advanced International Studies, Johns Hop-
kins University
Avner Greif
Bowman Family Professor in the Humanities and Sciences, Department of
Economics, Stanford University
Michael T. Hannan
StrataCom Professor of Management and Professor of Sociology, School
of Humanities and Sciences, Graduate School of Business, Stanford
University
Ko Kuwabara
Ph.D. Candidate, Department of Sociology, Cornell University

Christopher Marquis
Ph.D. Candidate, Sociology and Management & Organizations, University of Michigan Business School
Victor Nee
Goldwin Smith Professor of Sociology, Department of Sociology, Cornell University
Douglass C. North
Bartlett Burnap Senior Fellow, Hoover Institution, Stanford University *and* Spencer T. Olin Professor in Arts and Sciences, Department of Economics, Washington University
AnnaLee Saxenian
Department of City and Regional Planning *and* School of Information Management and Systems, University of California at Berkeley
Richard Swedberg
Department of Sociology, Cornell University
Viviana A. Zelizer
Department of Sociology, Princeton University

Index

capitalism (*continued*)
between, 289–91; spirit of, 26–27; theories of, 27–30; understanding of, need for, ix–x; unique conditions producing a dynamic, 47–50; venture capital and (*see* venture capital)
capital markets, 148–50
caregivers, 307–14
Carroll, Glenn R., 195
CASPA. *See* Chinese American Semiconductor Association
Castells, Manuel, 227
Chang, Carmen, 337–38
Chang, Ha-Joon, 106n.7
Chang, Morris, 336
Chiapello, Eve, 26
Chile, corporate governance, convergence of in U.S.-listed firms, 365–66, 371–74, 378–85
China, Democratic Republic of. *See* Taiwan
China, People's Republic of: institutional foundation of state capitalism in, 59–63; institutional incentive structures in, 51n.6; markets, emergence of and decline in redistribution, 58–59; market transition, institutional change and, xxxvii; organizational change, difficulties regarding, 63–71; Shanghai's Zhangjiang High Tech Park, 334–39, 345; Silicon Valley, brain circulation with, 339–48; Taiwan, technology transfers from, 332–34; transnational communities and growth of the information technology industry in, 325–28, 348–49
Chinese American Semiconductor Association (CASPA), 344–45
Chinese Institute of Engineers, 344
Christian democratic welfare states, 398–400, 404–6
Chunwei, Lu, 346
circuits: anthropologists confront, 295–96; capitalism and questions regarding, 314–15; caregiving, 308, 310–11; elements and functions of, 293–94; generalizations regarding, 315–16; ideologies in local currencies, 302–6; of intimacy and caring, 306–8; local currencies, 297–302; networks, distinguished from, 293–94
Cisco Systems, 133, 193
classes, the economic process and, 15
Coase, Ronald, 55, 81

Coffee, John C., Jr., 354, 360, 363
Cohen, Joseph, xliii
Coleman, James S., 17, 28, 153, 270
Collins, James C., 191
Collins, Randall, 293
commerce, circuits of. *See* circuits
commodity-based systems, 298
communications technologies. *See* Internet, the; television
communities of practice, 83
Company Law, 60–65, 71
comparative institutional advantage, 413
competitiveness, shareholder value and, 127
computer industry. *See* information technology (IT) industry
consumption, sociology of, 20–21
coordinated market economies, 396–98, 402–3
corporate governance: boards of directors, 361–63, 379–81; convergence of, discussion of findings, 382–85; convergence of, globalization of financial markets and, 352–61, 385–87; convergence of, methods for measuring, 365–70; convergence of, organizational theory approach to studying, 361–65; convergence of, results of analysis, 370–82; in Japan, 422; shareholder capitalism, 352–56, 360–61, 385. *See also* firms
corruption, 84–85
Crittenden, Ann, 309, 311–14
cultural capital, 14
culture: bit-based empires as shapers of, 100; capitalism and, 31–32; corruption and, 85; as determinant of economic behavior, 76–80, 86; the economy and, 25–27; at the Federal Reserve, 208; leveling the cultural playing field, 102–3; organizational, institutional change and, 64–65; organizational in Silicon Valley, 180–81, 186–89 (*see also* organizational entrepreneurship); social capital (*see* social capital)

Daft, Richard, 206
Daguid, Paul, 83
Daimler-Benz, 354, 360
DaimlerChrysler, 367, 371
David, Paul, 50–51
Davis, Gerald F., xliv, 127
Defense Department, United States, 130–32

and, 411–12; taxation race to the bottom theory, continued significance of, 414n.1; transnational communities and, 325–28 (*see also* transnational communities); the United States and, 409–11
Glover, Paul, 303, 305–6
Goffman, Erving, 31
government. *See* state, the
Granovetter, Mark S., xiv–xxxiv, 163
Greenspan, Alan, 205
Greif, Avner, xvii, xix, xxxix, 271
GSMC. *See* Shanghai Grace Semiconductor Manufacturing Corporation
Guthrie, Doug, 63

Hagen, Everett E., 77
Hamilton, W. D., 79
Hannan, Michael T., xlii, xlv, 56, 169, 194
Hannemyr, Gisle, 264n.6
Hart, Keith, 305
Hayek, Friedrich, xi, 4, 33n.4, 46
Heckathorn, Douglas D., 284
Heimer, Carol, 306
Hein, Laura, 440n.3
Heinze, Rolf, 305
Hewlett Packard, 130–31, 173
Hirsch, Fred, 80
Hirsch, Paul, 233
Hoff, Karla, 91, 106n.9
Houser, Daniel E., 273
Hua Yuan Science & Technology Association, 343–44
human capital, 15, 153
Hurst, James Willard, 23

IMF. *See* International Monetary Fund
inequality: comparing television to the Internet regarding, 241–46, 251; diffusion processes and, 228–29, 239–40, 261; Internet access and, 229–31, 237; new growth theory and, 98–100
information: inequality and, 229; within organizations, 81
information technology (IT) industry: brain circulation between China and Silicon Valley, 339–48; government and the evolution of, 127–35; Shanghai's Zhangjiang High Tech Park, 334–39, 345; the Silicon Valley-Taiwan connection, 330–32; Taiwan-China technology transfers, 332–34; technical communites

and industrial fragmentation in, 328–30; transnational communities and, 325–28, 348–49. *See also* Internet, the; organizational entreprenership
institutional change: in China (*see* China, People's Republic of); development theory and (*see* development theory); North's theory of (*see* North, Douglass C.); oppositional norms in response to, 64–65, 71–72; structural inertia and, 56–57, 63, 67–69, 71–72
institutions: of capitalism, evolution of approaches to understanding, xxxv–xxxix; change in (*see* institutional change); conceptions and definitions of, x, xii–xiv, xxiv, xxxviii–xxxix, xlvi, 5–6, 43, 55, 106n.7, 271; corporate governance (*see* corporate governance); corruption and the rule of law, 84–85; economic performance and modification of, 47; financial markets (*see* financial markets); game theoretic analysis of, xv–xxv; as incentive structures, 42–46, 48–50; Internet access and, 230; Japanese markets and, 420–22; perspectives on, x–xii; venture capital, required by, 149–51
Intel, 133
interests: capitalism and, 5, 31–32; globalization theory and, 413
International Monetary Fund (IMF), 406, 411
International Society of the New Institutional Economics, 43
Internet, the: Chinese start-up companies, 345; creation of, 130, 132; data for comparing diffusion processes, 246–48; eBay (*see* eBay); inequality and access to, 229–31, 237; markets created, advantages and problems of, 268–71; results of comparing diffusion processes, 248–60; as subject of social research, 284–85; tax policy and, 139–40n.2; television, compared to, 241–46. *See also* information technology industry
intimacy: definition of, 306; economics of, 307–14
Invisible Heart, The (Folbre), 312–13
Israel, corporate governance, convergence of in U.S.-listed firms, 365–66, 371–74, 382–85
Italy, Banca del Tempo (Bdt), 297, 300